Understanding Human Differences

Multicultural Education for a Diverse America

A CUSTOM EDITION FOR THE UNIVERSITY OF NEVADA, LAS VEGAS

Taken from:

Understanding Human Differences: Multicultural Education for a Diverse America, Third Edition
by Kent L. Koppelman, with R. Lee Goodhart

Multicultural Education in a Pluralistic Society, Eighth Edition
by Donna M. Gollnick and Philip C. Chinn

Teaching Strategies for Ethnic Studies, Eighth Edition
by James A. Banks

Learning Solutions

New York Boston San Francisco
London Toronto Sydney Tokyo Singapore Madrid
Mexico City Munich Paris Cape Town Hong Kong Montreal

Cover Art: *Simultaneous Formation*, by Robin McDonald-Foley

Taken from:

Understanding Human Differences: Multicultural Education for a Diverse America, Third Edition
by Kent L. Koppelman, with R. Lee Goodhart

Published by Allyn & Bacon
Boston, Massachusetts 02116

Multicultural Education in a Pluralistic Society, Eighth Edition
by Donna M. Gollnick and Philip C. Chinn

Published by Merrill Prentice Hall
Upper Saddle River, New Jersey 07458

Teaching Strategies for Ethnic Studies, Eighth Edition
by James A. Banks

Published by Allyn & Bacon
Boston, Massachusetts 02116

This special edition published in cooperation with Pearson Learning Solutions.

Pearson Learning Solutions, 501 Boylston Street, Suite 900, Boston, MA 02116
A Pearson Education Company
www.pearsoned.com

Printed in the United States of America

4 5 6 7 8 9 10 V202 15 14 13 12

000200010270596302

RH

PEARSON

ISBN 10: 0-558-84552-5
ISBN 13: 978-0-558-84552-0

Contents

Taken from: *Understanding Human Differences: Multicultural Education for a Diverse America*, Third Edition, by Kent L. Koppelman, with R. Lee Goodhart

Preface

Why Do We Need to Understand Diversity?

Americans live in the most racially, ethnically, and socially diverse country on earth. Yet too often we live, work, and play as if our own social, gender, or religious group is the only one that matters. To enjoy the advantages of our national diversity, it is necessary that Americans seek as many facts and consider as many issues as possible to enhance their ability to interact effectively with individuals from diverse groups. This book is not a collection of essays providing multiple perspectives on diversity—there are many books that already do that; instead, this book uses research to examine problems, perceptions, misperceptions, and the potential benefits of the diversity that exists in the United States. Understanding diversity is obviously a prerequisite for becoming an individual who values the diversity in American society.

If we are to value and respect the diversity represented by different groups in the United States, we can begin by learning how to value and respect opinions that differ from our own. It is not necessary to agree with everything a person might say, but it is necessary that when we disagree, we are able to express disagreement based upon a consideration of all available information and within a context of mutual respect.

The issues this book addresses are not new: Human beings have struggled with them in one form or another for centuries, as illustrated by the quotations from individuals of different eras that appear in each chapter. The quotations are not placed randomly in the text, but near a section of text that relates to each one. For example, near the section in Chapter 2 addressing the confusion about positive prejudices and explaining why prejudices are always negative, the quotation by Charles Lamb suggests that prejudices involve "likings and dislikings." Because Lamb was a respected writer of his era, his confusion about some prejudices being positive was not based on a lack of education or intellectual ability, but instead illustrates how ancient this misperception is.

Since the first edition of *Understanding Human Differences* was published, the rights of various minority groups in the United States have become common topics for debate. For example, the term "marriage" has now become a legislative and judicial football, and American perceptions about how we differ from one another have changed in many ways. Students used to come to diversity classes oblivious of the issues, but that is less likely now, even though many diversity topics are still misunderstood.

New to This Edition

With the appearance of the third edition of this textbook, it is no longer enough simply to provide content that addresses human differences; students should now be encouraged to examine nuances of time, place, precedent, and situation. Despite the changes, a study of the history of human differences in America is still necessary if students want to comprehend diversity issues, and that study, based on sources from multiple disciplines, remains the text's foundation.

A specific goal for this edition was to address issues that had been omitted in the previous two editions, such as the idea of a disability culture using the example of Deaf culture, the impact of ageism on the elderly and youth, and culturally responsive teaching. Another goal was to expand the discussion of certain issues that continue to be of major concern for members of minority groups within our diverse society.

As with any new edition, care has been taken to update statistics and sources, and to find more current examples that can be used to illustrate issues addressed in this textbook. With regard to specific additions of content, the third edition of *Understanding Human Differences* includes a substantial expansion of information on the following issues:

- Examining the growth of linguistic diversity in the United States and the value of this diversity for the nation (Ch. 4). This will benefit those who are not aware of the increased linguistic diversity and who may not understand why this diversity should be encouraged and maintained.
- Explaining the institutional racism represented by the disproportionate number of African American males in prison and the disproportionate number of people of color adversely affected by the recent sub-prime mortgage crisis (Ch. 8). Some students may be aware of the disproportionate number of black males in prison, but when the sub-prime mortgage crisis developed, there was little coverage in the news media of the disproportionate number of families of color who were affected by this issue.
- Discussing why "transgender" has become an inclusive term and examining the discrimination experienced by transgendered people in the workplace (Ch. 10). The concept and reality of transgender are still not well understood by most Americans.
- Defining ageism and exploring negative social and economic consequences of ageism not simply on elderly people but on young people as well (Ch. 11). The term "ageism" is relatively new and only referred to the elderly until it was expanded in recent years to include youth.
- Introducing the concept of a disability culture, then providing a framework of four primary components of culture and examining how Deaf culture satisfies all of these components (Ch. 12).
- Explaining why many teacher educators are advocating culturally responsive teaching and how it addresses the goals of multicultural education (Ch. 13). All students, but especially those in teacher education, should benefit from this discussion of an effective teaching approach for classrooms with culturally diverse students.
- Expanding the discussion of diversity in the military with a brief history of past military service by gays and lesbians and a review of the ongoing sexual harassment against women and the continuing debate over women being assigned combat roles (Ch. 13). Although the military services have made progress with regard to diversity issues, it is important to understand where more improvement is needed.

In addition to the major revisions cited above, the third edition also:

- Discusses stereotypes about violent behavior associated with people diagnosed with a mental illness.
- Presents a brief history of Muslim immigration to the United States and an expanded description of the ongoing prejudice and discrimination against American Muslims since 9/11.
- Provides examples to illustrate the reason for the perception that members of the English Only movement harbor anti-immigrant attitudes.
- Discusses how Barack Obama overcame an historic example of institutional racism during the 2008 presidential campaign.
- Expands the discussion of how gender contributes to the likelihood of women living in poverty.
- Addresses racial disparities in special education placement.
- Discusses the debate over the use of the term "queer" in the LGBT community.
- Explains how anti-immigrant attitudes have resulted in a militarization of the Mexican border.
- Responds to arguments from opponents of cultural pluralism.
- Analyzes diverse examples of sexist language and alternative non-sexist terms.
- Provides a brief history of the concept of inclusion in special education.
- Examines evidence for the impact of schools in addressing gender equity issues.
- Describes one corporation's evolution from being perceived as actively engaged in worker exploitation in the global marketplace into a model of corporate responsibility for multinational corporations.

Students should benefit from exploring all of these issues because each is relevant to the society we live in now and the future society that these students may influence. The first step in problem solving is to understand why a problem exists and how it is perpetuated; with that understanding, a person or a community, or a state or a nation can implement solutions to address root causes of persistent problems. Consistent with this book's first two editions, the additional content offers information to understand problems or issues in society in order to find solutions, or in some cases to describe solutions that have been proposed or implemented.

Inquiry Approach/ Organization

Chapter narratives in this book are presented in an inquiry format. After a brief introduction, each chapter consists of related questions with responses based on research from a variety of disciplines and on author expertise. As references illustrate, information for this book has been collected from studies in a broad array of behavioral sciences, including education, psychology, sociology, anthropology, history, science, and literature. Although sources cited are from relatively recent publications, some older sources are also included either because they are still highly regarded in the field or simply because an author expressed a conclusion replicated by other research but not stated with as much clarity.

Section 1 focuses on individuals and interpersonal relationships. Chapter 1 defines terms essential for discussing diversity issues: Being able to make clear distinctions between terms such as *bias, prejudice,* and *bigotry* is critical for a conversation about problems related to individual and group differences. Chapter 1 also introduces the concept of *values*. The values promoted by a particular culture shape the values, beliefs, and actions of individuals living within that culture. Our cultural values define who we are and what we think is important; they shape the ideals that we embrace.

Section 1 also examines issues affecting all individuals, especially those living in a diverse society: the causes of prejudice, how it is learned, and the impact of prejudice; communication, conflict, moral reasoning, and conflict resolution.

Section 2 provides a historical context to illustrate how cultural biases were reflected in our evolving society. This context must be understood prior to examining the issues in Section 3, which describes intergroup relations in our diverse society. Section 2 describes the foundations of oppression as observed in early interactions between the first European colonizers of America who created a new nation and the unceasing flood of immigrants coming to that nation. The attitudes of descendants of immigrants toward each successive wave of new immigrants reveal the difficulty of sustaining the ideal of America as a land of opportunity and freedom. Anti-immigrant sentiment was especially antagonistic toward immigrants of color, requiring an examination of the historical experiences of each of the four major racial groups. Anti-immigrant sentiment was also directed against new arrivals because of their religion, and eventually came to include blatantly anti-Catholic and anti-Semitic attitudes.

The final chapter in Section 2 reviews the development of alternative perspectives as expressed by Americans on immigrants and the diversity produced by immigration, including the idea (or ideal) of pluralism, also called *cultural pluralism*. The rationale for promoting pluralism in a diverse society is examined as well as the strategies that can be used to promote pluralism.

Section 3 describes various ways in which specific minority groups have been oppressed in our society. The description of relations between dominant and subordinate groups includes an analysis of current cultural, individual, and institutional behaviors. Examples illustrate cultural biases against certain groups; individual prejudices, myths, and stereotypes believed by members of the dominant group about members of subordinate groups; and institutional policies and practices that benefit dominant group members but disadvantage subordinate group members.

Section 4 discusses changes that have already occurred in various institutions in the United States, reflecting a shift toward pluralism. This final section describes efforts that will move individual attitudes and institutional practices toward an acceptance of pluralism as the most appropriate response of a diverse society. The final chapter includes implications for future changes as the United States struggles with the challenges inherent in its status as the most diverse society in the world.

Discussion Exercises

To assist in the examination of serious ethical questions, exercises for group discussion are provided at the end of each chapter. Based on specific issues, activities encourage readers to reflect on and discuss aspects of issues that involve ethical or moral dilemmas. The exercises are not designed to manipulate readers into making a "politically correct" solution, but to hear the variety of responses from others and to appreciate the complexity of individual, institutional, and cultural issues in America today.

The Conceptual Framework for This Book

Understanding human differences is an ongoing challenge. Initially, scholars focused on *individual attitudes and behaviors;* later, they described the influence of *cultural expectations* in shaping individual attitudes. Finally, scholars addressed *institutional policies and practices* in which either discrimination was intentional against minority groups or it was an unintentional outcome. Vega (1978) describes a conceptual framework incorporating these three elements to understand human differences and the oppression of minority groups by dominant groups. This conceptual framework provides the basis for the organization of this book as we examine individual attitudes and actions, the evolution of cultural biases, and the establishment of discriminatory institutional practices (see Figure F.1).

To understand human differences, Vega's conceptual framework allows us to analyze American cultural, individual, and institutional behaviors. In exploring culture, the objective is to describe *cultural norms and standards.* What images are associated with the ideal? Any culture associates particular images with the ideal woman, the ideal man, and the ideal family. For many Americans, those images are primarily white middle-class people living in a nuclear family. Norms and standards are powerful determinants of individual expectations and behaviors, represented by the arrow pointing from culture to individual. Once we understand norms and standards, we can begin to understand what is meant by *cultural biases.* In a multicultural society, cultural biases can be detrimental to minority groups whose norms or standards do not conform to those of the dominant culture.

Once we understand the influence of culture on individuals, we can analyze *individual beliefs, attitudes, values, opinions, actions,* and *inactions;* sometimes what a person chooses *not* to do reveals as much as his or her actions. Although individuals are influenced by their cultural norms and standards, the Vega conceptual framework portrays that arrow as double headed, meaning that when significant numbers of individuals accept cultural norms, express their agreement, and behave in accordance with them, the cultural norms and standards are reinforced. Any analysis of individual behavior must include the influence of *prejudice* on an individual's choices.

Finally, we analyze *institutional practices, policies,* and *standard operating procedures* that are influenced by cultural norms and standards as well as by individual attitudes and behavior. To the extent that they reflect cultural norms and standards as well as individual attitudes and behaviors, institutions also reinforce them. To relate institutions to human differences, the analysis must focus on discrimination, identifying both ways in which the institution intentionally discriminates against certain groups and ways in which the institution unintentionally advantages certain groups and disadvantages others.

FIGURE F.1 A Conceptual Framework for the Study of Intergroup Relations

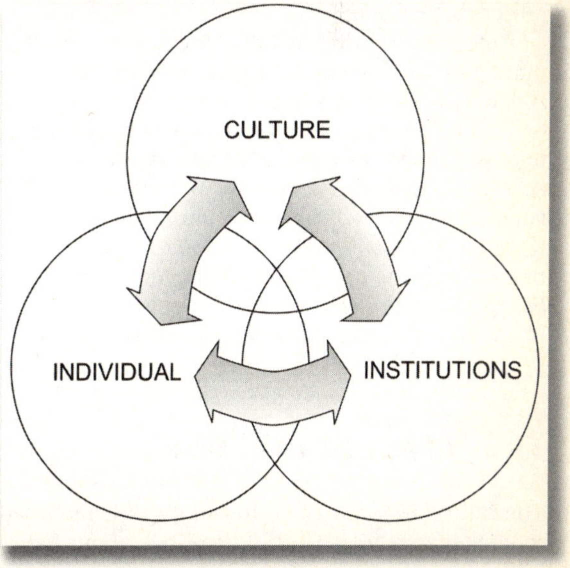

Although the Vega conceptual framework describes the intricate relationship among the three areas—cultural, individual, and institutional—chapter narratives of necessity deal with each discretely. Readers are asked to keep in mind the double-headed arrows signifying that all three areas are interlocked to create the following relationships:

1. Cultural norms and standards influence and are reinforced by individual attitudes and behaviors and institutional policies and procedures.
2. Individual attitudes and behaviors influence and are reinforced by cultural norms and standards and by institutional policies and procedures.
3. Institutional policies and procedures influence and are reinforced by cultural norms and standards and individual attitudes and beliefs.

Before concluding this explanation of Vega's conceptual framework, consider this example to illustrate how interreliant culture is with individual and institutional behaviors. Although many forms of family exist in the United States, our cultural bias is for the nuclear family (the norm). Influenced by this cultural bias, Americans tend to form nuclear families. Even when people with a cultural tradition of extended families immigrate to the United States, they tend to form nuclear families within a few generations, sometimes reversing convention with elderly parents receiving care in nursing homes rather than at home.

American institutions have encouraged the formation of nuclear families because they are more able to relocate in an age in which mobility of workers is highly desirable. In an analysis of discrimination, problems may emerge for minority subcultures that value extended families if they maintain that value rather than adjust to the cultural norm. As this example illustrates, Vega's conceptual framework helps clarify the complexity of intergroup relations by describing the related factors involved in the oppression of minority groups by a dominant group.

The Intent of this Book

The information provided in this book is intended to challenge readers to think and talk about issues that each of us must consider as citizens in a multicultural society; this book is not necessarily intended to change reader values, but to challenge attitudes based on incomplete or erroneous information (see Chapter 1 for a description of the difference between *values* and *attitudes*). Diversity brings benefit as well as challenge, but the surest way to enjoy the benefits is to meet the challenges with a firm foundation of knowledge and insight that is based on research from all behavioral sciences. Once students have read this textbook, the primary goal will be realized if they have gained a better understanding of the issues addressed. Whether or not that is accompanied by changes in attitudes is up to each individual, but there is an **Attitude Inventory in the Instructor's Manual** that accompanies this text, and your instructor may ask for your cooperation in taking this inventory before, during, or on completion of the course.

The intent of this book is to clarify our understanding of human differences and the role they play in interpersonal and intergroup relations. The Vega conceptual framework allows us to recognize how the interlocking circles of cultural biases, individual attitudes and actions, and institutional policies and practices have produced inequities that continue to polarize many Americans and that all too often prevent Americans from achieving ideals first expressed over two centuries ago when dreamers imagined a radical new concept, a nation where each person was given the freedom to be whoever he or she wanted to be.

Student Outcomes

To illustrate some desired outcomes, the following statements were written by students enrolled in a class using this book after the course was completed:

"If you had asked me whether I needed to know more (about diversity) at the beginning of the semester, I probably would have said no. . . . Now my views have changed. . . . I have been challenged to think about many issues and differences in society."

"I don't hear jokes with the same lightness that I did before this course. Too many jokes are at the expense of the race, ability, poverty, gender, or orientation of someone else."

"I am better able to consider the needs and situations of others in what I say and how I behave around others. Thanks. As I enter my profession, how I have changed my behavior . . . is a good career move!"

"I have learned a lot about myself and I have come to a better understanding of prejudice and white privilege."

"I did not fully understand that (as a white person) I have the odds in my favor when looking for housing, employment, or even shopping in a store. It is a strange feeling to know that I have an advantage over someone else simply because of what I was when I was born."

Supplements

The following ancillary materials have been created for the third edition. These instructor supplements are available for download from the password-protected Instructor Resource Center at HYPERLINK "http://www.pearsonhighered.com/irc" *www.pearsonhighered.com/irc*. Please contact your local Pearson representative if you need assistance.

Instructor's Manual/Test Bank

This resource provides instructors with a fundamental understanding of the text, its structure, format, and individual sections, including formal and informal assessment of student attitudes with regard to human differences. It also includes these features:

- *Fourteen Questions About Diversity in America*, each question represents a key concept in the corresponding chapter. Instructors can use these to prepare themselves for the course ahead and/or to use them as springboards for discussion on the chapter. Answers are included.
- Explanation of the objective activities: *Summary* and *Clarification Exercises* as well as *Community Involvement Opportunities* with answer keys.
- *Course and Instructor Assessment, Feedback and Evaluation* Worksheet
- Revised Multiple Choice, True/False, Fill-in-the-Blank and Matching questions from the Computerized Testbank.
- Attitude Inventory and instructions for instructor use to assess changes in students' attitudes from the beginning to the end of the course. This could also be used as a student self-assessment.

Computerized Test Bank/ MyTest

Pearson MyTest is a powerful assessment generation program that helps instructors easily create and print quizzes and exams. Questions and tests are authored online, allowing ultimate flexibility and the ability to efficiently create and print assessments anytime, anywhere! Instructors can access Pearson MyTest and their test bank files by going to *www.pearsonmytest.com* to log in, register, or request access. Features of Pearson MyTest include:

Premium assessment content

- Draw from a rich library of assessments that complement your Pearson textbook and your course's learning objectives.
- Edit questions or tests to fit your specific teaching needs.

Instructor-friendly resources

- Easily create and store your own questions, including images, diagrams, and charts using simple drag-and-drop and Word-like controls.
- Use additional information provided by Pearson, such as the question's difficulty level or learning objective, to help you quickly build your test.

Time-saving enhancements

- Add headers or footers and easily scramble questions and answer choices—all from one simple toolbar.
- Quickly create multiple versions of your test or answer key, and when ready, simply save to MS-Word or PDF format and print!
- Export your exams for import to Blackboard 6.0, CE (WebCT), or Vista (WebCT)!

PowerPoint® Presentation

PowerPoint® slides have been revised for the 3rd edition. Approximately 25 per chapter, they can be used "as is" but lend themselves well to customization to meet the instructor's specific needs. In addition to highlighting key points and information in each chapter, the presentation includes selected figures, tables, and cartoons.

MyEducationLab

myeducationlab

The power of classroom practice.

"Teacher educators who are developing pedagogies for the analysis of teaching and learning contend that analyzing teaching artifacts has three advantages: it enables new teachers time for reflection while still using the real materials of practice; it provides new teachers with experience thinking about and approaching the complexity of the classroom; and in some cases, it can help new teachers and teacher educators develop a shared understanding and common language about teaching. . . ."[1]

As Linda Darling-Hammond and her colleagues point out, grounding teacher education in real classrooms—among real teachers and students and among actual examples of students' and teachers' work—is an important, and perhaps even an essential, part of training teachers for the complexities of teaching in today's classrooms. For this reason, we have created a valuable, time-saving website—MyEducationLab—that provides you with the context of real classrooms and artifacts that research on teacher education tells us is so important. The authentic in-class video footage, interactive skill-building exercises and other resources available on MyEducationLab offer you a uniquely valuable teacher education tool.

MyEducationLab is easy to use and integrate into both your assignments and your courses. Wherever you see the MyEducationLab logo in the margins or elsewhere in the text, follow the simple instructions to access the videos, strategies, cases, and artifacts associated with these assignments, activities, and learning units on MyEducationLab. MyEducationLab is organized topically to enhance the coverage of the core concepts discussed in the chapters of your book. For each topic on the course you will find most or all of the following resources:

Connection to National Standards

Now it is easier than ever to see how your coursework is connected to national standards. In each topic of MyEducationLab you will find intended learning outcomes connected to the appropriate national standards for your course. All of the Assignments and Activities and all of the Building Teaching Skills and Dispositions in MyEducationLab are mapped to the appropriate national standards and learning outcomes as well.

Assignments and activities

Designed to save instructors preparation time, these assignable exercises show concepts in action through video, including classroom clips and ABC News footage, and then offer thought-provoking questions that probe your understanding of these concepts or strategies. (Feedback for these assignments is available to the instructor.)

Building teaching skills and dispositions

These learning units help you practice and strengthen skills that are essential to quality teaching. First you are presented with the core skill or concept and then given an opportunity to practice your understanding of this concept multiple times by watching video footage, reading scenarios, or interacting with other media and then critically analyzing the strategy or skill presented.

IRIS center resources

The IRIS Center at Vanderbilt University (*http://iris.peabody.vanderbilt.edu*—funded by the U.S. Department of Education's Office of Special Education Programs OSEP) develops training enhancement materials for pre-service and in-service teachers. The Center works with experts from across the country to create challenge-based interactive modules, case study units, and podcasts that provide research-validated information about working with students in inclusive settings. On your MyEducationLab course we have integrated this content where appropriate to enhance the content coverage in your book.

---

[1]Darling-Hammond, l., & Bransford, J.,Eds.(2005). *Preparing Teachers for a Changing World.* San Francisco: John Wiley & Sons

General resources on your MyEducationLab course

The *Resources* section on your MyEducationLab course is designed to help you pass your licensure exam, put together an effective portfolio and lesson plan, prepare for and navigate the first year of your teaching career, and understand key educational standards, policies, and laws. This section includes:

- *Licensure Exams*: Access guidelines for passing the Praxis exam. The Practice Test Exam includes practice questions, Case Histories, and Video Case Studies.
- *Portfolio Builder and Lesson Plan Builder*: Create, update, and share portfolios and lesson plans.
- *Preparing a Portfolio*: Access guidelines for creating a high-quality teaching portfolio that will allow you to practice effective lesson planning.
- *Licensure and Standards*: Link to state licensure standards and national standards.
- *Beginning Your Career*: Educate yourself—access tips, advice, and valuable information on: Resume Writing and Interviewing—Expert advice on how to write impressive resumes and prepare for job interviews; Your First Year of Teaching—Practical tips to set up your classroom, manage student behavior, and learn to more easily organize for instruction and assessment; and Law and Public Policies—Specific directives and requirements you need to understand under the No Child Left Behind Act and the Individuals with Disabilities Education Improvement Act of 2004.
- *Special Education Interactive Timeline*: Build your own detailed timelines based on different facets of the history and evolution of special education.

Visit *www.myeducationlab.com* for a demonstration of this exciting new online teaching resource.

Acknowledgments

I want to thank Greg Wegner for his assistance in researching and writing the addition to Chapter 11 on Ageism, and I also want to thank Robin DiAngelo for her assistance in researching and writing the addition to Chapter 13 on Culturally Responsive Teaching. In addition, Dr. Wegner and I are grateful to Larry White, the Director of the La Crosse County Office on Aging and James Schmidlkofer, State of Wisconsin Office on Aging for providing links to research resources on topics relating to ageism. I also want to extend a special thanks to Jan Koppelman for her assistance on numerous aspects of revising this textbook and improving both content and illustrations. I am most grateful to my editor, Kelly Villella Canton, for her wise counsel and assistance, and my appreciation also to her editorial assistant, Annalea Manalili for all of her help. Thank you also to the reviewers for this edition: Edward Garcia Fierros, Villanova University and Robert Lake, Georgia Southern University.

Individual Attitudes and Interpersonal Relations

Section 1 examines individual human differences. From the beginning, we human beings have been social animals; interpersonal relationships are the bedrock of our social nature. How we perceive and react to others is a complex combination of values, attitudes, beliefs, assumptions, and behaviors, including our communication skills.

Chapter 1 explores individual values in terms of our cultural context. We can be expected to share certain dominant cultural values, but we need to understand how individuals learn values in families and communities, and also how those values affect our individual behavior. The chapter also provides definitions for a number of important terms and concepts such as *race, ethnicity,*

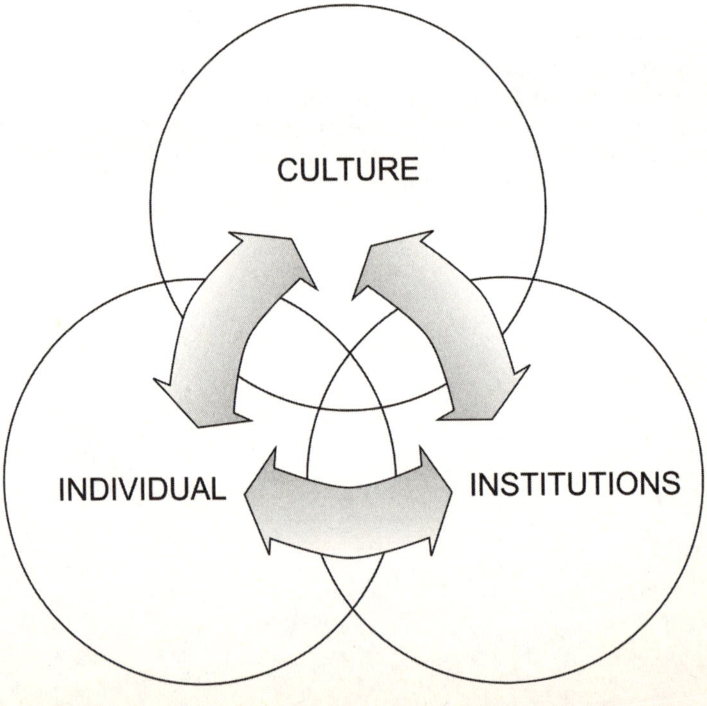

nationality, and *minority group*. Minority groups are often labeled, so this chapter explains how formal and informal labels are used to define and demean groups of people. It is essential to have shared meanings of important terms and concepts and to be aware of the influence of labels in order to understand human differences and perceptions of those differences.

Because the word *prejudice* is often confused with other terms, Chapter 2 explains distinctions between important and related terms: *bias, stereotype, prejudice, bigotry,* and *discrimination*. Because prejudice is not innate but is learned, the chapter describes how everyday language reflects and teaches negative attitudes toward groups of people. Although prejudice can lead to discrimination, other theories explaining discrimination are described that are not a consequence of prejudice. The chapter concludes by describing factors that promote prejudice in our society and the rationalizations that people employ to avoid identifying and confronting their prejudices.

Chapter 2 shows how perceptions of, or reactions to, human differences may result in negative behaviors creating conflict; however, conflict does not have to be a destructive force. Chapter 3 investigates interpersonal communication, beginning with an analysis of misperceptions about communication. With the help of a communication model, the chapter explains elements of communication, the origins of interpersonal conflict, and certain attitudes that promote conflict resolution. The chapter concludes with an explanation of how human beings develop moral reasoning and a look at the role of moral reasoning in conflict resolution.

Understanding Ourselves and Others: Clarifying Values and Language

"I have striven not to laugh at human actions, not to weep at them, nor to hate them, but to understand them."

Baruch Spinoza (1632–1677)

"May you live in interesting times" is a Chinese curse. It implies that life is easier and more enjoyable when nothing out of the ordinary or controversial happens. As Americans living in a complex, multicultural society, we certainly live in interesting times. Is it the best of times or the worst of times? Like the question about whether the glass is half empty or half full, the answer is the same: It's a personal decision. We can choose to be engaged in the challenges and opportunities of diversity issues, or we can retreat and resign ourselves to an attitude of indifference or even despair. Because America is not only a diverse society but also a democratic one, we have the freedom to choose our perceptions, assumptions, and behaviors.

If we take Spinoza's quote seriously, we need to understand all kinds of diversity—including opinions, appearances, values, and beliefs—as well as the categories of race, ethnicity, social class, gender, sexual orientation, and disability. The study of human diversity obviously requires an examination of social groups that encounter discrimination. However, in addition to focusing on the sociocultural differences between groups, we must also acknowledge the importance of *individual* differences. Each of us wants to be recognized as an individual. Our experiences are affected by multiple factors, including whether we are white or a person of color, female or male, from a low-, middle-, or upper-income family, or from a rural, suburban, or urban home. Each person's opinion offers a unique perspective that only the individual expressing it can fully understand. The task for us as listeners is to understand as best as we can the ideas, values, and beliefs articulated by the individuals we encounter.

What is the difference between beliefs and values?

Kniker (1977) suggests that **beliefs** are inferences about reality that take one of three forms: descriptive, evaluative, or prescriptive. A *descriptive belief* is exemplified by those who argued that the world was not flat but round because they observed boats sailing off to the horizon and recognized that the hulls disappear while sails are still visible. An *evaluative belief* is illustrated by Winston Churchill's conclusion about democracy based on his reading of history: He understood why some called democracy the worst form of government, but he found it to be better than all other forms of government that had been attempted thus far. An example of a *prescriptive belief* would be the recommendation that students take a role in creating classroom rules because research showed that students who help create rules are more likely to be cooperative and abide by them. All beliefs are predispositions to types of action. Rokeach asserts that a cluster of related beliefs creates an **attitude;** he defines **values** as "combinations of attitudes which generate action or deliberate choice to avoid action" (Kniker, 1977, p. 33).

The Role of Values in Human Differences

Rokeach is saying that values determine our choices: Values are the foundation for actions we choose to take—or to avoid (see Figure 1.1). What value do Americans place on wealth? For some, money and possessions are the primary measures of success. They admire others who are rich and successful, and they define their own worth by their income and wealth. For others, money is not a priority. Their main concern is to make enough money to support a comfortable lifestyle, however they choose to define it. There are also people who believe the biblical caution that love of money is "the root of all evil," and refuse to let wealth play an important role in their choices. Their behavior is a reflection of their values. While serving as vice president to John Adams, Thomas Jefferson was once turned away from a prominent hotel because his clothes were soiled and he had no servants with him. After the proprietor was told whom he had refused, he sent word to Jefferson, offering him any room in the hotel. Having been accepted into another hotel, Jefferson sent a reply politely refusing the offer of a room, noting that if the hotel proprietor did not have a room for a "dirty farmer," then he must not have a room for the vice president either (Botkin, 1957).

What is the relationship between a person's values and behaviors?

America has a history of social commentary on the role of values in people's lives, and scholars engage in research examining the relationship between expressed values and behavior. Searching for

FIGURE 1.1 The Relationship of Values, Beliefs, Attitudes, and Choices

From Charles R. Kniker *You and values education.* Published by Allyn & Bacon/Merrill Education, Boston, MA. Copyright © 1977 by Pearson Education. Reprinted by permission of the publisher.

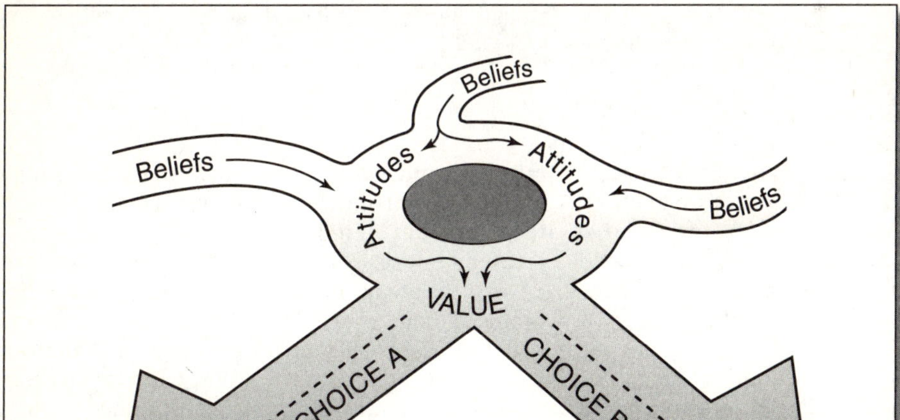

consistent patterns in values research is challenging. However, one theme from social critics has been repeatedly supported by research and case study: There is a *consistent inconsistency* between what we say we value and our actual behavior (Aronson, 2008; Lefkowitz, 1997; Myrdal, 1944; Terry, Hogg, & Duck, 1999).

The tendency for Americans to say we believe in a certain value and then engage in contradictory behavior is a curious and yet consistent pattern. Contradictory behavior by human beings has been criticized and even ridiculed by essayists, novelists, and observers of American society. In 1938, the Carnegie Foundation invited Swedish social economist Gunnar Myrdal to the United States to conduct a study on the "American Negro Problem." Myrdal (1944) went far beyond a study of racial relations: He attempted to identify and understand the core values of American society.

In his analysis of Myrdal's research, Risberg (1978) identified nine values that Americans perceived as defining their culture:

1. Worth and dignity of the individual
2. Equality
3. Inalienable rights to life, liberty, property, and the pursuit of happiness
4. Rights to freedom of speech, press, religion, assembly, and private association
5. Consent of the governed
6. Majority rule
7. Rule of law
8. Due process of law
9. Community and national welfare. (pp. 5–6)

These identified core values seem to be accurate, especially if we compare American culture to other cultures. For example, many nations around the world put great emphasis on the collective good, but in the United States we tend to focus on personal worth and to reward individual achievements. Expectations of equality and of having "inalienable rights" are expressed in founding documents such as the Declaration of Independence, and our various freedoms are guaranteed by the Bill of Rights to the U.S. Constitution. Our representative form of democracy is based on the assumption that local, state, and national governments will be elected by the majority, with an expectation that they will rule with the consent of the governed for the welfare of the community, state, and nation. Finally, being ruled by laws and being given a chance to resolve issues by making our case in court (due process) was established to protect our citizens from the whims of the wealthy and powerful (a reaction to oppressive behavior from aristocrats and monarchs in the past). These values have historically defined America as a society, and they represent beliefs that all Americans share.

Despite the consensus about them, Myrdal observed that all of the values were regularly contradicted by American behavior. He provided examples from his observations, primarily based on race relations, to illustrate his conclusion.

What inconsistencies exist between American values and American behaviors?

Although Americans have always tended to emphasize individuality, American society quite consistently has demanded conformity. We Americans always seem to be uncomfortable with differences, often minimizing or ignoring them. In the turbulent era of the 1960s, many young people protested the Vietnam War, challenging authorities on college campuses and elsewhere in American society. Young men and women defied traditional gender roles in their choice of lifestyles and music, but most Americans did not celebrate this youth counterculture as an expression of individuality; instead, many denounced their behavior. Families were sundered and social critics predicted the downfall of American values. The protests passed, and expectations that Americans should conform have continued.

> The primal principle of democracy is the worth and dignity of the individual.
>
> **Edward Bellamy (1850–1898)**

The influence of peers on individual behavior illustrates the seductive power of conformity. Social psychologists studying the influence of peer pressure have reported that people in groups engage in behaviors they would not undertake as individuals (Aronson, 2008; Haag, 2000; Terry, Hogg, & Duck,

1999). According to LeBon (1968), when individuals congregate, the group "presents new characteristics very different from those of the individuals composing it" (p. 27). In a study of young men who had assaulted homosexuals, Franklin (2000) found that many of the men she interviewed expressed tolerant attitudes toward homosexuality even though they admitted that when they were with friends, they participated in verbal or physical assaults on people perceived to be gay. When questioned, 35% said they were motivated by a desire to prove their "toughness" and to become closer to the friends who engaged in antigay behavior.

Contradictory behavior also is illustrated in the belief that Americans value equality. The Declaration of Independence proclaims that the United States is founded on the belief that "all men are created equal," and yet the man who wrote that statement owned slaves. During World War II, boxing champions Joe Louis and Sugar Ray Robinson signed up for military service. At a bus stop in Alabama, a military policeman insisted that the two "colored soldiers" move to the rear of the station. When they refused, they were arrested. After an officer had reprimanded them, Louis responded, "Sir, I'm a soldier like any other American soldier. I don't want to be pushed to the back because I'm a Negro" (Mead, 1985, p. 231). Although racial inequality has diminished to some degree in the United States, the gap between the wealthy and the poor has become greater than ever. A chairman of the board for the First National Bank of Chicago admitted that it was difficult to defend an economic system that permitted such a wide disparity of income as existed in the United States (Terkel, 1980, p. 23).

The United States also was founded on the rule of law and the belief in a justice system that would be fair to everyone, yet people with wealth and status are routinely able to circumvent our ideal. The view that our courts favor those who can afford the best lawyers is widely recognized and is often portrayed in films and on television. Despite the contradiction, Americans continue to believe that justice can prevail in a courtroom and they are resentful of cases where they believe it has not. For example, Claus von Bülow was a man of wealth and status who was tried and convicted for attempting to murder his wife. He subsequently hired the famous defense attorney Alan Dershowitz, who identified a legal technicality that necessitated a new trial for his client. At the retrial, the jury acquitted von Bülow of attempted murder (Wright, 1983). No one except von Bülow knows if he is guilty or innocent; however, there are poor people in prison today because they could not afford to hire a lawyer as skilled as Alan Dershowitz.

> The law, in its majestic equality, forbids the rich as well as the poor to sleep under bridges, to beg in the streets, and to steal bread.
>
> **Anatole France (1844–1924)**

What Myrdal observed and reported in the 1940s continues to be true today: Americans behave inconsistently and engage in actions that contradict their expressed values. Myrdal's observations reinforced what American social critics had been saying for many years and what research and case studies have documented since the 1940s. These observations require some explanation, and it seems logical to begin by examining how people choose their values.

Are values individually chosen or are we taught to accept certain values?

The way American values are taught plays a major role in the values we hold. Individuals, subcultures, and institutions are involved in teaching values; parents, teachers, peers, clergy, relatives, and youth counselors are just a few examples. By studying how individuals and organizations in America teach values to children and youth, Raths, Harmin, and Simon (1978) identified seven traditional approaches.

A first way to teach values is to (1) *set an example.* Parents and teachers are supposed to be role models for children and youth. Young people are also told to emulate various individuals—from historical leaders to contemporary athletes whose achievements are attributed to practicing certain values. In similar fashion, schools and other organizations use (2) *rules and regulations* to promote certain behaviors in children and youth (and adults) that represent important values. Learning punctuality is considered important enough that teachers send children to the principal's office for a tardy pass if they are late for class. This example is especially interesting because the child securing the tardy pass from the principal is kept away from the classroom for additional time while the other children engage in some kind of learning activity, which is supposedly the primary purpose for requiring students to attend school.

Another approach is to (3) *persuade or convince* others to accept certain values. Respectful discussions with reasonable arguments can be an effective means of convincing someone that the values being espoused are appropriate for living a good life. Related to this is an (4) *appeal to conscience* in which a parent or teacher may challenge a child or youth who seems to advocate an inappropriate value or belief. This approach is illustrated when a teacher responds to a student making an inappropriate comment by saying, "You don't really believe that, do you?" The point of such questions is not to give the student a chance to explain or defend what he or she said, but to bring a subtle and insistent form of moral pressure intended to coerce the student into rejecting an unacceptable point of view.

Parents often teach values by offering (5) *limited choices*. By limiting choices, parents intend to manipulate children into making acceptable decisions. If a mother values cooperation and tells her children that family members should share in household duties, what can she do if one of her children refuses? She asks one child to wash dishes twice a week, but the child hates to wash dishes and refuses. The mother might say, "Either you agree to wash dishes twice a week or you will not be allowed to play with your friends after school." The child is restricted to two options in the hope that he or she will choose to do the dishes, reinforcing the mother's original objective of wanting her children to learn the value of sharing domestic responsibilities.

Organizations have employed the approach of (6) *inspiring* people to embrace certain values, often by sponsoring a "retreat" with inspirational or motivational speakers or a social function where the combination of speakers, films, and activities is designed to have emotional or spiritual impact. Although religious groups employ this approach, corporations sponsor such events to inspire employees to work harder to achieve personal or group goals, and in doing so, contribute to the achievement of organizational goals.

Some religious groups and secular organizations emphasize (7) *religious or cultural dogma* to teach values. To accept beliefs without questioning them is to be **dogmatic.** If a Christian with dogmatic beliefs were questioned, he or she might say "That's what the Bible says," or, similarly, a dogmatic Muslim might say "This is what it says in the Qu'ran," even though for centuries people have interpreted the teachings of Jesus and Muhammad in different ways. Even early Christians held widely divergent views on the meanings of the life and words of Jesus (Pagels, 2006). Dogmatic beliefs stifle debate by emphasizing tradition: "This is what we have always believed."

Dogmatic beliefs also can be found in a secular context. When someone questions a value based on cultural beliefs, a dogmatic response might be "We've always done it this way." The appeal to tradition in opposing change has been employed in such controversies as using Native American mascots for school sports teams and including the Confederate flag in the official flags of some southern states. Only in 2003 did Georgia change its state flag to remove the confederate symbol.

> When people are free to do as they please they usually imitate each other.
>
> **Eric Hoffer (1902–1983)**

Understanding how values are taught provides some insight in answering the question about why people consistently behave in ways that contradict their expressed values. Each of the seven traditional approaches to teaching values seems to be based on a common assumption, and that assumption might explain the inconsistencies.

How does the way values are taught explain the inconsistency between values and behavior?

What do the seven traditional approaches to teaching values have in common? They are all based on an assumption that certain prescribed values are to be taught, and that the individuals being instructed should accept them. The person teaching values—the teacher, parent, scout leader, minister, priest, rabbi, imam, or employer—knows what values are appropriate. The goal is to persuade the student, child, parishioner, or worker to accept those values. In actuality, each approach is a form of **indoctrination,** where the intent is to dictate cultural values that must be accepted rather than assist people in deciding what is right and wrong (see Figure 1.2).

This assumption shared by all seven traditional approaches to teaching values in America caused Raths et al. (1978) to question whether all approaches were primarily successful in convincing people to *say* the right thing, yet not *do* the right thing. If this is true, there are important implications for how values should be taught. It is neither ethical nor prudent to teach values that are advocated but not practiced in our everyday lives. This does not teach values, but, rather, hypocrisy. If the goal of teaching is to help learners understand what they genuinely believe and choose values to incorporate into their behavior, those who teach must recognize the limitations of coercing children and youth to feign acceptance of prescribed values. For Americans to behave consistently with our expressed values, we must demonstrate authentic commitment to them.

FIGURE 1.2 Often found in public school textbooks, illustrations such as this one suggest that Native Americans and colonists had a peaceful, harmonious relationship, but the reality was one of consistent conflict as Indians were pushed off their lands and forced to move westward.

Source: "The First Thanksgiving," painting by Jean Leon Gerome Ferris (1863–1930). Library of Congress, Prints and Photographs Division (LC-D416-90423).

Why should anyone be concerned about inconsistencies between values and behavior?

If we understand our values and consistently act on them, it is more likely that our choices will reflect our highest ideals. We are constantly confronted with ethical dilemmas that challenge our values and require us to make moral choices. A *New York Times* reporter interviewed a national sales manager for Wachovia who was living in an upper-middle-class suburb of Atlanta—a homogeneous community where everyone was of the same race and social class, and even shared similar opinions on a variety of issues. At his corporate worksite, the manager said the importance of diversity was emphasized: "At work, diversity is one of the biggest things we work on." (Kilborn, 2007, p. 157) Yet in his private life, the manager admitted that he and his suburban neighbors were "never challenged" to learn about other groups, so they did not. The contrast between what happens at work and what takes place at home represents an inconsistency that could call into question the sincerity of the manager's commitment to diversity.

Another example of inconsistency that came up during the interview was when the sales manager said that his family attended church and Bible Study classes. Because they were secure in their own comforts, the manager admitted that he and his family didn't give much thought to other "economic groups," to families living in poverty. As a contrast, there is the example of Bono, lead singer for the rock group U2, who has used his position and wealth to lobby for human rights. Accepting an NAACP Image Award in 2007 for his work on poverty issues and the AIDS crisis in Africa, Bono identified Martin Luther King, Jr. as someone who inspired him, and he went on to say:

> The poor are where God lives. God is in the slums, in the cardboard boxes where the poor play house. God is where the opportunity is lost and lives are shattered. God is with the mother who has infected her child with a virus that will take both their lives. God is under the rubble in the cries we hear during wartime. God, my friends, is with the poor. God is with us if we are with them. This is not a burden. This is an adventure. (Gamber, 2007, p. 37)

Should parents rather than schools teach values to children?

The question of who should teach values is a rhetorical one. Both parents and schools in America are expected to contribute to the development of children's value systems. We constantly encounter people who reveal their values in everyday words and actions. Teachers model their values whether or not they consciously choose to do so. The question is not whether values should be taught, but how they should be taught.

Of the many approaches Kniker (1977) identified for teaching values, the most effective allow children and youth opportunity for discussion and debate, employing activities that stimulate them to think about their beliefs, hear other perspectives, and consider what effect different decisions could have for others as well as themselves. Discussing values, related behaviors, and possible consequences exposes young people to perspectives of others; evaluating arguments about values from their peers can help them decide which ones seem more attractive, compelling, and meaningful. In the process, they learn not only what values are important to them, but also to accept people with values different from their own.

As adults, we do not tend to make decisions about values at a particular point in time and then never change our minds. Our values are based on beliefs and attitudes that change frequently, resulting in an ongoing process in which decisions are made and reevaluated throughout our lives. Culture, geographical location, parents, and life experiences influence each person's decisions. Each individual must determine what he or she believes is best, and the cumulative decisions individuals make influence the evolution of our society (Bellah et al., 1991; Lappe, 1989; Zinn, 1990). School classrooms are part of this journey. Teachers must present stu-

> Consciously we teach what we know;
> unconsciously we teach who we are.
>
> **Don Hamachek (Contemporary)**

dents with moral dilemmas and trust that when our children and youth are given the freedom to choose, they will be capable of making ethical decisions.

What problems can interfere with making ethical decisions?

One of the main problems in making ethical decisions about human differences is confusion concerning the language employed to address those differences. Many essential words or phrases are either common terms with a history of misuse or unfamiliar terms. Confused language often reflects the discomfort people feel toward sensitive issues. For example, the word *racism* did not appear in most English dictionaries until the 1960s. As the civil rights movement gained momentum and attracted considerable attention from the media and people across America, we could no longer avoid using the term. Similarly, the word *sexism* did not appear in dictionaries until the early 1970s, as the women's movement became increasingly successful at bringing issues concerning the treatment of women to public attention (Miller & Swift, 2000).

> How often misused words generate misleading thoughts.
>
> **Herbert Spencer (1820–1903)**

Using inaccurate or ambiguous language creates problems when we are addressing sensitive, uncomfortable issues. To be coherent and meaningful in our discussion of human differences, we must clarify our vocabulary and agree to specific appropriate meanings for significant words and concepts.

Defining Terms Related to Human Differences

One would expect that consultation with any scholarly authority would provide definitions for a term such as *prejudice,* but the scholarly world is not free from confusion. Some textbooks have defined *prejudice* as a prejudgment that could be either positive or negative; this definition confuses prejudice with *bias,* a feeling in favor of—or opposed to—anything or anyone. *Stereotypes* always refer to people, and also can be positive or negative. As with stereotypes, prejudice always refers to people, but prejudice is always negative.

This chapter includes a series of definitions intended to clarify terms referring to human differences. Definitions throughout the text are based on the work of scholars from various fields in the behavioral sciences, including racial and ethnic studies, women's studies, education, sociology, and anthropology. Unless cited, definitions reflect a distillation of common themes identified in several scholarly sources (Andrzejewski, 1996; Feagin & Feagin, 2008; Herdt, 1997; Levin & Levin, 1982; Schaefer, 2008; Simpson & Yinger, 1985). The following series of definitions makes distinctions and indicates relationships between the terms.

Bias A preference or inclination, favorable or unfavorable, which inhibits impartial judgment.

Stereotype A positive or negative trait or traits ascribed to a certain group and to most members of that group.

Prejudice A negative attitude toward a group and persons perceived to be members of that group; being predisposed to behave negatively toward members of a group.

Bigotry Extreme negative attitudes leading to hatred of a group and persons regarded as members of the group.

Discrimination Actions or practices carried out by a member or members of dominant groups, or their representatives, that have a differential and negative impact on a member or members of subordinate groups.

Notice that each of the first four terms just listed represents attitudes of greater intensity than the previous one. Regarding bias and stereotypes, attitudes can be either positive or negative and can influence a person's perceptions of a person or group. Having a *bias* related to a group creates an inclination to favor or dislike an individual from that group. (See Table 1.1.) *Stereotyping* a group indicates an expectation that most members of the group will

TABLE 1.1 Examples of Bias

The following selection comes from a list of 27 biases:

1. *Family Bias:* Believing information provided by family members without seeking evidence to support the accuracy of their information.
2. *Attractiveness Bias:* Believing information provided by attractive people.
3. *Confirmation Bias:* Believing information that reinforces beliefs already held and ignoring information that contradicts these beliefs.
4. *Self-Serving Bias:* Believing information that is beneficial to self-interest and goals.
5. *In-Group Bias:* Believing information from people who are members of our group (e.g., friends, co-workers, same racial or ethnic group, etc.).
6. *Expectancy Bias:* Pursuing information and drawing conclusions that reinforce our beliefs when looking for information (or even conducting research).
7. *Pleasure Bias:* Assuming that pleasant experiences offer greater insights for strengthening one's beliefs than unpleasant experiences do.
8. *Perceptual Bias:* Assuming that one's own perceptions and experience of reality reveal objective truths to confirm one's beliefs.
9. *Perseverance Bias:* Perpetuating one's beliefs even after encountering information that contradicts those beliefs.
10. *Uncertainty Bias:* Choosing to believe or disbelieve information rather than remain uncertain because of discomfort with ambiguity.

–Adapted from Newburg and Waldman (2006) *Why We Believe What We Believe*

behave in certain positive or negative ways. No positive option exists for prejudice or bigotry because of the greater intensity of these attitudes. *Prejudices* are negative attitudes based on a prejudgment of a group; *bigotry* involves hatred and represents a harsher form of prejudgment against a person or group. Note that whereas bias, stereotype, prejudice, and bigotry relate to attitudes, discrimination refers to actions taken that demonstrate negative attitudes. A person can have a bias, a stereotype, a prejudice, or even be a bigot and still not engage in any kind of negative or positive behavior. Unless an individual's attitudes are publicly expressed, others may not be aware of them. Discrimination can be seen and documented, and it can cause physical and emotional harm.

How do negative attitudes develop?

We learn various biases, stereotypes, and prejudices as we grow up. We can be biased in favor of or against certain kinds of foods, categories of books, styles of clothing, or types of personalities. Bias can affect decisions about what we eat, read, or wear; it can influence our choice of friends. A stereotype assumes that individuals possess certain human traits simply because they are members of a particular group. Although some traits are regarded as positive—such as blacks have rhythm, Asians are good in math—other traits are viewed as negative—certain groups are lazy, shiftless, dishonest, or violent. Although negative stereotypes are regarded as unacceptable, many people accept positive stereotypes. The problem with positive stereotypes is that they cause us to have specific expectations for individuals and groups even though we have little or no evidence for these assumptions. A positive stereotype may sabotage the process of forming a realistic and accurate perception of an individual.

During a coffee break at a midwestern university, three Asian American women employed by a student services office reminisced about their undergraduate days. They complained about how difficult math classes had been and laughed as they recalled some of their coping strategies. The student services director, an African American, walked into the room, overheard what they were saying, and interrupted their discussion to chastise them for "putting yourselves down." He said they should stop. He also said he was disappointed in them and departed.

After the director left, the three women initially were too surprised to speak. Once they started talking, they realized they were angry because his comments suggested that he assumed they all had good math skills and were not being honest when discussing their lack of math ability. The women thought the director viewed them as individuals; they were angry and hurt when they realized that he had allowed a stereotype to distort his perception of them. They were especially upset because they had not expected a person of color to believe in a stereotype—even a positive one about the math abilities of Asians—but apparently he did.

If negative stereotypes reinforce negative biases, prejudices can develop, and prejudices are always negative. Although prejudice is only an attitude, negative attitudes often lead to negative actions against an individual or a group. Taking negative action might strengthen the prejudices of a person until they become the intense hatred of bigotry, which is the basis for white supremacist groups such as the Ku Klux Klan, neo-Nazis, and the Aryan nation. Because hatred is such a strong emotion, bigots are more likely to express their hatred with *actions,* including violence. Negative behaviors are often directed against individuals from social groups based on such differences as race, ethnicity, or nationality.

What is the difference between race, ethnicity, and nationality?

Race is not a scientific concept but a social reality dictated by the color of one's skin, even though skin color as a basis for human categorization is absurd. African Americans are identified as black, yet the skin color for many African Americans is more accurately described as brown. Contrary to the racist term "redskin," the skin color for Native Americans is not red. Yellow is an inaccurate description of skin color for those of Asian heritage. At an elementary school in Minneapolis, young children created a poster with the title "The Human Rainbow." The first band of their rainbow was colored with a light brown crayon, making a very pale brown band, and each band above it was a slightly darker shade of brown until the outer band, which was colored in such a dark brown color that it almost looked black. The children had created a realistic way of representing and understanding the effect of melanin on the color of human skin.

The concept of race is both easy and difficult to discuss. Most Americans believe they know the meaning of the term, yet we have no specific set of racial categories acceptable to the scientific community. In 1758, Carolus Linnaeus proposed the first racial classifications based largely on human geographical origins, but as Gould (2002) pointed out, J. F. Blumenbach has usually been credited as the originator of racial categories. It was Blumenbach who created the term *Caucasian,* and his taxonomy established a racial hierarchy with white people on top. This would be the foundation for much "scientific" theory and research in the eighteenth and early ninteenth centuries. In the 1930s, scientists such as anthropologist Franz Boas challenged theories describing a hierarchy of races (Gosset, 1997). In 1937, American historian Jacques Barzun bluntly denounced the spuriousness of race as a legitimate scientific concept:

> [Racial classifications] come and go and return, for the urge to divide mankind into fixed types and races is evidently endless. Each attempt only illustrates anew how race-groupings have been shaped not by nature but by the mode of thought or the stage of mechanical efficiency that mankind valued at the moment. The history of these attempts confirms . . . that race-theories occur in the minds of men for an ulterior purpose. (1965, p. 196)

The series of paintings on "Caste" from the Spanish colonial era (see Figure 1.3) supports Barzun's point about the historical effort to find ways to divide and label human beings. Current research on the human genome emphasizes human similarities

> In claiming the unity of the human race we resist the unsavory assumption of higher and lower races.
>
> **Alexander von Humboldt (1769–1859)**

FIGURE 1.3 Eighteenth-Century Paintings of "Castas"

A series of Mexican paintings from the eighteenth century identifies categories of people (such as Indian, Spanish, or African) and names the children of mixed marriages. For example, the child of a Spanish and African couple is a Mulatto, and the child of a Spanish and Mulatto couple is a Morisco. In these three paintings, the artist illustrates how descendants of a Spanish and Indian couple can regain status as a white person. The child of the Spanish and Indian couple is a Mestizo, the child of a Spanish and Mestizo couple is a Castiza, and the child of a Spanish and Castiza couple is considered Spanish.

Source: De Espanol, y India, na ce Mestiza (190.1996.1), De Espanol, y Mestiza, Castiza (190.1996.3), and De Espanol, y Castiza, Espanol (190.1996.2). c. 1775, Francisco Clapera, Frederick and Jan Mayer Collection, Denver Art Museum.

rather than differences. According to this research, every woman living today has the mitochondrial DNA of a single woman who lived approximately 150,000 years ago, and every man living today has the Y chromosome of a single man who lived approximately 59,000 years ago (Wade, 2006). Scientists involved in this research report that 85% of human genetic variation occurs *within* groups and only 15% of human genetic variation occurs *between* groups. And yet, as Olson (2002) acknowledges, "societies have built elaborate systems of privilege and control around these miniscule genetic differences" (p. 69).

Although race is based on perceptions of physical differences, **ethnicity** is based on cultural differences (Jones, 1997). Ethnicity refers to the historic origins of an individual's family. For immigrants to the United States, ethnicity identifies their country of origin or that from which their ancestors came: Poland, Mexico, China, Italy, Cuba, Ethiopia, Russia, or Iran. For those whose ancestors emigrated from different countries of origin, ethnicity can represent a choice about personal identity based on culture. As Dalton (2008) explains it,

> [Ethnicity] describes that aspect of our heritage that provides us with a mother tongue and that shapes our values, our worldview, our family structure, our rituals, the foods we eat, our mating behavior, our music—in short, much of our daily lives. (p. 16)

Most Americans identify more than one ethnic group as part of their heritage, and for that reason ethnicity may have little meaning because of a lack of strong cultural identification with one of those groups. Some of us with multiple ethnic heritages may claim a stronger cultural affinity with one of the groups. A person may be a mixture of Irish, German, and Swedish ancestry and yet, perhaps because her surname is Irish or because Irish traditions were more strongly promoted in her family, she identifies most strongly with being Irish (Banks, 1994).

For Native Americans, ethnicity generally refers to tribal affiliation: Apache, Kwakiutl, Cherokee, Seminole, Mohawk, Hopi, or Lakota. For most African Americans, ethnic identity was obliterated by the experience of slavery, making it practically impossible to trace one's heritage to a specific tribal group such as Hausa, Ibo, Tsutsi. The introduction of the term "African American" in the 1980s was intended to provide an "ethnic" label for black people as distinct from race (Dalton, 2008). Because of the unique preservation of his oral family history, Alex Haley (1976) was able to reconnect with his ethnic group as described in the book, *Roots*.

Nationality refers to the nation in which one has citizenship. To ask people about their nationality is to ask where they reside or what nation is identified on their passport. People curious about someone's ethnic heritage often ask, "What is your nationality?" instead of "What is your ethnic background?" Being asked about one's nationality may be considered quite insulting because it implies that the questioner does not perceive the other person as American but as belonging to another country (see Figure 1.4). What do the terms *race, ethnicity,* and *nationality* have in common? They each refer to people considered to represent minority groups in the United States.

What are minority groups and why are they called minority groups?

The term **minority group** does not necessarily imply anything about the number of people in the group; however, it does imply something about their power. Minority group members possess limited power compared to members of a dominant group. It is possible for a minority group to be larger than a dominant group because it is the group's lack of power that defines it. When the white minority held power in South Africa, black South Africans were the majority in terms of numbers, but they were considered a minority group because they lacked power under the racist system of apartheid. Women in the United States are included as a minority in affirmative action plans and equity proposals even though they are numerically the majority because historically they have not held as much power as have men.

A person in a minority group must overcome obstacles—handicapping conditions—related to her or his group identification based on such factors as race, ethnicity, gender, sexual orientation, socioeconomic status, religion, or disability. Some people refer to minority groups and diversity as if the two terms are synonymous, but **diversity** refers to the presence of human beings with perceived or actual differences based on a variety of human characteristics. Diversity exists both in classrooms having no minorities and in classrooms where all students are African American; too often, these differences can result in some children being stigmatized and marginalized by other children. The concept of diversity includes minority groups as well as groups identified according to differences based on age, marital status, parental status, educational status, geographic location, physical characteristics, and other factors that influence individual personality and behavior. As Banks (2006) has noted, it is imperative to recognize the interactions of all these variables in order to understand individual behavior.

How have minority groups been perceived by the majority?

The majority group has created derogatory names for members of minority groups. When a dominant group has the power to label a subordinate group, others will consistently associate that label with individuals from the subordinate group. The power to label results in the power to define the people in a group, not only for the dominant group, but sometimes for the members of the labeled group as well. In recognition of the power of such labels, many groups have engaged in efforts to label themselves in a positive way. In the 1960s, many in the group that the majority had labeled "colored people" or "Negroes" rejected the majority group's names and chose to call themselves "blacks." This was accompanied by calls for "black power" and claims that "Black is beautiful." Many black people continue to prefer that designation because they believe it makes a positive contribution to an individual's sense of identity. Since the 1960s, "African American" has also become a popular choice among black people and others as a positive label for this group.

When a majority group has the power to label and define those belonging to a minority group,

FIGURE 1.4 Nationalities of Ethnic Immigrants to America

Source: Schaefer, R.T. *Racial and ethnic groups, 10th Edition*, Copyright © 2006, p. 101. Reprinted by permission of Pearson Education, Inc., Upper Saddle River, NJ.

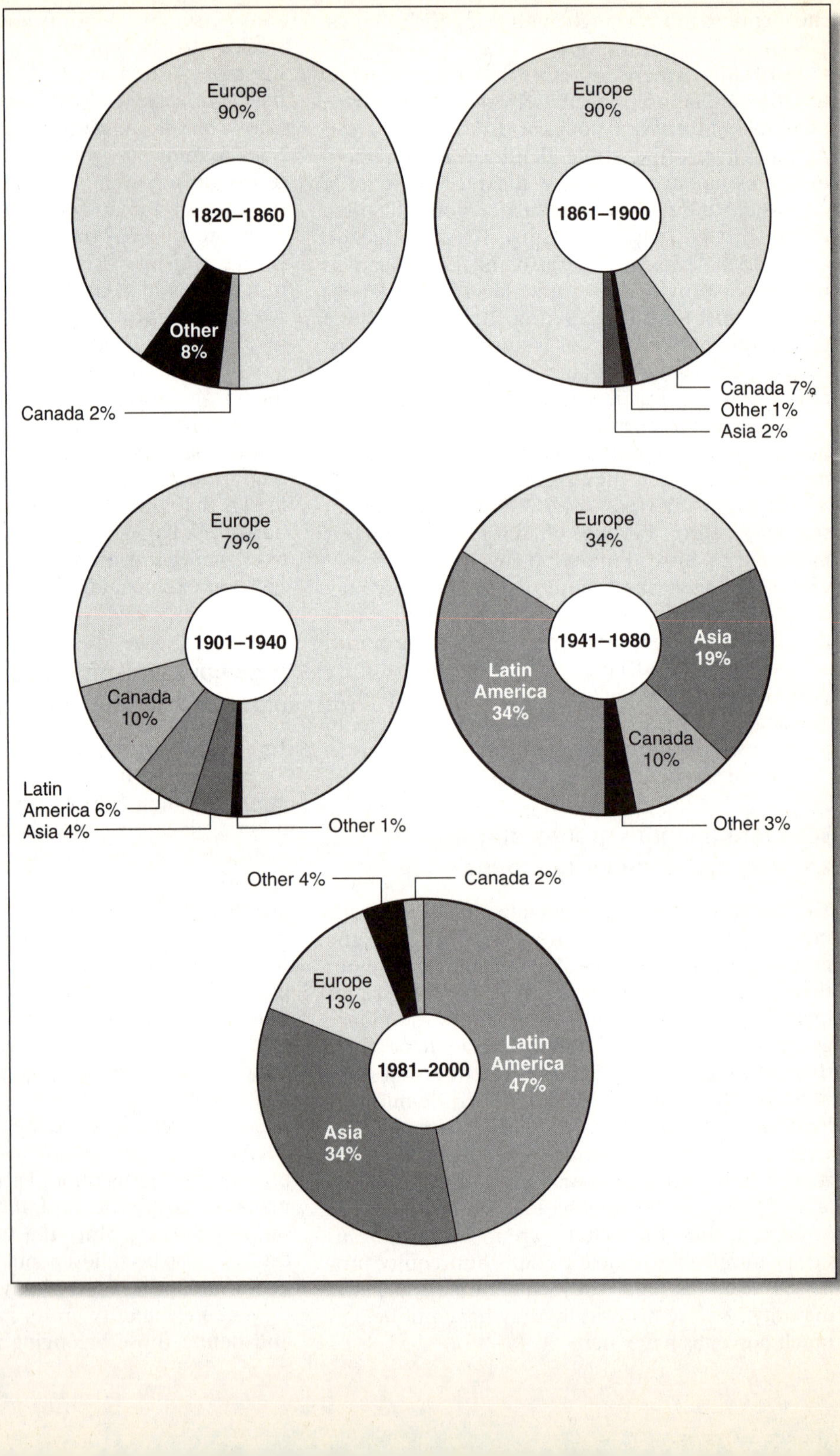

they also can control subordinate group members, obviously by limiting their opportunities, but sometimes in more subtle ways as well. Macedo and Bartoleme (2001) compare the term *migrant,* which most often labels Latinos seeking economic opportunity in the United States, with the term *settlers,* which is used to designate English and other Europeans immigrating to America to improve their economic opportunities. Reactions to the two terms are significantly different, even though both terms describe people engaged in a similar quest.

How have labels been used to define and control subordinate groups?

The idea that the power to label equals the power to define, which equals the power to control was illustrated by the 2007 media coverage of the incident at Virginia Polytechnic Institute in which South Korean student Seung-Chi Ho killed 32 students and wounded 25 others before taking his own life. The media reported Cho's history of mental illness and that he was hospitalized for a time, but the coverage never mentioned that Cho's violence was unusual for the 46% of American adults diagnosed with some form of mental illness at some point in their lives (Friedman, 2008). Perhaps the failure to report lack of violence from mentally ill people reflects the history of various forms of American media labeling and portraying mentally ill people as dangerous.

In American films, mentally ill characters are often presented as prone to violent acts, whether in classic films like Alfred Hitchcock's *Psycho* or in numerous low-budget "slasher" films. In addition, the news media tends to report incidents of violence when mentally ill people are responsible: A 2005 survey of 70 major U.S. newspapers found that almost 40% of the stories on mentally ill people emphasized how dangerous they are, and yet research indicates that mentally ill people are responsible for only 3–5% of the violence in the United States (Friedman, 2008). Since studies have found that drinking alcohol increases violent behavior, Friedman concludes: "You have far more to fear from an intoxicated businessman in a suit than from a homeless man muttering on the street corner" (2008, p. A3). This overemphasis on violent behavior and the lack of information on the reality of mental illness, including information about people who have achieved success despite having a mental disorder, has caused many Americans to accept the label and to stereotype mentally ill people as dangerous and violent. For this reason, many Americans believe that mentally ill people should not receive outpatient care, but be institutionalized for their own protection and for the protection of society.

Labels related to mental illness are official, formal, bureaucratic terms; others are informal and societal—terms used or heard by people in everyday life. The existence of **derisive labels**—terms reflecting a sense of contempt or ridicule based on factors such as race, class, disability, sexual orientation, and gender—and their variety suggest the extent to which prejudices exist. Words such as *nigger, spic, chink, buck,* and *squaw* represent only a few of the racist terms in English. Wessler (2001) described the observations of elementary educators who have heard children using such labels, especially during recess where children may feel they have more freedom to express themselves. Stephan (1999) insists that reducing prejudice requires that teachers help children become aware of the tendency to attach negative labels to others. After all, such words can be heard on the playgrounds of America, and some, for example, the word *squaw,* even show up in instructional materials such as maps, textbooks, or activities.

One theory of the origin of the word *squaw* is that it derives from a French word meaning vagina and was used by early French trappers to indicate that they wanted sex, usually followed by an offer to pay or barter something (Chavers, 1997). Other linguists claim that squaw has a more neutral origin, merely referring to a woman, but as Green (1975) demonstrated, its use has been consistently negative. The word *squaw* can still be found in elementary school materials and in names for lakes and other geographic sites around the United States.

Because they objected to the term, high school students in Minnesota successfully lobbied the state legislature to change the names of state geographical sites containing "squaw," yet at least one white community in Minnesota, Squaw Lake, refused to change. Chavers (1977) reports that students have lobbied other state legislatures to delete squaw in geographic sites or town names because the word is offensive and insulting to Native American women.

The power of labels was the focus of a study that asked subjects to supervise groups whose task was to make a collective decision on various issues (Zimbardo, 2007). The "supervisor" listened to the group's conversation from an adjacent room, and was asked to evaluate the group's decision-making process using criteria provided that was supposed to describe good decision-making. If the group made a bad decision, the supervisor was supposed to give them an electric shock ranging from a mild shock at level one to the maximum level of ten. No one was actually shocked, but supervisors heard a recording that simulated people being shocked.

The researcher was interested in how supervisors would be affected by overhearing labels ascribed to a group. The subjects "overheard" the researcher talking to his assistant over the intercom, describing the group that the subject was asked to supervise as an "animalistic, rotten bunch," or as a "perceptive, thoughtful group," another group was not labeled either positively or negatively. Supervisors tended to give minimal shocks to all groups after the first trial, but as the experiment went on and groups continued to make bad decisions, the "punishment" chosen for the groups began to diverge. Supervisors tended to shock the group labeled "animalistic" with more intensity and they increased the shock level on subsequent decision-making exercises, whereas those teams labeled positively were given the smallest amount of shock and the neutral group fell in between. The study suggested that labels can enhance or diminish the human qualities we ascribe to others, and when human qualities are diminished, our concerns for not harming an individual or group may also be diminished.

What is the impact of labels on individuals who are labeled?

Wright (1998) believes that young children are only minimally aware of skin color and often unaware of race. Asked what color she was, a three-year-old black girl wearing a pink and blue dress responded, "I'm pink and blue. What color are you?" At about the age of four, children begin to understand that skin color is permanent, yet they do not regard it as negative. At five years of age, children are likely to become more interested in differences of skin color and may ask teachers many questions; they also begin to be aware of race and societal attitudes about racial differences. However, true racial awareness does not tend to become a significant issue until children are eight or nine years old. Because of children's growing awareness of skin color and racial attitudes, teachers must consciously confront name-calling and other forms of prejudice in their classrooms and on the playground.

Racist name-calling usually involves blatant, ugly words that carry harshly negative connotations: *coon, jungle bunny, gook, greaser, wetback, timber nigger.* What impact does it have on a child to hear such words? Sometimes members of a subordinate group believe and internalize myths, stereotypes, and prejudices expressed about their group by the dominant group. Even for those who do not internalize the negative messages, being called derisive names, especially by other children, has an impact on children and youth. Anthropologist Jamake Highwater, who was orphaned, Native American, and gay, commented on the many derisive terms he heard as a child:

> At first, the words had no meaning to me. Even when I was told their meaning, I couldn't easily grasp why they were supposed to be shameful . . . [They] were whispered in the classroom and remorselessly shouted when adults were not around. On the playground. In the locker room. In the darkness of the balcony at Saturday movie matinees. Those were the words that filled my childhood.
>
> They were words that aroused a sense of power and self-aggrandizement for those who shouted them; they brought shame and humiliation in those at whom they were shouted. Words were weapons, fired in rapid succession in order to hold back an intrusion of outsiders—the "them"—aliens, deviants, perverts, and barbarians. Words were a psychological Great Wall of China, staunchly guarding the frontiers of conformity and an unrelenting notion of the superiority of insiders. (2001, pp. 24–25)

Highwater believes that derisives, derogatory terms, damage individuals in the dominant group as well as those in subordinate or minority groups because derisive language creates boundaries. Derisive terms define the oppressor as superior and the oppressed as inferior. Herbst (1997) agrees that such terms create suspicion, fear, and contempt in members of dominant groups and arouse frustration and anger in individuals from subordinate groups. In his struggle for social justice, Martin Luther King, Jr. (1963) insisted that his followers not hate oppressors, but instead hate oppression. Some groups have tried to take over certain words, to "own" them and reshape them to make them less hurtful. African Americans, especially urban blacks, have taken the word *nigger* for their own purposes, as can be heard in their rap music (Kennedy, 2002). Gay men and lesbians, especially young people, are using the word *queer* as a generic term for the gay community, and courses in queer studies have sprung up on college campuses in an attempt to change formal, bureaucratic language (Jagose, 1996).

How are negative bureaucratic terms as harmful as social derisive terms?

When we think of derisive terms, we usually think of informal, social labels. Derisive terms for social class, such as *hillbilly* or *redneck,* often have a regional origin but may become widespread as in *white trash,* a term that evolved into a variety of forms including *trailer park trash.* Yet some argue that the most harmful derisive terms for low-income people come from formal sources such as government reports and scholarly studies; these terms include *culturally deprived, culturally disadvantaged, welfare households, inner-city residents.* What images do such terms conjure? Derisive bureaucratic terms are powerful purveyors of negative images primarily because they have the sanction of authority behind them.

In addition to negative images, derisive bureaucratic terms send a negative message. Being labeled culturally deprived represents a form of blaming the victim. What group are we talking about? What do they lack? The term *cultural deprivation* suggests that poor people lack an ability to appreciate arts and humanities; it does not acknowledge the reality that they are economically deprived and need financial assistance for such things as job training, employment, and better health care. Labeling poor people *culturally deprived* implies that a deficiency in cultural qualities, perhaps certain values, is the cause of their problems.

People with disabilities are labeled with derisive social and bureaucratic terms. Around the world people have heard and told "moron jokes" as children, and Linton (1998) argues that when children insult others by calling them *retard, dummy, cripple,* or *gimp,* they are asserting a claim to normalcy and rejecting those who are deviant and unacceptable because of disability. In a bureaucratic setting, the term *handicapped* labels people as deviant. Since the 1950s, people with disabilities have objected to the term *handicapped* and have lobbied with some success to have it removed from common bureaucratic usage. Derisive bureaucratic terms are also represented by such phrases as the retarded and the disabled. These terms isolate one adjective for a disabled person and make it a noun to label the group. According to Charlton (1998), people with disabilities persistently object to the practice of labeling them with such adjectives because "their humanity is stripped away and the person is obliterated, only to be left with the condition— disability" (p. 54).

> One may no more live in the world without picking up the moral prejudices of the world than one will be able to go to Hell without perspiring.
>
> H. L. Mencken (1880–1956)

To understand what Charlton means, imagine a person who is either active or acquiescent, bold or bashful, cynical or compassionate, devilish or devout, and now add disabled to the description. If the last adjective is singled out and made a noun, that word defines the person being imagined. Using a term like *the disabled* defines and diminishes people with a disability because it focuses on only one aspect of their existence. Historically, nondisabled people in America all too often have viewed people with disabilities as unable to care for themselves. *The retarded* and *the disabled* have been institutionalized and the action was justified by claims that it was "for their own good." The history of institutionalized people with disabilities illustrates the power of everyday language labels to define and ultimately control the quality of life for those who have been labeled.

How has our society responded to social problems experienced by minority groups?

Ryan (1976) described two radically different approaches involved in addressing social problems. The **exceptionalistic perspective** focuses on individuals; it perceives all problems as local, unique, and unpredictable. Because problems are viewed as a consequence of *individual* defect, accident, or unfortunate circumstance, proposed remedies must be tailored to fit each individual case that is an "exception" to the general situation. A criticism of this approach is that it treats only *symptoms* of problems and not causes; exceptionalistic remedies have been derided as "Band-Aid solutions" that alleviate but do not solve problems.

Ryan describes an alternative approach, a **universalistic perspective** that views social problems as systemic, beginning in fundamental social structures within a community or a society. Because social structures are inevitably imperfect and inequitable, the problems that emerge are predictable and preventable because they do not stem from a situation unique to one individual but rather from conditions common to many. The universalistic perspective emphasizes engaging in research to collect and analyze data and to identify patterns that predict certain outcomes. Once patterns and root causes are identified, appropriate solutions can be created and implemented through public action, institutional policy, or legislation. Research takes time, so the universalistic approach has been criticized because it does not address the immediate consequences of particular problems or assist people who are currently suffering.

To illustrate the difference between exceptionalistic and universalistic perspectives, Ryan describes two responses to the problem of smallpox. An exceptionalistic approach would be to provide smallpox victims with medical care to help them recover; a universalistic approach would first demand legislation to fund inoculation of the population to prevent the disease from spreading. The contrast is similar to a metaphor from Kilbourne (1999) about bodies floating down a river and ambulances being called to rescue the drowning people. Although rescuing people from the river is important, it is also important to send someone upstream to investigate how people are falling in (p. 30).

The metaphors illustrate a need for both approaches. While people are engaged in studying problems, help must be provided to those who are suffering right now. If everyone goes upstream to discover how people are falling into the river, no one is left to save people who are drowning; if everyone stays downstream to rescue drowning people, the cause of the problem will never be found. Neither perspective can be neglected in the efforts employed to solve social problems.

AFTERWORD

The chapter began by discussing diversity and individuality. Holding differing values is part of both diversity and individuality. The values we choose are influenced by our membership in groups defined by such factors as race, ethnicity, gender, and social class; however, the ultimate decision to embrace certain values is up to the individual. Almost everyone holds some values similar to those of their parents, and almost everyone holds some values different from those of their parents. We share values with friends, yet we hold some values that are different from theirs. Values, and the attitudes and beliefs that determine them, are part of the landscape of human differences. But beliefs and attitudes change as we learn more information that helps us to understand

> Freedom is the right to choose: the right to create for yourself the alternatives of choice. Without the possibility of choice and the exercise of choice, human beings are not human but instruments, things.
>
> **Archibald MacLeish (1892–1982)**

and appreciate diversity. For those interested in exploring their own attitudes concerning diversity issues, an Attitude Inventory is available on the MyEducationLab web site (www.myeducationlab.com). Respond to the statements now, and when you have finished reading this book, you may want to return to the Attitude Inventory and respond to the statements about these issues again.

Language is the primary tool we use to pursue understanding. When we use language that labels a group of people, we create misunderstanding. It is important to observe and evaluate the behaviors of others, but we will never understand them without interacting with them or reading what they have written. Confusing or ambiguous language is like a smudge on the lens of a microscope; it prevents us from having a clear understanding of our subject. This chapter has tried to clarify some confusing terms so that our view is not distorted as we begin our study of human differences.

When Jewish author Isaac Bashevis Singer was asked if he believed people had free will, he replied, "Of course we have free will, we have no choice." As citizens of a democracy, we have many choices. As human beings living in a diverse society surrounded by diverse global cultures, trying to understand human differences would seem to be a necessary choice. For every reader who has already made that choice, this book offers insights and information to enhance your understanding. For readers who have not made that choice, this book may help to create an understanding of why the choice is necessary. But it is still each person's choice to make; as Singer said, we have no choice about that.

TERMS AND DEFINITIONS

Attitude A cluster of particular related beliefs, values, and opinions

Beliefs Inferences a person makes about reality that take one of three forms: descriptive, evaluative, or prescriptive

Bias A preference or inclination, favorable or unfavorable, that inhibits impartial judgment

Bigotry Extreme negative attitudes leading to hatred of a group and persons regarded as members of the group

Derisive labels Names that reflect attitudes of contempt or ridicule for individuals in the group being named

Discrimination Actions or practices carried out by a member or members of dominant groups, or their representatives that have a differential and negative impact on a member or members of subordinate groups

Diversity The presence of human beings with perceived or actual differences based on a variety of human characteristics

Dogmatic To accept beliefs one has been taught without questioning them

Ethnicity Identification of an individual according to his or her national origin and/or distinctive cultural patterns

Exceptionalistic perspective Views social problems as private, local, unique, exclusive, and unpredictable, a consequence of individual defect, accident, or unfortunate circumstance, which requires that all proposed remedies be tailored to fit each individual case

Indoctrination Instruction whose purpose is to force the learner to accept a set of values or beliefs, to adopt a particular ideology or perspective

Minority group A subordinate group whose members have significantly less power to control their own lives than do members of a dominant, or majority group

Nationality The nation in which an individual has citizenship status

Prejudice A negative attitude toward a group and persons perceived to be members of that group; being predisposed to behave negatively toward members of a group

Race A social concept with no scientific basis that categorizes people according to obvious physical differences such as skin color

Stereotype A positive or negative trait or traits ascribed to a certain group and to most members of that group

Universalistic perspective Views social problems as public, national, general, inclusive, and predictable; a consequence of imperfect and inequitable social arrangements which require research to identify their patterns and causes so that remedial institutional action can be taken to eliminate these problems and prevent them from reoccurring

Values Combinations of attitudes that generate action or the deliberate choice to avoid action

DISCUSSION EXERCISES

Discussion exercises are provided in which groups of three to five students can delve deeper into the content presented in the chapter.

Clarification Exercise—My Values: What I Believe

Directions: Create personal responses to each of the ten items below. Share your responses individually with several others and listen to their responses to those same items.

1. *Past and future:* Assume that you will have children. Why (or why not) will you treat your children the same way that your parents treated you?
2. *Success and achievement:* If you could wake up tomorrow morning having gained any one ability or quality, what would it be? Why would you choose that ability or quality?
3. *Friendship and personal life:* If you made up your mind to do something, but when your friends heard about it, they strongly advised you not to, why might you do it anyway?
4. *Possessions and priorities:* If you could have a wonderful new experience that you would remember for the rest of your life or be given something you have always wanted, which would you choose?
5. *Money and values:* Would you rather be given $100,000 for your own use or $1 million to give anonymously to strangers? If you prefer the former, what would you do with the money? If you prefer the latter, how would you arrange to contribute it?
6. *Living and dying:* Has your life ever changed dramatically as the result of some seemingly random event over which you had no control? To what degree, or in what ways, do you feel you have control over the course of your life?
7. *Physical well-being and disabling conditions:* Would you like to have a child much smarter than you? Much more handsome or beautiful than you? Would it bother you to have a child who had a disability or was physically unattractive?
8. *Leadership and responsibility:* If you were given full responsibility for creating a one-hour television show that millions of people would watch, about anything you wanted, what would it be about?
9. *Individuality and choices:* If you could be granted one magical power, what would you ask for?
10. *Social and personal responses:* When should it be illegal to help a terminally ill person to die? If someone is not dying but has chronic pain, should that person be assisted to commit suicide? What if the person is in emotional rather than physical pain?

Selected and adapted from Gregory Stock, *The Book of Questions* (1987) and *The Kid's Book of Questions* (1988) (New York: Workman Publishing).

Intergroup Exercise—A Mutual Support Dilemma

Directions: Examine the case situation explained below. Discuss it with those in your assigned group. Respond to each of the questions. Then, explain your group position to the class.

The Story of Mary and Luke: A Mutual Support Dilemma

Mary and Luke were married during their senior year in college. After their graduation, Mary took a secretarial job in the registrar's office of the university where Luke was attending graduate school. Mary worked for five years while Luke completed his doctoral degree. Their first and only child was born the second of the five years and Mary missed only two months of work at that time.

Luke has now been offered an assistant professorship at a prominent eastern school and is eager to accept it. Mary has applied and been accepted into graduate school at the University of Chicago. She is eager to accept the assistantship that she has been offered.

Mary argues that Luke should give her the chance for an education now that he has completed his. She also reminds him that he has been offered a job at the Chicago Junior College. Luke says that he intends to take the job in the east and that Mary can find someplace out there to go to school.

If Mary refuses to follow him, Luke promises to file for a divorce and seek custody of their three-year-old daughter.

Questions for discussion:

1. What would you do if you were Mary?
2. What advice do you have for Luke?
3. How could this situation be handled so that neither Mary nor Luke loses?
4. Does your group agree that either Mary or Luke loses?

REFERENCES

Andrzejewski, J. (Ed.). (1996). Definitions for understanding oppression and social justice. *Oppression and social justice: Critical frameworks.* Boston, MA: Pearson Custom Publishing.

Provides definitions for a variety of terms essential for discussing intergroup relations.

Aronson, E. (2008). *The social animal* (10th ed.). New York, NY: Worth Publishers.

Presents an overview of research in social psychology and describes people behaving inconsistently with their expressed attitudes in Chapter 2 on conformity.

Banks, J.A. (1994). The complex nature of ethnic groups in modern society. In *Multiethnic education: Theory and practice* (3rd ed.). Boston, MA: Allyn & Bacon.

Describes ethnic diversity in the United States, assimilation issues that have historically confronted ethnic groups, and how ethnicity influences individual identity in contemporary society.

Banks, J.A. (2006). Multicultural education: Characteristics and goals. In J.A. Banks & C.A. McGee Banks (Eds.), *Multicultural education: Issues and perspectives* (6th ed.). New York, NY: Wiley.

Describes the evolution of multicultural education, the importance of group identification, and how implementation of multicultural education meets the needs of diverse students.

Barzun, J. (1965). *Race: A study in superstition* (rev. ed.). New York, NY: Harper & Row.

Explains why race is a pseudoscientific concept with an appendix of racial (mostly racist) quotes from authors, scientists, and mystics.

Bellah, R., Madsen, R., Sullivan, W., Swidler, A., & Tipton, S. (1991). *The good society.* New York, NY: Vintage.

Presents quantitative and qualitative data from interviews with Americans talking about what values and behavior are necessary for creating a good society.

Botkin, B.A. (1957). *A treasury of American anecdotes.* New York, NY: Bonanza Books.

Includes over 300 anecdotes about famous, infamous, and ordinary Americans; the Jefferson anecdote originally appeared in a German Almanac published in Pennsylvania.

Charlton, J.I. (1998). *Nothing about us without us.* Berkeley: University of California Press.

Examines the status of people with a disability in various cultures.

Chavers, D. (1997). Doing away with the "S" word. *Indian Country Today, 16*(37), 5.

Describes efforts of high school students to force Minnesota to change the names of state geographic features that include the word *squaw.*

Dalton, H. (2008). Failing to see. In P. Rothenberg (Ed.), *White privilege: Essential readings on the other side of racism* (3rd ed.). New York, NY: Worth.

Discusses race and ethnicity and how white has been defined as the norm in the United States, making white people oblivious to the role of race in the formation of their identity.

Feagin, J., & Feagin, C. (2008). Basic concepts in the study of racial and ethnic relations. In *Racial and ethnic relations* (8th ed.). Upper Saddle River, NJ: Prentice Hall.

Explains major terms and concepts in intergroup relations and includes a glossary for all terms used in the book.

Franklin, K. (2000). Anti-gay behaviors among young adults. *Journal of Interpersonal Violence, 15,* 339–363.

A survey of 484 young adults concerning their participation in name-calling, physical violence, or threats against homosexuals.

Friedman, R.A. (2008, July/August). Media and madness. *The American Prospect, 19*(7), A2–A4.

Discusses media portrayals and descriptions of people with mental illness as violent and cites research refuting these stereotypes.

Gamber, F. (2007, March/April). Stars come out for NAACP Image Awards. *The Crisis, 114*(2), 36–37.

Identifies the recipients being honored at the 2007 NAACP Image Awards.

Gosset, T.F. (1997). *Race: The history of an idea in America.* Dallas, TX: Southern Methodist University Press.

Describes attitudes about race in colonial America, the evolution of this concept into a pseudo-scientific theory in the nineteenth century, and its debunking by scholars in the 1930s.

Gould, S.J. (2002). The geometer of race. In *I have landed: The end of a beginning in natural history* (pp. 356–366). New York, NY: Harmony Books.

Describes the origins and influence of J. F. Blumenbach's theory of racial classifications.

Green, R. (1975). The Pocohontas perplex: Images of Indian women in American cultures. *Massachusetts Review, 16,* 698–714.

Discusses the historic use of the term *squaw.*

Haag, P. (2000). *Voices of a generation: Teenage girls report about their lives today.* New York, NY: Marlow.

Examines responses of more than 2,000 females, ages 11 to 17, to six questions revealing a variety of explicit and implicit issues related to their public and privates lives.

Haley, A. (1976). *Roots.* Garden City, NY: Doubleday.

Describes the author's use of family stories to establish his ethnic background in Africa.

Herbst, P. (1997). Ethnic epithets in society. In *The color of words: An encyclopedic dictionary of ethnic bias in the United States* (pp. 255–259). Yarmouth, ME: Intercultural Press.

Describes the purpose of ethnic slurs and their effect on those who use them.

Herdt, G. (1997). *Same sex, different cultures: Exploring gay and lesbian lives.* Boulder, CO: Westview.

Reviews anthropological and cross-cultural evidence on attitudes toward sexual orientation and provides a glossary of essential terms.

Highwater, J. (1997). *The mythology of transgression: Homosexuality as metaphor.* New York, NY: Oxford University Press.

Describes the impact of derisive language directed against a child perceived by others as "different" in Chapter 2, "Inside the Walls" (pp. 23–30).

Jagose, A. (1996). *Queer theory: An introduction.* Washington Square, NY: New York University Press.

Explains why the term "queer" has evolved from derogatory slang to an umbrella term for people with diverse sexual self-identifications.

Jones, J. (1997). *Prejudice and racism* (2nd ed.). New York, NY: McGraw-Hill.

Integrates data from psychology, sociology, and history to explain the relationship between prejudice and racism in their appropriate sociocultural historical context.

Kennedy, R. (2002). *Nigger: The strange career of a troublesome word.* New York, NY: Pantheon Books.

Discusses the various historical uses of the term "nigger," including the more recent attempts by some African Americans to use the word in positive ways.

Kilborn, P.T. (2005). The five-bedroom, six-figure rootless life. In *Class matters* (correspondents of the *New York Times*) (pp. 146–165). New York, NY: Times Books.

Examines the increasing geographical isolation for middle/upper-middle class Americans as suburbs segregate not only by class but also by race, religion, and ethnic origin.

Kilbourne, J. (1999). *Deadly persuasion: Why women and girls must fight the addictive power of advertising.* New York, NY: The Free Press.

Argues that advertising is a pervasive cultural phenomenon that encourages people to objectify each other in a way that diminishes the quality of human relationships.

King, M.L., Jr. (1963). *Strength to love.* Philadelphia, PA: Fortress.

Contains many sermons addressing the idea of not hating oppressors, including "Loving Your Enemies."

Kniker, C.R. (1977). *You and values education.* Columbus, OH: Charles E. Merrill.

Summarizes theory and research concerning values and describes alternative approaches to teaching values in schools.

Lappe, F.M. (1989). *Rediscovering America's values.* New York, NY: Ballantine.

Presents a dialogue with one perspective emphasizing individualism and the other perspective emphasizing communitarianism and egalitarianism.

LeBon, G. (1968). The mind of crowds. In R. Evans (Ed.), *Readings in collective behavior.* Chicago: Rand McNally.

Examines the general characteristics of crowds and crowd behavior, especially the influence of emotional and moral factors on the behavior of crowds.

Lefkowitz, B. (1997). *Our guys: The Glen Ridge rape and the secret life of the perfect suburb.* Berkeley: University of California Press.

Explains the contradictions reflected in the upbringing and behavior of "All American" boys from the suburbs who gang rape a mentally retarded girl.

Levin, J., & Levin, W. (1982). *The functions of discrimination and prejudice* (2nd ed.). New York, NY: Harper & Row.

Describes the functions of prejudice for both the majority and minority groups; describes causes and effects of prejudice; and provides definitions of critical terms.

Linton, S. (1998). Reassigning meaning. In *Claiming disability: Knowledge and identity* (pp. 8–33). New York, NY: New York University Press.

Discusses "nice words" and "nasty words" for disabled people, and explains why some people with disabilities have begun to use the word *crip* in a positive way.

Macedo, D., & Bartolome, L.I. (2001). *Dancing with bigotry: Beyond the politics of tolerance.* New York, NY: Palgrave.

Examines issues concerning language, race, ethnicity, and limitations of teaching tolerance; the discussion of migrant versus settlers is in Chapter 1.

Mead, C. (1985). *Champion: Joe Louis—black hero in white America.* New York, NY: Charles Scribner.

Describes the life and boxing career of Joe Louis and his struggles with racism.

Miller, C., & Swift, K. (2000). *Words and women.* San Jose, CA: iUniverse

Analyzes sexism in the English language and provides many examples; discusses the inclusion of racism and sexism in dictionaries on page 141.

Myrdal, G. (1944). *An American dilemma: The Negro problem and modern democracy.* New York, NY: Harper & Row.

Describes values and contradictions in American culture and how they relate to the pervasive prejudice in American society.

Newberg, A., & Waldman, M.R. (2006). *Why we believe what we believe: Uncovering our biological needs for meaning, spirituality, and truth.* New York, NY: Free Press.

Proposes a new way of thinking about how convictions develop and influence individuals, based on recent research on how the brain perceives (and transforms) reality.

Olson, S. (2002). *Mapping human history: Discovering the past through our genes.* Boston, MA: Houghton Mifflin.

Describes human history as revealed by recent research on DNA that has concluded that human beings share a common African ancestor and do not consist of separate races.

Pagels, E. (2006). *The Gnostic gospels.* London, England: Phoenix.

Examines Gnostic beliefs as related to debates among early Christians regarding beliefs about Christ's resurrection and divinity, monotheism, and gender roles in the church.

Raths, L., Harmin, M., & Simon, S. (1978). *Values and teaching: Working with values in the classroom* (2nd ed.). Columbus, OH: Charles E. Merrill.

Addresses the issue of traditional approaches to teaching values as forms of indoctrination and describes these approaches.

Risberg, D.F. (1978, June 18). *Framework and foundations: Setting the stage and establishing norms.* Paper presented at the first annual National Conference on Human Relations, Minneapolis, MN.

Describes the development of human relations as an academic discipline incorporating knowledge from other disciplines but creating its own structure, paradigms, and language.

Ryan, W. (1976). *Blaming the victim* (2nd ed.). New York, NY: Vintage.

Explains exceptionalistic and universalistic perspectives on pages 17–20.

Schaefer, R.T. (2008). *Racial and ethnic groups* (11th ed.). Upper Saddle River, NJ: Pearson.

Provides information on racial and ethnic minorities, but also includes chapters on women, religious diversity, immigrants, and cross-cultural comparisons.

Simpson, G.E., & Yinger, J.M. (1985). *Racial and cultural minorities: An analysis of prejudice and discrimination* (5th ed.). New York, NY: Plenum.

Examines causes and consequences of prejudice and discrimination in the United States and includes definitions of important terms and concepts.

Stephan, W. (1999). *Reducing prejudice and stereotyping in schools.* New York, NY: Teachers College Press.

Reviews theories of prejudice and stereotyping, examines conditions to promote changes in negative attitudes, and describes techniques for improving race relations in schools.

Terkel, S. (1980). *American dreams: Lost and found.* New York, NY: Ballantine.

Interviews diverse people about their perceptions of America, including First National Bank board member Gaylord Freeman.

Terry, D., Hogg, M., & Duck, J. (1999). Group membership, social identity, and attitudes. In D. Abrams & M. Hogg (Eds.), *Social identity and social cognition* (pp. 280–314). Malden, MA: Blackwell.

Examines how attitude–behavior consistency is influenced by both congruence of individual attitudes with group norms and the significance to the individual of group membership.

Terry, R.W. (1993). *Authentic leadership: Courage in action.* San Francisco, CA: Jossey Bass.

Examines six leadership styles by defining leadership as the ability to frame issues correctly and to respond to issues by using power legitimately and ethically.

Wade, N. (2006). *Before the dawn: Recovering the lost history of our ancestors.* New York, NY: The Penguin Press.

Reviews recent scientific discoveries in biology and the social sciences and describes the increasingly detailed information now available on human evolution.

Wessler, S.L. (2001, January). Sticks and stones. *Educational Leadership, 58*(4), 28–33.

Describes the degrading and even violent language children use in schools and the impact of this language on its victims.

Wright, M.A. (1998). *I'm chocolate, you're vanilla: Raising healthy black and biracial children in a race-conscious world.* San Francisco, CA: Jossey-Bass.

Describes the changing awareness of skin color and social attitudes about race during child development and recommends strategies to preserve children's resilience and optimism.

Wright, W. (1983). *The Von Bulow affair.* New York, NY: Delacorte.

Provides a detailed review of the case; also of interest is the film "Reversal of Fortune" (based on Alan Dershowitz's book) available on videotape (Warner Brothers, 1990).

Zimbardo, P. (2007). *The Lucifer effect: Understanding how good people turn evil.* New York, NY: Random House.

Describes research in which college students role playing prison guards became abusive to those role playing prisoners and relates that study to the abuses at Abu Ghraib prison.

Zinn, H. (1990). *Declarations of independence: Cross-examining American ideology.* New York, NY: Harper-Collins.

Examines American beliefs and inconsistencies between behavior and ideals.

CHAPTER 2

Understanding Prejudice and Its Causes

"No one has ever been born a Negro hater, a Jew hater, or any other kind of hater. Nature refuses to be involved in such suicidal practices."

Harry Bridges (1900–1990)

No credible studies have concluded that prejudice is part of human nature, an innate outcome of being human. Instead, as Bridges suggests, prejudice is learned. It is also important to remember that prejudice is an attitude, not an action. Whether you are looking at definitions in a dictionary or reading scholarly writing, you will inevitably encounter puzzling uses of the term *prejudice.* Some people believe that prejudice involves a hatred of others, but hatred is bigotry. Based on their study of world cultures, anthropologists have argued that people everywhere in the world have prejudices, yet they do not claim that hatred—or bigotry—is widespread.

Confusion—not clarification—is caused by a definition suggesting that prejudice is synonymous with bigotry. Such a definition may cause many of us to deny that we are prejudiced: A bigot hates, and we are certain we don't hate anyone. In addition, we deny the pervasiveness of prejudice because we don't observe widespread hatred in the world; thus confusing prejudice with bigotry creates misunderstanding about the nature and extent of prejudice.

Conceptions and Misconceptions of Prejudice

What are examples of misconceptions about prejudice?

We confuse prejudice with bias, stereotypes, and bigotry. As defined in Chapter 1, bias is a mildly positive or negative feeling about someone or something; and to stereotype is to associate positive or negative traits with a group of people. **Prejudice** is a stronger feeling, but it is always negative, and it always refers to a group of people. Prejudice predisposes us to behave negatively toward certain others because of a group to which they belong. And when prejudice reaches the intensity of hatred, it becomes bigotry.

Some dictionaries define *prejudice* as the process of forming opinions without looking at relevant facts, yet people with prejudices may examine relevant facts and simply interpret them to confirm their prejudices. Other definitions describe prejudice as being irrational, implying that those we acknowledge as rational could not possibly be prejudiced. The problem here is that rational people also hold prejudices; we know this from reading what they wrote. Aristotle claimed that a woman was an inferior man. Abraham Lincoln believed black people were intellectually inferior to white people. Carroll (2001) quoted Martin Luther warning German Christians, "do not doubt that next to the devil you have no enemy more cruel, more venomous and virulent, than a true Jew" (p. 368). However, their prejudices did not deter any of these men from achieving significant improvements in human rights.

It is easy to smile at ancient racist or sexist attitudes and to denounce past prejudices as absurd, yet often we do not acknowledge current widespread prejudices that future generations may find just as absurd. In fifty or one hundred years, what will people think about the programs for the poor in the United States today? Or how people with disabilities were so often isolated or ignored? Or how gay men and lesbians were condemned by so many people?

How widespread is prejudice?

Although this book focuses on attitudes in the United States, prejudices are not limited to one country or one race. People living in nations around the world possess negative attitudes toward others within their own borders or close to them. Prejudices have been ignored, promoted, or tolerated, but rarely challenged. When prejudice has been challenged, the case often has become a *cause célèbre,* as when Emile Zola published "J'accuse," an essay denouncing anti-Semitism in France's prosecution of Alfred Dreyfus for treason (Bredin, 2008). Persistence of prejudice was illustrated by Jean-Paul Sartre's (1995) 1945 description of French anti-Semitic attitudes as Jews returned to France following World War II, even though French people were aware of the existence of Nazi concentration camps and of the genocide against the Jews.

> There are, in every age, new errors to be rectified, and new prejudices to be opposed.
>
> SAMUEL JOHNSON (1709–1784)

Today, nations around the world are being forced to confront historic prejudices because of economic globalization and population migrations that have created major demographic changes. Some responses to immigration have revealed the persistence of historic prejudices. In the opening paragraph of their book on prejudice and discrimination, Simpson and Yinger (1985) describe this phenomenon:

> Western European nations discovered that "guest workers," whom they have employed by the millions, are something more than cogs in an economic machine.
>
> And, for example,
>
> England, with a steady migration of people from India, Pakistan, Bangladesh, Africa, and the West Indies, found herself faced with problems of a color bar and passed an unprecedented law limiting immigration. Pressures against persons of Indian descent in the new nations of East Africa not only reshaped intergroup relations in those lands but influenced Britain's restrictive immigration policy (p. 3).

As long as people lived in relative isolation from others, prejudice against those who were far away was not necessarily harmful. In a global economy requiring functional and respectful relationships between nations, prejudice can be a destructive force both in the world and in individual societies, especially diverse societies (Gioseffi, 1993). Language is an important source for understanding a culture because analyzing language reveals a culture's assumptions, beliefs, values, and priorities, as well as examples of prejudice. Some countries are now addressing their historic prejudices by changing or eliminating media images and language that have promoted negative attitudes, especially toward racial or ethnic groups.

How are prejudices reflected in American media?

To understand how prejudices are transmitted in our culture, we need only observe some of the prevalent images of racial or cultural groups in society. As Giroux (1998) said,

> My concern with such representations . . . lies not in deciding whether they are "good" or "bad" but in analyzing them in relation to the pedagogical work they are doing. That is, what knowledge, values, and pleasures do such representations invite or exclude? (p. 27)

Look for magazine advertisements that depict Native Americans, Asian Americans, or Hispanic Americans. Why is it that most advertisements seem to use African American models to reflect diversity? If people of color are included in advertisements, why are they often featured in ways that reflect historic stereotypes? Native Americans are almost never portrayed as contemporary people but as nineteenth-century warriors; Asian Americans are often shown working at computers or in math-related professions; Mexican Americans are presented as gardeners or servants. Problems of omission and stereotyping affect other groups as well: People with disabilities are invisible, blue-collar workers are usually stereotyped, if they appear at all, and women appear frequently in advertisements as sex objects to sell products. Still, we typically don't recognize these advertisements as stereotypes because these images are so familiar that they seem not to be stereotypes at all, but rather to portray reality. This is one reason so many white Americans do not understand why Native Americans find offensive the use of Indian mascots for sports teams. (See Figure 2.1.)

Media portrayals of Muslim Americans represent the most recent example of pervasive stereotyping. Although anti-Muslim attitudes in the United States have a long history, Ansari (2004) insists that ever since the 1979 Iranian hostage crisis, the media has focused on activities of militant Muslims. Since then, media portrayals have often presented Muslims as "irrational, undemocratic (and) opposed to equality, freedom, and peace" (Khan, 2004, p. 100). According to McCloud (2006), the stereotype of Muslims as evil terrorists existed prior to 9/11, but such representations in the media have increased, and these portrayals have most likely contributed to the results reported in a 2004 opinion poll, where 25% of Americans said they had negative attitudes about Muslims and 50% supported the federal government restricting the civil liberties of Muslim Americans (Barrett, 2007). McCloud (2004) concluded that American media "have declared Islam and Muslims as violent, irrational, and anti-modern" (p. 79).

FIGURE 2.1

Source: John Branch, *San Antonio Express-News.*

Although the media bears some responsibility for reinforcing a variety of stereotypes, there are other sources that foster negative attitudes. One reason why many Americans may not even recognize portrayals of certain groups as stereotypical is because of the prejudices embedded in our language.

What examples of prejudice exist in our language?

One pattern observed in the English language has been called the **black/white syndrome**. Scholars report that this language pattern emerged in English long before the British knew that people described as black were living in Africa (Moore, 2006). Although the pattern likely originated in biblical language referring to Satan, evil, and hell as black or dark, it has been argued that a consistently negative pattern for references to black affected British perceptions of Africans and that negative connotations for blackness were readily applied to all dark-skinned people they encountered. A negative pattern for black has persisted in the English language, as can be seen in familiar phrases: black deed, black day, black hearted, black mass, black magic, the Black Death, black thoughts, black looks, and blacklist. Such words and phrases illustrate the point made by linguist Skuttnab-Kangas (2000), "Dominant groups keep a monopoly of defining others, and it is their labels we see in dictionaries" (p. 154).

Skuttnab-Kangas also argues that labeling others includes "the power to define oneself" by not having to accept the definitions others have for your group. It should not be surprising that references to "white" in the English language follow a consistently positive pattern: telling little white lies, having a white wedding, cheering white knights (in shining armor), indicating approval by saying "that's really white of you," and even engaging in white-collar crime (perceived as less harmful than other crimes). Some authors have exploited the pervasive black/white pattern by deliberately using white as a negative term, invoking images of sterility, death, or evil to shock readers with unexpected associations. Robert Frost employed this reversal in some of his poems, and it was no accident that Herman Melville chose to make Moby Dick, the symbol of evil in Ahab's obsession, a white whale.

Sometimes prejudice is not obvious, as in the expression, "Where there's a will there's a way." At first glance, this expression seems nothing more than an attempt to encourage children and youth to try hard, but it has another meaning: If all that it takes to be successful is to have the will to succeed, then those people who are not successful are at fault for their failure because they just didn't "try" hard enough. This belief leads to blaming the victim, providing an ethical escape for middle-class people. After all, if they were successful because they worked hard, then someone who is poor must not have worked hard enough, perhaps because they are lazy or incompetent.

Such stereotypes for "the poor" reinforces the conclusion that poor people are responsible for their poverty, and the rest of us are under no obligation to help them. Other stereotypes may be revealed in expressions. When people negotiate with the seller on the price of a product they might say, "I Jewed him down," alluding to an old stereotype. Parents and teachers have been overheard telling children to stop behaving "like a bunch of wild Indians."

> You can tell the ideals of a nation by its advertisements.
>
> NORMAN DOUGLAS (1868–1952)

Teenagers who say, "That's so gay" do not intend it as a compliment. Boys are still ridiculed by comments such as "he throws like a girl" or "he's a sissy." Children are no longer limited to the term *sissy.* Today, even elementary children can be heard calling one another a *faggot.* They may not be certain what the word means, but they know it is a negative term (Wessler, 2001).

And then there are jokes, based on racial, ethnic, gender, or other prejudices. When we complain that these jokes aren't funny, we are likely to be told we don't have a sense of humor: "It was a joke!" Just a joke. Although people are more careful today about telling racist jokes, sexist jokes are frequently told at work and in school. Perhaps the numerous examples of sexist words and phrases in our language make it easier to express sexist attitudes publicly.

How does gender prejudice in our language promote sexist attitudes?

Unlike many other languages, English does not have a neutral pronoun that includes both men and women, so the word *he* is used to refer to someone of indeterminate gender. *Man* has traditionally been used in words or phrases where the referent could be female (even though there are neutral nouns such as *human* and *people*). Some people continue to insist that *man* is generic when used in words such as *businessman, chairman, congressman, fireman, layman, mailman, policeman, salesman, spokesman,* and *statesman,* but studies do not support the claim. Arliss (1991) described studies using subjects ranging from elementary children to adults; all concluded that generic language invoked mental images of males.

In a study reported by Miller and Swift (2000) involving 500 junior high students, one group of students received instructions to draw pictures of "early man" engaged in various activities and to give each person drawn a name (so researchers could be certain that a man or woman was the subject of the drawing). The majority of students of both sexes tended to draw only males for every activity identified except the one representing infant care, and even for that activity, 49% of boys drew a male image. A second group of students was instructed to draw pictures of "early people" engaged in the same activities and to give each human figure drawn a name; once again, the majority of the humans drawn by both sexes were male. It is possible that the phrase *early people* sounded strange and that many students translated it as "cave men" and drew male pictures. The third group of students was asked to draw pictures of "early men and early women," once again giving names to human figures. Only in this group did the figures drawn by students include a significant number of female images, but even with these instructions, some students of both sexes drew only male figures.

> I am, in plainer words, a bundle of prejudices—made up of likings and dislikings.
>
> **Charles Lamb (1775–1834)**

What sexist terms for men could be considered derisive?

Although a plethora of derisive terms exist for women, derisive language directed at men often sends a mixed message. It may be intended as an insult to call a man a *prick* or a *bastard,* but it can also be interpreted as the speaker being envious of the man's power or position. Men may feel that they have to be tough, ruthless, and relentless if they are going to be successful in a "dog eat dog world"; such language could be regarded as a compliment to a man's prowess, his masculinity.

In American English, unambiguously derisive terms for men often accuse a man of being feminine. No little boy wants to be called a *sissy;* no man wants to be called a *wimp* or a *pussy.* Although a man may not like being called a name that implies he acts like a woman, according to Baker (1981), it is even more insulting to be called a name suggesting that a woman controls him, that he's *pussy whipped.* Men often use such language in a joking manner, but the message is serious.

That it is an insult for a man to be compared to a woman was illustrated at a recent summer festival. The dunking booth was not open yet, but a man and his son were getting it ready. Three young men came up to the booth and volunteered to be dunked. The man thanked them but said he had all the volunteers he needed. Animated by the alcohol they had consumed, the three of them badgered the man for several minutes before they gave up. As they walked away, the man at the booth said, "Good-bye, girls!" One of the young men turned around quickly and shouted, "What the fuck did you call me?" The vehemence of the young man's response was both surprising and disturbing as he came storming back. Even though the father had his son next to him, the young man was prepared to use violence to defend his manhood against such a degrading insult.

A mother and daughter were standing nearby in a line for face painting. Having observed this confrontation, the mother shouted sarcastically to the young man, "Oh, what a terrible thing to be called!" He looked over at the face-painting line, and other mothers standing with their daughters shouted similar comments. As the young man looked at them, his face betrayed his confusion. His body had swelled up with anger, but now it seemed to deflate.

His shoulders drooped and his expression became almost sheepish. As he approached the man at the dunking booth, he was still angry but not to the point of engaging in violence. After a brief conversation, a security officer appeared to escort the young man away. Considering the hostility aroused by such a flippant remark, one has to wonder about the attitudes males are being taught concerning women. Is it possible for a man to hate the idea of being called a female and not subconsciously hate women as well?

Aren't some prejudices positive?

Some people misuse the term *prejudice* by saying they are prejudiced *for* something, but a prejudice is always a negative attitude. A milder attitude of liking or disliking anything or anyone is a bias; however, the concept of prejudice involves learning to fear, mistrust, and strengthen stereotypes we have been taught about other groups of people. Once we learn to be prejudiced against a certain group, we tend to *behave* in negative ways toward others who appear to be members of that group. Negative behavior is discrimination: We no longer merely hold a negative attitude—we have acted on that attitude.

Consequences and Causes of Prejudice

With regard to discriminatory actions, Allport (1979) identified five negative behaviors caused by prejudice: (1) *verbal abuse* against others that occurs among friends or results in name-calling directed at others from a particular group. Name-calling can escalate into (2) *physical assaults*. The victim doesn't even have to be a member of the despised group to be assaulted; anyone could be a victim by being perceived as one of "them." When a large group of ethnic Hmong from Southeast Asia settled in a Wisconsin community of 50,000 people, some local citizens did not accept them. A Japanese foreign exchange student who attended a college in that community was severely beaten by a white man in the mistaken belief that his victim was Hmong. Another common example of violence based on misperceptions is that heterosexual men have been physically assaulted because they were perceived to be gay.

If prejudice evolves into bigotry, one's hatred can lead to (3) *extreme violence*, including the desire to commit murder. Such behavior is now called a "hate crime." In 1982, two Detroit men lost their jobs at an automobile factory and believed it was related to the popularity of imported Japanese cars. When they encountered Vincent Chin, a Chinese American, they mistakenly thought he was Japanese. Motivated by hatred and rage, they brutally murdered him. If homicidal rage spreads, it might lead to the extreme form of violence called **genocide**—the systematic and deliberate extermination of a nationality or a racial or ethnic group (Feagin & Feagin, 2008). A person can play a passive role that still supports genocide. After World War II, most Germans (also Poles, Austrians, and others) claimed they didn't know that six million Jews were killed in concentration camps; persuasive evidence has been gathered to argue that they knew but were not concerned enough to do anything about it (Goldhagen, 2002).

In contrast to confrontational negative behavior stemming from prejudice and bigotry, a more passive negative response to prejudice is to avoid members of other groups. We do this by (4) *limiting our interactions* with people from racial or ethnic groups other than our own. Measuring attitudes about avoiding others was the focus of research by Bogardus; this study used a Social Distance Scale in which people encounter a list of racial, ethnic, and religious groups and are asked to rank them in order of preference (Schaefer, 2008). People consistently reveal a preference for those groups most like their own, and they have less regard for people from groups they perceive as least like themselves.

Another way to avoid certain groups is (5) to *engage in or condone discrimination* in such areas as education, employment, and housing. To illustrate this behavior, consider how people choose what sort of neighborhood they want to live in. In the 1960s, when courts ordered urban school districts to desegregate, many school administrators responded by busing students to different schools, a controversial solution that caused massive movement of white families from urban neighborhoods to racially segregated suburbs, the **white flight** phenomenon (see Figure 2.2). Despite the passage of the 1968 National Fair Housing Act, studies have documented the preference of most white Americans to live in racially segregated neighborhoods (Farley, 2005; Massey, 2001). As Massey noted, the Fair Housing Act "theoretically put an end to housing discrimination; however, residential segregation proved to be remarkably persistent" (p. 424).

FIGURE 2.2

Neighborhood Preference of White Respondents

In a study cited by Farley (2005), subjects were shown diagrams of neighborhoods consisting of 15 homes with an X on the home in the center of the neighborhood indicating the subject's home. Each shaded home represented an African American family. White respondents were asked: How comfortable would they feel in each neighborhood? If they were uncomfortable, would they leave? Would they move into such a neighborhood? The percentage not willing to live in those neighborhoods where only a fifth or a third of homeowners were African Americans illustrates attitudes that produced white flight.

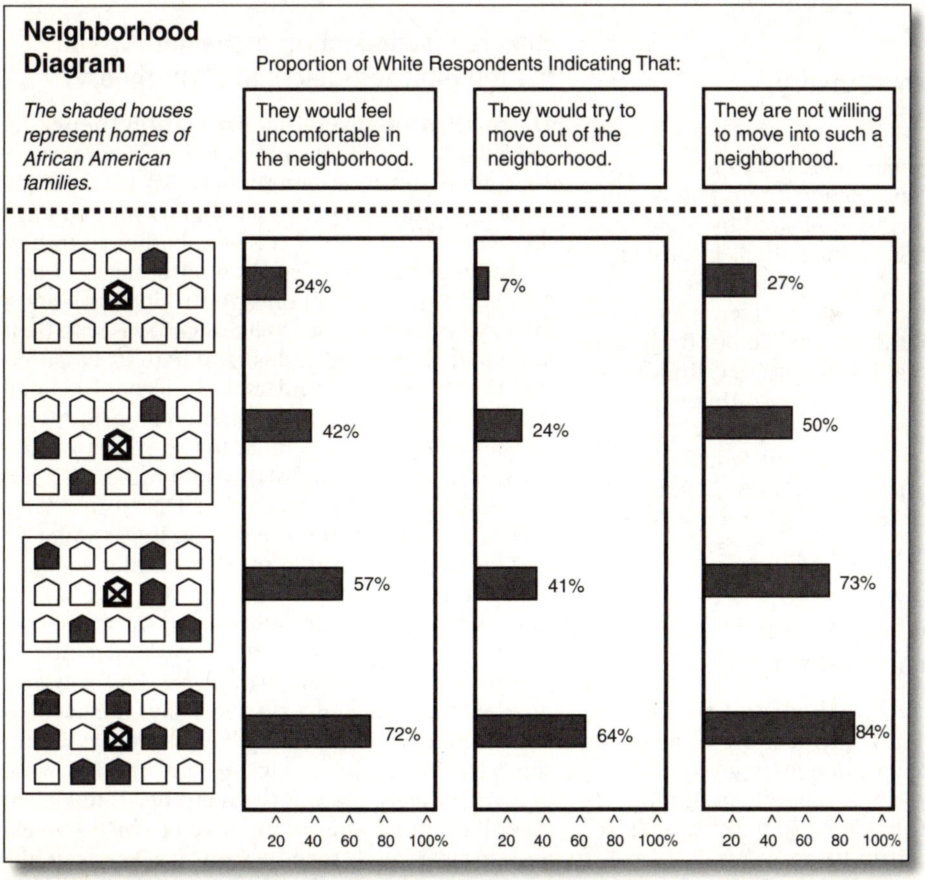

Is prejudice the main cause of discrimination in society?

For years we believed that discrimination was caused by prejudice; therefore, the way to reduce discrimination was to reduce prejudice. Efforts were made in schools and in popular culture to address and reduce prejudice, and they produced positive results. In recent years, research has shown a significant decrease in prejudice; however, studies have reported little decrease in discrimination (Astor, 1997). Based on efforts by scholars seeking alternative explanations, Feagin and Feagin (1986) described three theories of discrimination: the interest theory, the internal colonialism theory, and the institutionalized discrimination theory, all of which identify historic and contemporary forces responsible for inequities being perpetuated without the involvement of prejudice.

How does the interest theory explain discrimination?

The **interest theory** describes discrimination resulting from people protecting their power and privilege. Instead of being motivated by prejudice, people discriminate against individuals from subordinate groups because of self-interest. For example, white men may object to affirmative action programs not because of their prejudice but from fear of policies that might reduce their opportunities to be hired, retained, or promoted. Homeowners might persuade neighbors not to sell their home to a family of color because they are worried about what will happen to property values. Discrimination is a function of protecting one's interests; this is similar to the internal colonialism theory.

How is self-interest involved in the internal colonialism theory?

The **internal colonialism theory** of discrimination is an analysis of how privilege was created in the United States when the dominant group—white male Europeans—exploited subordinate groups to assume control of America's resources: land from American Indians, unpaid labor by African slaves, and wages and property of wives. Furthermore, by gaining control over resources and exploiting them to their advantage, certain white male Europeans achieved positions that provided them access to technological developments and control of industrial developments in the United States, including military technology. Once they are in a position of power, people will do what they can to maintain their advantage and stay in power.

Although initially established by force, unequal distribution and control of economic and political resources eventually became institutionalized. The theory of internal colonialism asserts that continued domination of nonwhites and women by white men is maintained by the way that institutions function in the United States. Internal colonialism theory creates the foundation on which the theory of institutionalized discrimination was built.

How is discrimination explained by the institutionalized discrimination theory?

The **institutionalized discrimination theory** accepts the history of internal colonialism but focuses on contemporary discrimination. This theory describes institutional policies and practices that have different and negative effects on subordinate groups. It examines how privilege and advantage are embedded in an organization's norms, its regulations, informal rules, and roles—social positions with their attendant duties and rights. An analysis based on this theory seeks to understand mechanisms and methods that lead to discrimination in institutional policies and practices. Similar to the other two theories, institutionalized discrimination theory is not concerned with prejudice (what U.S. courts have called "evil intent") but is based on the assumption that much discrimination today is unintentional.

When a number of women in city government in an urban area were interviewed for a research project, one department head explained how a group of female department heads had solved a problem. At the end of a workday, the women tended to leave immediately because of family responsibilities such as picking up children and preparing meals. Male department heads tended to meet for a drink after work once or twice a week, and to play golf together on weekends while women department heads spent that time with their families. At meetings where they had to make decisions about funding for programs, female department heads were frustrated by their inability to be as effective as their male counterparts in supporting each other.

The women understood why the men had an advantage. Because of their social activities, male department heads knew more about each other's departments, so they could make informed arguments in support of each other's programs. To create a similar advantage for themselves, the women started meeting together one evening every month (child care provided) to talk about their programs and needs, and to prepare for debates on funding priorities. As a result of their efforts, a greater amount of funding was distributed to departments headed by women (Koppelman, 1994).

The institutionalized discrimination theory provides a realistic basis for understanding discrimination: The actions of the male department heads were not based on a prejudice against women; rather, they were doing their job in accordance with historic practices that benefited their departments. The women understood that the solution was not to berate the men but rather to devise a strategy to offset advantages already established for male department heads. Even though informal institutional procedures favored the men, the women found a way to "play the game" more effectively. Discriminatory actions can still be a direct result of prejudice on the part of people making decisions, but it is more likely that causes for discrimination stem from reasons far more subtle and complex. Although prejudice may not be the main cause of discrimination, we should continue with research to understand what causes prejudice and do what we can to reduce it.

What factors promote the development of prejudice?

Considerable research has been conducted addressing the question of how individuals become prejudiced. Some studies suggest that elitist attitudes foster prejudice. **Elitism** is the belief that the most able people succeed in society and form a natural aristocracy while the least able enjoy the least success because they are flawed in some way or lack the necessary qualities to be successful. This condescending attitude promotes the belief that those in the lower levels of society deserve to be where they are and that successful people have earned their place in society. Unsuccessful people are often held responsible for their failure. Elitist attitudes are a major factor in studies based on social dominance theory (Howard, 2006; Stephan, 1999).

The eugenics movement beginning in the late 1800s argued that an individual's genetic inheritance determined his or her fate and that environment played little or no role in human development (Selden, 2006). Based on this argument, proponents of the eugenics movement in the United States were promoting elitist attitudes. Selden quotes American biologist George W. Hunter, author of several biology textbooks widely used in schools between 1914 and 1941, who expressed this elitist attitude clearly:

> Those of low grade intelligence would do little better under the most favorable conditions possible, while those of superior intelligence will make good no matter what handicaps they are given. (p. 75)

Other studies suggest a link between prejudice and attitudes about power. Some people express a **zero-sum** attitude, a highly competitive orientation toward power based on the assumption that the personal gains of one individual mean a loss for someone else; therefore, to share power is regarded as having less power. According to Levin and Levin (1982), an individual with a zero-sum orientation toward power tends to be a person with strong prejudices. Thurow (2001) has described the adverse consequences for society when a zero-sum orientation is prevalent. Studies also suggest that people with authoritarian personalities tend to be more prejudiced, although other studies refute the idea

> Everyone is a prisoner of his own experiences. No one can eliminate prejudices—just recognize them.
>
> **Edward R. Murrow (1908–1965)**

(Farley, 2005). Some have even proposed that prejudice is innate, but there are no scientific studies to support that claim.

To be as pervasive and persistent as it has been, prejudice must serve some purpose and offer some benefit to individuals or to society. Having reviewed research concerning causes of prejudice, Levin and Levin (1982) identified four primary causes, and within these causes, functions of prejudice that sustain it. The four causes include (1) personal frustration, (2) uncertainty about a person based on lack of knowledge or experience with the group to which they belong, (3) threat to one's self-esteem, and (4) competition among individuals in our society to achieve their goals in relation to status, wealth, and power.

How does frustration cause prejudice?

The frustration-aggression hypothesis maintains that as frustration builds, it leads to aggressive action. Frustration causes tension to increase until a person chooses to act on the frustration to alleviate the tension. Jones (1997) and others have called this the "scapegoat phenomenon." The word **scapegoat** derives from an ancient Hebrew custom described in Leviticus 16: 20–22, where each year the Hebrew people reflected on their sins during days of atonement. At the end of that time, a spiritual leader would stand before them with a goat, lay his hands on the goat's head, and recite a list of the people's sins, transferring the sins of the people to the goat—which was then set free. In modern America, the term generally refers to blaming a person or group for problems they did not cause.

When we take aggressive action—from verbal abuse to physical violence—we inevitably cause harm to others. Because most individuals define themselves as "good" according to some criteria, they will usually find a way to rationalize their actions as being good or at least justified. When southerners lynched black people in the late nineteenth and early twentieth centuries, they justified their actions by insisting that all blacks were lazy, lustful, or liars. Using the Kafkaesque reasoning that all blacks were guilty and therefore it didn't matter what crime a black person was accused of committing, they executed victims with no regard for whether that specific black person was guilty of a crime.

Ironically, data from some studies have shown that aggressive action may not alleviate frustration, but instead may exacerbate it. In one study, two groups of subjects were asked to allow medical technicians to take physical measurements of their bodies. After taking the measurements, the technicians made derogatory comments intended to make the subjects angry. One group was taken to the technician's "supervisor" if they wanted to complain; the other group was not. The researchers thought that members of the group being allowed to "vent" their anger would feel less hostile toward the technician afterward, yet those who complained reported stronger feelings of hostility than the subjects who were not allowed to complain (Aronson, 2008). The findings suggest that identifying a scapegoat on which to vent one's frustration does not solve a person's problems, and it may make matters worse.

The implication that finding a scapegoat does not solve problems is illustrated in domestic abuse cases. When a man takes out his frustrations by abusing his partner, he has to justify his actions. It is common for men arrested for domestic abuse to explain their behavior by saying, "She made me do it," or "She kept nagging and wouldn't shut up." This not only depicts the man as a victim (the suffering husband), but also it reinforces the stereotype of nagging wives, providing the husband with an excuse for assaulting the woman he once claimed to love. Because violence escalates with each domestic abuse complaint from the same home, it is obvious that blaming one's spouse or partner doesn't solve the problem; it may possibly cause the abuser to become more violent toward those interfering with his actions.

Because of the high rates of injury and death to police officers responding to domestic abuse cases, many American cities, counties, and states require officers to file abuse charges directly, even over the objections of the one abused. Courts often mandate counseling for abusers to address and understand how gender prejudices and stereotypes created negative attitudes leading to abuse, and to teach abusive men effective, nonviolent strategies for managing anger. The role of gender stereotypes in contributing to domestic abuse illustrates another major cause of prejudice—uncertainty.

What do stereotypes have to do with uncertainty and how do they cause prejudice?

Most of us only have knowledge of the groups to which we belong; often we do not know much about other groups. In the United States, schools have historically implemented curricula reflecting perspectives, contributions, and experiences of the dominant (white) group; many of our neighborhoods still tend to be segregated by race or social class. The result is that people from different racial and ethnic groups have few opportunities to learn about one another. Because of our lack of accurate information, we may believe in stereotypes as a way to convince ourselves that we know about certain groups. (See Figure 2.3.) Our stereotypes can be reinforced by images or information contained in such media as advertisements, textbooks, and films.

For an example of ignorance promoting prejudice, how many Americans know that Muslims have been in the United States from colonial times because many slaves brought to America from West Africa were Muslim? The evidence is in the names that "read like a Who's Who of traditional Muslim names"—Bullaly (Bilali), Mahomet (Muhammad), Walley (Wali), and Sambo meant "second son" to Muslim Fulbe people (Abdo, 2006, p. 66). While Americans tend to stereotype all Arabs as Muslims, the majority of Arabs immigrating to the United

FIGURE 2.3

This drawing has been used for research and in classrooms. One person is shown this picture and whispers a description of the entire scene to another person, who then whispers the description to another person until each person in the room has heard it. The last person is asked to describe the scene to everyone. Typically, the person describes a poorly dressed black man with a weapon preparing to attack a well-dressed white man, thus illustrating the power of racial stereotypes.

States in the late nineteenth century were Christians. How many Americans know that in the 1920s a small group of Muslims settled in Ross, South Dakota, and built the first mosque in the United States, or that the oldest continuously functioning mosque is in Cedar Rapids, Iowa (Abdo, 2006)?

Even if they don't know this history, how many Americans know that Muslim Americans today own over 200,000 businesses and that there are over 2,000 mosques in the United States (Ansari, 2004)? How many Americans know that Muslim American adults are better educated than the average American (59% have college degrees compared to 27% of other Americans) and wealthier (a median annual income of $60,000 compared to the national median annual income of $50,000) (Barrett, 2007)? Muslims have done what America expects of immigrants. But unaware of this information, and surrounded by stereotypes and media's focus on Islamic terrorists, how many Americans harbor negative views of both the Islamic faith and Muslims? According to a 2004 survey by the Pew Forum on Religion and Public Life, nearly 50% of Americans perceived the Islamic faith as more likely to promote violence than other religions (a percentage that doubled compared to the results of a similar survey conducted two years earlier) and nearly 40% expressed a negative view of Muslims (Abdo, 2006).

When a person actually encounters individuals of a different race, ethnicity, or social class, selective perception of the behaviors of those individuals often reinforces his or her stereotypes. Stephan (1999) reported on one study where subjects were presented with equal amounts of positive and negative information about a group to which they belonged (in-group) and a group to which they did not belong (out-group). Subjects tended to recall more positive information about the in-group and more negative information about the out-group. According to Stephan, negative attitudes in our memory tend to increase over time.

Selective perception was illustrated in another study where two groups of subjects viewed consecutive videotapes: The first videotape was of a fourth-grade girl playing with friends, and the second videotape was of the same girl taking an oral test in school where she answered some difficult questions correctly but missed some easy questions. Although the second videotape was the same for both groups, the first videotape shown to one group was the girl playing in a low-income neighborhood, and first videotape shown to the other group was the girl playing in a high-income neighborhood. After watching both videotapes, subjects were asked to judge the girl's academic abilities. Those who saw her playing in the low-income neighborhood rated her academic ability lower than those who saw her playing in the more affluent neighborhood. Whether the subjects focused more on the girl's correct or incorrect answers appeared to have been influenced by the neighborhood where they believed she lived and stereotypes associated with affluence and poverty (Aronson, 2008).

Researchers have also shown that becoming more knowledgeable about others helps people overcome stereotypical perceptions. In a psychiatric hospital with an all-white staff, patients acting violently were either taken to a "time-out room" or subjected to the harsher penalty of being put in a straitjacket and sedated. In the first month of a research study, both black and white patients were admitted. Although the black patients admitted were diagnosed as being less violent than the whites, they were four times more likely to be put in a straitjacket and sedated by the staff if they became violent. The discrepancy in the white staff's use of restraints suggests that they believed in the stereotype that black people were more prone to violence. As they became better acquainted with the patients, the staff responded to violent incidents with more equal use of restraints for both black and white patients (Aronson, 2008). Stereotypes that portray a group as being prone to violence, lazy, or less intelligent can influence a person's behavior; stereotypes can also play a part in a person's self-

> **Sometimes (prejudice) is like a hair across your cheek. You can't see it, you can't find it with your fingers, but you keep brushing at it because the feel of it is irritating.**
>
> **Marian Anderson (1897–1993)**

esteem being threatened, which is another major cause of prejudice identified in research.

How does threat to self-esteem cause prejudice?

In the United States, people are encouraged to develop self-esteem by comparing themselves with others. We do so by grades in school, music contests, debates in speech, and athletic competitions. But what happens when positive self-esteem is achieved by developing feelings of superiority to someone else? Or when we achieve our sense of superiority by projecting our feelings of inferiority onto another person or group? If we believe in the innate superiority of our group compared to other groups, then we believe we are better than anyone who is a member of the inferior group. If members of an inferior group become successful, their achievements threaten those whose self-esteem was based on feelings of group superiority and unconsciously transforms a condescending attitude into prejudice.

People of color confront the issue of self-esteem based on race as a cause of prejudice when they encounter white people whose self-esteem is threatened by their achievements or success. The first African American to teach at Harvard University Law School commented,

> You have to simultaneously function on a high level and try not to upset those whose racial equilibrium is thrown off when they recognize that you are not incompetent, not mediocre, and don't fit the long accepted notions about persons of color that serve as unrecognized but important components of their self-esteem. (Bell, 2002, pp. 66–67)

When we possess this kind of self-esteem, we are insecure and easily threatened. Coleman (2007) argued that people perceiving others as inferior "are more likely to identify and maintain negative stereotypes about members of stigmatized groups" (p. 222).

Studies suggest that part of the self-esteem for many men derives just from being male. In Michigan, over a thousand children wrote essays about what their lives would be like if they were the opposite gender. Although almost half the girls found many positive things to say about being male, 95% of the boys could find nothing positive to say about being female (Sadker & Sadker, 1994). Similar attitudes appear among adults. In their research on self-esteem, Martinez and Dukes (1991) reported that males displayed higher self-esteem than did females, and that white males had the highest self-esteem of all groups.

When male self-esteem derives from perceiving one's gender as superior, it is easily threatened by women's achievements. American men often rationalize female achievements by attributing women's success to reasons other than competence. Their rationalizations may be characterized by resentment or anger, which intensifies the prejudice that created the initial illusion of superiority. If a woman receives the promotion a man wanted, he might complain that she is "sleeping her way to the top." Because self-esteem based on a belief in gender superiority is an illusion, it is ultimately inadequate because the individual has done nothing to earn it. Fearing that an "inferior" person might receive rewards the "superior" individual desires is related to the fourth primary cause of prejudice: competition for status, wealth, and power.

How does competition for status, wealth, and power cause prejudice?

There is evidence that competition fosters prejudicial attitudes. Jones (1997) described a study at a summer camp where Boy Scouts were given time to become acquainted and to develop friendships before being divided into two groups and housed in separate bunkhouses. The groups were divided so that approximately two thirds of each boy's friends were in the other bunkhouse. The two groups were encouraged to play a series of competitive games such as tug-of-war, football, and baseball. Boys who had liked each other began to intensely dislike each other and to engage in name-calling. Although there was solidarity within groups, friendships that had been established with boys from the other group no longer existed. After competitive games were concluded, researchers brought the boys together, but animosity remained until the boys were given tasks that required them to cooperate with each other. Working together to achieve a common goal reduced the hostility and resulted in the boys again making friendships with individuals from the other group.

The Perpetuation of Prejudice

People want to be successful and will try to promote their own self-interests. When members of one group believe that individuals from another group are becoming more successful than they are, they may become angry at those individuals—even hostile toward the entire group—by rationalizing an advantage other than talent or skill that is responsible for their success. White American men sometimes resent affirmative action because they believe it provides women and racial or ethnic minorities with an advantage in being hired and promoted. Resentment from economic competition for good jobs with high salaries and status fosters prejudice. Because humans are intelligent enough to identify these various causes of prejudice, it seems logical to assume that people should be able to recognize that they have prejudices and attempt to eliminate them.

How are prejudices perpetuated?

A major factor in the perpetuation of prejudice is the tendency to rationalize prejudices and the negative behaviors prejudices promote. As Gioseffi (1993) has noted, "Just as individuals will rationalize their hostile behaviors . . . so nations do also" (p. xvii). Vega (1978) described rationalizations taking three forms: denial, victim-blaming, and avoidance. To unlearn our prejudices and develop effective ways of confronting prejudices expressed by others, we need to recognize these rationalizations so we can make an appropriate response when they are expressed.

Denial rationalizations

In making **denial rationalizations,** we refuse to recognize that there are problems in our society resulting from prejudices and discrimination. Such claims are astonishing in their ignorance, yet they continue to be made. In response to assertions of racism, the most common denial rationalization is the reverse discrimination argument that claims that women and minorities receive the best jobs because of affirmative action programs. Is there any truth to this claim?

According to population demographics, women now comprise almost half of the workforce; another 10% consists of men of color, which means that white men constitute about 40% of the workforce (Daft, 2003). A job paying an annual salary of $50,000 or more is a criterion to identify which jobs involve some degree of authority, status, and decision-making power. How many of these jobs are in the hands of white men? It would be consistent with their proportion of the workforce if white men had slightly less than half of these jobs, yet according to the Bureau of Labor Statistics (2001), white men hold over three fourths of these positions, about twice as many as the percentage of white men in the workforce. Claims that white men are unfairly discriminated against as a result of affirmative action policies would appear to be dubious (see Table 2.1).

The most common denial rationalization related to sexism is the "natural" argument, which denies gender discrimination, claiming that it is natural for women to do some things better than men, and for men to do some things better than women. This denial rationalization is offered as an explanation for why men and women have historically held certain types of jobs. The argument does not explain the difference between the skills of a tailor (predominantly men) compared to a seamstress (predominantly women) to justify the differences in their compensations. Nor does it explain why construction workers (mostly men) should be compensated at a greater rate than college-educated social workers (mostly women). Historically, women have been paid less than men for doing the same work, and occupations dominated by women still receive lower wages than occupations dominated by men (Bureau of Labor Statistics, 2001). This is the reality, but denial rationalizations have little to do with reality.

The most subtle denial rationalization is personal denial illustrated by the man who says, "How can I be sexist? I love women! I married a woman. I have daughters." This seems a reasonable statement: Someone denying he has gender prejudices does not appear to deny the existence of widespread prejudice against women—but the statement actually does imply a more sweeping denial. Psycholog-

TABLE 2.1 Annual Incomes of Full-Time Workers in the United States

	Median Weekly Earnings	
Race/Gender	1994	2004
White males	$690 (100%)	$732 (100%)
Black males	$505 (73.2%)	$569 (77.7%)
Hispanic males	$433 (62.8%)	$480 (65.6%)
White females	$514 (74.5%)	$584 (79.8%)
Black females	$437 (63.3%)	$505 (69.9%)
Hispanic females	$384 (55.7%)	$419 (57.2%)

Source: U.S. Census Bureau (2004). *Statistical abstract of the United States.*

ically, most people feel they are normal, average people. If a person denies being prejudiced, he or she is actually denying that most other normal, average people are prejudiced as well. The real meaning of such a statement is that the speaker does not believe prejudice and discrimination are serious problems in society. If someone argues this point, the person making this denial rationalization might resort to victim-blaming responses because the two are closely related.

> Prejudice blinds, ignorance retards, indifference deafens, hate amputates. In this way do some people disable their souls.
>
> MARY ROBINSON (1944–)

Victim-blaming rationalizations

People employing **victim-blaming rationalizations** reject the notion that prejudice and discrimination are problems in society, even though they admit that problems exist. The problems they identify, however, are typically deficiencies or flaws in members of minority groups (Ryan, 1976). Victim-blamers focus on the group being harmed by societal prejudices and insist that society doesn't need to change: The group needs to change. Victim-blamers urge individuals to stop being so sensitive or so pushy, to work harder, and to quit complaining. Group members are told they are responsible for whatever problems they must overcome.

Victim-blaming often occurs among people who want to believe in a just world. In one study, subjects observed two people working equally hard at a task. By a random decision, researchers gave one of the workers a significant reward when the task was completed; the other worker received nothing. When asked to rate how hard the two people had worked, the subjects tended to describe the person who received nothing as not working as hard as the person receiving the reward. Aronson (2008) concluded his analysis of this study by suggesting that "we find it frightening to think about living in a world where people, through no fault of their own, can be deprived of what they deserve or need" (p. 323).

People who engage in victim-blaming rationalizations often go beyond blame to propose solutions. By defining the problem as a deficiency existing in the victimized group, every solution proposed by a victim-blamer involves what *they* need to do because *they* are the problem. The rest of us need do nothing. Rape is increasing on college campuses? That's a woman's problem, so what they need to do is to wear less provocative clothing, avoid going out late at night, and learn to defend themselves by taking martial arts classes or carrying pepper spray. What to do about the men who rape isn't addressed. Because victim-blamers offer solutions, it is easy to confuse victim-blaming with some avoidance rationalizations.

Avoidance rationalizations

Unlike people who employ denial and victim-blaming, those who promote **avoidance rationalizations** recognize the problems in society as stemming from prejudice and discrimination. This is a significant difference from the previous rationalizations. Even though a person making avoidance rationalizations admits there are problems, he or she will not address them and will rationalize a reason to avoid them. Ways to avoid confronting issues include offering a solution that addresses only part of a problem, or suggesting a false solution that does not address the problem at all.

If college administrators decide to confront prejudice by requiring students to take an ethnic studies course, that requirement will address a small part of the problems caused by racial prejudice and discrimination. Learning more about ethnic groups is a good idea, but if colleges are serious about actively opposing racism and improving race relations, administration and faculty must recruit diverse students, hire diverse faculty, and promote cultural diversity through workshops and seminars both on campus and in the community.

A false solution that does not address the problems of sexism whatsoever is the proposal that "sexism would just disappear if we didn't pay so much attention to it." Problems created by sexism did not suddenly appear and they won't disappear unless people engage in actions to confront, challenge, and change sexist attitudes, policies, and laws. The only way any society can solve problems and improve conditions is to analyze a problem, create appropriate solutions, implement the solutions that seem most likely to be effective, and, after time passes, assess the impact of these solutions.

Another form of avoidance rationalization involves making an argument that distracts attention from the issue or question being discussed. Imagine a group of people discussing efforts that could be made to increase social justice in our society. Suddenly someone says, "You're being too idealistic. We are never going to solve this problem because we're never going to have a utopia." The speaker was not arguing for the creation of a utopia, a perfect society, but for ways to improve society. By making the reasonable statement that utopias are not possible, the speaker has shifted the focus of the conversation to a different topic that avoids the issue. It is not realistic to believe that it is possible to create a perfect society, but it is possible—in fact, essential—to believe that any society can be improved.

In a discussion about the need for child-care centers at work sites, someone might say, "I support the idea, but it takes time; it's not going to happen overnight." A reasonable response, except if the discussion ends with that comment, what has been achieved? To implement any solution successfully, it is necessary to clarify what is entailed: What needs to be done? Who will do what? Which actions should be taken next month? What can we expect in the next six months? Who will determine whether the solution is working, and how will that be determined? Saying a solution takes time may be true, but it is still necessary to discuss what must be done to implement it. To avoid that discussion is to avoid the problem. Problems are not solved by talk or the passage of time but by taking some kind of action.

Conservatives are often accused of engaging in denial and especially victim-blaming rationalizations. Their solutions tend to concentrate on perceived flaws in victims of prejudice rather than addressing the prejudice and discrimination that create many of these difficult circumstances. On the other hand, liberals are more likely to be criticized for engaging in avoidance rationalizations in which they acknowledge and express sympathy for the problems faced by oppressed groups, but never do anything to address the causes of these problems. As long as significant numbers of individuals continue to employ such rationalizations, Americans are not likely to perceive or confront persistent structural causes of inequities based on race, gender, and other human differences.

AFTERWORD

If prejudice were part of human nature, people would be justified in feeling despair because the implication would be that human beings eventually will destroy each other. But no evidence supports the idea that prejudice is innate. Instead, studies have consistently concluded that prejudice is learned. The fact that prejudice is learned offers hope because anything that can be learned can be unlearned. Education can confront negative attitudes both in the media and in our language to help students unlearn prejudices they have been taught,

> [There is a] strangely irrational notion that there is something in the very flow of time that will inevitably cure all ills. Actually time is neutral. It can be used either destructively or constructively.
>
> **Martin Luther King, Jr. (1929–1968)**

and also understand why it is in everyone's best interest not to act on prejudices.

In their study of brain research, Newberg and Waldman (2006) found that people could "interrupt" prejudicial beliefs and stereotypes and generate new ideas, and that these new ideas "can alter the neural circuitry that governs how we behave and what we believe. Our beliefs . . . aren't necessarily static. They can change; we can change them" (p. 9).

Prejudice can be reduced by accurate information, by formal and informal learning, and by establishing equitable workplace policies and practices. Prejudices can also be unlearned by friends challenging one another's negative attitudes. Even though some people may not be able to give up their prejudices, they do not have to act on them. It is not inevitable that our prejudices control us. When we can identify our prejudices and understand how we learned them, we can choose to limit their influence on our behavior. We can control them instead of letting them control us.

When we make positive choices, we affirm the basis for having hope for the future. Positive choices that individuals have made throughout history have resulted in genuine human progress. If our society is to benefit from its diversity, it will be because enough Americans have chosen to regard diversity as an asset and to confront their prejudices. Those who make such positive choices today will shape the nature of the society in which our children and their children must live.

TERMS AND DEFINITIONS

Avoidance rationalization A response to a social problem—such as injustice toward a minority group—that acknowledges the existence of a problem but avoids confronting the problem by offering partial or false solutions or by using arguments that do not address the situation as in "Yes, but you should have seen how bad it was last year."

Black/white syndrome A pattern in the English language consisting of negative meanings for phrases including the word *black* and positive meanings for phrases including the word *white*

Denial rationalization A response to a social problem—such as injustice toward a minority group—that does not acknowledge the existence of a problem but insists instead that no injustice has occurred as in "That's not discrimination, men have always been the boss; it's just the way things are meant to be."

Elitism The belief that the best people ascend to a place of superiority in society and represent a natural aristocracy, whereas those who are not successful are viewed as lacking the necessary qualities to be successful within society

Genocide The deliberate and systematic extermination of a particular nationality, or racial, ethnic, or minority group

Institutionalized discrimination theory Institutional policies and practices that have differential and negative effects on subordinate groups in a society

Interest theory People engaging or acquiescing in discriminatory actions based on a desire to protect their power or privilege

Internal colonialism theory Explains contemporary discrimination as the maintenance of inequities resulting from historic exploitation of subordinate groups by the dominant group

Prejudice A negative attitude toward a group and anyone perceived to be a member of that group; a predisposition to negative behavior toward members of a group

Scapegoat An individual or a group of people blamed for another person's problems or difficulties; identifying a scapegoat is often employed to justify one's taking a negative action against that individual or group

Victim-blaming rationalization A response to a social problem—such as injustice toward a minority group—that identifies the problem as a deficiency in the minority group and not a societal problem, as in "If poor people want to escape poverty they just have to be willing to work harder."

White flight The migration of white families from an urban to a suburban location because of court rulings to desegregate urban schools

Zero sum An orientation toward power and resources based on assumptions of scarcity, as when struggling to achieve goals, one person gains at the expense of another. The belief that sharing power means a reduction of power

DISCUSSION EXERCISES

Clarification Exercise—Rationalizations: Victim-Blame, Denial, and Avoidance

Directions: This exercise provides everyday statements we might hear; each one is a specific kind of rationalization. Based on the text and on your group discussion, identify the statements below according to one of the three types of rationalizations. First, select which passages would most likely represent an **avoidance** of a problem. Then select those in which the speaker employs a **denial** rationalization—that the problem either does not exist or that the speaker is suggesting "That's just the way things are." Finally, locate **victim-blame** statements where a specific person or group is being charged with its own downfall or problem.

Rationalizations for Our Prejudices

Directions: Decide whether the following statements represent a **denial** of the problem (D), a **victim-blame** that it is the speaker's problem (D/VB), or an **avoidance** of the problem (A).

_____ 1. Women and minorities are getting everything their way. They are taking away our jobs and pretty soon they are going to take over everything.

_____ 2. What we have here, basically, is a failure to communicate. We must develop better programs in interpersonal communications to address this issue.

_____ 3. This is the way these people want to live. You can't change poor people; they can't help the way they are.

_____ 4. We must move with deliberation on these issues. Real change takes time. We have to educate people.

_____ 5. All those women on welfare have it made. All they do is stay home and make babies while the rest of us have to work and pay taxes to support them.

_____ 6. I can't figure out what to call all these people. Why can't we all just be human instead of black, Chicano, Latino, Native American, or Asian American?

_____ 7. Indians are their own worst enemy. They should stop fighting among themselves and get together on whatever it is they really want.

_____ 8. If blacks want to make it in our society, they are going to have to get rid of those dreadlocks and other weird hairstyles, the baggy clothes, funny handshakes, and they better start speaking better English.

_____ 9. Yes, but in the old days, race and sex discrimination were much worse. And even today, women and minorities are much better off in this country than anywhere else in the world.

_____ 10. Women are just too sensitive about sexism. They need to look at these things less emotionally and much more rationally.

_____ 11. We need more programs in African American studies, Latino studies, Native American studies, and Asian American studies to learn about all the contributions these groups have made to our society.

_____ 12. Feminists are pushing too hard for the changes that they demand. They are hurting themselves more than they are helping.

_____ 13. I understand that some people face more difficulties than others, but this is a free country and I believe that anybody who is willing to work hard enough can be successful.

Follow-Up: Select any two from each of the three categories—D, VB, and A—and rewrite them to be the fourth kind of statement—those *without* rationalization. Explain why you chose to rewrite them as you did.

Exercise—The Liver Transplant Problem

Background: Today, the only medical procedure available to save the lives of persons suffering from diseases of the liver is an organ transplant. Unfortunately, there are not enough livers to take care of all cases now, and there will not be enough in the near future to save the lives of all those in need.

Your Role: The decision about which people can be saved must be made on criteria other than medical criteria. Your hospital has decided that the best way to select persons for a transplant is by setting up a volunteer citizens panel to make the decisions. You are on the panel and receive a Profile Sheet of applicants for transplants (see the table). Doctors have screened all patients, and all have equal prognosis for medical success.

Problem: There is a liver available for one person on the list. All those not served will die. The availability of other livers cannot be anticipated, although if other livers become available, additional persons on the list could receive transplants.

Directions: Your panel must make a *unanimous* decision regarding the person to be the liver recipient. A lottery violates institutional ethics and is not an acceptable strategy. As you deliberate, discuss your values and consider those of others related to the process being utilized and the criteria that you propose:

1. The criteria you develop for choosing the recipient.
2. Why you believe that the person you chose best fits your criteria.
3. How your panel arrives at a single selection of a recipient.

Please see the next page for more detailed notes about the recipients.

Liver Transplant Recipient Profile Sheet

Code	Age	Race	Sex	Marital Status	Religious Affiliation	Children	Occupation
A	24	Black	M	Married	Muslim	None	Postal worker
B	45	White	M	Married	Atheist	2	Executive
C	39	Asian American	F	Divorced	Buddhist	None	Medical doctor
D	40	White	F	Married	Jew	3	Housewife
E	23	White	M	Unmarried	Episcopal	None	PhD student
F	40	White	F	Unmarried	Pentecostal	9	Welfare mother
G	28	Native American	M	Unmarried	Native	3	Seasonal worker
H	30	Latina	F	Married	Catholic	7	Housewife
I	19	White	M	Unmarried	Baptist	None	Special student

Notes about Recipients:

A. Devotes time to volunteer work for black organizations
B. Possible candidate for U.S. Senate
C. College physician and feminist speaker
D. Active in local synagogue and charitable activities
E. Middle states chair of a gay rights task force
F. Advocate and organizer of welfare mothers
G. State chair, Indian Treaty Rights Organization
H. Blind and physically disabled
I. Cognitively disabled

REFERENCES

Abdo, G. (2006). *Mecca and main Street: Muslim life in America after 9/11.* Oxford, England: Oxford University Press.

Describes the efforts of a variety of Muslim Americans to live in the United States and to maintain their faith while being confronted by stereotypes, prejudice, and discrimination.

Allport, G. (1979). *The nature of prejudice.* Reading, MA: Addison-Wesley.

Examines prejudice and its consequences for individuals who act on prejudice as well as those victimized by prejudice.

Ansari, Z.I. (2004). *Islam among African Americans: An overview.* In Z.H. Buhhari, S.S. Nyang, M. Ahmad, & J.C. Esposito (Eds.), *Muslims' place in the American public square* (pp. 222–267). Walnut Creek, CA: Altamira Press.

Provides a history of Islam in African American communities and examines the recent revival of interest in Islam represented by increasing numbers of African American converts.

Arliss, L.P. (1991). *Gender communication.* Englewood Cliffs, NJ: Prentice Hall.

Analyzes sexist language in Chapter 3, "Debates About Language and Sexism."

Aronson, E. (2008). *The social animal* (10th ed.). New York, NY: Worth Publishers.

Presents an overview of research in social psychology and describes patterns and motives revealed in these studies concerning human behavior.

Astor, C. (1997, August). Gallup poll: Progress in black/white relations, but race is still an issue. USIA electronic journal, *U.S. Society & Values, 2*(3), 19–212.

Highlights information from a Gallup Poll Special Report on "Black/White Relations in the United States"; access the complete poll at http://www.gallup.com

Baker, R. (1981). "Pricks" and "chicks": A plea for persons. In M. Vetterling-Braggin (Ed.), *Sexist language: A modern philosophical analysis* (pp. 161–182). Lanham, MD: Littlefield, Adams.

Explores sexist attitudes in our society as expressed in sexual slang.

Barrett, P.M. (2007). *American Islam: The struggle for the soul of a religion.* New York, NY: Farrar, Straus and Giroux.

Describes the perceptions and experiences of a variety of Muslim Americans based on interviews conducted after the terrorist attacks on 9/11.

Bell, D. (2002). *Ethical ambition: Living a life of meaning and worth.* New York, NY: Bloomsbury.

Discusses six factors that are critical in determining the quality and meaningfulness of one's life: passion, courage, faith, relationships, role models, and humility.

Bredin, J. (2008). *The affair: The case of Alfred Dreyfus.* Bethesda, MD: Gryphon Editions.

Describes the historical background and the ensuing controversy surrounding this notorious example of anti-Semitism.

Bureau of Labor Statistics. (2001). Chapter 1: Counting Minorities: A brief history and a look at the future. *Report on the American workforce.* Washington DC: U.S. Department of Labor. Retrieved December 20, 2008, from http://ww.bls.gov/opub

Analyzes statistics pertaining to the American workforce and the role and nature of the participation in that workforce by women and minorities.

Carroll, J. (2001). *Constantine's sword: The church and the Jews, a history.* Boston, MA: Houghton Mifflin.

Examines the history of relations between the Catholic Church and the Jews and explains the basis for the historic pattern of anti-Semitism that still exists in the church.

Coleman, L.M. (2007). Stigma. In L. Davis (Ed.), *The disability studies reader* (2nd ed., pp. 216–233). New York, NY: Routledge.

Discusses the origin of the concept of stigma and analyzes the reasons why some differences in human beings are valued and others are stigmatized.

Daft, R.L. (2003). Managing diverse employees. *Management* (6th ed., pp. 436–468). Versailles, KY: Thompson Southwestern.

Discusses diversity in the workforce and how corporate culture is accommodating diversity.

Evans, S. (1989). *Born for liberty: A history of women in America.* New York, NY: The Free Press.

Provides evidence of the influence of women on the colonies and in the nation that emerged.

Farley, J. (2005). *Majority-minority relations* (5th ed.). Upper Saddle River, NJ: Prentice Hall.

Discusses the research on authoritarian personalities in Chapter 2 and racial segregation in U.S. neighborhoods in Chapter 10.

Feagin, J., & Feagin, C. (1986). *Discrimination American style* (2nd ed.). Malabar, FL: Krieger.

Describes the three alternative theories of discrimination on pages 7–12.

Feagin, J., & Feagin, C.B. (2008). Glossary. *Racial and ethnic relations* (8th ed.). Upper Saddle River, NJ: Prentice Hall.

Provides definitions of major terms and concepts in intergroup relations.

Gioseffi, D. (Ed.). (1993). *On prejudice: A global perspective.* New York, NY: Anchor.

Contains excerpts from historic and contemporary authors from around the world describing the existence and consequences of human prejudice.

Giroux, H. (1998). *Channel surfing: Racism, the media, and the destruction of today's youth.* New York, NY: St. Martin's.

Analyzes media images, especially films, and their impact on children and youth.

Goldhagen, D.J. (2002). *Hitler's willing executioners: Ordinary Germans and the Holocaust* (2nd ed.) New York, NY: Knopf.

Presents evidence for the controversial thesis that Germans readily collaborated in the Nazi Holocaust.

Howard, G.R. (2006). *We can't teach what we don't know: White teachers, multiracial schools* (2nd ed.) New York, NY: Teachers College Press.

Integrates theory, research, and personal experiences to describe problems created by racism and white privilege and discusses actions to bring about positive changes.

Jones, J. (1997). *Prejudice and racism* (2nd ed.). New York, NY: McGraw Hill.

Integrates data from psychology, sociology, anthropology, biology, political science, and history to explain prejudice and racism and the relationship between them.

Khan, M.A.M. (2004). Living on borderlines: Islam beyond the clash and dialogue of civilization. In Z.H. Buhhari, S.S. Nyang, M. Ahmad, & J.C. Esposito (Eds.), *Muslims' place in the American public square* (pp. 84–113). Walnut Creek, CA: Altamira Press.

Addresses conceptual and practical issues facing American Muslims and describes the influence of two groups—idealists and realists—on Muslims in the United States and worldwide.

Koppelman, K. (1994). *Race and gender equity in urban America: The efforts of six cities to define the issues and provide solutions.* Paper presented at the national conference of the Renaissance Group in San Antonio on October 15, 1994.

Describes policies and programs of public and private agencies in six urban areas to address racial and gender inequities.

Levin, J., & Levin, W. (1982). *The functions of discrimination and prejudice* (2nd ed., p. 202). New York, NY: Harper & Row.

Examines the causes and effects of prejudice summarized on two flow charts.

Martinez, R., & Dukes, R.L. (1991, March). Ethnic and gender differences in self-esteem. *Youth & Society, 22*(3), 318–339.

Presents findings from a study of self-esteem in a multiracial population of students in grades 7–12 who attended the largest school district in Colorado Springs, Colorado.

Massey, D.S. (2001, January). Residential segregation and neighborhood conditions in U.S. metropolitan areas. In N. Smelser, W. Wilson, & F. Mitchell (Eds.), *America becoming: Racial trends and their consequences.* (ERIC Document Reproduction Service No. ED449286)

Describes how segregation has increased in recent years, especially for blacks, as well as the nature of segregation for Hispanics and Asian Americans.

McCloud, A.B. (2004). Conceptual discourse: Living as a Muslim in a pluralistic society. In Z.H. Buhhari, S.S. Nyang, M. Ahmad, & J.C. Esposito (Eds.), *Muslims' place in the American public square* (pp. 73–83). Walnut Creek, CA: Altamira Press.

Examines the role of the media in creating negative images of Muslims and discusses the inconsistency between American responses to Muslims and American values.

McCloud, A.B. (2006). *Transnational Muslims in American society.* Gainesville, FL: University of Florida Press.

Examines the experiences of Muslims who have recently become citizens of the United States and explores the success of their various strategies for adapting to American culture.

Miller, C., & Swift, K. (2000). *Words and women.* San Jose, CA: iUniverse.

Explains the study of junior high students' drawings of "early man" along with other studies concerning the sexism of generic terms in Chapter 2, "Who Is Man?"

Moore, R.B. (2006). Racism in the English language. In K. Rosenblum & T. Travis (Eds.), *The meaning of difference: American constructions of race, sex and gender, social class, and sexual orientation* (4th ed., pp. 451–459). Boston, MA: McGraw-Hill.

Examines the origins and implications of many racist words and phrases.

Newberg, A., & Waldman, M.R. (2006). *Why we believe what we believe: Uncovering our biological needs for meaning, spirituality, and truth.* New York, NY: Free Press.

Proposes a new way of thinking about how convictions develop and influence individuals based on recent research about how the brain perceives (and transforms) reality.

Ryan, W. (1976). *Blaming the victim* (2nd ed.). New York, NY: Vintage Books.

Describes and analyzes victim-blaming attitudes toward blacks in the inner cities.

Sadker, D., & Sadker, M. (1994). *Failing at fairness: How America's schools cheat girls.* New York, NY: Charles Scribner.

Discusses how boys are favored and girls are discriminated against in schools; describes the Michigan study in Chapter 3, "The Self-Esteem Slide," on pp. 83–85.

Sartre, J.P. (1995). *Anti-Semite and Jew.* New York, NY: Schocken.

Describes French anti-Semitism expressed after World War II despite French people's awareness of the Nazi Holocaust.

Schaefer, R.T. (2008). *Racial and ethnic groups* (11th ed.). Upper Saddle River, NJ: Pearson.

Reviews changes in the composition of U.S. immigrants and anti-immigrant sentiments in Chapter 4, "Immigration and the United States"; discusses findings of research using the Social Distance Scale in Chapter 2, "Prejudice."

Selden, S. (2006). *Inheriting shame: The story of eugenics and racism in America.* New York, NY: Teachers College Press.

Examines the development of the eugenics movement in the United States and what lessons should be learned from it.

Simpson, G.E., & Yinger, J.M. (1985). *Racial and cultural minorities: An analysis of prejudice and discrimination* (5th ed.). New York, NY: Plenum.

Provides an in-depth examination of prejudice and discrimination, including studies that used the Social Distance Scale.

Skuttnab-Kangas, T. (2000). *Linguistic genocide in education—or worldwide diversity and human rights?* Mahwah, NJ: Lawrence Erlbaum Associates.

Uses contemporary theory and research to examine the impact of linguistic imperialism on human rights in general and the assault on linguistic diversity in particular.

Stephan, W. (1999). *Reducing prejudice and stereotyping in schools.* New York, NY: Teachers College Press.

Reviews theories of prejudice and stereotyping, examines conditions to promote changes in negative attitudes, and describes techniques for improving race relations in schools.

Thurow, L. (2001). *The zero-sum society.* New York, NY: Penguin.

Describes economic implications when a society accepts and acts on zero-sum thinking.

United States Bureau of the Census. (2008). *Statistical abstract of the United States.* Retrieved October 15, 2008 from http://www.census.gov/compendia/statab.

Provides historic and current statistical data on the demographics of the U.S. workforce.

Vega, F. (1978). *The effect of human and intergroup relations education on the race/sex attitudes of education majors.* Unpublished doctoral dissertation, University of Minnesota, Minneapolis.

Discusses the development of individual racist and sexist attitudes from cultural and institutional influences and measures the impact of a course on those attitudes.

Wessler, S. L. (2001). Sticks and stones. *Educational Leadership, 58*(4), 28–33.

Describes the degrading and even violent language children use in schools and the impact of this language on its victims.

CHAPTER 3

Communication, Conflict, and Conflict Resolution

> "If I were to summarize the single most important principle I have learned in the field of interpersonal relations it would be this: Seek first to understand, then to be understood."
>
> **Stephen Covey (1932–)**

Communication seems simple. One person talks, and other people listen to understand what the speaker is saying; when the first person stops talking, another person responds, perhaps to agree or disagree with the first speaker. Nothing seems complicated here, so why are there misunderstandings that so often lead to conflicts among individuals, groups, organizations, and nations? One answer was suggested in the 1960s film *Cool Hand Luke,* in which Paul Newman as Luke, an inmate, keeps breaking the warden's rules. As he prepares to punish Luke once again, the warden says, "What we have here is a failure to communicate." Actually it's not that Luke doesn't understand the rules; the problem is he doesn't *respect* the rules, so he violates them. By referring to a failure in *communication,* the warden means that Luke has not demonstrated his understanding that he must conform to the rules.

Communication and Conflict

In communication, more is going on than speaking, listening, and comprehending one another's words. Understanding communication requires some knowledge of the purpose served by that communication and what attitudes support it. Spitzberg (2008) reported that we interact with other people 70% of the time we are awake. Communicating effectively is an asset in one's personal and professional life, especially when conflicts occur. And conflicts are likely to be resolved only if those people involved communicate effectively.

What is an appropriate definition of communication?

Most people assume that the term *communicate* refers to interpersonal communication, but mass media represent another form of communication. Kougl (1997) offers a practical definition of **interpersonal communication:** "A dynamic process of interaction between people in which they assign meaning to each other's verbal and nonverbal behavior" (p. 7). Two features of this definition provide clues about how communication can lead to conflict: *assign meaning* and *nonverbal behavior.*

How does assigning meaning lead to conflict?

We not only listen to words; we also make assumptions about what the other person means. If our assumptions are accurate, there is no problem, but if they are not, the result is likely to be a misinterpretation of the message.

When interaction occurs between members of different groups, individuals may interpret the meaning of a statement in terms of the perceived influence of stereotypes or prejudices. During the second presidential debate in 2008 between John McCain and Barack Obama, McCain referred to an energy bill endorsed by President George W. Bush and Vice President Dick Cheney that came before the Senate. McCain claimed that the bill included significant funding for oil companies and stated, "You know who voted for it? You might never know. That one (pointing to Obama). You know who voted against it? Me."

The interpretation of Senator McCain's use of the phrase "That one" to refer to his Senate colleague was immediate, and overwhelmingly negative. The web site for CNN News soon posted a number of responses suggesting that the phrase was considered rude at the very least, if not racist: "Next he'll probably call (Obama) boy." An Executive Director of the Republican Party defended the party's candidate by saying: "I think McCain didn't mean anything negative. I think he was in the middle of his speech and was just getting passionate." But most of the respondents appeared to share the view of a woman from Chicago who wrote: "As soon as McCain referred to Obama as 'that one' my husband and I looked at each other in astonishment. John McCain's disdain for Obama is palpable . . . and incredibly ugly." According to some pundits, McCain may have appeared to show disdain for Obama to reinforce the campaign theme that Obama was inexperienced and not ready to be President, but his attitude was not well received by many viewers.

Another example of assigning meanings to statements occurred during a college ethnic studies class discussion of offensive words, phrases, and images based on ethnic and racial differences. An Asian American college student described his visit to a local middle school. As soon as he entered the building, he saw a few white male students put their fingers next to their eyes and pull their skin to create a "slant-eyed" look, and they began talking with a stereotypical Asian accent. The Asian American college student was appalled that these middle school students would taunt a visitor to their school with such blatant stereotypes, but another college student said this did not necessarily reflect their prejudice, just their immaturity. He argued that students at that age, especially boys, tend to be very insecure and they make fun of everyone and everything to get attention.

An American Indian student disagreed, saying that when he was in middle school and high school he heard a lot of students talking in terms of stereotypes. That was one of the reasons he was opposed to using Indians as mascots for sports teams because such images reinforced stereotypes for American Indians. A white woman in the class who was a nontraditional student said she didn't think there was anything wrong with Indian mascots because they had an Indian mascot at her high school and she felt that it was used to honor Indian people. That led to the following dialogue among the white female (WF), American Indian (AI), and Asian American (AA) students:

> *AI:* How am I supposed to be honored by an image like the Cleveland Indians mascot? These things are caricatures, cartoon figures! Even images that try to be respectable are just "noble savage" stereotypes that do not realistically depict real Indian people today . . . or at any time actually.
>
> *WF:* Well, I suppose if you look at something long enough you can always find something to be offended about.
>
> *AA:* Hold on, wait a minute! Are you saying that the problem is just in his head? That some people just make up stuff to be offended about but there's really nothing offensive there, nothing going on?
>
> *WF:* No, no, I'm not saying that. I just meant that . . . like with the Indian mascots . . . I don't think anyone intends to offend anyone, but some people are offended.
>
> *AA:* But you seem to be saying that the problem isn't real; that it's only a problem because of the way some Indian people look at this issue.
>
> *AI:* Yeah, it sounds like you don't think Indian mascots are stereotypes, and if we would just stop saying they were, then there'd be no problem.
>
> *AA:* Isn't that just another example of what we've talked about before? . . . You know, blaming the victim?
>
> *WF:* But that's not what I'm saying!

AA: Maybe not, but that's what it sounds like, and if we keep talking like that, then no one will ever confront the stereotypes that kids have learned about Asians or Indians or Blacks or any other group. It's not about immaturity or good intentions. It's about what people are doing, you know, it's about certain behaviors that should be confronted, especially in schools, and how to go about doing that.

The white woman continued to defend her position, but she was frustrated that she could not seem to get the other students to understand what she was saying—yet they felt they understood her meaning all too well. They perceived that she was denying the problem of stereotypes affecting white people's perceptions of people of color; they also believed that she blamed people of color for being offended about things that were never meant to be offensive. The white woman wanted to emphasize intent, but the other two students were focused on the consequences for people of color no matter what was intended. In both of the examples just given, the conflicts resulted from the meanings assigned to verbal statements. People make assumptions and interpretations about the meaning of another person's statements, regardless of whether it was what the other person intended. When the meaning assigned to a speaker's words becomes significantly different from what was intended, a conflict is likely to occur. Similarly, nonverbal communication can also lead to conflict based on someone's interpretation of the meaning of a nonverbal message.

> The meanings of words are not in the words; they are in us.
>
> **S. I. Hayakawa (1906–1992)**

How does nonverbal communication lead to conflict?

Hecht and DeVito (2008) define **nonverbal communication** as "all the messages other than words that people exchange" (p. 4). Estimates of how much meaning is taken from interpretations of nonverbal communication have been as high as 93%, although Burgoon (2002) estimated that 60% to 65% is more realistic. Children don't tend to find as much meaning from nonverbal behavior as do adults; still, parents and teachers must be conscious of their nonverbal cues, especially when they express disapproval or take disciplinary action. For a child to understand what adults mean, messages must not be contradicted or confused by nonverbal messages (Kougl, 1997).

Disciplinary action may be required in response to a child's unacceptable behavior—perhaps the child is teasing or taunting other children. The adult says, "Teasing is bad. It hurts people's feelings. It may make them angry and it certainly makes me angry. You must stop doing this or no one will like you and no one will want to play with you." The message is clear and provides good reasons, including self-interest, for the child to change his or her behavior. However, if this message is accompanied by angry looks, a loud voice, and gestures such as the adult pointing or jabbing a finger at the child, the good advice may get lost. The message the child gets is not that the behavior is bad but that "I'm bad" or "She hates me." (See Figure 3.1.)

Children receiving this message are not likely to change their behavior, but to persist in it, either as a way of rebelling against the adult who has made this negative comment about them or as a self-fulfilling prophecy: "She says I'm bad so I might as well be bad." Being told that certain *behavior* is unacceptable implicitly offers a child the power to choose. Children may not think they can change who they are, but they know they can change their behavior. If they hear an adult make a negative judgment about who they are, they can do nothing about that. Conflicts arising from such misinterpretations of nonverbal messages also occur among adults.

The need to assign meaning and the influence of nonverbal messages address two misconceptions about communication: (1) that communication simply means telling people something and (2) that communication is a verbal process to transmit messages using only words. Teachers who are committed to being good communicators understand the need to seek constant feedback from students to ensure that the knowledge they impart is being under-

FIGURE 3.1 According to Ekman (2003), expressions of contempt and disgust are often used to indicate hatred of another. Prior studies have indicated that expressions of hatred and anger are often confused. In these two photographs from Ekman's research, one expression represents contempt and the other is anger. Try to identify the emotion represented in each facial expression. (For the answer, see the Ekman annotation in the References at the end of the chapter.)

Source: Used by permission of Paul Ekman.

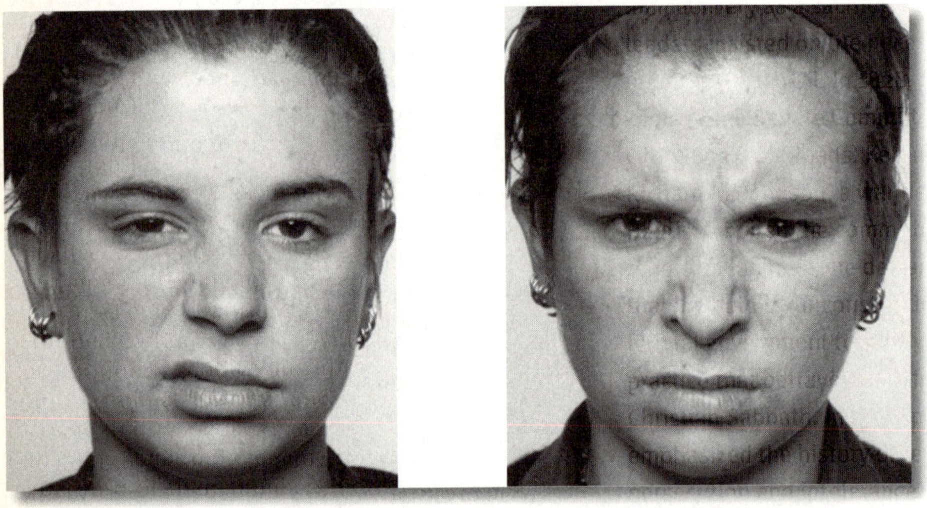

stood. Postman and Weingartner (1987) criticized educators for taking an "inoculation approach" in which teachers communicate information to students as if inoculating them against ignorance. When grades on tests reveal that students didn't retain much information, often the teacher's reaction is similar to that of a physician who doesn't understand why a vaccine had no effect when she knows she injected it. In discussing classroom communication, Kougl (1997) emphasized that teaching is not just talking; it involves more than words, as is true of all communication.

> Communication is something so simple and so difficult that we can never put it into simple words.
>
> **T.S. Matthews (1901–1991)**

What are other misconceptions about communication?

Of the many misconceptions about communication identified by Stone, Singletary, and Richmond (1999), the following five examples are especially important to recognize:

> Communication is a natural human ability.
> Communication is a good thing and should be encouraged.
> Communication will solve all our problems.
> Communications can break down.
> Communication competence is equal to communication effectiveness. (pp. 56–61)

Communication is a natural human ability. In a longitudinal study of three communities in the Piedmont Plateau region of the Carolinas, Heath (2006) described the way children learned communication skills and how skills varied depending on how the children had been taught. Heath found that low-income white parents taught language to children by reading storybooks with a moral for each tale. Parental communication style was didactic and authoritarian; their children memorized Bible verses, learned strict rules for right and wrong, and were severely punished for lying. When the children went to school, they did well initially because learning activities and communication styles of teachers were similar to what they had experienced at home. The children obeyed teachers, looked for a single meaning—the moral—of a story, and memorized material as required.

As the children from low-income white families progressed through elementary school, however, they encountered activities requiring critical thinking and creativity. They had trouble making up stories because it seemed like lying. They struggled to make sense of stories with multiple meanings and to identify and analyze different perspectives for strengths and weaknesses. Their life experiences had not prepared them for reading, thinking, and communicating at any level of complexity. As they approached middle school their grades declined, as did their confidence. The majority never achieved academic competence in school, and some dropped out before finishing high school.

Heath described the language learning of black children from low-income homes as a more creative process where children listened to adults tell stories that often had no particular moral point; these stories related what happened at work or in the neighborhood or gossip about "crooked politicians . . . or wayward choir leaders" (p. 168). Adults often told stories with a basis in fact, but with embellishment. When the stories got too far removed from reality, the teller was accused of "talkin' junk." In addition to hearing stories, boys developed language skills to respond to teasing based on "feigned hostility, disrespect and aggressive behavior" while girls became proficient in language by making up songs when skipping rope (p. 85). Both boys and girls practiced telling stories and, like adults, learned to embellish their stories with fictional details.

Black children from low-income homes came to school with highly creative communication skills, but they did not do well in the early elementary classes because they were not as adept at memorization or sticking to the facts. They saw many meanings to a story other than the simple moral the teacher wanted. As the students struggled with their assignments and growing feelings of inadequacy, they lost confidence in themselves as learners. When they finally encountered the more creative and complex learning activities later in elementary school, they were not successful because they had given up the possibility of success.

Heath noted that the children who succeeded in school at all levels were from middle-class homes, black as well as white, where their parents had read to them and had asked for didactic meanings of stories but also encouraged engagement in creative and analytical activity. A parent might read a story and then ask, "Would you have liked to go fishing with Little Bear? What do you think you would have caught?" (p. 250). Middle-class children came to school with a range of communication and language skills: They were successful at memorization and didactic activities during early elementary years; they were also able to adjust to activities emphasizing creativity or critical thinking in later years. Heath's research demonstrated that learning to communicate is not a natural human ability but rather is a product of the cultural and social context one experiences as a child.

Communication is a good thing and should be encouraged. Communication is a tool, and tools can be employed for good or bad purposes. Hitler used oratorical skills to arouse feelings of Aryan superiority and to deepen the anti-Semitic prejudices of Germans into a hatred that condoned persecution and execution. Martin Luther King, Jr., employed his oratorical skills to urge nonviolent resistance to oppression, warning his followers not to hate oppressors but to focus on the cause of justice. With any communication it is essential to ascertain the speaker's purpose and then determine whether that purpose is a good one. As Skuttnab-Kangas (2000) says, language is "a tool for domination (or) a tool for change and self-determination" (p. 134).

> Think like an active person; act like a thoughtful person.
>
> **Henri Bergson (1859–1941)**

It is also important to recognize when additional communication is not necessary—when the time has come to take action. Martin Luther King, Jr., deplored the "paralysis of analysis" as when people continue to talk about problems without ever doing anything. Of course it is essential to be thoughtful before acting, taking time to consider alternatives and consequences before deciding on a course of action, but there comes a time when one must stop analyzing every possible outcome and take action. After taking action, it is important to consider the consequences to determine whether to continue or choose another tactic. It is what Freire (2004) meant by the term **praxis**—taking action to address injustice and then reflecting on the effectiveness of the actions taken as the person or group continues their activities.

Communication will solve all our problems. Communication has the potential to solve problems, but it also has the potential to create them. In a speech to college students, poet Maya Angelou noted that whenever anyone asks, "Can I be brutally honest?" she always says "No" because she does not want to encourage anyone to do anything brutally. Whether information is accurate or inaccurate, truthful or distorted, if communication is delivered brutally it will be hurtful, and hurting people will create problems rather than solve them. We can communicate honestly without being brutal; we can show respect and sensitivity to the feelings of any person or group we encounter.

Ironically, some communication addresses problems with no *intent* of solving them. Berne (2004) described such interaction as playing "games." In the "Ain't It Awful" game, two people talk about a problem, not to solve it but to affirm each other's perceptions, sometimes at the expense of another. Imagine two teachers discussing a student. One describes Danny's misbehavior; the other responds with a similar story about something Danny did in her class, and they continue to exchange stories. The teachers are not trying to understand the boy's behavior to help him; instead, each is telling the other, "You and I are all right. Danny is the problem." When their conversation ends, both teachers walk away believing they are not to blame or obligated to do anything. Their communication has not solved Danny's problem, but it has made them feel better.

Another game Berne has described is "Yes, but . . . ," where one person comes to another asking for advice but actually wanting something else. For example, Luis is a teenager who is having problems with his parents. He goes to his best friend for advice. His friend suggests several strategies, and each time Luis says either (a) he tried that (or something similar) and it didn't work, or (b) he thought about doing that but explains why the suggestion wouldn't work. After the friend has exhausted all possible strategies he can think of, he may say something like, "Well I don't know what else to tell you. I don't know what else you can do." At this point, Luis walks away saying, "That's okay." The friend may be frustrated that he could not help solve the problem, but for Luis, the point of the conversation was to hear that he had done everything he could and there was nothing more for him to do. Now he can say the problem is not his responsibility; it is up to his parents. Both "Ain't It Awful" and "Yes, but . . ." involve a "solution" only in the sense that someone gets what he or she wants from the interaction, but the communication is not intended to solve the problem.

Communications can break down. Most of us have used this particular misconception about communication to justify ongoing conflicts. Rebellious teenagers say their parents don't understand them; husbands and wives complain that their partners don't appreciate them; workers may go on strike claiming that management isn't bargaining in good faith. In such cases, we may rationalize that our conflict cannot be resolved because communication has broken down. When machines break, they stop; however, communication cannot break down because it never stops, even if people stop talking to each other. Their communication could be hearsay

> Information voids will be filled by rumors and speculation unless they are preempted by open, credible, and trustworthy communication.
>
> **Jean Keffeler (Contemporary)**

or it could be nonverbal; it could consist of interpretations by one person about perceived decisions and actions of another.

Communication occurs because one person wants or needs to know what the other is thinking about or doing; a person may make decisions to do (or not to do) something based on assumptions about someone else. One person may decide not to attend a Christmas party so that a co-worker will know he is still angry with her, or he may decide to attend the party but not speak to the co-worker or make eye contact. In an extreme example, Dylan Klebold and Eric Harris had stopped responding to the taunts of some classmates and endured the verbal abuse at Columbine High School in silence, but when they went home, they left written and videotaped records of their repressed rage and their plans for revenge (Brown & Merritt, 2006). Communication can be ineffective or effective, but communication does not stop. If *verbal* exchange ceases, communication in some other form—whether words or actions—will replace it.

Communication competence is equal to communication effectiveness. This is a misconception few college students should believe because almost every college student is familiar with professors who are knowledgeable about their subject matter but ineffective at communicating that knowledge. We are competent to communicate on a topic if we have sufficient knowledge of it; however, possessing knowledge does not mean that we can communicate in a way that is easily comprehended.

A major function of teacher education programs consists of preparing people to be effective at organizing and communicating information. Whether they are lecturing or using alternative means of delivering information, teachers must understand what studies have concluded about effective ways of helping people learn. To assess how effectively they deliver information, teachers must also evaluate how well students learn. Tests and other forms of assessment may measure student learning; more importantly, they reveal how effectively the teacher communicated.

Except for those in teacher education, most college professors learn how to communicate from mentors or self-study. Many professors have acquired the skills to become good teachers, yet the misconception that communication competence equals communication effectiveness is often the basis for student complaints that they aren't learning because a professor is incompetent. Professors may have **communication competence** because they have the knowledge needed for communication and may even have published articles and books on their specialty, yet they may not display **communication effectiveness** because they lack the appropriate skills to communicate effectively in a classroom.

How does effective communication occur?

Numerous excellent models have been developed that examine the communication process and analyze communication to ascertain why misunderstandings occur (Narula, 2006; Stone et al., 1999). The following model describes four factors involved in interpersonal communication. Each instance of a person interacting with another is influenced by these four cumulative factors (see Figure 3.2).

A Circular Model of Communication

1. Attitudes toward people or groups
2. Observations and assumptions
3. Conclusions and judgments
4. Verbal and nonverbal action

First, the communication process is grounded in an individual's *attitudes toward people or groups.* All people develop a general attitude about their interactions with others. Some of us are trusting, others are suspicious; some are willing to share ideas, others are reserved; some are motivated by dominance and control, others function with an egalitarian view. Our attitudes may change because of those involved in our interactions. Our interactions with family are different than they are with strangers. We communicate differently within same-gender groups than in mixed groups or with people of the opposite gender. Our behavior is different with others of our own race or ethnic group as opposed to being in mixed groups or with individuals from another race or ethnic group. Having prejudices or stereotypes about a particular minority group will certainly influence our interactions with a member of that group.

Second, our *observations and assumptions* about another person shape the communication between us before anything is said. Our initial reaction may be friendly and accepting, aloof and suspicious, or even hostile and rejecting, depending on the appearance

FIGURE 3.2
The Circular Model of Communication

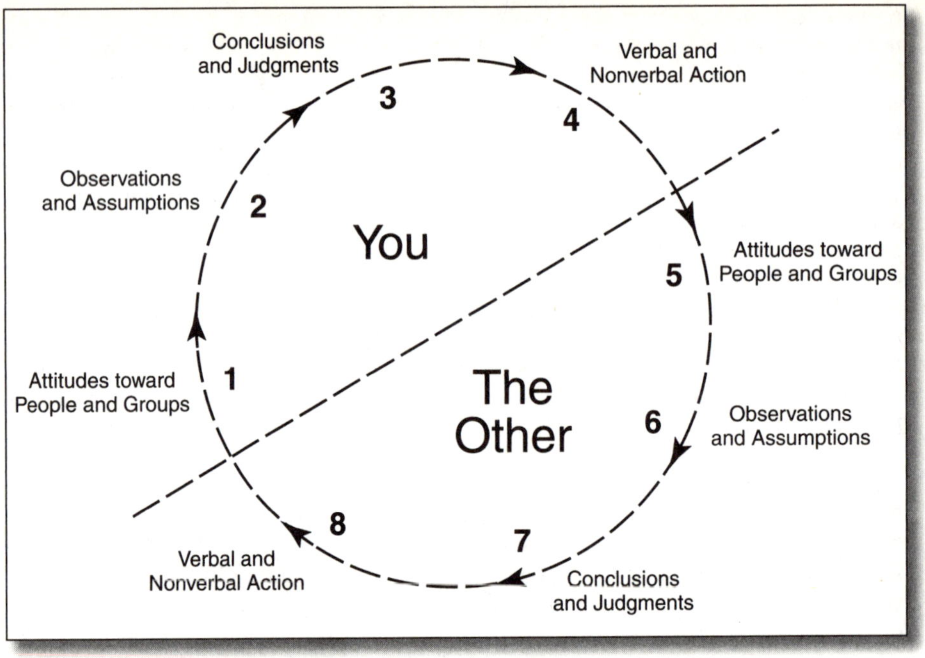

of the other person and sometimes on which behaviors we choose to observe—a phenomenon known as **selective perception.** If an individual believes a stereotype about someone from a certain group, that stereotype is likely to be reinforced by selective perceptions.

How do our observations influence our assumptions? What if a person were introduced to a long-haired young white male who was dressed in torn overalls and wore a red bandana around his head? Based on observation, one might assume that the young man has rejected our materialistic society by imitating college students from the 1960s who questioned authority figures and rebelled against middle-class values, conformity, and the Vietnam War. These observations and assumptions are now taken to the next level.

The third step, *conclusions and judgments,* refers to the values and beliefs we employ to draw conclusions or to judge others. In the example of the young man with long hair, various people observing him and making reasonable assumptions could come to different conclusions. One person may have been in college in the 1960s and remember it as an exciting time that had a profound influence on his life. His initial reaction may be a positive conclusion: "That young man reminds me of myself when I was his age." Conversely, someone who was taught to respect authority and appreciate the material comforts of our society and whose goal is to acquire those material comforts may make a negative judgment, perhaps generating additional assumptions about the young man smoking marijuana or using other illegal drugs. Prejudice and negative stereotypes lead to negative assumptions, which result in a negative judgment of another person.

The fourth and final step in the process is *verbal and nonverbal action.* When individuals meet, one person will say or do something to initiate interaction. Doing something might be as simple as smiling or frowning, making eye contact with the other or looking away. Nonverbal behavior employing such body language can initiate communication as much as words, often just as powerfully.

What does this communication model suggest about conflict resolution?

If conflict occurs during interaction, how can we resolve it? Our most common response is to focus on the action taken, on the words or behavior that initiated the conflict. For example, elementary teachers often witness conflict during recess where one child insults or hurts another. Some teachers respond by making the perpetrator apologize: The problem was the child's action, so the teacher forces the child to take another action to offset the first. This response focuses on the symptoms of the conflict and not the cause, so it is not likely to result in a resolution. Because the child may not feel genuinely sorry, what is learned from such an apology is a lesson in hypocrisy—being forced to say something that is not true.

Effective conflict resolution rejects superficial attention to actions and analyzes other factors to identify probable causes of the conflict. As Schramm (1973) stated, "The full significance of acts of communication is seldom on the surface" (p. 23). For this reason, most strategies for resolving conflicts are intended to get past surface meanings: Expressing "I" messages (Gordon, 2000); engaging in transactional analysis (Harris, 2004); using empathy to promote understanding (Rogers, 1995); and negotiating "Win/Win" strategies (Jandt, 1985). Still, even a proven approach may be ineffective if the people involved do not accept the value of the techniques employed.

The table on page 56 offers an analysis that employs the four factors of communication that preceded the conflict to understand the cause of a father/ daughter conflict. The situation concerns a father and Abby, his daughter. Abby is talking on the telephone and making plans to meet with some friends whom her father doesn't like.

If Abby and her father were to resolve their conflict by focusing on what each one said and did, resolution would be unlikely, but resumption of the quarrel would be quite likely. Instead, they could analyze factors involved prior to their argument to determine common ground on which to create a resolution. The cause of their quarrel stems from the father exercising his authority as a parent in conflict with Abby's desire for greater independence. They will need to discuss their conflicting assumptions and desires. The father must understand that adolescents typically resent parental authority and not take her rebelliousness personally. Abby must recognize her father's authority as legitimate. A resolution is likely to come from agreements about the father supporting Abby's desire to be more independent and Abby recognizing his concern to protect her from the consequences of what he perceives as bad decisions. The causes of an interpersonal conflict will rarely be found in an analysis or discussion of individual behaviors; they are more likely found in observations, assumptions, conclusions, or judgments made about each other, and sometimes in contrasting attitudes toward people and groups.

How can attitudes toward people or groups create conflict?

When people involved in interpersonal communication identify themselves—or are identified by others—as part of a specific group (such as by race or ethnicity), individual attitudes can be significantly influenced. In a multicultural society such as the United States, it is probable that people, especially in urban areas, will interact with others who are different by race, ethnicity, nationality, or religion (see Figure 3.3.). How much the cultures of different nationalities or people of different racial or ethnic groups affect communication will depend on the level of cultural awareness that the person has.

What are the levels of cultural awareness?

Kimmel (2006) identified levels of cultural awareness:

Cultural chauvinism Belief that one's culture is the best, superior to all other cultures; feeling no need to learn about other cultures.

Tolerance Awareness of cultural differences, recognition that differences stem from the country of origin for that person (or his or her ancestors); no judgment of cultural differences as inferior, simply as different ways of thinking or behaving.

Minimalization Minimizing cultural differences by emphasizing a universality of human needs and behaviors as a means of creating a stronger sense of relationship or connectedness with culturally different people.

Understanding Recognizing that reality is shaped by culture and that each person's reality is different from that of a person from a different culture; having no judgment of different

	Father	Abby
Interpersonal and Intergroup Attitudes:	Loves his daughter and wants her to be happy.	Loves her father but resents the authority he has over her.
Observations and Assumptions:	Remembers Abby as an obedient child, but she has been rebellious since becoming a teenager; she has been challenging his authority and questioning his decisions rather than giving him the respect he deserves.	Perceives her father as using his authority to control her and not being fair to her; expects him to interfere with decisions that she believes she has the right to make by herself.
Conclusions and Judgments:	Believes that Abby's behavior is a personal rejection of him; he has also concluded that Abby's friends have encouraged her to reject him by disobeying him.	Values independence and wants more freedom; regards her father as hypocritical for denying her what he values; ready to rebel against attempts to control her.
Nonverbal and Verbal Action:		Hangs up the phone and says, "I'm bored so I'm going out to meet my friends."
	Questions her choice of friends—"Why are you always hanging out with that bunch? Can't you find any other friends?"	
		"You are always criticizing my friends! You have no right to tell me who to be friends with!"
Conflict:	Becomes angry at her disrespectful tone of voice (which he expected to hear); tells her she cannot leave the house and orders her to her room.	Becomes angry about his attempt to control her (which she expected), shouts "Just leave me alone!" and runs out of the house, slamming the door behind her.

cultural realities; accepting and respecting cultural differences (cultural relativism).

Communication conflicts occur readily between people at the cultural chauvinism level, and they also may occur at the tolerance and minimalization levels. Only when people understand cultural differences and practice cultural relativism is it likely that conflicts between people from different cultures can be avoided or resolved.

Culture, Communication Style, and Conflict

Differences in cultural norms can cause misunderstanding and conflict. In the United States, business executives usually engage in minimal personal conversation before discussing a proposal at a group meeting. In some other cultures, communication is commonly expected to focus first on personal mat-

FIGURE 3.3 United States: Present and Future

As ethnic diversity increases in the United States, being aware of cultural differences will become increasingly important.

Source: Uncle Sam image, courtesy Library of Congress. Data from U.S. Census.

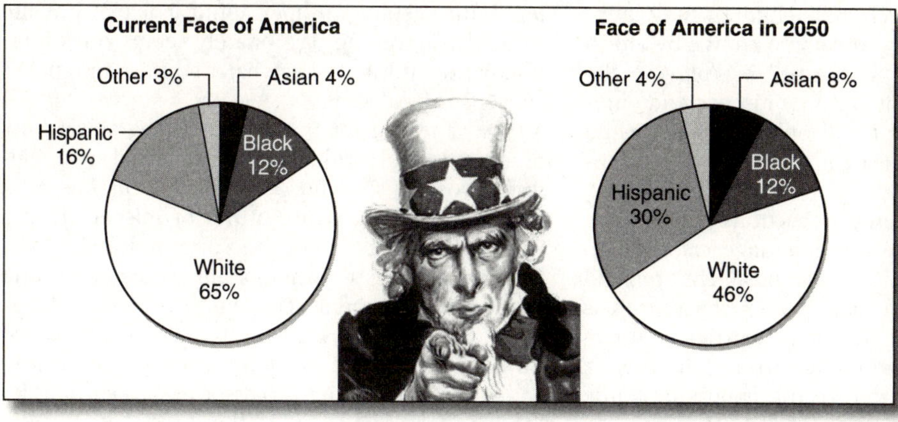

ters—questions about the person's health, family, or interests—before business is discussed. Ismail (2001) stressed how the global marketplace requires business executives to be knowledgeable about and employ appropriate communication strategies concerning use of direct speech, acceptable levels of informality, attitudes about time, and expressions of emotion to negotiate successfully with people from other cultures.

> The test of a first rate intelligence is the ability to hold two opposed ideas in the mind at the same time, and still retain the ability to function.
>
> **F. Scott Fitzgerald (1896–1940)**

What are some communication style differences that are based on culture?

In the United States, it has become acceptable to take a direct approach to conflict resolution, with each party openly expressing their concerns. In other cultures, people are expected to show sensitivity to the feelings of others by taking an indirect approach to resolving conflicts. In some cultures, people tend to speak in a linear progression, going from one idea to the next, but in other cultures, people digress, often telling stories or anecdotes to illustrate their point. Cultures also reflect differences in nonverbal behavior. In Arab cultures, people tend to stand much closer in conversation than do Americans. In the United States, men greet one another with a firm handshake; in France, anything other than a quick handshake is considered rude; in Ecuador, greeting a person without offering one's hand is a sign of special respect. In the United States, the forefinger to thumb gesture means "okay"; in France, it signifies that something is worthless; and in Brazil, the gesture is considered obscene (Jandt, 2003).

Differences in communication styles have also been identified in subcultures in the United States. Kochman (1981) described how black and white children learn to express aggression. For most middle-class white people, aggressive language is viewed as a harbinger of aggressive behavior. "Fighting words" are words that may provoke a physical confrontation. (Meltzoff, 2007). Most white children learn to repress aggressive feelings and maintain a calm demeanor even though they may be furious. If they begin using language aggressively, it is likely that a fight is imminent. For some black males, however, words can be used aggressively without a conflict. Foster (1986) described how urban black male children may taunt one another in a playground game known by different names including "sounding" or "playing the dozens." Situations may become intense and emotional; however, a fight will only occur if a child gives an obvious signal such as making a fist to indicate that he is angry.

The contrast between the reactions of black and white people to aggressive language can lead to misunderstanding. Imagine two black children still playing the insult game as they come back to their classroom after recess. The teacher tries to intervene, but the boys continue to insult each other. A black teacher may recognize the childhood game and firmly tell them to stop, but a white teacher may perceive the boys as engaged in a hostile quarrel and order them to the principal's office. If the principal asks them why they were sent, they are likely to say they don't know. When the principal says their teacher saw them fighting, they will vigorously deny it, insisting that they were just teasing each other. Because the teacher has made this "false accusation," they might think she doesn't like them and become hostile to her in return.

Kochman (1981) describes another difference in communication styles concerning the conduct of arguments. White people are encouraged to present unbiased, objective arguments, but black people tend to accept the existence of bias and are skeptical of claims of objectivity. Although white people have been taught to argue in a calm, dispassionate manner, people in many black communities defend their beliefs passionately. In debates, black people do not expect impersonal or dispassionate arguments and may distrust people who are not passionate. Expressing ideas passionately during an argument is regarded as a measure of sincerity. In white society, the norm in debating issues is to repress emotions because they are believed to interfere with keeping an open mind. For many white Americans, arguing passionately seems confrontational; they think it exacerbates conflict and makes consensus less likely.

> Misunderstandings and inertia cause perhaps more to go wrong in this world than slyness and evil intent.
>
> **Johann Wolfgang von Goethe (1749–1832)**

The potential for misunderstanding about how arguments are conducted was revealed in a televised program showing academics discussing racial issues in which a white professor misperceived a black professor based on his communication style. The black professor was making an eloquent and passionate argument. The white professor sitting beside him appeared uncomfortable, yet displayed no emotion. As the black professor paused before concluding, the white professor remarked in a defensive tone of voice but without facial expression, "Well you don't have to be so angry." Startled by the interruption, the black professor looked over at his white colleague and said, "Excuse me, you are mistaking intensity for anger."

In describing communication style differences, the intent is not to find fault with any group or person, nor is it to say that one communication style is better than the other. What is important is to understand that communication styles are influenced by cultural heritage; we should not make assumptions about others based on their communication style. If a conflict occurs in a group whose members are different races or cultures, individuals in the group must articulate their perceptions about the cause of the conflict to see if everyone has a similar perception. Understanding our perceptions of others provides a basis for resolving cultural misunderstandings and conflicts. Meanwhile, research suggests that differences in communication styles create misunderstandings between men and women as well.

How does gender influence communication styles?

Communication differences based on gender are said to originate in differences in the way boys and girls are socialized. Traditionally, Americans have encouraged boys to be aggressive and girls to be nice; this has been documented in studies of children's play activities. American boys tend to play outdoors, typically in competitive games that require groups and involve aggressive behavior; they resolve disputes by engaging in debates in which everyone participates. In contrast, girls tend to play indoor types of games in small groups or with a friend; these games involve conversation and collaboration, and a quarrel will usually disrupt the game (Dow & Wood, 2006; Honig, 2006).

Gender differences persist even as children leave childhood behind. Some scholars believe that male aggressiveness in conversation is revealed in studies where men interrupt women more than women interrupt men (Dow & Wood, 2006), but Tannen (1994) argued that it is simplistic to say such behavior is always a dominance issue. Reviewing communication research on gender differences, Burgoon (2002) reported that women are more competent than men at giving and understanding nonverbal messages. Grumet (2008) found that women tend to have more eye contact than men and to pay more attention to their conversational partner.

Differences in degree of eye contact and face-to-face interaction often reflect differences in how women and men express intimacy. Tannen (2007) described differences in male and female communication styles originating in childhood and continuing into adult years. In one study with subjects ranging from children to young adults, two people of the same age and gender were taken to a room, seated in chairs placed side by side, and asked to talk about a serious topic. The younger boys had trouble with the task; they didn't move the chairs, did not make eye contact, and spent much of their time shifting restlessly and talking about not wanting to talk. Males of all ages would sit in the chairs in their original position with minimal face-to-face interaction. At all age levels, female partners either moved the chairs or positioned themselves to face each other; they began talking immediately on a serious topic as requested.

High school boys express intimacy through aggressive behavior. Pushing, shoving, even punching each other is an indication of a close friendship. As adults, men transform aggressive physical behavior into aggressive verbal behavior. For example, American men are careful about expressing disagreement with someone they don't know very well, but they bluntly disagree with and even use sarcasm with a close friend. It is a sign of intimacy and trust when men don't have to "pull their punches" with each other.

From childhood through adulthood, American women tend to express intimacy by engaging in face-to-face interactions and expressing concern for the other person's feelings. For most, outright disagreement is regarded as a threat to intimacy, a lack of sensitivity or respect. When a woman disagrees with another woman, she will often begin by saying something positive or something they agree on, and then address the issue about which they disagree. The difference in male and female communication styles creates opportunities for misunderstanding. If a man and a woman have an intimate relationship and discuss an issue on which they disagree, he may make direct, honest comments because he feels so close to her, but she may interpret his harsh comments as insensitive, disrespectful, and even contemptuous of her opinions.

With such an emphasis on competition and aggression, boys become men who directly express wants, needs, or demands. With such an emphasis on cooperation, being nice, and caring about how others might feel, girls become women who are concerned about not imposing their wants or demands, preferring consensus. A man might attempt to convince someone to do what he wants, but a woman is more likely to ascertain whether the other person is interested in doing what she wants to do. Tannen (2007) argues that this difference may be a basis for historic gender stereotypes that have contributed to misunderstandings and conflict: men perceiving women as devious and cunning, and women perceiving men as arrogant and intimidating.

How do gender differences in communication styles lead to misunderstanding and conflict?

Imagine a woman coming home from work, greeting her husband, and then remembering, "Oh John, I meant to stop at the store and pick up a few things, but I am so tired I forgot to do it. This has been such a rotten day." She is indirectly asking him to go to the store for her, yet he may not get the message. Even if he tries to be sympathetic—"I'm sorry to hear that"—she will be upset if he doesn't offer to go to the store. If he wanted her to go to the store he would ask her directly; he needs to understand that her socialization and her communication style does not allow her to make demands as he would.

In a similar example, after leaving early for a long trip, a couple has been driving all morning on the interstate and it's almost noon. She sees a sign advertising a restaurant she likes at the next exit, points it out to him, and says, "Would you like to stop there and get something to eat?" He hears her comment not as an indirect request, but as a genuine question. He wants to drive for another hour before stopping to eat, so he says "No" and drives on. When he realizes that she is upset, they discuss the reason, and he criticizes her for not stating explicitly what she wanted. She thinks he should be able to understand that she did tell him in a manner that took account of his feelings. She believes that she has been sensitive and he has not. He believes she was being dishonest while he was being straightforward with her.

The reason for identifying gender differences is not to blame men or women, nor to say that one communication style is better than another. It is important to recognize the diverse ways people communicate so that differences in communication styles do not result in conflict. Knowing the influence on communication style of such factors as gender or culture provides a basis to prevent misunderstandings. If people recognize problems as possibly stemming from a difference in communication styles, they can modify their interaction to communicate more effectively (Jandt, 2003; Prince, 2004).

Conflict Resolution

Sometimes resolving conflicts seems hopeless. Groups have been in conflict for centuries; individuals take unresolved conflicts to their graves. Obviously, conflict resolution is not easy, and most people approach conflict with apprehension. In a study by McCorkle and Mills (1992), every metaphor chosen by participants to describe conflict was negative, often involving feelings of helplessness and of being an innocent victim.

Because K–12 schools are an environment for children and youth with adult supervision, we would expect to find less conflict, and yet studies find that considerable conflict occurs there. According to Wessler (2003), these conflicts usually stem from human differences such as race, mental disability, sexual orientation, and gender. Sexual orientation alone appears to result in many instances of harassment and conflict. According to an NMHA survey, students who were both gay and straight reported 20 or more incidences a day of hearing slurs and insults that were directed at their peers who were openly gay or simply perceived as gay. One third of the gay students in that survey had been threatened or actually injured at school in the previous 12 months (Roberts Jr., 2006). Garrett (2003) cites research documenting the consequences of harassment and conflicts between students:

10% of students drop out of school
20% of students avoid going to restrooms during the school day
54% of students say it would be easy for them to get a gun
30% of students have heard a peer threaten to kill someone
25% of students know a peer who has brought a gun to school (p. 12)

With so much conflict occurring, how are conflicts resolved?

Conflict offers opportunity for constructive change, if all parties are prepared to make concessions and to establish a context conducive to resolution. Deutsch (2006) identified values that participants must share if they want to resolve conflict: fallibility, equality, reciprocity, and nonviolence.

Fallibility refers to accepting the possibility of being wrong. In conflict, people are customarily presented with evidence and arguments. However, presenting evidence will not help resolve a conflict if participants refuse to acknowledge that their position could be wrong. During deliberations in a jury room, the foreman of a jury said he believed the defendant was guilty and that he would not change his mind. Another jury member pointed out that such an attitude violated the jury process that requires discussing and debating evidence, listening to arguments with an open mind, and changing one's mind if justified by the weight of evidence or arguments. Although still believing the defendant guilty, the foreman admitted the jury member was right, and he agreed to listen with an open mind. Ultimately he changed his mind.

Equality refers to the belief that every human being, regardless of status, occupation, or wealth, deserves to be treated respectfully, with consideration for his or her values, beliefs, and behavior. It is an acknowledgment that every human life has value and that no one should be treated unjustly. In another jury trial, some members of the jury began to criticize testimony of two overweight and casually dressed female witnesses, based on their appearance rather than on what they said. Another juror chastised them for their negative attitudes and argued that if the jury was to render a just verdict, they should focus on the evidence the women presented, not on how they looked. Other jurors agreed.

Reciprocity means that participants in a conflict must behave toward others with the same sense of fairness and attentiveness that they would want for themselves—a restatement of the golden rule that appears as an ethical principle in practically all cultures, or as modified by Confucius: "Do not do to others what you would not like yourself" (Waley, 1938, p. 162). Apparently Confucius believed one did not have to be good to others as long as no harm was done to them. Either way, the feeling of reciprocity is essential for participants in a conflict if they hope to negotiate a resolution to it.

To value *nonviolence* is to believe that the only genuine solutions are peaceful ones. As Deutsch explained in his fourth shared value, coercing others into accepting an imposed solution winds a long and tragic path through human history marked by brutality and blood, civil and global wars, leaving little evidence that solutions imposed by the strong on the weak are effective—or lasting—solutions.

> The man who strikes first admits that his ideas have given out.
>
> **Chinese Proverb**

In the context of the four shared values proposed by Deutsch, conflict need not be a destructive event; it can be a constructive opportunity. Appleton (1983, p. 185) quotes educational philosopher John Dewey: "Conflict is the gadfly of thought. It steers us to observation and memory. It instigates to invention. It shocks us out of sheep-like passivity." If participants use effective negotiation strategies, they may be able to identify sources of conflict and determine appropriate solutions leading to improved relations between people.

Johnson, Johnson, and Tjosvold (2006) identified effective negotiation strategies to engage in what they termed **skilled disagreement.** Their first strategy for engaging in skilled disagreement is similar to what the jury member described in the fallibility anecdote: that all parties (1) agree to emphasize rationality, seek the best possible answer based on the available evidence and arguments, and be willing to change their position when justified by the evidence. Another strategy is that participants (2) agree that criticizing an idea is not criticizing those who propose the idea—that their worth as human beings is separate from their ideas.

It is also important that participants (3) make a conscious commitment to encourage others to contribute to discussion and to listen thoughtfully to the contributions they make. To ensure the process is effective, it is helpful when participants (4) restate ideas if they're not clear on what was said so that everyone understands the issue from all perspectives being presented. Finally, it is essential that participants (5) remember that the problem and any recommended solution will affect everyone; they must not be focused on winning a debate but upon arriving at a collaborative solution everyone can support. These conflict resolution skills are not difficult to learn, and many educators say they can and should be taught in schools, even to young children. Based on her review of research, Garrett (2003) argues that "Conflict resolution skills . . . learned by all students will help to change a school's atmosphere" (p. 135). By teaching these skills, educators may foster the development of not only cognitive abilities but also moral reasoning abilities.

How do people develop moral reasoning abilities?

Different theories of moral reasoning have been described, but some have not been carefully researched; others do not seem widely applicable to different cultures or genders. Perry (1999) has described a theory of moral reasoning that develops along a continuum, providing an accurate description of moral reasoning engaged in by people of different ages, from different cultures or subcultures, and from both genders (Belenky et al., 1997; King & Kitchener, 1994). Using this theory, teachers can provide students with moral dilemmas and controversial issues, then analyze student discussions and engage students with questions intended to challenge and improve the quality of their moral reasoning. What is this theory of moral reasoning that Perry has developed?

Perry's theory is based on the assumption that changes in moral reasoning are related to cognitive development: Increased cognitive ability allows individuals the possibility of increasing the complexity of their moral reasoning. Although there are nine developmental positions in Perry's continuum, as an introduction to the theory, it is sufficient to understand two major areas Perry has identified—dualism and relativism—and the mental shift that occurs within each: A dualistic thinker transitions into multiplicity, a relativistic thinker transitions into making commitments (see Figure 3.4).

Dualism All human beings begin as dualistic thinkers when confronted with moral decisions; children tend to operate simplistically with absolute categories of right and wrong. In **dualism,** every moral issue is a question of either/or: Either it's right or it's wrong, it's true or it's false, it's good or it's bad. This is also called "black and white" thinking because there are no "shades of gray" for dualistic thinkers. To be dualistic is to believe that what is true must be regarded as an absolute truth: It has always been and will always be true. Newberg and Waldman (2006) say that brain research offers a biological explanation for dualistic thinking: "The brain tends to reduce cause-and-effect cognition into dualistic scenarios because they are an easy, neurologically efficient way to make sense of the world" (p. 88).

Believing in absolutes is challenged when a person is confronted with problems that don't lend themselves to the either/or style of thinking. A popular moral dilemma exercise is to ask people what they would have done if they were hiding Jews in the early 1940s and Gestapo officers came to their home to ask if they knew where there were any Jews. For the person who believes "honesty is the best policy," this is a difficult question to answer. Another problem with dualistic thinking is that the cognitive process of simplification and generalization inevitably leads to stereotyping others because the process does not consider individual differences. As studies have reported, the "'us-versus-them' mentality can be easily converted into racism" (Newberg & Waldman, 2006, p. 89). Complex issues that challenge dualistic thinking may not occur until a student enters high school or college, but when students confront such issues, they often feel

FIGURE 3.4 A Continuum of Moral Reasoning

Source: Perry, W. (1970). *Forms of Intellectual and Ethical Development in the College Years: A Scheme.* New York: Holt, Rinehart & Winston.

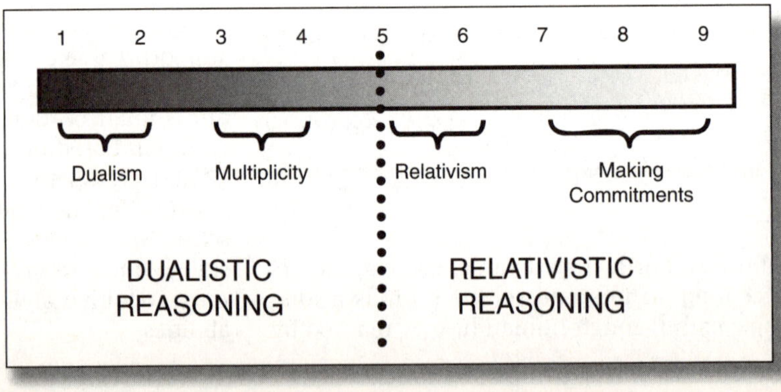

compelled to move away from rigid dualistic thinking and engage in the kind of moral reasoning called multiplicity.

Multiplicity The perspective of **multiplicity** recognizes the difficulty of knowing "the right answer" in every situation. When the right answer is not obvious, the only recourse is for the individual to examine various opinions or multiple perspectives without being certain which one is right. Each person must consider the different perspectives and decide which one seems best. This is not satisfying for people at the multiplicity position because they are still influenced by dualistic thinking. They would prefer to know the answer or the truth in a given situation, and often complain that all we have are opinions. Because of the influence of dualistic thinking, people at a multiplicity position still believe the truth can be known and will be known some day, but for the moment, they reluctantly accept that they do not know the answer for a number of issues.

> The question should never be who is right, but what is right.
>
> **Glenn Gardiner (Contemporary)**

Relativism When people move beyond multiplicity to relativism, they tend to exhibit a change in attitude from reluctantly accepting the existence of multiple perspectives to becoming intrigued by the idea that each person must decide what is right. **Relativism** is based on the assumption that there are no absolute truths, and truth is relative, a concept reflected in the familiar phrases: "One man's meat is another man's poison" and "One person's treasure is another person's junk." The relativist is stimulated by differences of opinions, is interested in debates, and may enjoy playing the devil's advocate in a discussion by articulating arguments and ideas to defend a particular perspective without really believing in it.

Relativism requires an individual to be comfortable with ambiguity and not demand specific answers that are right for everyone. Many people are uncomfortable living in a world where they have to accept many points of view without regarding any of them as the right one. The difficulty of accepting such ambiguity causes some people to "retreat" (as Perry calls it) by resuming a dualistic thinking process. Other people who never progress beyond relativistic thinking sometimes adopt a cynical attitude toward life because relativistic thinking does not often result in becoming passionate about or personally invested in any issue or cause. However, some people who have also felt a sense of dissatisfaction with relativism's moral ambiguity have identified questions they wanted answered and are engaged deliberately in efforts to find their own answers.

Commitment Relativistic thinkers who continue to develop their moral reasoning are attracted to the idea of making **commitments** to certain personal truths, ideals, or causes that seem to give meaning to their lives. Most people need to believe in something and to feel a sense of satisfaction that their belief enhances the quality of their lives. Commitments may include being active in a political party or joining a church, an advocacy group, or some other organization. A commitment may result in volunteer work or influence a person's career decision. Whatever the choice, it is made from among many alternatives and the individual makes the commitment because it reflects his or her values.

Once people make commitments, they often become advocates for that particular cause or perspective. Because commitment is made in the context of relativistic thinking, people who reflect this perspective do not advocate like dualistic thinkers whose arguments are based on a sense of certainty. Relativistic thinkers may emphasize the sense of satisfaction they feel that their commitment provides a stronger sense of meaning and purpose in their lives, and they invite others to join them. In contrast, when dualistic thinkers advocate for truths they believe are absolute, they tend to view those who agree with them as right and those who disagree as wrong. There is no other option. When people at the commitment level argue on behalf of their commitments, they do not tend to judge those who agree or disagree. They recognize that it is an individual's obligation to make his or her own choices, and they respect the person's right to choose. Someone at the commitment level does not reject relativism and its view of reality as ambiguous, but this person does recognize the satisfaction that may be gained by making commitments to provide a sense of meaning and purpose to his or her life. Being able to respect individual choice is not only important for moral reasoning, it is also essential for engaging in successful conflict resolution.

AFTERWORD

Even if we say exactly what we want to say, we can never assume that the meaning is heard and understood in the way we intend. Miscommunication happens when people do not check with others to ensure that they were understood. When misunderstandings are not clarified at the time they occur, they can cause people to become antagonistic toward others, thereby laying the foundation for an eventual conflict.

> Wrongdoing can only be avoided if those who are not wronged feel the same indignation at it as those who are.
>
> **Solon (640–558 BCE)**

Some efforts to reduce conflict in schools have been successful, and there is much to be learned from them. In elementary classrooms, teachers must emphasize respect and nonviolence in their work with students. At the middle and high school levels, schools can empower students to intervene in conflicts by sponsoring workshops and providing other opportunities to develop mediation skills. At all levels it is important for students to work in groups and to have other experiences (e.g., peer tutoring) where they become better acquainted. According to Garrett (2003), studies have reported a reduction of conflict in schools when children and youth have more opportunities to get to know each other.

Conflict resolution is not easy, yet it's better than coping with unresolved conflict. It is in everyone's interest to embrace the values that make conflict resolution possible and to practice communication strategies necessary for engaging in skilled disagreement. Conflict—from intimate disagreements between husbands and wives to global disputes among nations—is inevitable. The resolution of conflicts, however, is not inevitable. Teachers must challenge and enhance the moral reasoning abilities of our children and youth, and all of us must choose to engage in and be committed to the process of conflict resolution. The quality of individual lives and the quality of life for communities and for countries depends on the willingness of people to choose to resolve conflicts rather than hopelessly perpetuate them.

TERMS AND DEFINITIONS

Commitment Moral reasoning in a relativist context that recognizes the importance of becoming actively committed to certain personal truths to strengthen and deepen the meaningfulness of one's life experiences

Communication competence Having sufficient knowledge of a subject to communicate accurate information about that subject

Communication effectiveness Having the skills to communicate information in order to be easily understood

Cultural chauvinism An attitude that one's culture is the best, superior to other cultures

Dualism Moral reasoning involving a belief in absolute truths and unambiguous categories of right and wrong behavior; also called "either/or reasoning"

Interpersonal communication A dynamic process of interaction between people in which they assign meaning to each other's verbal and nonverbal behavior (Kougl, 1997)

Minimalization An attitude about other cultures that reduces importance of cultural differences and emphasizes the universality of human needs and behaviors to create a stronger sense of relationship with all people

Multiplicity Moral reasoning in a dualistic context recognizing that it isn't possible to know what is the right behavior in certain situations, in which case opinions from multiple perspectives must be examined; a person can't be confident of the final decision in such instances because he or she can't be certain of having made the right choice

Nonverbal communication Those messages other than words that people exchange, also called "nonverbal behavior" or "nonverbal messaging"

Praxis Taking action to address injustice and then reflecting on the effectiveness of the actions taken as the person or group continues their activities

Relativism Moral reasoning that rejects absolute truth and is based on the assumption that all truth is relative and determining the right behavior depends on the individual and the situation

Selective perception Paying attention to behaviors of another person that reinforce our expectations for that person

Skilled disagreement Strategies that have been proven effective in achieving a successful resolution to conflicts

Tolerance Aware of cultural differences without judging cultures as superior or inferior

Understanding Recognizing that culture shapes individual reality including acceptance of and respect for cultural differences

DISCUSSION EXERCISES

Exercise 1: Statements Illustrating Perry's Continuum

Directions: Conversations can be categorized according to Perry's concepts. Identify each of the following statements according to the four broad areas in Perry's continuum of moral development. You will find three examples from each area. Record your answers as (a) dualism, (b) multiplicity, (c) relativism, or (d) commitment.

Statements Illustrating Perry's Continuum

_____ 1. In areas where even the experts disagree, everyone has a right to his own opinion. I mean, if answers aren't given, like in lots of things, then it has to be just anyone's opinion.

_____ 2. Understanding another point of view, especially a contrary one, helps me understand my own point of view. So trying to see through the other person's eyes helps my own understanding of the issue.

_____ 3. I came here from a small town in the Midwest where everyone believed the same things and everyone is, like, Methodist and Republican. But here, there is a variety of Protestants and Catholics and a Chinese boy who follows the teaching of Confucius. . . . Some people are quite disturbing; they say they're atheists, but I don't think they are.

_____ 4. I'm not sure how to make any decision at all. When you are here and having the issues thrust at you and reading about the people who pushed their thought to the absolute limit and seeing how that did not result in an all-encompassing answer . . . , you begin to have respect for how great their thought could be even though it did fall short.

_____ 5. The science lectures are all right. They sort of say the facts, but when you get to a humanities course, they are awful! The lecturer is just reading things into the book that were never meant to be there.

_____ 6. This place is full of bull. If you turn in a speech or a paper that is well written, whether it has one single fact in it or not is beside the point. . . . So you sit down and write a paper in an hour, just because you know that whatever it is isn't going to make any difference to anyone.

_____ 7. I get frustrated in class when the teacher only looks at things from her point of view. There are other ideas to consider. What is important to me is trying to understand and evaluate ideas and to come up with my own. I dislike discussions in which everyone just voices an opinion without backing it up. What good are opinions unless you put them to the test?

_____ 8. When I have an idea about something and it differs from the way another person is thinking about it, I will usually try to look at it from that person's point of view, see how they could say that, why they think they are right, why it makes sense.

_____ 9. In science you don't really want to say that something is true. We're dealing with a model and models are always simpler than the real world, which is more complex than anything we can create. We simplify so we can work with it. When we try to describe things, we leave out the truth because we are oversimplifying.

_____ 10. About the only thing I guess I would say to a prospective student is that if you come to this college, you had better do everything you are supposed to do and then you will be all right. That's just about all.

_____ 11. As soon as someone tells me his point of view, I immediately start arguing in my head the opposite point of view. When someone is saying something, I can't help turning it upside down.

_____ 12. I can't really say that one opinion is better than another. It depends on your beliefs. I am the type of person who would never tell someone that their opinion is wrong. If they have searched, well, even if they haven't searched, if they just believe it, that's cool for them.

Exercise 2: Words and Phrases That Hurt

Directions: Our conversations carry implications that reflect personal understanding, values, or beliefs. The 10 statements here contain implications that can offend others. Considering who the communicants are, why might the statements have been made in the first place? What are the implications in each? How does the context in which each is spoken make it offensive or hurtful?

1. A white person to a black person: "We must have law and order."
2. In a discussion of inequitable school funding, a suburban parent to an inner city parent: "You can make your schools as good as ours."
3. A Korean American to a black acquaintance: "You're different from most blacks."
4. A white employer announcing the intention of integrating the workplace: "Of course, we will make sure we only hire a *qualified* minority applicant."
5. In a discussion of racial discrimination in America, a black person to a Japanese American: "Asians have done well in America; you shouldn't have anything to complain about."
6. A white person to a Chicano: "I don't understand what you people want."
7. A white person to a black person: "Our old neighborhood used to be good when I was a kid, but it's gone downhill since it was integrated."
8. A Chinese American to a black person: "The death of Martin Luther King was a terrible loss to your race."
9. A black Christian to a Jew: "Oh, you're Jewish? I didn't realize you were Jewish—you sure don't act like one."
10. A white person to a Native American: "I think your people have made great progress."

REFERENCES

Appleton, N. (1983). *Cultural pluralism in education: Theoretical foundations.* New York, NY: Longman.

Examines how the United States has become pluralistic, how American education has responded to pluralism, and what our pluralistic society might look like in the future.

Belenky, M.F., Clinchy, B.M., Goldberger, N.R., & Tarulle, J.M. (1997). *Women's ways of knowing: The development of self, voice, and mind.* New York, NY: Basic Books.

Describes the ways of gaining knowledge that women have developed and the obstacles women must overcome in developing their intellectual abilities.

Berne, E. (2004). *Games people play: The psychology of human relationships.* New York, NY: Ballantine. (Originally published in 1964)

Examines the purposes behind conversational "games" and analyzes a number of them, then provides suggestions to promote more honest interactions.

Brown, B., & Merritt, R. (2002). *No easy answers: The truth behind death at Columbine.* New York, NY: Lantern Books.

Describes the bullying and taunting of Dylan Klebold and Eric Harris by other students that resulted in their murder spree and suicides at Columbine High School.

Burgoon, J.K. (2002). Nonverbal signals. In M. Knapp & G. Miller (Eds.), *Handbook of interpersonal communication* (3rd ed., pp. 344–390). Beverly Hills, CA: Sage.

Reviews research to describe the nature, structure, and social functions of nonverbal communication including the impact of cultural norms, gender, and social status.

Deutsch, M. (2006). Cooperation and competition. In M. Deutsch, P. Coleman & E.C. Marcus (Eds.), *The handbook of conflict resolution* (2nd ed., pp. 21–40). San Francisco, CA: Jossey-Bass.

Describes constructive and destructive forms of competition and the implications of a cooperative orientation for more effectively resolving conflicts.

Dow, B.J., & Wood, J.T. (2006). *The SAGE handbook of gender and communication.* Thousand Oaks, CA: Sage Publications.

Reviews gender research on a range of communication issues such as perception, self-image, sex roles, language, and media images.

Ekman, P. (2003). *Emotions revealed: Recognizing faces and feelings to improve communication and emotional life.* New York, NY: Times Books.

This cross-cultural study of nonverbal communication reveals the effectiveness of facial expressions in communicating meaning. [The picture on the left was anger; on the right, contempt.]

Foster, H.L. (1986). *Ribbin', jivin', and playin' the dozens* (2nd ed.). Cambridge, MA: Ballinger.

Describes verbal and nonverbal communication of urban black youth to prevent misunderstandings and to provide teachers with effective interaction strategies.

Freire, P. (2000). *Pedagogy of the oppressed.* New York, NY: Continuum. (Originally published in 1970)

Analyzes the dynamics of oppression including the role of the oppressor, the responses of the oppressed, and the consequences of oppression for both.

Garrett, A.G. (2003). *Bullying in American schools: Causes, preventions, interventions.* Jefferson, NC: McFarland & Company, Inc.

Defines and discusses characteristics of bullies, identifies myths about bullies while reviewing research that refutes those myths, and describes successful interventions.

Gordon, T. (2000). *Parent effectiveness training: The proven program for raising responsible children.* New York, NY: Crown.

Describes a variety of strategies for parents to use not only to resolve conflicts with their children but also to teach children how to make responsible choices.

Grumet, G.W. (2008). Eye contact: The core of interpersonal relatedness. In J. DeVito & M. Hecht (Eds.), *The nonverbal communication reader* (3rd ed., pp. 126–139). Long Grove, IL: Waveland.

Presents an overview of research related to the significance of eye contact on relationships and the function of eye contact in interpersonal communication.

Harris, T. (2004). *I'm OK—you're OK.* New York, NY: Morrow/Avon.

Uses Berne's theory of transactional analysis (TA) to explain how TA can become an analytical tool to understand interactions with others and resolve conflicts.

Heath, S.B. (2006). *Ways with words.* Cambridge, UK: Cambridge University Press.

Describes how children learn language in three distinct communities and the consequences of the way they have learned language with regard to their ability to be successful in school.

Hecht, M.L., & DeVito, J.A. (Eds.). (2008). Perspectives on defining and understanding nonverbal communication: Classic and contemporary readings. In *The nonverbal communication reader* (3rd ed., pp. 3–17). Long Grove, IL: Waveland.

Reviews research to describe the characteristics of nonverbal communication and to explain the relationship between verbal and nonverbal communication.

Honig, A.S. (2006). Socio-cultural influences on gender-role behaviors in children's play. In D.P. Fromberg & D. Bergen (Eds.), *Play from birth to twelve and beyond: Contexts, perspectives, and meanings* (2nd ed., pp. 328–347). New York, NY: Routledge.

Describes gender differences in play activities, stereotyping in toy preference, and the influence of parents, peers, and television on children's play.

Ismail, N. (2001, September). Communicating across cultures. Victoria, BC: Pertinent Information. Available at http://pertinent.com/pertinfo/business/yaticom.html

Examines factors that affect communication between people from different cultures and offers suggestions for improving such cross-cultural interactions.

Jandt, F.E. (1985). *Win-win negotiating: Turning conflict into agreement.* New York, NY: Wiley.

Provides examples of conflicts that failed to reach a satisfying conclusion and describes alternative strategies that have proven to be more successful in resolving conflicts.

Jandt, F.E. (2003). *Intercultural communication: An introduction* (3rd ed.). Thousand Oaks, CA: Sage.

Describes how cultural norms and values create a context for communication and how understanding different cultures is necessary for successful intercultural communication.

Johnson, D.W., Johnson, R.T., & Tjosvold, D. (2006). Constructive controversy: The value of intellectual opposition. In M. Deutsch, P. Coleman & E.C. Marcus (Eds.), *The handbook of conflict resolution* (2nd ed., pp. 65–85). San Francisco, CA: Jossey-Bass.

Explains how conflict can be constructive and reports on the positive results of research involving people who were taught to use the strategies for "skilled disagreement."

Kimmel, P.R. (2006). Culture and conflict. In M. Deutsch, P. Coleman & E.C. Marcus (Eds.), *The handbook of conflict resolution* (2nd ed., pp. 453–474). San Francisco, CA: Jossey-Bass.

Describes the influence of culture on individual communication and the need to practice cultural relativism to avoid conflict in intercultural communication.

King, P.M., & Kitchener, K.S. (1994). *Developing reflective judgment: Understanding and promoting intellectual growth and critical thinking in adolescents and adults.* San Francisco, CA: Jossey-Bass.

Reviews research on the development of reflective judgment from childhood through adult years and includes cross-cultural and gender comparisons.

Kochman, T. (1981). *Black and white: Styles in conflict.* Chicago, IL: University of Chicago Press.

Explains differences in communication styles commonly used by black and white people in urban America and how those differences can lead to conflict.

Kougl, K. (1997). *Communicating in the classroom.* Prospect Heights, IL: Waveland.

Analyzes the dynamics of communicating in a classroom, including communication problems that often occur, and describes optional strategies for responding to those problems.

McCorkle, S., & Mills, J.L. (1992). Rowboat in a hurricane: Metaphors of interpersonal conflict management. *Communication Reports* 5(2), 57–67.

Examines the relationship between the metaphor selected by an individual to describe conflict and how that individual addressed conflict situations.

Meltzoff, N. (2007, Spring). Use another word. *Rethinking Schools. 21*(3), 46–48.

Reports on the success of a student initiative to reduce name-calling at school and references the U.S. Supreme Court's ruling concerning "fighting words."

Narula, U. (2006). *Handbook of communication models, perspectives and strategies.* New Delhi, India: Atlantic.

Provides an overview of communication research, describes various communication models, and analyzes the functions of contemporary communication.

Newberg, A., & Waldman, M.R. (2006). *Why we believe what we believe: Uncovering our biological needs for meaning, spirituality, and truth.* New York, NY: Free Press.

Proposes a new way of thinking about how convictions develop and influence individuals, based on recent research on how the brain perceives (and transforms) reality.

Perry, W.G., Jr. (1999). *Forms of intellectual and ethical development in the college years: A scheme.* San Francisco CA: Jossey-Bass, Inc.

Describes nine positions in the development of moral reasoning based on interviews with Harvard students and including interview excerpts illustrating developmental positions.

Postman, N., & Weingartner, C. (1987). *Teaching as a subversive activity.* New York, NY: Dell Publishing. (Originally published in 1969)

Advocates that teachers use the inquiry method in their teaching and provide a relevant curriculum so that students become critical thinkers who are interested in their learning.

Prince, D. W. (2004). *Communicating across cultures.* Greensboro, NC: Center for Creative Leadership.

Examines factors that affect communication between people from different cultures and offers suggestions for improving cross-cultural interactions.

Roberts, Jr., W. B. (2006). *Bullying from both sides: Strategic interventions for working with bullies and victims.* Thousand Oaks, CA: Corwin Press.

Describes characteristics of bullies and victims and successful intervention strategies.

Rogers, C. (1995). *A way of being.* New York, NY: Mariner Books. (Originally published in 1980)

Describes the philosophical basis for his professional practice and provides examples from his person-centered approach to therapy; Chapter 7 focuses on the value of empathy.

Schramm, W. (1973). *Men, messages, and media: A look at human communication.* New York, NY: Harper & Row.

Provides a historical overview of communication and uses research to analyze the functions of contemporary communication; communication models are explained in the appendix.

Skuttnab-Kangas, T. (2000). *Linguistic genocide in education—or worldwide diversity and human rights?* Mahwah, NJ: Lawrence Erlbaum Associates.

Uses contemporary theory and research to examine the impact of linguistic imperialism on human rights in general and the assault on linguistic diversity in particular.

Spitzberg, B.H. (2008). Perspectives on nonverbal communication skills. In J. DeVito & M. Hecht (Eds.), *The nonverbal communication reader* (3rd ed., pp. 18–22). Prospect Heights, IL: Waveland.

Describes how nonverbal communication contributes to communicating effectively and provides a rating scale to measure nonverbal communication skills.

Stone, G., Singletary, M., & Richmond, V.P. (1999). *Clarifying communication theories: A hands-on approach.* Ames: Iowa State University Press.

Explains the theoretical foundations for communication, examines aspects of interpersonal communication and mass communication, and describes communication research methods.

Tannen, D. (1994). *Gender and discourse.* New York, NY: Oxford University Press.

Six essays on language and gender including such topics as conversational strategies, issues of power, and the impact of culture and status on linguistic strategies.

Tannen, D. (2007). *You just don't understand: Women and men in conversation.* New York, NY: Harper Collins (Originally published in 1990)

Discusses how gender influences communication styles and explains how conflicts between men and women can result from these communication style differences.

Waley, A. (Ed.). (1938). *The analects of Confucius.* New York, NY: Vintage.

Provides the social and political background for the philosophy of Kongfuzi (Confucius) and an annotated translation with explanations of references to events and individuals.

Wessler, S. L. (with W. Preble). (2003). *The respectful school: How educators and students can conquer hate and harassment.* Alexandria, VA: Association for Supervision and Curriculum Development.

Describes the impact of degrading language and the pattern (and escalation) of abuse, and discusses strategies for reducing harassment and promoting positive student interaction.

Cultural Foundations of Oppression in the United States

Section 2 examines the history of oppression in the United States as experienced by immigrants who came to America in pursuit of the American dream. Immigrants encountered discomfort, rejection, even persecution because they arrived as "foreigners" with different customs, traditions, attitudes, and beliefs. Immigrants of color also experienced oppression based on their race, and certain religions have been oppressed for their beliefs. The forms that this oppression have taken are identified in the definition of oppression provided in Andrzejewski (1996):

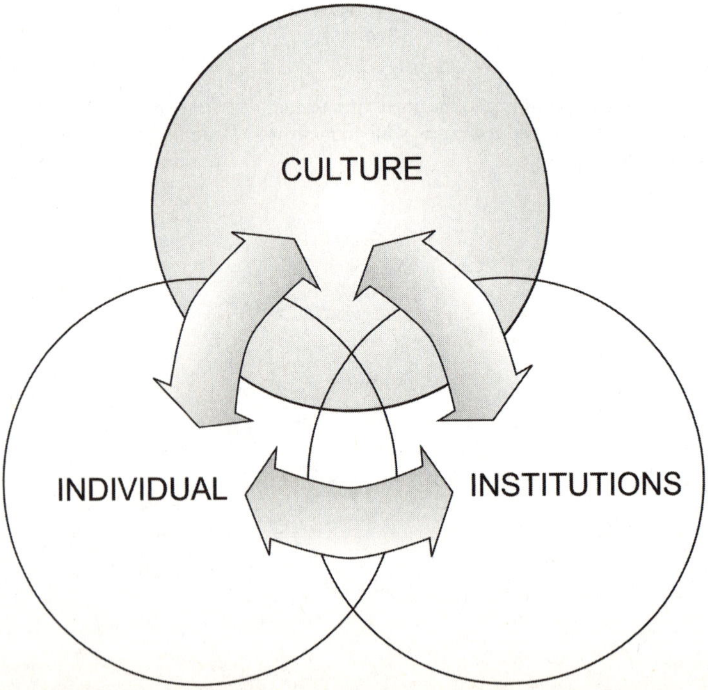

> Oppression exists when any entity (society, organization, group, or individual) intentionally or unintentionally distributes resources inequitably, refuses to share power, imposes ethnocentric culture, and/or maintains unresponsive and inflexible institutions toward another entity for its supposed benefit and rationalizes its actions by blaming or ignoring the victim. (p. 56)

Chapter 4 describes how ethnic diversity of immigrants historically has been perceived as threatening to white supremacist attitudes of the majority group. Historic attempts have been made to curb immigration to America, especially of immigrants perceived as not being satisfactorily white enough, and to justify anti-immigration efforts through the early twentieth-century quasi science of eugenics. Because of the reform of immigration laws in 1965, ethnic diversity of immigrants has dramatically increased. The chapter examines issues stemming from the increased cultural and linguistic diversity, especially in our elementary and secondary schools. The chapter concludes with a description of anti-immigrant activities that underscores the persistence of these attitudes on the part of a significant percentage of the American population.

Chapter 5 describes negative attitudes and actions of Americans of European descent toward people of color coming in the United States, beginning with their conquest of American Indians, the importation of Africans as slaves, the rejection of Asian immigrants, and the exploitation of Spanish-speaking ethnic groups. The oppression of these groups took different forms, but the common denominator was that they were not white. Race would sustain the oppression against individuals from these groups long past the period of time when they arrived as strangers in a strange land.

Chapter 6 focuses on the religious diversity of immigrants and the challenge that diversity has always represented to the creation of a free society. The religious diversity of people who settled in America eventually led to a shared concern that religious differences not be used to justify persecution, and the concept of religious freedom was included in the first amendment to the Constitution. Although members of different Protestant faiths began to accept one another as equals, Catholic, Jewish, and atheist immigrants were discriminated against. Although Catholics and Jews finally achieved a status as equals, the 1965 immigration reform resulted in an unprecedented increase in persons of other religions—such as Buddhists, Hindus, Muslims, and Sikhs. Once again the United States is being challenged to live up to its principle of providing religious freedom that acknowledges and accepts people from diverse faiths as equal partners in our religiously diverse nation.

In response to the cultural history just described, Chapter 7 identifies four perspectives that describe individual reactions to racial, ethnic, and religious diversity in America. The most recent perspective, pluralism, emerged in the 1920s and today is challenging this history of oppression by calling for Americans to recognize the value of diversity and the contributions diverse groups have made, and continue to make, to American society. Because the problems related to this diversity are ongoing and are discussed in the next section, this chapter emphasizes pluralism as a force for change, for a new direction in our society in response to the diversity that not only exists but is increasing.

CHAPTER 4

Immigration and Oppression: The Assault on Cultural and Language Diversity

"We are all citizens of one world; we are all of one blood. To hate someone because he was born in another country, because he speaks a different language or because he takes a different view on a subject, is a great folly."

John Comenius (1592–1670)

As British colonists settled in America, they struggled with the issue of ethnic diversity because the need for more people to settle this new land conflicted with their **xenophobia**—the fear of or prejudice against people from other nations. There was no such struggle with racial diversity. As Kammen (1972) noted, European colonists came to America with racist notions of primitive Africans and savage Indians that justified enslaving them; seeds of white supremacy were sustained—and nurtured—on American soil. Ethnic diversity, however, was different. As the dominant ethnic group, British immigrants witnessed people from other European nations coming to the colonies, creating the difficult task of coexistence in a diverse community of immigrants. The challenge of devising an appropriate response to diversity has never been fully resolved. Instead, America has been enmeshed in an ongoing paradox of established immigrants fearing each wave of newcomers.

As the dominant ethnic group, how did British colonists react to diversity?

Part of the dilemma of ethnic diversity was the determination of British colonists to retain their identity. The French who settled to the north in Canada had readily adapted to Indian ways, especially with regard to economic practices such as trapping and through intermarriage with Native American women. The Spanish came as conquerors, but after their conquest, they still required Indian labor to sustain their control of conquered territory. Like the French, the Spanish borrowed cultural elements from conquered peoples, and intermarriages produced what would eventually be termed a new race: "La Raza."

Those who settled the English-speaking colonies tended to emigrate in family groups. Although some immigrants came to seek their fortune and return home, most came to establish permanent settlements. The British came as subjects of the English king, prepared to create an English colony as an extension of Britain. Although settlers occasionally used information gained from Indians about such things as edible plants and food preparation, their goal was to recreate as much of the Old World as was possible in the New World.

The problem with recreating the Old World was that it was not possible to make the colonies into a *New England.* In addition to British colonists (English, Scottish, and Irish), significant numbers of

Dutch, German, and French colonists arrived, as well as small groups from other European countries and adventurers from parts of the world other than Europe. Germans in particular were as adamant as the English about maintaining their cultural heritage. They lived together in communities, spoke to each other in German, posted signs in German, imported books from Germany, and founded schools where their children were taught in German.

By the beginning of the eighteenth century, British colonial leaders became so alarmed by German behavior that some called for restricting or excluding Germans from further immigration. Benjamin Franklin believed it was necessary to Anglicize the Germans because of the size of their population. As their numbers continued to grow, he feared that the Germans would "shortly be so numerous as to Germanize us instead of us Anglifying them" (Feagin, 1997, p. 18). Although Franklin obviously shared the desire of British colonists to Anglicize the colonies, he also recognized positive attributes of German immigrants and the contributions they were making to colonial development: "All that seems necessary is to distribute them more equally, mix them with the English, and establish English schools where they are now too thick settled" (Brands, 2000, p. 219).

Franklin was concerned with Anglicizing Germans and all immigrants who were not from Britain and, therefore, unfamiliar with British customs and language. In 1749, he sponsored the establishment of a school that included no foreign language instruction. His desire to Anglicize foreign colonists was also reflected in the views of President George Washington: "The more homogeneous our citizens can be made . . . the greater will be our prospect of permanent union" (Kammen, 1972, p. 74). Perhaps the desire for a more homogeneous citizenry was the reason the New American Congress passed a law in 1790 that limited citizenship in the United States to immigrants who were "white" persons. This early expression of xenophobia would lead to the growth of nativism in the United States.

> Law is a reflection and source of prejudice. It both enforces and suggests forms of bias.
>
> **Diane Schulder (1937–)**

Causes of Xenophobia and Nativism in the United States

Assimilation refers to a process in which immigrants adopt cultural traits from their host country and are absorbed into society (note Figure 4.2 on page 77). British colonists preferred a homogeneous population of immigrants who could be assimilated into a dominant Anglo culture, but immigrants from other countries often demonstrated a persistent wish to maintain their own ethnic heritages. Their desires contributed to the development of xenophobia in response to the constant infusion of ethnicities among immigrants to America. When established immigrants, who considered themselves "natives," felt threatened by the many non-British immigrants in their midst, organizations based on nativist concerns would appear. Feagin and Feagin (1996) define **nativism** as "an anti-immigrant ideology that advocates the protection of native inhabitants of a country from [new or potential] immigrants who are seen as threatening or dangerous" (p. 503). Nativists have been the primary group engaging in the oppression of immigrants consistent with the definition of *oppression* (Andrzejewski, 1996) quoted in the section introduction.

Franklin's desire to Anglicize non-British immigrants and Washington's desire for a homogeneous population can be described as a benign form of nativism based on nationalistic concerns. Although nationalism represents one of the primary themes of nativist activities in the United States, two additional themes have characterized many nativist attitudes and actions: anti-Catholicism and anti-radicalism.

Nativism as anti-Catholicism

Although the religious beliefs of Benjamin Franklin, Thomas Jefferson, and other founders of the American republic were quite different from those of most Christians today, at its birth the United States was a nation strongly influenced by Protestant Christianity. The presence of Catholics had been tolerated throughout the colonial period, but by 1820, the 200,000 Catholics in the United States stimulated anti-Catholic sentiment, especially in urban areas. (See Figure 4.1.) By 1850, there were almost two million Catholics in the United States; the Irish alone constituted 42% of that foreign-born population (Fuchs, 1990).

During George Washington's presidency, immigrants had to be U.S. residents for a minimum of five years to be eligible for citizenship. The Nationalization Act signed by President John Adams changed the requirement to fourteen years of residency, but it was returned to five years after Thomas Jefferson became president. A nativist group calling itself "Native Americans" began forming in some of the larger cities; the party lobbied vigorously against immigrants becoming eligible for citizenship after five years. The Native American party insisted on a residency of twenty-one years before an immigrant was eligible for citizenship. Their main concern was voting, arguing that immigrants coming from nations governed by monarchs were not prepared to be self-governing. Since an immigrant came with:

> all his foreign habits, prejudices and predilections . . . can it be believed that he can disburden himself so completely of these, and have so learned to fulfill the duties of a citizen of the United States, in the very short term of five years? (Myers, 1960, p. 111)

At first, the Native American party encouraged people to welcome immigrants and only opposed their eligibility for citizenship after five years; however, by 1843, the movement had become hostile to continued immigration of both Irish and Catholics. In Philadelphia, the Native American party held a meeting in an Irish district of the city, initiating a confrontation between Protestants and Catholics; the violence that followed culminated in an angry mob setting fire to many buildings, reported in newspapers around the country. Federal troops were called in to restore order, which was no easy task, and peace prevailed for a little more than a

FIGURE 4.1

A major factor in the anti-Catholic sentiment was the fear that Catholics would try to convert Protestants, especially children. The cartoonist, Thomas Nast, made Catholic bishops into alligators coming to U.S. shores, reflecting such fears.

Source: 1876 cartoon from Harper's Weekly Magazine, by Thomas Nast.

month before mobs attacked a Catholic church and troops fired at the crowd to force them to disperse. Two more days of violence resulted in two soldiers being killed and twenty-six soldiers wounded.

Being confronted with such extreme violence was unusual, but American Catholics employed a number of strategies in response to anti-Catholic activities. To avoid having their children subjected to anti-Catholic sentiments in public schools, Catholics created their own privately funded K–12 schools nationwide, eventually establishing Catholic colleges and universities as well. To counter anti-Catholic rhetoric in mainstream and Protestant newspapers, Catholics published their own newspapers. Hennesey (1985) described how Bishop John Hughes submitted several anti-Catholic articles to a Protestant newspaper under the name of "Cranmer," then publicly announced that he was the author and that the articles included lies and distortions that the editors had not bothered to question or confirm. In addition, several Catholic organizations were founded in the 1800s, including the Knights of Columbus, which engaged in political activism but also provided centers for recreational activities and chapels for meditation and prayer. By the 1920s, church leaders adopted a different strategy, encouraging Catholics to become involved with "general reform groups in society and not limit their exertions to narrowly conceived partisan issues" (Hennesey, 1985, p. 247).

Nativism as anti-radicalism

Both anti-Catholicism and prejudice against the Irish fueled the nativism movement that flourished briefly in the 1850s, but the other negative sentiment contributing to the success of nativism was anti-radicalism. Most immigrants admitted to the United States in the first decades of the nineteenth century were overwhelmingly impoverished European laborers with minimal skills and little education. Some were sponsored by American capitalists to be contract laborers paid less than the wage native workers would accept. As new immigrant workers adapted to life in the United States, they came to realize how they were being exploited; many joined or helped create unions to demand better wages and benefits by engaging in strikes, marches, and protests. Nativists saw union actions as un-American, especially when the "foreigners" expressed socialist, anarchist, or other radical ideas. The antagonism toward what was regarded as radical activities by recent immigrants was clearly and frequently expressed on the editorial pages of urban newspapers (Higham, 1955):

> "Our National existence and . . . our National and social institutions are at stake."
>
> "These people are not Americans, but the very scum and offal of Europe."
>
> "There is no such thing as an American anarchist."
>
> "Europe's human and inhuman rubbish." (p. 55)

The first quotation illustrates the nationalism often expressed in nativist sentiments; the other quotations reveal hostility and a dehumanized view of the perceived "radicals." The un-American implication in each statement is central to the nativist perspective. Nativist concerns at that time also had to do with the decreasing amount of land available for immigrants in the Midwest and West; as a result, immigrants increasingly settled in urban areas. Because many immigrants were moving from southern and eastern Europe, land reformer Henry George commented, "What, in a few years more, are we to do for a dumping ground? Will it make our difficulty the less that our human garbage can vote?" (Higham, 1955, p. 42). The issue of immigrants becoming eligible for citizenship and voting continued to fuel individual xenophobia, and nativist political actions document a fear of the potential political power of incoming immigrants.

Nativism, Politics, and Social Change

The Native American party never gained political dominance, yet by the 1850s it had prepared the way for the rise of the "Know-Nothings," a somewhat secret movement whose members were told to respond to any question about the organization by saying that they knew nothing about it. Staunchly anti-immigrant and anti-Catholic, Know-Nothings were concerned with what they perceived as the growing political influence of Catholics; these fears were confirmed by President Franklin Pierce's appointment of a Catholic, James Campbell, to be the nation's attorney general.

How successful were the nativists in their political activities?

The Know-Nothings fielded candidates for the American Party, and in 1854 elected 9 governors, 8 (of 62) senators, and 104 (of 234) members of the House of Representatives (Myers, 1960). In the 1856 elections, Know-Nothing members used force and threats to keep immigrants from voting and encouraged election-day riots in Louisville, Kentucky, and St. Louis, Missouri. When the Whig Party refused to nominate Millard Fillmore for a second term as president, the American Party nominated him as their candidate. Despite the success of other American Party candidates, Fillmore received only eight electoral votes.

Reaction to the political success of the Know-Nothings was swift. In Congress a resolution was submitted, then voted down, condemning secret organizations and citing the Know-Nothings as a specific example. Political and religious leaders across the nation denounced the activities of the Know-Nothings, including the young political aspirant Abraham Lincoln, who wrote in a letter to a friend,

> As a nation we began by declaring that "all men are created equal." We now practically read it, "all men are created equal except Negroes." When the Know-Nothings obtain control, it will read: "All men are created equal except Negroes, foreigners, and Catholics." (Myers, 1960, p. 146)

Why did nativists fail to form a major political party?

The political success of nativism in the 1850s was brief because the issue of slavery began to take precedence over anti-Catholic prejudice and fears, and it divided the Know-Nothings. By the end of the Civil War, the Know-Nothings and the American Party were no longer a political force, although the nativist fears that fueled their activity persisted as a major influence in the United States. As the American people debated the issue of slavery, American capitalists continued to sponsor importation of labor from overseas to keep wages low and profits high.

Throughout U.S. history, a significant percentage of Americans consisted of recent immigrants or children of immigrants who appreciated the opportunities in America and vigorously opposed attempts by nativists to restrict immigration. Meanwhile, there was constant pressure from society to promote the **Americanization** of immigrants, and public schools carried out societal expectations by encouraging immigrants to abandon their heritage and conform to American ways (Pai & Adler, 2006). Nativist attitudes in the United States continued to wax and wane, with xenophobia historically balanced by those who believed in America as a place for oppressed people to achieve freedom and fortune.

The demand for Americanization of immigrants intensified in the late 1800s as the majority of immigrants were not northern Europeans—Greeks, Italians, Slavs, and Jews—people who did not conform to the Anglo ideal. Because of an economic downturn in the 1890s, nativism experienced a renewed popularity with American people; then in the ebb and flow of xenophobia, nativist fears succumbed to a confidence inspired by the U.S. triumph in the Spanish-American War and by heroes such as Teddy Roosevelt. Although nativists never again succeeded in sponsoring an independent political party, events in the early twentieth century would establish the foundation for their greatest political triumphs.

> There is no room in this country for hyphenated Americans.
>
> **Theodore Roosevelt (1858–1919)**

What influenced twentieth-century nativist attitudes in America?

It seemed certain to most Americans that if the United States was going to become a dominant political and economic power in the world, immigrants were needed in the labor market of its dynamic economy. But when World War I began, attitudes changed. Nativism surged again, driven by feelings of nationalism and anti-radicalism. German Americans were singled out for especially opprobrious treatment, and their loyalty to the United States was questioned. Rumors abounded that German Americans were spying for Germany.

Because German Americans insisted on maintaining their dual identity as Americans of German descent, people of influence such as Teddy Roosevelt admonished them by denouncing all immigrants who claimed a dual identity. German Americans were surprised by such criticisms. From colonial times they had maintained their culture, language, and traditions through separate schools, organizations, and newspapers. Because of their industriousness, efforts to preserve their German heritage had been tolerated by American society until World War I, when nativist individuals and organizations attacked German Americans for keeping themselves separate and not assimilating to an Anglo ideal.

During World War I, surging patriotism intensified the demand that immigrants be Americanized quickly. Although this nationalism was a less abrasive form of nativism, it became more virulent when reinforced by anti-radical attitudes. Radical organizations were attacked as un-American, especially radical unions like the International Workers of the World, the "Wobblies." Nativists accused certain immigrants of espousing ideas that were disloyal to the country and demanded their deportation.

German Americans were not the only targets of anti-American accusations. **Anti-Semitism**—having prejudices, stereotypes, or engaging in discrimination against Jews—increased with the success of the Russian Revolution in 1917. Jews were associated not only with communism, but also with international financiers who profited from the war. After World War I, nativists continued to complain that the Anglo ideal for America would disappear if diverse European ethnic groups continued to emigrate; however most Americans seemed to believe that those who came eventually would assimilate into the dominant culture.

By the 1920s, a revised perspective was being expressed. In settlement houses such as Hull House in Chicago, people providing social services began to appreciate the diversity of the immigrants. Social activist Jane Addams, cofounder of Hull House, and University of Chicago philosopher John Dewey described the advantages of diverse cultures and the value of people maintaining their heritages while

FIGURE 4.2 Assimilation Issues?

still learning, as Benjamin Franklin had recommended, the language and customs of American culture. Although resentment toward Germans slowly dissipated after the war, anti-Semitism persisted as part of a new development in xenophobic attitudes in the United States.

What new development affected xenophobic attitudes in the United States?

In 1899, William Z. Ripley, an economist from the Massachusetts Institute of Technology, published a so-called scientific study identifying and describing three European races: Teutonic, Alpine, and Mediterranean (Higham, 1955). Based on emerging theories about race, Nativists argued that for U.S. citizenry to achieve unity, immigrants of the blue-eyed, blond-haired Teutonic type (also called "Nordic" or "Anglo Saxon") should be given preference. Senator Henry Cabot Lodge of Massachusetts called for an end to all further immigration to the United States, and Teddy Roosevelt chastised Anglo Saxon women in America for contributing to the possibility of "race suicide" by not producing as many children as immigrant women (Brodkin, 2002). In the aftermath of World War I, pessimism about diverse groups being able to assimilate into an Anglo Saxon American culture fueled racist sentiments expressed in widely read books such as Lothrop Stoddard's *The Rising Tide of Color.* (See Figure 4.3.)

Madison Grant (1916/1970) provided the most influential expression of this pessimism in *The Passing of the Great Race, or the Racial Bias of European History.* Grant rejected the idea that immigrants from other than Nordic heritage could achieve the Anglo Saxon ideal; thus the "Great Race" of Anglo Saxons was doomed to disappear in America. Claiming that his ideas were grounded in the emerging science of genetics, Grant concluded that intermarriage between races produced degraded offspring who would revert to lower qualities contained in their parents' genes. Referring to Ripley's three European races, Grant stated, "The cross between any of the European races and a Jew is a Jew" (p. 16). Confirming Grant's assertion, the eugenics movement provided "scientific" evidence of the human degradation caused by miscegenation, and 30 states passed laws banning interracial marriage (Stubblefield, 2007). Many well-known and respected Americans such as automaker Henry Ford expressed beliefs consistent with Madison Grant's theories and the findings of eugenics, and racism—including anti-Semitism—was incorporated into traditional xenophobic attitudes.

FIGURE 4.3

This advertisement from a 1923 *Time* magazine warns its readers that the days of white supremacy may be numbered and urges white people who want to do something about it to read Stoddard's book, *The Rising Tide of Color.*

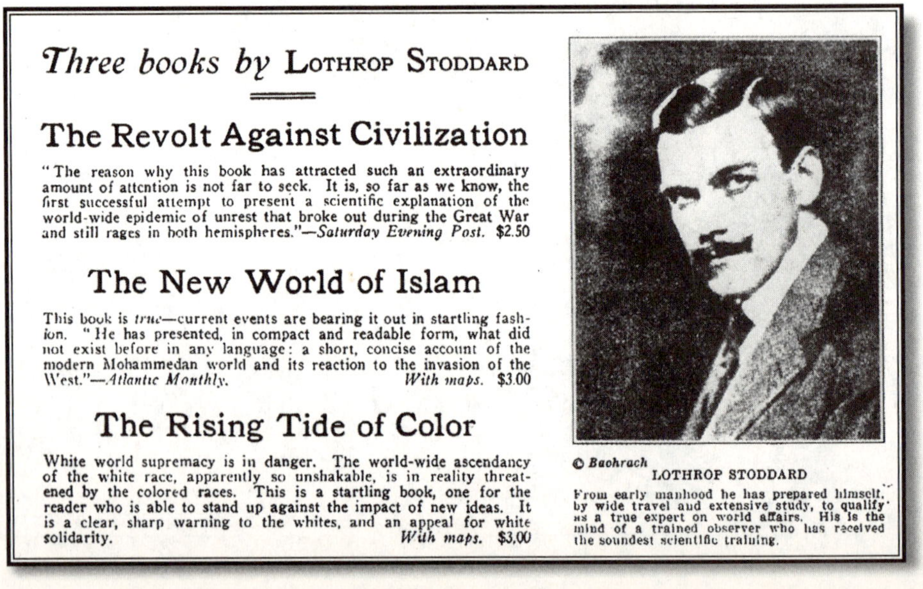

Three books by LOTHROP STODDARD

The Revolt Against Civilization

"The reason why this book has attracted such an extraordinary amount of attention is not far to seek. It is, so far as we know, the first successful attempt to present a scientific explanation of the world-wide epidemic of unrest that broke out during the Great War and still rages in both hemispheres."—*Saturday Evening Post.* $2.50

The New World of Islam

This book is *true*—current events are bearing it out in startling fashion. "He has presented, in compact and readable form, what did not exist before in any language: a short, concise account of the modern Mohammedan world and its reaction to the invasion of the West."—*Atlantic Monthly.* *With maps.* $3.00

The Rising Tide of Color

White world supremacy is in danger. The world-wide ascendancy of the white race, apparently so unshakable, is in reality threatened by the colored races. This is a startling book, one for the reader who is able to stand up against the impact of new ideas. It is a clear, sharp warning to the whites, and an appeal for white solidarity. *With maps.* $3.00

© *Bachrach*

LOTHROP STODDARD

From early manhood he has prepared himself, by wide travel and extensive study, to qualify as a true expert on world affairs. His is the mind of a trained observer who has received the soundest scientific training.

How did racism affect nativist attitudes and actions?

Nativists used the new racist concern for preserving the nation's Anglo Saxon heritage to sound the alarm about the numbers of immigrants from southern and eastern Europe—80% of all U.S. immigrants from 1900 to 1910. Stanford University's Ellwood P. Cubberley echoed their concerns in his history of education textbook (1919):

> These Southern and Eastern Europeans were of a very different type from the North and West Europeans who preceded them. Largely illiterate, docile, lacking in initiative, and almost wholly without the Anglo-Saxon conceptions of righteousness, liberty, law, order, public decency, and government, their coming has served to dilute tremendously our national stock . . . our national life, for the past quarter of a century, has been afflicted with a serious case of racial indigestion. (p. 338)

Nativists triumphed in 1924 with the passage of an immigration law establishing quotas for immigrants based on country of origin. The quotas ensured that immigrants from northern Europe (the so-called Nordic type) would constitute the majority of U.S. immigrants, guidelines that remained largely unchanged for the next four decades. Although people of color were the primary targets of nativists, other groups were also affected by racist attitudes.

> [America can have] a unity created by drawing out and composing into a harmonious whole the best, the most characteristic, which each contributing race and people has to offer.
>
> JOHN DEWEY (1859–1952)

What groups were affected by the addition of racism to xenophobia?

This new racist form of nativism was directed not only against people of color, but also against white people perceived as not being white enough, which often meant not sharing the common prejudices of the white majority. This was especially observed in southern states. In 1898, debates at Louisiana's state constitutional convention focused on who would be denied the right to vote. Although blacks were the main targets, Italians were considered "as black as the blackest negro in existence" (Barrett & Roediger, 2002, p. 32). Because of such perceptions, some Italians were victims of southern violence in the nineteenth century. In Tallulah, Louisiana, five Sicilian immigrants owned businesses that served primarily black customers. Local whites resented the immigrant storekeepers because they treated black people as equals. Before long, the locals fabricated a quarrel over a goat and lynched the five Sicilians (Higham, 1955).

> We gave [immigrants] disparaging names: Micks, Sheenies, Krauts, Dagos, Wops . . . until [each group] became sound, solvent . . . whereupon each group joined the older boys and charged down on the newest ones. . . . Having suffered, one would have thought they might have pity on the newcomer, but they did not.
>
> JOHN STEINBECK (1900–1969)

The idea of perceiving Italians, Irish, or others as separate races based on their national origins seems strange today; yet most Americans, including members of identified "races," accepted this designation. In the 1930s, an Irish campaign manager representing an Irish politician made the following speech at an Italian neighborhood meeting to ask the Italian men to vote for his candidate in the upcoming election:

> Maybe I'm the only Irishman here, but this is not a racial contest. You don't select your man because of his race. There are too many who cry him down because of that. But these people that sit behind closed doors and discriminate against a man because of his race have no place in American life. . .

FIGURE 4.4

Source: David Horsey © 2007. Tribune Media Services. Reprinted by permission.

> This district don't house men and women that vote only because of their racial strain. For the immigrants of your race and my race, I have no apology. In the time of need, we answered the call of our country. One of the largest quotas of men was sent out from this district. At that time there was no discrimination because of a man's race, there was no turning men back for that reason. We sent out boys by the thousands in order that we might enjoy the blessings of free government. Here we never turn down a man because of his race or creed. (Whyte, 1955, p. 227)

The idea of national origin defining separate races declined as skin color became the primary determinant of racial identity, and racism would prolong the oppression of people of color beyond the time normally experienced by white ethnic groups. The experiences of the four major racial groups are the focus of Chapter 5.

As the civil rights movement gained momentum, allegations of racism were made in many areas. President John Kennedy admitted to inequities in immigration policies based on the 1924 law. Attorney General Robert Kennedy characteristically stated the issue more bluntly, "As we are working to remove the vestiges of racism from our public life, we cannot maintain racism as the cornerstone of our immigration laws" (Eck, 2001, p. 7). In 1965, Congress amended immigration laws to eliminate the racially biased National Origins Quotas. From 1968 to 1993, 80% of the people immigrating to the United States came from Central or South America, the Caribbean, and Asia (Roberts, 1997). The influx of Latino immigrants spawned a renewed xenophobia, especially in California (see Figure 4.4).

The Paradox of Xenophobia and Nativism in a Nation of Immigrants

Daniels (2002) noted the absurdity among Americans to regard the people who first came to the United States as "colonists" or "settlers" and then to identify the people who came later as "immigrants." Social observers such as author John Steinbeck (1966) have described how immigrants were initially reviled only to be accepted later: "the surges of the new restless, needy, and strong . . . were resisted, resented, and accepted only when a new and different wave came in" (p. 14). Part of being accepted involved the former immigrants expressing xenophobic sentiments against current immigrants. In fairness, Americans have not consistently expressed such sentiments; instead, Daniels (2002) has observed the following pattern:

> When most Americans are generally united and feel confident about their future, they seem to be more willing to share that future with foreigners; conversely, when they are divided and lack confidence in the future, nativism is more likely to triumph. (pp. 265–266)

As previously mentioned, nativists used the work of scholars and scientists within the growing ranks of the eugenics movement in support of their efforts to limit immigration. British scientist Francis Galton coined the term **eugenics** as "the study of agencies under social control that may improve or repair the racial qualities of future generations, either physically or mentally" (Lynn, 2001, p. 4). American scholars endorsing the eugenics movement were concerned about the perceived degeneration of mental abilities among Americans. Many believed there was a racial component to the problem represented by immigrants whom they regarded as the primary cause of this decline of intelligence in America. As Stubblefield (2007) noted, many scholars believed that "White people were 'civilization builders,' while members of other races supposedly lacked the ability to produce civilization" (p. 163). Scholarly support for the eugenics movement would decline precipitously after the Nazis tainted it with their emphasis on race purification and their implementation of genocidal practices.

Although the eugenics movement in the United States never attracted a majority of academics, some in the eugenics camp were influential scholars: Robert Yerkes of Harvard (president of the American Psychological Association), Lewis Terman of Stanford, and Edward Thorndike from Teachers College, Columbia University (Selden, 2006). Because of their academic interests, Yerkes, Terman, and Thorndike were responsible for developing early intelligence tests (see Table 4.1). When Henry Goddard implemented intelligence tests with the immigrants at Ellis Island, he reported that 80% were "feeble minded" (Brodkin, 2002).

Because some respected scholars supported it, the eugenics movement flourished from 1910 to 1940, shaping the content of biology textbooks, reinforcing popular views concerning white supremacy, and contributing to the growth of anti-immigrant attitudes. One legacy of the eugenics movement is the standardized testing used to measure academic achievement that students still take today—but testing is not the only legacy of the eugenics movement.

Established in 1937 to promote eugenics policies, the Pioneer Fund advocated the forcible removal of "American Negroes" to Africa. The first Pioneer Fund President, Harry Laughlin, wrote the Model Eugenical Sterilization Law, adopted by thirty states in the United States and Nazi Germany. Laughlin proposed that Adolf Hitler be given honorary membership in the American Eugenics Society. The Pioneer Fund continues to support scholars working on race-based IQ theories, including work employed in support of the controversial comments about race made in *The Bell Curve* (Herrnstein & Murray, 1994). The Pioneer Fund also supported a recent book by Lynn (2001) arguing in favor of eugenic principles, and has continued to be a major funding source for the English Only movement (Tatalovich, 1997).

How is the English Only movement an example of xenophobic behavior?

Nativists have always been critical of immigrants who maintain their native language. They lobbied for literacy tests primarily as a strategy to reduce immigration, but for almost two decades Congress

TABLE 4.1 Sample Questions from the World War I Army Mental Tests

Alpha and Beta Tests developed by psychologists Robert Yerkes, Lewis Terman, and Henry Goddard assisted by Carl Campbell Brigham, founder of Educational Testing Service (ETS)

These sample questions reveal how culturally biased and inappropriate the early tests of "intelligence" could be; yet such tests were used with immigrants to determine which ones were of acceptable intelligence and which were "feeble minded."

From Alpha Test 8:				
2. Five hundred is played with:	rackets	pins	cards	dice
3. The Percheron is a kind of:	goat	horse	cow	sheep
7. Christy Mathewson is famous as a:	writer	artist	baseball player	comedian
10. "There's a reason" is an "ad" for a:	drink	revolver	flour	cleanser
19. Crisco is a:	patent medicine	disinfectant	tooth-paste	food
29. The Brooklyn Nationals are called the:	Giants	Orioles	Superbas	Indians
32. The number of a Kaffir's legs is:	two	four	six	eight
35. The forward pass is used in:	tennis	hockey	football	golf
38. The Pierce Arrow car is made in:	Buffalo	Detroit	Toledo	Flint

Source: Owen, David. *None of the above: The truth behind the SATs,* 1999, p. 176.

rejected the idea. When Congress finally passed such legislation, both Democratic and Republican presidents vetoed these laws until 1917, when Congress passed this requirement over President Wilson's veto (Delgado, 1997). Nativist opposition to immigrants maintaining their native language was evident in their criticisms of German immigrants, and culminated during World War I with state and local laws that forbade public displays of signs with German words and banned the teaching of German in public schools. In some communities German textbooks were burned as an act of patriotism (Crawford, 2000). The percentage of students taking German in U.S. high schools went from 25% in 1915 to 0.6% by 1922 (Baron, 2000). Today, **English Only** advocates demand that English be declared the "official language" of the United States, and they are working toward that goal on a state-by-state basis. English Only supporters claim that their desire to establish English as the official language of the United States is simply a response to the large number of immigrants who refuse to learn how to speak English.

The problem with this claim is the lack of supporting evidence. English Only proponents point to the existence of dual language street signs, billboards and government brochures and to bilingual instruction in schools. They believe that the use of non-English languages, especially in bilingual instruction, legitimizes these languages and elevates their status as well as the status of those who speak these alternate languages. Yet studies do not indicate a threat to the widespread use of English, reporting that well over 90% of U.S. residents speak English fluently (Crawford, 2000; Wiley, 2005). Critics of English Only activities argue that it is no coincidence that the current movement was initiated just 15 years after the 1965 immigration reform that resulted in the majority of U.S. immigrants becoming people of color, and there is some evidence of a xenophobic motivation behind English Only organizations. For example, Crawford (2000) reports on an investigation of US English, a major English Only organization, that found evidence of their real agenda: "determination to resist racial and cultural diversity in the United States" (p. 23). Baron (2000) argues that the history of such organizations "often masks racism and certainly fails to appreciate cultural difference" (p. 447). Latino immigrants appear to be the main targets; in a survey asking financial supporters of US English why they contributed to the organization, 42% of respondents agreed with the statement: "I wanted America to stand strong and not cave in to Hispanics who shouldn't be here" (Crawford, 2000, p. 24). Such attitudes support criticism that English Only activities disguise xenophobic attitudes by insisting that their goal is to promote assimilation by encouraging immigrants to learn English. Reviewing historic and current efforts to pass English Only legislation, Baron (2000) concludes: "no matter how idealistic or patriotic its claims . . . (it has) a long history of nativism, racism, and religious bigotry" (p. 451).

Immigrants have always tended to learn English out of necessity for economic and social well-being. Today, fewer than 14% of Americans speak a language other than English: Less than 6% of Americans speak no English (Wiley, 2005). Despite these facts, the English Only movement has been successful in promoting state legislation to establish English as the official language. Almost half the states have existing laws declaring English as the official language. Some laws are largely symbolic, no penalties are enforced, and there is no prohibition against teaching foreign languages or implementing and supporting bilingual programs. However, some state laws prohibit their governments from printing materials in other languages.

Because Spanish is the first language of a significant percentage of immigrants, English Only laws prevent recent immigrants who are trying to learn English from having access to useful information. Such laws may also prevent legally eligible people from voting (Tatalovich, 1997). Whether symbolic or harmful, English Only laws reflect the xenophobic reaction of a great many people in the United States against many of our recent immigrants, primarily people of color whose first language is not English and who may not yet be literate in English. English Only laws justify the antagonism some individuals feel toward people speaking a different language; at times this antagonism even results in violence.

How have xenophobic attitudes promoted violent behavior?

Today, immigrants or people who appear to be immigrants have been victims of violence. Recent Cambodian, Vietnamese, and Hmong immigrants can attest to this. White shrimp fishermen in Texas threatened Vietnamese fishermen when shrimp became scarce. In Wisconsin, a young white man attacked a Japanese exchange student whom he mistakenly believed was a Hmong immigrant. Xenophobia encourages individuals to see recent immigrants as "foreign"; instead of applauding their hard work and success, xenophobia causes people to criticize immigrants for taking "our" jobs. This kind of prejudice against foreigners and the stereotypes that accompany it can foster animosity and even violent behavior.

> We must get rid of fear; we cannot act at all till then. A man's acts are slavish, not true but specious; his very thoughts are false, he thinks as a slave and coward, till he have got fear under his feet.
>
> THOMAS CARLYLE (1795–1881)

Such violence has occurred many times, but an especially outrageous example occurred in 1997 in Rohnert Park, California. What made this incident especially deplorable was that police officers were responsible for the violence that resulted in the death of an Asian immigrant. An engineer of Chinese descent had gone to a bar with co-workers to celebrate his new job. At the bar, some patrons taunted him with racist slurs and insults. When he arrived home, he was still angry and still under the influence of alcohol as he raged about the bar incidents. Neighbors heard his shouts and called the police. When police officers arrived, the father of three young children walked out of his garage holding a long stick approximately one-eighth of an inch thick. When he waved the stick at the police, they shot him. Although the man's wife was a nurse, the police officers wouldn't let her help her husband; instead, they handcuffed the wounded man as he lay in a pool of blood in his driveway and bled to death. According to Martinez (2000), the police officers justified the shooting by saying that because he held a stick, they anticipated that: "the man would use 'martial arts' against them" (p. 95). Even the "model minority" stereotype was not enough to overcome prejudice and negative stereotypes.

What American nativist attitudes are evident today?

By the early 1990s, 73% of Americans surveyed believed the United States needed to strictly limit immigration, and surveys since then find that this sentiment continues to be widely supported (Ramos, 2002). The brunt of anti-immigrant backlash is largely directed at Latinos, especially Mexicans in areas such as Southern California where the Mexican population is expected to increase by two thirds from 2000 to 2020. Scherer (2005) quotes one Southern Californian's reaction: "Migration from Mexico is the catalyst that's starting the demise of America" (p. 57). This is not an isolated opinion. According to a 2005 NBC News/Wall Street Journal poll, almost half of Americans polled agreed with the statement: "Immigration detracts from our character and weakens the United States" (Scherer, 2005, p. 53).

Since the 1990s, anti-immigrant activity in America against Spanish-speaking immigrants has steadily increased, especially against illegal immigrants. Because immigrants from Spanish-speaking ethnic groups, referred to as Hispanics or Latinos, have constituted more than 50% of all U.S. immigrants, it is not surprising that they are the primary targets of anti-immigrant activity (Lee, 2004). Today nearly 40 million Latinos live in the United States, with perhaps one out of six arriving illegally as undocumented workers. Latinos are currently 12% of America's workforce, a figure expected to double in just two generations, in part because today one of every five babies born in the United States is Latino (Grow, 2004).

Still, many Americans accept immigrants coming to the United States. The NBC News/Wall Street Journal poll reported that 41% of those surveyed felt that immigrants made America a better place. Some Americans argue that racism is behind much of the anti-immigrant sentiment today, just as in the past. Buchanan and Kim (2005) profiled twenty-one leaders of anti-immigrant groups and described evidence of overt racist behavior for many of them: One was a member of the Council of Conservative Citizens, a white pride group that opposes "race-mixing"; one had published numerous articles reflecting a white supremacist perspective; the Web site of another claimed that the Mexican government was plotting to take over the southwestern United States; and a group founded by one leader was identified as a hate group by the Southern Poverty Law Center, an organization that tracks activities of hate groups in the United States.

Some of the harshest comments are directed at "illegal aliens." Scherer (2005) quoted the leader of an Arizona anti-immigrant group who said America "was being flooded with illegals, people that are substandard humans" (p. 57). Jim Gilchrist, one of the founders of the Minuteman Civil Defense Corps, a vigilante group sponsoring "border patrols" of armed citizens to prevent illegal entry into the United States, helped found his group because "Illegal immigrants will destroy this country" (p. 32). Gilchrist has not expressed concern about the increasing involvement by white supremacist groups to recruit people for the Minuteman organization. In the wake of this hostility toward illegal immigrants, which is constantly reinforced by some talk show hosts on radio and cable television, it should not be surprising to learn that the FBI reported a 40% increase in hate crimes against Latinos from 2003–2007 (O'Grady, 2009).

In response to anti-immigrant hostility, Shorris (2001) argues that illegal immigrants make an important contribution to the U.S. economy by taking "the worst of jobs, the ugly work, the dangerous work, the backbreaking debilitating work, the jobs that even the jobless reject" (p. 272). Some of these jobs are extracting innards from slaughtered chickens on a conveyor belt; cultivating and harvesting mushrooms in damp caves; doing fieldwork as contract laborers (digging onions, picking beans, or harvesting other fruits and vegetables); skinning, gutting, and butchering animals at meatpacking plants; and working in manufacturing sweatshops for Third World wages. Despite complaints about illegal immigrants, it is not clear that Americans would be willing to pay the price, literally, if they were absent. (See Figure 4.4.) Scherer (2005) quotes one Arizona resident: "I don't want to pay five bucks for a can of string beans" (p. 56).

At the University of California, Los Angeles, the North American Integration and Development Center analyzed the work performed by 3 to 4 million undocumented workers in the United States. Their report stated that undocumented workers generated $154 billion toward America's gross domestic product, including $77 billion toward the state domestic product of California alone. Anti-immigrant leaders insist that illegal immigrants are receiving services such as welfare and health care that deplete limited resources of state and local governments. According to a University of California, Davis study, however, the vast majority of undocumented workers do not enroll in government assistance programs because (1) many are not adequately fluent in English, (2) many are not aware of such programs, and (3) many are reluctant to ask for help for fear of being detained by authorities and deported (Ramos, 2002).

Another criticism directed at Spanish-speaking immigrants is that they aren't learning English fast enough and are changing American culture from Anglo to Spanish. Scherer (2005) quotes a Southern Californian arguing that where he lives has changed "literally overnight into a foreign country. The Fourth of July was not being celebrated but Cinco de Mayo was. All the billboards [were] in a foreign language" (p. 55). Although the Census Bureau reports that 78% of U.S. Latinos tend to speak in Spanish even if they can speak English, a study by HispanTelligence found that the number of Latinos fluent in both English and Spanish had increased to 63% (Grow, 2004). Ramos (2002) cites a University of Southern California research project reporting that 7 of 10 Latino children write and speak English fluently.

It is true that Latino children are more likely to maintain their native language than are other immigrant children, but that is consistent with past practices of immigrating groups. Germans, Italians, Norwegians, Chinese, Jews, and Japanese immigrants established schools, which children usually attend after public school, to maintain their native language and culture. It is also true that Latinos have changed U.S. society. It is easy to identify Latino influences on American music, entertainment, literature, business, scholarly activity, and even on the English language (see nearby box). Mexican cuisine can be found almost everywhere from fine restaurants to fast food; salsa recently surpassed ketchup as the most popular American condiment. Addressing Latino influences, Shorris (2001) insists that they are not "signs of conquest. . . . Civilization need not be a zero sum game. The victories of Latino culture are victories of pluralism, additions" (p. 47). They are also victories for the American economy, even though anti-immigrant critics don't seem to understand the significance of their contribution.

Spanglish?

Many commonly used words in American English are direct or slightly modified borrowings from the Spanish language. There are many place names, including cities such as San Diego, Los Angeles, San Francisco, and Santa Fe, and states such as Arizona, California, Colorado, Florida, Montana, and Nevada. This list includes just a few of the many Spanish contributions to American English:

adios, adobe, amigo, bronco, burro, canyon, chili, cigar, coca, cola, coyote, guerrilla, hacienda, hombre, hurricane, lasso, loco, macho, mesquite, mosquito, padre, peon, pinto, plaza, poncho, ranch, rodeo, savvy, sombrero, vista

How do immigrants contribute to the American economy?

The anti-immigrant argument, directed primarily against Mexican Americans, is that they don't contribute to our economy but to the Mexican economy, because they tend to send much of their money home to families and relatives in Mexico. Ramos (2002) cites a study by the National Academy of Science finding that legal and illegal immigrants spend more than $10 billion each year within the U.S. economy. As they were becoming the largest minority group in the United States with almost 40 million people, Latinos' disposable income increased from 2001 to 2003 by about 30% to a total of $652 billion (Grow, 2004). As this population continues to increase, so will their purchasing power, estimated to exceed $1 trillion by 2010. Latinos are currently about 13% of the U.S. population, and demographers predict that they will constitute 18% by 2030 and 22% by 2050 (Ramos, 2002).

Private sector businesses have started courting Latino consumers. Surveys report that Latinos tend to purchase high-quality brand-name products and maintain loyalty to those brands. Procter & Gamble spent $90 million in one year, 10% of its budget, on an advertising campaign targeting Latinos. Kroger Company, the nation's leading grocery store chain, spent almost $2 million creating a *supermercado* in a Houston neighborhood that had become 85% Latino. In addition, more Latinos are becoming entrepreneurs. According to the Internal Revenue Service, from 1988 to 2003, Latino entrepreneurs increased by 30% (Grow, 2004). Perhaps inspired by Cuban success, entrepreneurs from other Latino groups have discovered that their fluency in Spanish gives them an advantage in working with their counterparts in Central and South America. Despite this commercial success, most Americans still don't seem to appreciate the potential and immediate benefits of having a linguistically diverse citizenry.

The Value of Cultural and Linguistic Diversity

Cultural and linguistic diversity have evolved in human societies around the world, and each manifestation of a distinctive culture and language illustrates the complexity and richness of human creativity. Although human beings occupy the same planet, each language demonstrates how diverse groups interpreted and understood their world, and the differences between languages reveal that despite our similarities, human beings tend to see that world in distinctive ways. The four languages spoken by the most people in our global population are Mandarin Chinese (16%), English (8%), Spanish (5%), and Arabic (4%), but over 200 languages today are spoken by more than a million people (Skutnabb-Kangas, 2000). Taken together, these different worldviews provide a dynamic perspective on human beings accommodating to diverse environments.

Skutnabb-Kangas (2000) defines **linguistic diversity** as "the range of variation exhibited by human language" (p. 70), and she reports that there are between 6500 and 10,000 languages throughout the world, as well as a number of different sign language systems. A more precise estimate is impossible because so many languages are disappearing. In the United States alone there used to be more than 300 indigenous languages, but only 175 still remain and many are becoming extinct. Linguists have identified 43 indigenous languages that are on the verge of extinction, and as for the rest, they are only confident that three indigenous languages will survive: Cree, Ojibway, and Inuktitut (Crawford, 2000). When 93-year-old Helen Sater died in a Canadian hospital in 1996, she was the last living person who was fluent in her native Tuscarora language (Skutnabb-Kangas, 2000). The Tuscarora were once part of the powerful alliance known as the Six Nations of the Iroquois Confederacy. With over 300 indigenous languages already present and with the arrival of people speaking diverse European languages, the history of North America should be regarded as an ongoing chronicle of communities that were multilingual as well as multicultural; yet Americans continue to be ambivalent about linguistic and cultural diversity. The reality of linguistic diversity in the United States today can best be appreciated by visiting our urban classrooms.

Do Americans support or oppose linguistic diversity?

According to Gort (2005), 25% of all K–12 students in the United States currently come from a home where a language other than English is spoken. Although more than three fourths of these students are Spanish-speaking, the following list includes other languages spoken by children in U.S. schools:

Southeast Asia:	Hmong, Khmer, Lao, and Vietnamese
South Asia:	Hindi, Punjabi, and Urdu
Asia:	Cantonese, Japanese, Korean, Mandarin, and Russian
Europe:	Armenian, French, Polish, Portuguese, and Serbo-Croatian
Other:	Arabic, Haitian Creole, Tagalog, and Navajo

Continuing the pattern of using nationalistic justifications for nativist attitudes, some Americans argue that immigrants and their children should not be encouraged to maintain fluency in their native languages, but should instead focus on learning English and assimilating into American society. They often cite other countries such as Canada, the former Yugoslavia, India, or the former Soviet Union to illustrate their concern that social disruptions can occur when groups within a nation maintain their cultural and linguistic heritage, but as Baron (2000) has written, "where multilingualism has produced civil strife . . . (it) invariably occurs when minority-language rights are suppressed" (p. 451). Another argument against promoting bilingualism or multilingualism is based on the perception that it is normal for a nation's citizens to be monolingual, yet most individuals in the world today are either bilingual or multilingual. As Skutnabb-Kangas (2000) has noted, those of us who are monolingual are the abnormal ones.

A primary motivation for maintaining one's native language is to preserve one's sense of identity and ability to function within a linguistic community. The Latino parents that Villanueva (1997) interviewed were committed to helping their children become bilingual and bicultural so that the children could communicate with their grandparents and participate meaningfully in cultural celebrations in their community. In addition, an individual's identity is often grounded in his or her religious faith, and Skutnabb-Kangas (2000) has described the intimate relationship between language and religion. She reports that people who have learned to pray in their native language have established their sense of connection to their God in a way that often makes it difficult for them to pray in their second language. Despite these and many other reasons for maintaining one's native language, most immigrant families in the United States tend to learn English and eventually cease to be fluent in their native language.

Why do immigrant families tend to lose their native language?

In contrast to American fears concerning the failure of immigrants to learn English and assimilate into American culture, studies document a pattern of the loss of linguistic diversity in subsequent generations of immigrant families. In her review of this research, Gort (2005) concludes that fluency in the native language is usually lost by the third generation and cites some studies suggesting that the loss of language among U.S. immigrant families is accelerating rather than diminishing. Tse (2001) provides the following description to illustrate the typical pattern among immigrant families. Adult immigrants with or without children come to the United States and learn enough English to function in their daily lives while retaining fluency in their native language. They teach the native language to their children, but once these children begin attending K–12 schools, they learn English, speak English with their peers not only at school but in their community, and tend to prefer using English by the time they leave elementary school. When these children become adults and have children of their own, English is usually the only language spoken at home, resulting in grandchildren who are only able to talk to their grandparents in English.

Some Americans insist that this pattern does not accurately describe what is happening in the families of recent Latino immigrants, but Portes (2007) has reviewed studies of second generation Latino families in the United States reporting that 98% of the members of these families are fluent in English, whereas only 35% retain their fluency in Spanish. This loss of language is consistent across Western nations in which the dominant group (speaking English or French or German) demands that immigrants abandon their own language and heritage and adopt the language and cultural traditions of the dominant group. This can be most clearly seen in the education of immigrant children. After describing this form of assimilation that demands cultural and language conformity, Skutnabb-Kangas (2000) concludes: "This is the preferred Western strategy in the education of ethnic minority children. It amounts to linguistic genocide" (p. 174). Some educators in the United States and elsewhere have been sensitive to this issue and have advocated a different approach.

What alternative pedagogical strategy have American educators proposed?

American educators have advocated for bilingual education in an effort to preserve linguistic diversity in the United States; after some initial success, they have been losing ground over the past three decades. As part of the reform efforts of the 1960s, Congress overwhelmingly passed the Bilingual Education Act in 1968. To understand why bilingual education soon attracted critics, it is important to understand the rationale for the passage of this Act. The bill's chief sponsor offered the following argument to his Senate colleagues:

> It is not the purpose of this bill to create pockets of different languages throughout the country. It is the main purpose of the bill to bring millions of school children into the mainstream of American life and make them literate in the national language of the country in which they live: namely, English (Crawford, 2000, p. 88).

Ralph Yarborough (D-Texas) made this argument to convince his Senate colleagues that this bill would serve the needs of Mexican Americans like those in his district where adults with limited English skills were trying to find jobs while their children struggled to learn English. He portrayed the Bilingual Education Act as an anti-poverty program for a constituency he believed had largely been overlooked in other "Great Society" programs. This means that from the beginning, most politicians and Americans viewed bilingual education not as a way to achieve bilingualism but as a more effective means of encouraging assimilation. If students learned better by teaching them in Spanish, then some instruction could be delivered in Spanish so that students would not fall behind in their content learning. The assumption was that bilingual education was a transitional program that would temporarily maintain fluency in a native language until the student's English skills were sufficient to allow all of his or her instruction to be in English.

Many advocates for bilingual education disagreed with this interpretation, arguing that students had a right to maintain not only their native language but also their cultural heritage while they learned English and adapted to their new culture. These advocates were not opposed to assimilation, but they believed that it should be done in a more culturally pluralistic fashion. In the early 1970s, Massachusetts and several other states had to repeal their English Only laws to establish "transitional bilingual education," but these states and Americans across the country were disturbed when a nationwide study in the late 1970s reported that 86% of bilingual programs retained Spanish-speaking students after they had become fluent in English. This caused considerable consternation among state and federal lawmakers who had believed that bilingual education programs would take a transitional approach (Crawford, 2000). In 1978, Congress voted to allow federal funds to be used only for "transitional" bilingual education programs. Lost in this controversy was another finding from the same study that half of all bilingual teachers were not proficient in the students' native languages, raising doubts about whether bilingual education programs could produce students who were genuinely fluent in their native language as well as English. In 1980, a report by the President's Commission on Foreign Language and International Studies encouraged advocates for bilingual education by stating: "The melting pot tradition that denigrates immigrants' maintenance of their skills to speak their native tongue still lingers, and unfortunately causes linguistic minorities (in the U.S.) to be ignored as a potential asset" (Tse, 2001, p. 51).

Even so, the nationwide study raised doubts that would continue to plague bilingual education programs, and early research did not diminish these doubts. Shorris (1992) described numerous conflicting studies that reported findings that were both supportive and critical of bilingual education. Increasingly, critics of bilingual education portrayed it as a language-maintenance program rather than as a way for children of immigrants to learn English and academic content more effectively. In the midst of this debate, the Reagan administration chose to promote and fund the implementation of English-only approaches to teaching students learning English as a second language (Crawford, 2000).

As the controversy continued, it became obvious that this was not simply an educational debate, but that there were social and political aspects as well. Advocates for bilingual education were interested in more than language learning; they argued for the value of teaching diverse "viewpoints, histories, sociopolitical realities and languages, and to promote the intrinsic worth of diversity in general" (Gort, 2005, p. 34). Opponents were adamant that such goals went beyond the original mandate of helping non-English speaking students to learn English, and they also criticized bilingual programs for separating their students from students in the regular classes, isolating them from the kinds of interaction with their American peers that might enable their assimilation into American society. Critics of bilingual education were more successful in their efforts to persuade Americans that bilingual education programs were not working.

By the 1990s, many Americans perceived bilingual education as being more likely to promote students' maintenance of their native language and culture rather than their learning English and assimilating into American society, even though ongoing research began to make a stronger case for the efficacy of bilingual education programs. Salas (2005) cites a number of studies finding that students whose first language was not English achieved more academic progress in English when they also had instruction in their first language. Salas also referred to a review of research on bilingual education programs concluding that students in these programs "do as well as or better on standardized tests than students in comparison groups of English-learners in English-only programs" (p. 34). Still, the five million English language learners (ELLs) in K–12 public schools today are unlikely to be enrolled in bilingual programs because the federal Bilingual Education Act was not renewed in 2002, and, despite research supporting bilingual education, federal policies continue to emphasize English-only educational programs for ELLs.

Have research studies identified effective approaches to ELL instruction?

English-only programs have often involved a total immersion approach in which only English is spoken in the classroom, yet advocates for this approach can produce no credible studies to support it; instead, they usually offer anecdotal evidence. By contrast, there are numerous studies documenting the diverse outcomes achieved in bilingual education programs. Gort (2005) reviewed these studies and reported: ". . . a growing body of research points to the educational, social, and psychological benefits associated with educating bilingual learners in their native language as they develop skills in English" (p. 25). In 2006, the National Literacy Panel published its review of research on programs educating ELLs, and in that same year the Center for Research on Education, Diversity and Excellence published its review of these programs. Literacy expert Claude Goldenberg of Stanford University engaged in a meta-analysis of these two major reviews of literacy studies to determine what conclusions could be reached.

Goldenberg (2008) began by providing some demographic data: Of the five million ELLs in U.S. schools, 80% are Spanish-speaking. Approximately 60% of ELLs are receiving some form of English-only instruction. Test results reveal that ELLs tend to have low scores on measures of academic achievement, but there is no way of knowing if these low scores reflect poor content knowledge or the limitations of the students' proficiency in English because the tests taken by ELLs were in English. Although that question cannot be answered, Goldenberg (2008) reports that one of the major findings emerging from both studies was that "Teaching students to read in their first language promotes higher levels of reading achievement in English" (p. 14). Goldenberg also noted that this finding was consistent with four previous meta-analyses of research on ELLs. He emphasized the significance of this finding: "No other area in educational research with which I am familiar can claim five independent meta-analyses based on experimental studies, much less five that converge on the same finding" (p. 15). Further, both research reviews that Goldenberg analyzed reported that ELLs in bilingual education programs tended to develop sufficient literacy skills to be not only fluent in speaking two languages, but also fluent in reading and writing in both languages (i.e., not only bilingual but biliterate).

Why should educators be advocates for bilingual programs?

Tse (2001) suggests that American educators should refer to the report from the 1980 President's Commission on Foreign Language and International Studies, which stated: "Our vital interests are impaired by the fatuous notion that our competence in other languages is irrelevant" (p. 50). In addition, Gort (2005) argued that there is support for bilingual education in the No Child Left Behind Act of 2002 because it identified learning a foreign language as a "core academic subject" (p. 33). As the global economy becomes an increasingly important factor for our national economy, it is advantageous for the United States and any nation today to have citizens fluent in one or more languages other than their native language. There is evidence that this advantage has been apparent at the federal level for decades. Since 1946, when it was first established, the largest foreign language school in the United States has been the Defense Language Institute for military and government personnel.

Tse (2001) addresses the reason for establishing the Defense Language Institute in the first of her three arguments describing the advantages of increasing the number of bilingual or multilingual Americans. The first advantage is for *diplomacy/security*—having fluent speakers of the world's languages enables the United States to play a major role in global affairs and negotiate peaceful solutions to political conflicts. Bilingual Americans also strengthen our ability to gather credible intelligence with regard to issues affecting our national security. The second advantage is *economic*—because of globalization, businesses increasingly need employees who can not only speak another language, but also understand the culture where the language is spoken. Businesses that are able to navigate the linguistic and cultural terrain will be able to establish better relations with trading partners around the world. The third advantage is *educational*—promoting bilingualism in our children and youth will inevitably increase the numbers of college students majoring in a language, and that will likely result in increasing the numbers of bilingual students choosing to enroll in teacher training courses. For many years now, it has often been difficult for our K–12 schools to find teacher candidates who are both fluent in a language and have teaching certification.

For all of these reasons, educators who are advocates for bilingualism may be more successful today if they renew their efforts to implement bilingual education programs in our K–12 schools. There are also various forms of bilingual education approaches such as dual language (also known as two-way immersion) that have experienced great success with students and parents. Dual language programs pair ELLs with students who want to learn another language in the same classroom. A bilingual teacher may provide instruction in two languages and the students serve as resources for each other. In a program with Spanish-speaking students, the students learning Spanish use their ELL peers as language tutors, and ELLs use their partners to tutor them in English. The growing need in the United States and in the world for linguistic diversity and cultural competence should be a catalyst for a more pluralistic attitude toward diverse languages and cultures. If Americans develop greater respect for the linguistic and cultural diversity of immigrants to the United States, it could dispel some of the myths about immigrants that too many Americans still believe.

What myths about immigrants do many Americans believe?

Myths about "foreigners" who legally or illegally enter the United States have long fueled negative attitudes toward immigrants. Many Americans have expressed anti-immigrant sentiments openly, and immigrants and their children cannot help but hear them. As part of a longitudinal study, immigrant youth in high schools were asked what most Americans think about "people from my country"; 65% of their responses were negative—being stupid, lazy, thieves, and gangsters (Suarez-Orozco & Suarez-Orozco, 2001).

Although most myths about immigration refer to all immigrants, some refer specifically to immigrants with refugee status. According to the United Nations, a *refugee* is a person "unable or unwilling to return to his or her country because of a well-founded fear of persecution . . . based on race, religion, nationality, or membership in a particular social group or political party" (Pipher, 2002, p. 18). The myths highlighted in this chapter reveal current nativist attitudes about immigrants and refugees.

MYTH #1: Immigrants arrive ignorant, penniless, with very little formal education and immediately have to go on welfare.

Macedo and Bartolome (2001) record an example of this myth being expressed by a former president of Boston University complaining about the number of Cambodians in Massachusetts: "There has to be a welfare magnet going on here. . . . Why should Lowell be the Cambodian capital of America?" (p. 11). In fact, immigrants often have been professionals in their country of origin—doctors, professors, and engineers. Although the figure varies each year, in 2007, 28% of U.S. immigrants had a college degree (Just the Facts, 2008). Still, even those arriving with college educations may take minimum wage jobs because institutions or professional organizations in the United States may not recognize their practices, skills, or degrees, forcing them to return to school to be certified in their profession or retrained in related fields. Despite obstacles of language and culture, the percentage of immigrants, including refugees, receiving welfare is approximately the same as native residents (Levinson, 2002). The statistics about modern immigrants to the United States document that they rarely become permanent recipients of public assistance.

Immigrants are consumers who pay rent and buy groceries and other products that help strengthen the economy. Most studies of the economic impact of immigrants report that they ultimately benefit local economies, even taking into account the services that may be required to assist them during their first few years in the country. With regard to undocumented immigrants, they are not eligible to receive most forms of public assistance beyond admitting their children to public schools or to the emergency room of a hospital, but they do pay taxes. The *New York Times* reported that illegal undocumented immigrants contribute approximately $7 billion each year to Social Security, and since they can never claim this money, it will be used to fund the benefits of other workers in the Social Security system (Scherr, 2008). Despite such contributions, many Americans express negative attitudes toward recent immigrants, especially the majority who are Spanish-speaking. Baron (2000) observes that some Americans appear to equate bilingualism with a lack of patriotism. Perhaps this was the basis for the animosity expressed by one caller to a Massachusetts radio talk show who referred to Spanish-speaking immigrants as "bilinguals" in a clearly derisive manner (Macedo & Bartolomé, 2001). It is ironic to see the ability to speak fluently in more than one language transformed into a racial slur.

> All the people like us are We.
> And every one else is They,
>
> **Rudyard Kipling (1865–1936)**

MYTH #2: Immigrants cling to their culture, language, and traditions, and refuse to assimilate into the American "melting pot."

New immigrants have always maintained their cultural heritage, in part because their identity has been profoundly shaped by the native culture. When immigrant children become adults, they typically integrate their cultural heritage with American culture, producing a hybrid of traditions and values taken from both. As for learning English, it is not unusual to find that immigrants are multilingual when they arrive; often English is one of the languages they know.

Immigrants pay taxes, send children to schools, serve in the military, and are affected by local political decisions. Recent immigrants have demonstrated their desire to be actively engaged in our democratic society by participating in voter registration efforts and transporting voters to the polls for elections. Because the Constitution leaves the issue of voting qualifications up to the local government, some cities have responded by giving voting rights to immigrants who are not yet citizens. The assimilation of immigrants is further complicated by a backlog of those pursuing naturalization, a process that can take years if not decades before they are granted legal permanent resident status, and the process has been delayed even further since the 9/11 tragedy (Wucker, 2003).

MYTH #3: The United States is taking more than its fair share of immigrants; other countries need to take more.

In many European countries, immigrants represent over 10% of the population. In Germany, this percentage is predicted to rise to 30% by 2030. The countries accepting more immigrants than the United States include Canada, Australia, Germany, and Switzerland (Ramos, 2002). The main difference between U.S. immigration and that of other countries is that more diverse groups are admitted to the United States than are accepted by other countries. Between 70% and 80% of immigrants around the world are refugees. The United States accepts less than 1% of the refugees; several other countries admit a higher percentage. According to the 2000 Census, immigrants constituted 10% of the U.S. population, whereas in 1900, they constituted 15% (Passel & Edmonston, 1994; Pipher, 2002).

People who express concerns about excessive admission of immigrants to the United States often refer specifically to Mexicans, who constituted 25% of all legal immigrants in the 1990s, and an undetermined number of illegal immigrants. Current xenophobic attitudes have demanded restrictions on Mexican immigration and more money for border patrols to keep out illegal immigrants. Mexican immigration has not diminished, but increased border scrutiny has caused legal Mexican immigrants to stay in the United States rather than return home for fear they might not be allowed reentry: The number of those returning to Mexico plummeted in the 1990s. Although stricter border enforcement has not kept illegal immigrants from coming, it has resulted in three times as many deaths of those attempting to enter the United States (Massey, 2003).

MYTH #4: The main problem with U.S. immigration is the large number of illegal immigrants getting into the country.

Illegal immigrants make up 20% of the immigrant population and about 2% of the U.S. population. According to the U.S. Citizenship and Immigration Service, the number of illegal immigrants in the United States is relatively stable, increasing slightly since 1996 (USCIS, 2005). The popular image of illegal immigrants is that of Mexicans illegally crossing the border into the United States. In fact, over 41% of illegal immigrants in the United States entered legally, often recruited by employers, and only become illegal by remaining after their work visas expire.

The United States has a visa waiver program for residents of twenty-two selected countries, mostly in Western Europe, whose citizens can come to America for up to 90 days simply by purchasing a round-trip travel ticket. The Immigration and Naturalization Service (INS) reports that many people who come with such visas stay well beyond the 90-day limit, also becoming illegal aliens. According to the INS data, major abusers of the privilege come from France, Sweden, and Italy (Hernandez-Truyol, 1997). So why is it that only Mexicans are viewed as "illegals"? The stereotype of Mexicans sneaking across the U.S. border illustrates not only xenophobia, but racism.

MYTH #5: Illegal immigrants are responsible for increased crime, disease, and terrorism in the United States.

This allegation appeared in a 34-page booklet on illegal immigration published by the American Legion and disseminated to its nearly three million members. It included the false assertion that illegal immigrants infected more than 7,000 Americans with leprosy, even though this myth had already been proven false through investigations by many sources, including the news program *60 Minutes* (Scherr, 2008). Further, the source for the claim that immigrants were bringing various diseases into the United States came from an article written by a lawyer with a history of anti-immigrant attitudes and no medical expertise. According to Scherr (2008), there is no medical research reporting an increase in the numbers of Americans with diseases stemming from the presence of immigrants.

Unlike the disease myth, the myth about immigrants engaging in criminal acts seemed to be supported by a *New York Times* article claiming that 21% of all crime in the United States was committed by undocumented workers; however, after the researcher making the claim was confronted with evidence of errors in his interpretation of the data, he corrected his calculations and reduced his estimate to 6.1% (Wilson, 2008). In addition, estimates of criminal behavior often come from data about people in prisons, and many immigrants are in prison for violating immigration laws, not for violent crimes. As Wilson (2008) reported, research on criminal activities over several decades has consistently concluded that: "Immigrants aren't a crime problem" (p. 21). Finally, with regard to the terrorism aspect of this myth, Scherr (2008) cites a 2005 study by the Nixon Center reporting that this allegation was patently false, concluding that ". . . not a single (terrorist) entered from Mexico" (p. 34).

MYTH #6: Immigrants are taking jobs away from Americans.

For as long as there has been immigration, business owners have insisted and continue to insist that immigration is necessary to sustain U.S. economic growth. According to a Cato Institute study, immigrants do not increase joblessness, even in lowest-paid worker categories. A 2006 study found that states with large increases in immigration did not experience more unemployment for native-born workers (Scherr, 2008). Studies have also found that an influx of immigrant labor may create new jobs: One Los Angeles County study of a decade of immigration reported that Mexican immigrants created 78,000 new jobs (Cole, 1996). A 2005 study by the Kenan-Flagler Business School found that Hispanics accounted for 35% of the increase in the North Carolina workforce, and the increased number of Hispanic workers created 89,000 new jobs in the state (Wiggins, 2006).

As in the past, it is employers who are demanding immigrant labor for available jobs. In 1986, the U.S. government made it a crime for an employer to hire undocumented workers; now, many employers hire subcontractors to supply them with workers, thus placing the risk of arrest on the subcontractors for hiring undocumented workers. Unions have begun to accept the reality of immigrant labor and have been attempting to organize workers—especially laundry workers, janitors, hotel housekeepers, and waiters. These unions have become the main voice representing immigrant concerns (Massey, 2003).

A new and possibly growing problem may be the fault of businesses that urge opening immigration to more workers: the use of H1(b) visas and professional visas for entry into the United States. During the labor shortage of the 1990s, American companies increased their use of H1(b) visas to recruit qualified workers for vacant jobs, and there have been allegations of abuse concerning the use of these visas. Trade pacts signed by the Bush administration relax H1(b) rules to allow into the United States additional thousands of workers from countries with whom the United States has free trade agreements. If this problem continues, immigration laws in the United States will likely be revised once again. Maintaining fairness in addressing the diversity and complexity of immigration issues in the American economy is an ongoing challenge, but the goal should be to provide opportunity to immigrants, no matter when they came to the United States.

AFTERWORD

This history of immigration demonstrates that there have been and still are diverse but clearly defined attitudes toward immigration on the part of American citizens, political leaders, and representatives of business and industry. Although entrenched workers sometimes resent the economic competition, our society has always benefited from the willing labor of immigrant workers. We have also benefited from the cultural diversity represented by immigrants from so many different nations. Although some have complained that immigrants do not assimilate and have repeatedly insisted that immigrants should rid themselves of their old culture, history teaches us that there is no royal road for

America, it would seem, is miraculously both singular and plural, organized and scattered, united and diffused.

Henry Kariel (1924–)

immigrants trying to adjust or adapt to a new culture; in reality, there are diverse pathways. Each immigrant may take a different route, but each will end at the same destination—becoming an American.

myeducationlab

Now go to Topics #1, 4, and 10: **Ethnicity/Cultural Diversity, Language,** and **Immigration** in the MyEducationLab (www.myeducationlab.com) for your course, where you can:

- Find learning outcomes for these topics along with the national standards that connect to these outcomes.
- Complete Assignments and Activities that can help you more deeply understand the chapter content by viewing classroom video and ABC News footage.
- Apply and practice your understanding of the core teaching skills identified in the chapter with the Building Teaching Skills and Dispositions learning units.

TERMS AND DEFINITIONS

Americanization The demand that immigrants to the United States reject their ethnic or cultural heritage and conform to American ways as defined by the dominant group

Anti-Semitism Having anti-Jewish prejudices or stereotypes, or engaging in discrimination against Jews

Assimilation A process whereby immigrants adopt cultural traits of the host country in order to be identified with that country and integrated into the immediate society

English Only A movement in various states demanding that legislatures make English the official language of the state, with the eventual goal of having the federal government make English the official language of the United States

Eugenics The study of agencies under social control that may improve or repair the racial qualities of future generations, either physically or mentally

Linguistic diversity The range of variation exhibited by human language (Skutnabb-Kangas, 2000)

Nativism An anti-immigrant ideology advocating the protection of "native" inhabitants of a country from new or potential immigrants who are viewed as threatening or dangerous (Feagin & Feagin, 1996)

Oppression When any entity (society, organization, group, or individual) intentionally or unintentionally distributes resources inequitably, refuses to share power, imposes ethnocentric culture, and/or maintains unresponsive and inflexible institutions toward another entity for its supposed benefit and rationalizes its actions by blaming or ignoring the victim (Andrzejewski, 1996)

Xenophobia Fear of or prejudice against people from nations other than one's own

DISCUSSION EXERCISES

Exercise #1 What I Know Is . . . What Do We Know about Hyphenated Americans?

Directions: In a society as diverse as that in many parts of the United States today, immigrant cultures are sometimes strongly demonstrated, as in those described here. After reading each item, explain what you know and how you tend to feel about the subcultural diversity illustrated within each category. If possible, explain what knowledge you have and/or the feelings you hold about those differences. Finally, attempt to explain any animosity or frustration that could result from experiencing those cultural differences.

1. Differences in social interaction:
   A. How loudly some racial or ethnic groups seem to talk in conversation.
   B. Direct eye contact between conversants is prohibited in some cultures.
   C. Some family sizes are large and seem to be happy living together, even in smaller spaces than actually needed.
   D. Physical contact in public between men and women is forbidden, and neither is walking together allowed.
2. Differences in dress:
   A. Women from a number of countries wear a traditional sari, many of them of exquisitely beautiful fabrics.
   B. The Sikh male turban is part of culture and religion.
   C. The burqua for Muslim women may be required by cultural and religious policy.
   D. Male Hasidic Jews wear black suits, hats, and payess (uncut sideburns).
3. Differences in cultural traditions:
   A. Preparing foods from many countries involves ingredients that are not familiar to many of us whose parents and grandparents have more thoroughly integrated customs and foods into a standard American fare.
   B. National celebrations such as Cinco de Mayo and Syttende Mai are often unknown to a majority of Americans, even though American citizens with heritages from different countries work to keep their homeland traditions alive.
   C. The significant events of a culture can be observed through seasonal rituals, religious occasions, wedding ceremonies, and family activities and vary according to ethnicity, religion, and country, such as gathering for H'mong New Year and for funeral rites.

Exercise #2 The Immigration Letter to the Editor

Directions: This letter appeared in newspapers across the United States, each signed as if written locally. Discuss your understanding of its message, and then move to the Questions for Discussion. As you read, consider which of the four ethnic perspectives presented in this chapter is illustrated.

> I am tired of this nation worrying about whether we are offending some individual or their culture. . . . I am not against immigration, nor do I hold a grudge against anyone who is seeking a better life by coming to America. Our population is almost entirely made up of descendants of immigrants. However, there are a few things that those who have recently come to our country, and apparently some born here, need to understand.
>
> This idea of America being a multicultural community has served only to dilute our sovereignty and our national identity. As Americans, we have our own culture, our own society, our own

language and our own lifestyle. This culture has been developed over centuries of struggles, trials, and victories by millions of men and women who have sought freedom.

We speak ENGLISH, not Spanish, Portuguese, Arabic, Chinese, Japanese, Russian or any other language. If you wish to become part of our society, learn the language! "In God We Trust" is our national motto. This is not some Christian, right wing, and political slogan. We adopted this motto because Christian men and women, based on Christian principles, founded this nation, and this is clearly documented. It is certainly appropriate to display it on the walls of our schools. If God offends you, then I suggest you consider another part of the world as your new home, because God is part of our culture.

We are happy with our culture and have no desire to change, and we really don't care how you did things where you came from. This is OUR COUNTRY, our land, and our lifestyle. Our First Amendment gives every citizen the right to express opinions and we will allow you every opportunity to do so. But once you are done complaining, whining, and griping about our pledge, our national motto, or our way of life, I highly encourage you to take advantage of one other great American freedom, THE RIGHT TO LEAVE.

God Bless America

Questions for Discussion

1. What do you think the writer means in saying that the view of America as a multicultural community "has served only to dilute our sovereignty and our national identity"?
2. Are large numbers of immigrants not learning English?
3. Should Spanish-speaking immigrants who are learning English be criticized for trying to maintain fluency in Spanish or other native languages spoken by other immigrants?
4. Are immigrants complaining about the use of "God" in the Pledge of Allegiance?
5. If "God is part of our culture," do you have to believe in God to be an American?
6. Who is intended to be included in the "We" of the last paragraph?
7. How could the letter be written to reflect any of the other ethnic perspectives?

REFERENCES

Andrzejewski, J. (1996). Definitions for understanding oppression and social justice. In J. Andrewski (Ed.), *Oppression and social justice: Critical frameworks* (5th ed., pp. 52–59). Needham, MA: Simon & Schuster.

Provides definitions for a variety of terms essential for discussing intergroup relations.

Baron, D. (2000). English in a multicultural America. In K.E. Rosenblum & T.C. Travis (Eds.), *The meaning of difference: American constructions of race, sex and gender, social class, and sexual orientation* (pp. 445–451). Boston, MA: McGraw-Hill.

Reviews the history of linguistic diversity in the United States and its implications for concerns expressed by people in the English-Only movement.

Barrett, J.R., & Roediger, D. (2002). How white people became white. In P. Rothenberg (Ed.), *White privilege: Essential readings on the other side of racism* (pp. 29–34). New York, NY: Worth.

Discusses the process of Americanization of immigrants to the United States with attention to the use of white privilege as an inducement for immigrants to conform to the majority.

Brands, H.W. (2000). *The first American: The life and times of Benjamin Franklin.* New York, NY: Doubleday.

Describes Franklin's development as a scholar, entrepreneur, political leader, and the influence he had on the emerging nation.

Brodkin, K. (2002). How Jews became white folks. In P. Rothenberg (Ed.), *White privilege: Essential readings on the other side of racism* (pp. 35–48). New York, NY: Worth.

Discusses the racism and anti-Semitism that has characterized anti-immigrant sentiment and the factors that resulted in the ultimate acceptance of white ethnic immigrants.

Buchanan, S., & Kim, T. (2005, Winter). The nativists. *Intelligence Report, 120,* 25–42.

Profiles twenty-one leaders of anti-immigrant groups in the United States and describes their attitudes and the actions they and their groups have taken.

Cole, D. (1996). The new Know-Nothingism: Five myths about immigration. In J. Andrzejewski (Ed.), *Oppression and social justice: Critical frameworks* (5th ed., pp. 152–154). Needham, MA: Simon & Schuster.

Describes some popular myths about immigration and provides information disproving each of these myths.

Crawford, J. (2000). *At war with diversity: US language policy in an age of anxiety.* Clevedon, England: Multilingual Matters LTD.

Discusses reasons for decreased linguistic diversity in the United States, especially the demise of indigenous languages, the growth of the English-only movement, and bilingual education.

Cubberley, E.P. (1919). *Public education in the United States.* Boston, MA: Houghton Mifflin.

Describes how schools were established in the United States and the influences that shaped the development of American public schools.

Daniels, Roger. (2002). *Coming to America: A history of immigration and ethnicity in American life* (2nd ed.) New York, NY: Perennial (HarperCollins).

Describes U.S. immigration patterns from the colonial period to the present, paying particular attention to the ethnic minorities who immigrated.

Delgado, R. (1997). Citizenship. In J.F. Perea (Ed.), *Immigrants out!: The new nativism and the anti-immigrant impulse in the United States* (pp. 318–323). New York, NY: New York University Press.

Discusses recent proposals directed toward making U.S. citizenship more difficult to obtain.

Eck, D.L. (2001). *A new religious America: How a "Christian Country" has become the world's most religiously diverse nation.* New York, NY: HarperCollins.

Examines the growth of diverse religions in the United States, especially with regard to immigration patterns since 1965, and describes its impact and potential.

Feagin, J. (1997). Old poison in new bottles: The deep roots of modern nativism. In J.F. Perea (Ed.), *Immigrants out!: The new nativism and the anti-immigrant impulse in the United States* (pp. 13–43). New York, NY: New York University Press.

Presents an overview of the development of nativist sentiment in the United States from the early 1800s to the present.

Feagin, J., & Feagin, C. (1996). Basic concepts in the study of racial and ethnic relations. In *Racial and ethnic relations* (5th ed., pp. 6–26). Upper Saddle River, NJ: Prentice Hall.

Provides definitions of essential terms and concepts for intergroup relations.

Fuchs, L.H. (1990). *The American kaleidoscope: Race, ethnicity and the civic culture.* Hanover, NH: University Press of New England.

Argues that immigrant groups have been successful in embracing and practicing basic social and political principles of U.S. society.

Goldenberg, C. (2008, Summer). Teaching English Language Learners. *American Educator 32*(1), 8–23, 42–43.

Provides a meta-analysis of two major reviews of research on English Language Learners.

Gort, M. (2005). Bilingual education: Good for U.S.? In T. Osborn (Ed.), *Language and cultural diversity in U.S. schools: Democratic principles in action* (pp. 25–37). Westport, CT: Praeger.

Discusses misconceptions about bilingual education, describes quality bilingual programs, and explains why bilingual education is necessary for educational equity.

Grant, M. (1970). *The passing of the great race, Or the racial basis of European history* (Rev. ed.). New York, NY: Arno Press. (Original work published 1916)

Expresses fears that the white race may be losing its position of supremacy in the world.

Grow, B. (2004, March 15). Is America ready? *Business Week,* pp. 58–70.

Describes current Latino population and its projected growth and the economic implications currently and in the future.

Hennesey, J. (1985). *American Catholics: A history of the Roman Catholic community in the United States.* New York, NY: Oxford University Press.

Provides a comprehensive description of the experience of Catholics in America from the colonial period to the present.

Hernandez-Truyol, B.E. (1997). Reconciling rights in collision: An international human rights strategy. In J.F. Perea (Ed.), *Immigrants out!: The new nativism and the anti-immigrant impulse in the United States* (pp. 254–276). New York, NY: New York University Press.

Discusses the basis for advocacy of human rights globally and in the United States.

Herrnstein, R.J., & Murray, C. (1994). *The bell curve: Intelligence and class structure in American life.* New York, NY: Free Press.

Analyzes research to argue that differences in intelligence stem from race/ethnicity and are genetically determined and that economic success or failure is determined by intelligence.

Higham, J. (1955). *Strangers in the land: Patterns of American nativism, 1865–1925.* New Brunswick, NJ: Rutgers University Press.

Describes the growth of anti-immigrant sentiment in the United States, culminating in significant anti-immigrant policies and legislation of the 1920s.

Just the Facts. (2008, June). Immigrants and education. Retrieved on June 14, 2009, from the Public Policy Institute of California at www.ppic.org (Publications).

Provides data on educational attainment of recent immigrants.

Kammen, M. (1972). *People of paradox: An inquiry concerning the origins of American civilization.* New York: Vintage.

Analyzes and attempts to reconcile contradictory aspects of American culture as revealed in the history of the colonial experience and in the emerging nation.

Lee, E. (2004). American gate keeping: Race and immigration law in the twentieth century. In N. Foner & G.M. Frederickson (Eds.), *Not just black and white: Historical and contemporary perspectives on immigration, race and ethnicity in the United States* (pp. 119–144). New York, NY: Russell Sage Foundation.

Examines changes in racial composition of immigrants since 1965.

Levinson, A. (2002). Immigrants and welfare use. Retrieved on May 15, 2009, from the Migration Policy Institute at www.migrationinformation.org/US-Focus.

Describes the extent and nature of immigrants using welfare services.

Lynn, R. (2001). *Eugenics: A reassessment.* Westport, CT: Prager.

Provides background on the historical formulations of eugenics, gives examples of how eugenics has been implemented, and discusses the role that eugenics could play in the future.

Macedo, D., & Bartolome, L.I. (2001). *Dancing with bigotry: Beyond the politics of tolerance.* New York, NY: Palgrave.

Examines issues of language and limitations in multicultural education; the first quote is from John Silber, who was chair of the Massachusetts State Board of Education at the time.

Martinez, E. (2000). Seeing more than black and white. In M. Adams, W.J. Blumenfeld, R. Castañeda, H.W. Hackman, M.L. Peters, & X. Zuñiga (Eds.), *Readings for diversity and social justice* (pp. 93–98). New York, NY: Routledge.

Discusses the need to go beyond the focus on black people and white people in addressing problems of racism in the United States.

Massey, D.S. (2003). Closed-door policy. *American Prospect 14*(7), 26–28.

Analyzes recent trends in Mexican immigration to the United States and the impact of U.S. government reactions taken in response to these trends.

Myers, G. (1960). *History of bigotry in the United States.* New York: Capricorn.

Describes the historic targets of bigotry since colonial days, with emphasis on Catholics, Jews, and immigrants, and the actions taken against these minorities by the majority.

O'Grady, C. (2009, May). Hate speech, media activism and the first amendment. *Extra! 22*(5), 8–9.

Reviews racist rhetoric against illegal immigrants in the media and the efforts of activists to challenge such hate speech.

Pai, Y., & Adler, S. (2006). Schooling as Americanization: 1600s–1970s. In *Cultural foundations of education* (4th ed., pp. 55–91). Upper Saddle River, NJ: Merrill Prentice Hall.

Describes the evolution of the Americanization concept and its implementation in schools.

Passel, J., & Edmonston, B. (1994). Immigration and race: Recent trends in immigration to the U.S. In B. Edmonston & J. Passel (Eds.), *Immigration and ethnicity: The integration of America's newest arrivals* (pp. 31–71). Washington DC: Urban Institute Press.

Examines 1980s immigration and compares it to immigration trends from 1880 to 1920.

Pipher, M. (2002). *The middle of everywhere: The world's refugees come to our town.* New York, NY: Harcourt.

Presents stories about a variety of recent immigrants, including the conditions that forced them to immigrate and the difficulties they encounter trying to adjust to American culture.

Portes, A. (2007, October). The fence to nowhere. *The American Prospect 18*(10), 26–29.

Discusses historic cyclic migration of Latino workers into the United States and confronts various misconceptions about recent Latino immigrants.

Ramos, J. (2002). *The other face of America.* New York, NY: Rayo.

Provides statistics and describes studies on U.S. immigrants, focusing on the contributions of Latinos and the implications of Latino immigration.

Roberts, D. (1997). Who may give birth to citizens: Reproduction, eugenics, and immigration. In J.F. Perea (Ed.), *Immigrants out!: The new nativism and the anti-immigrant impulse in the United States* (pp. 205–219). New York, NY: New York University Press.

Discusses proposals to deny citizenship to children of undocumented immigrants, relating this to the eugenics movement and other historical examples of racism.

Salas, K.D. (2006). Defending bilingual education. *Rethinking Schools, 20*(3), 33–37.

Discusses criticisms of bilingual education, implications of NCLB for bilingual programs, and studies documenting the effectiveness of bilingual programs.

Scherer, M. (2005). Scrimmage on the border. *Mother Jones, 30*(2), 50–57.

Describes current anti-immigrant controversy, especially in Southern California, with comments from immigration critics and supporters.

Scherr, S. (2008, Fall). Legionnaires' Disease. *Intelligence Report,* 131, 28–35.

Reviews several anti-immigrant myths reported in a publication by the American Legion and debunks all of them.

Selden, S. (1999). *Inheriting shame: The story of eugenics and racism in America.* New York, NY: Teachers College Press.

Analyzes the development of the eugenics movement in the United States in the early twentieth century and what lessons should be learned from this development.

Shorris, E. (2001). *Latinos: A biography of the people.* New York, NY: W.W. Norton.

Provides a personal narrative of the diverse Latino groups in the United States using many personal stories told within a historical context.

Skutnabb-Kangas, T. (2000). *Linguistic genocide in education—or Worldwide diversity and human rights?* Mahwah, NJ: Lawrence Erlbaum Associates.

Describes how the education of indigenous and ethnic minority children contributes to the loss of linguistic diversity in Western societies including the United States.

Smedley, A. (2007). The arrival of Africans and descent into slavery. *Race in North America: Origin and evolution of a world view* 3rd ed. Boulder, CO: Westview.

Describes the arrival of Africans to America and how they lost their equal status with other immigrants.

Sorenson, E., & Enchautegui, M.E. (1994). Immigrant male earnings in the 1980s: Divergent patterns by race and ethnicity. In B. Edmonston & J. Passel (Eds.), *Immigration and ethnicity: The integration of America's newest arrivals* (pp. 139–161). Washington DC: Urban Institute Press.

Examines how the earnings of immigrants are affected by trends in skill composition and the length of time immigrants have lived in the United States.

Steinbeck, J. (1966). *America and Americans.* New York, NY: Viking Press.

Includes observations of America with regard to politics, democracy, values, contradictions, consumerism, diversity, environment, global perceptions, and the future.

Stubblefield, A. (2007, Spring). "Beyond the pale": Tainted whiteness, cognitive disability, and eugenic sterilization. *Hypatia 22*(2), 162–180.

Explains how eugenicists manipulated the concept of "feeblemindedness" at the start of the 20th century to label people of color, poor people, and women as inferior.

Suarez-Orozco, C., & Suarez-Orozco, M. (2001). *Children of immigration.* Cambridge, MA: Harvard University Press.

Describes the lives of recent immigrants based on the authors' longitudinal study and other studies, and examines the difficulties they face as they try to assimilate.

Takaki, R. (2000). *A different mirror: A history of multicultural America.* Boston, MA: Little Brown.

Describes the experience of diverse racial and ethnic groups in the United States.

Tatalovich, R. (1997). Official English as nativist backlash. In J.F. Perea (Ed.), *Immigrants out!: The new nativism and the anti-immigrant impulse in the United States* (pp. 78–102). New York, NY: New York University Press.

Examines the English Only movement as an example of the new nativism.

Tse, Lucy. (2001). *"Why Don't They Learn English?": Separating fact from fallacy in the U.S. language debate.* New York, NY: Teachers College Press.

Explains causes and consequences of language loss in the United States and debunks myths about English language learning among immigrant children.

United States Citizenship and Immigration Services (USCIS). (2005). *Illegal Alien Resident Population.* Retrieved July 5, 2006, from http://www.uscis.gov

Provides data on illegal residents in the United States, formerly the Immigration and Naturalization Service (INS) until merged with Homeland Security.

Villanueva, I. (1997). The voices of Chicano families: Life stories, maintaining bilingualism and cultural awareness. In M. Seller & L. Weis (Eds.), *Beyond Black and White: New faces and voices in U.S. schools* (pp. 61–79). Albany, NY: SUNY Press.

Describes the efforts of several Latino families who believe in the importance of being bilingual and bicultural, and how they are helping their children achieve both goals.

Whyte, W.F. (1955). *Street corner society: The social structure of an Italian slum.* Chicago, IL: The University of Chicago Press.

Presents an ethnographic study of an urban Italian neighborhood in the 1930s.

Wiggins, L.D.R. (2006). Will the immigration debate impact black employment? *The Crisis, 113*(3), 6–7.

Discusses African American attitudes concerning the current immigration debate, especially with regard to employment opportunities.

Wiley, T.G. (2005). Literacy and language diversity in the United States (2nd ed.). Washington DC & McKinney, IL: Center for Applied Linguistics & Delta Systems.

Provides statistics and commentary concerning language diversity in the United States.

Wilson, D.L. (2008, October). The illusion of immigrant criminality. *Extra! 21*(5), 21–22.

Reviews allegations of criminal behavior by immigrants and evidence used in support of such claims to refute the claims and show how data has been misused or misinterpreted.

Wucker, M. (2003). Civics lessons from immigrants. *American Prospect 14*(7), 45–46.

Examines efforts of recent immigrants to express political concerns and play an active role in addressing local issues.

CHAPTER 5

Race and Oppression: The Experiences of People of Color in America

> "Everyone likes to give as well as to receive. No one wishes only to receive all the time. We have taken much from your culture. I wish you had taken something from our culture for there were some good and beautiful things in it."
>
> **Chief Dan George (1899–1991)**

The categorizing of human beings into racial groups has resulted in a history of racial oppression in America, beginning with the colonial period and continuing as rebellion against England created a new nation. Although all immigrants to the United States encountered obstacles and opposition, being perceived as white initially or eventually proved an enormous benefit. Whether they came voluntarily as immigrants or were brought involuntarily as slaves, people of color had to contend with blatant forms of oppression. Some of these experiences were similar for all groups, but other forms of oppression were unique to a particular group.

The quotation from Chief Dan George describes a problem for **indigenous people,** those who were established in the New World, in their encounter with European colonists. All immigrants of color would experience some version of this problem. Although perceived as different because of "race," the real difference that defined people of color was the different culture of each particular ethnic group. In rejecting them because of race, the majority also rejected the cultural gifts each group could have shared. The diversity created by people of color in the United States began with the American Indians, whose culture and knowledge were ignored first by the colonial settlers, and later by the citizens of the new nation called the United States.

Native Americans

The Arawaks were one of more than 500 nations of indigenous people in the Americas when Columbus "discovered" a Caribbean island he called Hispaniola. Columbus created the pattern of oppression repeated by those who followed. After a brief period of peaceful relations, the Columbus party exploited the Arawaks and their natural resources. Columbus kidnapped a number of Arawaks to auction as slaves in Spain. When most of them died on the voyage back to Spain, Columbus looked for other ways to profit when he returned.

Columbus noticed gold jewelry worn by Arawaks, so he told them to bring him gold. They insisted that there was only a little gold on the island, but Columbus did not believe them. He demanded gold and warned them not to return without it. If any Arawaks came back empty-handed, Columbus had his men cut off their hands as punishment to intimidate the rest into complying (Zinn, 2003). By such brutal behavior, Columbus and his followers almost eradicated the Arawaks. Europeans eventually exterminated nearly half of the 500 nations of indigenous people in the Americas, and they almost eradicated the cultures of many of the nations that still remain today (Josephy, 2005).

What did Europeans learn from Native Americans?

English settlers in America tended to build on existing Indian settlements and walked on Indian paths, many of which eventually became the roads of the new nation. Benjamin Franklin studied the governance structure of the Iroquois League and borrowed heavily from it to create his "Albany Plan," the basis for the Articles of Confederation that was the first form of government implemented in the United States (Weatherford, 1988). Although he borrowed ideas from the Iroquois League, Franklin's prejudice against Indians appears in a letter to James Parker:

> It would be a very strange Thing, if six Nations of ignorant Savages should be capable of forming a Scheme for such an Union and be able to execute it in such a Manner, as that it has subsisted for Ages, and appears indissoluble; and yet that a like Union should be impracticable for ten or a Dozen English Colonies, to whom it is more necessary. (Le May, 1987, p. 444)

Unlike Franklin, most colonists did not care to learn from Indians. Their ethnocentric goal was to establish the culture and traditions of their own European heritage in America. **Ethnocentrism** is the belief that one's own race, nation, or culture is superior to all others, illustrated by colonial choices for settlement names. Dutch settlers called their town New Amsterdam until the English captured it and renamed it New York. Many settlements were named without even adding the term *new,* which can be seen by comparing city names on current maps of New England states with city names on maps of England. Williams (1954) described an example of ethnocentrism when English colonists called a bird a robin because it reminded them of an English robin. We still call this bird a robin today, but it's not an English robin, nor is it related to the English robin.

What's in a Name

Although the term *Native American* has become widely used, there is still not a consensus among native peoples about the generic term they prefer. Popular author Sherman Alexei is adamantly against the term, preferring to be called an American Indian. Some prefer to be called "indigenous people"; others are content with the traditional label of "Indian." In this chapter, all of the terms are used to reflect this diversity of preferences. The only consensus among all of the indigenous people is their preference to be identified by their tribal affiliation such as Hopi, Apache, Sioux, Mohican, Kwakiutl, or Inuit. In conversations with individual American Indians, one would do well to follow Beverley Tatum's advice—ask the individual what his or her preference is, then use that term.

What did European settlers fail to learn from Native Americans?

If Europeans had been willing to listen, they could have learned much from Native Americans. The following five areas provide a few examples.

Foods and Medicines. European settlers did not want to eat food initially unfamiliar to them such as potatoes, peanuts, corn, squash, tomatoes, peppers, and pumpkins. Later, these foods came to be exported around the world and had a major influence within countless nations. As Weatherford (1988)

> God teaches the birds to make nests, yet the nests of all birds are not alike.
>
> **Duwamish Proverb**

wrote, "It is difficult to imagine what Ireland would be today without the potato" (p. 64). Similarly, it is difficult to imagine what Italian food was like before the American tomato became part of its cuisine.

Europeans did not try to learn the indigenous people's knowledge of medicinal properties of plants. (See Figure 5.1.) For example, scurvy is a disease resulting from vitamin C deficiency, causing bleeding gums and fatigue; it often afflicted people voyaging on ships because fruit didn't last long at sea. Native Americans knew how to cure scurvy long before Europeans found a cure by noticing that German sailors on boats stocked with sauerkraut did not tend to get this illness (Weatherford, 1988). Suzuki and Knudtson (1992) estimate that 75% of prescription drugs derived from plants were discovered based on clues stemming from the healing practices of the indigenous peoples of the world. According to Harvard botanist Richard Schultes, every time a shaman dies, "it is as if a library had burned down" (Gell-Mann, 1994, p. 339).

Hygiene. According to Spring (2001), European descriptions of Indians as "filthy savages" had nothing to do with hygiene but with their "seemingly unrepressed sexuality" (p. 10). American Indians practiced frequent bathing while Europeans did not. Europeans believed that exposing one's body to the air could cause colds and other health problems. Christian church leaders also disapproved of public bathing, fearing that nude people mingling in a public bath might inspire lust. Instead, throughout Europe, many, including the aristocracy, would dry-rub themselves with sand, ashes, or pumice stone. For the rich or royal, perfume disguised body odor. According to Smith (2001), England's Queen Elizabeth I took a bath once a month, and Spain's Queen Isabella proudly claimed that she had only taken two baths in her life: when she was born and when she was married. No wonder perfume was so expensive and so highly valued!

Governance and Gender Equality. In 1642, Virginians met with a Cherokee delegation led by Cherokee leader Outacite to negotiate for a peaceful resolution of their recent conflicts. As he approached the colonial delegation, Outacite asked why he saw no women. Hearing that the colonists had brought no women, Outacite returned to his people saying he could not negotiate because the colonists did not have half of their people. Perdue (1998) also described a 1757 meeting of the South

FIGURE 5.1 The use of Indian images on medicine bottles in the 1800s suggests that Americans were aware that Indians understood the medicinal value of plants. Instead of acquiring that knowledge, entrepreneurs created concoctions (usually including alcohol), put an image of an Indian on the bottle, and sold the bogus medicine to naïve customers.

Source: Pictures of Record, Inc.

> Take only what you need and leave the land as you found it.
>
> **Arapaho Proverb**

Carolina Governor's Council to which the noted Cherokee leader Attakullakulla had been invited. His first comment was to ask why no women were on the council. If Indian women owned property, it remained in their control regardless of marital status (White, 2001). Indian women belonging to the Iroquois League did not serve on the governing tribal council, but they selected the men who served (Woodward, 1988).

Childcare. Europeans might also have benefited from learning childcare practices from American Indians. Children of European immigrants, like children in Europe, were expected to work on domestic chores at an early age. If they misbehaved, they were punished severely with beatings and whippings to teach them obedience to parental authority, just as parents had to be obedient to their superiors. Children were rarely shown overt affection and were allowed little freedom. By contrast, European observers of American Indian societies were surprised by the amount of freedom given to Indian boys and girls. Young children were not expected to assist their parents with farming, hunting, or household tasks. There were few restrictions on their activities as they became intimately familiar with their surroundings. Instead of punishing with straps or rods, Indian children were scolded and made to feel a sense of shame about misbehaving. The parents' goal was to promote a sense of personal pride and an independent, courageous spirit. They believed that threats and physical punishment would cause children to become passive and fearful (Mintz, 2004). European children who were captured and raised by Indians were called "white Indians." Even if offered a chance to return to their families, many of these children refused to leave. When "white Indian" children were returned to colonial society, most preferred to return to their Indian families. Benjamin Franklin addressed this phenomenon in 1753 (Mintz, 2004):

> When white persons of either sex have been taken prisoners young by the Indians, and lived awhile among them, tho' ransomed by their Friends, and treated with all imaginable tenderness to prevail with them to stay among the English, yet in a Short time they become disgusted with our manner of life . . . and take the first good Opportunity of escaping again into the woods, from whence there is no reclaiming them. (p. 8)

Ecology. Native Americans have expressed the belief that human beings share a spiritual kinship with the natural world and are obligated to live in harmony with it. Suzuki and Knudtson (1992) cite a declaration by the Iroquois Confederacy deploring the destruction of forests by entrepreneurs, the depletion of wildlife by sports hunters and pesticides, the pollution of the air by factories, the pollution of water and poisoning of fish by industry and agribusiness, and toxic wastes deposited in chemical dumps across the country. The Iroquois declaration calls on people to preserve life around us, to "carry out our function as caretakers of the land" (pp. 240–241).

What relationships did colonists have with native people?

Instead of learning lessons from Native Americans, colonists practiced lessons already learned about conflict, conquest, and survival. Europeans usually began by being friendly toward Indians until they no longer needed them. For example, colonists at an early Connecticut settlement had good relations with the Pequot and Narragansett Indians until Fort Saybrook was built and stocked with munitions. The Pequots and Narragansetts did not understand why the fort was built. They had helped the settlers and signed treaties with them. Fortunes changed, however, when Narragansetts killed a colonist, John Oldham, in revenge for an unnamed outrage, probably holding him responsible for the outbreak of smallpox that took the lives of 700 of their people. With military might sufficient to ensure victory and Oldham's death as an excuse, General John Endecott was sent to Fort Saybrook to attack not only Narragansetts but also innocent

Pequots. After initial skirmishes, some Pequots met with Lieutenant Lion Gardiner to determine if they could resume peaceful relations, but Gardiner was not willing to stop fighting. Having heard of Dutch brutality, the Pequots asked Gardiner if it was true that Europeans did not just kill warriors, but women and children. They expected him to deny such a harsh accusation; Gardiner replied, "they should see that hereafter" (Jennings, 1976, p. 212). They understood his meaning and returned to tell their people of this threat from their formerly friendly neighbors.

What was the main source of conflict between Europeans and Indians?

The primary contention between European colonists and Indians was land ownership. In school, children are often taught that Columbus planted Spain's flag in the New World to claim the land for Spain, implying that Spanish and Indian representatives would resolve the competing claims by negotiating a treaty or by warfare. Engaging in war based on claims to land was common in European history. Nations gained or lost inhabited land through conquest because only uninhabited land could be claimed, a principle identified as *vacuum domicilium* (Berkhofer, 2004). Even in 1492, international law recognized the rights of indigenous people to own the land where they lived. Explorers were given charters to allow them to claim land under the legal principle of *terra nullius,* an ambiguous term suggesting lands without people, but interpreted as including land inhabited by a people not possessing religions and customs equal to that of Europeans.

When Columbus planted the Spanish flag, he was establishing the legal right for Spain to possess uninhabited land or to purchase the land if indigenous people had a legitimate claim to it. But most legal claims for land inhabited by Native Americans were not made under the principle of *vacuum domicilium* because natives made it clear that the land where they lived belonged to them collectively, and they belonged to the land. To resolve the ambiguity of making a *terra nullius* claim, European nations wanting to take possession of Indian land created a new concept called *occupatio bellica,* referring to peaceful seizure of land underutilized by the indigenous people. Although indigenous people might not agree with what was viewed as "underutilized," the principle allowed Europeans to take possession of land by peaceful means, such as by erecting crosses throughout the land marked with the royal seal or by bribing a few indigenous individuals to sign an agreement conceding the land.

> They made many promises, so many I can't remember, but they only kept one. They promised to take our land, and they took it.
>
> **Red Cloud (1822–1909)**

Nomads were the exception. Defined as "pastoral people" wandering on the land and never staying in one place, **nomads** were not granted legal claim to land. In making land claims, colonists described indigenous people as "nomadic" because they would move their villages every few years because of soil depletion and decreasing crop productivity. After many years at another site, they might move again, eventually returning to a site abandoned decades before where the soil would now be replenished (Berkhofer, 2004). Such a pattern does not fit the definition of nomadic. Although Plains Indians, such as the Sioux or Cheyenne, were nomadic and followed historic migratory patterns, most indigenous people lived in villages. If villagers resisted encroachment on their land, the result was often armed conflict ending with a treaty mandating the loss of land and Indian resettlement.

Why are Indian treaties still important today?

A **treaty** is a legal document negotiated between two (or more) sovereign nations involving terms of peace, trade, and other matters. Indian treaties document the cession of Indian lands to the U.S. government that were then made available for settlement. Land was also confiscated for resources. As described in Gedicks (1993), historian David Wrone has calculated that 19.5 million acres of land taken from one indigenous group alone, the Chippewa, resulted in the United States gaining significant wealth. Besides taking possession of the land, the resources from the land included "100 billion board feet of timber; 150 billion tons of iron ore; 13.5 billion pounds of copper" (p. 51). Other resources taken from Indian land included water, ports, fish, fowl, and game, all contributing to a profitable tourism industry that has yielded considerable wealth to members of the dominant society who gained access as a result of treaties.

A treaty signed by an Indian nation and the United States was an agreement between sovereign nations. Treaties were written with provisions to be maintained in perpetuity, yet the U.S. government has violated virtually every treaty made with indigenous peoples, often during the lifetimes of those who signed the treaty (Josephy, 2005; Wilson, 1998). Yet treaties continue to be important documents because they affirm the status of Indian Sovereignty. Deloria (2001) described **Indian Sovereignty** as a principle affirming the legal right of Indian nations to define themselves on their own terms and to behave as unique cultural and legal entities.

Why were Native American treaties consistently violated?

When Indian treaties were signed, the land designated for indigenous people was often regarded as expendable, yet if the land became desirable, Indians were forced to surrender it. When settlers migrated to Wisconsin, Winnebago Indians were removed to Nebraska and Kansas. Many refused to leave and hid from authorities; others left but eventually returned (Bieder, 1995). As colonists and settlers demanded land, treaties with Indian nations were renegotiated, often forcefully.

The Cherokee possessed legal deeds to Georgia land where they had built homes and businesses. When ordered to go to Oklahoma territory, they took their case to the U.S. Supreme Court, which ruled in their favor; however, President Andrew Jackson refused to enforce the ruling. In 1838, he ordered federal troops to march the Cherokee to Oklahoma, a journey now called the Trail of Tears because of numerous deaths that occurred on the way (Wallace, 1993).

Because of treaties, several Indian nations were forced to occupy Oklahoma territory until white demands for cheap land led the United States to renegotiate the treaties, restricting Indians in Oklahoma to the least desirable land and allowing settlers to claim the rest. Americans had little interest in Indian land in Oklahoma—until oil was discovered. The treaty was renegotiated. Similarly, an 1868 Treaty of Fort Laramie declared that the Sioux would permanently retain lands sacred to them in the Black Hills—until gold was discovered. The treaty was renegotiated (Josephy, 2005; Wilson, 1998). This pattern has continued.

Many treaties signed over a century ago relegated Indians to small reservations but affirmed their right to hunt and fish on tribal lands beyond reservation boundaries. For native people, being able to hunt and fish on former tribal land was a critical concession that may have seemed an innocuous benefit to the other side when the treaty was signed. As hunting and fishing became profitable tourism activities, complaints that the treaties should be abrogated or renegotiated have increased. People promoting outdoor recreational activities have protested Indian hunting and fishing privileges, even though treaties guarantee such privileges. Indigenous people have responded by insisting on maintaining the treaties and respecting their rights as sovereign nations.

What are other contemporary issues affecting indigenous people?

Regarding the origin of indigenous peoples in the Americas, anthropologists have called Indians the first immigrants, claiming that they crossed a land bridge along the Bering Straits 15,000 years ago, but American Indians insist that they have always been here. Increasing archaeological evidence makes it difficult to ignore the conclusion that indigenous people appear to have been living in both North and South America for more than 30,000 years, long before the land bridge (Chatters, 2001; Parfit & Garrett, 2000).

Many schoolchildren are not taught about the multiplicity of Indian cultures that existed in early America. The diversity that existed among more than 500 Indian nations encompassed political governance, economic structures, and cultural patterns. For example, diversity was apparent in Indian homes: the long houses of Northeastern woodland

Indians such as the Wampanoag, Pawnee earth homes later copied by Midwest pioneers as sod houses, grass houses of the Wichita, adobe houses of the Navajo, log houses of Kwakiutl and other Northwestern Indians. Ask American children about Indian homes, and they will likely say Indians lived in "tepees." Instead of educating youth about Indian diversity, teachers have tended to promote a stereotype based on the Plains Indians, which is reinforced by the use of Indian mascots.

Many Native Americans and tribal councils have spoken out against Indian logos and mascots for sports teams, saying they are racist and offensive (Connolly, 2000). They have asked schools and colleges displaying such images to discontinue this practice! (See Figure 5.2.) Most sports fans say they don't see what is so offensive, insisting that mascots are meant to honor and show respect for Native Americans. But how can we "honor" a people in a manner that they find objectionable? We argue that Indian mascots honor a proud, fighting spirit; meanwhile we criticize or ignore Indians who proudly fight to eliminate the use of Indian mascots.

FIGURE 5.2

> All wars are civil wars because all men are brothers. . . . Each one owes infinitely more to the human race than to the particular country in which he was born.
>
> **Francois Fenelon (1651–1715)**

The response of non-Indians to Indian mascots illustrates how contemporary Indians are perceived. According to Berkhofer (2004), Americans tend to hold one of the following two images of Indians: the noble savages who lived long ago and were exterminated, or contemporary Indians who have lost their culture and been degraded by white people's ways. Many school textbooks reinforce the former by presenting information about Native Americans only up to the nineteenth century; twentieth-century Indians don't appear. Students are left to assume that Native Americans lived long ago and then ceased to exist, except perhaps for a few living on reservations (Hawkins, 2005). Critics of American education charge that children and youth are not regularly taught about Indians living in urban areas or about current issues such as resistance by reservation Indians to the use of their land as sites for dumping toxic wastes or other forms of environmental exploitation (Hendry, 2003).

One of the few facts about contemporary Indians that seems to be widely known is that they operate casinos, even though less than 1% of the total Native American population makes substantial revenue from gambling profits. If a state sanctions gambling activity, then by federal law it is legal for Native Americans living on reservations in that state to have gambling facilities. Although American Indians have been criticized for operating casinos, profits often have been employed to purchase land, build or improve schools, offer academic scholarships, support job-training programs, create jobs, and fund an array of projects intended to improve opportunities for Indian people and to perpetuate their culture.

Despite the financial gains from casinos on a few reservations, many living on reservations still confront consequences of their forced assimilation into the dominant society, including extremely high unemployment rates, low school completion rates, widespread domestic abuse, and considerable alcoholism. Tribal elders have witnessed the deterioration of cultural traditions and ancient beliefs, and they fear the survival of their people is in jeopardy. Despite the need for economic resources on reservations, many American Indians oppose corporate enterprises that have identified resources on reservation land and tried to purchase mineral or water rights (Gedicks, 1993; Matthiessen, 1993).

Legal action is a critical part of the ongoing struggle of indigenous people with the U.S. government. A recent class action suit accuses the Department of the Interior of mismanaging Indian lands and funds, denying Indian tribes an estimated $176 billion. The judge has delivered several rulings in favor of the Indian tribes. According to Whitty (2005), the U.S. government is continuing to appeal the case using resources at its disposal including "35 of the country's most expensive private law firms" (p. 58). This largest class action suit ever filed may eventually provide Native Americans with needed economic resources.

African Americans

The first Africans in the New World came not as slaves but as soldiers and explorers. Although we do not have individual names, records indicate that Africans came with Cortez and Pizarro in the early 1500s, that 30 Africans sailed with Balboa, and 200 accompanied Alvarado to Quito. The names of a few black adventurers have survived. In the early sixteenth century, Estevanico (from Morocco) explored the American Southwest, preparing the way for later Spanish conquest. In the late eighteenth century, Jean Baptist Point du Sable (from Haiti) came with French explorers and founded a permanent trading post in a settlement called Chicago (Painter, 2005).

The first Africans in the American colonies arrived in 1619. A Dutch ship traded twenty Africans to Jamestown settlers for food and water (Reiss, 1997). The seventeen men and three women were not slaves but indentured servants, able to gain their freedom after specified years of servitude. During the seventeenth century, 75% of American colonists came as servants, many of them indentured servants (Takaki, 1993), but Zinn (2003) argues that English colonists regarded African indentured servants as inferior to white servants and treated them accordingly.

How were the black indentured servants treated differently?

A few Africans were able to earn their freedom, and some had to resort to courts to free them from unwilling owners, but most were never free. A few free blacks bought property, including slaves, but by the mid-1800s, the colonies were establishing different rules for white and black servants. Based on assumptions of black inferiority, Africans were often forced to accept permanent servitude status. A 1662 Virginia statute decreed that children born to a woman who was a permanent indentured servant must take her status (Reiss, 1997). Not surprisingly, 70% of Africans in Virginia at this time were permanent indentured servants (Takaki, 1993).

As southern agriculture gravitated toward large plantations for the export of crops, the use of slaves became increasingly attractive. Indian workers knew the area and easily escaped, and white indentured servants escaped and passed as free whites. Blacks could be easily identified, captured, and returned to their owners. Because England was already invested in the slave trade, exporting Africans to America was simply an expansion of an existing business. From the late 1500s to the early 1800s, more than 10 million Africans were brought to America.

Where and how did the British procure Africans?

In the sixteenth century, European traders had marveled at West African civilizations in Mali, Timbuctu, and Ghana. By the seventeenth century, British merchants had established strong trade relations in West Africa, including the export of slaves (Smedley, 2007). Spivey (2003) says that 90% of all African Americans are descended from West African ancestors.

> Until lions have their historians, tales of the hunt will always glorify the hunter.
>
> **African Proverb**

Historically, slaves have been victims of conquest. African slaves tended to be prisoners of war, and some were sentenced to slavery for crime or debt, but the removal of 15 to 18 million Africans to America, as Franklin and Moss (2000) have stated, was "one of the most far-reaching and drastic social revolutions in the annals of history" (p. 49). Not all Africans sent to the New World arrived; a third are believed to have died during what is called the **Middle Passage.**

Why did so many Africans die during the Middle Passage?

Conditions on slave ships were horrendous. According to Reiss (1997), a full-grown man was allotted a space 6 feet long and 18 inches wide in the hold. Women and children were given even less. There was no room to sit up. Slaves were chained together and packed into the hold in a "spoon" position to maintain maximum space. Reiss quoted Lord Palmerston, "They had less room than a corpse in a coffin" (p. 34).

Enroute, slaves were fed twice a day and given buckets to relieve themselves; the buckets were seldom emptied and frequently overflowed. Many were unable to get to the buckets and soiled themselves where they lay. Not surprisingly, disease was a major cause of death, including typhoid, smallpox, yellow fever, and malaria (Painter, 2005).

Because bodies of the dead were tossed overboard, sharks routinely accompanied slave ships. As slaves were brought up on deck during the day, some took the opportunity to escape by leaping into the shark-infested waters. Scholars estimate that from 5 to 6 million Africans died during Middle Passage, and some who survived the voyage were left permanently disabled (Reiss, 1997). As bad as conditions were on slave ships, slavery was even more brutal.

What was it like to be a slave?

Although slavery existed throughout all the colonies, it never led to the economic advantage in the North that it did on southern plantations where work was backbreaking and punishments severe. Working days were as long as 18 hours during harvest, with brief rest periods to eat. Overseers punished those who didn't appear to be working hard enough, usually by whipping. Other tasks included clearing land for planting, chopping wood, digging drains, or improving roads. At night, seven or eight slaves might be crowded into dirt-floor one-room cabins. Women worked with men, performed domestic chores, and often suffered sexual assault from masters and overseers. As former slave Harriet Jacobs (1861/1987) said, "Slavery is terrible for men, but it is far more terrible for women" (p. 77). But slavery enriched slave owners. A British visitor once asked future president James Madison how much profit he made from slaves. Madison replied that he only had to spend $12 to $13 annually for one slave who could produce almost $260 of profit each year (Zinn, 2003). Despite these huge profits, many people opposed slavery.

How did Africans resist the oppression of slavery?

African captives engaged in a range of activities in their resistance to slavery. Some cut off their toes or mutilated themselves in other ways so they would be less useful workers for their masters. In addition, some slaves murdered their masters; many slave owners lived in fear of being poisoned by their slave servants (Franklin & Moss, 2005). Some slaves learned to read and write either by tricking their masters into teaching them or by converting to Christianity and persuading their master to give them the literacy skills needed to read the Bible (Cornelius, 2000). They perceived competent literacy skills as a useful tool to assist themselves and other slaves, and as an important asset if they managed to escape from slavery.

When slaves converted to Christianity, their owners tried to use aspects of the faith to manipulate them into being more docile and obedient, but slaves usually resisted. For example, although white owners exhorted slaves to obey the commandment against stealing, slaves continued to steal. They justified their thefts by regarding their owners as hypocrites with no moral authority on this issue: White people were responsible for stealing Africans from their homeland and their families, and slave owners continued the offense by maintaining possession of this stolen property. The captive Africans also rejected many "moral" precepts emphasized by white ministers. Raboteau (2000) described a service for slave converts in which a white clergyman used a passage from the Apostle Paul in a sermon condemning slaves who ran away. During the sermon, the clergyman reported that, "one half of my audience deliberately rose up and walked off" (p. 31).

Who opposed slavery and what did they do?

Africans, enslaved or free, adamantly opposed slavery. Thousands of slaves ran away and many successfully escaped. Former slaves Harriet Jacobs and Frederick Douglass gave speeches and wrote books denouncing slavery. In addition, from 1750 to 1860, there were an estimated 250 slave rebellions, each involving ten or more slaves (Zinn, 1999), and numerous smaller rebellions. Perhaps the best-known rebellion was inspired by a solar eclipse in February 1831, that Nat Turner interpreted as an omen (Franklin & Moss, 2005). Six months later he led a slave rebellion that began with the killing of Turner's owner and family, and went on to result in the deaths of 60 other slave owners before the slaves were overpowered by federal troops.

As early as the 1770s, free blacks petitioned colonial legislatures to emancipate slaves. Using the words of revolutionary leaders, they challenged whites to live up to their ideals of democracy and equality by making them a reality for all (Painter, 2005). As colonial leaders considered issues related to self-government, they recognized "a marked inconsistency in their position as oppressed colonists and slaveholders" (Franklin & Moss, 2000, p. 80). The Declaration of Independence denounced slavery as an "execrable" practice until the Continental Congress deleted that particular passage at the insistence of southern slaveholders. Even the participation of blacks in the Revolutionary War did not resolve conflicting opinions about slavery.

Why did blacks fight on the American side during the Revolutionary War?

When the war began, George Washington and his aides agreed that the Continental Army would not recruit blacks. Alexander Hamilton warned that if they did not, the British would (Chernow, 2004). In November 1775, Washington issued his policy against recruiting blacks, and British supporters quickly recruited slaves by promising emancipation for military service. Washington issued a new policy in December, permitting free blacks to serve in the Continental Army. Meanwhile, colonial militias were already recruiting slaves as well as free blacks. According to Franklin and Moss (2000), 5,000 of the 300,000 colonial troops were Africans, primarily free blacks from northern colonies. The bravery of black soldiers refuted the pervasive stereotypes, but their achievements were betrayed when the U.S. Constitution was drafted.

How did the U.S. Constitution address the issue of slavery?

Although slaves represented 20% of all Americans at this time, the word *slave* does not appear in the Constitution of the United States (Painter, 2005); instead, it refers to "unfree persons." Article II, section 9, states that "importation of such persons as any of the States now-existing shall think proper to admit, shall not be prohibited by Congress prior to the year 1808." In other words, in deference to southern plantation owners and businesses, the new nation had agreed to ignore the slave trade for twenty years; however, taxes were to be collected on imported slaves. Even northern states that had abolished slavery profited from the continued importation of slaves.

Another issue in drafting the Constitution concerned the question of whether slaves should count in determining political representation. With 300,000 slaves representing 40% of its population, Virginia wanted slaves counted, as did North and South Carolina with over 100,000 slaves in each state (Painter, 2005). The constitutional compromise was to count each slave as three fifths of a person, giving significant political power to southern states: Ten of the first fifteen American presidents were slaveholders. Nevertheless, anti-slavery organizations became increasingly influential.

Were these anti-slavery organizations widely supported and effective?

In 1775, Quakers organized the first anti-slavery society in Philadelphia; ten years later another was formed in New York. Anti-slavery societies soon formed throughout New England (Chernow, 2004). In 1777, Vermont abolished slavery in its state constitution, and in 1783, New Hampshire and Massachusetts did the same. In two decades, all northern states had abolished slavery or legislated a timeline for its extinction. Some organizations lobbied to end the slave trade and others wanted to deport slaves, but all agreed on the principle of abolishing slavery. When the twenty-year constitutional hiatus ended, anti-slavery groups successfully lobbied Congress to pass a law that prohibited importation of slaves to the United States. The law was primarily a moral victory because the American coast was too long and the U.S. Navy too small to stop the smuggling of slaves. Meanwhile, slaves continued to rebel against slavery, and many were able to escape by using the Underground Railroad.

What was the Underground Railroad?

Named in the 1800s because of the popularity of steam railroads, the **Underground Railroad** existed as early as the late 1700s as a network of people helping slaves escape. Franklin and Moss (2000) quote a 1786 letter from George Washington complaining that one of his slaves escaped and went to Philadelphia where "a society of Quakers, formed for such purposes, have attempted to liberate (him)" (p. 205). By 1804, this informal network had become more organized and had established "stations" 10 to 20 miles apart for runaways to rest and eat after traveling all night. In the 1830s, the steam railroad's popularity was responsible for the name of the Underground Railroad. The organization eventually included over 3,000 people of all races (Painter, 2005). They had to be careful because helping slaves escape was a criminal activity, violating federal fugitive slave laws that compelled the return of any runaway slave.

Some slaves had a "conductor" to help them escape; one of the best known was Harriet Tubman who made 19 trips and freed over 300 slaves. Plantation owners offered $40,000 to anyone who caught her, but they never did (Painter, 2005). Although it is impossible to determine how many slaves escaped using the Underground Railroad, one southern governor estimated that from 1810 to 1850 the South had lost 100,000 slaves worth $30 million (Franklin & Moss, 2000). Still, all enslaved Africans in America would not gain their freedom until the end of the Civil War.

Did slaves and free blacks fight for the Union during the Civil War?

Slaves supported the North during the Civil War by disrupting southern productivity. Many refused to work even though they were severely punished; others engaged in subversive tactics such as supplying information to approaching Union troops. When Union soldiers came near a plantation, slaves would abandon it. Early Union victories in western states liberated slaves, but the federal government had not allocated resources to assist them. In northern cities, relief societies formed to raise money for food, clothing, and shelter and provided some education and job training for newly freed blacks.

When the war began, free blacks offered to enlist, but once again they were rejected. Few people believed the conflict would last long, but when it did, the need for more soldiers intensified. In September of 1862, the **Emancipation Proclamation** freed blacks in rebellious states, but slave owners in Delaware and Kentucky kept slaves until the 13th Amendment was ratified. Issued in January 1863, the final version of the Emancipation Proclamation allowed free blacks to enlist in the army. Over 200,000 blacks enlisted. By August, 14 black regiments were trained and ready for service, with 20 more regiments in preparation (Franklin & Moss, 2000).

Black soldiers protested the Congressional Enlistment Act that established lower compensation for them. Two black regiments from Massachusetts refused their wages rather than be paid less than white soldiers. When the Massachusetts legislature offered them money to make up for the difference, the black soldiers refused that offer. They were fighting for the Union, and they insisted that the Union pay them fairly. In 1865, the War Department finally approved equal pay for black and white soldiers (Painter, 2005), even though it came too late for the 38,000 black soldiers who had died. For those who survived the war, the next task was to create a new society in the South that would include a significant number of free blacks.

Did blacks play a role in shaping the new South?

Black males (but not females) could vote and run for office, and over 600 were elected to state legislatures. Although black legislators never became a majority, free black people participated in drafting new state constitutions. In response, angry southern whites formed secret societies such as the Knights of the Ku Klux Klan to bribe or intimidate blacks and ostracize those whites who seemed to support the developing new social order. Many racist groups began to use violence to reestablish white supremacy in the South, usually engaging in activities at night.

Blacks who registered to vote were harassed; some were forced to leave their communities and some were lynched. In 1871, blacks elected to the South Carolina legislature were given fifteen days to resign. State laws prohibited such harassment, but even Union troops stationed throughout the South were ineffective to stop it. The U.S. Congress passed laws giving the president broad powers to punish anyone interfering with a citizen trying to vote. Hundreds were imprisoned, but violence persisted.

Throughout the 1870s, the Democratic Party, led by white southerners, elected majorities to state legislatures. Congress no longer required federal troops at all southern polling places during elections, and even the U.S. Supreme Court refused to rule on cases involving protection of black voting rights (Franklin & Moss, 2000). By 1877 when President Harrison withdrew federal troops, the transformation to white control in the South was almost complete.

> The basic race hatred in the United States is a matter of the educated and distinguished leaders of white civilization.
>
> **W. E. B. Du Bois (1868–1963)**

How did black citizens in the South respond to this transformation?

Southern blacks did not accept the threats and harassment passively, yet without support from the federal government or northern organizations, they did not have the resources to combat white supremacists. They regarded education as the best way to acquire resources and power on their own, but with minimal state funding for schools, educational opportunities were limited. As late as the 1890s, southern states supported segregated private schools, spending an average of less than $2 annually per student in public schools compared to $20 per student provided in northern states (Lewis, 1993).

In 1881, Booker T. Washington came to Tuskegee Institute and created an educational approach that appealed to whites and many blacks. Washington wanted blacks to carve out a niche in the southern economy, and he knew that white people could accept black people doing agricultural, domestic, and factory work. Washington cultivated good relations with local leaders by having his students provide food and services to the community, and he promoted his school as a model for black education in the South. Eventually Washington attracted interest and funding from northern whites, many of them industrialists who wanted a better trained workforce in the South.

At the Atlanta Cotton Exposition of 1895, Washington declared that he believed black people would be willing to accept social inequality in exchange for economic opportunity. White politicians, business leaders, and the press claimed that Washington spoke for black Americans, but some blacks, notably W. E. B. Du Bois, believed black Americans deserved more.

What did Du Bois want for black Americans?

Based on his own experience as the first black graduate from Harvard, Du Bois felt that blacks could demonstrate academic ability if given an opportunity. Du Bois rejected the idea that social inequality for blacks was acceptable under any conditions. He supported vocational training for black students but not for those who demonstrated academic ability. Du Bois's approach was overt and confrontational. Although Washington worked within the status quo, secretly donating money in support of legal efforts opposing racial segregation, Du Bois challenged the status quo, publicly denouncing all racial discrimination, as in the following statement (Lewis, 1993):

> Such discrimination is morally wrong, politically dangerous, and industrially wasteful and socially silly. It is the duty of whites to stop it, and to do so primarily for their own sakes (p. 208).

In 1910, Du Bois helped found the **National Association for the Advancement of Colored People (NAACP)** and for twenty-five years he served as editor of its main publication, *The Crisis*. For eighteen years he hosted a conference on race problems at Atlanta University, and he helped found the American Negro Academy for black intellectuals. Throughout his life, Du Bois attacked racism and promoted racial equality in his research, reports, essays, and even fiction (Lewis, 2000).

FIGURE 5.3 Cartoonist Albert Smith illustrated "The Reason" for blacks to migrate north in the 1920s.

What were black Americans doing to cope with race problems?

In the late 1800s, southern blacks began to migrate to northern cities, driven by economic need and persistent violence in the South, especially lynching. (See Figure 5.3.) For more than thirty years, Ida Wells-Barnett ignored death threats to take a public stand against lynching. In 1914, *The Crisis* published the names of 2,732 blacks lynched between 1885 and 1914, and the NAACP challenged Congress to pass anti-lynching laws (Lewis, 1993). According to Feagin and Feagin (2008), at least half of all lynchings were not recorded, so the total number is estimated to be over 6,000. The House of Representatives passed anti-lynching bills in 1922, 1937, and 1940, but southern senators blocked them. It was not until June 2005 that the Senate finally took a stand, voting to issue a public apology for its failure to pass an anti-lynching law.

Southern migration to the north was not dramatic until the twentieth century. According to Feagan and Feagin (2008), 90% of all black Americans still lived in the South in 1900. Migration increased significantly between 1914 and 1918 when World War I created labor shortages because so few Europeans immigrated. By the time the war ended, a million southern blacks had moved to northern cities. In addition, over 360,000 out of more than 2 million registered blacks served in World War I, and many returning southern black soldiers settled in northern cities (Franklin & Moss, 2000). In 1900, Chicago had 30,000 blacks; by 1920, it had over 109,000. By 1930, 2 million southern blacks had migrated to northern cities (Takaki, 1993).

As Americans welcomed war heroes from World War I, buried the dead, and cared for maimed and suffering veterans, they were ready for a new era. As F. Scott Fitzgerald said, "The uncertainties of 1919 were over—there seemed little doubt about what was going to happen—America was going on the greatest, gaudiest spree in history" (2005, p. 188). Prohibition drove drinking into the shadows of speakeasies. Jack Dempsey drew the first million-dollar gate in boxing. Babe Ruth became the highest paid baseball player in history. And in New York City, black people began a cultural and literary development called "the Harlem Renaissance."

What was the Harlem Renaissance?

Whites came to Harlem in the 1920s to enjoy the clubs, the dancing, and the jazz, creating an open community where people from all races would dance to Duke Ellington at the Cotton Club or listen to Louis Armstrong at the Savoy. As Americans enjoyed a variety of new music, new dances, new artists and new writers, Harlem contributed the novels of Jean Toomer, the poetry of Langston Hughes, and many others who expressed the uniqueness of the black experience in America. Although it was a racially segregated community, Harlem was home to diverse black peoples including newly arrived southern blacks, Africans, and West Indians. Spivey (2003) notes that this mix of people produced a new kind of black individual, quoting Alain Locke's description of how this "New Negro" emerged: "Each group has come with its own separate motives and its own special ends . . . but their greatest experience has been the finding of one another" (p. 165).

> Had it not been for our art and our culture, when all else was ripped from us, we would never have been able to survive as a people.
>
> **Harry Belafonte (1927–)**

Was there a decrease in discrimination against blacks after World War I?

Many African Americans were upset that the U.S. military did not recognize the achievements of black soldiers during World War I. For more than six months, the black first battalion of the 369th infantry endured continuous fire while fighting in France. The French awarded the Croix de Guerre to the battalion, but the U.S. Army did not invite the first battalion (or any black units) to Paris for the victory parade in August 1918 (Lewis, 1993). Many black mothers received Gold Stars symbolizing the loss of a son, but when the French government invited American Gold Star mothers to France to honor them, the army only paid for the white mothers. Black mothers who attended had to pay their own way (Painter, 2005).

The 1920s saw the rebirth of the Ku Klux Klan, reaching a peak of 5 million members in 1925. In 1921, a white mob in Tulsa, Oklahoma, set fire to all of the buildings in the black community and burned them to the ground. In 1923, whites also destroyed the black community of Rosewood, Florida. It is not surprising that the NAACP experienced dramatic growth at this time, expanding from 50 chapters to more than 500 between the two world wars (Woodward, 1966).

The 1920s were not "good times" for American farmers, especially black farmers in the South because two thirds of them did not own their own land (Painter, 2005). During the Great Depression, black farmers suffered even more than white farmers, with many being ejected from their land. As for black workers in northern cities, over twenty-six unions did not accept black members in 1930, and black unemployment was three to four times higher than that of whites (Feagin & Feagin, 2008).

In October 1933, 18% of blacks were receiving government assistance ("relief") compared to 10% for whites, and relief programs often provided black families less than was given to whites (Takaki, 1993). In urban areas, some civic and religious organizations refused to serve black people in their soup kitchens. The best hope for black people seemed to be the nominee of the Democratic Party, Franklin Delano Roosevelt, but many black Republicans were still loyal to "the party of Lincoln." The "New Deal" would eventually convert most into Democrats.

Did the New Deal programs help black Americans?

Millions of black people benefited from New Deal programs, yet millions did not. The Social Security Act provided financial security for older Americans and the Fair Labor Standards Act established a minimum wage, but both excluded agricultural and domestic work, jobs largely held by blacks (Lui, 2004). Black union leader A. Philip Randolph threatened to organize a march on Washington until President Roosevelt issued Executive Order 8802 banning racial discrimination in defense industries and creating a Federal Employment Practice Commission. He was criticized, however, for appointing a white Mississippian to head the commission (Lewis, 2000).

Despite the president's mixed record, blacks appreciated the social activism of Eleanor Roosevelt and her close relationship with black activist Mary McLeod Bethune. In 1936, while heading the Division of Negro Affairs, Bethune helped create the Federal Council on Negro Affairs, an advisory group to the president consisting of thirty black professionals. Media soon referred to them as FDR's **Black Cabinet.** FDR appointed blacks to serve in the Federal Housing Authority, Department of the Interior, and other federal agencies, and black Americans were increasingly changing their allegiance to the Democratic Party, but their participation in the nation's economic recovery was not meaningful until World War II began.

What gains did black Americans make during World War II?

With so many men enlisting in the military, including more than a million who were black, jobs were available for black men and women, especially in defense industries. Blacks in the military were selected for programs that had not been permitted before, such as the engineer corps, pilot training, and officer training. For the first time in its history, the Marine Corps recruited African Americans. When the navy restricted blacks to mess hall duties, they protested, and within a year they were given general assignments and included in officer training programs (Franklin & Moss, 2000). In 1948, President Truman issued Executive Order 9981, officially desegregating the U.S. Armed Forces.

> There is nothing quite so effective as a refusal to cooperate economically with the forces and institutions which perpetuate evil in our communities.
>
> **Martin Luther King, Jr. (1929–1968)**

What happened to African Americans after the war?

Americans seemed to regard the defeat of Nazi Germany as a victory over Nazi beliefs of racial superiority. By the war's end, half of the major unions had accepted black members (Feagin & Feagin, 2008). In business and industry however, the percentage of black men and women laid off during the postwar period was considerably higher than that for whites, suggesting a possible return to "business as usual" attitudes with regard to racial discrimination.

As the United Nations was being formed, W. E. B. Du Bois objected to its lack of representation for "750 million people, a third of mankind, [who] live in colonies" (Lewis, 2000, p. 504). People of color were engaged in a global struggle to free themselves from European domination. In 1947, Mahatma Gandhi's success in gaining India's independence from Britain encouraged African Americans who demanded their rights as citizens of the United States. Court cases involving transportation and education ruled against racial segregation, and in 1954, the ***Brown v. Board of Education*** decision overturned decades of legal discrimination based on race. It was a victory more in principle than in practice as segregation in America persisted; nevertheless, in the context of these national and global events, the civil rights movement was born, and Americans were challenged to recognize their prejudices and stereotypes. (See Figure 5.4.)

With more black people demanding their rights as American citizens, the response from southerners became more violent. In August 1955, a 14-year-old black youth from Chicago came to Mississippi to visit relatives. After Emmett Till showed a group of black friends a picture of a white girl he knew in Chicago, one of the boys dared him to go into the nearby store and talk to the white woman working there. After buying candy in the store, Emmett turned before leaving and said, "Bye, Baby." The woman's husband was out of town, but soon

FIGURE 5.4 Despite the commercial advantage of maintaining a familiar face on one's product, Quaker Oats felt that the old image (B) of Aunt Jemima was too much of a stereotype and updated her image in the 1960s. (A)

(A)

returned. It was shortly after midnight when he and two friends came to the home of Mose Wright where Till was staying and dragged the boy out of bed. They brutally murdered him and threw his body in the Tallahatchie River. When his corpse was found three days later, it was so badly mutilated that Mose Wright could only identify the boy by a ring on Emmett's finger (Williams, 1987).

Emmett's mother demanded an open casket at his funeral so that mourners could see what had been done to her son. Americans were shocked and revolted by the photographs of the boy's mangled face that appeared in newspapers across the nation. The three men responsible were arrested and brought to trial. Despite the courageous testimony of Mose Wright, who identified the accused men as the ones who took Emmett Till from his house, the all-white jury acquitted all three men of kidnapping and murder. People of all races across the nation expressed outrage at the violence and the injustice, and the civil rights movement grew in number and increased in resources as more people rose up to challenge racist attitudes and practices in America (Williams, 1987).

What did the civil rights movement achieve for African Americans?

In Montgomery, Alabama, Rosa Parks and Martin Luther King, Jr., inspired African Americans to conduct a boycott of city bus services to end racial segregation. The boycott lasted over a year; then in 1957, the U.S. Supreme Court upheld a federal court ruling to desegregate public bus transportation systems. Although Congress passed civil rights laws in 1957 and 1960, they were ineffective in addressing problems of segregation and racial discrimination.

In February 1960, as a practical demonstration of civil rights, four black college freshmen in Greensboro, North Carolina, entered a Woolworth store and deliberately sat at a lunch counter that served only whites. When refused service, the black students opened their textbooks and read. They eventually left, but they returned, and other students came with them. The idea spread across the nation as 70,000 students, mostly black but some white, staged more than 800 sit-ins in over 100 southern cities. As more than 4,000 students were arrested, whites stayed away from lunch counters, and many would not shop in stores where sit-ins were occurring. The economic losses forced many businesses to begin offering services to blacks (Lomax, 1963).

Although Martin Luther King, Jr., encouraged nonviolent tactics, younger, radical black leaders encouraged black Americans to return violence for violence. The passionate oratory of Malcolm X may have predisposed some whites to be more comfortable listening to the peaceful rhetoric of change expressed by King and his followers. Even after Malcolm X ended his association with the extremist Nation of Islam to pursue a more authentic Islamic faith, he still insisted that black people should demand the same rights that white Americans enjoyed—not just civil rights but their human rights (Malcolm X, 2000):

> When you expand the civil-rights struggle to the level of human rights, you can then take the case of the black man in this country before the nation in the U.N. . . . You can take Uncle Sam before a world court. . . . Civil rights keeps you in his pocket. Civil rights means you're asking Uncle Sam to treat you right. Human rights are something you were born with. Human rights are your God-given rights. (p. 596)

Another militant voice came from the Black Panther Party founded in 1966 by Huey Newton and Bobby Seale. The Black Panthers attracted black youth, especially in urban areas. Despite the Panthers' sponsoring community service activities such as a free breakfast program for black children, they were viewed by white authorities as a paramilitary organization. The FBI Counterintelligence program targeted its leaders for surveillance, and Panther members were subjected to police raids. Newton's 1967 arrest and imprisonment on murder charges weakened the Panthers, as did the violent assaults on party members that left 28 dead (Carson & Carson, 2000). By the mid-1970s, most of the Panther leaders either had been expelled from or had voluntarily left the organization.

Throughout the 1960s, the South was the primary scene for marches, protests, and demonstrations. In 1963 alone, the Department of Justice recorded over 1,400 events in three months (Zinn, 2003). As usual, the white response was immediate and violent, but now some of the violence was recorded by a national press and witnessed by a national audience. The images of law enforcement officers using dogs, fire hoses, and clubs to assault unarmed black people left many white viewers appalled, yet even more violence took place. Mississippi civil rights leader Medgar Evers was shot and killed on his front porch. Four black children were killed by a secretly planted bomb in the basement of their Birmingham church, and Martin Luther King, Jr., was assassinated in Memphis.

Being white did not protect protestors from southern wrath. When Freedom Riders rode integrated buses to test southern compliance with desegregation laws, mobs attacked the buses, assaulting whites and blacks as local law enforcement and the FBI observed the violence but did nothing (Zinn, 2003). In Mississippi, authorities found the bodies of three young civil rights workers who had been murdered. During a Selma-to-Montgomery march in Alabama, a white minister was beaten to death, and a white housewife transporting marchers to Selma was shot and killed (Painter, 2005).

Amid this turmoil, Congress passed the Civil Rights Act of 1964 and the Voting Rights Act of 1965, forbidding discrimination in public accommodations, federally assisted programs, public facilities, education, and voting. In 1952, 20% of eligible southern blacks were registered to vote, but because of this legislation, 40% of eligible southern black voters were registered in 1964, and by 1968, 60% of blacks were registered, the same percentage as for whites (Zinn, 2003). Although some problems in the South were being addressed, 1960s race riots in urban areas demonstrated that racial problems also existed in northern cities. The Kerner Commission's investigation of this outbreak of urban violence concluded that the major cause of the riots was the persistence of white racism. Naming the problem did not solve it, and discrimination against African Americans in the United States has persisted and continues to contradict our American ideals.

Asian Americans

The first Asian immigrants to the United States were from four villages in the Canton province of China. Arriving in 1850, they set the Chinese pattern of predominantly male migration to America with a ratio of 10 men for every 1 woman (Lowe, 2000). Chinese immigrants tended to be young and married, lured to California by the thought of finding gold and returning to China. San Francisco welcomed the new arrivals by inviting them to participate in California's statehood ceremonies, but by 1870, 63,000 Chinese immigrants had arrived, with more than 75% in California, representing 25% of the state's workforce (Fong, 2000). Chinese immigrants quickly became the targets of Nativist sentiments expressed in slogans such as "California for Americans."

What actions did Nativists initially take against the Chinese in America?

Nativists lobbied the California legislature for a tax on people mining for gold who were not U.S. citizens (Takaki, 1993). Although the tax penalized any immigrant, the passage of the "foreign miners" act was a major setback for the Chinese. Most had borrowed money and were expected to repay their debts on arriving in America. In addition to paying for their passage, they were expected to send money home to support their wives and families, and two thirds of them managed to earn enough money to take care of their financial obligations and return to China (Glenn & Yap, 2000). Because of the 1790 law restricting U.S. citizenship to "whites only," there was little incentive to remain in the United States.

Why didn't Chinese men bring their wives and families?

In places like Singapore and Hawaii, Chinese men who chose to remain either married local women or sent for their wives, but neither option was possible in America. California law forbade interracial marriage, and entrepreneurs imported Chinese women to work as prostitutes. In 1870, the California legislature passed the Page Law to stop the immigration of Chinese prostitutes, but this resulted in the exclusion of almost all Chinese women. By 1890, the ratio of Chinese men to women was 26 to 1 (Fong, 2000).

Who employed Chinese immigrants?

Unable to mine for gold, many Chinese men found work as laborers on the western portion of the transcontinental railroad. Railroad owners paid the Chinese less than other workers and forced them to work during the winter of 1866, despite snowdrifts as high as 60 feet. They had to tunnel under the snow, digging shafts to allow for air so they could work. After that winter, Chinese workers went on strike for higher wages, only to be denounced by local newspapers and literally starved into submission when railroad owners cut off food supplies (Takaki, 1993). After the railroad was completed, most Chinese laborers returned to China, but some chose to stay, particularly in the area of San Francisco.

Wherever they settled, Chinese men continued to be paid low wages. In addition to agricultural jobs, they worked in factories or were employed as houseboys, gardeners, and cooks, and a few started small businesses. Starting a laundry was especially tempting because it required minimal investment for equipment and minimal English skills. Being self-employed enabled them to avoid exploitation by employers as well as competition with hostile white laborers.

What kind of hostile actions did the Chinese encounter?

The resentment of white laborers was not the only source of hostility; the white population in general tended to perceive the Chinese as refusing to give up their "foreign" identity and become "Americanized." Some white men would occasionally target Chinese men who maintained traditions such as the "queue," a long single braid of hair worn down their back. (See Figure 5.5.) Chinese laborers complained of white men grabbing or even cutting off their queue. It wasn't long before such hostility escalated to violent confrontation.

The U.S. economy experienced a depression in the 1870s, yet the numbers of Chinese increased, and many were becoming visibly prosperous. Looking for a scapegoat, white politicians and labor leaders blamed economic problems on the Chinese, and newspapers published and disseminated their views. In 1871, mob violence resulted in the deaths of 21 Chinese men in Los Angeles; in 1885, 28 Chinese railroad workers were killed in Rock Springs, Wyoming (Fong, 2000; Wu, 1972). Although Chinese immigrants constituted less than 1% of the U.S. population in 1882, Congress passed the **Chinese Exclusion Act** to prohibit Chinese immi-

FIGURE 5.5 Newspapers often expressed their hostility to Chinese immigrants in cartoons.

gration for the next ten years; it was renewed for another ten years in 1892, and renewed indefinitely in 1902. The door to the "Gold Mountain" closed.

During another economic recession in the 1890s, unemployed white workers rioted, beating and shooting Chinese workers. Such violence often discouraged the Chinese from continuing to work as laborers except for Chinese employers. The Chinese created their own communities in urban areas—Chinatowns—where they felt safe establishing businesses and homes, and less vulnerable to white discrimination and violence. Chinese entrepreneurs often pooled their resources to start a business, and they would employ other Chinese. By 1890, 6,400 Chinese workers employed in California laundries constituted 69% of all laundry employees in the state (Takaki, 1993).

Although they were willing to live in separate communities, most Chinese who remained in America were unwilling to be perceived as foreigners in the land. By 1924, Andrew Kan had lived and worked in the United States for over forty years, and he took his case to court to insist on his right to be an American citizen; the courts disagreed. Anti-Asian sentiment would intensify during World War II as the United States fought a Japanese enemy portrayed as treacherous and brutal.

> If we believe absurdities we shall commit atrocities.
>
> **Voltaire (1694–1778)**

How did Americans view the Japanese before World War II?

Initially Japanese immigrants settled in Hawaii to work on plantations. By 1880, only 148 Japanese lived in the United States (Fong, 2000); however, 150,000 Japanese immigrated to the mainland between 1880 and 1908. By the 1920s, the Japanese population in America was twice as large as the Chinese (Zia, 2000). Unlike the Chinese, Japanese immigrants tended to include women. By 1920, women constituted 46% of the Japanese in Hawaii and 35% in California (Takaki, 1993). Based on their awareness of the hostility toward the male Chinese immigrants; Japanese government officials screened immigration applications to ensure that those approved included married couples and to eliminate anyone who might engage in prostitution, gambling, or other vices that had been used to justify American anti-Chinese attitudes.

Despite these efforts, in 1905, California newspapers initiated a campaign against the **Yellow Peril** based on the belief that the Japanese, like the Chinese, could not or would not adopt the American culture (Feagin & Feagin, 2008). In reality, many Japanese immigrants had assimilated and desired to become American citizens. In 1922, Takao Ozawa challenged the 1790 law restricting U.S. citizenship to white people. Ozawa had been educated in American schools, belonged to a Christian church, and spoke only English at home. Ozawa's argument to the U.S. Supreme Court was that he had done everything that any immigrant could be asked to do to assimilate into the culture, and the only thing that prevented his citizenship was his race. The Supreme Court said that was all that mattered, and rejected his appeal.

Before the Supreme Court made their decision, California legislators in both houses passed a resolution calling for the prohibition of further Japanese immigration. Responding to such nativist sentiment, President Theodore Roosevelt met with Japanese officials in 1908 and reached the **Gentleman's Agreement** that Japan would prohibit further immigration except for the close relatives of those already in the United States. Japanese immigrants could use this loophole until 1920 to bring family members—including "picture brides"—to join them in America.

What was a picture bride?

Japanese culture regarded marriage as an affair negotiated between families. In the **picture bride** system, matchmaking resulted from an exchange of photographs. Combining those who came with their husbands and those who came as picture brides, 60,000 Japanese women immigrated to America (including Hawaii) and gave birth to almost 30,000 children. These children, **Nisei,** were Americans by right of birth. Most Japanese immigrants still lived in Hawaii, constituting 40% of the population; they were less than 2% of California residents (Zia, 2000).

Where were Japanese immigrants employed?

The Japanese often worked in canneries and took a variety of jobs, but many became agricultural laborers as they had been in Japan. Some began to contract for land, negotiating a share of the profits with the owner or guaranteeing a set price after the crop was sold. The owner provided seed and equipment, so with minimal investment and intense labor, Japanese farmers were able to be quite successful. Some saved enough money to secure a loan and lease or purchase land, giving them the opportunity for higher profits. By 1910, Japanese farmers in California owned or leased about 200,000 acres of land, producing almost all of the state's celery and snap beans, three quarters of the strawberries, and almost half of the onions and green peas (Takaki, 1993).

In 1913, California legislators passed the Alien Land Law to prohibit any immigrant ineligible for citizenship from owning land or leasing land for more than three years. Because their children, the Nisei, were American citizens, the Japanese leased or purchased land in their children's names; those who had no children paid other families for the right to use their children's names as their "landlords" (Zia, 2000). This prompted the California legislature to pass a new Alien Land Law in 1920, prohibiting the use of children's names to lease or purchase land.

Japanese immigrants were disappointed that their success, their efforts to assimilate, and their children's citizenship status did not reduce hostility against them. Even when possessing a college diploma, their children were not likely to find work.

Many returned to the family business, and those who were doctors or dentists tended to work in the Japanese communities (Takaki, 1993). Then World War II began, and Japan became America's enemy.

How did the war affect American attitudes toward Japanese families living in the United States?

Given the history of anti-Japanese sentiment, it is not surprising that rumors of spying and sabotage began circulating immediately. Japanese farmers were accused of planting flowers in a particular pattern to guide airplanes carrying bombs to their target (Feagin & Feagin, 2008). Fearing a broad anti-Asian backlash, many Asian-owned businesses posted signs saying that the owners were Asian but not Japanese. Some shops sold buttons that said, "I am Korean" or "I am Chinese" so Americans would not confuse them with Japanese (Koppelman, 2001).

What actions were taken against the Japanese during World War II?

Barely two months into the war, President Roosevelt issued Executive Order No. 9066 that was the basis for taking Japanese Americans from their communities and relocating them in federal "camps." Japanese families were given a week or less to sell property and possessions, packing what remained into their suitcases. More than 100,000 people, two thirds of them American citizens, lost almost everything as they were evacuated to ten federal camps. The path to these relocation camps was paved with widespread prejudices that were affirmed by political leaders at all levels of state and national government. (See Figure 5.6.)

Once at the camps, Japanese families were informed that the U.S. government required them to take a loyalty oath renouncing their allegiance to Japan. The Nisei were already American citizens, so this was not an issue for them, but for their parents, renouncing Japanese citizenship with no chance of becoming an American citizen meant that they would become a people without a country. When 4,600 of them refused to sign the oath, they were sent to federal prisons (Zia, 2000). Despite such treatment, 23,000 Japanese men joined the army to prove their loyalty. The army segregated its troops by race, and a Japanese American regiment, the 442nd, became the most highly decorated unit of the war. Yet, until the war's end, Japanese families continued to be kept in camps with barbed wire and armed soldiers. It is a tribute to the tenacity of Japanese Americans that so many were able to rebuild their lives and their finances after the war.

FIGURE 5.6 The Japanese American relocation camps of World War II illustrate the perception of these American citizens as "foreign." Rumors that there were spies from Japan circulating among them were enough to justify confiscating their property and keeping them behind barbed wire for the duration of the war.

Source: The Japanese American Citizens League.

What other Asian immigrants faced anti-Asian attitudes?

Between 1907 and 1910, large numbers of Filipinos immigrated primarily to Hawaii as agricultural laborers. When the 1924 immigration law prohibited Asian entry into the United States, Filipinos immigrated, not as Asians but as "nationals" because the Philippines had become American territory after the Spanish-American War. Of the 45,000 who had entered the United States by 1930, most were young men who worked as agricultural workers or domestic servants. Filipinos tended to be active in labor unions, causing resentment among both white landowners and other laborers (Fong, 2000).

In 1934, Congress passed legislation restricting Filipino immigration to 50 people annually. Filipinos were prohibited from entering many professions and were declared ineligible for federal aid during the Great Depression. Yet, during World War II, the army recruited 30,000 Filipinos to fight the Japanese in the Philippines. Although Filipino soldiers were promised full citizenship, the promise was not kept until 1990, long after many had died (Feagin & Feagin, 2008).

> Almost all people have this potential for evil, which would be unleashed only under certain . . . social circumstances.
>
> **Iris Chang (1968–2004)**

Koreans first began immigrating to the United States in the early 1900s to work in agriculture or as domestic servants. Like other Asian immigrants, they encountered oppression. They were refused entrance into some restaurants, not allowed access to some public places, and restricted to racially segregated neighborhoods. Because Japan had conquered Korea in the late 1930s, Koreans hoped that the allies would defeat their historic enemy during World War II; instead, the U.S. government classified Koreans as "Japanese" during the war because Japan governed Korea (Feagin & Feagin, 2008).

After the war, the total ban on Asian immigration was slightly modified, but the number of Korean immigrants was minimal until the Korean War. Because the U.S. army maintained a presence in South Korea, many American soldiers returned with Korean wives who were exempt from Asian immigration quotas. As with other Asian groups, the number of Koreans in America has increased dramatically since the Immigration Reform Act of 1965. There have also been significant increases in the numbers of other Southeast Asian immigrants such as Vietnamese, Cambodians, Laotians, and Hmong. Even though they have encountered prejudice, most refugees emigrated to escape violence in their native countries. Living safely with their families, they tend to be more optimistic about overcoming difficulties here (Pipher, 2002).

In the early 1900s, Sikh farmers were the first Asian Indian immigrants to America. Landowners employed them instead of Asians who had been targets of nativist outrage. In 1923, a Punjabi immigrant named Bhagat Singh Thind applied for U.S. citizenship using "scientific" race theories to prove he was white. Having cited race theories to deny citizenship to previous nonwhite applicants, the U.S. Supreme Court nevertheless chose to ignore "science" in this case, asserting that Thind was not white because they did not believe him to be white (Zia, 2000).

Most Asian Indian immigration has occurred since 1965, with 80% of Indo-Americans being the first generation of immigrants. Yet Asian Indian immigration has involved significant numbers of people, producing an Indo-American population that is the fourth largest among all Asian groups (after Chinese, Japanese, and Filipinos). Asian Indians are notable for linguistic and religious diversity, and they are culturally diverse, more likely to identify with a province such as Bengal or Punjab than with India. Migrating Asian Indians often have academic qualifications in fields such as engineering, medicine, mathematics, and computer management. In one study of Asian immigrants employed as physi-

> America has traveled and is still traveling a long, hard road . . . littered with persistent intolerance and bigotry. However, our progress as a nation has been marked by a succession of civil rights laws . . . (but) without proper enforcement, these laws are merely empty promises.
>
> **Bill Lann Lee (1949–)**

cians, over half were Asian Indians (Kar et al., 2000). Their success has contributed to the "model minority" myth that has been used to counter claims of discrimination by other minority groups.

What is the model minority myth?

Beginning in the 1960s, white Americans praised Asian Americans as a **model minority** because they had overcome all obstacles and achieved success. People of color were told that if they were willing to work as hard as Asian Americans, they could be just as successful, and if they failed it was their own fault. The model minority myth has created resentment among people of color, particularly African Americans, toward Asian Americans. Takaki (1993) suggests that this was the intent of those promoting the model minority myth: "Our society needs an Asian American 'model minority' in an era anxious about a growing black underclass" (p. 416). The model minority myth has often been criticized as a distraction that avoids the reality of ongoing discrimination against Asian Americans.

How does the model minority myth distort reality?

As a group, Asian Americans exist on both extremes of social status, but the model minority myth focuses on the upper extreme. Data that seems to document their financial success needs to be put in context. Asian Americans tend to live in urban areas of states where cost of living is high, inflating salary data. One study said 60% of all Asian Americans lived in three states—Hawaii, California, and New York (Woo, 2000). Asian American incomes are also inflated because they are reported as household incomes. Although most American households consist of dual wage earners, Asian American households often have additional earners.

At the other extreme are Asian Americans working for low wages. In San Francisco, Asian American women constitute 80% of all garment workers averaging 10 to 12 hours a day, 6 to 7 days a week (Louie, 2000). Their wages are low because they are competing against Third World workers who are hired by companies outsourcing jobs or establishing factories in other countries, making multiple incomes a necessity for many Asian American households. Although it is appropriate to celebrate the success of those who overcome oppression, the model minority myth actually harms Asian Americans, as Fong and Shinagawa (2000) have explained:

> [It] diverts attention away from serious social and economic problems that affect many segments of the Asian American population, detracts from both the subtle and overt racial discrimination encountered by Asian Americans, places undue pressure on young Asian Americans to succeed educationally and professionally, and fuels competition and resentment between Asian Americans and other groups. (p. 191)

Hispanic Americans/ Latinos/as

There is no clear consensus on an appropriate term that includes all diverse Spanish-speaking ethnic groups in the United States, but the immigration of Mexicans, Puerto Ricans, Cubans, Central Americans, and South Americans has created a need for an inclusive generic term. In 1980, the U.S. Census Bureau suggested *Latino* as the generic term; however, some critics said that sounded like "Ladino," an ancient form of Castilian Spanish spoken by Spanish Jews. The Bureau chose *Hispanic,* a label rejected by many Spanish-speaking people as a contrived, bureaucratic term (Shorris, 2001). Although *Hispanic* seems to be the preferred term in the southeastern United States and Texas, it is rejected in many other places, including most of California and much of the Midwest. Given this lack of consensus, both *Hispanic* and *Latinos* are used in this final section.

What was the first Spanish-speaking group to come to the United States?

The Spanish established the first permanent U.S. settlements in 1565 at St. Augustine, Florida, and in 1598 at Santa Fe, New Mexico, yet rarely do American history books mention this. Historically, school textbooks have focused on the English settlements in 1607 at Jamestown, and in 1620 at Plymouth (Loewen, 2008). When the U.S. annexed Texas, Mexicans living there (Tejanos) found themselves in America; as the Tejanos like to say, "We didn't cross the border; the border crossed us" (Shorris, 2001, p. 37). After the Mexican-American War, Mexico signed the Treaty of Guadelupe Hidalgo, giving up a million square miles of land, half of its territory. Mexicans living there were given six months to decide either to stay and become U.S. citizens or to return to Mexico. Of the more than 82,000 Mexicans who had to choose, about 80,000 chose to stay (Duignan & Gann, 1998).

> Poor Mexico, so far from God, so near to the United States.
>
> **Porfirio Diaz (1830–1915)**

Article X of the treaty promised to honor the land claims of Mexicans who became citizens, but when the American Congress ratified the treaty, they rejected Article X. To reassure Mexico that land titles and civil rights of Mexicans would be respected, American representatives presented a "Statement of Protocol" to the Mexican government with assurances that the U.S. government would not annul Mexican land grants and that these claims would be considered legitimate in American courts (Vento, 1998). That promise proved to be false.

Only a few **Anglos,** as Mexicans called white settlers, came to the new territory at first, but after gold was discovered in California, they flooded the land. Anglos settled on Mexican American land, refusing to move, and authorities took no action against the "squatters." When Anglos made legal claims to the land, Mexican Americans were forced to retain white lawyers to represent them because court proceedings were conducted in English. Although courts confirmed land grants for more than 2 million acres owned by Mexican Americans, they rejected Mexican American claims for almost 34 million acres (Vento, 1998). Even when the courts affirmed their claims, landowners often had to sell portions of their land to pay legal fees. Aggressive Anglo efforts soon created a society in former Mexican territory consisting of Anglo landowners and entrepreneurs and a pool of primarily Mexican laborers. What Shorris (2001) said of California was true for all of the former Mexican territory: "In less than a quarter of a century California changed from Spanish to Anglo" (p. 31); it was an enormous transfer of wealth and culture.

What was the experience like for Mexicans immigrating to the United States?

In the 1880s, Mexicans began crossing the border into the United States, recruited by American employers after the Chinese Exclusion Act was passed in 1882. Mexican immigrants tended to take jobs in agriculture, mining, and construction; they constituted 70% of workers laying track for Southern Pacific and Santa Fe railroads. Although American businesses actively recruited them, many Anglos perceived Mexicans as inferior. Mexicans were refused admission to public places such as beaches and restaurants. Takaki (1993) quotes the wife of an Anglo rancher arguing that a Mexican "is not as good as a white man. God did not intend him to be; He would have made him white if He had" (p. 327). All members of Mexican families participated in agricultural work; child labor laws were not enforced. Experienced workers might make up to $1.50 per day compared to $4 to $5 a day earned by miners (Duignan & Gann, 1998).

Mexicans did not passively accept such exploitation. In 1903, Mexican and Japanese farm workers formed the Japanese-Mexican Labor Association (JMLA) and engaged in a strike to increase hourly wages. They were successful, but they couldn't survive without support from national labor organizations. They petitioned the American Federation of Labor (AFL) to accept JMLA members, but AFL president Samuel Gompers insisted that the JMLA would be granted a membership charter only if it excluded Asian members. The Mexicans refused to betray their Japanese co-workers, so the charter was not granted (Takaki, 1993). Although the JMLA did not survive, Mexican farm workers continued to strike and protest against low wages.

Because of the Gentleman's Agreement of 1908 and the restrictive 1924 immigration law, Mexico was regarded as an excellent source of cheap labor. By 1910, 222,000 Mexicans lived in the United States, some as far north as Montana. Many migrated to escape the violence of the Mexican Revolution from 1910 to about 1920. When the revolution was over, only 10% of Mexico's citizens were landowners, and the northern migration continued (Vento, 1998). By 1930, 90,000 Mexicans lived in Los Angeles, representing about 10% of the city's population. Smaller numbers settled in Denver, Pittsburgh, and St. Louis, and over 20,000 Mexicans lived in Chicago (Duignan & Gann, 1998). Only a small number of these immigrants applied for citizenship, perhaps because the proximity of Mexico made it easier to consider returning.

To promote Latino immigrants applying for citizenship, the **League of United Latin American Citizens (LULAC)** was formed in the 1920s. In addition to being American citizens, members promoted assimilation by encouraging the use of English and affirming the virtues of citizenship. Although criticized for its middle-class bias, for many years LULAC was the only Latino organization to have a national presence. LULAC worked to improve education for Latino students, to protest discrimination, and to promote civil rights for Hispanic Americans (Vento, 1998). LULAC also encouraged Latinos to become citizens so they would be less vulnerable to Nativist activities.

What did Nativists do to keep Mexicans from immigrating?

Nativists were upset that no quotas were established for Mexicans in the 1924 immigration law. During the widespread unemployment of the 1930s, Nativists persuaded Congress to pass legislation restricting Mexican immigration, and the Immigration and Naturalization Service (INS) pursued Mexicans not living in the country legally. By 1935, almost 500,000 Mexicans had been deported, including some who were U.S. citizens (Duignan & Gann, 1998). When World War II began, however, attitudes about recruiting Mexican workers changed.

Why did attitudes toward Mexicans change during World War II?

When the United States entered the war, the government began negotiations for Mexicans to replace the workers who had joined the military and the Japanese workers who had been taken to relocation camps. The U.S. proposed a **Bracero Program,** *braceros* referring to contract laborers. The U.S. government offered transportation and jobs, and the Mexican government felt that this program would also provide Mexicans with an opportunity to learn about American agricultural practices. In 1942, the Bracero Program was implemented.

The U.S. government had guaranteed that Mexican workers would be paid the "prevailing wage" for their labor, but supervision of the program was inadequately funded, and many growers abused it by failing to pay the promised wages. In Texas, growers with a history of employing illegal immigrants continued to use them because they were less costly to hire. Although the Bracero Program was criticized on both sides of the border, it lasted well beyond World War II. When it ended in 1964, the program had issued almost 5 million contracts to Mexican workers (Vargas, 2000). In addition to the contribution of Mexican workers, more than 500,000 Spanish-speaking soldiers, primarily Mexican Americans, joined the American armed forces, the highest percentage of soldiers from any ethnic community (Takaki, 1993). Despite their willingness to fight for the country, Latino soldiers encountered prejudice from fellow soldiers and in communities where they were stationed. One of the most publicized examples was the **Zoot Suit Riots.**

What were the Zoot Suit Riots?

On June 3, 1943, eleven sailors on shore leave in Los Angeles claimed to have been attacked by a gang of Mexican youth. Local media often stereotyped young Mexicans in flamboyant "zoot suits" as criminals and gangsters. (See Figure 5.7.) On June 4, soldiers and sailors rented twenty taxicabs and cruised the barrio, attacking those who looked Latino, especially anyone wearing a zoot suit. At the Carmen Theater, sailors charged in and grabbed youth wearing zoot suits, ripping off their clothes

> I believe cruelty is the inability to assign the same feelings and values to another person that you harbor in yourself.
>
> **Carlos Fuentes (1928–1999)**

FIGURE 5.7 After the Zoot Suit Riots, servicemen justified attacking Mexican youth by claiming that it was unpatriotic to wear zoot suits requiring so much cloth when cloth was being rationed because of the war.

Courtesy: J.S. Koppelman.

and beating them severely. The police arrested several Mexican American youth, and the local media portrayed the sailors as heroes (Banks, 2003; Vento, 1998).

The following night sailors and soldiers marched into the barrio invading bars and businesses, destroying property and attacking patrons. Local police refused to charge them with destruction of private property or assault. On June 7, civilians and serviceman formed a mob of thousands, attacking anyone who looked Latino, including several Filipinos and blacks. Some were left naked and bleeding on the streets. Los Angeles police arrested 600 Mexican American youth. Eleanor Roosevelt declared in her newspaper column that the riots were the result of "long standing discrimination against Mexicans" (Vento, 1998, p. 187). Los Angeles police and city government denied the accusation, but as they followed the events in the newspapers, Latinos, especially Latino soldiers, were angry that they were still not accepted in their adopted land.

Was it better for Latinos after the war?

Latino communities felt a great deal of pride in their returning veterans. Latino soldiers earned numerous bronze and silver stars given for bravery in battle, and seventeen Latino soldiers received the nation's highest military award—the Congressional Medal of Honor (Duignan & Gann, 1998). Because Latino soldiers had not been segregated, they not only served with white soldiers, some also rose to positions of command. As Shorris (2001) stated, "Men who had commanded Anglo troops in battle did not cringe before them in civilian life" (p. 97).

Although they had encountered difficulty getting home loans before the war, Latino soldiers now had their loan applications approved. The G.I. Bill allowed many to pursue college educations. These soldiers represented only a small portion of Latinos, but their experiences demonstrated that Latinos could receive equitable treatment. Yet the majority of Latinos still encountered prejudice and discrimination, even those who had served in the military. At Three Rivers, Texas, a funeral home director refused to bury Felix Longoria, a Mexican American who had been decorated for heroism in World War II. After Mexican Americans protested, Longoria was finally buried with military honors at Arlington National Cemetery (Shorris, 2001).

How did Mexican Americans respond to discrimination after the war?

Challenging racially segregated schools, Mexican Americans brought *Mendez v. Westminster School District* to California courts in 1946; the judge ruled it was unconstitutional to segregate Mexican American children. This case and others would create a legal context that helped the NAACP to bring *Brown v. Board of Education* to the Supreme Court in 1954. Recognizing the need for a legal organization similar to the NAACP, an attorney in San Antonio named Pete Tijerina persuaded the Ford Foundation to provide $2.2 million to establish the **Mexican American Legal Defense and Educational Fund (MALDEF).** MALDEF continues to be involved in confronting discrimination and addressing civil rights issues affecting Mexican Americans.

To establish a fair wage for agricultural workers in California, Cesar Chavez assisted farm workers in creating a union. Chavez led a strike lasting from 1965 until 1970, resulting in a contract with one of the major growers. After another seven years of activism, the remaining growers agreed to pay farm workers standardized wages and benefits. Also in the 1960s, Reies Tijerina came to New Mexico in his quixotic pursuit of restitution for descendants of Mexicans who lost millions of acres of land they owned prior to the Treaty of Guadalupe Hidalgo (Tijerina, 1971). In Crystal City, Texas, Mexican Americans who were a large majority of the residents formed a third party called La Raza Unida and won control of the city council and the school board. They instituted bilingual education programs and hired numerous Mexican American administrators and teachers.

In 1957, El Paso citizens elected Raymond Telles to be the first Mexican American mayor in the United States. In 2005, Antonio Villaraigosa was the first Mexican American elected as mayor of Los Angeles. Political candidates in the Southwest, in urban areas, and in California eagerly court Mexican American voters. Mexican Americans have been elected to local, state, and national offices. Today, Mexican Americans are two thirds of all Latinos, the largest Spanish-speaking ethnic group in the United States followed by Puerto Ricans and Cubans (Shorris, 2001). Unlike other Latino immigrants, Puerto Ricans came to America already claiming U.S. citizenship.

How did Puerto Ricans become citizens of the United States?

When Spanish ships arrived in 1493, they called the island San Juan Batista and the harbor Puerto Rico; over time the names reversed and the "rich port" of San Juan became the capital of the island of Puerto Rico (Fitzpatrick, 1971). The 70,000 Tainos inhabiting the island were almost exterminated, so Africans were imported to work as slaves. Because Spain mainly sent soldiers, marriages and relationships took place between Spaniards, Tainos, and Africans, producing the range of skin colors from light to dark that can be found among Puerto Ricans today. In 1897, the Spanish government agreed to give Puerto Rico more autonomy, but the Spanish-American war made Puerto Rico a U.S. possession.

After almost twenty years of autocratic rule by the United States, Congress responded to Puerto Rican demands for more autonomy by passing the Jones Act in 1917. Puerto Ricans elected representatives to their two legislative bodies as well as a resident commissioner, but the U.S. president still appointed the governor and maintained veto power (Fitzpatrick, 1971). The Jones Act also provided the opportunity for Puerto Ricans to become U.S. citizens, giving them six months to decide. Although it made them eligible for military service, only 287 out of more than a million people rejected U.S. citizenship (Perez y Gonzalez, 2000).

> Come from where it may, racism divides.
>
> **Jose Marti (1853–1895)**

What effect did becoming part of the United States have on Puerto Rico?

When the United States assumed control, Puerto Rican farmers owned 93% of the farmland. By 1930, 60% of sugar beet production and almost all tobacco production came from farms with absentee owners, primarily American corporations. Although the United States built more roads and schools, the basis of the economy was transformed from small farms producing food to meet the local need to large farms hiring low-wage workers and exporting their products (Feagin & Feagin, 2008). Soon the island was not producing enough food for its own people, and malnutrition became common. Because of improved health care, Puerto Rico's population doubled by 1940, but jobs did not. Agriculture jobs paid as little as six cents an hour. By 1910, about 1,500 Puerto Ricans had come to America because of economic hardship, with a third of them living in Spanish Harlem in New York City (Duignan & Gann, 1998).

In the 1930s, Luis Marin formed the Popular Democratic Party (or "Populares") to address Puerto Rico's economic problems. They sponsored legislation to limit land that absentee owners could control; land returned to the government was redistributed to small farmers, but two thirds of American corporations refused to cooperate with the law (Perez y Gonzalez, 2000). Puerto Ricans expressed their frustration by demanding more autonomy from the United States.

In 1949, the United States allowed Puerto Ricans to elect their own governor, and they elected Luis Marin. Three years later, Congress approved the proposed Puerto Rican Constitution, giving the island the status of a commonwealth. Although it now had more autonomy, Puerto Rico also had significant economic problems. After sixty years of American rule, more than 50% of the total national income went to 20% of the people, and there was persistent unemployment and underemployment (Duignan & Gann, 1998).

Governor Marin proposed an ambitious economic plan called **Operation Bootstrap** that offered incentives such as a large supply of cheap labor and tax exemptions for businesses moving to Puerto Rico. Many corporations took advantage of this offer. Throughout the 1950s and 1960s, Operation Bootstrap expanded the island's industrial base and created 140,000 manufacturing jobs. Personal income rose from an annual average of $118 in 1940 to $1,200 by 1970 (Perez y Gonzalez, 2000). Tourism increased, and Puerto Rico was called the "Showcase of the Americas," but economic problems persisted. With so much land being used for industry, the number of agricultural jobs decreased, resulting in unemployment rates as high as 10%. So much land was given over for industrial use that Puerto Rico had to import food. Corporate tax exemptions required Puerto Ricans to pay higher taxes to fund the necessary improvements in sewers, roads, electricity, and water (Feagin & Feagin, 2003).

For many Puerto Ricans, the primary economic benefit was the opportunity to earn enough money to migrate to the United States. By the 1980s, more than 900,000 were living in New York City alone, comprising about 12% of the city's population, and the 3 million Puerto Ricans living in the United States represented 11% of all Latinos. Approximately 60% of Puerto Ricans lived in either New York or New Jersey, but with unemployment rates as high as 23%, nearly 60% of these Puerto Rican families lived in poverty (Banks, 2009; Duignan & Gann, 1998).

How do the experiences of Puerto Ricans in the United States compare to other Latino groups?

Puerto Ricans have encountered many obstacles in the United States. The percentages of Puerto Ricans unemployed or on welfare have been higher than for other Latino groups. In part, the high unemployment rate is the result of a decline in unskilled and semiskilled jobs in urban areas where they have settled. Puerto Rican children living in poverty have attended racially segregated urban schools without resources to provide the quality of education necessary for their students to compete for better paying jobs. One consequence of these economic and social problems is that Puerto Ricans have higher rates of drug use, drug addiction, and crime than other Latino groups. Single-parent families headed by women constitute a third of all Puerto Rican families, more than for any Latino group except Dominicans (Perez y Gonzalez, 2000). Shorris (2001) described the typical situation for many Puerto Ricans in New York City:

> Puerto Ricans work in marginal businesses; they have no unions, no benefits, nothing but the weekly paycheck, from which social security may or may not have been deducted and paid; when the marginal business goes broke after a few or even many years, . . . the loyal Puerto Rican employee is left with nothing. (p. 87)

Yet Puerto Ricans have succeeded in a variety of fields including literature, sports, politics, the arts, music, medicine, and more. For over forty years the Puerto Rican organization called Aspira has supported high school clubs to encourage Puerto Rican youth to graduate and go to college. Regardless of their success or failure, Puerto Ricans resent other Americans perceiving them as foreigners rather than regarding them as the fellow citizens that they are. If they migrate from Puerto Rico to a state, or from one state to another, Puerto Ricans should be viewed the same as a Minnesotan who moves to New York.

Today, the majority of Puerto Ricans living in the United States were born here. Puerto Ricans tend to be bilingual and bicultural, identifying themselves as Puerto Ricans but proud of their status as American citizens. Like other Latinos, they often speak Spanish at home, but young people are more likely to speak English to their peers (Perez y Gonzalez, 2000). Puerto Ricans encourage their youth to succeed, despite the difficulty of that goal. According to Shorris (2001), "Every Puerto Rican who survives and succeeds to any degree on the mainland is a miracle of love and will" (p. 144). Although they have not been as successful as other Latinos, especially Cubans, Puerto Ricans want to believe that such miracles are possible.

Why has the experience of Cubans been so different from that of Puerto Ricans?

The islands of Cuba and Puerto Rico have similar histories. Columbus and his men conquered the Taino Indians, inhabiting both islands and enslaving the residents. Yet by 1762, Cuba's capital city was twice the size of New York or Philadelphia; Havana was a port of such significance that the British captured the city and refused to give it back until Spain agreed to give up Florida in exchange. In addition to being a major trading center in the Caribbean, Cuba prospered because of its sugar production carried out by imported African slaves. By 1830, the combination of free and enslaved blacks was larger than the population of whites. By 1870, Cubans were trying to win independence from Spain; a few Cubans immigrated to the United States during the lengthy struggle that ended in 1898 when American troops prevailed in the Spanish-American War.

After four years of military rule, the United States agreed to make Cuba a sovereign nation, but the Platt amendment gave the United States the right to intervene in Cuba's affairs at any time to protect property and liberty in Cuba. For the next two decades, no Cuban who did not gain U.S. approval could be elected president nor stay in that office (Feagin & Feagin, 2008).

Even under American dominance, Cuba prospered; few Cubans immigrated to the United States until Fidel Castro's successful revolt against dictator Fulgencio Batista. After Castro announced that Cuba would be a communist nation, Cubans began leaving, most immigrating to Florida. The wealthiest Cubans left first. Those who followed in the 1960s were a heterogeneous group, but with a disproportionately high number of businessmen, professionals, and entrepreneurs. Many had been in the merchant navy; others were former government officials or were revolutionaries who were disillusioned with Castro (Duignan & Gann, 1998).

What happened to the Cubans who came to the United States?

A federally funded Cuban Refugee Program (CRP) was established to assist Cubans coming to Florida. CRP refugee centers provided resources rarely given to other immigrants (Portes & Bach, 1985). Cuban businessmen who had salvaged some of their wealth relied on traditional business methods called *socios* or *socioismo* where loans were approved not by an objective analysis but because the applicant was a friend. Cuban immigrants tended to be educated, and many had business experience. For the next two decades, Cubans used their resources to engage in business enterprises as well as to provide services such as grocery stores, legal assistance, and funeral homes. As Shorris (2001) stated, "The Cuban exiles, primarily middle- and upper middle-class, soon became middle- and upper middle-class again" (p. 67). Attracted by Cuban success in the United States and disenchanted with Castro's communism, more Cubans came.

The next wave of Cuban immigrants tended to be working-class people from urban areas (almost half from Havana alone). Many found work in businesses owned or managed by Cubans where they tended to earn higher wages. By the mid-1980s, Cuban Americans were the majority in Dade County and in Miami. Although 40% of Cuban immigrants settled in Florida, they also settled in New York, New Jersey, and California (Duignan & Gann, 1998). A 1953 Cuban census identified 72% of Cubans as white, but the 1970 U.S. census identified 95% of Cubans living in the United States as white (Portes & Bach, 1985).

Compared to other major Latino groups in the United States, Cuban Americans have recorded the highest median household incomes. One reason for their success is that, similar to Asian American families, they tend to have multiple wage earners in a household. According to a study of Cuban immigration from 1960 to 1980, about two thirds of Cuban American wives worked outside the home, and 27% of these households had additional family members earning income. The presence of Cubans in Florida has attracted an increasing number of tourists and entrepreneurs from both Central and South America, providing additional business opportunities.

Although Cuban immigrants have traditionally viewed themselves as a people in exile, that view is not shared by Cuban American youth. According to Shorris (2001), "Older Cubans say they will return to Cuba as soon as Castro dies or is deposed. The younger generation is interested only in going back to visit" (p. 75). Their attitudes are similar to Mexican American and Puerto Rican youth, as well as other Latinos living in the United States.

What other Latino groups live in the United States?

Other Hispanic immigrant groups coming to the United States in the twentieth century included Dominicans, Central Americans, and South Americans. Since the 1960s, there has been a small but steady stream of immigrants from the Dominican Republic, surging in the early 1980s because of the global recession that drove down sugar prices, creating a huge foreign debt and an unemployment rate of 30%. By the time the crisis was over, 10% of Dominicans had immigrated, primarily to the United States, with 90% settling in New York City (Duignan & Gann, 1998).

Immigrants from Central America have usually come to the United States to escape political turmoil and violence in countries such as Guatemala, Honduras, Nicaragua, and El Salvador. To address their needs, the Central American Refugee Committee (CRECE) was established to provide food, temporary shelter, work, and legal assistance. CRECE food distribution centers raise money to purchase food wholesale, and they ask for small contributions from those taking food to help pay for the purchase of more food, making the centers a collaborative endeavor, not merely a charitable one (Shorris, 2001). As Central Americans have tended to settle in urban areas, CRECE has been a critical resource for them. So many Salvadorans have settled in Los Angeles that it has now become the second largest Salvadoran city after the nation's capitol of San Salvador.

Unlike Central Americans, who tend to come from impoverished areas, South American immigrants tend to have had the advantage of a good education, many having a doctoral degree. Some Chileans immigrated because of political repression, but few South Americans are refugees. Reasons for immigrating usually involve a desire for better jobs, higher salaries, and greater opportunity. Because they come with such resources, South Americans are reported to have the highest educational attainment and higher incomes than any other Spanish-speaking group in the United States (Duignan & Gann, 1998).

Why have many Americans objected to Latino immigration?

The primary motivation for all Latino immigrants is economic opportunity, but many have resorted to illegal means of gaining entry to the United States. Mexican Americans are the largest source of foreign labor in the United States, especially for manual labor jobs (Portes, 2007). Although the North American Free Trade Agreement that was implemented in the 1990s resulted in American industries building many factories just inside the Mexican border, Mexican workers have migrated to these border towns in huge numbers, creating a labor pool larger than the available jobs require. As a consequence, wages at these factories continue to be low, and many unemployed workers have crossed the border illegally to find work in the United States (Acuña, 2004).

In 1990, the U.S. Defense Department built an 11-mile fence along the Mexican border near San Diego as a strategy for keeping illegal drugs from being brought into the United States. This initiated a "militarization" of the Mexican border that has continued and has been extended to include denying entry to illegal immigrants (Acuña, 2004). Sociologist Douglas Massey argues that the border militarization has failed to stop the flow of drugs and has been equally ineffective at stopping illegal immigration. Militarizing the border has caused smuggling to become professionalized (Portes, 2007). Although professional smugglers are expensive, the odds of their being caught are reduced. By making the process of entering the United States more difficult, illegal immigrants tend to remain here, resulting in an outcome opposite to what people supporting border militarization wanted to achieve. Experts predict that the problem of undocumented workers will never be resolved until the U.S. government recognizes and facilitates historic patterns of cyclic immigrations for seasonal work between Mexico and the United States (Portes, 2007).

> What the people want is very simple. They want an America as good as its promise.
>
> **Barbara Jordan (1936–1996)**

AFTERWORD

Human evolution is a story of survival, but once physical survival is assured, human beings create culture. The struggle to maintain one's culture while living in a new homeland with its own culture is no easy task, especially because physical and cultural differences have been used to create the concept of race. Race has then been used to divide human groups, creating subordinate races that are forced to struggle against a dominant race.

For the indigenous people in America, this struggle began when European colonists stepped on American shores. The roots of oppression expanded across the nation in the cultural and physical conflict that followed. The oppression eventually encompassed African slaves, Chinese and Japanese laborers, Mexican migrant workers, and other immigrants of color. This oppression was even directed against groups considered white today like Irish, Italian, and Slavic immigrants, but all European groups would eventually be offered the freedom and opportunity they sought in the United States while it continued to be denied to people of color.

Oppression based on race and related ethnic groups has been sustained by the descendants of the original European settlers, affecting people of color living in the United States and those who are coming with the same vision of freedom and opportunity that brought the first colonists. We are now a nation of nations with people from all over the world pursuing the happiness promised by a free society. If the United States is to be a pluralistic society embracing diverse groups, it must make sure that all people living in America are respected as part of our diverse national family.

By insisting on racial equality, Americans of color are simply demanding a chance to achieve the same American dream that has attracted so many immigrants to these shores. It is a dream not yet realized for far too many of them. In the poem "Let America be America Again," Langston Hughes (1994) speaks for all oppressed people who still pursue the American dream:

> America never was America to me,
> And yet I swear this oath—
> America will be! (p. 191)

myeducationlab

Now go to Topic #2: **Race** in the MyEducationLab (www.myeducationlab.com) for your course, where you can:

- Find learning outcomes for this topic along with the national standards that connect to these outcomes.
- Complete Assignments and Activities that can help you more deeply understand the chapter content by viewing classroom video and ABC News footage.
- Apply and practice your understanding of the core teaching skills identified in the chapter with the Building Teaching Skills and Dispositions learning units.

TERMS AND DEFINITIONS

Anglos A term identifying white people who settled in Mexican territory, eventually becoming a generic term for white people

Black Cabinet The Federal Council on Negro Affairs, consisting of thirty black professionals, served as an advisory group to President Franklin Roosevelt

Bracero Program Initiated during World War II, this program continued to import Mexicans into the United States for twenty-two years as manual laborers

Brown v. Board of Education The 1954 Supreme Court decision overturning *Plessy v. Ferguson* by declaring racial segregation as unconstitutional

Chinese Exclusion Act An 1882 law prohibiting Chinese immigration to the United States, renewed in 1892, and making exclusion permanent in 1902

Emancipation Proclamation Issued by President Lincoln to free slaves only in Confederate States and permitting free blacks to enlist in the Union Army

Ethnocentrism Believing one's race, nation, or culture is superior to all other; also individual actions or institutional practices based on that belief

Gentleman's Agreement The Japanese government assured the U.S. government it would issue no more passports (as of 1908) to Japanese workers except those already in the United States or their close relatives

Indian Sovereignty Legal rights of Indian nations, confirmed by treaties with the U.S. government, to define themselves and to act as unique cultural and legal entities.

Indigenous people A racial or ethnic group that is well established in an area before the arrival of a new group; a group that may be but does not need be native to the area in which it is established

League of United Latin American Citizens (LULAC) A national organization for members of Spanish-speaking ethnic groups who are American citizens that is dedicated to promoting the value of citizenship, protesting discrimination, and advocating for civil rights for Latinos

Mexican American Legal Defense Fund (MALDEF) An organization opposing discrimination and advocating for Mexican Americans' civil rights

Middle Passage The ocean crossing of slave ships resulting in the deaths of an estimated 5 to 6 million Africans being transported as slaves

Model minority The belief that Asian Americans have been successful because they have been willing to work hard, and that all other minorities could be just as successful if they emulated Asian American behavior

National Association for the Advancement of Colored People (NAACP) An organization opposing racism and advocating for black civil rights

Nisei The term for children of Japanese immigrants who were born in the United States and therefore possessed U.S. citizenship

Nomads A group of persons with no single fixed abode who move from place to place in search of food and water

Operation Bootstrap An economic plan for Puerto Rico during the 1950s and 1960s to boost its industrial base and create more manufacturing jobs

Picture bride A modification of the Japanese system for arranged marriages involving the exchange of photographs between families negotiating a marriage for Japanese men who had immigrated to the United States

Treaty A legal agreement between two or more nations involving terms of peace, trade, and other matters as agreed to by the negotiating parties

Underground Railroad An organization that established "stations" where runaway slaves could get food and rest as they escaped north to freedom

Yellow Peril The term for the belief that Chinese and Japanese immigrants could never be assimilated into American culture and therefore threatened the unity of American society

Zoot Suit Riots Several days of mob violence in 1942 in Los Angeles that demonstrated anti-American prejudice as U.S. servicemen (later joined by civilians) attacked Mexican American youth, especially targeting those wearing zoot suits

DISCUSSION EXERCISES

Exercise #1 Understanding Recollections of Larry Kobori Activity

Directions: Read to learn the feelings that Larry recounts having had about the incident that he describes. Then, respond to the Insight Builder Questions below.

Larry Kobori's School Story

When I was young I noticed I was a little different from my friends. My father told me I was Japanese and that I should never be ashamed of being Japanese. He has emphasized this for as long as I remember.

When I started school everything was perfect until the fourth grade. Some kids called me a "Chink." I told them I'm Japanese, not Chinese. If I was going to be called a dirty name, at least use the proper dirty name. My friends always told me to forget those kids, that those kids were stupid. I was glad to hear my friends say that.

After a while the fourth grade things straightened out. But in the seventh grade we started to read about World War I and World War II. I knew that in World War II Japan attacked Pearl Harbor. So I worked real hard on World War I. I answered every question I could. But when it came to World War II, I never answered any questions. I would just slouch in my chair.

I guess I was feeling ashamed and embarrassed at the atrocities of Japan during World War II. But what I didn't understand was why the textbooks and the teacher glorified America's bombing of Hiroshima and Nagasaki. My teacher said thousands of civilians, including women and children, were killed by the atom bombs, thus making Japan surrender. She then added that the bombings had saved many American lives.

I then asked my teacher, "Wouldn't that be considered an atrocity since so many civilians died? That's the way you describe Japanese atrocities." I'll never forget the way she stared at me and said, "There's a difference." Today that episode is still clear as a bell. It's something that I've never forgotten.

My three years in high school were the best years. I felt that now I was really being accepted. I was the varsity scorekeeper for three years in football, basketball, and baseball. I couldn't compete on the high school level so I did what I could to help. I learned the plays and found myself getting to know the other guys much better. I was then encouraged to write sport stories in the local newspaper. When these stories came out the sophomores and juniors wanted me to help them. As a result I got to know quite a few of them.

Outside of class sometimes it was a different story. Traveling with the basketball team, some blacks called me a "Jap." Remembering my promise I turned around and was about to call the blacks "Niggers." I restrained myself because I was sure it would lead to a fight. The same thing happened when some Mexicans called me a "Jap." Once again I refrained from retaliating.

I'll never understand why those people called me a "Jap."

Insight Builder Questions

1. What are your impressions of Larry Kobori?
2. Do you think Larry Kobori's responses to the racial incidents were appropriate ways to deal with the discrimination that he experienced?
3. Whether you agree it is appropriate or not, what alternatives did Larry have?
4. Which of them would you recommend as the best strategy?
5. In your opinion, how should teachers present the Japanese role in World War II? The use of atomic bombs on Hiroshima and Nagasaki?
6. What conditions were favorable in his school experiences?
7. What conditions were not favorable?
8. Suggest a generalization about Americans and race today.

Exercise #2 College Racial Incidents Activity

Directions: The following case studies illustrate a variety of incidents that occurred. Imagine that you are a college counselor or residence hall assistant when the student of color in each incident comes to you to report what happened. What sort of advice would you give to this student? Explain why your advice represents the best course of action for the student to follow.

1. A Puerto Rican American, Jorge, interviewed for a graduate assistantship position. The director discussed the role and responsibility of the assistantship position and indicated that the primary responsibility would be to supervise outreach activities for Hispanic students who were not using available student services. The director believed that Jorge would be a good role model and could convince students to use services since there were biological factors resulting in some people being able to learn more and to be more intelligent than others. Noting Jorge's negative response, the director said he just wanted to be open and honest about his opinions.
2. When in the Marine Corps, Leonard, a Lakota Sioux, had been stationed in the United States and Germany. After serving three years, he returned to his reservation and enrolled in a nearby college. Visiting a sweat lodge, Leonard's friends and older members of the tribe shared stories of their ancestors. When Leonard had been a child, he remembered listening to his father telling stories about his great-grandfather; he had always enjoyed learning about his family history. Now Leonard realized, however, that the stories had no meaning for him, and he could not understand the importance that his tribe placed on talking about individuals who no longer existed. Leonard found himself in conflict with his family and friends. He considered dropping out of college to get a job to earn enough money to leave and live elsewhere. But he knew there weren't many jobs for people with only a reservation high school diploma. Leonard became more depressed about the conflict he was experiencing and began to think that the only resolution was to drop out of college and reenlist for another full term.
3. Anthony, a Chinese American student transferring from community college to a four-year university, was invited to the new student orientation, where he met with his adviser. As he was leaving the adviser's office, the adviser said in a jovial and friendly tone of voice, "You know, the restaurant across the street sells the best wonton soup around." The more Anthony thought about it, the more upset he became.
4. Jessica, a 22-year-old Mexican American from central Illinois, left home to attend college in California. A few weeks into the semester she began to notice that the majority of the Hispanic students were able to speak both English and Spanish fluently. Although her parents spoke Spanish at home, they did not insist that their children become bilingual, so Jessica could understand Spanish if someone spoke to her, but she was not a fluent Spanish speaker. Jessica talked to the Chicano studies professor after class, who assured her that not all Mexican Americans share the same sociocultural experience, but that all people needed to understand and respect the values of others. He also suggested that if this situation continued to bother Jessica, she should consider seeing a counselor. In her English class, consisting primarily of white students, Jessica felt comfortable and relaxed; however, in a Chicano studies course, she felt out of place because she did not share the experiences of the other Hispanic students.

REFERENCES

Acuña, R. (2004). *Occupied America: A history of Chicanos* (5th ed.). New York, NY: Pearson Longman.

Presents a comprehensive overview of Chicano history beginning prior to the Spanish invasion of 1519 and subsequent occupation and ending with contemporary events.

Banks, J.A. (2009). *Teaching strategies for ethnic studies* (8th ed.). Boston, MA: Allyn & Bacon.

Describes history of racial and ethnic groups in the United States with additional information for teachers on developing a multicultural curriculum with teaching lessons and resources.

Berkhofer, R., Jr. (2004). *The white man's Indian: Images of the American Indian from Columbus to the present.* New York, NY: Vintage Books.

Examines legal manipulations by Europeans with regard to land claims in the new world. See especially "The Colonial Foundations of White Indian Policy."

Bieder, R.E. (1995). *Native American communities in Wisconsin, 1600–1960: A study of tradition and change.* Madison: University of Wisconsin Press.

Describes the history of Indian tribes in Wisconsin and examines the impact of efforts at the state and federal level to promote their assimilation.

Carson, C., & Carson, D.M. (2000). The Black Panther Party. In J. Birnbaum & C. Taylor (Eds.), *Civil rights since 1787: A reader on the black struggle* (pp. 618–620). New York, NY: New York University Press.

Provides a brief history of the Black Panther Party.

Chatters, J.C. (2001). Routes of passage. In *Ancient encounters: Kennewick Man and the first Americans* (pp. 239–264). New York, NY: Simon & Schuster.

Addresses archeological discoveries that place human beings in North and South America much earlier than can be accounted for by the Bering Strait theory of migration.

Chernow, R. (2004). *Alexander Hamilton.* New York, NY: Penguin Books.

Describes Hamilton's life, including his anti-slavery activities and his belief in racial equality.

Connolly, M.R. (2000, September/October). What's in a name?: A historical look at Native American-related nicknames and symbols at three U.S. universities. *Journal of Higher Education, 17*(5), 515–548.

Examines the Indian mascot issue by focusing specifically on efforts to change the mascots at the University of Illinois, Miami of Ohio, and Eastern Michigan University.

Cornelius, J.D. (2000). Literacy, slavery, and religion. In J. Birnbaum & C. Taylor (Eds.), *Civil rights since 1787: A reader on the black struggle* (pp. 85–89). New York, NY: New York University Press.

Describes how and why slaves tried to gain literacy skills, and how they used conversion to Christianity as a means of pursuing literacy.

Deloria, P. (2001). Sovereignty. In B. Ballantine & I. Ballantine (Eds.), *The Native Americans: An illustrated history.* North Dighton, MA: J. G. Press.

Defines and describes Indian sovereignty as a historical concept and explains why it continues to be an important concern for Native Americans.

Duignan, P.J., & Gann, L.H. (1998). *The Spanish speakers in the United States: A history.* Lanham, MD: University Press of America.

Describes the factors in their country of origin that motivated immigration and the experience in the United States of diverse Spanish-speaking ethnic groups.

Feagin, J., & Feagin, C.B. (2008). *Racial and ethnic relations* (8th ed.). Upper Saddle River, NJ: Pearson Prentice Hall.

Describes experience of major racial and ethnic groups in the United States.

Fitzgerald, F.S. (2005). Early success. In J.L. West (Ed.), *My lost city: Personal essays, 1920–1940* (pp. 184–192). Cambridge, UK: Cambridge University Press.

Describes the author's early years and initial success in writing.

Fitzpatrick, J.P. (1971). *Puerto Rican Americans: The meaning of migration to the mainland.* Englewood Cliffs, NJ: Prentice Hall.

Provides a historical overview of Puerto Rico and examines the migration of Puerto Ricans, especially to New York City, and what they have encountered.

Fong, T.P. (2000). A brief history of Asians in America. In T.P. Fong & L.H. Shinagawa (Eds.), *Asian Americans: Experiences and perspectives* (pp. 13–30). Upper Saddle River, NJ: Prentice Hall.

Provides an overview of immigration and their experience in the United States from the earliest arrivals to the most recent.

Fong, T.P., & Shinagawa, L.H. (2000). Employment and occupation. In T.P. Fong & L.H. Shinagawa (Eds.), *Asian Americans: Experiences and perspectives* (pp. 191–192). Upper Saddle River, NJ: Prentice Hall.

Describes content for the readings in the 5th chapter of their anthology after an opening comment (quoted) on the model minority myth.

Franklin, J.H., & Moss, A.A., Jr. (2000). *From slavery to freedom: A history of African Americans.* New York, NY: Alfred A. Knopf.

Begins with a description of the African cultures from which slaves came and presents a thorough description of the African American experience.

Gedicks, A. (1993). *The new resource wars: Native and environmental struggles against multinational corporations.* Boston, MA: South End Press.

Examines Indian resistance to corporate exploitation globally and efforts in Wisconsin to protect the environment by opposing mining plans of two multinational corporations.

Gell-Mann, M. (1994). *The quark and the jaguar: Adventures in the simple and the complex.* New York, NY: W.H. Freeman.

Integrates knowledge from research in the sciences, primarily physics, to explore various issues such as the need to preserve cultural and biological diversity (Chapter 21).

Glenn, E.N., & Yap, S.G.H. (2000). Chinese American families. In T.P. Fong & L.H. Shinagawa (Eds.), *Asian Americans: Experiences and perspectives* (pp. 277–292). Upper Saddle River, NJ: Prentice Hall.

Explains how Chinese American families have adapted to American society and identifies three family types that have emerged.

Hawkins, J. (2005). Smoke signals, sitting bulls, and slot machines: A new stereotype of Native Americans? *Multicultural Perspectives,* 7(3), 51–54.

Results of a review of seven popular middle and high school history textbooks as well as classrooms where the textbooks were being used.

Hendry, J. (2003). Mining the sacred mountain: The clash between the Western dualistic framework and native American religions. *Multicultural Perspectives,* 5(1), 3–10.

Contrasts patterns of Western thought with the perspective of Native Americans, especially with regard to their views of nature and the protection of the environment.

Hughes, L. (1994). Let America be America again. In A. Rampersad & D. Roellel (Eds.), *The collected poems of Langston Hughes* (pp. 189–191). New York, NY: Alfred A. Knopf.

A poem about the "dream" of America that was never fulfilled for people of color and poor whites.

Jacobs, H.A. (1987). *Incidents in the life of a slave girl.* Cambridge, MA: Harvard University Press.

Provides a personal account of the author's experience as a slave and her escape from slavery.

Jennings, F. (1976). *The invasion of America: Indians, colonialism, and the cant of conquest.* New York, NY: W.W. Norton.

Describes the conflict between the Pequot and Narragansett Indians in Chapter 13.

Josephy, A., Jr. (2005). *500 nations: An illustrated history of North American Indians.* London: Pimlico.

Provides information on conflicts between Indians and the dominant society.

Kar, S.B., Campbell, K., Jiminez, A. & Gupta, S.R. (2000). Invisible Americans: An exploration of Indo American quality of life. In T.P. Fong & E.H. Shinagawa (Eds.), *Asian Americans: Experiences and perspectives* (pp. 303–319). Upper Saddle River, NJ: Prentice Hall.

Presents the results of a survey and focus study research to identify the factors that have contributed to the quality of life for Indo-Americans.

Koppelman, K. (2001). Was Orwell wrong? In *Values in the key of life: Making harmony in the human community* (pp. 57–63). Amityville, NY: Baywood.

Discusses how language is used to label and divide people.

Le May, J.L. (Ed.). (1987). *Benjamin Franklin: Writings* (pp. 442–446). New York, NY: Library of America.

Franklin's comment is in "Securing the Friendship of the Indians: A letter to James Parker."

Lewis, D.L. (1993). *W.E.B. Du Bois: Biography of a race, 1868–1919.* New York, NY: Henry Holt.

Provides a thoroughly researched and detailed description of the first fifty years of the life of this African American scholar and social activist.

Lewis, D.L. (2000). *W.E.B. Du Bois: The fight for equality and the American century, 1919–1963.* New York, NY: Henry Holt.

Provides a thoroughly researched and detailed description of the last fifty years of the life of this African American scholar and social activist.

Loewen, J. (2008). *Lies my teacher told me: Everything your American history textbook got wrong.* New York, NY: The New Press.

Describes distortions and omissions of Americans of color in high school history textbooks.

Lomax, L.E. (1963). *The Negro revolt.* New York, NY: Signet Books.

Provides the historical context that was the foundation for the 1960s civil rights movement and explains the purpose and goals of this movement.

Louie, M.C. (2000). Immigrant Asian women in Bay Area garment sweatshops: "After sewing, laundry, cleaning and cooking, I have no breath left to sing." In T.P. Fong & L.H. Shinagawa (Eds.), *Asian Americans: Experiences and perspectives* (pp. 226–242). Upper Saddle River, NJ: Prentice Hall.

Describes the exploitation of Asian immigrant women working in the garment industry and their efforts to organize to improve work conditions.

Lowe, L. (2000). Heterogeneity, hybridity, multiplicity: Marking Asian American difference. In T.P. Fong & L.H. Shinagawa (Eds.), *Asian Americans: Experiences and perspectives* (pp. 412–421). Upper Saddle River, NJ: Prentice Hall.

Discusses the importance of recognizing differences between Asian American populations in their origins and in their American experience.

Lui, M. (2004). Doubly divided: The racial wealth gap. In C. Collins, A. Gluckman, M. Lui, B.L. Wright, & A. Scharf (Eds.), *The wealth inequality reader* (pp. 42–49). Cambridge, MA: Dollars & Sense.

Reviews the historical development of wealth in the United States to explain how people of color were not given the same opportunities as white Americans.

Malcolm X. (2000). The ballot or the bullet. In J. Birnbaum & C. Taylor (Eds.), *Civil rights since 1787: A reader on the black struggle* (pp. 589–603). New York, NY: New York University Press.

Presents a speech delivered in Cleveland on April 3, 1964 (after he had broken from the Nation of Islam) that is a call to work for human rights for all African Americans.

Matthiessen, P. (1993). *Indian country.* New York: Penguin.

Analyzes conflicts concerning land claims and land use between Indians and white people.

Mintz, S. (2004). *Huck's Raft: A history of American childhood.* Cambridge, MA: Belknap Press of Harvard University Press.

Describes historically shifting attitudes toward child raising in the United States and the diversity of approaches stemming from diverse cultural groups.

Painter, N.I. (2005). *Creating Black Americans: African-American history and its meaning, 1619 to the present.* Oxford, England: Oxford University Press.

Describes historical and aesthetic developments, using art work by blacks, to explain how certain people and events shaped black Americans.

Parfit, M., & Garrett, K. (2000). Hunt for the first Americans. *National Geographic, 198*(40), 40–64.

Explains how recent archaeological discoveries have changed the way anthropologists think about prehistoric Native Americans.

Perdue, T. (1998). *Cherokee women: Gender and culture change, 1700–1835.* Lincoln: University of Nebraska Press.

Examines the role of women in traditional Cherokee society and how that role was changed by contact with European colonists and ongoing relations with the dominant society.

Perez y Gonzalez, M.E. (2000). *Puerto Ricans in the United States.* Westport, CT: Greenwood Press.

Describes the history of Puerto Rico under Spanish and American rule, the causes of U.S. migration, and how Puerto Ricans have fared in the United States.

Pipher, M. (2002). *The middle of everywhere: The world's refugees come to our town.* New York, NY: Harcourt.

Presents stories about a variety of recent immigrants, including the conditions that forced them to immigrate and the difficulties they encounter trying to adjust to American culture.

Portes, A. (2007, October). The fence to nowhere. *The American Prospect, 18*(10), 26–29.

Discusses the attempts made to deny illegal immigrants entry into the United States and the factors that motivate that immigration; also suggests more effective ways to control it.

Portes, A., & Bach, R.L. (1985). *Latin Journey: Cuban and Mexican immigrants in the United States.* Berkeley, CA: University of California Press.

Provides historical context for Latino immigration, then describes an eight-year study of Cuban and Mexican immigrants and presents the results.

Raboteau, A. (2000). Slave religion, rebellion and docility. In J. Birnbaum & C. Taylor (Eds.), *Civil rights since 1787: A reader on the black struggle* (pp. 29–34). New York, NY: New York University Press.

Describes how Africans resisted slavery, even using Christianity as a tool to rebel against their slave owners.

Reiss, O. (1997). *Blacks in colonial America.* Jefferson, NC: McFarland.

Explains how slavery in the American colonies was different from historical antecedents and describes anti-slavery activities of both blacks and whites.

Shorris, E. (2001). *Latinos: A biography of the people.* New York, NY: W.W. Norton.

Provides a personal narrative of the diverse Latino groups in the United States using many personal stories told within a historical context.

Smedley, A. (2007). The arrival of Africans and descent into slavery. *Race in North America: Origin and evolution of a world view.* Boulder, CO: Westview.

Describes how Africans were procured for the slave trade, the arrival of Africans in America, and how they lost their equal status with other immigrants.

Smith, V. (2001). Cleanliness. In P. Sterns (Ed.), *Encyclopedia of European social history: From 1350 to 2000* (Vol. 4, pp. 343–353). New York, NY: Scribner.

Describes how attitudes and practices with regard to cleanliness have evolved since the Middle Ages (from a six-volume encyclopedia).

Spivey, D. (2003). *Fire from the soul: A history of the African-American struggle.* Durham, NC: Carolina Academic Press.

Presents African American history as an ongoing struggle against racism that takes different forms in different eras requiring different tactics.

Spring, J. (2001). *Deculturalization and the struggle for equality: A brief history of the education of dominated cultures in the United States* (3rd ed.). Boston, MA: McGraw-Hill.

Presents a concise history of racism in the United States with special attention given to the impact of school policies on members of subordinate groups.

Suzuki, D., & Knudtson, P. (1992). *Wisdom of the elders: Honoring sacred native visions of nature.* New York, NY: Bantam Books.

Provides information on Native American knowledge of herbal medicine, their perceptions of nature, and their efforts to interact harmoniously with nature.

Takaki, R. (1993). *A different mirror: A history of multicultural America.* Boston, MA: Little, Brown.

Describes the historical experience of diverse racial and ethnic groups in the United States.

Tijerina, R. (1971). Reies Tijerina's letter from the Santa Fe jail. In W. Moquin & C. Van Doren (Eds.), *A documentary history of the Mexican Americans* (pp. 484–487). New York, NY: Bantam Books.

Explains why the author is in jail for pursuing land claims based on the Treaty of Guadelupe Hidalgo (the treaty is also reprinted in this book).

Vargas, Z. (2000). Citizen, immigrant, and foreign wage workers: The Chicana/o labor refrain in U.S. labor historiography. In R.I. Rochin & D.N. Valdes (Eds.), *Voices of a new Chicana/o history* (pp. 153–165). East Lansing: Michigan State University Press.

Reviews research on the historic involvement of Chicano/a workers in the United States and their efforts to organize and confront their exploitation.

Vento, A.C. (1998). *Mestizo: The history, culture and politics of the Mexican and the Chicano.* Lanham, MD: University Press of America.

Describes the pre-Columbian cultures in Mexico, the conquest by Spain, and the evolution of Mexicans into Mestizos, Chicanos, and Mestizo-Americans.

Wallace, A. (1993). *The long, bitter trail: Andrew Jackson and the Indians.* New York, NY: Hill & Wang.

Describes the forced removal of the Cherokee to Oklahoma known as the "Trail of Tears."

Weatherford, J. (1988). *Indian givers: How the Indians of the Americas transformed the world.* New York, NY: Fawcett.

Identifies specific examples of Indian knowledge or products borrowed by Europeans and that in some instances have been associated with Europe (the Irish potato, German chocolate).

White, R. (2001). Expansion and exodus. In B. Ballantine & I. Ballantine (Eds.), *The native Americans: An illustrated history.* North Dighton, MA: J. G. Press.

Describes the failed efforts of Native Americans to reconstruct the world destroyed by contact with whites, and the institutions and values created to replace what was lost.

Whitty, J. (2005). Accounting coup. *Mother Jones, 30*(5), 57–63, 86.

Describes the efforts of a Blackfoot woman, a MacArthur Foundation Award recipient, to secure economic resources, especially by her class action suit.

Williams, J. (1987). *Eyes on the prize: America's civil rights years, 1954–1965.* New York, NY: Viking.

Describes the events that were responsible for an organized civil rights movement whose efforts resulted in the passage of the 1964 Civil Rights Act and 1965 Voting Rights Act.

Williams, W.C. (1954). The American background. *Selected essays of William Carlos Williams* (pp. 134–161). New York, NY: Random House.

Examines colonial ethnocentrism and provides several examples such as the robin.

Wilson, J. (1998). *The earth shall weep: A history of native America.* New York, NY: Atlantic Monthly Press.

Describes the history of Native American nations and relations with the dominant society.

Woo, D. (2000). The inventing and reinventing of "model minorities": The cultural veil obscuring structural sources of inequality. In T.P. Fong & L.H. Shinagawa (Eds.), *Asian Americans: Experiences and perspectives.* Upper Saddle River, NJ: Prentice Hall.

Describes the historical evolution of the model minority myth with an analysis of its popularity and persistence in the United States.

Woodward, C.V. (1966). *The strange case of Jim Crow.* Oxford, England: Oxford University Press.

Explains the origin and perpetuation of racial segregation in the South and the historic efforts of those opposed to it.

Woodward, G.S. (1988). *The Cherokees.* Norman: University of Oklahoma Press.

Presents the history of the Cherokee nation and their struggle to maintain culture and sovereignty despite the "trail of tears" and treaty violations.

Wu, C. (Ed.). (1972). *"Chink!" A documentary history of anti-Chinese prejudice in America.* New York, NY: World Publishing.

Reprints speeches, newspaper articles, and cartoons showing anti-Chinese prejudice; mob violence examples are in Chapter 3, "Chinaman's Chance."

Zia, H. (2000). *Asian American dreams: The emergence of an American people.* New York, NY: Farrar, Straus and Giroux.

Provides a personal perspective on the experiences of diverse Asian American groups and their encounters with prejudice and discrimination.

Zinn, H. (2003). *A people's history of the United States.* New York, NY: HarperCollins.

Presents historical events from the perspective of minority groups experiencing the events.

CHAPTER 6

Religion and Oppression: The Struggle for Religious Freedom

"I wish you had a religion, Peter . . . Oh, I don't mean you have to be Orthodox, or believe in heaven and hell and purgatory and things. I just mean some religion. It doesn't matter what. Just to believe in something!"

Anne Frank (1929–1945)

The character of Anne Frank makes her comment about religion in *The Diary of Anne Frank,* a play based on the journal she kept during World War II until the Nazis found her. Her story has frequently been used to introduce students to the horrors of the Holocaust. At the play's end, Anne's father reads her diary and the audience hears Anne say, "In spite of everything, I still believe that people are really good at heart" (Goodrich & Hackett, 1956). Both comments affirm the goodness of humanity, regardless of differences between people. Neither comment seems to be controversial, yet some Christians have demanded that children not read the play because the remark about religion suggests that all religions are equally valid. Usually those who complain believe that one religion, their religion, is the only true faith.

Religious Diversity in Colonial America

Americans have confronted religious controversy since early colonial times when immigrant groups arrived with an array of diverse beliefs and minority faiths contended with the power of a dominant faith to survive. Honoring the principle of **religious freedom/religious liberty**—the right to worship according to one's individual beliefs—has been an ongoing struggle in America, and the history of our efforts to achieve it is the focus of this chapter.

Although religious freedom does not deny an individual's right to disagree with the beliefs and practice of another religion, it does require acceptance of divergent beliefs, as long as they don't infringe on the rights of others. The constitutional separation of church and state principle was established to resolve the problem of diverse faiths in America, and although the principle is appropriate, efforts to achieve religious liberty and the freedom to worship have been a source of dramatic conflict throughout American history.

How did the first colonists deal with religious diversity?

Puritans came to the New World to practice their religion freely, yet they had no intention of allowing others the same freedom. When Anne Hutchinson expressed religious sentiments contrary to Puritan teaching, she was excommunicated and then exiled in 1637. Roger Williams was exiled as well because he advocated respect for all religious faiths and for separation of church from state, a principle not inherent in either Puritan cultural heritage or that of other European immigrants. To reestablish Old World practices, dominant religious groups such as the Anglicans in Massachusetts expected their faith to be designated the **established church** of their colony and to be supported by an allotment of local tax dollars. Miller (1976) described this perspective: "The established religion with its educated ministers and stately rituals was an important element in creating or re-creating the world they left behind" (p. 26).

English colonists discovered that it was difficult to create an established church in the New World. Parishioners wishing to take care of their families could not afford to give their churches much financial support; therefore, the need for support from colonial governments was greater than had been required in England, which placed a significant fiscal burden on scarce colonial revenues. Furthermore, immigrants represented diverse faiths—Presbyterians, Quakers, Baptists—who were resentful when colonial tax revenues were expended to support a church to which they did not belong.

Religious resentment was mutual. Northern colony Puritans particularly disliked Quakers because of their ecstatic worship and their practice of allowing women to be church leaders. In Massachusetts, blasphemy laws were enacted to force Quakers out, threatening them with death if they returned. When they did return, authorities promptly arrested them; four Quakers were executed between 1659 and 1661. The executions stopped only because authorities in Britain were embarrassed, insisting that Quakers be sent to London for proper trials (Miller, 1976).

Most American colonies enacted blasphemy laws directed at those who did not belong to the colony's majority faith. Blasphemy was defined as an individual denying the truth and authority of the Bible. If anyone denied the divinity of Christ he could be executed or at least lose his property. Although violating blasphemy laws usually did not result in death, punishments could be quite severe, especially for freethinkers and atheists. According to a 1699 Maryland law, blasphemers, typically people who were using language that degraded Christ, the Apostles, or the Holy Trinity, were to be branded with a "B" for a first offense, have a hole burned through their tongue with a red-hot iron for a second offense, and have their property confiscated for a third offense. In a humanitarian gesture, some colonies allowed blasphemers to avoid punishment by publicly asking to be forgiven (Myers, 1960).

As colonies designated "established churches," blasphemy laws also required ministers from other churches to register as "dissenters" and agree to practice only after receiving colonial approval. Dissenting ministers sometimes refused to register and preached whenever they wished; however, there were consequences. In 1771, a sheriff accompanied by an Anglican minister disrupted a church service by arresting the Baptist minister, taking him to a nearby field and whipping him (Waldman, 2006). Being a minority faith, Baptist ministers were often arrested, sometimes with an effect opposite of what was intended. At one point when Baptist ministers were being aggressively pursued, arrested, and jailed for unauthorized preaching, the number of Baptist converts increased dramatically (Miller, 1976). Conversion efforts were customarily focused on those colonists who attended but were not members of a church or on those not attending a church, a majority in the colonies.

By 1775, more than 150 years since the first colonists arrived, approximately 10% of Americans were church members (Lippy, 1994). Although groups such as Puritans and Quakers came to the colonies to plant the seeds of faith in fertile ground, most immigrants came instead to escape physical destitution and moral despair. They hoped to achieve material success: to own their own land and to provide for their families. They wanted a better life on earth, not in heaven. Preachers from minority faiths focused on those who attended church with little enthusiasm or those who may have found a better material life but longed for satisfaction of spiritual needs. The competition for converts intensified the desire for religious freedom.

How did the colonies promote the concept of religious freedom?

Because of the influence of Roger Williams, William Penn, and Lord Baltimore, the colonies of Rhode Island, Pennsylvania, and Maryland declared religious freedom for those of any faith. Puritans regarded their faith as a "light to the world," so they often forced people to accept it. Williams argued that people could not develop true faith through coercion, and expressed the need for a "wall of separation between the garden of the church and the wilderness of the world" (Nord, 1995, p. 135). With a Baptist majority in Rhode Island, the arrival of Quakers tested the colony's commitment to religious freedom. Williams personally disliked Quakers and attacked them in his writings, but general tolerance prevailed as religious freedom was maintained, attracting some intolerant Puritans and a small group of Jews settling in Newport. Quakerism eventually became the dominant religion in Rhode Island (Miller, 1976).

William Penn believed that God spoke directly to individuals through the conscience and that this was the basis for a commitment to religious freedom. Penn undertook deliberate efforts to bring to Pennsylvania people from diverse faiths: Anabaptists, Presbyterians, Puritans, Roman Catholics, and others who had no religious conviction. Pennsylvania was the first colony to experiment with the idea of denominational churches instead of an established church; no church received state assistance, nor did the state interfere in church affairs. Members of a denomination were not expected to withdraw from the world but to participate in it.

As might be expected, Pennsylvania's "holy experiment" was not without problems. Because Penn was a Quaker, Quakers had more government influence than other denominations, and for a time they functioned as an informal established church. Although Quaker dominance caused some friction, compared to other colonies, Pennsylvania and Rhode Island provided the clearest alternative to the Old World tradition of state support for an established church.

> (If) Papists and Protestants, Jews and Turks, may be embarked in one ship . . . none of the Papists, Protestants, Jews or Turks (should) be forced to come to the ship's prayer or worship nor compelled from their own particular prayer or worship, if they practice any.
>
> **Roger Williams (1603–1683)**

Founded by Lord Baltimore, Maryland was originally intended as a refuge for English Catholics. The principle of religious freedom was self-serving because Catholics constituted a minority even among the first contingent settling Maryland, and Catholicism remained a minority faith throughout the colonial period. Still, Baltimore's commitment to religious tolerance attracted immigrants from diverse faiths. But Maryland's experiment was not successful: The Church of England became its established church in 1702. Because three other faiths—Anabaptists, Presbyterians, and Quakers—had more members, the Church of England was established on condition that religious tolerance would be maintained. Such tolerance was reserved for the currently residing religious groups; incoming Jews and Unitarians were not allowed to settle in Maryland at that time (Hudson, 1973).

How was the principle of religious freedom established in all the colonies?

As the mid-eighteenth century approached, a significant event (later termed the "Great Awakening") promoted the principle of religious freedom, beginning with ideas in the widely read writings of Jonathan Edwards and other New England ministers. Concerned about the "extraordinary dullness" of people's faith, Edwards challenged individuals to demonstrate personal commitment to their faith in their everyday lives, and he spoke of the necessity of faith being emotional as well as rational. Edwards argued that we can be told honey is sweet, but to taste honey results in a knowledge that is "direct, intuitive, certain, and rests upon experience that can be neither doubted nor denied" (Gaustad & Schmidt, 2002, p. 59). Edwards believed that such "knowledge" was the substance of genuine faith.

In 1740, English preacher George Whitefield presented his similar challenge to colonial people, with dramatic results. (See Figure 6.1.) Although Protestant ministers throughout the colonies invited him, Whitefield avoided churches, preferring to speak in open fields. His sermons stimulated people's emotions as much as their intellect, and audi-

FIGURE 6.1
Whitefield's impact on colonial America is commemorated in this statue on the University of Pennsylvania campus.
Source: Photo courtesy of the University of Pennsylvania.

ences responded enthusiastically. Whitefield insisted that being a Christian was not about belonging to a particular church, but being committed to faith and demonstrating that commitment in everyday life. Ironically, his sermons resulted in a huge increase in church attendance and church members. Nord (1995) describes a sermon in Philadelphia where Whitefield looked up to the sky and shouted:

> Father Abraham, whom have you in heaven? Any Episcopalians? No! Any Presbyterians? No! Any Independents or Methodists? No, no, no! Who have you there? . . . We don't know those names here. All who are here are Christians . . . Then God help us to forget party names and become Christians in deed and truth. (p. 103)

The impact of the Great Awakening on religious freedom was that it denied the significance of differences between Protestant sects. Prior to the Great Awakening, Protestants belonged to one sect or another, each defining itself as the "true faith." This **sectarian** view of Christianity gave way to a consensus about what it meant to be Christian: accepting others, doing good deeds, and ignoring theological controversy. The Great Awakening replaced a sectarian approach to Christianity with a **denominational** view based on the perception of a singular Protestant church that is called—denominated—by many different names such as Anglican, Lutheran, or Baptist. Although the denominational view united Protestants, Catholics were not included.

The Emerging Concept of Religious Freedom

In the mid-eighteenth century, Europeans were making significant discoveries based on scientific inquiry. Isaac Newton alone was responsible for discovering the principles of gravitation and light; he also developed differential calculus and even had time to invent the reflecting telescope. The dissemination of ideas and inventions during this era, eventually called "the Enlightenment," created an increased respect for science and a diminished belief in miracles and the supernatural. Some argued that religious truths, like scientific truths, would be discovered by human reason, not through divine revelation. This thinking led to the birth of **Deism,** a

> I do not believe in the creed professed by the Jewish church, by the Roman church, by the Greek Church, by the Turkish church, by the Protestant church nor by any church that I know of. My own mind is my own church.
>
> **Thomas Paine (1737–1809)**

religious philosophy based on rationality that was devoid of mysticism. Deists acknowledged that God created the universe but insisted that human beings must use their intellects to understand the rational principles by which the universe functions. In response to the increased emphasis on rationality and the scientific method as the preferred means of ascertaining truth, many intellectuals rejected all religious faiths. Although some American colonists declared themselves **atheists,** denying the existence of God, the religious philosophy of Deism was more appealing than atheism to Christian intellectuals in the colonies.

What was the relationship between Deism and Christianity?

Deism dismissed much of what constituted traditional Christian beliefs. Deists believed God created the world and a system of natural laws that governed it. Although they believed that God would reward or punish the soul after death, they did not believe that God was an active force in the everyday world. Thomas Jefferson and Benjamin Franklin were among many who were attracted to Deism as a religious philosophy. Although Deists denied the divinity of Christ, they tended to admire his moral teachings; therefore, many Deists attended churches of various denominations while others never went to church. Although Deist views were not popular among the general public, the principles of Deism influenced several people who would write the documents that transformed the thirteen colonies into the United States of America. Curiously, these "enlightened" founders included little about religion in the Constitution.

Why was there so little reference to religion in the original Constitution?

Although the majority of men responsible for writing the U.S. Constitution were Protestant and of European descent, they chose to defy their European traditions and create the first secular government. For centuries, the governments of most European nations claimed to derive their authority from God; therefore, the state had both the right and the responsibility to intrude into religious issues and attempt to resolve religious controversies, usually in favor of a majority faith and against minority faiths. The Articles of Confederation had continued that tradition by referring to "the Great Governor of the World" (Jacoby, 2005, p. 30), but the authors of the U.S. Constitution cited "We the People" as the source of the government's power and authority, deliberately excluding any reference to God. When challenged to explain this omission, Alexander Hamilton's tongue-in-cheek response was "We forgot" (Chernow, 2004, p. 235).

> The government of the United States of America is not in any sense founded on the Christian Religion.
>
> **John Adams (1735–1826)**

They did not forget. When the delegates met in Philadelphia in 1787, they were well aware of the debate that had recently occurred in Virginia. In the early 1780s, Patrick Henry unsuccessfully lobbied to have Christianity declared Virginia's established religion. In 1784, he introduced a resolution calling for a tax on Virginians to promote Christianity but allowing them to designate their denomination or even a particular church as the recipient of their tax dollars. Those belonging to no church could contribute their taxes to a general education fund. This resolution gained wide support, even receiving George Washington's endorsement. On November 11, the Virginia legislature voted 47 to 32 in favor of the resolution, but the legislative session was dismissed shortly after this vote.

The opposition to this resolution and the legislation it called for was led by James Madison, soon to be a major contributor in drafting the U.S. Constitution. Madison saw the dangers inherent if such legislation would be enacted, and he wrote a pamphlet to describe them. Waldman (2006) cited Madison's major concern: "Who does not see that the same authority which can establish Christianity, in exclusion of all other Religions, may establish with the same ease any particular sect of Christians, in exclusion of all other Sects?" (p. 36). Madison's pamphlet was widely distributed and generated widespread support for his arguments. By the time the Virginia legislature reconvened, they were inundated with petitions and documents espousing staunch opposition to establishing Christianity as Virginia's state religion, some even coming from Christians—especially evangelical Christians.

Based on the previous passage of his resolution, Patrick Henry brought a bill to the Virginia legislature to establish Christianity as the state religion, but it was soundly defeated. Later, the legislators discussed Thomas Jefferson's "Statute for Religious Freedom," which they modified slightly before passing, making this legislation not only state law, but also a model for other states and for the first amendment that guaranteed religious freedom in the United States.

Why wasn't religious freedom guaranteed in the Constitution?

By the time of the Revolutionary War in 1776, four colonies had guaranteed the right of people to worship as they chose: Rhode Island, Pennsylvania, Delaware, and New Jersey. The Church of England remained the established church in other colonies; however, during the war one colony after another ceased providing church support. By the war's end, only Massachusetts, New Hampshire, Connecticut, and Virginia continued to have established churches. In 1786, the new nation was still struggling to function under its first constitution, entitled the Articles of Confederation, when the delegates met in Philadelphia to write the new Constitution. Especially after what had just transpired in Virginia, most of them did not question the issue of religious freedom, nor did they appear interested in debating it.

The delegates did debate other issues, however, such as what civil rights should be granted to those who were not Protestant. New Jersey's constitution stated that every officeholder had to be Protestant, a provision not revised until 1844. Some states required all those seeking public office to recite an oath that they had no allegiance to any foreign power—"ecclesiastic as well as civil" (Myers, 1960, p. 46). Of course, a devout Catholic could not take such an oath, which was the reason it was required. Some states merely demanded that an officeholder be a Christian; Maryland, which eventually permitted Jews to settle, stood alone as the only state that allowed Jews to vote and hold public office. Obviously, Jefferson's wall between church and state had yet to be built.

As they wrote the Constitution, the authors affirmed the principle of religious freedom by stating, "No religious Test shall ever be required as a Qualification to any Office or public Trust under the United States" (Article VI). When completed, this was the only reference to religion, and it was not widely supported. At the debate over ratifying the Constitution in North Carolina, a minister protested that Article VI was "an invitation for Jews and pagans of every kind to come among us" (Jacoby, 2005, p. 30).

To secure consensus for the Constitution, the question of having an established church was left to each state. Because religious freedom was a well-established principle in most states, the authors may have thought there was no need to include such a statement until it became obvious that several amendments would be necessary before enough states would ratify the Constitution. Eck (2001) describes how Jefferson used the "Statute for Religious Freedom" he had written for Virginia's legislature in 1786 when he drafted the First Amendment's explicit guarantee of religious freedom.

Nord (1995) argued that much of the impetus for religious freedom stemmed from the Enlightenment belief that "natural reason, operating in a free culture, was the way to the truth" (p. 108). Yet most church leaders supported the First Amendment for similar reasons, especially evangelical Christians. They were concerned about separating church and state because they had already been persecuted and harassed. Evangelicals equated religious persecution with political persecution and insisted that Christ called for separating church and state in the statement: "render unto Caesar that which belongs to Caesar." Jefferson's letter espousing a "wall of separation between church and state" was written to Connecticut evangelicals who were pleased by his comments, saying to him in response, "Religion is at all times and places a matter between God and individuals" (Waldman, 2006, p. 38). Ministers such as Ezra Stiles believed that through competition, truth would prevail: "Here Deism will have its full chance; nor need libertines . . . complain of being overcome by any weapons but the gentle, powerful ones of argument and truth" (Hudson, 1973, p. 110).

Did the First Amendment establish religious freedom in the new nation?

Although the freedom to worship according to one's personal religious beliefs was guaranteed in the Bill of Rights, it was guaranteed in principle more than in practice. Of the two states still supporting an established church, Connecticut ended its tax subsidies to the Congregational Church in 1817, and Massachusetts did the same in 1833 (Myers, 1960). Yet having a minority faith could still affect one's political rights. As the Constitution was being ratified by the thirteen states, only three of them—Pennsylvania, Maryland, and Delaware—permitted Catholics to vote. Within five years of the Constitution's ratification, three more states—South Carolina, Georgia, and New York—granted the vote to its Catholic citizens, and eventually the remaining states did the same (Myers, 1960).

Because of their numbers, Jews exercised limited political influence, encountering intolerance early in the colonial period when Jewish immigrants were forced to depart from Boston as soon as they arrived. More than three decades after the Constitution was approved, Maryland was the only state where Jews could vote or hold public office. During the Civil War, General Ulysses S. Grant expelled Jews from areas he had reclaimed by military conquest for the United States; however, President Lincoln rescinded Grant's order (Miller, 1976). North Carolina granted civil rights to Jews in 1868; New Hampshire granted Jews the right to vote in 1876.

A Challenge to the Separation of Church and State

In 1810, Congress mandated Sunday mail service. Conservative Christian leaders lobbied aggressively against it, denouncing Sunday mail delivery as a sacrilege, but business leaders insisted on the necessity of uninterrupted mail. In 1828, the controversy came to the Senate Committee on the Post Office and Post Roads. Kentucky senator Richard M. Johnson, a war hero and devout Baptist, chaired the committee, yet in his report to Congress, he declared unequivocally that it would be unconstitutional for the federal government to engage in policy or practice that betrayed a preference for the Christian Sabbath. In the report, Johnson emphasized the history of religious persecution and intolerance that had created the need for a line separating church and state, and that "the line cannot be too strongly drawn" (Jacoby, 2005, p. 31). In the 1840s, the telegraph ended the reliance of business on daily mail service, but the principle of separation of church and state had been upheld.

Was any group actively persecuted for their religious beliefs?

Religious freedom was violently denied to the followers of Mormonism, the Church of Jesus Christ of Latter-Day Saints, which was founded on the revelations of Joseph Smith in the early 1800s. After his *Book of Mormon* was published in 1830, Smith found followers captivated by his new vision of the past and his responses to major religious controversies of the day. He aroused animosity among traditional Christian denominations by his promotion of polygamy and other ideas deemed unconventional and unacceptable in American society. Smith's first church in Ohio was not welcomed, and when the members moved to Missouri, they were attacked and forced to leave, eventually settling in Nauvoo, Illinois. They lived there for only a few years before Smith was arrested and incarcerated at nearby Carthage, where a masked mob broke into his cell, and shot and killed him. Miller (1976) declared, "The rise of Mormonism tested the American dedication to religious liberty, and the nation ultimately failed the test" (p. 111).

FIGURE 6.2 The Mormon Trail

To escape persecution, the Mormons headed west and did not stop until they had left the United States and reached the safety of Mexican territory.

Source: © by Intellectual Reserve, Inc.

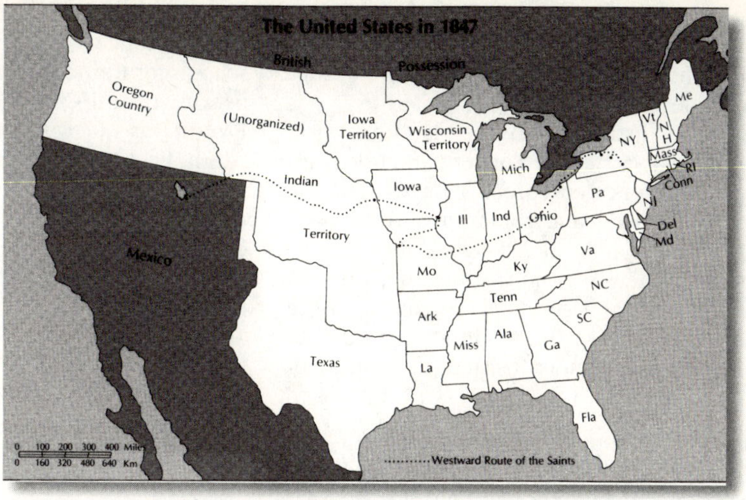

When Brigham Young was chosen to replace Smith, he was convinced that the Mormons would not be granted religious freedom anywhere in the United States, so he asked them to follow him "to a far distant region . . . where bigotry, intolerance, and insatiable oppression lose their power" (Gaustad & Schmidt, 2002, p. 178). In 1847, Young and his followers began an ambitious journey of a thousand miles, finally stopping to settle on land that belonged to Mexico. (See Figure 6.2.) One year later, as the Mexican-American War ended, the Great Salt Lake Valley where the Mormons had settled became part of the United States. Because there was no one close enough to persecute the Mormons, they successfully populated the territory of Utah and applied for statehood. Their application was denied six times until 1897, when they changed their state constitution to renounce polygamy (Kosmin & Lachman, 1993).

Religious freedom was also not extended to those who rejected religious beliefs. Atheists in Virginia could be arrested for publicly professing that God did not exist. In 1833, Abner Kneeland was arrested and incarcerated in Massachusetts for questioning the divinity of Jesus, his miracles, and his resurrection. Kneeland was convicted under the state's blasphemy law and sentenced to sixty days in jail; however, his conviction resulted in vigorous protests. Kneeland was the last person convicted of blasphemy in Massachusetts, although the law was not repealed for many years (Miller, 1976).

The Rise and Fall of Anti-Catholicism

In contrast to the slow but steady growth of members in Protestant churches, membership in the Catholic Church increased dramatically. By 1850, the number of Catholics in the United States had expanded from several hundred thousand to nearly 2 million. Between 1820 and 1865, of approximately 2 million Irish immigrants to the United States, over a million were Catholic (Kosmin & Lachman, 1993). Because of its assistance to Irish immigrants, the New York City political and labor organization known as Tammany Hall became a powerful force influencing the city and state of New York, which intensified anti-Catholic sentiments.

What was the impact of large numbers of Catholic immigrants?

Immigrants have almost always provoked hostility in some Americans, but the arrival of so many Catholics fueled Protestant fears and created an atmosphere of suspicion and distrust. Because the Catholic Church had persecuted, tortured, and even killed those who defied its authority in the past, Protestants believed that Catholics would not hesitate to employ any tactic that would convert Protestants to the Catholic faith. Several popular novels, including *The Awful Disclosures of Maria Monk,* described Protestant women being kidnapped and confined in underground cells in convents and subjected to unspeakable tortures.

Following a fistfight between laborers at a Charlestown, Massachusetts, convent and brickyard workmen, the workmen spread rumors that the convent had imprisoned a woman just as the novels suggested. Although published results of an investigation said there was no truth to the rumor, a mob gathered and set fire to the convent. No police or militia appeared. Ten fire engines responded to the call, but the fire brigades insisted they could not act without orders from a magistrate, so they watched as the convent was destroyed. A meeting of Protestants called by the mayor of Boston produced a formal statement denouncing the mob's actions, but the Catholic Church never received compensation for its losses (Myers, 1960).

> We have just enough religion to make us hate. But not enough to make us love one another.
>
> **Jonathan Swift (1667–1745)**

Why was hostility directed against Catholics?

The 1830s and 1840s was the era of Native American and Know-Nothing parties promoting **anti-Catholicism** and anti-immigrant sentiments. The Know-Nothings dedicated themselves to reducing a perceived growth of Catholic power and influence. Anti-Catholic prejudices were also reflected in public school textbooks in which priests were depicted as living in luxury, oblivious to the poor and hungry, and the Catholic Church was described as the enemy of freedom and knowledge because of its history of religious persecution and its suppression of the Bible (Miller, 1976). It is not surprising that at this time the Catholic Church felt compelled to create an alternative school system, increasing Protestant animosity toward Catholics.

Protestants were not opposed to separate schools for Catholics, but in 1840, Bishop Hughes of New York created controversy when he petitioned the New York Public Schools Society for funds to support Catholic schools. Hughes argued that separate schools for Catholic children had become necessary because of anti-Catholic materials in public schools. Protestants objected to using tax dollars to teach "Catholic dogma" and accused the bishop of trying to undermine public schools. Hughes provided excerpts from textbooks that ridiculed Catholicism, including one book in which the Catholic Church was accused of encouraging drunkenness to maintain its hold on church members who would reject the "Romish religion" if they could only think rationally (Myers, 1960). Although the New York Public Schools Society denied Hughes's petition for funds, they agreed to remove anti-Catholic content from textbooks and to exclude from school libraries books that clearly promoted anti-Catholic prejudice. Although this seemed to solve the problem in New York, growing anti-Catholic sentiment would lead to the shocking events of the Philadelphia Bible Riots.

What were the Philadelphia Bible Riots?

In 1844, the Philadelphia School Board approved the substitution of the Douay (Catholic) Bible for Catholic students when Bible reading was required. The Native American Party called for a meeting in Kensington, an Irish Catholic district in Philadelphia, to protest the use of the Catholic Bible in public schools. The meeting provoked area residents, who attacked participants and forced the meeting to end. Native American Party leaders insisted on a second meeting in Kensington, which resulted in violence that left one person dead and fifty wounded.

The following day, a large crowd gathered to approve a resolution in support of teaching the Protestant version of the Bible in public schools. The meeting soon became uncontrollable, and when the mob heard shots fired from a nearby building, they set fire to that building and went on a rampage. Troops were called in, but before they could restore order, several homes had burned, eight men were dead, and sixteen were wounded. The night was quiet, and there was no further violence the next morning. Most of the soldiers withdrew.

By midafternoon, a Protestant mob gathered once again, setting fire to a Catholic Church and a nearby row of houses whose tenants were Irish.

Troops were recalled, but before they arrived, the mob attacked another church. This time the police surrounded the church, but the mob drove them off with bricks and stones and set fire to that church and a Catholic school; then the fire spread to frame houses nearby. The troop commander summoned to Philadelphia declared martial law. Property losses from the riots included forty-five homes, two churches, and a school. Violence flared again a month later, and by the time the Philadelphia Bible Riots were finally over, 58 people had been killed and 140 wounded. The Native American Party blamed the Irish for the deaths and injuries and even for the destruction of churches and homes in Irish neighborhoods (Myers, 1960; Ravitch, 1999). Although anti-Catholic sentiment would remain strong for another decade, other issues and events would command the nation's attention.

What caused anti-Catholic sentiments in the United States to subside?

Nord (1995) concluded, "The politics of race and the Civil War put the politics of anti-Catholicism to rest" (pp. 73–74). Although the Great Awakening unified Protestant churches, they were split over the slavery issue. During the Civil War, Catholic soldiers fought and died as bravely as the Protestant soldiers beside them, and anti-Catholic sentiments declined. After the war, anti-Catholic prejudice still existed and flared up on occasion, yet it never reached the level that fostered the rise of the Native American and Know-Nothing parties. Another factor in the decline of anti-Catholic prejudice after the Civil War was that the Catholic Church was no longer the only serious opponent for Protestant churches. Religious diversity in the United States was about to increase dramatically.

How did religious diversity increase following the Civil War?

After the Civil War, immigration to the United States surpassed prewar levels. By 1900, there were 75 million Americans, 25 million of whom were foreign-born adults and their children. The number of Roman Catholics in the United States increased from 2 million in 1850 to 4 million in 1870 to 12 million by 1900. Although Protestants continued to be the dominant group, a third of Americans who claimed church membership in 1920 were members of the Catholic Church (Hudson, 1973).

Catholic immigrants came from Germany, Ireland, Poland, Italy, and Czechoslovakia, their ethnic diversity creating tension in the church. Not only did they speak different languages, but also they had different traditions and customs related to their worship. The church's inability to resolve ethnic differences led to the creation of the Polish National Catholic Church in the 1890s and the Lithuanian National Catholic Church in 1914. Protestant churches faced similar challenges. The majority of Protestant immigrants were Lutherans whose diversity resulted in Finnish, Icelandic, Swedish, Danish, German, and Norwegian Lutheran churches. According to Hudson (1973), there were at least twenty-four different kinds of Lutheran churches by 1900.

Diversity also resulted from missionaries proselytizing Native Americans and former slaves. Minimal efforts to reach either group had been made prior to the Civil War because both groups had been perceived as heathen. The Great Awakening had generated some enthusiasm for seeking Indian converts, but Native Americans who accepted Christianity usually blended new beliefs with their old ones. Following the Civil War, the federal government banned many tribal religions and provided missionaries with funding to build schools for Indian children. Protestants often established off-reservation boarding schools, whereas Catholics tended to establish boarding schools and day schools on reservations (Hendry, 2003).

Although Christian ministers were willing to evangelize and recruit slaves into the faith, many slave owners were reluctant to have their captives converted. They approved of conversion only if ministers emphasized the need for the slaves to submit to both divine and earthly authorities with the promise of eternal life as their reward for enduring slavery in this life (Lippy, 1994). After the Civil War, Protestant missionaries actively recruited the 3.5 million newly freed slaves. Former slaves who were Christians no longer wanted to attend the churches their owners had forced them to attend, especially when the church members still expected former slaves to sit in the back seats. Separate churches for freedmen were established, the majority being Baptist with Methodists a distant second. By 1916, 43% of blacks were members of a church, a higher percentage than for the white population (Hudson, 1973).

As racial and ethnic groups added to the diversity, so did the creation of new faiths. Mary Baker Eddy responded to the growing importance of scientific research by founding Church of Christ, Scientist. Eddy spoke of an Eternal Mind as the source of life, and believed that disease was a consequence of mental error. Christian Scientists sought to overcome the illusions that have been the source of all human troubles (Lippy, 1994).

William Miller was abandoned by "Millerites" in 1844 when his prediction about Jesus returning did not come true. Many of his former followers turned to Ellen Harmon White, whose spiritual revelations included hygienic practices and dietary restrictions for the faithful to ensure the return of Jesus; White's followers became Seventh-Day Adventists. Adding to the complexity of diverse faiths in the late nineteenth century, was the fact that all immigrants were not simply Christian.

What non-Christian religions were included among immigrants?

Immigrants to the United States included members of non-Christian religious groups. On the West Coast, Buddhists among Chinese and Japanese immigrants established a Young Men's Buddhist Association in 1898. On the East Coast, 1.5 million Jews came to America between 1880 and 1905 to escape anti-Semitism in Russia, Poland, Rumania, and Austro-Hungary. Hudson (1973) cites an adviser to the czar predicting the consequences of new Russian policies: "One-third of the Jews will emigrate, one-third will be baptized, and one-third will starve" (p. 332).

Diversity increased within the Jewish community as well. In 1880, most of the 250,000 Jews in the United States were descendants of German-speaking Jews from central Europe affiliated with reform Judaism; Jews emigrating later from Eastern Europe were more likely to be orthodox than reform. According to Hudson (1973), more than 3 million Jews had immigrated by 1920, with orthodox Jews outnumbering reform Jews. The largest Jewish group, larger than the total number of all religious Jews combined, comprised those not affiliated with any synagogue; many of them were Zionists whose activity was more likely to be political than religious.

America also experienced an increase in people professing no religion. Darwin's theory of evolution and other scientific advances caused many people to question the validity of religious faith. English scientist Thomas Huxley declared himself an **agnostic,** believing that one could neither prove nor disprove the existence of God. Lawyer and orator Robert Ingersoll published *Why I Am an Agnostic* in 1896 and traveled across America questioning many aspects of Christianity. Still, some scholars reconciled Darwin's ideas with religion by believing in God, just not in specific denominational doctrines. The Christian majority reacted by punishing those who strayed from conventional beliefs as well as nonbelievers. In 1878, Alexander Winchell publicly rejected the Genesis version of creation, and Vanderbilt University trustees asked him to resign. When Winchell refused, they abolished his position. In 1886, James Woodrow was removed from his faculty position at Columbia Theological Seminary for advocating the possibility of reconciling Darwin's ideas with those of the Bible (Hudson, 1973).

> A believer is a bird in a cage: a freethinker is an eagle parting the clouds with tireless wing.
>
> **Robert Ingersoll (1833–1899)**

Did increasing numbers of non-Christians cause anti-Catholic prejudice to diminish?

Although racial prejudice became more dominant than religious prejudice after the Civil War, a large Catholic immigration fueled anti-Catholic attitudes. Protestant leaders called for tolerance, yet others said tolerance meant a lack of religious commitment and an indifference to the true faith, and urged Protestants not to give equal status to any other religion.

Forced to disband by federal troops during Reconstruction, the Ku Klux Klan was revived in 1915. In their efforts to promote and maintain white supremacy in the United States, the Klan employed tactics of intimidation including threats and violence. Although their primary targets were blacks and foreigners, as a Christian group, its

FIGURE 6.3
The Ku Klux Klan had its highest membership when the group sponsored this 1925 march in front of the nation's capitol.

Source: Library of Congress, Prints and Photographs Division

members were also hostile to Catholics and Jews. Membership in the Klan increased every year for ten years, peaking at 2 million in 1925. (See Figure 6.3.) It fell to 100,000 by 1928. At a 1941 rally in Charleston, the Grand Dragon of North Carolina was heckled and booed by many of the 3,000 who attended (Myers, 1960). The last time the Klan's anti-Catholicism would be seen on the national stage was in the presidential election of 1928.

How did the 1928 election demonstrate anti-Catholic prejudice?

The Democratic Party nominated Alfred E. Smith, the first Catholic to run for president. Some political and religious leaders hailed the nomination as evidence of growing religious tolerance; others saw it as a threat to the social order. The Klan and other anti-Catholic organizations insisted that the Vatican was directing Smith's campaign with a Jesuit committee assigned to persuade Protestants to ignore Smith's religion as an issue. Presbyterians were urged to vote for the Republican candidate. Methodists were urged to vote for the man who prayed the same way they did. Myers (1960) quoted an excerpt from an anti-Catholic magazine claiming that Smith would get not only the Catholic vote, but also "the Jew and Negro vote . . . gamblers, the red-light and dope-ring vote . . . the Jew-Jesuit movie gang (vote) who want sex films and Sunday shows to coin millions through the corruption of youth" (p. 268).

Although anti-Catholic prejudice contributed to Smith's defeat, it is not clear how large a role it played. Democrats were the minority party, the economy was doing well, and Republican candidate Herbert Hoover was widely respected. Despite the anti-Catholic assault, Smith received 40% of the vote, more than the Protestant Democratic candidates had received in the two previous elections (34% in 1920, 28% in 1924). Smith had a higher percentage of votes than a majority of Democrats running for Congress in that election (Hudson, 1973).

After Franklin Roosevelt was elected president in 1932, Catholic participation in national politics became common, and the question of whether a Catholic could be elected president was answered in 1960 when Americans chose John F. Kennedy. It is possible that Kennedy's election was not so much a measure of increased religious tolerance as it was an indication of what has been called the "Americanization of religion." Since World War II, attitudes of

American Catholics gradually diverged from a strict recognition of Roman Catholic Church doctrine and more closely allied with attitudes of the Protestant majority. By the 1990s, polls documented Catholic attitudes as similar to Protestant attitudes on such issues as abortion, birth control, ordination of women, and marriage of priests (Kosmin & Lachman, 1993).

> Anti Semitism is a noxious weed that should be cut out. It has no place in America.
>
> **William Howard Taft (1857–1930)**

How were Jews affected by the "Americanization of religion"?

In the late 1880s, Jews contended that they should be regarded as another denomination and accepted in the same spirit as Methodists, Baptists, or Lutherans. They were unsuccessful partly because at that time Jews were defined as a race more than a religion, a transformation that began in 1451 when the King of Castile endorsed a blood purity statute (*limpieza de sangre*), declaring that Jews who converted to Christianity could not hold office in the Catholic Church. Carroll (2001) explained that the concern for blood purity was "a shift from a religious definition of Jewishness to a racial one" (p. 347). By the nineteenth century, the transformation in Europe of societal perceptions of Jews from religious to racial was complete. Nazi Germany could justify arresting Jews who had converted to Christianity because "once born a Jew, always a Jew" (Wegner, 2002, p. 152).

Anti-Semitism in America

By 1870, American public school textbooks referred to Jews as "a race" with traditional stereotypes of Jews as greedy, selfish, and manipulating. Jews were described as unethical entrepreneurs who tried to monopolize certain professions and as the devious power behind the throne in many European countries (Miller, 1976). In 1879, the term **anti-Semitism** was employed for the first time by a German journalist to express his opposition to the Jewish "race." In his essay, Wilhelm Marr made the paradoxical argument that although Jews were inferior to Aryans, they were a threat to Aryan world dominance (Carroll, 2001). Reacting against such pervasive stereotypes, one Jewish writer complained, "In the popular mind, the Jew is never judged as an individual, but as a specimen of a whole race whose members are identically of the same kind" (Eck, 2001, p. 303). This judgment would continue in the "popular mind" for many more decades.

From 1890 to 1914, Jews accounted for 10% of all immigrants. With increased numbers of Jews in America, anti-Semitism was at least as strong as earlier anti-Catholicism. Ironically, despite their experience of oppression, Catholics joined Protestants in vilifying Jews. In the popular press, Eck (2001) found Jews presented as undesirable aliens who could not assimilate because they were "incapable of grasping American ideals" (p. 50), although many Jews refuted the view by achieving extraordinary success, especially in higher education. As the number of Jews at Harvard escalated from 6% in 1908 to 22% in 1922, the president of Harvard proposed establishing a quota for the number of Jews Harvard would accept. Faculty rejected his plan, but Harvard still limited the number of Jews for many decades. Other colleges established quotas for Jewish enrollment at anywhere from 3% to 16% (Dinnerstein, 1994).

In what ways was anti-Semitism promoted?

Anti-Semitism had several popular advocates. In the 1920s, one was Henry Ford. In his role as publisher of a weekly newspaper, *The Dearborn Independent,* Ford printed the text of "The Protocols of the Elders of Zion," which documented the activities of a Jewish conspiracy plotting a revolution to undermine Christian civilization and establish Jewish supremacy throughout the world. Ford's popularity made it likely that his readers would take his warning seriously. In a poll taken in 1923, *Collier's* magazine reported that 260,000 people—over a third of those polled—endorsed Ford to run for president (Ribuffo, 1997).

Shortly after Ford published "Protocols," the document was exposed as a forgery concocted in the late 1890s by Russian loyalists supporting the czar. In response to this revelation and to a legal action for slander brought by a Jewish businessman, Ford wrote a letter of apology, promising not to publish anti-Semitic articles again, but the damage had been done. Ford ceased publishing his newspaper, yet he continued to maintain and express anti-Semitic attitudes. In 1938, Ford traveled to Germany to receive a medal from Adolf Hitler in honor of his anti-Semitic actions, and two years later in England during an interview with the *Manchester Guardian*, Ford insisted that "international Jewish bankers" caused World War II (Ribuffo, 1997).

In the 1930s, President Franklin Roosevelt invited many Jews into his cabinet, and over vigorous objections, he appointed a Jew to the Supreme Court, Felix Frankfurter. However, anti-Semitism found a spokesman in a priest named Charles Edward Coughlin. In his popular radio show, Father Coughlin attacked President Roosevelt, communists, and Jews. Although reprimanded for his attacks on the president, church superiors did not criticize Coughlin's anti-Semitism because he disguised it in anti-communist rhetoric (Myers, 1960).

In 1938, Coughlin revealed his anti-Semitic attitudes by reprinting "The Protocols of the Elders of Zion" despite the evidence of its forgery. Nineteen thousand people attended a gathering in Madison Square Garden where Coughlin gave a speech, surrounded by banners declaring "Smash Jewish Communism!" and "Stop Jewish Domination of Christian America!" Coughlin's use of rumor and distortions of fact to castigate Jews was challenged by Jewish groups, denounced by Protestants, and contradicted by his embarrassed superiors in the church. He was forced to abandon his radio program in 1940, but for the next three years, young men belonging to his "Christian Frontier" organization roamed the streets in several large cities, affixing obscene materials to Jewish businesses or synagogues and even assaulting Jews they chanced to encounter (Myers, 1960).

During World War II, anti-Semitism intensified. Dinnerstein (1994) quotes an Irish soldier who was disturbed by the anti-Semitism of soldiers who told him,

> All the Jews stay out of the army, or if they get in, they are given commissions—the President is a Jew—you can't get a defense contract unless you are a Jew—Jews own 80% of the nation's wealth—Jews got us into the war. (p. 137)

> (The Jew) always talks about the equality of all men, without regard of race or color. Those who are stupid begin to believe that.
>
> **Adolf Hitler (1889–1945)**

According to a poll conducted during the war, over half of Jewish soldiers in the armed forces had changed their names to generic American surnames to avoid anti-Semitic remarks from other soldiers. Even Jews in Roosevelt's cabinet were excluded from private clubs catering to people in power. By the end of the war, 58% of Americans agreed with the statement, "Jews have too much power in the United States" (Dinnerstein, 1994, p. 146).

What influence did the Holocaust have on American attitudes?

Learning about the horrors of the Holocaust changed American attitudes toward Jews after World War II. Many returning veterans deplored anti-Semitism and other prejudices they had witnessed. Hollywood produced films exposing the prejudice and bigotry of anti-Semitism in America, and one of them, *Gentleman's Agreement*, won the Oscar for best picture in 1947. Editorials in many newspapers and magazine articles reinforced the idea that anti-Semitism was no longer acceptable in the United States. Although it was in the 1950s that "under God" was added to the Pledge of Allegiance and "In God We Trust" to U.S. currency to emphasize U.S. opposition to "godless communism," being a Catholic, Protestant, or Jew was less important than being someone who believed in the Judeo-Christian God (Fraser, 1999).

In his analysis of religion in America, *Protestant-Catholic-Jew,* sociologist Will Herberg (1955) wrote that Catholics and Jews reflected American attitudes as much as Protestants did. An "Americanization" of religion meant that each faith "regards itself as merely an alternative and variant form of being religious in the American way" (p. 278). Herberg admitted that the majority of Americans were still anti-Semitic, but they knew it was inappropriate to act on their feelings. *Look* magazine reported that Hitler had made anti-Semitism unequivocally disreputable. A series of polls in the 1950s reported Americans expressing increasingly positive attitudes toward Jews. Discrimination against Jews still occurred, especially in such prestigious professions as law and medicine, yet doors had opened, especially to colleges and universities. By 1965, *Time* magazine reported that "anti-Semitism is at an all time low," and that overt expressions of anti-Semitism were "out of fashion" (Dinnerstein, 1994, p. 171). However, a national immigration law was passed in 1965 that would challenge Americans with a new religious dilemma.

The Impact of Immigration Reform on Religious Diversity

The 1924 U.S. immigration law had prohibited Asian immigration, and strict quotas ensured that the majority of American immigrants would be white and Christian. When President Lyndon Johnson signed the Immigration and Nationality Act of 1965, not only did the racial makeup of incoming immigrants change dramatically, but their religious affiliation did as well. From 1960 to 1990, Asians constituted more than 5 million of 15 million immigrants to the United States, and from 1990 to 1999, the Asian population grew 43% to total almost 11 million people. They increased the religious diversity within and outside of Christianity; among them were 4 million Buddhists and enough Korean Christians to form 2,000 congregations. Jainists have established 60 temples and centers and Sikhs have 80 temples (Gaustad & Schmidt, 2002). Of the more than a million Hindus in the United States, 170,000 live in New York City alone. Nationwide, America can claim over 6 million Muslims, more than the number of Presbyterians and equal to the number of Jews (Eck, 2001). There are increasing numbers of children from diverse faiths: About 20% of students attending public school in the United States identify as "religious minorities" (Clark et al., 2002).

Although proportions of those representing different religions have changed, what has not changed is the importance of religion. According to Elshtain (2001), data from the 2000 census report that 90% of Americans believed in God and 70% were members of a church, synagogue, or mosque. To appreciate this variety of faiths, Americans must confront stereotypes. We often make assumptions about an individual's religion based on his or her ethnicity, although there is religious diversity within any religion. An old stereotype is that Irish Americans are Catholic, even though the majority of Irish Americans are not. Most Asian Americans are not Buddhist or Hindu but instead are Christian, as are most Arab Americans, and most American Muslims are not Arabs (Kosmin & Lachman, 1993).

How have Americans responded to the increasing religious diversity?

Unfortunately, recent immigrants continue to encounter prejudice as Americans persist in their past religious animosities and revert to learned stereotypes. Muslim Americans have received the brunt of these negative reactions, in part because they are the largest religious minority in America. With 6 million Muslims now residing in the United States, including 4 million who were born here, Muslims have now surpassed Jews to become the second largest religious group in the nation (McCloud, 2006). But the primary reason for Barrett (2007) reporting that 75% of Muslims have personally experienced or know someone who has encountered anti-Muslim behavior is related to the terrorist activities carried out by extremist members of the Muslim faith. Americans have used the terrorist activities of some Muslims to stereotype all Muslims, including American Muslims. This has especially troubling implications for education, as illustrated by a study assessing how much pre-service teachers knew about the Islamic faith. Taggar (2006) reported the study's finding that one third of the pre-service teachers associated Islam with such negative words as "enemy," "Bin Laden," "terrorist," and "oppression of women." Only 5% of the future teachers said they would make sure their students understood that all Muslims were not terrorists.

Some American Muslims accuse television news programs of perpetuating Muslim stereotypes. Abdo (2006) has argued that: "television news programs (portray) Muslims as the new enemy of the West" (p. 5). This was illustrated following the 1995 bombing of the Murrah Federal Building in Oklahoma city when television broadcasts suggested that it was a terrorist attack and that authorities were pursuing "Middle Eastern-looking" men; the backlash was immediate. Islamic centers across the nation were sites for drive-by shootings and bomb threats. Muslim students on college campuses were assaulted. Muslim parents kept their children home for fear they would be taunted or even assaulted in school.

What the media did not report was the presence of Muslim firefighters rescuing victims of the bombing, Muslim physicians working to save victims' lives, and individual Muslims and Muslim organizations donating money to help the families of the victims. Despite their efforts, Muslims were denied an opportunity to participate in the nationally televised memorial service featuring words of consolation from President Clinton and representatives of Catholic, Jewish, and Protestant faiths.

Similar to the reaction following the Oklahoma City incident, media coverage of the 1996 crash of TWA Flight 800 prompted many Americans to suspect that Muslim terrorists were responsible despite the lack of any evidence to support their suspicions. According to Khan (2004), this was another example of American media promoting the "demonization of Islam . . . and the prejudice, hatred and intolerance it bred" (p. 100). Anti-Muslim behaviors have included arson at mosques in Minneapolis and Quincy, Massachusetts, and a shotgun attack on Muslims in Memphis.

Anti-Muslim activity increased after the destruction of New York City's World Trade Center on 9/11. More than 8,000 Muslim Americans and Arab Americans were immediately interrogated, and within a few weeks, approximately 1200 were incarcerated. This action was called a "preventive detention"; the prisoners were held without charges, they were denied the opportunity to post a bond, and they were not allowed any contact with their families (Abdo, 2006). Two months later, 600 were still held in custody, yet the FBI eventually admitted that they had no evidence linking any of the people incarcerated to terrorist activities. Of the 82,000 Muslim immigrants who were eventually fingerprinted and interrogated under the Patriot Act, officials could only find enough evidence to declare 11 of them as "suspected" terrorists (Lee, 2004). Such actions have caused McCloud (2006) to claim that no other religion has been treated in such fashion in the history of America, noting that, "Even the Christianity of Nazi Germany (was) not demonized but considered an abomination" (p. 6). According to Nimer (2004), in the thirty days following 9/11, Muslims filed 1,700 complaints of harassment and hate crimes. One man drove his car through the plateglass doors of an Ohio mosque, a Texas mosque was firebombed, and mosques were vandalized in Tallahassee, Cleveland, and Seattle. The violence has not been restricted to Muslims; Buddhist and Hindu temples were vandalized in Boston, Houston, and Detroit. An Egyptian businessman who had resided in the United States for twenty years was shot and killed in his California store. He was a Christian.

McCloud (2004) argues that while Muslims have been accused of violence and terrorism, it was the U.S. government that imprisoned Muslims without charging them with a crime, and individual Americans who have violently attacked mosques and Muslims. It is heartening that most Americans reject the violent discriminatory acts of bigots. Neighbors and community advocates for victims of violence directed at religious groups have responded with kindness, sympathy, and offers of support. Positive responses have consistently countered negative actions against recent immigrants of diverse religious faiths. American Muslims have tried to distance themselves from terrorist activities while emphasizing Islam as a religion of peace. In 2005, the Islamic Society of North America disseminated a statement not only condemning extremism and violence, but also calling on all American Muslims to openly denounce such actions (Barrett, 2007). Some Americans have been critical of other American Muslim organizations for not making a similar statement, but the reality is that every major Islamic organization in the United States has issued a statement condemning terrorist violence (Abdo, 2006). If Americans are not aware of this, it is probably because the American media has rarely reported on these proclamations, especially the national media. In addition to denouncing terrorism, Muslims in the United States have recognized the importance of interacting with people to clarify beliefs and practices of the Islamic faith. Smith (2004) cites a Bagby survey of American Muslims reporting that 65% of them had participated in an interfaith activity.

As the United States has become home to believers from diverse faiths, some American individuals and organizations have engaged in activities to recognize this diversity and to promote interactions among members of many faiths. Since 1991, Muslim and Hindu chaplains have joined Protestant, Catholic, and Jewish chaplains to open each session of the House of Representatives and the Senate with invocations. Administrators of the Mall of America in Minneapolis, the largest enclosed shopping facility in the United States, have created an interfaith group called the Mall Area Religious Council to promote interfaith dialogue and conversations between people of different religions and cultures. Is American interfaith support a harbinger of the future as business and community leaders come to terms with the implications of religious diversity? At a Whirlpool manufacturing plant in Nashville, Tennessee, a Muslim employee quit when he was refused permission to perform his midday prayers; those Muslim employees who remained prayed secretly. After a Muslim support group intervened, Whirlpool managers agreed to schedule afternoon coffee breaks to accommodate the Islamic prayer schedule (Eck, 2001).

> The First Amendment has erected a wall between church and state. That wall must be kept high and impregnable.
>
> **Justice Hugo Black (1886–1971)**

Universities and colleges have increasingly promoted interfaith dialogue. Wellesley College developed a Multi-Faith Council, Chapman (CA) University created an All-Faiths Chapel, and Johns Hopkins University instituted an Interfaith and Community Service Center; in each, faiths as diverse as Baha'i, Buddhist, Christian, Jewish, Muslim, and Hindu may come to worship or to talk with members of other faiths. Interfaith discussions not only address commonalities between faiths but encourage honest dialogue concerning differences in beliefs (Eck, 2001). It is essential that students at colleges and universities engage in religious discussions because religious freedom requires understanding of different faiths. Public and private educational institutions from elementary grades through high school must also play a critical role in fostering that understanding.

How have schools taught students about the concept of religious freedom?

The history of American education reveals a gradual secularization of public schools. Public schools in the United States originally did not teach about religious freedom; they reinforced Protestant beliefs, causing Catholics and Jews to establish schools for their children in addition to or instead of public schools. History credits Horace Mann with shaping public schools in the United States, yet he was denounced as the "archenemy of the Christian church" for advocating that the Bible should be read—but not interpreted—in school because biblical interpretation should be a parental prerogative (McMillan, 1984, p. 85). When Bible reading was eliminated, *McGuffey's Reader* became the most popular public school textbook. It referred to God and used Protestant perspectives to deliver its moral lessons. Later revisions of McGuffey eliminated overt religious language but maintained a sermonizing tone. By 1870, most Protestants agreed that a sectarian religious perspective should not be presented in public schools, but that a nonsectarian Christian perspective was essential (Nord, 1995).

Starting in the 1940s, U.S. federal courts wrote several decisions related to the constitutional guarantee of religious freedom being enforced or contradicted in schools (see Table 6.1). The next sixty years of court rulings would challenge schools to eliminate their Christian bias and to become more **secular,** reflecting the civic culture and not promoting any religious perspective. U.S. courts have ruled that schools are forbidden to force students to say the Pledge of Allegiance, compel students to pray, begin the day with devotional reading from the Bible, have a minister, priest, or rabbi give a prayer at graduation, post the Ten Commandments in

TABLE 6.1 Court Rulings on Religion in Public Schools (a selection of significant cases)

1943	*West Virginia v. Barnette* (brought by a Jehovah's Witness family): No child can be forced to recite the Pledge of Allegiance.
1947	*Everson v. Board of Education:* Students attending parochial schools could be transported to their schools on buses provided for public school students.
1962	*Engel v. Vitale:* Students attending public schools could not be forced to recite state written prayers.
1963	*Abington Township v. Schempp:* Public schools could not insist that students recite the Lord's prayer or any prayer nor require "devotional Bible reading."
1968	*Epperson v. Arkansas:* An Arkansas law forbidding the teaching of Darwin's theory of evolution in school was ruled unconstitutional.
1971	*Lemon v. Kurtzman:* Established that the separation of church and state principle was not violated if the statute, policy, or practice under consideration: (1) had a secular legislative purpose; (2) did not foster excessive government entanglement with religion; (3) neither advances nor inhibits religion as its primary purpose.
1980	*Stone v. Graham:* A Kentucky law requiring a copy of the Ten Commandments posted in every public school classroom was declared unconstitutional.
1985	*Wallace v. Jaffree:* Since the intent of an Alabama law requiring a moment of silence was "to return prayer to the public schools," it was unconstitutional.
1987	*Edwards v. Aguillard:* Schools could not teach creationism as an alternative to evolutionary theory because creationism was based on religious beliefs and did not satisfy the criteria to constitute a scientific theory.
1990	*Westside Community Schools v. Mergens:* If a public school allows community groups to use its facilities, religious groups must have equal access.
1992	*Lee v. Weisman:* Schools could not include prayers offered by religious leaders (of any faith) at graduation ceremonies; if a school policy or practice has a coercive effect, it is unconstitutional.
2000	*Santa Fe School Independent School District v. Doe:* Student-led prayers at football games violated separation of church and state.

Source: The religious history of America: The heart of the American story from colonial times to today by E. Gaustad and L. Schmidt, 2002.

classrooms or hallways, or teach religion disguised as science—"creationism"—as a scientific alternative to evolutionary theory (Allen, 1996; Fraser, 1999; McMillan, 1984).

In 2002, the Ninth Circuit court created a controversy in *Newdow v. United States Congress* by ruling that the inclusion of the phrase "under God" meant the Pledge of Allegiance served a religious, not a secular purpose. The court concluded that schools could not have students recite the pledge even if they are allowed to choose to not participate because the school setting is a coercive context that puts pressure on students to conform to the majority (Pauken, 2003).

How can public schools teach about religion in a way that respects all religions?

As federal and district courts ruled on what schools could not allow, they also provided guidelines for constitutional activities. Schools were encouraged to teach objectively about all religions, and even about the Bible. As Justice Clark wrote,

> It might well be said that one's education is not complete without a study of comparative religion or the history of religion and its relationship to the advancement of civilization. It certainly may be said that the Bible is worthy of study for its literary and historic qualities. (McMillan, 1984, p. 163)

Although schools cannot force students to pray, they cannot prevent a student from praying, as long as the prayer does not create a disruption. If students representing a religious group want to use school facilities, they have the same right of access as any community group.

In 1999, the U.S. Department of Education sent comprehensive guidelines on issues related to religion in public schools to every public school in the nation. A committee of diverse religious and educational leaders had developed the guidelines that include legal assurances for recommended practices (al-Hibri, 2001). Teaching *about* religions has now been incorporated into national and state standards for teachers (Douglass, 2002); following the guidelines will ensure that schools address those standards by providing accurate information about fundamental beliefs of the world's major religions.

AFTERWORD

Although historically the Protestant majority in the United States resisted accepting other faiths vigorously, at times even violently, Protestants of all denominations accepted each other on equal terms and eventually accepted Catholics and Jews. Will the faiths of new immigrants—Hinduism, Buddhism, Islam, and other non-Christian religions—become acceptable to the dominant Judeo- Christian groups in America? Although U.S. courts have consistently upheld the principle of religious freedom, schools will also have an important role to play.

In the past, public schools promoted Protestantism and reinforced anti-Catholic and anti-Semitic attitudes. As schools became more secular, they engaged less in proselytizing and contributed to the resolution of conflicts among Protestants, Catholics, and Jews. Because current immigration has increased non-Christian religious diversity in the United States, it is important that public schools continue to affirm court decisions and use the guidelines offered by the Department of Education. Students need to learn more about other religions.

If the United States is to be successful as a religiously diverse society, it is essential that "the principal religious groups not only claim freedom for themselves, but affirm equal freedom for others, whatever their beliefs may be" (Katz & Southerland, 1968, p. 269). As students learn about diverse religions they may also come to appreciate why religious freedom was guaranteed in the Bill of Rights, and why it has been so difficult to achieve that ideal.

> We establish no religion in (America), we command no worship, we mandate no belief, nor will we ever. Church and state are, and must remain, separate. All are free to believe or not to believe, all are free to practice a faith or not, and those who believe are free, and should be free, to speak of and act on their belief.
>
> **Ronald Reagan (1911–2004)**

myeducationlab

Now go to Topic #5: **Religion** in the MyEducationLab (www.myeducationlab.com) for your course, where you can:

- Find learning outcomes for this topic along with the national standards that connect to these outcomes.
- Complete Assignments and Activities that can help you more deeply understand the chapter content by viewing classroom video and ABC News footage.
- Apply and practice your understanding of the core teaching skills identified in the chapter with the Building Teaching Skills and Dispositions learning units.

TERMS AND DEFINITIONS

Agnostic A belief that human beings cannot prove or disprove the existence of God

Anti-Catholicism Expressing stereotypes about or prejudices against Catholics or discriminating against Catholics

Anti-Semitism Having anti-Jewish prejudices or stereotypes, or engaging in discrimination against Jews

Atheism Believing that God does not exist

Deism A belief that God created the world and the system of natural laws that governed the world, but was not a presence (and did not play a role) in everyday life

Denominations A perspective on diverse Protestant faiths that views all of them as a singular Protestant church with different names (denominations)

Established church When one church is declared the official faith of a political unit (a colony or state) and tax revenues are used to fund this church

Religious freedom/religious liberty The right to worship in any church of one's choice consistent with that church's beliefs and practices

Sectarian A perspective on diverse Christian churches or sects in which an individual regards his or her own sect as the "true faith"

Secular The civic culture of a society not reflective of religious perspective

DISCUSSION EXERCISES

Exercise #1 Separation of Church and State Activity

Directions: Read the situation below and decide which requests for changing school policy from the following list will be implemented (Agree) and which requests for change will be rejected (Disagree). On completion of your group's consideration of the twelve proposed rule changes, compare your recommendations with those of other groups.

The Situation: It is December 5. As a citizen and parent, you have been publicly assigned to a select committee to examine a list of new school district policies that has been proposed by a group of Jewish parents. Twenty-five percent of the students in the district are Jewish, 15% have no religious affiliation, and 60% declare some sort of Christian affiliation.

Proposed District Policies: Breaks and Absences

1. Vacation breaks during the school year will be established without regard to religious holidays.
2. Jewish children will be excused when they are absent on Jewish holidays.
3. Jewish teachers will not be charged with personal leave when they are absent during Yom Kippur and Rosh Hashana.

Religious Holidays

4. No celebration of Christmas as part of the school curriculum.
5. No celebration of Hanukkah as part of the school curriculum.
6. No creche will be displayed in school.
7. No Christmas trees will be displayed in school.
8. No gift exchanges or Christmas parties in class.

Curricular and Extracurricular Activity

9. Impact of religious values on historic or current events and issues will be examined and discussed in the classroom.
10. The Holocaust will be studied as part of the World War II unit and as part of the history of Western civilization.

11. No extracurricular activity will be scheduled on Friday evening.
12. No songs that refer to Jesus Christ will be sung in the winter music program.

Exercise #2 Religious Freedom in the United States: What Is Your Judgment?

Directions: The following list contains incidents that have actually occurred. Determine which items you believe violate the rights of people to behave in accordance with their chosen faith.

Religious Freedom in the United States

1. Should a Sikh be allowed to wear his turban on a hard-hat job even though it appears to be a violation of safety regulations?
2. Can a soldier who is a member of Wicca practice his or her religion on an army base?
3. Should Hindus be forced to build their temple with a "Spanish" architectural style that will match the other buildings in a Southern California community instead of building it based on their traditional temple architecture?
4. Because a Jainist student attends the high school, must the cafeteria staff clearly mark the contents of the meals prepared so that the student can be assured of eating only vegetables?
5. Can a Muslim woman teaching in a public school wear her traditional head covering in her classroom?
6. Should members of the Native American Church be allowed to ingest peyote because this drug has historically been part of their religious rituals?
7. Should a Florida city council allow members of the Santeria faith to engage in animal sacrifice because it is traditionally part of their religious practice?
8. Should a Sikh student come to school with the symbolic knife (*kirpan*) he is required to wear following his initiation?
9. Should Muslim employees be given time to perform obligatory prayers during the workday?
10. Do Seventh-Day Adventist or Jewish employees have the right to be excused from work on Saturday because it is their Sabbath?

REFERENCES

Abdo, G. (2006). *Mecca and Main Street: Muslim life in America after 9/11.* Oxford, England: Oxford University Press.

Describes the efforts of a variety of Muslim Americans to live in the United States and to maintain their faith while being confronted with stereotypes, prejudice, and discrimination.

al-Hibri, A.Y. (2001). Standing at the precipice: Faith in the age of science and technology. In A. al-Hibri, J.B. Elshtain, and C.C. Haynes (Eds.), *Religion in American public life: Living with our deepest differences.* New York, NY: W.W. Norton.

Explains how the Industrial Revolution produced a mechanistic model and how it has affected the United States, including how the country approaches issues such as the separation of church and state.

Allen, R.S. (1996). *Without a prayer: Religious expression in public schools.* Amherst, NY: Prometheus.

Provides the human story behind the Supreme Court cases on religion in public schools, including the consequences for those individuals who brought those cases forward.

Barrett, P.M. (2007). *American Islam: The struggle for the soul of a religion.* New York, NY: Farrar, Straus and Giroux.

Describes the perceptions and experiences of a variety of Muslim Americans based on interviews conducted after the terrorist attacks on 9/11.

Carroll, J. (2001). *Constantine's Sword: The church and the Jews, a history.* Boston, MA: Houghton Mifflin.

Examines the history of relations between the Catholic Church and the Jews and explains the basis for the historic pattern of anti-Semitism that still exists in the church.

Chernow, R. (2004). *Alexander Hamilton.* New York, NY: Penguin Books.

Describes Hamilton's life, especially his influence on the American Federal government.

Clark, C., Vargas, M.B., Schlosser, L., & Allmo, C. (2002, Winter). It's Not Just "Secret Santa" in December: Addressing educational and workplace climate issues linked to Christian privilege. *Multicultural Education,* pp. 53–58.

Describes the ways Christianity is affirmed or promoted in subtle and blatant ways at work and in schools, and provides a religious dilemma at a worksite for group discussion.

Dinnerstein, L. (1994). *Anti-Semitism in America.* New York, NY: Oxford.

Summarizes the experience of Jews in America and the various forms of anti-Semitism they have encountered from the colonial period to the present.

Douglass, S. (2002). Teaching about religion. *Educational Leadership, 60*(2), 32–36.

Reports findings from a study of the inclusion of religion in national and state teaching standards and discusses resources and strategies for implementing these standards.

Eck, D.L. (2001). *A new religious America: How a "Christian Country" has become the world's most religiously diverse nation.* New York, NY: HarperCollins.

Examines the growth of diverse religions in the United States, especially with regard to immigration patterns since 1965, and describes both its impact and its potential.

Elshtain, J.B. (2001). Faith of our fathers and mothers: Religious belief and American democracy. In A. al-Hibri, J.B. Elshtain, & C.C. Haynes (Eds.), *Religion in American public life: Living with our deepest differences* (pp. 39–61). New York, NY: W.W. Norton.

Defines the concept of the civil society in America while examining how responsibility for religious rights has become increasingly relegated to the courts in the United States.

Fraser, J.W. (1999). *Between church and state: Religion and public education in a multicultural America.* New York, NY: St. Martin's.

Describes the history of religious diversity in the United States from the colonial beginnings to the present, and examines the critical court cases on religious freedom.

Gausted, E., & Schmidt, L. (2002). *The religious history of America: The heart of the American story from colonial times to today.* New York, NY: HarperCollins.

Describes the diversity of American religions, the historical conflicts between religious faiths, and the growing acceptance of religious diversity.

Goodrich, F., & Hackett, A. (1956). *The diary of Anne Frank.* New York, NY: Random House.

Presents ideas and events recorded in Anne Frank's diary; this Pulitzer Prize–winning play was first performed on Broadway in the fall of 1955.

Hendry, J. (2003). Mining the sacred mountain: The clash between the Western dualistic framework and Native American religions. *Multicultural Perspectives, 5*(1), 3–10.

Contrasts patterns of Western thought with the perspective of Native Americans, especially with regard to their views of nature and the protection of the environment.

Herberg, W. (1955). *Protestant-Catholic-Jew: An essay in American religious sociology.* Garden City, NY: Doubleday.

Examines the status of religion in the United States in the early 1950s and explains how the three major religions have achieved equal status in American society.

Hudson, W.S. (1973). *Religion in America: An historical account of the development of American religious life* (2nd ed.). New York, NY: Charles Scribner.

Describes the religious life of Americans from separate faiths moving toward common principles and eventually toward the pluralistic attitudes necessary for religious liberty.

Jacoby, S. (2005). Original intent. *Mother Jones, 30*(7), 29–31, 74.

Examines the historical record to argue that the founders of America did not want to create a state based on religion but separate from religion.

Katz, W., & Southerland, H. (1968). Religious pluralism and the Supreme Court. In W. McLoughlin & R. Bellah (Eds.), *Religion in America* (pp. 269–281). Boston, MA: Beacon Press.

Examines the role played by the Supreme Court in moving the United States from a nation tolerating religious diversity toward the goal of promoting religious pluralism.

Khan, M.A.M. (2004). Living on borderlines: Islam beyond the clash and dialogue of civilization. In Z.H. Buhhari, S.S. Nyang, M. Ahmad, & J.C. Esposito (Eds.), *Muslims' place in the American public square* (pp. 84–113). Walnut Creek, CA: Altamira Press.

Describes actions taken against Muslims for practicing their religion and discusses the need for acceptance of religious diversity in America.

Kosmin, B.A., & Lachman, S.P. (1993). *One nation under God: Religion in contemporary American society.* New York, NY: Crown.

Analyzes results from the 1990 National Survey of Religious Identification with data from 113,000 Americans; this was one of the most extensive religious surveys ever conducted.

Lee, E. (2004). American gate keeping: Race and immigration law in the twentieth century. In N. Foner & G.M. Frederickson (Eds.), *Not just black and white: Historical and contemporary perspectives on immigration, race and ethnicity in the United States* (pp. 119–144). New York, NY: Russell Sage Foundation.

Examines changes in racial composition of immigrants since the 1965 immigration reform.

Lippy, C.H. (1994). *Being religious, American style: A history of popular religiosity in the United States.* Westport, CT: Praeger.

Describes religious beliefs and practices of Americans from colonial times to the present that supplement or replace beliefs and practices from traditional religions.

McCloud, A.B. (2004). Conceptual discourse: Living as a Muslim in a pluralistic society. In Z.H. Buhhari, S.S. Nyang, M. Ahmad, & J.C. Esposito (Eds.), *Muslims' place in the American public square* (pp. 73–83). Walnut Creek, CA: Altamira Press.

Examines the role of the media in creating negative images of Muslims and the inconsistency of American responses to Muslims with American values.

McCloud, A.B. (2006). *Transnational Muslims in American society.* Gainesville: University of Florida Press.

Examines the experiences of Muslims who have recently become citizens of the United States and the success of their various strategies for adapting to American culture.

McMillan, R.C. (1984). *Religion in the public schools: An introduction.* Macon, GA: Mercer University Press.

Examines the historical background of the separation of church and state principle and provides the written Supreme Court decisions on major cases with minimal editing.

Miller, G.T. (1976). *Religious liberty in America: History and prospects.* Philadelphia, PA: Westminster.

Provides a history of conflicts related to religious diversity in the United States and progress made toward religious liberty with an emphasis on the period prior to the twentieth century.

Myers, G. (1960). *History of bigotry in the United States* (rev. ed.), G. Christman (Ed.). New York, NY: Capricorn.

Describes the historic targets of bigotry since colonial days, with emphasis on Catholics, Jews, and immigrants, and the actions taken against these minorities by the majority.

Nimer, M. (2004). Muslims in the American body politic. In Z.H. Buhhari, S.S. Nyang, M. Ahmad, & J.C. Esposito (Eds.), *Muslims' place in the American public square* (pp. 145–164). Walnut Creek, CA: Altamira Press.

Discusses the violence against Muslims after the Oklahoma City bombing and after 9/11, and the growing political activism of American Muslims.

Nord, W.A. (1995). *Religion and American education: Rethinking a national dilemma.* Chapel Hill: University of North Carolina Press.

Addresses current dilemmas involving religion in public schools and establishes a middle ground to accommodate religion while maintaining the principle of religious liberty.

Pauken, P. (2003, January). *I Pledge Allegiance to the Curriculum: The establishment clause and the legal balance between educational authority and individual rights.* Presented at the Hawai'i International Conference on Education, Honolulu.

Reviews court cases concerning the First Amendment's guarantee of religious liberty and the legal principles that have evolved, especially with regard to religion in the schools.

Ravitch, F.S. (1999). *School prayer and discrimination: The civil rights of religious minorities and dissenters.* Boston, MA: Northeastern University Press.

Provides an overview of the history of religious intolerance and currently legal religious practices in public schools and provides a model statute to promote religious freedom.

Ribuffo, L.P. (1997). Henry Ford and the international Jew. In J. Sarna (Ed.), *The American Jewish experience* (2nd ed., pp. 201–218). New York, NY: Holmes & Meier.

Traces Henry Ford's involvement in anti-Semitism through a series of articles in his newspaper and describes Ford's impact on anti-Semitic attitudes around the world.

Smith, J.I. (2004). Muslims as partners in interfaith encounter. In Z.H. Bukhari, S.S. Nyang, M. Ahmad, and J.L. Esposito (Eds.), *Muslims' place in the American public square* (pp. 165–197). Walnut Creek, CA: Altamira Press.

Describes seven models for interfaith dialogue and examines the problems and benefits of such dialogues in general and for Muslims specifically.

Taggar, S.V. (2006). Headscarves in the headlines! What does this mean for educators? *Multicultural Perspectives 8*(3), 3–10.

Examines teacher responses to Muslim students since 9/11, focusing on three urban high school teachers who represent distinctly different ideological perspectives.

Waldman, S. (2006). The framers and the faithful. *Washington Monthly, 38*(4), 33–38.

Discusses historical evidence that evangelical Christians were among the major supporters of the separation of church and state principle.

Wegner, G.P. (2002). *Anti-Semitism and schooling under the Third Reich.* New York, NY: Routledge Falmer.

Describes the Nazi educational philosophy and the anti-Semitic curriculum and pedagogy developed by German educators to promote Nazi ideas about race and racial purity.

CHAPTER 7

Rejecting Oppressive Relationships: The Logic of Cultural Pluralism for a Diverse Society

"In the United States, we have the richest mix of ethnic groups, of racial groups, of global experience that the world has ever known and it is this richness of this mix that yields our incredible creativity and innovation. We have not even begun to experience the real potential of our fantastic human resource mix—our competitive edge in the global economy."

James Naisbitt (1929–)

James Naisbitt, author and respected consultant, provides corporate clients with analyses of data and trends to facilitate corporate decision making related to many pertinent social issues. In his remarks quoted at the opening of this chapter, Naisbitt is describing the possibilities for America because we have become the most diverse society in the world, and most demographic projections about the United States predict even greater diversity in the future. Because demographic changes have not yet occurred in many areas of the United States, it is possible for some people to have difficulty believing in these projections, but even if we focus on the present, the obvious changes in many states, especially in bellwether states such as California and Texas, make it impossible to ignore the reality of the change in the U.S. population toward increased diversity.

Diversity in the United States

In 2005, Texas became the fourth state to have more people of color in the state's population than white people (the others are New Mexico, Hawaii, and California). Hispanic Americans constitute the largest group among people of color in all of these states except Hawaii, where Asian Americans are the largest group. In six additional states, people of color represent approximately 40% or more of the population—Arizona, Florida, Georgia, Maryland, Mississippi, and New York. And people of color are the majority of the population in the 100 largest cities in the United States (U.S. Census Bureau, 2005). White people have been the majority group in the United States since the founding of the nation, but demographers are saying that this is going to change before the end of the twenty-first century. As early as 2050, non-Hispanic whites will constitute only 53% of the U.S. population; white men will represent about 26% of the population and many of them will be retired, resulting in about half of the workforce consisting of people of color (Schaefer, 2008). For the social security system to continue to provide its promised benefits, people of color will need jobs that pay living wages. All Americans must care about diversity because in our complex, technological society we are already highly dependent on each other.

Based on data from the 2000 census, Pipher (2002) reported that one in ten people in the United States was born in another country and that one in five children in school is a child of recent immigrants. Historically, immigrants tended to settle in urban areas of a few states, primarily New York, California, and Florida, but immigrants now live in smaller cities of all states. Pipher illustrates this point by observing that in a Lincoln, Nebraska, newspaper "Our obituary column . . . is filled with Hrdvys, Andersens, Walenshenkskys, and Muellers. But the births column . . . has many Ali, Nguyen, and Martinez babies" (p. 6).

Demographers track movement of people in society, yet none can predict accurately what the mix of people will be in the future. Demographers tend to be conservative in their speculations, yet the harbingers of change to come surround us. Pipher (2002) provides this example: Police in Nashville, Tennessee, have computers that explain laws and basic words for simple requests or demands in twenty languages. Rather than debate demographic predictions, it is more pertinent to consider how the current white majority responds to population changes.

How have members of the majority responded to diverse groups?

In any society, there is often a group hierarchy where preferred groups occupying superior positions disregard groups that are devalued by that society. As we have already seen in previous chapters, the history of the United States reveals that the white majority has never been consistently respectful of the rights of diverse groups. Terry (1993) described the relationship of dominant and subordinate groups by using an "up/down" metaphor. To determine who is up or down in a society, one must discover which groups have the most wealth, status, and power, and which have the least. In the United States, a person becomes an up by belonging to these groups: white, male, middle or upper class, Christian, heterosexual, or nondisabled. A down belongs to one or more of these groups: people of color, female, lower class, non-Christian, homosexual, bisexual, transgender, or disabled. Most individuals represent a mixture of memberships in these up or down groups.

With reference to his metaphor, Terry suggests that ups don't know much about downs, and they think they don't need to know about them because downs are not regarded as socially important. Such ignorance is one cause of prejudice as Eck (2001) noted when she described prejudice as "being down on something you're not up on" (p. 300). Ups do not compete with downs; they move in different circles. The only time ups become concerned about downs is when downs start getting "uppity" by challenging the power structure or the status quo by engaging in marches, demonstrations, or some other kind of protest about an issue. The response of ups is likely to be "What do these people want?" because they genuinely do not know. They are "dumb ups" when it comes to understanding issues affecting downs. By contrast, downs know a great deal about ups because they must; it is essential for their survival and for their success. To achieve whatever goals they have set for themselves, downs have to understand ups so that, as Terry says, they know what the ups are up to (pp. 194–196).

It is tempting to assume that if someone is a down in one category, that person will be more sensitive to downs in a category in which he or she functions as an up. Unfortunately it doesn't seem to work that way. When people are behaving as part of an up group, they tend to be "dumb ups." It's as if there are separate file folders; their experiences in one category stay in that file and don't influence other files. People living in poverty can be racist; people of color can be homophobic; gays and lesbians can be prejudiced against immigrants; immigrants can be sexist; women can be prejudiced against people with disabilities; and people with disabilities can be prejudiced against welfare recipients. Terry's "up/down" metaphor provides a useful way of thinking about the complexity involved in a society that includes diverse minority groups.

When the topic of diversity, especially racial and ethnic diversity, is addressed in the media, pundits and scholars often use negative terms rather than the positive terms that James Naisbitt used. Columnist George Will has criticized education's efforts to advocate for diversity, chastising institutions for engaging in "political correctness." Skeptical of attempts to emphasize diversity, scholars such as Arthur Schlesinger, Jr. (1991) have argued that promoting multiculturalism would lead to the "balkanization" of the United States. Others refer to ethnic conflict in the former Yugoslavia as an example of the dangers of promoting ethnic affiliations. In the wake of the destruction of New York's World Trade Center, Americans assaulted and killed Arab Americans and vandalized mosques in several cities despite appeals from religious and political leaders. Misguided responses do not bode well for our future as the nation with the most diverse population on earth.

> It is well to remember that the entire universe, with one trifling exception, is composed of others.
>
> **John Andrew Holmes (1789–1876)**

It is imperative that Americans understand how we benefit from diversity and that we learn more about about previous and current contributions of diverse groups in our society because the real threat to our nation is not diversity but ignorance. Some Americans are choosing to focus on opportunities in a diverse society rather than on problems in areas such as business, community, and education. This issue does not simply affect the United States; rather, it is global. Naisbitt and Aburdene (1990) were among the first to describe global societies becoming culturally homogenized in the 1980s. Looking ahead to the twenty-first century, they predicted a "backlash against uniformity" as people struggled to "assert the uniqueness" of their culture in the global village: "As our outer worlds grow more similar, we will increasingly treasure the traditions that spring from within" (p. 120).

Attitudes about Diversity

Historians have long maintained that to understand the present, we must understand the past. In terms of diversity, the best way to understand historic attitudes toward societal diversity is to examine how Americans have responded to immigration, the primary source of our diversity. Although some Americans have been (and still are) guilty of anti-immigrant sentiments, many have expressed positive beliefs about immigrants assimilating into society. By reviewing past and present attitudes concerning immigration, Gordon (1964) described consistent ideological perspectives with regard to ethnic diversity: Anglo conformity, melting pot, and pluralism. Brooks (1996) and others have described a fourth perspective: separatism. Taken together, the four perspectives represent historic and contemporary American views on ethnic diversity. Curiously, despite the persistence of these ideological points of view, Anglo conformity has been and continues to be the dominant perspective on racial and ethnic diversity in the United States.

What does it mean to have an Anglo conformity perspective?

Cole and Cole (1954) first identified **Anglo conformity** as the efforts of English colonists to institute American values, norms, and standards perpetuated ever since. Anglo conformity is an extension of English culture and European civilization. It rejects diversity in favor of homogeneity, maintaining that everyone should conform to values, norms, and standards determined by the Anglo founders of the country and modified by a continuing white majority.

Anglo conformity requires that immigrants stop speaking native languages and use only English as soon as possible. Anglo conformity requires immigrants to abandon their ethnic heritages—the customs, ceremonies, clothing, and traditions of their former culture. Even if their native lands are European, immigrants have been expected to adopt American ways and to become similar to everyone else. Barrett and Roediger (2002) explained that people of color have found Anglo conformity to be a problem because it "took place in a nation obsessed by race. For new immigrant workers the processes of 'becoming white' and 'becoming American' were connected at every turn" (p. 30). Because immigrants of color could never become white, they could never completely achieve the goal of Anglo conformity: to look and act just like the members of the white majority.

When referring to individuals assimilating into society, social scientists often use the term *Americanization,* yet it still refers to Anglo conformity. Early in our nation's history, Americanization was a process of assimilation applied even to children of indigenous people. In the late 1800s, as public schools were expected to be responsible for the Americanization of immigrant children, schools created by the Bureau of Indian Affairs (BIA) were expected to "Americanize" Native American children. Indians had long been viewed as an obstacle to U.S. expansion and occupation of new territories; Adams (1995) quoted a liberal reformer who argued that "We must either butcher them or civilize them, and what we do we must do quickly" (p. 2). The insistence on Americanizing Indian children led to the creation of BIA boarding schools. As illustrated in the photographs of Navajo student Tom Torlino (Figure 7.1), BIA boarding schools were a dramatic example of the Anglo conformity ideal.

How did the BIA boarding schools promote Anglo conformity with Indian children?

At first, Indian schools were established on reservations, but being close to parents meant Indian children would return home and go "back to the blanket"—back to Indian values and behaviors. Parental influence defeated one of the major purposes of BIA schools, which was, as Adams (1995) explained, to teach values: "to respect private property . . . to realize that the accumulation of personal wealth is a moral obligation" (p. 22). For the BIA to be more confident of success in its Americanization efforts, Indian children were taken to boarding schools away from reservations, where they were not allowed to return home even on weekends. Although years passed before anyone recognized the absurdity of trying to Americanize Native Americans, the boarding school experiment ultimately failed. Their emphasis on conformity, uniformity, and individual achievement were too contrary to intrinsic Indian values.

FIGURE 7.1

Anglo conformity is vividly illustrated in these two pictures of a Navajo student, Tom Torlino, before and after being enrolled in a BIA boarding school.

Source: Western Americana Collections. Manuscripts Division. Department of Rare Books and Special Collections. Princeton University Library.

> Two deer, two owls will behave differently from each other. I have studied many plants. The leaves of one plant, on the same stem, none is exactly alike. . . . If the Great Spirit likes the plants, the animals, even little mice and bugs to do this, how much more will he abhor people being alike, doing the same thing.
>
> **John Lame Deer (1903–1976)**

Which immigrant groups benefited from Anglo conformity?

Northern European ethnic immigrants to the United States could more easily achieve Anglo conformity. To insist that people Americanize—dress, talk, think, behave, and conform fully to the white majority—is an advantage for those with white skin. However, white advantage created frustration and anger for people of color, who rejected their heritage and native language and who imitated white behavior but could not overcome the disadvantage of skin color; they could not be as successful as their white peers. As Americans of color were denied rewards given to white ethnic groups, individuals with lighter skin sometimes opted to claim white skin—"passing for white"—although some who succeeded paid a psychological price. Their success illustrated the power of Anglo conformity and contradicted the concept of America as a melting pot.

What does it mean to describe America as a melting pot?

The **melting pot** perspective is that immigrants to America need not relinquish their entire racial or ethnic heritage. Instead, the idea was that ethnic differences would blend into the dominant culture to create a new identity, an American identity, made up of cultures and customs carried to America by all immigrants. This perspective was first articulated by eighteenth-century French immigrant Hector St. John de Crèvecoeur, who said of the United States: "Here individuals of all nations are melted into a new race of men" (Schlesinger, 1991, p. 12). Others such as Ralph Waldo Emerson also alluded to a melting pot concept, but Americans scarcely responded.

It was in 1908 when Israel Zangwill established this engaging and popular metaphor in the American imagination as his successful play, *The Melting Pot,* opened in Washington, D.C., during a tidal wave of immigration. The melting pot has been especially attractive in intellectual, artistic, and political circles with its compelling image of Americans as a blend of cultures. In the following excerpt, the character David, a Russian Jew, describes the metaphor but also defines the limits of the melting pot:

> America is God's Crucible, the great Melting Pot where all the races of Europe are melting and re-forming! Here you stand, good folk, think I, when I see them at Ellis Island, here you stand in your fifty groups, with your fifty languages and histories, and your fifty blood hatreds and rivalries. But you won't be long like that, brothers, for these are the fires of God you've come to—these are the fires of God. A fig for your feuds and vendettas! Germans and Frenchmen, Irishmen and Englishmen, Jews and Russians—into the Crucible with you all! God is making the American! (1915, p. 33)

Despite rhapsodic oratory, notice the absence of references to people of color. Blacks, Latinos, Asians, and Native Americans are excluded. Only northern Europeans are invited to this highly selective melting pot; even members of certain white ethnic groups such as Greeks or Italians need not apply! As Laosa (1974) noted, the melting pot favored "the white Anglo-Saxon Protestant (WASP) group and . . . [neglected] certain 'culturally different' groups" (p. 136). Anglo conformity was ac-

> The energy of the Irish, Germans, Swedes, Poles, and Cossacks, and all the European tribes—and of the Africans, and of the Polynesians—will construct a new race, a new religion, a new state, a new literature.
>
> **Ralph Waldo Emerson (1803–1882)**

tually reflected in government policy and educational programs, but the idea of America as a melting pot remained an idea—a belief about America embraced by some, rejected by others.

People of color first questioned the melting pot concept, criticizing it as a myth that had nothing to do with the reality of America's diversity. People of color were not only excluded from the melting pot, they weren't sure they wanted to be included. To them, melting meant giving up their ethnic identification, along with its history and traditions, to be accepted in America. Although the melting pot was supposed to be the combination of all subcultures into a new and superior culture, Laosa (1974) described the process as a "melting away of subcultures [and] the preponderance of the dominant group over the others" (p. 136). People could talk about a melting pot, but Anglo conformity was the reality.

FIGURE 7.2

A political cartoon illustrating the idealistic image of the melting pot. Even though Japanese and blacks are included in the pot, anti-Irish prejudice is revealed in the caricature of an Irishman with a knife in one hand, the Irish flag in the other, and the caption that reads, "The Mortar of Assimilation—and the One Element That Won't Mix."

Source: Courtesy of Michigan State University Museum.

The melting pot perspective deemphasized differences and emphasized instead the need to disregard diversity and accept immigrants as Americans as long as they learned to speak English and became citizens. The most common expression of the melting pot perspective today is the argument that people should be **color blind,** that people should ignore a person's skin color. Americans will often say, "When I look at you I don't see color, I just see an American (or a student or a neighbor)."

People of color often are offended by the color-blind approach, arguing that it implies a negative attitude about race. When white people say they don't notice the color of anyone's skin, people of color find it difficult to believe: White Americans seem to advocate being color blind only when it relates to skin color. People of color question why someone should be oblivious to skin color but not to other colors in the world—flowers, sunsets, animals, rainbows? Seldon (1996) believes the answer indicates a discomfort with those whose skin color is not white. To be color blind is to pretend that a person is white in order to be able to associate with them, work with them, or view them in a positive way.

Foner (2000) offers historical evidence that America has never been color blind, even before the passage of the 1790 naturalization law that limited citizenship to white immigrants; yet many Americans still lobby for a color blind society. Advocacy of a color blind approach in education is especially problematic. Nieto (2008) describes the U.S. Supreme Court's 1974 decision in *Lau v. Nichols,* in which the San Francisco schools were sued for not providing an equal education for Chinese students. The schools' lawyer argued that Chinese students had the same curriculum, teachers, and instruction as other students. The Supreme Court ruled that taking the same approach with diverse students, as if all of them had the same needs, did not fulfill the goal of providing an equal education since students

> We are not fighting for integration . . . We are fighting for recognition as human beings.
>
> **Malcolm X (1925–1963)**

whose first language was Chinese would not benefit from curriculum and instruction provided in English, as would students who were native speakers. And if being color blind results in problems at the institutional level, it is even more disastrous at the individual level. After describing teachers who took a color blind approach in teaching diverse children, Sleeter (1993) asked: "What does it mean to construct an interpretation of race that denies it?" (p. 161). The answer to this critical question illustrates why many people of color view a color blind attitude toward skin color as being just as negative as anything advocated by the people who represent a separatist perspective.

How is the separatist perspective negative?

Separatism is the most pessimistic of the four perspectives, yet it may also be the easiest to recognize. Separatists believe that different racial and ethnic groups ought to be apart; they should have their own places and "be with their own kind." The goal of separatism is for diverse groups to tolerate each other. Separatism is based on the premise that ineradicable differences exist between groups of people and that differences inevitably cause hostility. The logical outcome is to believe that different groups must have their own places separate from others and should interact only when necessary. The best a person can hope for is peaceful coexistence.

At different times, both majority and minority group members have advocated for the separatist perspective. Before the Civil War, white separatists advocated for African Americans being relocated to Africa, and some Americans assisted a number of former slaves in creating a new African nation called Liberia. Even President Lincoln considered the idea, but he abandoned the project after hearing a vehement rejection of the proposal at a White House meeting with a group of prominent African Americans including Frederick Douglass (Martin, 1984). In the 1920s, Marcus Garvey promoted the goal of supporting black entrepreneurs to create a self-reliant black society (Cronon, 1955). For a more contemporary example, Appleton (1983) described Switzerland as a "segregated pluralism where the country is divided into four distinct cultures" with four languages (p. 26). Although German speakers in the northern and eastern cantons constitute 70% of the population, 21% live in western cantons and speak French, 8% live in south-central cantons and speak Italian, and 1% living in the Alps speak Romansh.

Although there are separatist groups in the United States today, they attract few followers and most are perceived as hate groups such as the Aryan Nation or Black Muslims. Although not all separatists advocate hatred, they tend to subscribe to the pessimistic separatist premise. Some call for a separate state for African Americans; others reject the concept of integrated schools in favor of returning to the *Plessy v. Ferguson* principle of separate but equal education for white children and children of color. Contrasting views will continue to be part of the mix of voices reacting to diversity; however, pluralism is now challenging the dominance of Anglo conformity.

What attitudes about diversity does pluralism promote?

Pluralism (also known as **cultural pluralism**) refers to the equal coexistence of diverse cultures in a mutually supportive relationship within the boundaries of one nation (Pai & Adler, 1997). When Horace Kallen coined the term in 1906, his focus was on ethnic diversity, advocating that the cultural differences of immigrants were essential to American democratic life. Alain Locke advocated a pluralism that encompassed racial groups as well. In the 1920s, based on the work of Kallen and Locke, pluralists insisted that people in a diverse society such as the United States should have the right to preserve their cultural heritage and not be forced to abandon it to conform to a dominant culture (Hattam, 2004; Menand, 2001). Pluralism is based on the belief in "equality of opportunity for all people, respect for human dignity and the conviction that no single pattern of living is good for everyone" (Pai & Adler, 1997, p. 102). Beginning in the 1960s, the National Association for the Advancement of Colored People and professional organizations such as the National Education Association have actively promoted pluralism.

Advocates for pluralism believe that diversity is not a difficulty to be overcome but a positive attribute of a society. American pluralists do not refer to being tolerant of others; to pluralists, tolerance is an inadequate response in a nation as diverse as the United States. As Eck (2001) writes, "Tolerance can create a climate of restraint but not one of understanding. . . . It is far too fragile a foundation for a society . . . [as] complex as ours" (p. 72). In a society guided by pluralistic beliefs, people appreciate differences because everyone is enriched by a diverse society. To pluralists, individuals have the right to maintain and be proud of their racial, cultural, ethnic, or religious heritage.

Separatists say that human differences will never disappear and will always cause conflict. Melting pot advocates ignore differences to avoid problems arising from them. Anglo conformity advocates demand the elimination of differences based on the assumption that a homogeneous society will be a more harmonious one. By contrast, pluralism encourages individuals to identify themselves in terms of their heritage in addition to identifying themselves as American. Individuals who embrace pluralism tend to identify themselves as Italian American or Polish American, as African American or Arab American, as Mexican American or Cuban American, as Chinese American or Hmong American. The identification means they perceive their identity as being shaped by their racial or ethnic heritages as well as by a more homogeneous American culture. A recent adaptation in response to persistent criticisms of "hyphenated Americans" has been to refer to "Americans of Japanese (or other) descent." With regard to preserving one's cultural heritage, some have asked how Italian must an Italian American be? From a pluralist perspective, it is up to each individual to decide how much of the customs, traditions, and language of an ethnic heritage he or she wants to maintain.

Because pluralism promotes bilingual education and maintenance of one's native language, those in the English Only movement seem to misunderstand the pluralist position as a rejection of the need for English as a common language for all Americans. English Only groups in various states have organized to lobby for legislation establishing English as the official language of that state, with the ultimate goal of eliminating the use of all other languages. Of course, a society including diverse language groups needs a common language, and English has been and continues to be the common language for the United States. Can people become fluent in English without losing the language spoken in their home? Students the world over are taught to be fluent in more than one language. Should children and youth in America who are fluent in a language learned at home be taught English at school while maintaining their first-language fluency? Pluralists argue that speaking different languages is a fundamental part of a diversity that enriches our society: People proud of their heritage should not be forced to give up the language associated with it. The concept of pluralism is consistent with American values about individuality and freedom, and as the diversity in our nation increases, it becomes increasingly necessary for Americans to reject Anglo conformity in favor of pluralism.

What are some arguments from people who are opposed to pluralism?

Opponents of cultural pluralism insist that promoting pluralistic attitudes contradicts the American emphasis on the individual by placing more importance on group membership in the creation of individual identity. They argue that emphasizing groups in a society will encourage individual identification with a group rather than with the nation, and that such group identification will lead to animosity between individuals who identify with a group and those who simply perceive themselves as "American." But for a number of years, pluralist advocates have said that this criticism is a misinterpretation of pluralism (Appleton, 1983; Greeley, 1975; Pai & Adler, 1997). One of the goals of pluralism is to empower individuals to shape their own identity. Cultural pluralism does not require mindless adherence or conformity to a group's cultural heritage; instead, pluralism fosters a dynamic process that allows individuals to decide the extent to which they choose to embrace their cultural heritage exclusively or to integrate certain aspects of other cultures or the dominant culture into that heritage. Pluralists would support both individuals who have chosen to maintain their heritage as well as those who choose to adopt other cultural ways while retaining important aspects of their cultural heritage.

Opponents maintain that there is still a problem with pluralism because it places so much emphasis on being proud of your cultural group. They argue that any level of individual identification with a cultural group inflates the importance of the group and exacerbates the potential for conflict between groups. They believe that the best way to avoid such conflicts is for all people living in the United States to identify themselves as Americans. Without this common bond, pluralism's critics believe that the group conflicts are inevitable and will lead to the fragmentation and ultimately the destruction of our society. Yet when Chua (2007) examined the historical record to understand the reasons for the achievements of the most successful nations, she discovered that a common thread connecting all of them was the promotion of pluralistic attitudes toward their diverse people. From the Roman empire to the Mongol dynasty to the British empire, the central government encouraged all of the people under its rule, including people they conquered, to maintain their culture and religion. In addition, the most gifted people from all groups were solicited and employed in ways that allowed the empire to benefit from their talents, and the government provided opportunities for diverse individuals to achieve, regardless of their background or their differences.

At the end of her book, Chua acknowledges that the United States is now a superpower, and she insists that "Tolerance played a critical role in every dimension of the United States' rise to superpower status" (p. 254). But tolerance is not enough; Chua argues that the United States will not benefit from its diverse population until it begins to promote pluralistic attitudes. For those critics who remain skeptical, pluralist advocates have tried to assure them that pluralism is consistent with both democratic principles and American values related to individuality and freedom. As diversity in the United States increases, it will become even more necessary for Americans to change our attitudes and our historic practice of demanding Anglo conformity in favor of promoting cultural pluralism.

Why should American society become pluralistic?

Anglo conformity remains the dominant perspective among Americans, even though numerous individuals and organizations advocate pluralism and question the appropriateness of Anglo conformity in a society as diverse as the United States. Although these advocates encounter resistance, they have articulated persuasive arguments in support of the practice and promotion of pluralism in America. Here are five of their compelling reasons:

1. *The failure of Anglo conformity* has been described by many social critics. Although a majority of Americans have historically endorsed Anglo conformity, this effort has been ineffective because its demand for conformity contradicts the historic identity of the United States. Eck (2001) observed, "America is a nation formed not by a race or a single people, but by the ideals articulated in the succession of founding documents, beginning with the Declaration of Independence" (p. 74). American immigrants have succeeded because they have accepted and embraced the civic culture of the United States as described by those founding documents; to require conformity based on race, religion, or other human differences in a society with such diversity is by nature unrealistic and illogical (Fuchs, 1990).

Sociologists who note that Anglo conformity has failed in America argue that it is inherently unjust to those who cannot conform adequately because they are not white or Protestant (or at least Christian). People unable to conform have endured oppression, and many are still being oppressed today. Racial and ethnic minority groups are still disproportionately represented in the data on human suffering such as infant mortality rates, unemployment statistics, welfare rolls, inadequately funded schools, and unsafe neighborhoods. The availability of goods and services and accessibility to education and opportunity have been inequitably distributed in the United States based on factors of race, gender, social class, sexual orientation, and disability. Respect and self-respect have also been inequitably gained, an issue that goes beyond equity to raise an ethical question about a lack of human compassion.

2. *The impact on self-consciousness and self-determination* refers to the impact of being perceived as "different" on one's efforts to develop the kind of positive self-consciousness that is essential for individuals to be confident in their ability to determine goals and to achieve them. If people consciously feel proud of who they are, it is easier to set goals and to believe they can be reached. Appleton (1983) argued that a primary purpose of democracy is to "provide an opportunity for individuals to choose who and what they will become" (p. 57). It is difficult for people to develop a sense of personal pride and to believe they can achieve their goals when they feel their abilities are constantly being doubted.

In one study, researchers reviewed the Graduate Record Examination (GRE) taken by undergraduates across the country to get into graduate school. Twenty questions from the GRE were selected to create a "test" that was given to black and white undergraduate students. In testing sessions where they were asked to identify their race on a pretest questionnaire, black students only answered half as many questions correctly as compared to testing sessions where they were not asked to identify their race. After the test, African American students were asked if anything had occurred to create a problem for them doing well on the test. They would typically say, "No." Even when asked specifically if identifying their race on the pretest questionnaire bothered them, they answered that it did not. Yet several African American students also admitted that they questioned their ability to achieve academic success at the graduate level (Gladwell, 2005). It is essential that people function in a context where their abilities are clearly respected if they are to develop a positive consciousness of self and a belief that they can determine their own goals and achieve them.

3. *The necessity for human interdependence* concerns the extent to which people depend on others. Individuals interact in any society; as a society becomes more complex, people inevitably become more dependent on each other. A complex society relies on technology, cooperation, and division of labor. Some people grow food, some build homes and furniture, some sell and service cars, and so on. People rely on others to provide the goods and services needed in their daily lives. It is also essential that those in the workforce are paid well enough to support the social security system for retired workers. In any society, but especially in a democratic society, people rely on each other. According to Pai and Adler (1997), "a democratic society is necessarily pluralistic . . . because it is founded on a belief in the intrinsic worth of individuals and their unique capacities to become intelligent human beings" (p. 109); therefore, becoming a pluralistic society promotes positive relations between individuals in all areas and from all groups within that society.

> **Pluralism is the greatest philosophical ideal of our time.**
>
> **John Dewey (1859–1952)**

The lack of a pluralistic perspective concerning racial and ethnic interdependence in the United States contributed to problems in the past. When drug use began to increase in urban ghettos and barrios in the 1950s and 1960s, the larger society ignored it. No one seemed to care what "those people" did to themselves because we did not understand that interdependence means that social problems cannot be confined. By the 1970s, drug use by urban and suburban white people increased significantly, and today the entire society is confronted with an enormous health and economic problem because of the availability and use of illicit drugs. Drug use became a significant problem in the United States because the majority did not appreciate the interdependence of diverse groups in American society.

White people are not alone in misunderstanding social interdependence. When AIDS first appeared, most people, including people of color, ignored the disease because it seemed to affect only the gay community. Some people said—and some still say—that AIDS was a punishment from God on homosexuals. It was only when the virus spread to heterosexuals in highly publicized cases that the U.S. government began providing funds for research to find a cure. In the meantime, thousands of human beings died.

Human interdependence exists everywhere, but in a diverse, democratic society such as the United States, citizens must advocate and practice pluralistic attitudes to ensure that our society functions as effectively as possible to be a good place for all (Locke, 1989). The Boy Scout study described in Chapter 3 illustrates this point. When boys competed with each other, hostility developed between groups, but hostility was eliminated when they cooperated to achieve a mutual goal. As Aronson (1999) concluded, "The key factor seems to be mutual interdependence—a situation wherein individuals need one another and are needed by one another in order to accomplish their goal" (p. 332). This is not a new insight. More than three centuries ago, poet John Donne wrote, "Any man's death diminishes me . . . therefore never send to know for whom the bell tolls; it tolls for thee" (Simpson, 1967, p. 101).

4. *The recognition of diversity as an ideal* implies that people must promote the idea that our diversity constitutes the best possible situation. We need only consider what has already occurred as a result of the diversity in the United States: Some of the best art, music, and literature ever created in America was a consequence of borrowing from different cultural traditions. Our modern English language has evolved by adopting words from languages of other cultures as diverse as those of Spain, Germany, France, Italy, Mexico, as well as from African and from Native American dialects (Claiborne, 1983). A major argument for promoting English as a world language is its ability to accommodate infusion of words from other cultures—proving its flexibility and accessibility.

Diversity is regarded as positive when people engage in solving problems. If we all examined problems the same way, we would generate similar solutions. Williams (2003) described a problem-solving conference in which a chemical company invited 50 employee women and people of color along with the company's top 125 predominantly white male managers. When divided into problem-solving teams, half of the groups consisted of white males only and half included diverse members by both gender and race. Afterward, the company CEO said, "It was so obvious that the diverse teams had the broader solutions. They had ideas I hadn't even thought of. . . . We realized that diversity is a strength as it relates to problem-solving" (pp. 442–443).

Diversity is also valued in the natural world: The more diversity there is in nature, the more likely it is that human life will adapt as new conditions arise. We have become concerned about endangered species and the destruction of rain forests: If diversity in nature is diminished, whatever potential usefulness we find in a species of plant or animal will be lost permanently. If diversity in nature can be appreciated and valued, should it be so difficult to appreciate diversity in human beings?

5. *The current existence of diversity* is perhaps the most compelling argument for promoting pluralism. If some quality is characteristic of a society, it makes sense that we value it rather than deny it or try to pretend that it didn't exist. If most of the players on a basketball team are tall, a coach will take advantage of their height to create offensive and defensive strategies. If the tall players graduate and next year's team is short and fast, the coach will take advantage of speed and quickness by creating new offensive and defensive strategies. As the most multicultural society in the world today, we must realize the advantages of diversity and embrace pluralism to capitalize on our advantages.

> **Commandment Number One of any truly civilized society is this: Let people be different.**
>
> **David Grayson (1870–1946)**

Other arguments for pluralism challenge us to think about how our society is changing and what sort of society it could become. To maintain Anglo conformity is to perpetuate the current fear and hostility of certain groups for each other and the conflicts between them. However, changing societal attitudes to a pluralistic perspective offers hope. Human beings have always encountered problems and conflicts, but in a diverse society, conflicts and problems are more likely to be resolved if everyone demonstrates pluralistic attitudes.

Valuing Individual Differences

The evidence that Americans already value diversity becomes most apparent when people are asked, "Would you want to live in a society where everyone was the same?" Americans often reply that they would not want to live in such a society. It is an American belief that each person is unique, and most of us are proud of those factors that establish our individuality. The United States has always consisted of people from different races, cultures, and religions. If we value our own uniqueness, it is logical and consistent to value what is unique in others. Pluralists value human differences. Sooner or later, all Americans should embrace pluralism because no other perspective regards differences as an asset for a society. Still, to be a pluralist requires more than claiming to value diversity; pluralism must be practiced. As Eck (2001) noted, "diversity alone is not pluralism. Pluralism is not a given but must be created. Pluralism requires participation and attunement to the life and energies of one another" (p. 70). Individuals and organizations committed to pluralism are actively working to bring about social change in the United States and to transform social attitudes from our traditional acceptance of Anglo conformity to acceptance and promotion of pluralism.

Must one be actively involved in change to be a pluralist?

Terry (1975) has developed a matrix (see Figure 7.3) based on the idea that people can be either prejudiced against one or more groups (racist, sexist, homophobic) or they can demonstrate pluralistic attitudes toward diversity. According to Terry, people also can be active or passive in their prejudices or their acceptance of diversity. The matrix

FIGURE 7.3
Matrix for Oppressive and Anti-Oppressive Behaviors

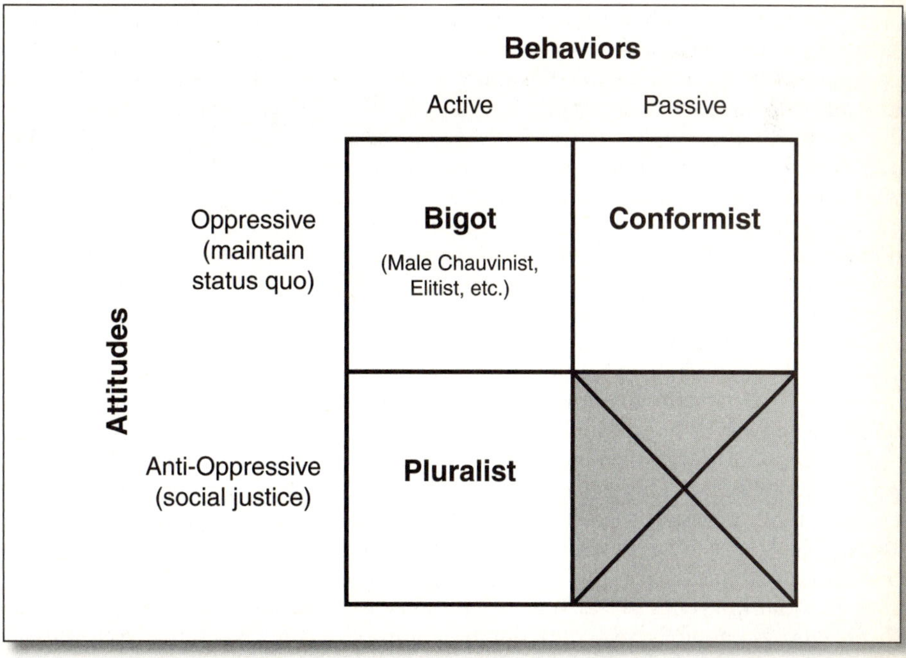

identifies four different positions: (1) people may actively assert and promote their prejudices; those with such strong prejudices are typically perceived as extremists (such as a bigot or a male chauvinist). (2) People may be prejudiced without expressing those ideas or behaving in ways that obviously reflect prejudice; they do not disagree with bigots or chauvinists, but do not tend to articulate their ideas on behalf of causes. People in this group passively accept the status quo that has been shaped by past prejudice and thereby perpetuate injustice in our society. They are conformists. They like things as they are and they would like to see them stay that way.

In another position (3) people may reject prejudiced ideas and sympathize with victims of social injustice but not express their views. Although opposed to prejudice and discrimination, they don't want to risk causing trouble or upsetting anyone, so they say nothing—and do nothing. Similar to those who are passive in their prejudice, people in this group conform to the status quo. By their conformity they help perpetuate problems that are known to be part of the status quo. There is little difference between prejudiced people and people opposed to prejudicial ideas and actions if they are both passive in their behavior. It is not possible to claim to have pluralistic attitudes and be passive, because passivity perpetuates social injustice.

Tatum (1997) describes the existence of prejudice and its benefits for the dominant group as similar to a moving walkway at an airport. People who actively engage in prejudice not only step on the walkway, but keep walking as well. People who are passive, whether their attitudes are prejudiced or opposed to prejudice, merely step on the walkway and let it carry them along. To be actively opposed to prejudice and the benefits it brings to the dominant group, people must step off the walkway as soon as they recognize its function. Using Tatum's metaphor, to escape the moving walkway means to be actively involved in promoting social justice.

To promote social justice, (4) people must reject prejudiced ideas, articulate pluralistic attitudes, and act on a new consciousness of human differences. To be a pluralist requires not only positive attitudes, but also a commitment to engage in activities to change social injustices in our society. Contrary to those who promote being color blind, pluralists argue that it is not consciousness of color that is the problem, but that people's consciousness of color and other differences has tended to be negative. Whites may feel uneasy around someone who is not white. Middle- or upper-class people may have contempt for welfare recipients. Nondisabled people feel pity for people with disabilities. Men may be condescending to women. What is needed is not to ignore differences but to consciously develop a positive attitude toward human differences. Put simply, unless we are part of the solution, we are part of the problem.

What kinds of activities can create social change?

If one has power to address a problem, one need only decide how to use that power to solve the problem. If individuals or groups do not have power to make a desired change, they may employ tactics to persuade those with power to implement the solutions they advocate. The tactics—deliberate and conscious strategies—employed to achieve social change in the United States are as old as the birth of our country, as illustrated in the Declaration of Independence and in the writing of John Adams, Thomas Jefferson, Thomas Paine, and others responsible for revolution against England and for eventual American independence. Terry (1975) identified six tactics historically employed to promote social change.

The most basic tactic is to engage in (1) a *dialogue* with those in power to convince them to implement a proposed change. If dialogue fails, people might organize (2) a *confrontation* of some kind: a march, a sit-down strike, or a rally. Confrontation dramatizes the need for change by public demonstration to show that people are concerned about an issue. The goal of confrontation is either to revive a dialogue that had been terminated or to pressure those in control to develop a greater sense of urgency about finding a solution.

If both dialogue and confrontation fail, those advocating change might (3) apply *economic pressure* to those individuals or organizations unwilling to change. Pressure usually takes the form of a **boycott** of products or services related to the issue in dispute. During the sit-ins at lunch counters in the 1960s, the youthful protestors were arrested and jailed, and their angry parents closed their charge accounts at these stores and encouraged others to do the same. In addition, white shoppers tended to avoid the stores because of the conflict. The economic hardship caused many store owners and managers to change their racist policies.

The best known example of this tactic was the Montgomery bus boycott that lasted more than a year and ended only when the courts ruled in favor of desegregation of public transportation. The bus boycott launched the career of Martin Luther King, Jr., and brought national attention to the civil rights movement (Williams, 1987; Wright, 1991). Nestlé Corporation was the target of a boycott based on concerns about the marketing strategies Nestlé had employed to sell infant formula in developing countries (Infact Canada, 2009).

In addition to boycotts, economic pressure can be applied through discrimination litigation calling for major economic penalties. In the 1990s, 1,300 African American employees at Coca-Cola brought a class-action lawsuit charging the corporation with discrimination in performance reviews, pay, and promotions. They won the case and were awarded $192 million. To improve the corporate image in the aftermath of the lawsuit, Coca-Cola committed additional resources to diversity issues including "increasing its use of minority suppliers, instituting a formal [diversity] mentoring program, and instituting days to celebrate diversity with its workforce" (Jones & George, 2003, p. 130).

People demanding change often initiate or support (4) *research* designed to examine data relevant to the issue being confronted. Research of a specific issue or problem might define the nature of the problem and perhaps identify its causes. Researchers may or may not recommend specific solutions to address problems, but the purpose of research is to provide information in support of a persuasive argument about changes being proposed to those in control.

Another tactic is to establish (5) an *inside-outside alliance* in which a member of a decision-making body (such as a board of directors, city council, or school board) collaborates with a group demanding change. This tactic may involve persuading someone who is already in the decision-making group of the benefits of the changes advocated, or it may mean working to elect a candidate or influence an appointment to the decision-making group of someone who is sympathetic to the need for change. Once elected or appointed, the person selected can represent and articulate arguments for change advocated by outside groups. Jones and George (2003) provide the example of an insurance and annuity company committed to diversity that owned almost a million shares of Nucor Corporation; they exerted pressure on Nucor to add more women and people of color to its board of directors.

> A nation without the means of reform is without the means of survival.
>
> **Edmund Burke (1729–1797)**

When all else fails, people resort to (6) *violence* to demonstrate their frustration and to dramatize the need for change. This tactic might involve destruction of property or an assault on people or both. The use of violence is typically an unplanned and spontaneous reaction such as the Los Angeles riots of 1992 in response to the acquittal of the police officers who had been videotaped beating a black man, Rodney King. When violence is planned, most often it is meant primarily to be a symbolic gesture, such as the Boston Tea Party of 1773.

In the past, violence erupted when frustration over an issue reached a point where the people most affected could no longer control their rage, usually responding destructively to a specific incident. During the Civil War, if wealthy young men were drafted, they avoided military service by paying poor and often unemployed men to take their place. The poor knew that these young men were being exploited and that most of them would probably be killed in the war, and their anger resulted in the 1863 Draft Riot in New York City. More recently, riots occurred in several cities in 1968 following the assassination of Martin Luther King, Jr., and the 1992 Los Angeles riot erupted after the acquittal of police officers caught on videotape brutally beating an African American named Rodney King.

Violence rarely resolves problems primarily because incidents igniting riots are typically only symptoms of larger problems. Even if symptoms are addressed following a riot, the causes of those symptoms will eventually create new problems.

In the last half of the twentieth century, people of color participated in riots, especially in urban areas. This has caused many Americans to associate violent tactics for change with people of color, but many groups have resorted to violence at one time or another. In fact, the history of riots in the United States reveals that white people have most often been the group causing riots (see Table 7.1). Jones (1997) reported on the historical record: "With few exceptions . . . previous racial riots had consisted of interracial fighting or the destruction of black communities by white mobs" (p. 46).

In identifying tactics, Terry noted that the first five not only represented nonviolent approaches but also illustrated *the critical role education must play*

TABLE 7.1 Riots in America: A Selected List of Riots in the United States Since the Nation Began

Year	Name/Location	Cause
1788	Doctors' Riot/New York City	Medical students digging up bodies
1834	Election Riots/Several cities	Allowing recent immigrants to vote
1835	Abolition Riots/Several cities	Opposing abolitionist efforts
1844	Bible Riots/Philadelphia	Use of Catholic Bible in public schools
1863	Draft Riots/New York City	Corruption and injustice in draft laws
1877	Railroad Riots/Baltimore, Pittsburgh, Chicago, others	Workers striking for fair pay riot in response to militia being called in
1885	Anti-Chinese Riots/Rock Springs, Wyoming	Opposing the railroad's use of Chinese labor
1908	Race Riot/Springfield (IL)	(False) allegation by a white woman of being raped by a black man
1917	Race Riot/East St. Louis	Blacks hired to replace white workers on strike
1921	Race Riot/Tulsa (OK)	(False) allegation by a white woman of an attempted rape by a black man
1942	Zoot Suit Riot/Los Angeles	Allegation that sailors were assaulted by *pachucas* in zoot suits leads to sailors attacking Mexican Americans
1965	Watts Riot/Los Angeles	"Routine" traffic stop sparks protest against unjust treatment by police and legal system
1967–1968	Race Riots/Detroit, Newark and other cities	Protesting police brutality against black suspects, other local racial injustices, and the assassination of Martin Luther King, Jr.
1992	Race Riot/Los Angeles	Protesting white jury acquitting white police officers caught on videotape beating a black man (Rodney King)

if individuals and groups are to engage in nonviolent change. The skills and means necessary to engage in nonviolent tactics are related to what we teach in our schools. To be persuasive in dialogue requires the kinds of communication and problem-solving skills students are taught in school. To engage successfully in confrontation, it is essential to understand how to work effectively in groups; from elementary school through college, students are provided opportunities to participate in collaborative activities and projects. In addition, students are taught how to deliver an effective public speech in school, and skillful confrontation requires one or more individuals with an ability to articulate the group's concerns to the public.

Although economic pressure may not seem to relate to schools but simply to the economic resources one controls, studies show that people earn higher salaries based on the level of education they have completed (Bonilla-Silva, 2001; U.S. Department of Labor, 2000). Organizing a successful boycott requires sufficient numbers of people in a community with economic resources to create pressure on those resisting change, and that largely depends on how much education the people have completed. The level of education an individual has completed is also a major factor in employing the tactic of an inside-outside alliance. The perception of an individual's credibility as a legitimate candidate for election or appointment to a decision-making body is typically influenced by his or her educational achievements.

> Be the change you want to see in the world.
>
> **Mohandis K. Gandhi (1869–1948)**

Finally, education also plays a pivotal role in research. Although studies can be conducted by anyone with a basic knowledge of principles of effective research, those results that are widely disseminated and that influence public and corporate policies tend to come from studies conducted by people with college experience. Violence is the only tactic that does not require education; as Jefferson wrote in the Declaration of Independence, it is the approach people will choose when they believe no other options exist. It is essential that schools provide people with the skills and means for engaging in nonviolent tactics to address issues of social injustice.

> We are all Americans who, because of our cultural heritage, contribute something unique to the fabric of American life. We are like the notes in a chord of music—if all the notes were the same, there would be no harmony, no real beauty, because harmony is based on differences, not similarities.
>
> **Rosa Guerrero (1934–)**

AFTERWORD

The United States today is a society struggling with its internal diversity at the same time that it is attempting to understand and adjust to the external diversity of the global village. Americans have much to learn from other nations' experiences with diversity. Historically, societies dominated by Western Europeans have been intolerant of differences, persecuting those who did not think or act in accordance with what religious or political authorities deemed acceptable, causing conflicts between religions, ethnic groups, and countries. Even when tolerance was practiced, Zeldin (1994) argued that it was for the wrong reasons: "Not out of respect for other people's views, not out of deep knowledge of what they believe, but in despair of finding certainty. It meant closing one's eyes to what other people believed" (p. 272).

Being more diverse than all of Europe, the United States is engaged in a debate between maintaining Anglo conformity or promoting pluralism in response to diversity. Zeldin (1994) explained why advocating tolerance is inadequate: "The tolerated are increasingly demanding to be appreciated, not ignored, and becoming more sensitive to [the] contempt lurking behind the condescension. They do not want to be told that differences do not matter" (p. 272). Pluralism goes beyond tolerance, requiring understanding and acceptance of differences. Many American institutions are responding positively to diversity and taking public positions on the issue. Eck (2001) praised the following statement from the Girl Scouts:

> Pluralism means being inclusive and respectful of people or groups with different backgrounds, experiences, and cultures . . . although you can have diversity without pluralism, you cannot have pluralism without valuing diversity. (pp. 76–77)

If Americans are to demonstrate pluralistic attitudes, educators must teach all students about diversity, and how individuals from diverse groups have contributed to our society. If the changes needed to improve and sustain this society are to come as a consequence of nonviolent tactics for change—from discussion and debate in the context of mutual respect—teachers must help students develop the abilities to use nonviolent tactics effectively. How schools can fulfill this role and what pluralistic policies and practices illustrate the changes happening in the United States will be the focus of the final section of this book, but first it is necessary to understand the problems experienced by diverse groups in our society.

myeducationlab

Now go to Topics #1 and 10: **Ethnicity/Cultural Diversity** and **Immigration** in the MyEducationLab (www.myeducationlab.com) for your course, where you can:

- Find learning outcomes for these topics along with the national standards that connect to these outcomes.
- Complete Assignments and Activities that can help you more deeply understand the chapter content by viewing classroom video and ABC News footage.
- Apply and practice your understanding of the core teaching skills identified in the chapter with the Building Teaching Skills and Dispositions learning units.

TERMS AND DEFINITIONS

Anglo conformity Views the values, norms, and standards of the United States as an extension of English culture because the English were the dominant group during the colonial era and when the new nation was emerging

Boycott To abstain from using, buying, or associating with a group, organization, or nation to protest an injustice and to force the other to address this injustice

Color blind A response to race based on the belief that a person should not notice or consider the skin color of another

Melting pot The conceptual belief that when immigrants from diverse racial/ethnic backgrounds come to the United States they blend into the culture and, mixed together with those who have come before, develop into a new, distinctly American identity

Pluralism (cultural pluralism) The equal coexistence of diverse cultures in a mutually supportive relationship within the boundaries of one nation

Separatism The conceptual belief in the notion of establishing entirely separate societies for each distinct racial, ethnic, or other groups that exist within a society

DISCUSSION EXERCISES

Exercise #1 Differing Views: America's Ethnic Composition Activity

Directions: Do you hear or participate in conversations that reflect your perspectives about American racial and ethnic relationships? Identify each statement by its perspective on ethnic diversity.

AC = Anglo Conformity	MP = Melting Pot
P = Pluralism	S = Separatism

_____ 1. My parents decided not to teach us Laotian. They hoped that this would enable us to move more quickly through the process of becoming an American.

_____ 2. More and more I think in family terms, less ambitiously, on a less than national scale. The differences involved in my being from an Italian family, and Catholic, and even growing up in a lower middle-class home seem more and more important to me.

_____ 3. The reliance of our race on the progress and achievements of others for a consideration in sympathy, justice, and rights is like a dependence on a broken stick: Resting on it will eventually consign you to the ground. The Negro needs a nation and a country of his own, where he can best show evidence of his own ability in the art of human progress.

_____ 4. Now listen to me, Nikki, you are beginning to understand our American ways, so the sooner you drop your Puerto Rican notions, the more successful you will be.

_____ 5. Our blood is as the flood of the Amazon, made up of a thousand noble currents all pouring into one. We are not a nation, so much as a world.

_____ 6. The Japanese race is an enemy race, and while many second- and third-generation Japanese born on United States soil possess U.S. citizenship and have become "Americanized," the racial strains are unchanged.

_____ 7. Outwardly I lived the life of the white man, yet all the while I kept in direct contact with tribal life. While I learned all that I could of the white man's culture, I never forgot that of my people. I kept the language, tribal manners and usages, sang the songs, and danced the dances.

_____ 8. A few years ago, these Greek immigrants had nothing, and now most of them have made it. They're all well off. Of course, the richest ones have left the Greek neighborhoods and live in the suburbs.

_____ 9. Teachers must teach our children what they need to know, but the teachers must also have a profound knowledge of our culture when they work with our children. This is of paramount importance to the preservation of the Cherokee nation.

_____ 10. The Amish keep to themselves. They are tied together by religion, by kinship, and by custom, and they want to keep it that way.

_____ 11. That's right, I was ashamed of my name. Not only that, I was ashamed of being a Jew. There you have it. Exit Abraham Isaac Arshawsky, Enter Art Shaw! You see, of course, how simple this little transformation was. Presto, Change-o! A new name, a new personality. As simple as that!

_____ 12. Indian children are taught to "be like a white man, and think like a white man." They completely lose their self-identity as Navajos.

_____ 13. What I should like to do is come to a better and more profound knowledge of who I am, whence my community came, and where my son and daughter, and their children's children, might wish to head in the future: I want to have a history.

_____ 14. I only ask of the government to be treated as all other men are treated. If I cannot go to my own home, let me have a home in some country where my people will not die so fast.

_____ 15. It makes no difference to me whether my students are black, white, brown, green, red, yellow, or purple. They are *students*, and I treat them all the same. After all, we are all human beings. Why can't we forget about color entirely and just treat each other like human beings?

Adapted from *Education in a Multicultural Society* By Fred Rodriguez University Press of America (1983)

Exercise #2 Are You an Advocate for Gender Equality?

Directions: In our everyday language we make implicit comments that signal oppressive relationships. Read each of the following statements; then respond Yes or No and write a brief comment of explanation. Check for assumptions that are contained in the item before writing your response. What issues of culture, bias, stereotype, and prejudice arise?

1. Should a husband help his wife most of the time with homemaking and child care?

   Yes _____ No _____ Comment:

2. Should a husband usually ask his wife's opinion before making decisions about major purchases or investments?

   Yes _____ No _____ Comment:

3. Should a husband approve of his wife's working outside of the home, although it interferes with her homemaking and child-care duties?

   Yes _____ No _____ Comment:

4. Should a husband be willing to let his wife take the initiative sexually?

   Yes _____ No _____ Comment:

5. Should a husband be pleased when his wife expresses informal opinions about political or intellectual matters, even if her views differ from his?

   Yes _____ No _____ Comment:

6. Should a husband agree to baby-sit the children when his wife is unable to do so?

   Yes _____ No _____ Comment:

7. Do you rate yourself relatively liberated?

   Yes _____ No _____ Comment:

REFERENCES

Adams, D.W. (1995). *Education for extinction: American Indians and the boarding school experience, 1875–1928.* Lawrence: University Press of Kansas.

Describes the establishment of the Bureau of Indian Affairs boarding schools and examines their impact on the Indian students who attended them.

Appleton, N. (1983). *Cultural pluralism in education: Theoretical foundations.* New York, NY: Longman.

Examines how the United States has become pluralistic, how American education has responded to pluralism, and what our pluralistic society might look like in the future.

Aronson, E. (1999). *The social animal* (8th ed.). New York, NY: W. H. Freeman.

Presents an overview of research in social psychology and describes patterns and motives revealed in these studies concerning human behavior.

Barrett, J.R., & Roediger, D. (2002). How white people became white. In P. Rothenberg (Ed.), *White privilege: Essential readings on the other side of racism* (pp. 29–34). New York, NY: Worth.

Discusses the process of Americanization of immigrants to the United States with attention to the use of white privilege as an inducement for immigrants to conform to the majority.

Bonilla-Silva, E. (2001). *White supremacy and racism in the post-civil rights era.* Boulder, CO: Lynne Rienner.

Examines why blacks and other racial minorities remain behind whites financially, and in terms of occupation, health, educational attainment, and other social indicators.

Brooks, R.L. (1996). *Integration or separation?: A strategy for racial equality.* Cambridge, MA: Harvard University Press.

Explains why racial integration and separatist movements have not been successful in the United States, and discusses how a "limited separation" approach could be a successful alternative.

Chua, A. (2007). *Day of empire: How hyperpowers rise to global dominance–and why they fall.* New York, NY: Doubleday.

Summarizes and analyzes the historic rise and fall of major world empires and describes the role religious and racial tolerance played in their rise and the role intolerance played in their demise.

Claiborne, R. (1983). *Our marvelous native tongue: The life and times of the English language.* New York, NY: Times Books.

Describes the evolution of English as a language and the influences and contributions from cultures around the world that shaped it.

Cole, S.G., & Cole, M.W. (1954). *Minorities and American promise.* New York, NY: Harper Brothers.

Provides a framework for discussing diversity; critiques Anglo conformity and melting pot models; and describes how interactions between groups can produce cultural unity.

Cronon, E.D. (1955). *The story of Marcus Garvey and the universal Negro Improvement Association.* Madison: University of Wisconsin Press.

Describes the ideals and aspirations—the rise and fall—of Marcus Garvey.

Eck, D.L. (2001). *A new religious America: How a "Christian Country" has become the world's most religiously diverse nation.* New York, NY: HarperCollins.

Examines the growth of diverse religions in the United States, especially with regard to immigration patterns since 1965, and describes its impact and its potential.

Foner, E. (2000). Affirmative action and history. In J. Birnbaum & C. Taylor (Eds.), *Civil rights since 1787: A reader on the black struggle* (pp. 697–699). New York, NY: New York University Press.

Describes how an affirmative action bias has worked to the advantage of white males in the United States and explains how these historic practices have contemporary consequences.

Fuchs, L.H. (1990). *The American kaleidoscope: Race, ethnicity and the civic culture.* Hanover, NH: University Press of New England.

Argues that immigrant groups have been successful in embracing and practicing basic social and political principles of U.S. society.

Gladwell, M. (2005). *Blink: The power of thinking without thinking.* New York, NY: Little, Brown.

Examines evidence for thought processes that do not appear to be conscious and yet affect a person's choices and behavior.

Gordon, M. (1964). *Assimilation in America: The role of race, religion, and national origins.* New York, NY: Oxford University Press.

Reviews research on immigration and assimilation, and discusses the emerging perspectives on ethnic diversity: Anglo conformity, melting pot, and cultural pluralism.

Greeley, A. (1975, summer). On ethnicity and cultural pluralism, *Change,* pp. 38–44.

Responds to the criticism that pluralism promotes divisiveness and explains some of the main principles and goals of cultural pluralism.

Hattam, V. (2004). Ethnicity: An American genealogy. In N. Foner & G.M. Frederickson (Eds.), *Not just black and white: Historical and contemporary perspectives on immigration, race and ethnicity in the United States* (pp. 42–60). New York, NY: Russell Sage Foundation.

Discusses varying responses to ethnic diversity in the United States.

Infact Canada. (2009). Nestle Boycott. Retrieved June 12, 2008, from http://www.infactcanada.ca

Provides information about the organization including their participation in the Nestlé boycott.

Jones, G.R., & George, J.M. (2003). Managing diverse employees in a diverse environment. In *Contemporary management* (3rd ed., pp. 112–149). New York, NY: McGraw-Hill.

Describes increasing diversity among consumers and in the workforce.

Laosa, L. (1974). Toward a research model of multicultural competency-based education. In W.A. Hunter (Ed.), *Multicultural education through competency-based education* (pp. 135–145). Washington, DC: American Association of Colleges for Teacher Education.

Discusses the value of cultural diversity and the need for competency-based programs to prepare teachers to work with culturally diverse students.

Locke, A. (1989). *The philosophy of Alain Locke: Harlem renaissance and beyond,* L. Harris (Ed.). Philadelphia, PA: Temple University Press.

Discusses the relevance of pluralism for democracy in several essays including "Pluralism and Intellectual Democracy" and "Pluralism and Ideological Peace."

Martin, W., Jr. (1984). *The mind of Frederick Douglass.* Chapel Hill: University of North Carolina Press.

Describes influences on Frederick Douglass's intellectual development.

Menand, L. (2001). *The metaphysical club.* New York, NY: Farrar, Straus, & Giroux.

Discusses the evolution of ideas that led to the philosophy of pragmatism and explains how this influenced Horace Kallen and Alain Locke's concept of cultural pluralism.

Naisbitt, J., & Aburdene, P. (1990). Global lifestyles and cultural nationalism. In *Megatrends 2000* (pp. 118–153). New York, NY: William Morrow.

Discusses the assertion of cultural uniqueness in response to homogenization caused by globalization.

Nieto, S. (2008). *Affirming diversity: The sociopolitical context of multicultural education* (5th ed.). Boston, MA: Pearson.

Provides a comprehensive analysis of how schools fail to meet the needs of students of color and suggests strategies for more effective teaching based on research and practice.

Pai, Y., & Adler, S. (1997). *Cultural foundations of education* (2nd ed.). Upper Saddle River, NJ: Merrill/Prentice Hall.

Discusses the relationship between pluralism and democracy in Chapter 4, "Cultural Pluralism, Democracy, and Multicultural Education: 1970s–1990s" (pp. 93–136).

Pipher, M. (2002). *The middle of everywhere: The world's refugees come to our town.* New York, NY: Harcourt.

Describes the nature of current immigration to America using some statistical data; the book is primarily based on interviews with immigrants.

Schaefer, R.T. (2008). *Racial and ethnic groups* (11th ed.). Upper Saddle River, NJ: Pearson.

Provides information on racial and ethnic minorities but also includes chapters on women, religious diversity, immigrants, and cross-cultural comparisons.

Schlesinger, A., Jr. (1991). *The disuniting of America: Reflections on a multicultural society.* Knoxville, TN: Whittle Books.

Provides an overview of the various historical perspectives on ethnic diversity.

Seldon, H. (1996). On being color-blind. In J. Andrzejewski (Ed.), *Oppression and social justice: Critical frameworks* (5th ed., pp. 297–298). Needham, MA: Simon & Schuster.

Analyzes the implications of asserting a "color-blind" perspective.

Simpson, E. (Ed.). (1967). Meditation 17. *John Donne: Selected prose* (pp. 100–101). London: Oxford University Press.

Considered one of the most profound statements about the connectedness of human beings.

Sleeter, C. (1993). How white teachers construct race. In C. McCarthy & W. Crichlow (Eds.), *Race identity and representation in education* (pp. 157–191). New York, NY: Routledge.

Describes the assumptions and perceptions of white teachers concerning racial identity and the consequences this has when they are teaching students of color.

Tatum, B.D. (1997). *"Why are all the black kids sitting together in the cafeteria?" and other conversations about race.* New York, NY: Basic Books.

Explains the development of racial identity in adolescents and the subtle and overt racial barriers that inhibit the cross-racial dialogues Americans need to initiate and sustain.

Terry, R.W. (1975). *For whites only* (2nd ed.). Grand Rapids, MI: William B. Eerdmans.

Discusses the need for white people to embrace pluralism and describes the tactics to be used to promote social change.

Terry, R.W. (1993). *Authentic leadership: Courage in action.* San Francisco: Jossey-Bass.

Examines six leadership styles by defining leadership as the ability to frame issues correctly and to respond to issues by using power ethically.

U.S. Census Bureau. (2005). Florida, California and Texas to Dominate Future Population Growth. Retrieved July 10, 2006, from http://www.census.gov

Provides information about current and future population trends in the United States.

U.S. Department of Labor. (2009). Education pays. Retrieved on April 10, 2009, from www.bls.gov/emp/emptab7.htm.

Provides data on 2008 earnings in the United States based on educational attainment.

Williams, C. (1968). *Manifesto.* Ann Arbor: Michigan Education Association.

Presents a rationale for advocating for cultural pluralism in our schools.

Williams, C. (2003). Managing individuals and a diverse work force. In *Management* (2nd ed., pp. 343–371). Versailles, KY: Thomson Southwestern.

Explains why diversity is being promoted in the corporate world, discusses the benefits of diversity, and discusses principles for being an effective manager of diverse employees.

Williams, J. (1987). *Eyes on the prize: America's civil rights years, 1954–1965.* New York, NY: Viking Penguin.

Describes the Montgomery bus boycott in Chapter 3 (pp. 59–89); also of interest is Episode 1, "Awakenings: 1954–1956," of the PBS documentary "Eyes on the Prize: America's Civil Rights Years" (Blackside, Inc., 1986).

Wright, R.H. (1991). *The birth of the Montgomery bus boycott.* Southfield, MI: Charro Press.

Provides a first-person account of the crucial first four days of the boycott.

Zangwill, I. (1915). *The melting pot.* New York, NY: Macmillan.

Presents the melting pot perspective. [Also of interest, *Moscow on the Hudson,* a contemporary melting pot perspective available on video (Columbia Pictures, 1984).]

Zeldin, T. (1994). *An intimate history of humanity.* New York: HarperCollins.

Examines private lives and relationships but expands to explore a universal human history through a variety of perspectives, employing a wide range of knowledge.

Contemporary Dilemmas for Intergroup Relations

Section 3 examines oppression currently experienced by members of diverse groups based on differences of race, gender, sexual orientation, social class, and disability. Although institutional discrimination is emphasized, cultural biases and individual prejudices and negative behaviors also are addressed.

Although white supremacist attitudes described in Section 2 are no longer the cultural norm, Chapter 8 describes how white privilege is reflected in American culture. Ongoing individual racial prejudices have resulted in increased racial segregation in neighborhoods and schools. Overt and covert institutional discrimination is

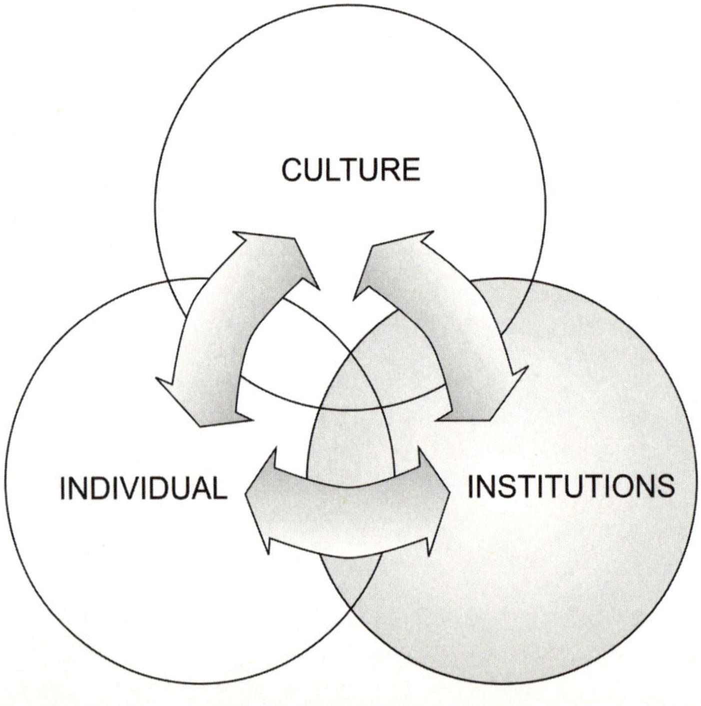

described in such diverse practices as word-of-mouth hiring, tracking plans in schools, realtors steering clients to specific neighborhoods, and communities employing at-large elections to diminish or deny representation of racial minority groups.

Chapter 9 examines the sexist messages inherent in everyday words and phrases and provides nonsexist alternatives to language that has historically promoted sexist cultural attitudes. Not only does language present attitudinal disparity, but the nature of violence against women in the United States ranges from domestic abuse to rape: Institutional sexist inequity is reflected in salary disparity between men and women, exploitation of women as part-time workers, and sexual harassment in the workplace.

Chapter 10 provides an overview of historical influences shaping the European and American cultural bias against homosexuality and the myths that have emerged from that bias. Although many of these myths are contradicted by scientific studies of sexuality, many individual Americans maintain derogatory beliefs about gays and lesbians that justify their homophobia. Institutional discrimination is apparent in such areas as the workplace, the legal system, the military, and in schools; the campaign for "gay rights" represents the efforts of activists to demand equal legal status for all Americans regardless of sexual orientation.

Chapter 11 describes how American cultural values historically promulgate negative influences on individual perceptions of poor people in terms of their deficiencies and personal responsibility for their own poverty. American cultural influence was interrupted in the 1930s when the Great Depression forced many Americans to demand that the federal government become involved in addressing the widespread problems of poverty. Even though many of those 1930s poverty programs are still in place, the previous negative attitudes have reappeared and are reinforced by derogatory beliefs concerning the poor, including myths about the capability of welfare recipients. Institutions contribute to the exploitation of the poor through government economic policies that favor the wealthiest Americans, resulting in a growing disparity between rich and poor. Vulnerable low-income families are also subjected to economic manipulation by banks and merchants, as illustrated by redlining practices, high interest rates, rent-to-own stores, and pawnshops.

Chapter 12 presents an overview of historical perceptions of people with disabilities and how these impressions contributed to a cultural bias in America that resulted in the institutionalization of these individuals. Being kept apart from society reinforces negative perceptions of people with disabilities, especially the attitude that people with disabilities are unable to care for themselves, and results in discrimination against them even when they are living in one's community. Although many states have passed laws to reduce or eliminate these institutions today, people with disabilities encounter various forms of discrimination even when they require minimal accommodations for personal needs.

CHAPTER 8

Racism: Confronting a Legacy of White Domination in America

"The problem of race remains America's greatest moral dilemma. When one considers the impact it has upon the nation, its resolution might well determine our destiny."

Martin Luther King, Jr. (1929–1968)

We have always divided people into categories based on physical differences: However, the concept of **racism,** which involves the creation of racial categories of human beings with one group superior to others, was not widely accepted until the nineteenth century. Even today, young children learn the lessons of difference.

When a city in the northwestern United States became home to a large Gypsy community, the elementary school teachers noted animosity between Gypsy children and other children. The teachers decided to implement curricula concerning Gypsy history and culture. The school district hired a consultant, Carlos Cortes, to assist them.

Cortes (2000) asked the teachers to find out what the children already knew about Gypsies, especially negative information or stereotypes. The teachers were confident that the children were too young to have learned stereotypes and believed that because the Gypsies had only recently arrived, it was highly unlikely that the children had heard much about them. Nevertheless, Cortes insisted that teachers talk to the children to find out what they knew about Gypsies. If they expressed prejudices or stereotypes, their misinformation would need to be addressed and corrected before new information could be accepted. When the teachers implemented Cortes's suggestion, they were shocked by what their children said about Gypsies: They were dirty, they were thieves, and they kidnapped babies. It is sad to realize how easy it is for young children in America to learn to be racist; they have learned some of these lessons from their culture.

Cultural Racism

Cultural racism is the practice of recognizing activities and contributions of one racial group in preference to others within a multiracial society. From its earliest days, America had a mix of races; however, the dominant culture that emerged did not tend to include all racial groups. Andrzejewski (1996) described one aspect of oppression as an **ethnocentric** group imposing its culture on others. Because schools are regarded as institutions that instill cultural knowledge and values in the next generation, our schools are an appropriate place to begin an analysis of cultural racism.

How is racism taught to children and youth in our schools?

One misinterpretation that could be taken from the Cortes experience is that schools work to confront and reduce racial prejudice. Although this is true to some degree, too many schools do not discuss issues

> At the start of the twentieth century, over 98 percent of blacks in the United States were native-born—a much higher percentage than for whites. Blacks are as American as you can get.
>
> **Marguerite Wright (Contemporary)**

of race, and all too often, they misrepresent the role of race in the history of the United States and in contemporary American life. Students may be taught that the slave trade began because Europeans viewed Africans as a primitive and inferior people. Although some Europeans had this view, it was not shared by everyone. Evidence from English merchants engaged in trade with Africans reveals that they knew they were "dealing with people from well-organized sociopolitical systems, people who were sophisticated and intelligent" (Smedley, 1999, p. 92).

In addition, some schools celebrate African American accomplishments by identifying the first black person to achieve a particular goal or status. Providing such information may persuade students that America allows all individuals to pursue their goals, but as Smith (2004) notes, such achievements can also be viewed as a lesson in racism. Students are rarely told why a particular black person was the first to achieve a goal because that would require providing information about how the opportunity for a black person to strive for such an achievement had been denied by past racist policies and/or practices.

Cultural racism is also evidenced when teachers and textbooks largely overlook indigenous people. If students are asked who settled the country now called the United States, the answer we have been taught to give is most likely "Pilgrims" or possibly "English colonists." We don't think of—or don't know about—Africans brought to South Carolina by the Spanish and left to establish a settlement in 1526. We tend to overlook Spanish settlements (in what are now Florida and New Mexico) that existed prior to English settlements at Jamestown and Plymouth. And ironically, American elementary and secondary students are unlikely to consider American Indians as "settlers." Loewen (1995) comments,

> Part of the problem is the word *settle*. "Settlers" were white, a student once pointed out to me. "Indians" didn't settle. Students are not the only people misled by *settle*. The film that introduces visitors to Plimoth Plantation tells how "they went about the work of civilizing a hostile wilderness." (p. 67)

Apparently "civilizing the wilderness" included stealing and desecrating graves. Loewen cited a colonist's journal reporting that on only their second day after arriving, two men from the Mayflower came upon an Indian dwelling where no one was at home and stole several items, noting in their journal that they intended to pay the Indians back later.

Pilgrims also took from caches where Indians stored food. During that first harsh winter when the Pilgrims were desperate for food, they dug up several Indian graves, knowing that food was buried with the bodies; then they thanked God for assisting their survival. Loewen (1995) explains the irony that Thanksgiving was never intended to be a holiday celebrating harmony between Indians and Pilgrims; it was declared a holiday by President Lincoln in the midst of the Civil War to foster patriotism. In spite of stereotypical textbook images showing Pilgrims and Indians sharing food at Thanksgiving, many Native Americans consider this holiday a form of cultural racism and do not participate in Thanksgiving celebrations.

How does society reinforce the cultural racism taught in school?

Sometimes racist messages are communicated in subtle ways. Citron (1969) identified what he called a **rightness of whiteness** concept, meaning that children learn to regard being white as normal, and to make negative judgments of those who deviate from white norms. Children grow up seeing primarily white faces on television, in movies, in advertisements. They read fairy tales and stories about Snow White and Peter Pan, request Christmas presents from a white Santa Claus, and revere white heroes in history or literature. White children and youth usually attend schools with predominantly white students, learning a curriculum that emphasizes white people's perspectives and achievements.

George (2006) argues that "Schools propagate and nurture whiteness by providing students with a steady diet of white ideology . . . [that] has resulted in a system that thinks, acts, and teaches 'white as right'" (p. 51). Consequently, white children are likely to unconsciously regard nonwhite people as less important.

In recent years, scholars have expanded Citron's insight into the concept of **white privilege,** referring to choices and behaviors white people take for granted that people of color cannot. McIntosh (2001) described white privilege as "an invisible package of unearned assets" and she identified many specific examples (p. 164). See Table 8.1 for some examples. Akbar (2010) defined white privilege as a set of options, opportunities, and opinions that are gained and maintained at the expense of people of color. To Akbar, white privilege can be as arrogant as people believing in a God who looks exactly like them or as poignant as a child reading Superman or Spiderman comic books and not needing to color the faces to identify with the heroes. Unless confronted, white privilege may create an unintended sense of white supremacy in white youth and adults, and white supremacy includes racist attitudes ranging from paternalism to antagonism.

White privilege not only fosters self-esteem and an attitude of superiority toward others, but also has provided tangible benefits. Initially excluding agricultural and domestic workers from the social security program denied hundreds of thousands of people of color a benefit that most white people enjoyed. Kivel (2002) cites a report concluding that black veterans were denied many of the benefits given to white veterans following World War II, and that veterans of color who did receive benefits were often given fewer benefits compared to white veterans. Even today, being white means a greater likelihood of being paid a higher salary, receiving promotions, and having loans approved. Hughes (2004) reports that white men are only 30% of the U.S. population, yet they have 75% of the most highly paid jobs.

White privilege is not just about economic benefits; it offers cultural benefits such as being able to shape American conceptions of reality. In our schools, white people have determined when and where philosophy begins, or mathematics or classical art. American history is said to begin when white people arrived; anything that happened prior

TABLE 8.1 White Privilege

Because of white privilege, the following activities illustrate assumptions white people can make that people of color cannot make:

1. If I should need to move, I can be pretty sure of renting or purchasing housing in an area which I can afford and in which I would want to live.
2. I can be pretty sure that my neighbors in such a location will be neutral or pleasant to me.
3. I can go shopping alone most of the time, pretty well assured that I will not be followed or harassed.
4. When I am told about our national heritage or about "civilization," I am shown that people of my color made it what it is.
5. I can be sure that my children will be given curricular materials that testify to the existence of their race.
6. Whether I use checks, credit cards, or cash, I can count on my skin color not to work against the appearance of financial reliability.
7. I can arrange to protect my children most of the time from people who might not like them.
8. I can swear, or dress in secondhand clothes, or not answer letters, without having people attribute these choices to the bad morals, the poverty, or the illiteracy of my race.
9. I can be pretty sure that if I ask to talk to "the person in charge," I will be facing a person of my own race.
10. If a traffic cop pulls me over or if the IRS audits my tax return, I can be sure I haven't been singled out because of my race.
11. I can easily buy posters, postcards, picture books, greeting cards, dolls, toys, and children's magazines featuring people of my race.
12. I can choose blemish cover or bandages in "flesh" color and have them more or less match my skin.

Source: McIntosh, P. *White Privilege: Unpacking the Invisible Knapsack.* In P. Rothenberg (Ed.), *Race, Class, and Gender in the United States: An Integrated Study.*

to that time is relegated to a largely irrelevant category termed *prehistory.* In classrooms reflecting white privilege, textbooks, bulletin boards, classroom discussions, and assignments typically focus on white people; the contributions and concerns of other racial or ethnic groups may be minimally represented or omitted. Because understanding racial and ethnic groups has not been emphasized, white students entering college may be surprised and possibly annoyed to find requirements for courses in racial and ethnic studies.

As a consequence of receiving an ethnocentric education, white Americans may regard certain people of color as foreign. Howard (2006) and others have described white people who meet Asian Americans or Latinos and ask, "Where are you from?" When a hometown such as Chicago or Miami is identified, the next question often will be, "Okay, but where are you *from?*" If the person of color responds by saying he or she has always lived in Chicago or Miami, the white person may respond: "Okay, but I mean, where did you come from?" In an attempt to ascertain the person's ethnicity, the questioner implies a perception that the other person is from outside the United States, especially because the response about their American hometown was ignored. The questioner is suggesting, "You don't look like an American." And the message that "You don't belong here" is clear to the Latino or Asian American being questioned.

Consequences of racist attitudes promoted by our culture can range from mildly annoying to tragic. A few days after the terrorists' destruction of the World Trade towers in New York City, a white man walked into a convenience store in Mesa, Arizona, and shot and killed the store clerk because he wore a turban and looked Muslim and Middle Eastern. The murder victim was not foreign, but American; he was not Muslim, but a Sikh who had emigrated from India. The killer justified his act by rationalizing that he was not racist, that his behavior was an expression of patriotism.

Individual Racism

Individual racism includes both racial prejudice and racist behavior. Racial prejudice refers to negative attitudes a person holds based on racial categories, and it is learned in many ways: from stereotypes in films to myths passed on from one generation to the next. Racist behavior occurs when someone responds to his or her racial prejudices by saying or doing something degrading or harmful toward a person or group. The murder of the Sikh man was an extreme example of individual racism; it is also illustrated by name-calling or by refusing to hire a person of color. In discussing individual racism, it is important to include an analysis of the attitudes and rationalizations used to justify racist behavior.

What denial rationalizations justify individual racism?

Although studies report a decline in racial prejudice among Americans, acts of individual racism are still prevalent. The 1954 *Brown v. Board of Education* decision said segregated schools were inherently unequal and ordered the desegregation of American schools. Communities were slow to respond to this mandate, but by the 1960s, school desegregation plans were finally being implemented. In response to legal and social pressures, school districts throughout the United States continued to develop and implement desegregation proposals. But in the 1980s, Supreme Court decisions backed away from the desegregation mandate, and the lack of aggressive political pressure brought desegregation efforts to a halt. Based on data gathered by the Harvard Civil Rights project (Orfield & Lee, 2006), schools have now become even more racially segregated than they were in the past. Yet many Americans deny that school segregation is still a problem.

Denial rationalizations often reject a reality that is well documented, and denying the resegregation of America's schools is an illustration. In 1968, almost 55% of Latino students attended segregated schools. By 1986, that percentage had risen to over 71%, and by 1998, it was at 76% and it was 77% in 2003 (Orfield & Lee, 2006; Wells, 1989). Latino students attend predominantly minority schools because the 1960s desegregation effort only succeeded in integrating students of color in urban schools. Few white students attended urban schools because their families had moved out of urban areas in a massive migration to segregated suburbs, a phenomenon called **white flight** (Thompson, 1999). Massey (2003) analyzed multiracial societies around the world and found that the only nation as segregated as the United States is today was South Africa under apartheid.

Similar to Latino students, African American students are also likely to attend segregated schools, but some states are more segregated than others. According to Orfield and Lee (2006), the states where the highest percentages of black students attend segregated schools are California (87%), New York (86%), Illinois (82%), and Texas (78%). Obviously, segregation is not just an issue for southern states. Although 29% of North Carolina's students were African American, only 37% attended segregated schools. The North Carolina percentage is still too high, but many states outside of the South are even higher. These comparisons clearly suggest the impact of white flight on public schools in America.

Some white Americans believe school desegregation ended in the 1960s, and that the passage of the 1964 Civil Rights law ended the major problems associated with racial discrimination. This denial rationalization has prompted the argument that there is no longer any need for affirmative action plans to address racial discrimination. A majority of voters in California in 1997 ended the state's affirmative action mandate; one year later the state of Washington did the same, and in the 2008 election, Nebraska voters approved a similar proposal. These voters believed that there was no longer any reason to give preference to any group because of their race or gender. Whether white or nonwhite, male or female, individuals from all groups now are supposedly competing on equal terms and with objective, unbiased criteria for scholarships, admission to college or vocational programs, and employment.

As with all denial rationalizations, this belief in a "level playing field" crumbles before even a cursory examination of the American reality. As Kozol (2005), Spriggs (2008), and Powell (2008) have documented, families of color overwhelmingly tend to live in racially segregated neighborhoods and send their children to segregated schools, which are often deteriorating facilities. A disproportionate number of people of color live in poverty, and even when people of color earn a college degree, they do not gain the same financial reward for that achievement as a white person. Further, Rehmeyer (2007) described a study that demonstrated how economic forces arising from racial segregation created economic inequities even when there was no history of discrimination between two groups. The study also concluded "even when social groups are economically equal, continued segregation may result in inequality over time" (p. 2).

In the United States, racially segregated neighborhoods and schools are not economically equal. In contrast to the deteriorating schools previously mentioned, middle- and upper-middle class white students will likely attend schools with excellent facilities and programs because of generous funding resources. Mainly white suburban school students can enjoy state-of-the-art equipment in well-financed districts, sometimes including swimming pools, tennis courts, and other luxuries that urban schools cannot afford. Meanwhile, teachers in metropolitan schools often struggle to have minimally equipped chemistry or biology laboratories and reasonably current textbooks and instructional materials. In spite of these disparities, all students take the same standardized tests to qualify for admission to colleges, technical schools, and training programs.

Another denial rationalization white people use to justify their opposition to affirmative action is to deny that racism exists. Because a disproportionate number of Americans of color live in poverty, some white people argue that poverty is the real issue, that it affects white people as well as people of color. In reality, race plays a role in *creating* poverty conditions. When white families moved to the suburbs, businesses abandoned inner cities, taking resources and jobs with them. As a result, urban schools are challenged to educate a diverse population of primarily students of color and to address problems based on disproportionate numbers of students living in poverty. Kozol (2005) cites the research finding that in 86% of schools with primarily black and Latino students, more than half of the students qualify for free or reduced-price meals.

To address the needs of students adequately, urban schools must be provided with funding equal to or greater than that for suburban schools. Instead, urban schools historically have operated with far less funding, creating a self-fulfilling prophecy for failure. When low-income students—especially students of color—are not successful in school, white people all too often insist that "those students" just aren't willing to work hard in school, a rationalization that moves beyond denial to become victim-blaming.

What victim-blaming rationalizations justify individual racism?

Surveys conducted by scholars at the University of Chicago have reported a high percentage of comments from white people that appear to blame black people and regard them as deficient. Researchers randomly selected hundreds of households in 300 different communities and conducted surveys concerning racial attitudes, especially white people's perceptions of African Americans (National Opinion Research Center, 1998).

> Most of the people I meet in America are compassionate. Why is it that individually we can be so compassionate and collectively we can be so harsh? . . . I don't have an answer to that.
>
> **Jonathan Kozol (1936–)**

A 1991 survey reported that 62% of white respondents believed that black people were more likely to be lazy than white people, 53% believed that black people were less intelligent than white people, and 56% believed that black people were more likely than white people to commit acts of violence. A 1998 survey found that 56% of white people still thought blacks were lazy. Believing blacks are lazier or less intelligent than whites can be used to justify the individual racism of an employer refusing to hire a black applicant.

Although fewer white people in 1998 thought black people were less intelligent than whites (down from 50% to 35%), white people perceiving blacks as more likely to be more violent than whites increased from 56% in 1991 to 79% in 1998. Regarding black people as violent has contributed to whites demanding more prisons and tougher sentences for violent crimes; it also affects how police officers respond to black suspects and contributes to racial profiling.

For example, Kivel (2002) cites two major reports on juvenile and adult crime in America that seem to document racial profiling. Although black youth constitute only 15% of those under eighteen, they represent 26% of youth arrests. Although a similar number of white and black adults use drugs, there are far fewer arrests of whites than of blacks, and blacks represent two thirds of those convicted of drug use. Racial disparities continue as people move through the criminal justice system. Black youth make up 40% of those in juvenile prisons, 46% of youth tried in adult criminal courts, and 58% of juveniles incarcerated in adult prisons. The disparity continues when they become adults. In a study of thirty-seven states, black men went to prison at a rate that averaged "between 27 and 57 times the rate of white men" (p. 215).

Perhaps the most curious response to the 1991 survey was to a question eliminated from later surveys: 51% of white respondents said black people were less patriotic than white people, which is surprising because a conventional measure of patriotism in America is the willingness to risk one's life in service to the country. Buckley (2001) described African Americans who volunteered, fought, and died in every war in which the United States was involved: the Revolutionary War, Civil War, Spanish-American War, and all conflicts, large and small, in the twentieth century. (See Figure 8.1.)

What avoidance rationalizations justify individual racism?

Avoidance rationalizations propose partial or false solutions or are intended to distract attention from racism as a cause of some problem. A common avoidance rationalization stems from white people's belief that the passage of the 1964 Civil Rights Act, affirmative action plans, and a variety of other policies and programs since then have resulted in significant progress toward achieving the goal of eliminating racial prejudice and discrimination. Based on this belief, many white people have opposed a variety of programs intended to assist people of color—from recreational basketball activities to bilingual education.

Because of the highly visible role of African Americans in the civil rights movement, one would assume that they were the major beneficiaries of policies and programs developed in response to that movement, but an examination of African Americans' economic circumstances contradicts this rationalization. The good news according to Wellner

FIGURE 8.1

This photograph shows the black members of the Rough Riders who fought in the Spanish-American War; African American soldiers have rarely been acknowledged in films or in history books.

Source: North Wind Picture Archives.

ON THE BATTLE-GROUND OF LAS GUASIMAS—TROOPS GOING TO THE FRONT.

(2000) is that more than 40% of all black families today are middle class. The bad news is that almost 49% of black families earn approximately $15,000 a year or less, and they still face significant barriers stemming from race and class prejudice.

Black children are 3.5 times more likely to be part of a family living in poverty than are white children. Further, blacks are twice as likely as whites not to have health care insurance. Studies show that blacks are less likely than whites to graduate from high school or college, and about twice as likely to be employed in low-paying, low-status jobs (Morin, 2001). Despite such statistics, Morin cited a national survey conducted by the *Washington Post,* the Henry J. Kaiser Family Foundation, and Harvard University reporting that 40% to 60% of white Americans believe great progress has been made to reduce racial discrimination and that black people are almost economically equal to white people in the United States today.

> As long as you keep a person down, some part of you has to be down there to hold him down, so it means you cannot soar as you otherwise might.
>
> **Marian Anderson (1897–1993)**

When white Americans acknowledge problems of Americans of color, they often express no sense of responsibility. History provides numerous examples of the white majority in the United States discussing "the Negro problem" as if it had nothing to do with the white population. Novelist Richard Wright contradicted that assertion: "There isn't any Negro problem; there is only a white problem" (Lipsitz, 2008). Wright meant that the racial attitudes and behaviors of white people were the problem—that racism in America meant white racism. It is neither ethical nor practical for Americans of any color to avoid issues stemming from racism.

Institutional Racism

Jones (1997) defined **institutional racism** as "established laws, customs, and practices that systematically reflect and produce racial inequities in American society" (p. 438). We rely on institutions in America. Although individual racism is damaging, institutional racism is far more devastating because of the broader impact institutions have on people.

Institutional racism can be intentional when it is a result of a prejudiced person making a conscious decision about a person or group based on their race. Williams (2007) described a study in which pairs of black and white males, and pairs of Hispanic and white males applied for the same jobs. Identical qualifications were created on their résumés. The men were trained to present themselves in similar ways to minimize differences during interviews; still, white men received three times as many job offers as did black or Hispanic men.

We also know that institutional racism can be unintentional. Although studies have reported that people of color pay more to purchase a car than white people, especially white men, representatives of car dealerships deny that they engage in discrimination, but perhaps they are simply not conscious of it. Gladwell (2005) cites a Chicago study where 38 people dressed and identified themselves as professionals to purchase an automobile: fifteen white men, seven white women, eight black women, and five black men. They visited 242 car dealers and negotiated for a car according to strict instructions so that their behavior would be similar. The initial offers that sales representatives made to white men tended to be about $725 above dealer's invoice compared to initial offers of about $935 above invoice given to white women. The initial offers to black women tended to be $1,200 above invoice, and for black men it was $1,690. Even after negotiating with the sales representatives, the average price of the car for black men was $1,550 above invoice, more than double what white men were offered without any bargaining.

Because most Americans seem to agree that it is wrong to discriminate based on race, ethnicity, gender, or other factors, it is important to understand how institutional racism occurs. Whether intentional or unintentional, institutional racism results in negative consequences for people of color. Unemployment statistics document how race makes a difference when decisions are made about hiring people.

> The sad truth is that most evil is done by people who never make up their minds to be either good or evil.
>
> **Hannah Arendt (1898–1989)**

How is institutional racism reflected in statistics on employment?

Disproportionate numbers of people of color work in low-paying, low-status jobs, and people of color tend to have significantly higher unemployment rates compared to whites. The data for black youth is staggering. Tyson (1997) reported a 34% unemployment rate for black teenagers compared to 14.2% for white teenagers, and as high as 60% for black teenagers in some cities. According to Foster (2001), the employment discrepancy continues after graduation from high school. Higher percentages of African Americans are unemployed in the year after they graduate from high school than white graduates. It did not matter if the graduates were from rural or urban schools. The unemployment rate for black graduates was higher than whites regardless of socioeconomic status, the type of high school attended, or the type of academic program in which they were enrolled. Foster argued that racism is the obvious explanation of these consistently different rates.

Despite affirmative action programs, studies by the U.S. Bureau of Labor Statistics (2001) document that disparity between unemployment rates for people of color compared to whites was slightly worse in 1990 (11% versus 4%) than it was in 1960 (10% versus 5%). In 2009, the disparity in unemployment continued with an 8.4% rate for whites, 12.7% for Latinos, and 14.9% for African Americans (Bureau of Labor Statistics, 2009). Yet even with a strong economy, urban areas showed larger disparities in jobless rates for white and black workers. In a study by the Center for Economic Development at the University of Wisconsin-Milwaukee, Levine (2008) compared black and white jobless rates in Milwaukee with those in selected cities such as Chicago, Buffalo, Detroit, and St. Louis. Levine looked at jobless rates rather than unemployment rates because the latter does not include adult people in the workforce who have given up on finding a job, often because no jobs appear to be available. This is especially a problem in urban areas. Levine's data (see Table 8.2) reveals that urban black workers are almost twice as likely not to have a job as urban white workers. Milwaukee had the most significant problem with 51.1% of its black workers jobless and a disparity of 32.5% between black and white workers. Such data clearly suggests that race, whether intentional or unintentional, was a factor in hiring employees.

TABLE 8.2 Black/White Jobless Rates in Selected Metropolitan Areas

	Jobless Rates for Working-Age Men		
	Black	White	Disparity
1. Milwaukee	51.1	18.6	32.5
2. Buffalo	51.4	25.3	26.1
3. Detroit	50.6	25.6	25.0
4. St. Louis	46.3	21.4	24.9
5. Chicago	45.1	20.4	24.7

Source: Center for Economic Development, University of Wisconsin-Milwaukee (2008).

How does institutional racism influence hiring decisions?

To understand why disparities in black and white unemployment exist, examine how hiring decisions are made. Studies repeatedly show that one of the most important methods used to recruit and hire employees is **word-of-mouth hiring.** If job seekers have relatives or friends already working for the company to recommend them, those job seekers have a better chance of being hired. Research suggests that 60% to 90% of blue-collar workers were hired because of recommendations from family or friends—and the same pattern has been observed in hiring decisions for white-collar jobs.

Employers feel they benefit from the word-of-mouth approach. If a trusted employee recommends someone, the employers believe that the risk in determining the quality of the person being hired is greatly reduced. Another benefit is that hiring costs are minimal; jobs are filled without paying to advertise them. Because of word-of-mouth hiring, Lipsitz (2008) found that 86% of available jobs never appeared in the classified ads of local newspapers.

Word-of-mouth hiring disadvantages people of color because of the history of segregation and discrimination in the United States. In the past, white male employees were blatantly favored over applicants who were women or people of color. At one time the preference was so obvious that state and federal governments passed anti-discrimination laws to address the problem; still, white men constituted a disproportionate share of the workforce. Schaefer (2008) reviewed social distance studies indicating that people consistently indicate a preference for people most like themselves; therefore, white people may recommend other white people simply to make sure they will be with people with whom they are comfortable.

Furthermore, because of ongoing housing segregation, white Americans have not tended to become friends with people of color. When white workers recommend a friend or relative for a job, they may insist that they are not trying to prevent a person of color from being hired but instead are helping someone they know. Intentional or not, word-of-mouth job recruitment offers a distinct advantage to white job applicants and contributes to discrimination documented by statistics on unemployment disparities between black and white workers.

Another way to secure employment is to join a labor union. However, admission policies of many unions still discriminate against people of color, particularly in unions for skilled trades that are historically dominated by white workers and have records of past discrimination against people of color. Unions typically accept new members based primarily on recommendations of current members. As with word-of-mouth hiring, white union members may or may not recommend people of color, but they are more likely to know and recommend someone who is white (Feagin & Feagin, 1986; Lipsitz, 2008).

Discrimination also occurs in decisions regarding company location. Because neighborhoods in the United States still reveal a pattern of racial segregation, a company's decision to locate in a white suburb means that the employees hired will be primarily or exclusively white. Studies show that when a new company selects a location or an established company expands to a new location, employees who live within a 30- to 40-mile radius of the worksite tend to be hired.

In the 1990s, Wilson (1996) reported a trend toward the *suburbanization of industry,* especially among retail trade companies. The trend has continued. White suburbs are advantaged because they tend to be more affluent than urban areas and usually offer more incentives to influence a company's decision to relocate. Wilson reported that when a number of low-income blacks were placed in suburban apartments, they were significantly more likely to find work than the low-income blacks placed in apartments in the city; the reason was the higher availability of jobs in the suburbs. Leondar-Wright (2009) cites a study of forty-five urban areas reporting that 25% to 50% of black unemployment was a result of jobs being shifted to the suburbs. A company's reasons for selecting a location may have more to do with economic incentives than with race, but the consequences of that decision have a racial impact.

How has institutional racism influenced the development of segregated neighborhoods?

Studies report that neighborhoods in the United States continue to reveal a pattern of racial segregation (Bonilla-Silva, 2001; Farley, 2010; Massey, 2001; Orser, 1990). Although there has been some improvement since the 1980s, Massey (2003) describes the level of black and white segregation in urban areas:

> The most common measure of residential segregation is an index that ranges from 0 to 100, where 0 indicates that blacks and whites are evenly distributed among neighborhoods and 100 means that blacks and whites share no neighborhood in common. Scores greater than 50 are considered to be "high"; those above 70 are "extreme." . . . The most segregated U.S. metropolitan area is Detroit, with an index of 85, followed by Milwaukee (82), New York (81), Newark, N.J. (80), and Chicago (80). Other areas with "extreme" segregation scores include Buffalo, Cincinnati, Cleveland, Kansas City, Philadelphia, and St. Louis. (p. 22)

Past practices of discrimination were overt, including the use of covenants by which homeowners guaranteed other homeowners in their neighborhood that if they sold their home it would not be sold to a family of color. Today such tactics are illegal, but other discriminatory practices still occur.

Some people believe American attitudes are changing. Foster (2001) cites a 1958 study in which white people were asked if they would leave their neighborhood if a black family moved in next to

> An illustration of the craving people have to attach favorable symbols to themselves is seen in the community where white people banded together to force out a Negro family that had moved in. They called themselves 'Neighborly Endeavor' and chose as their motto the Golden Rule.
>
> **Gordon Allport (1897–1967)**

them: 44% of them said they would, but in a 1997 study only 1% of white respondents said they would move. In the 1958 study, 80% of white respondents said they would leave their neighborhood if a large number of black families moved in, but in the 1997 study, only 18% said they would leave. Yet Foster and others have cited studies documenting that white families will stay in a neighborhood as long as black families do not exceed 7% or 8% of its residents. Once that percentage is exceeded, white families leave (Bonilla-Silva, 2001).

Neighborhood segregation is assured when realtors engage in a practice known as **steering.** The term refers to keeping files of homes for sale in white neighborhoods separate from those for sale in areas consisting predominantly or exclusively of families of color. Realtors show their clients homes in neighborhoods based on their race (Jenkins, 2007). Clients may be shown homes in integrated neighborhoods, if there are any, in response to a specific request. If accused of racism, realtors may claim that white homeowners who don't want people of color moving into their neighborhoods will not list their home with a realtor whom they believe will show their home to people of color. Realtors could insist that they are not being racist but are simply respecting the wishes of their clients.

Zoning ordinances might also contribute to racial segregation of neighborhoods. City councils often approve ordinances excluding multifamily dwellings in certain residential areas. The cost of homes in such areas is usually well beyond the means of many families of color. The rental price of units in a multifamily dwelling might be affordable to many clients of color. So the passage of a zoning ordinance expressly prohibiting multifamily housing virtually eliminates the possibility of families of color moving into the neighborhood.

Segregation aside, it is often more difficult for people of color to finance the purchase of homes. A study of the Federal Reserve Bank of Boston reported almost three times as many mortgage loans in low-income neighborhoods consisting of white homeowners than in those consisting of African American homeowners. Home loan officers seem more willing to dismiss the credit record problems of white applicants. Lipsitz (2008) also cites a Los Angeles study that found different standards of eligibility for white and black loan applicants. A study of a Houston bank reported that 13% of middle-income white applicants were denied loans compared to 36% of middle-income black applicants; a study of home loan institutions in Atlanta found that they approved five times as many loans to whites as to blacks.

Between 1998 and 2008, banks and other lending institutions began to approve more home loans to people of color as part of the infamous sub-prime mortgage fiasco. During the financial collapse that took place in 2008, many critics blamed the lenders for making too many bad loans to people, especially people of color, whose finances were inadequate to pay off the home loans they received. Yet data was collected over the same ten-year period from the Community Advantage Program that facilitated loans to families with low incomes or single-headed households, and the data reveals that even though these clients presented a greater risk, they were no more likely to default on conventional home mortgage loans than the rest of the population (Oliver & Shapiro, 2008). The problem with sub-prime mortgage loans was that they involved hidden costs, wildly adjustable rates, and severe pre-payment penalties. Adding insult to injury, African American families who qualified for conventional mortgages often were steered to the more profitable sub-prime home loans. As a consequence, three times more families of color were given sub-prime mortgages than white families, and twice as many African American and Latino homeowners ended up losing their homes because they defaulted on the sub-prime loans. One estimate of the loss of wealth to African American homeowners was somewhere between $72–$93 billion (Oliver & Shapiro, 2008). These foreclosures not only harmed families who lost their homes, but also diminished the value of surrounding homes in the neighborhood. Since U.S. neighborhoods tend to be racially segregated, homeowners who were people of color were more likely to suffer a loss in the value of their homes because of foreclosures in their neighborhood. And reductions in home values result in fewer tax dollars to support the schools in these areas.

How does institutional racism occur in schools?

As the statistics given earlier in the chapter illustrate, American schools are racially segregated, in fact, more segregated than ever. The last significant effort by the U.S. Congress to support racial integration in schools was a 1972 law providing funds for schools attempting to desegregate. According to Gary Orfield of the Harvard Civil Rights Project, schools in the United States were desegregating in compliance with court-ordered desegregation for slightly more than two decades, and data from that period show that the numbers of students of color graduating from high school increased significantly and the racial divide in test scores decreased substantially (Kozol, 2005). As schools began resegregating in the 1990s, racial test scores widened once again. Orfield's research shows that this ongoing process of resegregation has resulted in 75% of African American and Latino students attending schools with predominantly minority populations, with more than 2 million of them attending "schools which we call apartheid schools" (Kozol, 2005, p. 19).

Some school districts, especially in urban areas, have attempted to overcome the impact of racial segregation by implementing multicultural curricula to make subject matter more inclusive, yet most elementary and secondary schools do not address adequately issues concerning people of color. In part, this problem stems from textbooks that continue to demonstrate a Eurocentric bias in history, literature, art, and music (Kirp, 1991; Loewen, 1995; Sleeter & Grant, 1991). Indeed, textbook bias can be a problem at all levels of education. In a review of college economics textbooks, Clawson (2002) found African Americans were disproportionately described as low-income families and were not usually featured in contexts such as the 1930s depression where readers might be more sympathetic to the poor. Textbook bias requires that conscientious teachers develop supplementary materials to provide students with information about multicultural perspectives. This is a difficult task because the major function of teaching is delivering curriculum, and teachers have limited time and resources to develop new material.

Another example of racism in schools is **tracking**—grouping students into categories by ability and assigning them to specific, ability-related classes. Most public elementary, middle, and high schools in America engage in some form of tracking. Based on supposedly objective tests of intellectual ability, children whose first language is not English have been inappropriately placed in remedial classes or even classes for cognitively disabled students (Fattah, 2001). Students of color tend to be overrepresented in classes for slow learners, underrepresented in accelerated classes, and placed in vocational or remedial classes in disproportionate numbers (Kershaw, 1992; Oakes, 2005; Oakes & Wells, 1996; Oakes et al., 2004). Nieto (2008) explained how tracking children who are still going through puberty influences economic and occupational outcomes when they become adults.

> If we were to select the most intelligent, imaginative, energetic, and stable third of mankind, all races would be represented.
>
> **Franz Boas (1858–1942)**

Research has found that tracking provides minimal value for accelerated learners, and it harms students tracked at lower levels, especially those at the lowest level. Because a large percentage of low-income students are racial minorities, tracking usually results in both race and class segregation because low-income students are typically placed in different tracks than middle- or upper-class students. Tracking has been justified by the argument that it improves education for all students, allowing teachers to teach to the students' level so they learn more efficiently. Research does not support this assumption. Academic outcomes for high-achieving students do not appear to be compromised in heterogeneous classes. Middle- and low-achieving students appear to benefit by interacting with high-achieving students; scholastic development is curtailed significantly when they are stratified with other equally low-achieving students (Oakes, 2005; Oakes & Wells, 1996; Oakes et al., 2000).

It is difficult for people of color to confront institutional racism in jobs, housing, and schools because that requires political power at local, state, and federal levels. Institutional racism curtails opportunities to be elected to local governing bodies—school boards, city councils, county commissions—and makes it even more difficult to win party primaries or elections at the state and national levels.

How does institutional racism affect politics?

Although the situation is improving in some state legislatures, people of color still tend to be underrepresented in the House of Representatives and Senate at both state and federal levels (Bonilla-Silva, 1999). Although people of color constitute more than 35% of the U.S. population, only 17% of the members of the House of Representatives and 5% of the Senate are people of color (Amer & Manning, 2009). There are many problems for candidates of color to overcome.

> In a democracy the majority of citizens is capable of exercising the most cruel oppressions upon the minority.
>
> **Edmund Burke (1729–1797)**

In New Mexico, some Hispanic candidates have been successful emphasizing their Spanish (i.e., white) ancestry. Shorris (2001) noted that such candidates were elected to local and state offices "long before other Latinos could get past gerrymandering, ward politics, and at-large elections" (p. 167). The use of **at-large candidates** involves members of city councils or school boards being elected by the entire city, instead of by their respective districts or wards. If the majority of voters in a city are white, electing at-large candidates will assure all-white representation on councils or boards, despite having areas within the city consisting primarily or exclusively of people of color. Imagine a city that is composed of twelve wards, where three wards are predominantly Mexican American. If each ward elects its own council member, it is likely that three of the twelve city council members would be Mexican American. To reduce or even eliminate that possible outcome, a city can require at-large elections to fill any available position. Each year, when city council elections are conducted, voters in all twelve districts vote to fill all vacancies, with candidates receiving the most votes being elected. Because nine of the twelve wards consist predominantly of white voters, they can cast enough votes to elect white candidates at each election, making it very difficult for a Mexican American candidate to be elected to the city council.

In the 2008 presidential campaign, the Democratic Party exemplified the changing face of America by fielding three highly regarded candidates who were not white males. The Latino candidate, Governor Bill Richardson (New Mexico), dropped out of the race after the early primaries, but Hillary Rodham Clinton and Barack Obama competed for the nomination through the entire primary season. Perhaps the most significant achievement of Obama's campaign organization was its ability to overcome fundraising problems that have tended to disadvantage candidates of color at all levels in the past. For example, when Jesse Jackson ran for president in the Democratic primaries in 1984 and 1988, he used his celebrity status to compensate for his lack of funds because the national media gave extensive coverage to his campaign. Obama's phenomenal fundraising during the primaries was surpassed after he received the party's nomination for President, setting a record by raising $65 million in August and then shattering that record by raising $150 million in September. Much of the fundraising was done on the Internet as 3.1 million contributors gave an average of $86.

Despite Senator Obama's fundraising success and his impressive oratory, pundits still wondered if white voters would vote for an African American candidate or if they would merely tell pollsters they were voting for him but then vote for the Republican candidate, Senator John McCain, or one of the other white male candidates on the ballot. This phenomenon was called the *Bradley effect* because of the 1982 California Governor's race in which Tom Bradley, the popular African American Mayor of Los Angeles, was defeated despite being ahead in the polls. Despite the doubts and fears, Barack Obama emerged triumphant on election night, becoming the first African American and the first openly biracial individual to become President of the United States. His election was viewed by many as a stunning blow against institutional racism in the United States, and as a sign of hope that institutional racism may be challenged and diminished even more in the future.

FIGURE 8.2

President Barack Obama's nomination of Judge Sonia Sotomayor meant that she would become the first Latina to serve on the Supreme Court. Although widely regarded as one of the best qualified nominees in recent years, Republican opponents demonstrated the persistence of historic prejudices as they questioned her abilities and even accused her of being "a racist" for arguing that her ethnicity provided a valuable perspective for her judicial decisions.

Source: Whitehouse.gov, Stacey Ilyse Photography

How can institutional racism be reduced in the United States?

Institutional racism involves complex problems that are not easily solved. In the 1970s, scholars began to emphasize that *intent* was not necessarily relevant to the issue of whether institutional policies and practices created advantages for white people and disadvantages for people of color. In the 1980s, however, the U.S. Supreme Court ruled that to prove a claim of discrimination, plaintiffs had to demonstrate that the intended purpose of institutional policies or practices was to discriminate against a particular group. Producing statistics documenting racial inequities was not enough; plaintiffs had to prove that those who developed policies or engaged in practices alleged as discriminatory were guilty of an *evil intent.* As Bonilla-Silva (1999) noted,

> The standards that the Supreme Court enacted . . . on discrimination (plaintiffs carrying the burden of proof in discrimination cases and the denial of statistical evidence as valid proof of discrimination) help to preserve intact contemporary forms for reproducing racial inequality in America. (p. 85)

The Supreme Court's ruling illustrates the difficulties involved in making much progress on institutional racism unless the people of the United States and the legal system acknowledge that evil intent is not always the cause of discrimination. When courts are willing to examine the issue of who is advantaged or disadvantaged by institutional policies or practices—regardless of the original goals that these policies or practices were intended to address—then we may see progress in the United States against subtle but widespread institutional practices of racism. In the meantime, people of color must rely on affirmative action programs and legal recourse to respond to blatant discrimination within American institutions. Affirmative action has been effective to a degree, but it also has produced vigorous criticisms.

How do advocates and critics assess the effectiveness of affirmative action programs?

Advocates of affirmative action cite studies beginning in the 1960s showing that the number of workers of color decreased in their traditional occupations and increased significantly in other occupations. For example, the percentage of African Americans employed as domestic servants or other service occupations decreased while their numbers have increased in the ranks of bank tellers, firefighters, electricians, and police officers. Professionals of color have moved into high-status positions in larger numbers than ever before. Critics of affirmative action argue that gains have primarily benefited people of color who were already middle class. They propose changing affirmative action policies to focus on socioeconomic status rather than race, but Waller (2001) described extensive racism encountered by middle-class people of color despite their economic success.

Critics of affirmative action charge that these programs engender **reverse discrimination** by giving applicants of color preferential treatment over whites, especially white men. Studies do not support this allegation. Kivel (2002) summarizes a report reviewing opinions rendered by U.S. District Courts and Courts of Appeal for over four years. There were 3,000 discrimination cases of which 100 alleged reverse discrimination. The courts found merit in only 6 of the 100 claims and ordered restitution. Kivel concluded that charges of reverse racism were part of a strategy "to counterattack attempts to promote racial justice" (p. 61). Affirmative action advocates agree, and they also argue that white men have benefited from preferential treatment, beginning with the U.S. Constitution and sustained in most policies and practices implemented since then. Because racial discrimination still exists, they believe that affirmative action programs are essential to combat it.

Countering the historical argument, critics of affirmative action insist that it be eliminated because reverse discrimination is the more serious problem today. To support this allegation, studies have been cited showing that African Americans represented approximately 40% of new hires for police officers in U.S. cities from 1970 to 2000 (Reaves & Hickman, 2002). Because African Americans constitute only 12% of the population in the United States, this appears to justify the accusation that urban police departments are hiring an excessive number of African Americans.

African Americans actually constitute much more than 12% of the population in most urban areas, yet Jones (1997) reported that 95% of urban police officers in 1970 were white. To determine if hiring decisions by police departments have been fair, a useful measure would be to compare the percentage of officers of color with the percentage of people of color in an urban community. In police departments of many cities in the United States, the percentage of police officers of color still does not equal the percentage of the city's residents of color.

According to a Justice Department report, 63% of the police force in Detroit was African American, but African Americans comprise 82% of Detroit's population. Almost 39% of Baltimore's police officers were African American, but 65% of Baltimore's citizens are black. New York City's finest included 13.3% African American police officers, half of what it should be to equal the percentage of black people in New York City (Reaves & Hickman, 2002).

Such discrepancies do not just affect African Americans. Latinos represented 26% of New York City's population, but only 18% of NYPD. San Diego's police force was 16% Hispanic, but Latinos constituted 26% of the population; 18% of Houston's police officers were Hispanic, less than half of the percentage of Latinos living in Houston; and 12% of Phoenix police officers are Hispanic, but a third of its citizens are Latino (Reaves & Hickman, 2002). Although people of color have constituted a significant percentage of the police officers hired over the past thirty years, claims of reverse discrimination can be countered by the argument that the hiring decisions were a justifiable effort to correct a history of discrimination.

What are some consequences of racial discrimination?

One consequence that has been addressed by numerous critics is the incarceration of disproportionate numbers of African Americans, especially males. The Sentencing Project has calculated the racial disparity rates for each state in the United States (see Table 8.3). Many Americans still associate overt racism with southern states, but there is not a single southern state among the top states with the most disproportionate numbers of African Americans in prison. Researchers suggest two major reasons to explain this disparity: (1) different levels of involvement in criminal activity and racially biased penalties imposed during the judicial process, and (2) institutional biases resulting in different outcomes for minority defendants (Rome, 2008). For example, even the FBI's Universal Crime Reports Index (UCRI) reflects biases in our society. UCRI provides data on street crime, but excludes white-collar crimes, and white people are the majority of offenders with regard to white-collar crime. Rome (2008) also explains that police are given wide latitude in how they enforce the law and how they make arrests, and that police are likely to spend far more time monitoring minority neighborhoods than middle- or upper-class neighborhoods. Referring to findings from sociological research, Rome argues that class and race biases are revealed in police judgments about whom they are more likely to perceive as "troublemakers," and there is evidence that police are more likely to make an arrest if the complainant is white and less likely to arrest someone who appears to be white and middle class.

TABLE 8.3 Racial Disparities between Blacks and Whites in Prison

State	Disparity Index Rating*
1. New Jersey	13.15
2. Connecticut	12.77
3. Minnesota	12.63
4. Iowa	11.63
5. Wisconsin	11.59
6. Pennsylvania	10.53
7. New York	09.47
8. New Hampshire	09.26

Source: Cited in Rome (2008), data came from the Sentencing Project in Washington D.C.

*Index indicates the disparity between minorities and whites in prison as a percentage of their respective populations in that state.

Another consequence of racial discrimination can be seen in the asset inequalities based on race. According to Oliver and Shapiro (2007), for each dollar of net worth owned by white Americans, Hispanic Americans own only 9 cents and African Americans own just 7 cents. In addition, Packer (2005) provides the calculations of a Fannie Mae consultant about how life would be different for African Americans if the United States had achieved racial equality. In education, 2 million more African Americans would have graduated from high school, and another 2 million would have graduated from college. With regard to employment, almost 2 million more African Americans would have professional and managerial jobs, and they would have almost $200 billion more in income. In terms of housing, about 3 million more African Americans would own their own homes, with $760 billion more in home equity value. Finally, if racial equality existed in the United States, African Americans would have $120 billion more in their retirement accounts, $80 billion more in their bank accounts, and the wealth they controlled would be $1 trillion higher than it is today. This is an indication of only economic consequences of racism, but it is important that the cost to African Americans and other people of color in this country be understood and acknowledged. As Kivel (2002) says, all Americans "are responsible for the daily choices we make about how to live in a racist society. We are only responsible for our own part, (but) we each have a part" (p. 41).

> Washing one's hands of the conflict between the powerful and the powerless means to side with the powerful, not to be neutral.
>
> **Paulo Freire (1921–1997)**

What remedies have been proposed to address institutional racism?

To speak of remedies for problems as complex and widespread as those stemming from institutional racism is to speak of partial solutions and of good faith efforts. Ongoing research must be conducted on institutional racism because racist outcomes of policies and practices often are not easily identified and vary from one region and one institution to the next. Solutions will require cooperation and commitment, but whatever progress can be made represents a step forward. With each step, America comes closer to resolving race problems.

Remedies proposed to address problems stemming from racism have come from scholars such as Massey (2001); Wilson (1996); and Feagin and Feagin (1986). Among their proposed solutions for institutional racism are the following:

1. A national agency should be created that has regional offices to coordinate anti-discrimination activities across the nation. Such an agency would improve enforcement of anti-discrimination legislation and provide better documentation and dissemination of information. Most experts agree there are adequate laws against discrimination, but enforcement of those laws is not adequate because the responsibility for enforcement is currently assigned to the Justice Department, which has so many other areas of responsibility.
2. There must be a national and statewide commitment to stop the deterioration of inner cities in America. By providing resources, we could better address conditions that create misery and despair. Examples of resources include tax incentives to attract businesses to inner cities, federally funded jobs similar to the 1930s Works Progress Administration, training programs to give people skills related to available jobs, and day care subsidies to provide quality and affordable child care so that more people could work.
3. There must be active monitoring of real estate practices pertaining to advertising and marketing. Such oversight would ensure that practices are consistent with guidelines established in federal fair-housing legislation.
4. A commitment must be made to improve public elementary, middle, and high schools serving low-income students. Schools in low-income areas include many students of color who could be provided opportunities to develop the abilities and skills needed to function effectively in our highly technical, global economy. Resources will be required to remodel or build new schools, replacing the deteriorating buildings that low-income students often have to attend. Resources will also be required to develop and implement multicultural curriculum and to redesign teacher preparation programs.
5. Teachers must be taught how to work effectively with diverse student populations. They need to learn about the diversity of their students, not just students of color, but students with disabilities, low-income students, and students marginalized by the society or by other students. Teachers must learn how to support positive intergroup relationships between students in their classrooms. They also must be able to identify bias in instructional materials and to teach students how to recognize bias. Until textbooks reflect multicultural content, schools must have resources to purchase multicultural instructional materials to supplement textbooks.

AFTERWORD

In *The Souls of Black Folk* published originally in 1903, W. E. B. Du Bois (1994) wrote that the problem of America was the problem of the "color line," that skin color divided America as if it were a line drawn in the sand, never to be crossed. The color line continues to prevent Americans from being united by a common vision, strengthened by an appreciation of diversity. Du Bois challenged Americans to solve the problem of the color line in the twentieth century. That challenge still has not been met at the beginning of the twenty-first century.

What must Americans do to confront the problem of the color line? For people of color, the challenge continues to be the same as it was for Du Bois, to overcome barriers created by racism. The challenge for white Americans is first to acknowledge

> [America is] a vast and quarrelsome family, a family rent by racial, social, political and class division, but a family nonetheless.
>
> **Leonard Pitts (1957–)**

the existence of racism, then to understand blatant and subtle ways it operates in society, and, finally, to join with Americans of goodwill to reduce racism in America's schools, neighborhoods, and institutions. If those of us who will commit to this goal are successful, we will bring this society closer to the ideals for which it stands: freedom, equality, and the opportunity for all people to pursue their vision of happiness. When we come closer to that goal, it will not just be a victory for Americans of color, it will be a victory for America.

myeducationlab

Now go to Topic #2: **Race** in the MyEducationLab (www.myeducationlab.com) for your course, where you can:

- Find learning outcomes for this topic along with the national standards that connect to these outcomes.
- Complete Assignments and Activities that can help you more deeply understand the chapter content by viewing classroom video and ABC News footage.
- Apply and practice your understanding of the core teaching skills identified in the chapter with the Building Teaching Skills and Dispositions learning units.

TERMS AND DEFINITIONS

At-large candidates Refers to candidates for local offices being elected by an entire community rather than by districts or wards within that community

Cultural racism The societal recognition and promotion of activities and contributions of one racial group in preference to others within a multiracial society; the superimposition of history and traditions of one racial group over other racial groups

Ethnocentrism The belief that one's race, nation, or culture is superior to all others; also individual actions or institutional practices based on that belief

Individual racism Prejudiced attitudes and behavior against others based on skin color demonstrated whenever someone responds by saying or doing something degrading or harmful about people of another race

Institutional racism Established laws, customs, and practices in a society that allow systematic discrimination between people or groups based on skin color

Racism The creation of categories of human beings according to color, with one group establishing an artificial superiority to others; an attitude, action, or institutional structure that subordinates or limits a person on the basis of his or her race

Reverse discrimination The allegation that people of color are receiving preferential treatment with regard to decisions about hiring, promotion, participation, and admission to schools

Rightness of whiteness The belief that white people are the human norm against which all persons of color must be judged

Steering The practice of realtors of showing homes to prospective buyers in neighborhoods where residents are predominantly or exclusively of the same race

Tracking The process in which students are divided into categories so that they can be assigned in groups to various kinds of classes

White flight The migration of white families from an urban to a suburban location because of court rulings to desegregate urban schools

White privilege A set of options, opportunities, and opinions that are gained and maintained at the expense of people of color

Word-of-mouth hiring Employment of a job applicant based on the recommendation of current employees

DISCUSSION EXERCISES

Exercise #1 My Feelings About Race—A Personal Questionnaire

Directions: The twelve statements below could be a reaction that you might hear concerning another person's feelings about race. Create a response you think would be appropriate.

1. People should not be forced to integrate if they don't want to.
2. I don't believe I'm racist, but when it comes right down to it, I wouldn't marry a person of another race.
3. On the whole, the educated, the upper classes, the more sophisticated, or the more deeply religious people are much less racist.
4. I don't want to hear any more about the past and broken treaties; I should not be held responsible for what white people did to Indians a hundred years ago.
5. When I am around angry blacks, it makes me feel defensive because it's as if they want me to feel guilty or something.
6. Other ethnic groups had to struggle, so why should it be any different for Mexican Americans? Why should they get bilingual education and other special accommodations?
7. These days, whenever a black man sneezes, thirty-seven white people rush up to wipe his nose.
8. How can I be pro-Indian without being anti-white?
9. Don't tell me that blacks aren't more violent than whites. If you look at the statistics, you have to admit that there is a higher crime rate in the ghetto.
10. In many situations, minorities—especially Jews and blacks—are paranoid and oversensitive; they read more into a situation than is really there.
11. Because of the civil rights legislation passed in the mid-1960s, great opportunities are now available to racial minorities, and it is up to them to take more responsibility for exploiting those increased opportunities.
12. No, I'm not going to take the *Understanding Diversity* course because I'm not interested in learning about minorities; further, I've been told that it's a white-bashing course; male-bashing, too.

Exercise #2 My Experiences with Culture, Race, and Ethnicity

Directions: Reflect on what age(s) over your life span you have had personal, direct contact with someone of a different culture, race, and ethnicity. Begin with the earliest recollection and move forward to the present.

1. Identify your first personal experiences with people different from you. What was the setting: home, school, family? What was the basis for the contact: dinner guest, classmate, and playmate? What was your age at the time? Who and how was the person different?
2. Identify your earliest exposures to people who were different from you through movies or television shows, including newscasts. What was the story about? What was your age at the time? Who and how was the person different? What impressions did you gain from each of these visual media experiences?
3. Identify your earliest exposure to different others through newspapers, storybooks, novels, or magazines. What was the story about? What was your age at the time? Who and how was the person different? What did you learn about people different from you because of these reading experiences?

Follow-up: Explain to others the impressions these experiences made on you at the time and your reactions to them then and now. Have your reactions changed over time?

REFERENCES

Akbar, N. (2010). Privilege in black and white. In K. Koppelman (Ed.), *Perspectives on diversity*. Boston, MA: Allyn & Bacon.

Discusses white privilege and ways that blacks collaborate with white privilege.

Amer, M.L., & Manning, J. E. (2009). Membership of the 11th Congress: A profile. Retrieved on September 21, 2009 from www.senate.gov.

Provides demographic details on members of the House of Representatives and the Senate.

Andrzejewski, J. (1996). Definitions for understanding oppression and social justice. In J. Andrzejewski (Ed.)., *Oppression and social justice: Critical frameworks* (5th ed., pp. 52–58). Needham, MA: Simon & Schuster.

Provides definitions for a variety of terms essential for discussing intergroup relations.

Bonilla-Silva, E. (2001). *White supremacy and racism in the post-civil rights era.* Boulder, CO: Lynne Rienner.

Examines why blacks and other racial minorities remain behind whites financially, in educational attainment and other social indicators (see residential segregation on pp. 95–96).

Bonilla-Silva, E. (1999). The new racism: Racial structure in the United States, 1960s–1990s. In P. Wong (Ed.), *Race, ethnicity, and nationality in the United States: Toward the twenty-first century* (pp. 55–101). Boulder, CO: Westview.

Examines research on housing, education, politics, and social interactions to describe how the new racism perpetuates social and economic control of African Americans.

Buckley, G. (2001). *American patriots: The story of blacks in the military from the Revolution to Desert Storm.* New York, NY: Random House.

Includes statistics and stories about African Americans who fought in America's wars.

Citron, A. (1969). *The rightness of whiteness.* Detroit: Michigan-Ohio Regional Educational Laboratory.

Describes how cultural images create racial ethnocentrism in the United States.

Clawson, R. (2002, January). Poor people, black faces: The portrayal of poverty in economics textbooks. *Journal of Black Studies, 32*(3), 352–361.

Examines images of African Americans in college economics textbooks and relates findings to previous studies of how women and minorities are portrayed in college textbooks.

Cortes, C. (2000). *The children are watching: How the media teach about diversity.* New York, NY: Teachers College Press.

Analyzes media images, including news and entertainment, to identify themes and values related to diversity and describes media influence on public perceptions of diversity issues.

Du Bois, W. E. B. (1994). *The souls of black folk.* New York, NY: Dover.

Includes the famous "color line" phrase in "The Forethought" that precedes essays affirming African Americans and rejecting accommodations to white supremacy. For those interested in learning more about Du Bois, read David Lewis Levering, *W.E.B. Du Bois: Biography of a race (1868–1919)* (1993), and *W.E.B. Du Bois: The fight for equality and the American century, 1919–1963* (2000), both published by Henry Holt.

Farley, J. (2010). *Majority-minority relations* (6th ed.). Upper Saddle River, NJ: Prentice-Hall.

Provides an overview of racial segregation in the United States in Chapter 10, and examines the basis and consequences of busing in Chapter 12,

Fattah, C. (2001, October). *Racial bias in special education.* FDCH Congressional Testimony, Washington DC: eMediaMillWorks.

Testimony on special education issues, including a description of the boy placed in a low-functioning category who graduated from school and obtained a PhD.

Feagin, J., & Feagin, C. (1986). *Discrimination American style* (2nd ed.). Malabar, FL: Krieger.

Describes theories of discrimination and examples of discrimination in employment, housing, politics, education, and more.

Feagin, J., & Sikes, M.P. (1994). *Living with racism: The black middle class experience.* Boston, MA: Beacon.

Examines overt and subtle discrimination experienced by middle-class African Americans.

Foster, M. (2001). Education and socialization: A review of the literature. In W.H. Watkins, J.L. Lewis, & V. Chou (Eds.), *Race and education: The roles of history and society in educating African American students* (pp. 200–244). Boston, MA: Allyn & Bacon.

Reviews research on racial attitudes and interracial behaviors in school and society.

George, R.G. (2006). The race card: An interactive tool for teaching multiculturalism. *Multicultural Perspectives, 8*(3), 51–55.

Discusses how white is presented as the norm in schools and how whiteness functions as a system of institutional oppression, and describes a pedagogical tool to teach about race.

Gladwell, M. (2005). *Blink: The power of thinking without thinking.* New York, NY: Little, Brown.

Discusses evidence for cognitive activity below the level of consciousness.

Howard, G.R. (2006). *We can't teach what we don't know: White teachers, multiracial schools.* New York, NY: Teachers College Press.

Integrates theory, research, and personal experiences to describe problems created by racism and white privilege and discusses actions to bring about positive changes.

Hughes, R. (2004). The dwindling pool of qualified professors of color: Suburban legends. In D. Cleveland (Ed.), *A long way to go: Conversations about race by African American faculty and graduate students* (pp. 81–93). New York, NY: Peter Lang.

Discusses strategies for the recruitment and retention of students of color in higher education.

Jenkins, A. (2007, May). Inequality, race and remedy. *The American Prospect, 18*(5), A8–A11.

Examines the legacy of past racial discrimination in the present, evaluates the role of racial discrimination in promoting poverty, and suggests ways of addressing racial barriers.

Jones, J. (1997). *Prejudice and racism* (2nd ed.). New York, NY: McGraw Hill.

Integrates data from psychology, sociology, and history to explain the relationship between prejudice and racism in their appropriate sociocultural historical context.

Kershaw T. (1992). The effects of educational tracking on the social mobility of African Americans. *Journal of Black Studies 23*(1), 152–170.

Analyzes criteria used to determine student placement in tracking systems; explains how black students are discriminated against and the negative consequences of such decisions.

Kirp, D.L. (1991, Summer). Textbooks and tribalism in California. *Public Interest, 104,* 20–37.

Discusses the dissatisfaction expressed by various minority groups with textbooks being considered for adoption by California's curriculum commission.

Kivel, P. (2002). *Uprooting racism: How white people can work for racial justice.* (Rev. ed.). Gabriola Island, British Columbia: New Society Publishers.

Examines the dynamics of racism and white privilege in society and offers strategies to work for social justice.

Kozol, J. (2005). *The shame of the nation: The restoration of apartheid schooling in America.* New York, NY: Crown.

Examines evidence of segregation in American schools based on race and social class and discusses the moral and societal implications of maintaining this segregation.

Leondar-Wright, B. (2004). Black job loss deja vu. In C. Collins, A. Gluckman, M. Lui, B.L. Wright, & A. Scharf (Eds.), *The wealth inequality reader* (pp. 95–105). Cambridge, MA: Dollars & Sense.

Discusses low unemployment for blacks in the 1990s, the high percentage of blacks laid off during recessions, and other economic factors affecting income and wealth for black families.

Levine, M. (2008). *Research update: The crisis of male joblessness in Milwaukee, 2007.* Retrieved June 10, 2009 from www.uwm.edu/ced/publications.cfm

Explores unemployment and joblessness in Milwaukee and surrounding areas and compares the economic conditions for blacks in Milwaukee with other urban areas.

Lipsitz, G. (2008). The possessive investment in whiteness. In P. Rothenberg (Ed.), *White privilege: Essential readings on the other side of racism* (pp. 61–84). New York, NY: Worth.

Discusses the economic benefits of racism for white people in the United States.

Loewen, J. (1995). *Lies my teacher told me: Everything your American history textbook got wrong.* New York, NY: The New Press.

Describes distortions and omissions concerning the role of people of color in U.S. history.

Massey, D.S. (2001). Residential segregation and neighborhood conditions in U.S. metropolitan areas. In N. Smelser, W. Wilson, & F. Mitchell (Eds.), *America becoming: Racial trends and their consequences.* East Lansing, MI: National Center for Research on Teacher Learning. (ERIC Document Reproduction Service No. ED449286)

Describes how segregation has increased in recent years, especially for blacks, as well as the nature of segregation for Hispanics and Asian Americans.

Massey, D.S. (2003). The race case. *The American Prospect, 14*(3), 22.

Describes the current status of housing segregation in the United States, especially in urban areas.

McIntosh, P. (2001). White privilege: Unpacking the invisible knapsack. In P. Rothenberg (Ed.), *Race, class, and gender in the United States: An integrated study* (5th ed., pp. 163–168). New York, NY: Worth.

Describes how her understanding of white privilege emerged from a feminist analysis of male privilege and provides a list of twenty-six examples of white privilege.

Morin, R. (2001, July 11). Misperceptions cloud whites' view of blacks. *Washington Post.* Retrieved June 11, 2009, from http://www.washingtonpost.com

Presents the results of a poll of 779 randomly selected white Americans in terms of their perceptions of the economic status of and opportunities available to black Americans.

National Opinion Research Center. (1998). *Race surveys.* University of Chicago. Retrieved August 10, 2003, from www.norc.uchicago.edu/projects/gensoc4.asp

Access survey information dealing with racial attitudes on this Web site by going to "General Survey Data and Information Retrieval System."

Nieto, S. (2008). *Affirming diversity: The sociopolitical context of multicultural education* (5th ed.). Boston, MA: Pearson.

Provides a comprehensive analysis of how schools are failing to meet the needs of students of color and suggests strategies to improve schools.

Oakes, J. (2005). *Keeping track: How schools structure inequality.* New Haven, CT: Yale University Press.

Documents how tracking practices have perpetuated racial and social class inequalities.

Oakes, J., Quartz, K.H., Ryan, S., & Lipton, M. (2000). *Becoming good American schools: The struggle for civic virtue in school reform.* San Francisco, CA: Jossey-Bass.

Describes the effort of sixteen schools in five states to move away from tracked classes and implement other reforms to improve the education of all students.

Oakes, J., & Wells, A.S. (1996). *Beyond the technicalities of school reform: Policy lessons from detracking schools.* Los Angeles, CA: UCLA Graduate School of Education and Information Studies.

Describes problems affecting students in tracked classes and strategies for detracking schools.

Oliver, M.L., & Shapiro, T.M. (2008, October). Sub-prime as a black catastrophe. *The American Prospect, 19*(10), A9–A11.

Describes how families of color, especially African Americans, were adversely affected by the sub-prime mortgage crisis.

Oliver, M.L. & Shapiro, T.M. (2007, May). Creating an opportunity society. *The American Prospect, 18*(5), A27–28.

Discusses the need to implement asset-building strategies so that more Americans can acquire property and increase their wealth.

Orfield, G., & Lee, C. (2006). *Racial transformation and the changing nature of segregation.* Cambridge, MA: The Civil Rights Project at Harvard University.

Examines the transformation of the racial composition in American schools from 1954 to 2003, with special attention to the period from 1991 to 2003.

Orser, W.E. (1990). Secondhand suburbs. *Journal of Urban History, 16*(3), 227–263.

Describes blockbusting tactics and white flight occurring in Baltimore in the 1950s and 1960s and the economic consequences for black homeowners.

Packer, Z. (2005). Sorry, not buying. *The American Prospect, 16*(12), 46–48.

Analyzes efforts by political conservatives to attract black voters on moral issues and the difficulties they face because of their reluctance to address current racial inequities.

Powell, J.A. (2008, October). Race, place, and opportunity. *The American Prospect, 19*(10), A21–A23.

Describes current consequences of ongoing segregation for people of color in the United States and some of the historic efforts that have been made to address it.

Reaves, B.A., & Hickman, M.J. (2002). *Police departments in large cities, 1990–2000.* United States Department of Justice. Retrieved June 9, 2009, from http://www.ojp.usdoj.gov/bjs.

A special report from the Bureau of Justice Statistics agency that includes statistics in the text and in tables concerning police departments in major U.S. cities.

Rehmeyer, J.J. (2007). Separate is never equal. *Science News.* Retrieved Nov. 7, 2008, from http://blog.sciencenews.org (select Math Trek, search for separate_is_never_equal).

Highlights a study that applied a mathematical model to a segregated community to explore the interaction between segregation and inequality.

Rome, D. (2008, Spring). How stereotypes become acts of discrimination: A look at racial disparities in Wisconsin prisons. *Kaleidoscope II,* The University of Wisconsin Institute on Race and Ethnicity, pp. 2–5.

Examines issues related to the disparity between blacks and whites incarcerated in prisons nationally and specifically in the state of Wisconsin.

Schaefer, R.T. (2008). Prejudice. In *Racial and ethnic groups* (11th ed., pp. 37–65). Upper Saddle River, NJ: Pearson Education.

Discusses causes and consequences of prejudice including the findings from research using the Social Distance Scale.

Shorris, E. (2001). *Latinos: A biography of the people.* New York, NY: W.W. Norton.

Provides a personal narrative of the diverse Latino groups in the United States using many personal stories told within a historical context.

Sleeter, C.E., & Grant, C.A. (1991). Race, class, gender and disability in current textbooks. In M. Apple & L.K. Christian-Smith (Eds.), *The politics of the textbook* (pp. 78–110). New York, NY: Routledge.

A textbook analysis instrument was employed to examine forty-seven elementary and middle-school textbooks in social studies, reading, language arts, science, and mathematics.

Smedley, A. The arrival of Africans and descent into slavery. *Race in North America: Origin and evolution of a world view.* Boulder, CO: Westview.

Describes the arrival of Africans to America and how they lost their equal status with other immigrants.

Smith, W.A. (2004). Black faculty coping with racial battle fatigue: The campus racial climate in a post–civil rights era. In D. Cleveland (Ed.), *A long way to go: Conversations about race by African American faculty and graduate students* (pp. 171–190). New York, NY: Peter Lang.

Explores race relations in the United States and consequences for African Americans in higher education.

Spriggs, W.E. (2008, October). The economic crisis in black and white. *The American Prospect, 19*(10), A2–A5.

Analyzes trends in economic data concerning income and wealth of African Americans compared to white Americans.

Thompson, H.A. (1999). Rethinking the politics of white flight in the postwar city. *Journal of Urban History, 25*(2), 163–199.

Discusses the pattern of white flight in Detroit up to 1980 and explains how white flight has contributed to the economic devastation of Detroit's inner city.

Tyson, J.L. (1997). Jobless rate for blacks falls to 23-year low. *Christian Science Monitor, 89*(214), 8.

Describes the decline in unemployment for black Americans in the 1990s while noting problems that remain, such as high unemployment for black youth.

U.S. Bureau of Labor Statistics. (2009, June 5). Employment Situation. Retrieved on June 10, 2009, from www.bls.gov/cps/#news.

Provides unemployment data as recorded for May of 2009.

U.S. Bureau of Labor Statistics. (2001). Counting minorities: A brief history and a look at the future. In *Report on the American Workforce.* Washington, DC: U.S. Department of Labor (www.bls.gov/opub).

Analyzes statistics pertaining to the American workforce and the role and nature of the participation of women and minorities in that workforce.

Waller, J. (2001). *Face to face: The changing state of racism across America.* Cambridge, MA: Perseus Books Group.

Refutes myths about the decline of racism in America and describes various forms of contemporary racism in the United States.

Wellner, A.S. (2000). The money in the middle. *American Demographics, 22*(4), 56–64.

Examines the impact of the economic prosperity of the 1990s on incomes of racial and ethnic minorities and immigrant populations in the United States.

Wells, A.S. (1989). *Hispanic education in America: Separate and unequal.* ERIC Document Reproduction Service.

Presents data on the growth of the Hispanic population of the United States, the percentage of Hispanic students in segregated schools, and the need for desegregation.

Wilson, W.J. (1996). *When work disappears: The world of the new urban poor.* New York, NY: Knopf.

Discusses the causes of unemployment in inner cities and provides recommendations to address the problem. The study of blacks placed in suburbs is on pp. 38–39.

Williams, C. (2003) Managing individuals in a diverse workforce. In *Management* (2nd ed., pp. 434–471). Versailles, KY: Thompson Southwestern.

Explains the benefits of diversity in the corporate world and principles for managing diverse employees effectively.

CHAPTER 9

Sexism: Where the Personal Becomes Political

"Male supremacy has kept woman down. It has not knocked her out."

Claire Boothe Luce (1903–1987)

Segregation is the normal pattern for the relationship between dominant and oppressed groups. Most Americans have been segregated according to such differences as race, social class, and disabilities. Sexism, however, is a unique form of oppression because people who belong to the dominant and subordinate groups live together. Andrzejewski (1996) defines **sexism** as "an attitude, action, or institutional structure that subordinates or limits a person on the basis of sex" (p. 56). Although sexism is customarily regarded as the oppression and exploitation of women, the concept of sexism includes both men and women, and it is an oppression stemming from cultural norms for femininity and masculinity that prevent us from achieving our full potential as human beings. Racism and most other forms of oppression are influenced by the isolation and alienation of dominant and subordinate groups; yet because daily personal relationships exist between most women and men, we believe we have intrinsic, intimate knowledge about sexism.

How does daily interaction between men and women influence sexist attitudes?

Most people grow up in families where they are likely to have close relationships with someone of the opposite sex—brother/sister, parent/child, grandparent/grandchild—and they often enjoy some degree of affection between males and females. Because they believe they genuinely like women, men are more likely to take gender issues lightly, to joke about them and discuss them without the fear and discomfort that usually affects discussions of racism or other forms of oppression. Men in our society are also more likely to make insensitive comments about women that they would never make about people of color.

To illustrate male insensitivity, consider the use of the *natural* argument. White Americans used to say people of color were naturally—meaning genetically—inferior to whites; this belief persisted through the first half of the twentieth century but is now mostly relegated to the ranks of white supremacy groups. Yet many white men in the United States have employed the natural argument in discussing male and female differences, usually to defend their beliefs about male superiority. To justify their argument, men may claim that "the male animal" is always larger than the female, illustrating nature's intent to make males the aggressive protector of females. Gould (1983) corrected this assumption by explaining that larger males are only true for mammals, and not all of them, whereas in the entire animal world—think of insects and fish—the more typical pattern is that females are larger than males.

In conversation, Americans are often more comfortable talking about gender issues than racial issues; men and women joke about the "war between the sexes" where any strategy is acceptable because "all's fair in love and war." When Virginia congressman Howard Smith amended the Civil Rights Act of

1964 by adding gender, he was not expressing concern about gender discrimination in this country; as a southerner, he wanted the bill defeated. Smith gambled that the "absurd" addition of women as a group whose civil rights needed protecting would appear so ridiculous that it would prevent or at least delay the bill's passage. Needless to say, the tactic backfired. The majority of members of the House of Representatives and the Senate were committed to voting for civil rights and the bill was passed (Branch, 1998).

Cultural Sexism

Cultural sexism in the United States originated in the gender roles brought by the English and other European colonists. Historically, men were expected to be in a superior role as head of the household while women were assigned the subordinate role as the person responsible for domestic chores, including child care. English law stipulated that any property owned by a woman became her husband's property after marriage, and any money a wife earned had to be given to her husband. As Sir William Blackstone expressed it, "The husband and wife are one, and the husband is that one" (Collins, 2003, p. 12). These gender roles shaped our culture's ideals for masculine and feminine behavior in ways that have been modified but not radically changed since those early years. Men are still expected to be in control, the leaders and decision makers, while women are expected to play a supportive role both at home and in the workplace.

What gender biases did women confront in the earliest years of the United States?

Although men were expected to provide for the family's needs, from the beginning women went beyond the limits of their gender role. To support the family some women took in laundry or sewing, taught neighbor children, or made things to sell or barter. During the American Revolution—and all subsequent American wars—women assumed additional responsibilities while their husbands were away. Women joined together during the American Revolution to protest against certain merchants who were suspected of inflating prices. Angered by one exceptionally greedy merchant, a group of women attacked the man, took his keys, and helped themselves to the coffee stored at his warehouse (Riley, 1986a).

Because of women's active involvement during the war, it is not surprising that Abigail Adams urged her husband John to make sure women's rights were protected in the Constitution then being written. Although an unmarried woman could own property and engage in business activities on her own, a married woman could not. She could not sign a contract or request a loan without her husband's approval. In the early 1800s, American women continued to earn extra money at home, producing four times the textiles as were produced in textile factories. Women also began to protest against the common law stipulation that their property and earnings must be given to their husbands.

> And in the new code of laws . . . remember the ladies, and be more generous and favorable to them than your ancestors. Do not put such unlimited power into the hands of the husbands. Remember, all men would be tyrants if they could . . . [women] are determined to foment a rebellion and will not hold ourselves bound by any laws in which we have no voice or representation.
>
> **Abigail Adams (1744–1818)**

How and when did forms of discrimination change?

Women activists such as Elizabeth Cady Stanton and Susan B. Anthony lobbied successfully in many states for women's property rights, but they were not as successful in their demand for women's right to vote. By the 1830s, individual states began to pass legislation to grant women the right to own property and keep their earnings. In 1848, in Seneca Falls, New York, women—and men supporting women's rights—met and signed a declaration of women's rights claiming full citizenship rights for all women, including the right to vote.

As more textile factories were built and more young women employed, factory owners exploited them, forcing workers into unions to strike for better pay and working conditions. With the number of schools increasing and so few men willing to take the low salary of a teacher, public schools reluctantly began to hire women, reducing the salary even further. One Ohio superintendent boasted that he was able to hire twice as many female teachers as other school districts that hired only men (Collins, 2003).

In addition to demanding gender equality, women became active in the anti-slavery movement. The Grimke sisters shocked those who felt it wasn't women's place to speak in public, especially not passionately about political issues. Women who defied society's norms provoked harsh criticism, as illustrated by this explanation of their "unladylike" behavior: "Some of them are old maids, whose personal charms were never very attractive and who have been sadly slighted by the masculine gender" (Evans, 1989, p. 102). These unladylike women continued to lobby for gender equality and against slavery as the Civil War approached.

What effect did the Civil War have on women's demands for gender equality?

During the Civil War, the wives of soldiers once again had to provide for themselves and their children. Women were hired to be office workers, government workers, factory workers, teachers, and nurses, yet they encountered a gauntlet of critics. Their morals were questioned and they were said to be a distraction to male workers. After the war, women continued to work and to be active politically, lobbying for such diverse causes as women's suffrage, immigrant issues, and temperance.

After the Civil War, many people migrated west, more men than women. In 1869, Wyoming became the first state to give women voting rights. The legislators also passed laws to guarantee married women's right to own property and to require equal pay for female teachers. With so few women in Wyoming, the passage of this legislation gave the *Cheyenne Leader* some hope of seeing "quite an immigration of ladies to Wyoming" (Collins, 2003, p. 235). Perhaps the need for women explains why the first twelve states giving women the right to vote were all in the West.

In the late 1800s, Congress passed a bill outlawing contraception, perhaps hoping that women with children would be too busy to be politically active. American men usually did not appreciate women's political activities, especially those of college-educated women who provided much of the leadership. Studies warned women that only 28% of college-educated women would marry. A book by a professor at Harvard's medical school alleged that the rigors of a college education created a conflict between the brain and uterus, resulting in infertility (Faludi, 2006). Scientists like Paul Broca engaged in a study of brain size based on the theory that larger brains equaled greater intelligence. Not surprisingly, white male researchers reported that white males had the largest brains, with white women—and people of color—far behind. Based on his studies, Le Bon published his conclusions in 1879 about women's inferior intelligence:

> This inferiority is so obvious that no one can contest it for a moment; only its degree is worth discussion. All psychologists who have studied the intelligence of women . . . recognize today that they represent the most inferior forms of human evolution and that they are closer to children and savages than to an adult, civilized man. (Gould, 1981, pp. 104–105)

Still, new employment opportunities for women arose as the establishment of department stores required personnel who could assist predominantly female customers. By 1900, more than a third of all clerical workers were women; twenty years later, women would be the majority. Women already constituted the majority of teachers, and their numbers steadily increased among librarians, social workers, and nurses (Evans, 1989). But as women tried to redefine their "place" in the early twentieth century, they encountered strong resistance.

What progress and what resistance to women's rights occurred in the early twentieth century?

By 1910, 40% of college students were women, rising to 50% by 1920. Women held a third of all federal government jobs and pursued a greater variety of careers than ever before, but they tended to be unmarried women. In the 1890s, only 3% of married women worked outside the home, increasing to 10% by the 1920s (Collins, 2003). Nevertheless, many women were politically active, especially for the cause of women's suffrage, and a few began to call themselves *feminists.* Using recently created psychological language, critics called them *lesbians,* accusing them of hating men. Yet women's efforts on behalf of suffrage succeeded after almost a century of struggle. Women cast their first votes for president in 1920; ironically, one year later, the first Miss America Beauty Pageant was held in Atlantic City, New Jersey, reminding women of their place and purpose.

With the trauma of World War I becoming a memory and the economy booming, Americans seemed uninterested in social issues. The National Women's Party went to every state legislature to lobby for their proposed Equal Rights Amendment (ERA) stating, "Men and women shall have equal rights throughout the United States and every place subject to its jurisdiction" (Riley, 1986b, p. 81). In 1923, they even managed to get a congressional hearing on the ERA, but they seemed to encounter an unsympathetic audience wherever they went.

When the Great Depression of the 1930s arrived, men and women struggled simply to survive. With high unemployment and few jobs, employers preferred to hire men until World War II began. As men left the workforce to join the military, women continued the pattern from earlier wars by doing the work that men were not available to do.

Did women workers during World War II prove their competence?

During the war, women became the majority (57%) of the workforce for the first time (Faludi, 2006). Several scientific studies from the 1930s and 1940s proved how research could be manipulated to support the prevailing needs in American society: When jobs were scarce during the Great Depression, studies concluded that menstruation reduced women's ability to be effective at work. One researcher even described the effects as debilitating; later, that same researcher conducted a study of working women during World War II and reported that menstruation caused no adverse effects on their ability to perform their jobs (Tavris, 1999).

Wartime women workers were praised for the quality of their work (see Figure 9.1), including advertising campaigns like the one celebrating "Rosie the Riveter," but no one expected them to stay in those jobs permanently—no one except the women. Seventy-five percent of women surveyed wanted to keep their jobs after the war. But industry had other ideas: Businesses that had praised the women's work during the war suddenly found them to have "bad attitudes" or to be incompetent. The aircraft industry was one of the first to act, firing over 800,000 women two months after the war ended (Faludi, 2006). The aggressive actions of the business community and the blatant bias of the media forced women out of the jobs they had proved they could do well.

What role did the media play in women being forced out of their jobs?

In 1945, a *Fortune* magazine poll reported that a majority of Americans believed that if a husband earned enough money to provide for his family, his wife should not work—even if she wanted to (Evans, 1989). The media was telling women to stop taking the jobs that men should have and go home where they belonged. By 1946, more than 3 million women were eliminated from well-paying industrial jobs. More than 80% of them did not quit working, but took jobs with lower salaries instead. Three years after the war, the United States was the only nation in the Western Hemisphere that refused to sign a statement issued by the newly created United Nations that supported equal rights for women (Faludi, 2006).

> I'm just a person trapped inside a woman's body.
>
> **Elayne Boosler (Contemporary)**

From 1946 to 1952, there were huge increases in births, creating what is called the baby boomer generation. Women were reinforced in their role as wives and mothers. Evans (1989) described a 1950s *Look* magazine celebrating the "wondrous creature" who married young, had babies, and was still more

FIGURE 9.1

Advertisements like the one on the left glorified efforts of working women during World War II. Although the pictures such as the one above often depicted white women, a significant number of wartime workers were women of color.

Source: (left) N. S. National Archives; (right) Courtesy FDR Library, Hyde Park, New York.

feminine "than the emancipated girl of the 1920s" (p. 249). An additional factor that discouraged women from working was the growth of suburbs, which isolated them from cities, the site of most jobs. Still, women resisted these efforts to keep them in their place.

How did women respond to the pressure to stay home and not have a career?

After reaching a peak of 50% in 1930, the number of women college students decreased to 35%. In the 1950s, more women enrolled in college. Echoing research a half century earlier, a Cornell University study warned that 65% of college women were much more likely not to get married (Faludi, 2006). But women continued to enroll and continued to work, especially middle-class married women. Evans (1989) reported that middle-class married women "entered the labor force faster than any other group in the population through the 1950s and 1960s" (p. 254). By 1980, women represented 43% of the workforce and they were attending college in record numbers.

A 1986 Harvard–Yale study predicted that if women postponed marriage to get a college diploma, they would find few marriage partners available. According to the study, women had a 20% chance of marrying if they were thirty years old, a 5% chance at thirty-five, and a 1.3% chance at forty. But the prediction was based on an erroneous assumption: Earlier studies of marriage patterns had found that women tended to marry men two to three years older, and that assumption was used to produce the results of the Harvard–Yale study. By the 1980s, this pattern had changed as more women were marrying men closer to their age and even younger. Two other studies reported findings contradicting the conclusions of the Harvard–Yale study, but the popular press did not report on them (Faludi, 2006), once again revealing a sexist bias in our culture.

What other sexist messages exist in American culture?

In America as in other countries, gender roles are both consciously and unconsciously transmitted to children; also conveyed are the inequalities inherent in those roles. Feminists have been confronting gender roles in our culture—and others around the world—to demand equality. An evolving global economy is demanding change as well. As the number of women in the workforce has increased and the dual-career couple has become the dominant family form in the United States, one would assume that men and women share domestic duties. Domestic sharing, however, has not occurred. Too often, Badgett (2001) reports, men tend to do minimal housework if they are living with someone, and even less if they are married. It is not easy to change traditional gender roles.

> Culture is the medium through which children fashion their individual and collective identities.
>
> **Henry A. Giroux (1943–)**

Sexism is learned through images, especially everyday images in advertising where women have historically been presented in stereotypical roles or as sex objects to sell products. Citing surveys in which most women say their most important goal is to lose 10 to 15 pounds, Kilbourne (1999) argued that women's concern for weight loss is a consequence of cultural messages about beauty reinforced by the beauty industry to make profits. Sexist images illustrating cultural traditions are important influences in the development of sexist attitudes, yet perhaps the single most significant influence in the development of sexist attitudes is language.

How does learning sexist language influence attitudes and behavior?

For decades there have been (and continue to be) professions that are male dominated, and traditional terms such as *policemen, firemen,* and *mailmen* imply that these jobs are exclusively for men. Feminists have long recognized such gender prejudice in language, and they have been committed to changing the language by replacing sexist terms with nonsexist alternatives (Arliss, 1991; Nilsen, 1977a, 1977b). Their efforts are reflected in language changes that have become common usage, such as *police officer, fire fighter,* and *letter carrier.* In addition to including women, this language is more descriptive of the job responsibilities. Since these examples show that language has changed, have attitudes and behaviors changed as well?

Studies suggest some evidence of changing attitudes among youth. In the past, American high school senior boys listed more than twice as many possible career options as did their female peers; few careers appeared on both lists. In a longitudinal study, Wulff and Steitz (1997) reported that junior high school students indicated interest in 45 careers—12 of them (26.7%) identified by both girls and boys. Just before high school graduation, these same students expressed interest in 68 different careers, with 16 (23.5%) identified by both genders. According to data from the National Center for Educational Statistics, the number of women graduating with a degree in engineering has jumped from 1% in 1970 to 20% today. In addition, the number of women graduating with a degree in physical sciences and technology has gone from 14% to 41%, and women graduating with degrees in natural resources and agriculture increased from 9% to 49% (NCES, 2008).

Even with these impressive increases, traditional occupations continue to exert a strong attraction for both women and men. For example, women still constitute 75% or more of students graduating with degrees in education or health professions; therefore, even though high school graduates today, especially women, are more likely to pursue a nontraditional career than in the past, the numbers are still small—15% for women and 8% for men (Bernstein, 2004; NCES, 2008).

Increased use of nonsexist language may not be solely responsible for gender differences reported in career choice studies, but feminists continue to address changes in language that conveys a sexist perception that certain jobs are for men only or that men are more significant in our culture. Opponents question the impact of their efforts, insisting that changing sexist terms in our language is a trivial and ineffective way to change sexist attitudes. Yet there are examples of language being changed to accommodate men. After men won the right to work in the formerly all-female occupation of stewardess, airlines uniformly and rapidly revised the name to *flight attendant.* If it was so easy to change the language to be inclusive of men, why can't women be similarly accommodated?

To address sexism in our language, feminists have lobbied professional organizations, businesses, and institutions to promote the use of **inclusive language** (terms that include both men and women). In response, several organizations have changed the guidelines in their writing manuals to promote nonsexist language as preferred for their professional publications. The style manual of the American Psychological Association includes writing conventions employing language free of sexist implications (see Table 9.1). Despite such progress, feminist scholars continue to confront sexist language reflected in common words and phrases. Do we have a man-made product if it is manufactured in a factory employing only women? Can an organization "man the desk" with women? Does brotherly love include sisters? Does the opinion of the common man include women, or are women "uncommon"? Alternatives for sexist terms exist: a product is handmade, women can staff the desk, and the average person can give his or her opinion.

In addition to terms that exclude women, feminists also argue that sexist language often involves a distortion of reality. For example, using the common expression "founding fathers" denies the importance of women's historical role in the establishment of this country. The presence of immigrant families distinguished the settlements in what became the United States from New World settlements of the French (primarily men—trappers and hunters) and Spanish (primarily soldiers—conquistadores). Evans (1989) insists that compared to New World settlements of other nations, the presence of women and children in the English colonies had a definite impact on how American society evolved, and that an accurate picture of our nation's historical development is distorted by language denying women's presence. Although feminists have made a good effort to eliminate negative terms, there is still much to be done to change sexist language.

For example, there is a pattern of condescending language toward women illustrated by the use of diminutive endings such as "poet*ess*." Although the Academy Awards still has a "Best Actress" category, most women who receive the award refer to themselves as actors. American feminists have also explained that the term *coed* is a condescending reference from an era when men believed that women lacked the intelligence required for college studies—comparable to the condescending phrase *colored people* for African Americans. Colleges permitting women to attend were "coeducational"; therefore, the term *coed* reflects the historic perception of

TABLE 9.1 Language Recommended by the American Psychological Association

Problematic	Gender Preferred
man a project	staff a project, hire personnel, employ staff
man–machine interface	user–system interface, person–system interface, human–computer interface
manpower	workforce, personnel, workers, human resources
man's search for knowledge	the search for knowledge
mothering	parenting, nurturing [or specify exact behavior]
The authors acknowledge the assistance of Mrs. John Smith.	The authors acknowledge the assistance of Jane Smith.
cautious men and timid women	cautious women and men, cautious people, timid men and women, timid people

Source: Publication Manual of the American Psychological Association (5th ed.) pp. 71–72, 74–75.

women as intellectually inferior to men. Oberlin College became the first coeducational campus in 1833. Although the college deserves credit for offering the opportunity, women admitted to Oberlin were required to meet one condition in addition to those for men who were admitted: they had to agree to do the laundry for Oberlin's male students (Sadker & Sadker, 1994). This illustrates the reality that change is usually resisted, and rarely occurs without some sacrifice.

Another sexist pattern in American English is the consistent denigration of aging women, reinforcing the importance of female appearance: Women are valued only if they are beautiful. English novelist George Meredith argued that women die twice—their first death occurs when they lose their beauty. Attractive young women are referred to as "kittenish," but with age they become "catty." The sexy young "chick" becomes the "old biddy" who "henpecks" her husband. And speaking of marriage, a man is considered a "good catch," but a woman is a "ball and chain." Our cultural history shows a persistent tendency to portray marriage as bad for men, whereas women should get married as soon as possible. Although such attitudes are not as intense today and many young women are waiting much later to get married, the perception persists that the unmarried woman is to be pitied, whereas the bachelor is envied. Women still have a bridal shower to celebrate the marriage while men traditionally have a stag party to mourn the groom's last night of freedom. Is there any evidence that marriage is such a desirable state for women and such a terrible burden for men?

> The limits of my language are the limits of my world.
>
> **Ludwig Wittgenstein (1889–1951)**

What do studies say about who benefits from marriage in our culture?

Previously, studies found that married men tended to have fewer mental and physical health problems than single men; however, married women have more mental and physical health problems than single women (National Center for Health Statistics, 1999; Tavris & Wade, 1984). More women than men seek therapy for emotional problems, and the majority are married. Results from recent studies have challenged the previous studies, arguing that men and women both benefit from marriage. Simon (2002) reported that unmarried men and women were more likely to suffer from depression than men and women in stable marriages and that unmarried men were more likely to report alcohol abuse than married men. These studies would still seem to contradict the traditional belief that only women benefit from marriage.

Individual Sexism

As a result of learning sexist attitudes from our culture and from the sexist attitudes of others, people of both genders may engage in **individual sexism** involving prejudiced attitudes and actions against women or men because of rigid beliefs about gender and gender roles. Although both men and women can become "male chauvinists," they can also choose to be "feminists" in support of gender equality.

What does it mean to be a "male chauvinist" or a "feminist"?

The term "chauvinist" is reported to have originated with a Frenchman named Chauvin, a zealous soldier intensely loyal to Napoleon Bonaparte. To be a *chauvinist* has evolved to designate someone who believes in the superiority of someone or something (Partridge, 2009). In Chapter 3, Kimmel (2006) referred to people being chauvinistic about their culture. French scholars have been accused of being chauvinistic about their language, as demonstrated by their attempts to prevent foreign words, especially American phrases—"le hamburger" or "le week-end"—from polluting their native tongue. To call someone a *male chauvinist* is to accuse that person, who could be male or female, of believing men to be superior to women. A **male chauvinist** is a person who believes that men ought to be the leaders and decision makers and women should be subordinate. It is interesting that there are American men who publicly declare themselves male chauvinists yet would bristle at being called racists or bigots.

Confusion exists also with the word *feminist* and with those labeled as feminists. Too many people perceive a feminist as an angry woman; our media has reinforced that view by focusing on feminists who represent radical perspectives. In reality, a **feminist** is a woman—or a man—who advocates for the personal, social, and economic equality of women. The goal of feminist activists is to increase the opportunities available for both men and women as part of the larger goal of eliminating traditional, stereotypical gender roles. To eliminate gender stereotypes, feminists have advocated *androgyny,* a concept that promotes interchangeability of female and male roles or responsibilities in all areas beyond fundamental biological ones.

> People call me feminist whenever I express sentiments that differentiate me from a doormat or a prostitute.
>
> **Dame Rebecca West (1892–1983)**

What does it mean to be androgynous?

Androgyny has been confused with the unisex concept illustrated by unisex clothing, hair styling, and toilets, but the unisex concept denies differences between men and women and advocates treating members of both genders as if they were exactly the same. **Androgyny** is the belief that men and women share a variety of human traits that should be encouraged in both as opposed to fostering certain traits in each gender based on traditional cultural stereotypes about masculinity and femininity (Tavris & Wade, 1984).

Androgynous people respond to situations as needed, without being limited by their gender. If a situation calls for aggressive behavior, an androgynous person responds aggressively; if the situation requires a nurturing response, the androgynous person is nurturing. The person's gender does not matter because aggression and nurturance are traits every human being possesses. Does each androgynous person respond the same way in a given situation? No, because each *individual* is different, but if everyone in a society were androgynous, the differences between people would derive from their individual abilities and preferences, not from artificial differences created by teaching children to shape their identities and behavior to conform to rigid stereotypes about being male or female. Many feminists believe that promoting androgyny from childhood could have a positive impact on the traditional ideas about gender roles that contribute to a serious problem for women in this society: aggressive and abusive behaviors of men that are often harmful to women physically, socially, and psychologically.

What kind of abuse do women encounter in the United States?

According to a study by Tjaden and Thoennes (1998), over a million women in the United States are stalked each year (half of them by an intimate partner); 2 million American women are physically assaulted annually, and over 200,000 are sexually assaulted. A third of all women (and 20% of female high school students) are victims of physical or sexual abuse, usually from an intimate partner.

As high as these numbers are, experts say the actual number of incidents is even higher. According to Gonnerman (2005), 73% of domestic violence incidents are not reported; more than 60% of women who did not report such an incident said they did not think the police would believe them. This is unfortunate because police officers are much more likely to arrest an abusive husband today. Responding to domestic violence has proven to be a main source of injury to officers, especially when the abuser is a repeat offender, so many cities and states have passed laws calling for an aggressive police action in response to domestic violence. These laws typically call for the arrest and prosecution of the abuser based on evidence gathered by the police, and not on whether or not the victim presses charges (Catania, 2005).

In addition to physical abuse, rape is a significant part of the violence against women in America. Over 65,000 women are raped each year (that means a rape occurs every eight minutes), and young women are especially vulnerable. Almost half of the victims were raped before they turned eighteen; one out of four women attending college have been victims of rape or attempted rape (Rape, Abuse, and Incest National Network [RAINN], 2009; Sampson, 2003). There is often confusion when discussing rape because it has a history of being misrepresented. Simply put, **rape** is physical and psychological violence defined as forcing someone to submit to sexual intercourse or engaging in sexual intercourse without another's consent. Unfortunately, rape continues to be misunderstood by those who have inaccurate information.

> There is no difference between being raped and being run over by a truck, except afterwards men ask if you liked it.
>
> **Marge Piercy (1936–)**

How has rape been misunderstood in the United States?

As the twentieth century was ending, *Newsweek* released a cover story on rape. Three fourths of the article was about "stranger rape"; the last section addressed the issue of "acquaintance rape," including date rape. The emphasis was the reverse of what really happens: Stranger rape accounts for about a third of all reported rapes and only 10% of college rapes (Sampson, 2003). It is important to recognize misperceptions about rape to understand the reality of that experience. Some generally conceded myths and realities about rape are listed in the box to the right.

One in six American women have been victims of rape or attempted rape in their lifetimes. As high as that statistic is, as well as the other statistics cited earlier, law enforcement officials say this data would be even higher if all of the rapes and attempted rapes were reported.

MYTH: Rape is an act of sexual arousal caused by an attractive, sexy woman who stimulated such sexual tension and passion that the man could not control himself.

REALITY: Rape is an act of power and humiliation, and any woman of any age is a potential victim regardless of her physical appearance.

MYTH: Rapes usually occur in dark alleys or poorly lit parking lots where the woman is isolated and therefore vulnerable.

REALITY: More than 60% of rapes occur in the victim's home or in a place where the woman would normally feel safe—the home of a friend, relative, or neighbor.

MYTH: Rapes are usually committed by violent strangers concealed somewhere usually at night waiting for an unwitting and unknown victim.

REALITY: Almost 66% of rapes are committed by someone the victim knows, such as a lover, a friend, relative, or an acquaintance; other potential rapists may be trusted authority figures such as a teacher, a minister, a counselor, or therapist.

MYTH: Because many women read and enjoy romance novels that typically include rape scenes, these women must fantasize about rape and secretly want to be raped.

REALITY: Romance novels are exciting fantasy adventures that tend to portray sex in terms of seduction. Although women may fantasize about being seduced by some handsome man, such fantasies bear no relationship to the brutality, violence, and violation associated with rape. It is well documented that boys and men enjoy reading novels and watching movies and television shows filled with murder and violence. Does that mean they secretly want to be murdered or assaulted?

Why do women choose not to report a rape or attempted rape?

Rape is an underreported crime, and feminists have argued that the one out of six rate that is reported for rape is conservative. Because of changes in police departments' processing of rape cases and new guidelines for rape trials, this crime is now more likely to be reported. Still, fear affects a woman's decision to report a rape. According to MacKinnon (1987, p. 82), victims have given four reasons for not reporting a rape:

Threats: Rapists often threaten to return and to inflict even more violence if victims go to the police. Some rapists even threaten to kill their victims, and just by reading newspapers, women know this has happened to others.

Reactions: Some victims fear the reactions of their significant others. Women have been verbally abused, beaten, and even abandoned by partners who would not believe that the woman did nothing to incite the rape.

Disbelief: Some women fear that if they report the rape, the police might not believe her. Even if the police are convinced, some women fear they may not be able to persuade a jury. There is no guarantee of justice from the legal system.

Publicity: Some women fear the loss of privacy, and the feeling of being exposed and vulnerable, as well as being subjected to embarrassing allegations about their personal lives in court. They are also reluctant to recall and relive (in front of an audience) a painful, humiliating incident they would rather forget.

The concerns of rape victims are the reason law enforcement officials and other experts have generally agreed with feminists that the number of reported rapes is probably much less than the number of incidents. Rape and domestic violence are painful consequences of sexism played, principally by men, as a power game in our culture.

Institutional Sexism

Institutional sexism is the consequence of established laws, customs, and practices that systematically discriminate against people or groups based on gender. Institutional sexism takes many forms, but a persistent problem is the ongoing gender discrimination in hiring. Jones and George (2003) describe a study in Philadelphia where men and women applied for restaurant jobs offering good salaries. Although their résumés were carefully constructed to make them equally qualified, men were called in for interviews twice as often as women, and five times as many men as women received job offers. Jones and George also report that women constitute 46% of the workforce in 2000, yet:

> Only about 12 percent of corporate officers and boards of directors were women, less than 6 percent of employees with the highest status job titles are women, and only about 4 percent of women occupy positions with the highest earning levels. (p. 127)

Even if women are successful at finding jobs, another persistent problem is the salary inequity between men and women. Historically, there is ample evidence of inequities in the salaries of men and women, but attempts have been made to address this gender gap. There is disagreement about the extent to which gender salary inequities are being resolved, but most people concur that men earn more than women, even when they work in the same jobs (see Table 9.2).

Why are men earning more than women in the workforce?

Four arguments address the issue of salary inequity between men and women. The first argument is the claim that significant progress has been made in closing this income gap. According to the U.S. Bureau of Labor Statistics (2008), women earned approximately 60 cents for every dollar a man made from 1960 to 1980. Since then the gap narrowed, so that by 2007, American women were earning an average of 80 cents for every dollar a man earned. The answer to the salary inequity question would seem to be that men are still earning more, but that women must be getting more raises and promotions and are apparently catching up.

> The Glass Ceiling hinders not only individuals but society as a whole. It effectively cuts our pool of potential corporate leaders by half. It deprives our economy of new leaders, new sources of creativity.
>
> **Lynn M. Martin (1939–)**

TABLE 9.2 Statewide Comparison of Gender Salaries

Rank Earnings Gap	Median 2007 Earnings: Men	Median 2007 Earnings: Women	Female Earnings per Dollar of Male Earnings
1 Wyoming	$45,310	$28,540	63.0
2 Louisiana	$41,980	$27,469	65.4
3 West Virginia	$40,126	$26,719	66.6
4 North Dakota	$40,028	$27,554	68.8
5 New Hampshire	$51,385	$35,722	69.5
6 Montana	$38,230	$26,598	69.6
7 Michigan	$48,512	$34,849	71.8
7 Indiana	$43,410	$31,158	71.8
9 Utah	$43,035	$31,001	72.0
10 Alabama	$40,829	$29,756	72.9
10 Mississippi	$36,819	$26,838	72.9
12 Wisconsin	$44,105	$32,265	73.2
12 Idaho	$39,413	$28,846	73.2
14 Illinois	$48,562	$35,638	73.4
14 South Dakota	$36,726	$26,965	73.4
16 Arkansas	$36,379	$26,815	73.7
17 Alaska	$51,275	$37,835	73.8
18 Ohio	$44,443	$32,853	73.9
19 Kansas	$42,041	$31,145	74.1
20 Washington	$50,269	$37,454	74.5
21 Missouri	$41,347	$30,827	74.6
22 Pennsylvania	$44,755	$33,438	74.7
22 Iowa	$41,375	$30,925	74.7
24 Kentucky	$39,920	$29,957	75.0
24 South Carolina	$40,139	$30,124	75.0
26 Maine	$41,704	$31,496	75.5
27 Connecticut	$55,394	$41,868	75.6
28 Virginia	$48,142	$36,971	76.8
28 Oregon	$42,389	$32,538	76.8
30 New Jersey	$54,846	$42,221	77.0
30 Tennessee	$39,207	$30,178	77.0
32 Minnesota	$47,602	$36,707	77.1

	Median 2007 Earnings		
Rank Earnings Gap	Men	Women	Female Earnings per Dollar of Male Earnings
33 Rhode Island	$48,492	$37,475	77.3
34 Oklahoma	$37,884	$29,378	77.5
35 Nebraska	$39,070	$30,406	77.8
36 Massachusets	$53,602	$42,062	78.5
37 New Mexico	$38,366	$30,188	78.7
38 Texas	$40,344	$31,845	78.9
39 Hawaii	$44,802	$35,471	79.2
40 Georgia	$41,837	$33,351	79.7
41 Colorado	$46,230	$36,827	79.7
42 Nevada	$42,787	$34,164	79.8
43 Florida	$40,238	$32,150	79.9
44 Delaware	$47,964	$38,543	80.4
45 North Carolina	$39,447	$31,738	80.5
46 Maryland	$54,501	$44,022	80.8
47 Arizona	$41,308	$33,723	81.6
48 New York	$47,198	$38,830	82.3
49 California	$46,404	$38,903	83.8
50 Vermont	$40,834	$34,341	84.1
51 District of Columbia	$52,860	$49,364	93.4
52 Puerto Rico	$20,242	$19,812	97.9

Source: U. S. Census Bureau (www.census.gov)

Careful analysis of salary data tells a different story: The primary reason for the decreasing gap is that the salaries of male workers *have not been increasing;* they have even been decreasing in some areas. The claim that women's salaries are becoming closer to men's salaries is based on the reality of salary stagnation for men. In addition, 80% of working women still earn less than $20,000 a year. It seems debatable to say that "progress" is being made concerning men's and women's salaries if closing the gender gap is based on women making small wage gains while men are receiving no wage increases.

A second argument regarding gender salary inequity is based on data showing that young women entering the workforce are earning slightly more than 80 cents for every dollar a man makes. This statistic has been used to argue that the gender inequity problem is being solved and to predict that the salary gap will eventually disappear as more highly paid young women pursue their careers. Although entry-level salaries are becoming more equal, feminists argue that women who stay in the workforce lose ground to their male peers because they are not promoted as readily as men. The term **glass ceiling** was coined to refer to an upper limit, usually middle management, beyond which women are not promoted. Studies have confirmed that women are not being promoted at the same rate as men; few are promoted to top leadership roles (U.S. Bureau of Labor Statistics, 2006).

According to a recent report from the White House Project's Corporate Council, no more than 20% of women function in leadership roles in fields as diverse as business, politics, and journalism, and even fewer are leaders in the military, large law firms, and Fortune 500 companies. Using a global comparison for women's political representation, the United States ranks 69th, lagging behind such nations as Iraq and North Korea (Quindlen, 2008).

In addition, our dominant cultural expectation for women to perform housekeeping duties and raise children results in less opportunity for developing abilities, experience, contacts, and reputation. Businesses could do more to encourage women to maintain their careers while being a parent. According to Jeffery (2005), every industrialized nation except for the United States and Australia offers women paid parental leave and guarantees them a job when their leave is finished if they return to work. The reduction of the gap between men's and women's salaries for entry-level jobs is important, but the economic penalty women pay for bearing and raising children still contributes significantly to the disparity between men's and women's salaries.

A third argument about gender salary disparity is based on the fact that more American women earn college diplomas than ever before. Because more education is assumed to mean more access to careers with higher salaries, gender disparity is predicted to decrease further, and eventually to disappear. Yet statistics show that college-educated women are still paid less than men. A 2004 government study of census data reported that the average annual salary for a college-educated woman with a bachelor's degree was $35,000, but it was $36,000 for a male high school dropout. All women with college degrees (including master's and doctorate) averaged an annual salary of $42,000 compared to their male counterparts who earned an average of $77,000 (Bernstein, 2004).

A fourth argument for the gender salary inequity is that women tend to choose careers that pay lower salaries than the more highly paid professions men select. Although women account for 59% of low-paying jobs, including 70% of minimum-wage jobs, comparing the salaries of women and men within the same profession reveals that men are paid more—even in those professions where women constitute the majority of workers (U.S. Bureau of Labor Statistics, 2008; Kim, 2000).

What are economic consequences of institutional sexism for women?

Although people debate gender disparity in wages, Day and Newburger (2002) report that during their lifetimes women with high school diplomas can expect to be paid $450,000 less than men with high school diplomas. They also predict that women with bachelors' degrees will earn almost $900,000 less than men with similar degrees; women with professional degrees will earn $2 million less than men with professional degrees.

For middle- and upper-class women, these economic disparities make it difficult for them to pursue political power by campaigning for national or state offices. Such campaigns are expensive and require personal funds as well as aggressive fundraising. Currently, women constitute only 17% of the U.S. Congress, a percentage exceeded by fifteen African nations. In the new government of Iraq, almost a third of the members of its parliament are women (Amer & Manning, 2009; Jeffery, 2005). Another consequence of earning lower salaries over a lifetime is that women over sixty-five are twice as likely as men to be poor.

Part-time employment also illustrates the economic exploitation of women. For a variety of reasons, women constitute the majority of people working less than forty-hour weeks or working forty or more hours a week on a temporary basis. In either case, part-time workers are typically denied most or all fringe benefits provided to full-time employees, including day care, health insurance, life insurance, and employer contributions to retirement accounts.

> Whatever women do they must do twice as well as men to be thought half as good.
>
> **Charlotte Whitton (1896–1975)**

Another economic consequence of institutional sexism concerns child support payments. When the family unit is broken, mothers are most often awarded custody of children and, as part of legal divorce settlements, fathers are almost always required to provide child support for children under the age of majority. Despite their fiscal obligation, only 40% of American fathers are observed to pay full child support during the first year following a divorce. Another 26% of divorced fathers make partial payments for only the first year (Grall, 2000). After one year, almost half of paying fathers stop making payments altogether; of those who continue, few pay the full amount, even though most can afford to make the payments (Benokraitis & Feagin, 1995; Sorenson, 1997).

For low-income mothers, lack of child support often forces them to apply for public assistance, whereas middle-class mothers often return to college to upgrade their skills so they can compete for jobs in the labor market. If divorced custodial mothers applied for loans, they would likely be rejected because child support payments are not considered a reliable source of income! Lenders are familiar with the data on child support. Despite lower salaries, lack of child support, and other economic consequences, women often work for all the same reasons as men. And they do so regardless of discrimination in salaries and promotions, and despite another frustration encountered on the job: sexual harassment.

How is sexual harassment a significant problem for women in the workforce?

The behavior called *sexual harassment* is not new, but it wasn't until 1979 that Catherine MacKinnon created the term in her writings on workplace behaviors and gender discrimination (Wetzel & Brown, 2000). There were 13,867 sexual harassment complaints filed in 2008, and those making charges received $47.4 million. Sexual harassment in the workplace is not just a problem for women; men filed 15.9% of those complaints. Typically, **sexual harassment** is defined as unwelcome deliberate and repeated behavior of a sexual nature that is neither requested nor returned. Men tend to be responsible for sexual harassment, even when men are the victims. Sexual harassment is an issue of power, not sex. Most men do not engage in sexual harassment at work; it is estimated that only 5% to 10% of the American male workforce engage in harassment. Men who do harass are being pressured to change their behavior.

What are the most common behaviors that women regard as sexual harassment?

There are two common reasons that women complain about sexual harassment. The behaviors described can be regarded as illustrating a "cultural" conflict between men and women. One complaint: Men make a nuisance of themselves by persistently asking women for dates. In response, the explanation is that during childhood and adolescence, every American male is taught some version of the cliché "if at first you don't succeed, try, try again." Men taught to view persistence as a positive attribute are encouraged to be persistent in anything they do. Accused of harassment, some men have yet to understand that persistently approaching women for dates may initially be regarded as obnoxious, but eventually becomes threatening. American women tend to regard such harassment as a verbal form of stalking, and it is not surprising that many victims tend to describe harassers as disgusting, even ugly, regardless of the physical attractiveness of the harasser (Strauss & Espeland, 1992).

A second complaint has to do with men making unwelcome, sexually suggestive remarks to women, often in the form of sexual jokes sometimes told by men to each other. Now constituting almost half of the workforce, most women find this kind of humor unequivocally offensive. As our workforce continues to change, it is inevitable that some previously established norms and behaviors will also change. Men must recognize the need for reform and respond appropriately. Men must also recognize that respecting rather than resisting or criticizing reasons for reform demonstrates their respect for women.

Throughout the global economy, corporations are confronted with sexual harassment and must establish clear policies on what they consider acceptable and unacceptable behavior. The European Equal Opportunities Commission has ruled that flirting becomes harassment if it continues after the recipient has made it clear that it is offensive (Webb, 2000). How are employers at all levels supposed to monitor employee behavior in a way that is fair? The U.S. Equal Opportunities Commission has established some reasonable guidelines.

What are the workplace guidelines for sexual harassment in the United States?

If sexual harassment is not severe—persistent requests for a date or telling sexual jokes—victims must tell the harasser that they regard this behavior as offensive. If the harasser continues the offensive behavior despite the victim's repeated objections, the victim can contact a supervisor to ask that he or she intervene or file a sexual harassment complaint. In cases where the behavior is not considered severe, it usually must be repeated a number of times before a sexual harassment complaint should be filed.

How many times must the victim be subjected to the behavior before filing a complaint? The courts use a "reasonable person" standard, meaning how long a reasonable person should have to tolerate such behavior before it is considered intolerable. Conversely, if the behavior is considered severe, such as demanding sexual favors from an employee in return for a raise or promotion, it only has to occur once for the victim, or an advocate aware of the behavior, to file a sexual harassment complaint (Webb, 2000).

Are American employers following sexual harassment guidelines?

Most American employers have demonstrated a willingness to take aggressive action against sexual harassment. This is probably because of a consistent pattern of court cases that have ruled for individuals making sexual harassment allegations. Business owners and managers cannot claim ignorance of the harassment because courts have ruled that they have a "vicarious liability" for what happens at their worksite. The main defense against sexual harassment allegations is to have sexual harassment policies in place and prove that the victim did not take advantage of them (Baker, 2006).

As employers become aware of research findings, they have even more reason to follow workplace guidelines. Studies report that one effect of sexual harassment in the workplace is a reduction of profits, which is reason enough for any employer aggressively to enforce policies against sexual harassment. According to research, when sexual harassment is not stopped at worksites, the consequences include increased worker absenteeism, lower worker productivity, and higher training costs from employee turnover (Knapp & Kustis, 1996). As American employers take aggressive actions to eliminate sexual harassment in the workplace, educators must take similar steps to eliminate sexual harassment from our schools and address other gender equity issues.

How much of a problem is sexual harassment in the schools?

In 1993, the American Association of University Women (AAUW) commissioned a Harris poll to examine sexual harassment in schools. Over 1,600 students in grades 8 through 11 from seventy-nine school districts across the United States responded. The AAUW survey reported that 81% of girls and 76% of boys had experienced sexual harassment, and that for 30% of girls and 18% of boys, it was a frequent occurrence. The students described sexual harassment beginning in elementary school and continuing through middle school and high school. Although the most common form of sexual harassment involved only nonverbal and verbal behaviors such as sexual comments, jokes, and gestures, the second most common complaint involved being touched, grabbed, or pinched in a sexual way. The survey also reported that 13% of the girls had been forced to do something sexual other than kissing. The perpetrators of this sexual harassment were overwhelmingly peers (79%) rather than adults.

According to Wetzel and Brown (2000), studies conducted since 1993 have continued to find evidence of ongoing sexual harassment in schools. In 1999, the U.S. Supreme Court decision on *Davis* v. *Monroe County Board of Education* ruled that schools had a responsibility to take appropriate action to eliminate student sexual harassment and were legally liable. To reduce sexually harassing behavior, educators must make efforts to change sexist attitudes that encourage such behavior. Based on studies of attitude and behavioral change related to racial issues, Brandenburg (1997) recommended that educators confront sex role stereotypes as well as the issue of sexual harassment to increase student awareness of gender issues.

What are some other gender issues in schools?

Nonsexist educators have long advocated teaching strategies to confront sexist attitudes because gender problems in schools are not limited to sexual harassment. After collecting years of observational data on teacher–student interactions in K–12 classrooms, Sadker and Sadker (1994) reported consistent sexist patterns for both teacher and student behaviors. Boys were more likely to call out answers without raising their hands, and they interrupted when others gave answers. Because boys were more aggressive, teachers tended to call on them, praise them, and discipline them more often than girls. Teachers were more likely to challenge boys to finish their homework, whereas they would help girls finish theirs.

Are there gender equity issues for boys?

In recent years, the popular media has given attention to those who question whether schools have gone too far in promoting gender equity because boys are having more problems today. Gurian (2004) reports that girls are consistently earning higher grades than boys; they earn 60% of all A grades and boys are the recipients of 70% of all D and F grades. Approximately two thirds of all students in the top fifth of their class are girls, whereas boys constitute two thirds of all students diagnosed with a learning disability. Boys represent 90% of students with behaviors requiring disciplinary action in school and 80% of all dropouts. The federal government has considered modifying the Title IX act to permit single-sex schools, but when all-male schools have been tried previously, they did not produce the improved academic achievement they promised. As Sadker (2005) points out, they often became a "dumping ground" for boys with behavioral problems.

Gurian (2004) believes that schools need to provide teachers with a better background in recent findings from brain research so they can accommodate male ways of thinking and learning. He describes several specific teaching strategies stemming from the research that he believes will improve the academic achievement of boys. The central issue in this debate over gender equity in schools should be focused on whether both groups are being given the opportunity to learn and develop their talents and abilities so they can become confident and productive members of our rapidly changing society. Gender equity in education is not about winners and losers in a competition between boys and girls, but about the treatment of both boys and girls as they participate in school programs, both curricular and extracurricular. The goal of all educators should be to make that experience as fair and as equitable as possible for both boys and girls.

Many educators agree that there are gender equity issues for boys, but Sadker (2005) insists that most of these issues are not new. He believes the larger issue is that gender stereotypes for both boys and girls are still being reinforced in our schools and in society. For example, boys receive more math/science-related toys than girls, earn higher scores on most standardized achievement tests during high school and college, and continue to dominate high-paying occupations such as those in math- and science-related fields. We need to implement strategies both in schools and in society to address these ongoing gender equity issues.

What evidence indicates that gender equity issues are being addressed in schools and society?

One aspect of women's achievements that has evoked concern for males is access to higher education. Females are increasingly entering college, and they earn 55% or more of all college degrees (Collins, 2003). Of the women enrolled in college, 66% of them graduate with a bachelor's degree compared to 59% of men. Today, women constitute 60% of all biology/life science majors, 60% of all accounting majors, and 50% of all majors in math and business (NCES, 2004). Women currently constitute nearly half of students in law schools and medical schools (Collins, 2003). In addition to their academic achievements, women are increasingly involved in athletics; 32% of high school girls participated in sports compared to 45% of high school boys. Since 1981, the number of college women's teams nearly doubled and the number of women participating in collegiate athletics increased by 81% (Tanner, 2002).

As for the workplace, an ongoing problem for women workers is that so many of them are raising children; 65% of all families in the United States consist of either two parents or a single mom working full time. With so many working mothers, employers need to consider adopting changes such as flexible work hours to give these mothers the opportunity to respond to family needs. Companies such as Best Buy have implemented flexible work schedules in which individual workers can vary the time they come to work or leave work, and other companies such as J.C. Penney have experimented with online scheduling to allow workers to request certain hours or to trade shifts with other workers (Levin-Epstein, 2007). With these approaches, supervisors evaluate employee performance based on their productivity, and not simply by their hours at work. Early studies report that flexible scheduling reduces stress, increases productivity, and reduces the employee turnover rate.

An article in the April, 2006 issue of *The Economist* argued that women workers were the most underutilized segment of the workforce, and it recommended that governments work with businesses to address the difficulties preventing women with children from working (Williams, 2007). Some businesses have already implemented strategies such as offering childcare at the worksite and paid family leave. According to Levin-Epstein (2007), one study reported that such strategies resulted in higher worker productivity and retention rates. Since the pattern of U.S. families with dual wage earners or a single working parent is likely to persist, businesses competing for quality workers will feel increasing pressure to develop and expand on such "family-friendly" practices.

AFTERWORD

This description of cultural, individual, and institutional sexism is the tip of an iceberg. Gender discrimination occurs in our laws and in our court system, in the arts and in athletics, and in the images encountered in media and in school textbooks. Sexism permeates our institutions. Some men believe that sexism works to their advantage and resist efforts to promote gender equality, but sexism hurts men and women, boys and girls. Anything that prevents people from using their talents and abilities results in a loss for us all. When anyone is denied a chance to contribute to our society, the result is a nation that is less than it could have been. If Americans create a society that offers opportunities to all and receives the gifts each person has to offer, the male–female power game can cease—a victory for everyone.

> What is enough? Enough is when somebody says, 'Get me the best people you can find,' and nobody notices when half of them turn out to be women.
>
> **Louise Renne (1937–)**

myeducationlab

Now go to Topic #7: **Gender** in the MyEducationLab (www.myeducationlab.com) for your course, where you can:

- Find learning outcomes for this topic along with the national standards that connect to these outcomes.
- Complete Assignments and Activities that can help you more deeply understand the chapter content by viewing classroom video and ABC News footage.
- Apply and practice your understanding of the core teaching skills identified in the chapter with the Building Teaching Skills and Dispositions learning units.

TERMS AND DEFINITIONS

Androgyny The interchangeability of male and female roles and responsibilities in all areas beyond fundamental biological ones

Cultural sexism The societal promotion of negative beliefs and practices that reinforce rigid gender roles in which men are traditionally accorded a superior role in society while women are assigned to subordinate roles; the artificial superimposition of authority of one gender over another

Feminist A woman or man committed to the struggle for the social, economic, and personal rights of women and men; an advocate for equality between women and men

Glass ceiling An informal upper limit that keeps women and minorities from being promoted to positions of greatest responsibility in work organizations

Inclusive language Words or phrases that are not gender specific but inclusive of both genders

Individual sexism Prejudiced attitudes and behavior demeaning to women, or to men, because of beliefs about gender and gender roles, demonstrated whenever someone responds by saying or doing something degrading or harmful about persons of the other gender

Institutional sexism Established laws, customs, and practices in a society that allow systematic discrimination against people or groups based on gender

Male chauvinist A man or woman who believes that men ought to be the leaders and decision makers and women should be subordinate to them

Rape Forcing someone to submit to sexual intercourse or engaging in sexual intercourse without their consent

Sexism An attitude, action, or institutional structure that subordinates or limits a person on the basis of sex (Andrzejewski, 1996)

Sexual harassment Deliberate and repeated behavior that has a sexual basis and is not welcomed, requested, or returned

DISCUSSION EXERCISES

Exercise #1 Find the Problem: Analyzing Sexist Language

Directions: Determine why the language in each statement has been termed "sexist." Write an appropriate nonsexist message to replace the sexist one. [*Example:* The average American drinks his coffee black. Nonsexist revision: The average American drinks black coffee.]

1. Dear Sir:
2. Any student who is not satisfied with his performance on the pretest may take the posttest.
3. Mr. McAllister runs the garage in partnership with his wife, a striking blonde who mans the pumps.
4. The English teacher developed a wonderful thematic unit on "Man and His World."
5. Housewives are feeling the pinch of higher food prices.
6. A writer can become so involved in his work that he neglects his family.
7. NCTE convention-goers and their wives are invited to attend the gala event.
8. One of our prehistoric ancestors was the Neanderthal man.
9. We are asking all the mothers to send cookies for our field trip tomorrow.
10. Blacks finally received the vote in 1870.
11. While lunch was delayed, the women gossiped about last night's meeting.
12. A slave could not claim his wife or children as his own because the laws did not recognize slave marriages.
13. The average student is worried about his grades.
14. The ancient Egyptians allowed women considerable control over property.
15. One of the political debates in the racial struggle taking place in South Africa is over the concept of "one man, one vote."

Exercise #2 Sexual Harassment: Case Studies from Higher Education

Directions: Sexual harassment may take several forms: innuendo or overt action toward either gender by those of the same or opposite sex, unwanted sexual advances, sexual assault, or sexual coercion (rape). In each situation, respond to the following three questions:

- Is this a case of sexual harassment? If yes, when did the harassment begin to occur?
- What are the harassing behaviors in this situation?
- What can the individual(s) involved in each situation do to address the harassment?

1. Kevin is taking an introductory English course. His first writing assignment dealt with his uncertainties about being a new student in college, on his own for the first time. When the essays are returned, his has no grade and only the comment, "Please see me." Kevin goes to the teacher's office during the posted office hours. His teacher suggests that they go out for a drink to discuss the essay.
2. Connie is taking a math course that includes a unit on statistics. Connie has been having some difficulty understanding probability theory. She knows that this course is important to her career and a good grade in math can increase her chances of getting into graduate school. She contacts her teaching assistant and explains her concerns about the material and her wish to get a good grade to qualify for graduate school. They set up a series of tutoring sessions, and by the third session have not only become friends but have begun to date outside of the sessions.
3. Tamara, one of the few women in an engineering class, notices that her professor stares at her, especially while she takes quizzes. She is aware that the professor has a history of interrupting women students when they ask questions and even refusing to respond to their questions. In addition, during one class period the professor told a joke demeaning to women. Many of the men in the class laughed at the joke, which angered Tamara even more.
4. In her introductory psychology class, Sonia, a Latina, notices that her professor smiles and comments on her appearance as a greeting each morning, but that he does not greet any other student in that way. Before his lecture on contemporary sexual roles and behavior, he says to the class, "Sonia can probably help us understand this topic because she has to put up with macho types."
5. Near the entrance to the library, men using cards with the numbers one through ten "rate" the sexual attributes of women who enter the library, accompanied by much laughter and some ambiguous gestures. Their behavior causes many women to avoid going to the library.
6. In an undergraduate literature class, Professor Helmsley who is also the director of Graduate Studies, expresses his opinion that courses in literature offered under the Women's Studies Program are useless preparation for graduate study. He has recommended that all such courses be dropped from the list of acceptable courses for the undergraduate major in literature.

Adapted from *Sexual Harassment and the University: Seven Cases.*

REFERENCES

American Association of University Women. (1993). *Hostile hallways: The AAUW survey on sexual harassment in America's schools.* Washington, DC: Author.

Describes pervasive patterns of sexual harassment against both girls and boys in public schools in the United States.

Andrzejewski, J. (1996). Definitions for understanding oppression and social justice. In J. Andrzejewski (Ed.), *Oppression and social justice: Critical frameworks* (5th ed., pp. 52–58). Needham, MA: Simon & Schuster.

Provides definitions for a variety of terms essential for discussing intergroup relations.

Arliss, L.P. (1991). *Gender communication.* Englewood Cliffs, NJ: Prentice Hall.

Provides examples of sexist language in Chapter 3, "Debates About Language and Sexism."

Badgett, M.V.L. (2001). *Money, myths, and change: The economic lives of lesbians and gay men.* Chicago, IL: The University of Chicago Press.

Discusses the study of domestic duties in Chapter 6, "A Family Resemblance," page 147.

Baker, L.A. (2006). Sexual harassment by supervisors. *FBI Law Enforcement Bulletin, 75*(3), 25–33.

Reviews the history of sexual harassment and current obligations of employers as have been established by rulings from a variety of court cases.

Benokraitis, N., & Feagin, J. (1995). *Modern sexism: Blatant, subtle and covert discrimination* (2nd ed.). Englewood Cliffs, NJ: Prentice Hall.

Analyzes gender discrimination in society, including issues specifically related to women of color, and provides recommendations to eliminate gender discrimination.

Bernstein, A. (2004). Women's pay: Why the gap remains a chasm. *Business Week,* 3887, 58–59.

Examines the lack of progress in narrowing the gap between men's and women's salaries.

Branch, T. (1998). *Pillar of fire: America in the King years 1963–65.* New York, NY: Simon & Schuster.

Describes the civil rights movement in the United States and the leadership role played by Martin Luther King, Jr. (the second volume of a trilogy).

Brandenburg, J.B. (1997). *Confronting sexual harassment: What schools and colleges can do.* New York, NY: Teachers College Press.

Provides information and case studies to explore the psychology behind sexual harassment, examines the legal issues involved, and provides educators with a variety of educational strategies.

Catania, S. (2005). The counselor. *Mother Jones, 30*(4), 45–49, 88.

Discusses the issue of domestic abuse through the experience of one domestic abuse counselor and describes what has been done in recent years to address the problem.

Collins, G. (2003). *America's women: 400 years of dolls, drudges, helpmates, and heroines.* New York, NY: HarperCollins.

Describes the experiences of women in America collectively as well as providing individual stories of women who made unique contributions to American society.

Daft, R.L. (2003). Managing diverse employees. In *Management* (6th ed., pp. 436–468). Versailles, KY: Thompson Southwestern.

Discusses the current status of affirmative action, explores various dimensions of diversity in the workforce, and examines how corporate culture is changing to accommodate diversity.

Day, J.C., & Newburger, E.C. (2002, July). The big payoff: Educational attainment and synthetic estimates of work-life earnings. *Current Populations Reports.* Washington, DC: U.S. Department of Commerce. Retrieved June 11, 2009, from www.census.gov/www/abs/popula.html (Select p23–210)

Compares earnings of men and women and projects work-life earnings in today's dollars.

Equal Employment Opportunity Commission (EEOC). Retrieved on September 24, 2009 at www.eeoc.gov

Provides information and statistics on EEOC policies and enforcement of policies.

Evans, S. (1989). *Born for liberty: A history of women in America.* New York: The Free Press.

Describes the experiences of women in America beginning with indigenous women and including women of color as well as European women immigrants.

Faludi, S. (2006). *Backlash: The undeclared war against American women.* New York, NY: Three Rivers Press.

Describes the backlash against the women's movement that has undermined and manipulated women in the media, the legal system, the fashion industry, politics, and business.

Gonnerman, J. (2005). The unforgiven. *Mother Jones, 30*(4), 38–43.

Examines the issue of domestic violence by providing recent data and describing experiences of specific women.

Gould, S.J. (1981). *The mismeasure of man.* New York, NY: W.W. Norton.

Discusses the belief in human intelligence as an entity that can be measured and quantified in each individual, producing a number to judge individuals as superior or inferior.

Gould, S.J. (1983). Big fish, little fish. In *Hen's teeth and horses toes* (pp. 21–31). New York, NY: W. W. Norton.

Examines assumptions about "natural" differences between genders in the animal world.

Grall, T. (2000, October). Child support for custodial mothers and fathers. *Current Population Reports.* Washington, DC: U.S. Department of Commerce.

Provides demographic and economic data on custodial parents from census reports.

Gurian, M. (2004). With boys and girls in mind. *Educational Leadership, 62*(3), 21–26.

Discusses results of brain research in terms of gender differences and recommends teaching strategies to facilitate learning among boys.

Jeffery, C. (2005). Why women can't win for trying. *Mother Jones, 30*(4), 22–23.

Provides statistics on diverse gender issues including economics, politics, and violence.

Jones, G.R., & George, J.M. (2003). Managing diverse employees in a diverse environment. In *Contemporary management* (3rd ed., pp. 112–149). Boston, MA: McGraw Hill.

Describes increasing diversity among consumers and in the workforce and provides strategies for managers to work effectively with diverse employees.

Kilbourne, J. (1999). *Deadly persuasion: Why women and girls must fight the addictive power of advertising.* New York, NY: The Free Press.

Argues that advertising is a pervasive cultural phenomenon that encourages people to objectify each other and diminishes the quality of human relationships.

Kim, M. (2000, September). Women paid low wages: Who they are and where they work. *Monthly Labor Review,* pp. 26–31.

Uses a national data set from the 1998 *Current Population Survey* (March) of 60,000 households in the United States to analyze salaries for women in the workforce.

Kimmel, P.R. (2006). Culture and conflict. In M. Deutsch & P. Coleman (Eds.), *The handbook of conflict resolution.* San Francisco, CA: Jossey-Bass.

Describes the influence of culture on individual communication and the need to practice cultural relativism to avoid conflict in intercultural communication.

Knapp, D.E., & Kustis, G.A. (1996). The real "Disclosure": Sexual harassment and the bottom line. In M. Stockdale (Ed.), *Sexual harassment in the workplace: Perspectives, frontiers, and response strategies* (pp. 199–213). Thousand Oaks, CA: Sage.

Examines the cost of sexual harassment including a "comprehensive behavior costing model" to determine economic consequences of tolerating sexual harassment.

Levin-Epstein, J. (2007, March). Responsive workplaces. *American Prospect, 18*(3), A16–A18.

Discusses the need for workplace flexibility for women workers and proposes solutions that are "family-friendly" and create a positive work environment.

MacKinnon, C.A. (1987). A rally against rape. In *Feminism unmodified: Discourses on life and law* (pp. 81–84). Cambridge, MA: Harvard University Press.

Discusses why women do not report rapes and calls on men to be supportive.

National Center for Educational Statistics. (2004). *Trends in education equity of girls and women: 2004.* Retrieved October 14, 2008, from http://nces.ed.gov/pubs2005/equity/index.asp

Select "Persistence and Attainment" to access data, and at that location, select "figure k" for an excellent chart on increasing numbers of women in selected college majors.

National Center for Health Statistics. (1999). *National Vital Statistics* 47(21). Retrieved July 12, 2003, from http://www.cdc.gov/nchs

Provides statistics on a variety of health issues including those related to marriage; studies are periodically updated and made available at this Web site.

Nilsen, A.P. (1977a). Sexism as shown through the English vocabulary. In A.P. Nilsen, H. Bosmajian, H.L. Gershuny, & J.P. Stanley (Eds.), *Sexism and language* (pp. 27–41). Urbana, IL: National Council of Teachers of English.

Examines how sexism is implicit in many words and phrases in American English.

Nilsen, A.P. (1977b). Sexism in the language of marriage. In A.P. Nilsen, H. Bosmajian, H.L. Gershuny, & J.P. Stanley (Eds.), *Sexism and language* (pp. 131–140). Urbana, IL: National Council of Teachers of English.

Examines the nature of sexism in words and phrases pertaining to marital relations.

Partridge, E. (2009). *Origins: A short etymological dictionary of modern English* (p. 92). New York, NY: Routledge.

Citation notes that Nicolas Chauvin was often ridiculed for his loyalty to Napoleon.

Quindlen, A. (2008, October 13). The Leadership Lid. *Newsweek,* 86.

Describes the current status of the glass ceiling for women in leadership positions.

RAINN (2009). Rape, Abuse, and Incest National Network. Retrieved June 12, 2009, from http://www.rainn.org

Provides statistics from the 2005 National Crime Victimization Survey conducted by the U.S. Department of Justice (at the web site, Select "Get Information"). Also go to National Domestic Violence Hotline (www.ndvh.org) for additional statistics.

Riley, G. (1986a). *Inventing the American woman: A perspective on women's history, 1607–1877: Vol. 1.* Arlington Heights, IL: Harlan Davidson.

Describes women's experiences from the colonial era to post–Civil War Reconstruction.

Riley, G. (1986b). *Inventing the American woman: A perspective on women's history, 1865–present: Vol. 2.* Arlington Heights, IL: Harlan Davidson.

Describes the experiences of women in the United States from the Civil War to the 1980s.

Sadker, D. (2005). Gender bias lives, for both sexes. *Education Digest, 70*(8), 27–30.

Discusses gender equity issues in schools and the influence of gender stereotyping.

Sadker, D., & Sadker, M. (1994). *Failing at fairness: How America's schools cheat girls.* New York, NY: Charles Scribner.

Discusses sexist practices and their consequences in American schools; describes conditions women had to meet to attend Oberlin College in Chapter 2, pp. 21–22.

Sampson, R. (2003). Acquaintance rape of college students. *Problem-Oriented Guides for Police,* No 17. Retrieved June 6, 2009, from www.cops.usdoj.gov.

Analyzes data concerning acquaintance rape on college campuses.

Simon, R.W. (2002, January). Revisiting the relationships among gender, marital status, and mental health. *American Journal of Sociology, 107*(4), 1065–1097.

Describes survey data on differences in mental health for those married and unmarried.

Sorenson, E. (1997, November). A national profile of nonresident fathers and their ability to pay child support. *Journal of Marriage and the Family, 59*(4), 785–798.

Describes demographic characteristics and child support paid by nonresident fathers.

Strauss, S., & Espeland, P. (1992). *Sexual harassment and teens: A program for positive change.* Minneapolis, MN: Free Spirit.

Addresses sexual harassment at the worksite, but focuses on sexual harassment in schools, including a program for implementing sexual harassment policy and procedures.

Tanner, J. (2002). *Women in sports, issues in race, ethnicity and gender.* Washington, DC: CQ Press, 225–242.

Describes college compliance with Title IX, documents the increasing numbers of women playing college and professional sports, and discusses current related issues.

Tavris, C. (1999). *The mismeasure of woman.* New York, NY: Peter Smith.

Analyzes scientific studies of women to expose the biases in them that have been used to justify the status quo by perpetuating sexist stereotypes and the devaluation of women.

Tavris, C., & Wade, C. (1984). *The longest war: Sex differences in perspective* (2nd ed.). New York, NY: Harcourt Brace Jovanovich.

Examines an array of gender issues by reviewing research in anthropology, biology, human sexuality, education, psychology, and sociology.

Tjaden, P., & Thoennes, N. (1998). *Prevalence, incidence, and consequences of violence against women: Findings from the National Violence Against Women Survey.* Washington, DC: United States Department of Justice. Retrieved June 10, 2009, from http://eric.ed.gov (ERIC # E0934980).

Provides data on domestic violence that is regularly updated.

Trusty, J., Robinson, C.R., Plata, M., & Ng, K. (2000, Fall). Effects of gender, socioeconomic status, and early academic performance on postsecondary educational choice. *Journal of Counseling and Development, 78*(4), 463–473.

Analyzes national data on academic performance and educational choices of eighth-grade students and recent high school graduates to determine the influence of gender and class.

U.S. Bureau of Labor Statistics. (2008). Highlights of Women's Earnings in 2007. Retrieved June 11, 2009, from www.bls.gov

Provides information and tables concerning women's and men's salaries in 2007.

U.S. Bureau of Labor Statistics. (March 2006). Women still underrepresented among highest wage earners. *Issues in Labor Statistics.* Retrieved July 15, 2006, from www.bls.gov

Provides data on the increasing number of women managers and the continuing lack of women in top management positions.

Webb, S. (2000). *Step forward: Sexual harassment in the workplace* (2nd ed.). New York, NY: Mastermedia.

Reviews the history of sexual harassment, offers solutions to prevent sexual harassment, and examines sexual harassment in the global workplace. For more information, read *Women's International Network News, 28*(1).

Wetzel, R., & Brown, N.W. (2000). *Student-generated sexual harassment in secondary schools.* Westport, CT: Bergin & Garvey.

Describes legal rulings on sexual harassment, theories explaining why sexual harassment occurs, and guidelines for secondary schools to develop effective sexual harassment policies.

Williams, J.C. (2007, March). The opt-out revolution revisited. *American Prospect, 18*(3), pp. A12–A15.

Discusses several studies dealing with the problem of inflexibility at the workplace pushing women out and the difficulties women face when they return to work.

Wulff, M.B., & Steitz, J.A. (1997). Curricular track, career choice, and androgyny among adolescent females. *Adolescent, 32*(125), 43–50.

Describes their study of androgyny among twenty high school girls from a college-track upper-level math class and twenty girls from a vocational-track cosmetology class.

Heterosexism: Transforming Homosexuality from Deviant to Different

"The only abnormality is the incapacity to love."

Anais Nin (1903–1977)

The word *homosexual* and the concept of homosexuality appear to have originated in the 1860s in the German medical writing of Dr. Karl Ulrichs. Homosexuality does not seem to enter into public discourse in a formal and explicit way until 1892, when scholars such as Havelock Ellis and Magnus Hirschfield published essays and books describing theories and research concerning human sexuality. In a highly regarded book published in 1886, Richard von Krafft-Ebing chose not to use "sexual inversion," the common term in America, but Ulrich's word, translated to English as *homosexuality.* Krafft-Ebing described a **homosexual** as someone sexually attracted to members of the same sex. Although same-sex liaisons had been documented throughout human history, the new term challenged the Western world's traditional heterosexual assumption.

What is the heterosexual assumption?

Non-Western cultures have a history of acknowledging and accepting sexual variation in human beings (Herdt, 1997; Williams, 2001). Western cultural attitudes about sexuality have been based on a **heterosexual assumption:** that all people were born **heterosexual** and that being attracted to opposite-sex partners was the natural condition of human beings. People who engaged in any sexual activity not conforming to heterosexual norms were assumed to be making deviant and unnatural choices, especially when sexual activity took place with a same-sex partner. The Bible was often used to justify beliefs about normal or deviant sexual behavior, and even twentieth-century psychologists reinforced the assumption by regarding homosexuality as a mental illness. Homosexuals were widely perceived as aberrations in need of correction (a cure) to bring them back to their true heterosexual nature (Duberman, Vicinus, & Chauncey, 1989).

When was the heterosexual assumption challenged?

Krafft-Ebing provided the term that challenged the heterosexual assumption. Although he still believed that homosexuality was immoral and unacceptable, he defined it as one of many forms of sexual desire. Like fetishism or masochism, Krafft-Ebing argued that homosexuality was a condition, a mental defect that could be cured (Halperin, 1989).

Although the general public would not become familiar with the idea of homosexuality for another sixty years, Krafft-Ebing established the idea that there were various forms of sexual desire, and that one of these involved a desire for same-sex partners. His assertion was addressed by the evolving field of psychology as its practitioners searched for a way to remedy deviant behavior. The suggested "cures" included castration, sterilization, electric shock, and occasional lobotomies; however, none proved practically successful (Katz, 1985).

Although conventional wisdom among psychologists continued to regard homosexuality as deviant and unnatural—a mental defect—the failure of recommended remedies in the clinical setting caused a number of respected people in the field, including A.A. Brill, Magnus Hirschfield, and even Sigmund Freud, to conclude that homosexuality could not be cured and was probably a permanent condition. As psychologists became convinced that deviant sexual desires could not be redirected, they adopted approaches such as adjustment therapy to control homosexual behavior. These practices were the norm when the Kinsey Report was published in 1948.

How did the Kinsey Report challenge the heterosexual assumption?

With funding from the Rockefeller Foundation and Indiana University, a zoologist named Alfred Kinsey and his research staff engaged in a study of human sexual behavior from 1938 to 1956. The Kinsey Report issued in 1948 was controversial for many reasons, not the least of which was its proposition that **sexual orientation** was not a singular phenomenon, but a continuum of multiple possibilities ranging from exclusive heterosexuality to exclusive homosexuality, with a variety of bisexual orientations in between (see Figure 10.1). Based on self-reports of dreams and fantasies as well as behavior, Kinsey and his staff concluded that only a small percentage of their research subjects were exclusively heterosexual or exclusively homosexual (later a figure of 10% became widely used). Most appeared to have some potential for **bisexual** behavior—being sexually attracted to members of either gender—although sexual attraction might be biased more toward one gender than another.

The 1948 Kinsey Report (and the 1953 report focusing on women) challenged the general assumption that all human beings possessed a heterosexual orientation. Americans were confronted with the radical concept of sexual orientation: that every human being is not heterosexual, but that human sexuality encompasses categories of different sexual attractions and behaviors, including an attraction to and a desire for same-sex partners.

What was the impact of the Kinsey Report?

The term *homosexuality* provided a label for what Oscar Wilde's lover had called "the love that dare not speak its name," but most Americans were uncomfortable with the subject and refused to discuss it. Most psychologists still regarded homosexuality as a defect, a form of mental illness, but homosexuals themselves began to reconsider their situation. There were, and always had been, same-sex–oriented people who were comfortable with their sexuality while being discreet in their behavior. These men and women became convinced that attitudes in America needed to change, but they weren't sure how that could happen.

Homosexual friends of psychologist Evelyn Hooker argued that psychologists persisted in regarding homosexuality as a mental illness because the homosexual patients who sought treatment were not comfortable with their own sexuality. These individuals were often filled with guilt and anxiety because of society's condemnation or their religious upbringing. One gay man urged Dr. Hooker to engage in research involving well-adjusted gay men, and he volunteered a number of such men for the research (Marcus, 1992).

Hooker subsequently conducted a study involving thirty homosexual men and thirty heterosexual men. She administered three different personality tests to each subject—Rorschach, Thematic Apperception, and Make a Picture Story—and submitted the results to a panel of internationally respected psychologists. None of the panelists could discern heterosexual from homosexual subjects, and they gave two thirds of the subjects from each group a score of average or higher, clearly refuting the belief that homosexuality was associated with inherent mental problems. Hooker presented the findings of the panel evaluations in her research at the national conference of the American Psychological Association (APA) in 1956. It would take another seventeen years for APA members to admit they had been wrong and take appropriate action.

In 1973, the American Psychological Association voted to remove homosexuality from its list of mental illnesses. The American Medical Association (AMA) would later join the APA in declaring that homosexuality was not a mental illness, affirming that gay men and lesbians could be just as healthy,

FIGURE 10.1

The Kinsey Continuum of Sexual Orientation

Based on dreams and fantasies as well as behavior, the continuum of sexual orientation ranges from exclusively heterosexual to exclusively homosexual with the majority of people between the two exclusive positions.

Source: Figure based on data from *Sexual Behavior in the Human Male*, by A. Kinsey, W. Pomeroy, and C. Martin, 1948.

The Kinsey Continuum of Sexual Orientation

0 = Exclusively heterosexual
1 = Predominantly heterosexual, only incidentally homosexual
2 = Predominantly heterosexual, but more than incidentally homosexual
3 = Equally heterosexual and homosexual
4 = Predominantly homosexual, but more than incidentally heterosexual
5 = Predominantly homosexual, only incidentally heterosexual
6 = Exclusively homosexual

competent, and capable of functioning effectively in society as heterosexuals. The decisions of the APA and AMA sent a clear message to people who believed they were justified in discriminating against people who were not heterosexual. This resulted in the concept of **heterosexism**—the oppression or exploitation of human beings not biologically heterosexual.

> In my relationship with others, I have found that it does not help, in the long run, to act as if I am something I am not.
>
> **Carl Rogers (1902–1987)**

What has current research reported with regard to homosexuality?

Research on human sexuality has continued and, based on the studies, researchers seem to agree that sexual orientation has a significant biological basis. Using anthropological evidence and studies in child development, Pillard (1997) proposed that sexual orientation is an innate characteristic, a deeply embedded personality trait that can be observed in young children:

> There seems to be a fundamental bias toward either a heterosexual or a homosexual developmental path, prefigured early in life, neither taught nor learned, and profoundly resistant to modification. (p. 233)

Le Vay (1996) argued that the influence of sex hormones on brain functioning at the primary drive center, the hypothalamus, appears to be a significant biological factor. Although not denying the importance of biological factors, anthropologists have described cultural influences on behavior and attitudes concerning human sexuality (Herdt, 1997). Researchers widely agree that there is no single cause for the sexual orientation of each individual, but that multiple factors are responsible (Le Vay, 1996; Stein, 1999).

Reinforcing the idea of sexual variation among humans, studies of animal behavior have reported sexual activities between same-sex animals (Stein, 1999). Money (1988) described research that experimentally manipulated prenatal hormones af-

Research with an Agenda Is Not Research: The Story of Paul Cameron

In 1982, Dr. Paul Cameron, an assistant professor of psychology at the University of Nebraska, opposed a change being considered by the Omaha city council to add lesbians and gay men to its civil rights ordinance. In a speech at a Lutheran church, Cameron claimed that a homosexual had recently kidnapped and castrated a local boy. The Omaha police and local hospitals had no record of the incident, but people were outraged. The proposal was defeated four to one.

In 1983, Cameron formed the Institute for the Scientific Investigation of Sexuality, announcing that he would conduct a national sex survey. Although it is considered unscientific for a researcher to predict results prior to conducting a study, Cameron said his study would show that sexually adventurous people contract more diseases, are less happy, and are more inclined to attempt suicide. Cameron's findings were consistent with his predictions, but legitimate researchers identified many flaws in his statistical analysis and research methodology. This study continues to be cited by Christian fundamentalist organizations and individuals who want research to justify their anti-gay attitudes.

Based on data from a 1978 study by Nicholas Groth, Cameron published a study in 1983 claiming that homosexuals are ten to twenty times more likely to molest children. Groth interviewed 175 convicted child molesters and reported that more boys than girls were victims; he also reported that the men either identified themselves as heterosexual or had no interest in adult sex. Groth filed a complaint with the American Psychological Association (APA) accusing Cameron of misrepresenting data from his study. The APA stripped Cameron of his professional accreditation.

In 1992, as director of what he now called the Family Research Institute, Cameron moved to Colorado to assist supporters of a state constitutional amendment to ban civil rights protection for gay men and lesbians. Amendment supporters distributed thousands of copies of Cameron's anti-gay research a week before the election. A majority of the state's voters approved the proposed ban on civil rights protection for gays and lesbians.

In 1994, Cameron published his "Gay Obituary Study." Based on 6,000 newspaper obituaries of gay men, Cameron calculated the *average life span of all gay men* as 43. Because this figure was cited on radio and television talk shows, a Manhattan Institute scientist pointed out that the average age for AIDs victims was 40, so if the *average life span for all gay men* was 43, those without AIDs could not live past 46. The average age of 43 for gay men is a statistic still cited in anti-gay literature.

In a 2004 decision upholding a state law banning adoption by same-sex couples, the Florida Supreme Court cited a Cameron "study" as justification for their decision. After Cameron began claiming that his research was sociological, the American Sociological Association said he had misinterpreted sociological research and insisted that he cease claiming to be engaged in sociological study. Despite his "success," most scientists agree with Nicholas Groth's assessment of Cameron: "He disgraces his profession" (p. 14).

Source: **David Holthouse (2005), "The Fabulist," *Intelligence Report*.**

fecting the sexual pathways of the brain to successfully influence animals (other than primates) to engage in exclusively homosexual or heterosexual behavior during mating. Money did not claim that scientists could have the same success with humans, explaining that prenatal hormones are thought to have a less absolute influence on primates, but he did conclude that manipulation of sex hormones can create a predisposition for sexual activity with same-sex or opposite-sex partners.

Research regarding human sexual variation would seem to parallel the role that variation plays throughout nature. Gould (1983) provides an illustration in his explanation of the variety in striping patterns for zebras. One striping pattern has numerous, narrow, parallel stripes configured relatively straight up and down the body. Another pattern has fewer, thicker stripes on the body and three broad slightly curved stripes on the haunch. A third pattern has even fewer and thicker stripes on the front of the body, and even broader stripes starting from the middle of the belly and curving back to the haunch (see Figure 10.2).

The three striping variations result from the striping mechanism being initiated at different times during fetal development. Because variation occurs in something as simple as the striping pattern for zebras, it is difficult to maintain that all human beings possess the same heterosexual orientation, given the complexity of factors involved with the sexual development of the human fetus. It is far more logical to expect the kind of sexual variation described in the *Kinsey Report,* in the research conducted since 1948, and as recorded in human history.

Cultural Heterosexism

Cultural heterosexism refers to a dominant culture defining heterosexuality as the norm and anything else as deviant. The heterosexual assumption is an example of cultural sexism. Although science has attempted to explain the complexity and variations in human sexual response, some people insist that the only acceptable way to love and make love is to be a heterosexual couple. History tells us,

> I can't understand any discussion of gays and lesbians as if they were something immoral or unsatisfactory. They're just doing what nature wants them to do.
>
> **R. Buckminster Fuller (1895–1983)**

FIGURE 10.2

A simple genetic striping mechanism occurring at different times during fetal development produces these three striping patterns.

Source: From *Hen's Teeth and Horse's Toes: Further Reflections in Natural History* by Stephen Jay Gould. Copyright © 1983 by Stephen Jay Gould. Used by permission of W. W. Norton & Company, Inc.

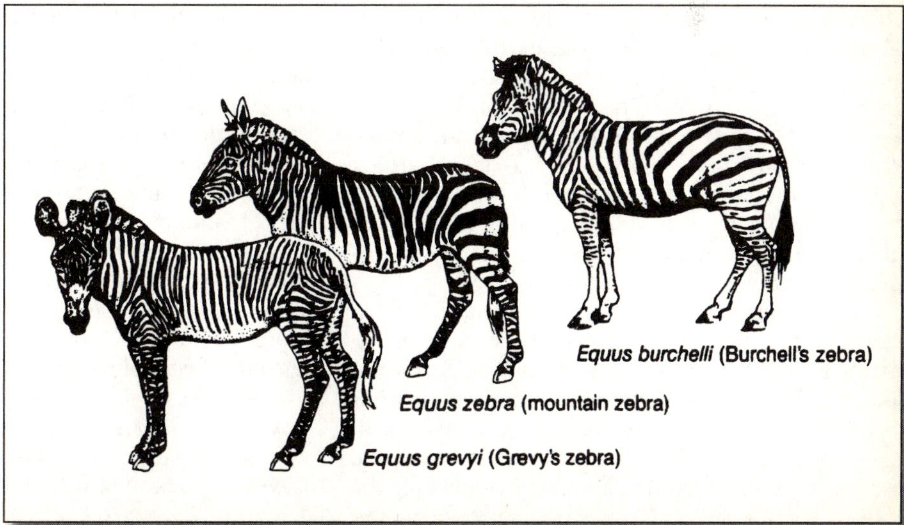

however, that homosexual feelings are not a contemporary aberration, but have been reflected in human behavior in all cultures, in every era.

What historical evidence has described the existence of homosexuality?

Love and sexual desire between men was accepted and widely practiced in ancient Greece. Greeks openly wrote about the love of one man for another. Although Sappho's poetry described women's love for other women, men were the primary authors of Greek literature that has been preserved. Approving of same-sex attraction wasn't an Athenian idiosyncrasy; it was also widely accepted in Sparta and other city-states. One of the most famous military units in Greek history was the Band of Thebes—150 pairs of lovers, a fighting force of 300 men; each pledged to stand by his lover in battle until death took one or both. The unit played a heroic part in Sparta's siege of Thebes: Fewer than 6,000 Theban defenders defeated more than 10,000 Spartan soldiers, a defeat from which Sparta never recovered, paving the way for the conquest of Greece by Philip of Macedonia. Philip's son, Alexander the Great, would become famous for conquering the known world during his lifetime and, according to contemporary accounts, was known to engage in sexual activity with male partners (Rowse, 1977).

One of the ironies of the history of homosexuality was recorded in nineteenth-century England. At a time when English society was extremely homophobic, wealthy families sent their sons to male-only boarding schools, where they learned to read Latin and Greek texts, some with homosexual themes. Many memoirs recall upper-class boarding school experiences where English boys are described as engaging in homosexual behavior that they called **Greek love,** a euphemism for homosexual activity (Crompton, 1998).

Anthropologists have observed that culture often determines societal attitudes toward homosexuality. Some Native American cultures believed that a homosexual is a special human being, possessing traits of both males and females, and thus endowed with great power. Katz (1976) provided historical and anthropological documentation as evidence of the acceptance of homosexuality in various Native American cultures.

Some Polynesian and Caribbean cultures also view same-sex attraction and homosexual behavior as acceptable. The Mediterranean region, including southern Italy and countries such as Greece, Morocco, and Turkey, has historically been a haven for European homosexuals because same-sex relationships were tolerated. Aristocratic homosexuals traveled there primarily to act on their sexual attraction to same-sex partners (Crompton, 1985; Williams, 2001). According to Zeldin (1994), homosexuality has been accepted at one time or another by about two thirds of human societies.

Early on, the Catholic Church played a major role in the denunciation of homosexuality in Europe. The church regarded homosexuality as a sin, yet in 1102, the Archbishop of Canterbury called for lenient punishments for people engaging in same-sex activity because, "this sin has been so public that hardly anyone has blushed for it" (Zeldin, 1994, p. 123). As part of investigations by the Inquisition, church persecution of homosexuals began in the thirteenth century as the Vatican sought to eliminate various heresies. The Inquisition lasted about 400 years, but homosexuals continued to be persecuted in Europe for the next 600 years (Boswell, 1994; Duberman, Vicinus, & Chauncey, 1989).

Medieval churchmen executed both male and female homosexuals, although women were equally likely to be executed as witches, also justified in the Bible. The persecution and execution of men has suggested the origin of the term *faggot* as derived from *fagot,* referring to sticks tied in a bundle for kindling. When medieval judges condemned men to death for engaging in sexual activity with another man, the executioner sometimes tied up and piled the men on top of one another like bundles of kindling and burned them (Kantor, 1998).

Even royalty were not immune from persecution. Kings and queens were permitted a variety of sins as long as they were discreet, but English monarch Edward II was not discreet. His coronation festivities were almost disrupted by public reaction to the king's obvious preference for his friend Piers Gaveston rather than his queen. Offended by the king's outrageous behavior, English nobles sent Gaveston back to France. Edward could not bear to be separated from his lover and pleaded that Gaveston be allowed to come back. Shortly after Gaveston returned to England, he was murdered, which led to a civil war that ended with Edward's death at the hands of Queen Isabella and her lover, Mortimer (Rowse, 1977). Still, Edward II was the exception. For royalty or aristocrats, or perhaps an artist under their protection, it was possible to escape persecution for having homosexual feelings or behaviors.

Despite some degree of tolerance for occasional royal family and aristocratic dalliances, England continued to reflect homophobic attitudes that forced those with fame and fortune, like the poet Lord Byron, to seek sexual pleasure outside the boundaries of Britain for fear of punishment in the country. Indeed, popular playwright Oscar Wilde was tried and sent to prison (1895–1897) for his homosexual activity.

By the twentieth century, cultural attitudes about homosexuality in England had mellowed; this was true for most of Europe, but not for the United States. The contrast between European and American attitudes was illustrated by the appointment of James Hormel as U.S. ambassador to Luxembourg during the Clinton administration. Officials in Luxembourg raised no objection to Hormel, who was openly gay, but his appointment was stalled in the Senate for two years because of objections from influential conservative senators.

> Whenever I behold someone who possesses any talent or displays any dexterity of mind, who can do or say something more appropriately than the rest of the world, I am compelled to fall in love with him, and give myself away to him so entirely that I am no longer my own property but wholly his.
>
> **Michelangelo [Buonarroti] (1475–1564)**

How have attitudes of the American people changed concerning homosexuality?

As it did with racial minorities, World War II had an impact on American homosexuals returning from the war. The 1948 *Kinsey Report* had refuted the heterosexual assumption, and many gay and lesbian veterans thought their military experience earned them the right to be accepted regardless of sexual orientation. Because California courts had upheld the right of openly gay men and lesbians to patronize certain bars and businesses, it seemed the safest place to live. San Francisco had been a major port of departure for men and women sent to the Pacific, and many returning gays and lesbians chose to remain there. As their numbers grew, so did their political activism; by the 1970s, mayoral candidates such as George Moscone were openly courting gay voters.

San Francisco was one of many cities across the United States to witness gay and lesbian political activism, yet when Harvey Milk, an openly gay candidate, was elected San Francisco city supervisor in 1977, national media reported the story. One year later, a city supervisor who objected to serving with a gay man murdered both Milk and Mayor Moscone. As an indication that anti-gay prejudice had not disappeared, the jury convicted Dan White of the minimal penalty possible in such a case, manslaughter. The White verdict sparked a riot that lasted more than two hours in gay areas of San Francisco; police responded by shouting homophobic slurs and brutally beating any gay man or lesbian they encountered (D'Emilio, 1989).

The San Francisco riot on the West Coast, like the Stonewall riot a decade earlier in New York City, were two of many events in the late twentieth century that would force Americans everywhere to acknowledge the presence of homosexuals (see Table 10.1). The word **gay** became accepted as the self-chosen label of the homosexual community, although usage eventually was limited to men. The identification of homosexuals in popular culture and the acceptance of gays and lesbians by prominent people were important factors in changing historical anti-gay attitudes. By the 1970s, columnist Abigail van Buren ("Dear Abby") responded to questions about homosexuality based on her understanding of scientific research, emphasizing the need to accept it. In 1975, David Kopay, a retired National Football League running back, published an autobiography in which he not only admitted

TABLE 10.1 A Timetable of Important Events in the Twentieth Century for the Recognition of Gay Rights in the United States

1924	Formation of the first recognized activist group for gays and lesbians (Chicago).
1962	Illinois is the first state to repeal its sodomy laws.
1969	Police raid of the Stonewall Inn (a gay bar in New York City) results in riots that spark the beginning of the gay rights movement.
1970	First "Gay Pride" march (New York City) commemorates the Stonewall Riot.
1975	Retired NFL running back, Dave Kopay, is the first professional athlete to admit that he is gay.
1978	Harvey Milk, San Francisco's first openly gay city supervisor, is assassinated.
1981	The Centers for Disease Control and Prevention reports on the first case of what later becomes known as AIDS (initially called the "gay plague").
1982	Wisconsin is the first state to prohibit discrimination based on sexual orientation.
1982	Harvey Fierstein's play about a drag queen called *Torch Song Trilogy* opens on Broadway and wins the Tony Award for best play.
1984	Hollywood's legendary leading man Rock Hudson admits to being gay.
1987	Formation of ACT UP, which advocates for more funding for AIDS research.
1993	U.S. military adopts "don't ask, don't tell" policy as a compromise to address the problem of harassment of gay and lesbian soldiers.
1993	Hundreds of thousands participate in a march for equal rights for gays and lesbians (Washington, D.C.).
1996	U.S. Supreme Court declares equal rights for gays and lesbians.
1997	The popular television show *Ellen* is the first program to have a main character who admits to being gay (as does the actress, Ellen DeGeneres).
1998	The murder of Matthew Shepard gains national attention and is the catalyst in many states to include gays and lesbians in hate-crime legislation.
1999	Vermont's Supreme Court rules that same-sex couples have the same legal right to get married as heterosexual couples.
2003	U.S. Supreme Court rules that sodomy laws are unconstitutional, reversing its 1986 decision in *Hardwick v. Bowers.*

his own homosexuality but also alleged that many professional athletes were gay. With the sexual identity of popular stars from the 1950s and 1960s such as Rock Hudson and Liberace being revealed to the public, gays and lesbians increasingly encountered more tolerant attitudes, especially in urban areas.

Most Americans tended to ignore the AIDS epidemic that arose in the early 1980s, although some radio and television ministers blamed homosexual behavior for causing this "gay disease." As Sontag (1989) explained, "The unsafe behavior that produces AIDS (was) judged to be more than just weakness. It is indulgence, delinquency—addiction to chemicals that are illegal and to sex regarded as deviant" (p. 25). As the epidemic continued, Americans were forced to confront the American historic cultural bias against gays; people increasingly recognized HIV as a virus, not a punishment from God. The fact that a young boy, Ryan White, could contract this fatal disease from a blood transfusion illustrated the point dramatically. (See Figure 10.3.) For seven of his eight years as president, Ronald Reagan never publicly acknowledged the spread of AIDS (Shilts, 1987). It took another presidential election before Congress passed the Ryan White Comprehensive AIDS Resources Emergency Act in 1990. But anti-gay attitudes in the United States have persisted, in part because of religious and cultural beliefs.

What are some anti-gay cultural and religious beliefs?

Many Americans still cling to the cultural belief that homosexuality is unnatural, an accusation that calls for reasonable people to consider what it would mean for something to be natural. Some sexual activity, such as incest, is forbidden in every known culture, yet homosexual behavior is—or has been—accepted in most world cultures. Scientists have argued that anything observed and documented in nature should be considered natural. Stein (1999) found that scientific studies of animals in their natural habitat report occurrences of sexual activity between animals of the same sex in every group studied, suggesting that sexual activity between same-sex partners normally occurs in nature.

> God loves homosexuals as much as he loves everybody else.
>
> **Ryan White (1971–1990)**

Although the Catholic Church accepts that homosexuality is a natural predisposition (that is, one is born with it), it continues to denounce homosexual activity as a sin—the only instance of the church forbidding something it admits to be natural. The struggle within the Catholic Church over this issue is reflected in a letter from American bishops urging Catholic parents to accept and love their gay and lesbian children regardless of whether they refrain from acting on their homosexuality (Christian Century Foundation, 1997).

Protestant churches are divided on the issue of accepting homosexuality. Some Protestant theologians continue to condemn homosexuality. Others argue that certain biblical passages have been mistranslated to justify regarding homosexual behavior as a sin—these passages actually denounce male and female prostitution, not homosexuality. Some feel biblical criticism of men engaging in homosexual acts was based on the biblical authors assuming everyone was heterosexual, and that anyone engaging in a homosexual act betrayed human nature (Doupe, 2001). Another argument that has arisen is that since biblical injunctions against eating pork or making clothes out of two types of material are now

FIGURE 10.3

Ryan White returns to school after being sent home by school authorities who feared that having AIDS would make him a danger to the lives of the other students. Based on medical testimony, the courts disagreed.

Source: © Bettman/CORBIS.

regarded as historic but no longer relevant, any biblical passage interpreted as an injunction against homosexual acts should also be regarded as an example of historic prejudice. Protestant debates about accepting homosexuality certainly will continue as we have seen in the controversy in the Episcopal Church over the ordination of the first openly gay bishop. Time will tell if various Christian denominations will respond to research on sexual orientation and accept people who are not heterosexual.

Individual Heterosexism

Despite increasing acceptance of homosexuality in Western cultures outside the United States, as well as research findings discussed earlier, many Americans still regard homosexuality as unnatural and sinful. Sociological study confirms that **individual heterosexism,** negative attitudes and behaviors based on the belief that sexual orientations other than heterosexual are unnatural, is a major factor promoting one of the most common hate crimes in the United States, the physical assault of a person perceived to be gay known as **gay bashing.** Herek and Berill (1992) report that more than 75% of gay men and lesbians have experienced verbal abuse, almost half have been subjected to violent threats, and for 20% or more, the threats were carried out. Young men are the primary perpetrators of anti-gay violence, and most of them do so as part of a group. Although personal prejudice is ascribed as a major factor, studies of motivations for anti-gay violence have revealed that young men often believe cultural myths about homosexuality that justify their verbal abuse and physical attacks (Franklin, 1998). Each of us must confront myths that promote anti-gay behavior, and, because gay bashers tend to be young men in high school, vocational school, or college, educators must play a role in giving our youth accurate information to refute these myths.

What are some myths about homosexuality?

Myths regarding homosexuality contribute to individual prejudice and homophobia in the United States (Blumenfeld, 2001; Hollier, 2004). **Homophobia** is a stronger feeling than prejudice, usually defined as fear or hatred of homosexuals. Following are some examples of myths still perpetuated in American society about gays and lesbians along with refutations based on reality.

> **MYTH:** Anyone who has ever engaged in a homosexual act at any time is a homosexual.
>
> **REALITY:** To be identified as a homosexual means that a person demonstrates a persistent erotic attraction for people of the same sex. Gays and lesbians are not attracted to every same-sex person they see, but when they feel physically and emotionally attracted to someone, that person is consistently someone of the same sex.

Some people engage in sexual activity with a person of the same sex one time and never again. Some people have only engaged in homosexual acts during unusual and temporary circumstances, such as being in situations where there is no easy access to members of the opposite sex (such as in prison or in the military). Men or women who engage in sexual acts with a partner of the same sex in an unusual situation generally do not persist in this behavior when circumstances return to the more typical situation and thus should not be identified as homosexual.

> **MYTH:** Homosexuals tend to engage in criminal activity and are especially likely to prey on children and molest them.
>
> **REALITY:** Studies of criminal activity report that homosexuals are no more likely to engage in criminal activity than heterosexuals, and studies of child molesters reveal that over 99% are male and nearly 80% are white heterosexual men who are married or were formerly married (Abel & Harlow, 2001).

Child molesters are **pedophiles**—adults who desire sexual contact with children. There are heterosexual pedophiles who desire children of the opposite sex and homosexual pedophiles who desire children of the same sex. As the data show, children are at greater risk from heterosexuals than from gays and lesbians. Pedophilia has nothing to do with being homosexual.

MYTH: Homosexuals attempt to seduce vulnerable adolescents and recruit them into their lifestyle.

REALITY: Individuals who engage in homosexual behavior during adolescence tend to do so with other adolescents, not adults.

This accusation is an ancient one, as we know from the life of Socrates, who was accused of corrupting the youth, found guilty, and ordered to drink a poisonous cup of hemlock for his punishment. Because the primary group responsible for gay bashing in the United States is adolescent males, gays are risking violence if they approach adolescents for sexual purposes.

MYTH: Homosexuals do not have loving relationships but are only interested in sex and engage in sexually promiscuous behavior.

REALITY: Americans have historically denied gay men and lesbians the right to marry and refused to recognize domestic partnerships; they have tolerated sexual activities of gays and lesbians who are discreet but have not sanctioned their activity.

This myth is especially egregious because American society has created conditions that promote the behavior being condemned. Gays and lesbians have been allowed to engage in sexual activity in gay bars and bathhouses, but they are not allowed to declare their affection publicly or to have their relationships acknowledged. Americans have vigorously resisted gays and lesbians who have sought public sanction for their relationships by demanding the right to marry or to be recognized in domestic partnerships. Although heterosexuals may engage in public displays of affection, gay men or lesbians are often verbally or physically assaulted for the same behavior.

Heterosexuals are encouraged to marry and be monogamous, yet the percentage engaging in premarital sex with many partners has increased, and it has been estimated that two thirds of all marriages in the United States will end in separation or divorce (Cushner, McClelland, & Safford, 2008). Given such projections, it is hypocritical for the heterosexual community to accuse gays and lesbians of promiscuity and to insist that marriage is sacred and should be reserved exclusively for heterosexual couples. According to psychologists, gays and lesbians have the same need as heterosexuals for long-term stable relationships. Because of the 2003 decision by the Massachusetts Supreme Court that gay and lesbian couples ought to have the same legal right to marry as heterosexuals, gay men and lesbians may have an opportunity to demonstrate their ability to have successful monogamous marital relationships.

> If . . . marriage can keep you in touch with your past, your emotional self, and your humanity, the notion that this should be any less true for gay or lesbian couples than it is for heterosexuals is absurd.
>
> **Derrick Bell (1930–)**

MYTH: People become homosexual because they had a bad experience while involved in heterosexual activity; therefore gay men or lesbians could change their sexual behavior if they had a positive heterosexual experience.

REALITY: Many gay men and lesbians have been involved in heterosexual relationships, including marriage, because of the hostility directed against homosexuality.

Many gays and lesbians have engaged in heterosexual activities in an effort to convince themselves of their normality, but sexual orientation is not a choice. Some people still refer to *sexual preference* as if lesbians and gays prefer to love same-sex partners. But human sexuality is not a matter of preference, and past efforts to reorient an individual's sexuality have not been successful. Studies of human sexuality have concluded that sexual orientation is determined early in human development.

Once we become aware of our sexual feelings, our only choice is to accept these feelings and act on them or to reject and repress them. Some gays and lesbians have accepted their sexual orientation but—as with some heterosexuals—have chosen to be chaste. Sexual abstinence is a choice any individual can make, but it is no more likely to lead to happiness for homosexuals than for heterosexuals.

Displays of affection between men and between women are common in many cultures. In American culture, women are allowed some degree of public intimacy with each other such as holding hands, dancing together, or even kissing (as long as they don't kiss on the lips). Men are not allowed to engage in similar public behaviors with other men without being perceived as homosexual; this creates a burden for American men who have the same human need for affection and intimacy as do women.

Myth: Close personal relationships between adolescents or adults of the same sex could stimulate homosexual feelings and behavior, so intimate friendships should be avoided, especially between men.

Reality: It is perfectly normal for a man or a woman to feel and express love and affection for a person of the same sex as can be observed in other cultures.

Because of myths such as these, it should be easy to understand why most people would be reluctant to identify with such a reviled and persecuted group. Civil rights activists often claim that gays and lesbians encounter more blatant discrimination than any other group. In response to this discrimination, gays and lesbians have intensified their efforts to promote the concept of gay rights across America. (See Figure 10.4.)

Institutional Heterosexism

Although Kinsey suggested that the sexual orientation of approximately 10% of Americans is exclusively homosexual, surveys report approximately 3% of men identify themselves as gay and about 1.5% of women identify themselves as lesbian (Jones & George, 2009). It is impossible to have a census of gay men and lesbians because of the number who conceal their sexual identity—or deny it—to protect themselves from other people's negative attitudes and behaviors. Hollier (2004) provides estimates of from 7 to 21 million gay and lesbian workers in the U.S. workforce, constituting anywhere from 3% to 12% of one's employees. **Institutional heterosexism**—established laws, customs, and practices that systematically discriminate against people who are not heterosexual—has been so prevalent and so blatant that activists have increased their efforts to combat discrimination across America. They are promoting **gay rights,** insisting that gays and lesbians should have the same rights and privileges as heterosexual Americans.

Is the demand for gay rights really a demand for special privileges?

The goal of gay rights is to make it possible for gays and lesbians to be honest about their sexual orientation without being deprived of civil rights. These rights do not entail special privileges, but rather the rights of citizens in our democracy. It is a question of tolerance: One can support civil rights for gays and lesbians without necessarily condoning homosexual behavior. It does require us to agree that if gays and lesbians identify their sexual orientation publicly, they should not be discriminated against in being hired for jobs, renting or purchasing a home, running for political office, enlisting in the military, attending their church of choice, or any other rights that heterosexuals take for granted. Gay rights means having the same—not special—rights and responsibilities as other citizens of the United States. In most of the United States, gays and lesbians are often not extended the civil rights that heterosexu-

> Tolerance is the positive and cordial effort to understand another's beliefs, practices, and habits without necessarily sharing or accepting them.
>
> **Joshua Liebman (1907–1948)**

FIGURE 10.4

Parents, Families and Friends of Lesbians and Gays (PFLAG) is an advocacy organization that started when the mother of a gay man participated in a 1972 gay pride march in New York City after her son had been assaulted because of his sexual orientation. Today PFLAG has a national office in Washington, D.C., with 500 affiliates that promote respect for human differences and the acceptance of all people regardless of sexual orientation or gender identity.

Source: Photo Courtesy of PFLAG.

als enjoy unless they are **in the closet,** meaning they deny or disguise their sexual orientation.

According to Van Den Burgh (2003), one third of gay men and one fourth of lesbians surveyed said they had personally encountered discrimination at their work site. About 17% of them either were fired from a job or were denied employment when the employer became aware of their sexual orientation. When the research included the broad range of individuals included in the term **transgender**, discrimination remained at the same level, but a hostile work environment became more likely. A national study of lesbian, gay, and transgender employees reported that 17% had been fired or pressured to quit a job, and 25% had experienced harassment at work. For transgender people, the harassment could range from a co-worker not wanting to share a bathroom with them to being unfairly evaluated and denied a promotion. According to a study by the Transgender Law Center, half of all transgender employees have experienced some form of discrimination at work (Broadus, 2006). In the 1990s, only one state included gender identity in its nondiscrimination policies, but in the first decade of the 21st century, transgender advocates have been successful in getting transgender people included in four of the six states that revised their nondiscrimination policies to address sexual orientation (see Table 10.2).

Only 15 states have laws against discrimination based on sexual orientation. In the other 35 states, it is legal for a business to refuse to hire or to be able to fire someone simply for being gay. Numerous examples exist of gays and lesbians who have been dismissed from jobs, not because they were inefficient or incompetent but because employers discovered their sexual orientation. A Baltimore civil rights advocate told the story of a lesbian manager of a diner who hired a gay dishwasher. When the owner of the diner realized the sexual orientation of the dishwasher, he insisted that the manager fire the man because he did not want gay employees on his payroll. The woman enjoyed a good relationship with her boss and had certainly proven her competence as a manager over the past ten years. She took a chance. She told the boss he already had a gay employee and he was looking at her. She also was fired. The civil rights advocate who related the

TABLE 10.2 States with Nondiscrimination Policies That Include Sexual Orientation

Wisconsin—1982
Massachusetts—1989
Connecticut—1991
Hawaii—1991
New Jersey—1992
Vermont—1992
Minnesota*—1993
New Hampshire—1997
Nevada—1999
Rhode Island*—2001
Maryland—2001
New York—2002
New Mexico*—2003
California*—2003
Illinois*—2005

*States including Gender Identity as well as Sexual Orientation in these policies.

Source: Rankin (2005), p. 9.

incident insisted the story was not unusual. The only way gays and lesbians can be certain of keeping their jobs is to stay in the closet. And so they do, but even then they do not avoid discrimination.

How can homosexuals be discriminated against if they don't reveal their identity?

If gay men and lesbians are in the closet—not perceived by their employers, supervisors, and coworkers as homosexual—it seems logical to assume that they should not experience discrimination, but that assumption is only accurate for blatant kinds of discrimination. Subtle forms of discrimination can affect such concerns as job advancement. According to a Harvard Business School study, gays and lesbians who did not identify themselves at work were not promoted as readily as their heterosexual peers. Because of the need to keep their personal lives secret, gay men and lesbians often maintained their personal privacy at work, not engaging frequently in casual conversations and not socializing with others after work or on weekends. The study concluded that social isolation in protection of one's identity is a major factor for gays and lesbians not being promoted (Badgett, 2001).

Another form of discrimination based on sexual orientation involves employee benefits. According to Hollier (2004), almost 40% of employee compensation is offered in benefits such as insurance (life, health, and dental), retirement (pension, health care), and leaves (bereavement, family). Employees who receive such benefits for their spouses are being compensated significantly more than coworkers who may be in committed domestic partnerships. A legal **domestic partnership** is defined as "An intimate, committed relationship between two individuals of legal age who are financially and emotionally interdependent, share the same residence, and intend to remain together indefinitely" (Badgett, 2001, p. 82).

Being unable to claim these benefits is a substantial financial loss for gay and lesbian employees who have a domestic partnership but are in the closet. In addition, openly gay and lesbian employees suffer the same loss when employers refuse to implement policies including domestic partners in employee benefits. At this time, about 90% of American businesses refuse to recognize such partnerships. If policies of Fortune 500 companies are emulated by other businesses, gay and lesbian workers may be treated more equitably in the future: 95% of the Fortune 500 have nondiscrimination policies that include sexual orientation, and 70% have benefit policies that include domestic partnerships. In addition, 7,000 other employers nationwide currently offer benefits to domestic partners (Badgett, 2001; Edwards, 2003).

Why do homosexuals want legal recognition for domestic partnerships?

Many gays and lesbians are willing to let marriage remain an exclusively heterosexual arrangement as long as the law recognizes domestic partnerships. The purpose of legal recognition for domestic partnerships is to provide gay couples with the same legal rights married couples enjoy: being able to inherit a partner's property, being eligible for a partner's survival benefits, or having the right to make decisions for an incapacitated partner. Advocates for recognizing domestic partnerships emphasize the existence of such laws in Belgium, Denmark, Finland, France,

Germany, Hungary, Iceland, the Netherlands, Norway, Portugal, and Sweden (Galeano, 2004).

A dramatic example of the importance of recognizing domestic partnerships was illustrated in Minnesota. A head-on collision with a drunk driver left Sharon Kowalski paralyzed and unable to speak. Her long-term partner visited her at the hospital for as many as eight hours a day to read aloud to her, massage her, and make sure Sharon received rehabilitative therapy. At first appreciative, Sharon's parents began to question the behavior of Sharon's friend until they were finally told that their daughter was a lesbian and that the friend was actually her domestic partner. Sharon's father immediately took steps to prevent Sharon's partner from seeing his daughter, even though hospital personnel confirmed that Sharon was improving largely because of the therapy her partner had been providing (Griscom, 2009).

Even though it offered minimal rehabilitation services, Sharon's father committed her to a nursing home. Sharon's partner pursued every possible course of action, and after eight years, the courts recognized that Sharon Kowalski was competent to make her own decisions and that it was her desire to be cared for by her partner. Since that incident, Minnesota legislators have added homosexuals to the list of protected groups in its civil rights law. With the U.S. Supreme Court's 2003 decision in *Lawrence v. Texas* that it is unconstitutional to criminalize gay sexual activity, opponents feared that the decision represents the first step toward sanctioning gay marriages.

> If what we think is right and wrong divides still further the human family, there must be something wrong with what we think is right.
>
> **William Sloan Coffin (1924–)**

If domestic partnerships were recognized, why would homosexuals wish to marry?

Gays and lesbians who desire state-recognized marriage give reasons similar to those of heterosexuals: to make public statements about their commitment to each other, including the pledge to maintain a monogamous relationship. Rather than a special privilege, marriage is a decision to participate in a legally and socially sanctioned activity. Church leaders may insist that marriage is a sacred rite reserved exclusively for people in heterosexual relationships; however, many gays and lesbians want to participate in a secular marriage ceremony performed in accordance with state law, not necessarily a religious marriage. To assert that marriage is a legal contract available exclusively for heterosexual couples is to engage in discrimination based on sexual orientation. Even so, 17 states have passed constitutional amendments prohibiting same-sex marriage (Zemsky & Sanlo, 2005).

In recent years, gays and lesbians have taken legal action to force the courts to rule on the legality of same-sex marriage. In 1996, a Hawaii Circuit Court found no legitimate legal basis for denying homosexuals the right to obtain marriage licenses, but the state court reversed that ruling three years later. In 1999, Vermont's Supreme Court ruled that denying gay and lesbian couples the opportunity to participate in legal, secular marriage violated the state constitution. In many states, the reaction to such rulings has been to pass legislation defining marriage as a legal contract between "a man and a woman," refusing to recognize same-sex marriages performed in other states. The California Supreme Court decision in May of 2008 in support of gay marriage followed by Californians voting for Proposition 8 which prohibits gay marriage has made it even more likely that the U.S. Supreme Court will soon have to address the issue of whether gay men and lesbians have the legal right to get married. In the meantime, many gays and lesbians continue to enjoy stable, monogamous relationships, some choosing to have children, while they wait for state and federal law to acknowledge the reality of their relationships.

What harm is done to a child raised by gay parents?

It is harmful and immoral for a child to be abandoned, untouched, unloved, ridiculed, and physically or sexually abused. It is usually not harmful for a child to be cared for by his or her biological mother or father or to be adopted by loving parents, regardless of their sexual orientation. Yet Gilgoff

(2004) cites a national poll reporting that 47% of Americans do not believe that gay and lesbian couples should be allowed to adopt children; 43% responded in support of their right to adopt.

There are over 160,000 same-sex couples raising children. According to Badgett (2001), approximately 30% of lesbians have children in their homes and 27% of gay men are fathers, with 15% of them raising their children in their homes. In the past, these children were from a previous marriage, before an individual understood and acknowledged his or her sexual orientation, but half of the children today being raised by same-sex couples were adopted or are the result of reproductive technologies. Regardless of the reason for having children, studies suggest that same-sex couples are conscientious parents.

According to Johnson and O'Connor (2002), research concludes that gay and lesbian couples are effective parents, providing for their children's physical and emotional needs to ensure a healthy and positive childhood. In evaluating children raised by gays or lesbians, studies have explored such factors as social interaction, intelligence, self-esteem, and ability to express feelings. Children of gays and lesbians not only appear to develop self-confidence and social skills, but also are more tolerant of differences than are other children (McLeod & Crawford, 1998). Research does not support the exclusion of gays and lesbians from any occupation or activity in which other U.S. citizens participate. For that reason, the American Psychological Association, American Academy of Pediatrics, National Association of Social Workers, and the American Bar Association have released statements that support the right of gays to be parents.

Why have homosexuals always been excluded from military service?

Historic evidence indicates that gays and lesbians have served in the military in the United States and in other countries. In addition to the Greek Band of Thebes, historic warriors such as Alexander the Great and Richard the Lion-Hearted had male lovers. As attitudes in the Western world have become more negative toward homosexuality, same-sex behavior in the military became more carefully concealed. Activities occasionally would be exposed, as in Germany's Eulenberg Affair where from 1907 to 1909, accusations of homosexual behavior were directed against officers in the German army, the diplomatic corps, and the cabinet of Kaiser Wilhelm (Steakley, 1989). Allegations were well documented, which led to several resignations by cabinet members and military officers.

In America, a navy investigation at Newport Naval Training Station following World War I similarly revealed widespread homosexual activity (Chauncey, 1989). During World War II, the army conducted an investigation of alleged lesbian activity in the Women's Army Corps (WAC) in which a WAC officer testified about a letter she received from the Surgeon General's Office that said "homosexual relationships should be tolerated" as long as they were discreet and did not lead to disruptions in the unit (Bérubé, 1989, p. 384).

Homosexual participation in the armed forces is not new. What is new is periodic blatant discrimination against gays and lesbians by the U.S. military. In 1981, the Pentagon instituted a policy banning all gays and lesbians from the armed forces because the leaders believed that homosexuality was incompatible with military service. Patriotic gay and lesbian soldiers serving their country could be discharged, not for incompetence or misbehavior, but because they were homosexual. The first Clinton administration modified the policy, forbidding the military to inquire about a person's sexual orientation; neither recruits nor gays and lesbians already in the armed forces could be asked about their sexual orientation.

> You don't have to be straight to shoot straight.
>
> **Barry Goldwater (1909–1998)**

The "Don't Ask, Don't Tell" policy was intended to discourage attempts to identify and remove homosexuals from the military. According to the policy, gays and lesbians were required to keep quiet or lie about their identity, and they could be discharged if their sexual identity were discovered or they admitted to being homosexual. Perhaps because of the increased militancy in the gay community or because of a growing reluctance to conceal their identity, the number of gays and lesbians dis-

FIGURE 10.5 Annual Gay Discharges Under "Don't Ask, Don't Tell, Don't Pursue. Don't Harass"

Update: In 2001, 1227 gays and lesbians were discharged from the military services, but in 2003, only 770 gays and lesbians were discharged. Of the nearly 10,000 people discharged for their sexual orientation since 1994, 71% were men.

Source: Courtesy of Servicemembers Legal Defense Network (www.sldn.org), based on Department of Defense Figures.

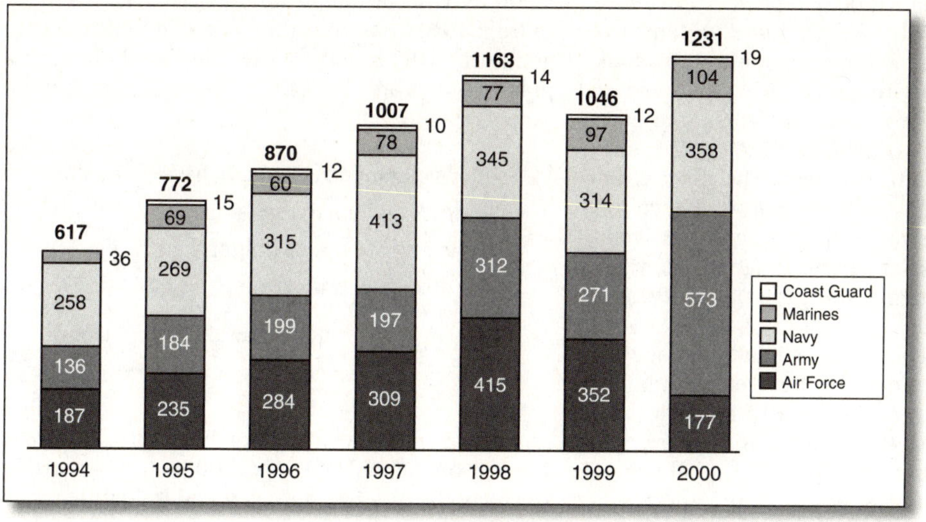

charged from the military actually has increased under the new policy (see Figure 10.5).

As the United States has hardened its resistance to gays in the military, attitudes in other countries have become more tolerant. Armies in Australia, France, Ireland, and the Netherlands actively recruit and train openly homosexual soldiers, many of whom worked with U.S. armed forces as part of the UN peacekeeping forces in Bosnia (Palmer, 1997). Gay activists are demanding that gays and lesbians be accepted not only in the military but in other professions, such as education, where they have been excluded because of past prejudice.

Why should homosexuals be allowed to become teachers?

During the early 1990s, the Republican governor of Massachusetts was concerned enough about the safety of gay youth to initiate an investigation. In its final report, the Governor's Commission described a disturbing pattern of abuse: Testimony from gay and lesbian youth and their parents described a constant barrage of taunts and slurs, being spit on, and physical attacks. One boy left all his classes late and arrived late to every class so he could walk through empty hallways to avoid constant harassment. Another student *who was not gay* was assaulted every day at school simply because other students thought he was homosexual. Having heard such painful testimony of widespread anti-gay violence, the commission's recommendations included implementing school policies to protect gay and lesbian youth from harassment and violence, establishing support groups for gay and lesbian students, and providing information in school curriculum and in school libraries on gay and lesbian issues (Massachusetts Governor's Commission on Gay and Lesbian Youth, 1994).

In the report issued by the Governor's Commission, more than 50% of the gay and lesbian students said that they had heard at least one teacher make a homophobic comment. When adults are in a position of authority, such as a teacher, and express prejudicial attitudes to children or youth, they are legitimizing those negative attitudes. To correct this problem, the Governor's Commission recommended hiring lesbian and gay teachers and providing additional training for teachers and counselors to be more accepting of gay and lesbian students. The same issue occurs on college campuses. A national study by Rankin (2005) reported that more than one third of LGBT undergraduate students experienced anti-gay behaviors—most often this took the form of derogatory remarks (89%) followed by threats (48%), derogatory graffiti (39%), and even physical assaults (11%). Almost 80% of the time, the harasser was another student. The most effective way to address this problem is for K–12 schools and college campuses to become more aggressive in defending both the safety and the rights of not just gay and lesbian students, but bisexual and transgender youth as well.

Various studies report that the average age for gays and lesbians to identify themselves publicly, called **coming out,** dropped from 14 for males and 17 for females in the 1960s to 10 and 12, respectively, in the 1990s. According to a National School Climate Survey of lesbian, gay, bisexual and transgendered youth (**LGBT**), 74% of these students had heard homophobic remarks in school, and 86% were subjected to verbal harassment because of their sexual orientation. The students also reported that when faculty overheard homophobic comments, about half of them were reluctant to respond and only intervened some of the time; a third of the faculty never intervened. Not surprisingly, more than a third of these students said they did not feel comfortable bringing up LGBT issues with their teachers (Gay, Lesbian, and Straight Education Network [GLSEN], 2008).

Being confronted with such hostility while receiving little support from teachers or others can result in feelings of worthlessness and despair. D'Augelli (1998) reported that over half of gay youth consider committing suicide, and that 30% attempt to commit suicide at least once. These statistics are a measure of the homophobia LGBT students encounter in their everyday lives, including when they are at school. According to the National School Climate Survey, over 60% of LGBT students said they did not feel safe at school, and almost a third admit to staying home from school because they felt it was especially unsafe to attend on a particular day (GLSEN, 2008).

There was some good news from the National Survey; almost one in ten high schools have a Gay-Straight Alliance (GSA) support group, and they appear to help. A GSA consists of gay and lesbian students and gay-friendly straight students. LGBT students who attended schools with a GSA were more likely to say that they felt safe in schools. In addition, LGBT students attending a school with a policy that protected LGBT students from harassment and violence were much less likely to stay home from school (GLSEN, 2008). It is important that schools hire not only gay and lesbian teachers but also straight teachers who are comfortable with and supportive of LGBT students. Such teachers can be role models for all of their students and can establish a more positive learning climate for everyone. LGBT youth deserve that as much as any other student.

> I believe all Americans who believe in freedom, tolerance and human rights have a responsibility to oppose bigotry and prejudice based on sexual orientation.
>
> **Coretta Scott King (1927–)**

Why are the terms *bisexual* and *transgender* being linked to gays and lesbians?

All of these terms relate to the issue of sexual orientation, and although the terms are new, the issues are not. As Sullivan (2003) noted, "Although the terms transsexual and transgender have been coined only relatively recently, a variety of forms of gender ambiguity can be found throughout history" (p. 99). Introduced in 1949, *transsexual* was one of the first terms for a category eventually classified as "Gender Identity Disorder." A transsexual was someone who could not psychologically identify with his or her biological gender—a male identifying as a female or a female identifying as a male. By the 1960s and 1970s, the medical profession came to regard transsexuals as different from homosexuals as they established gender identity clinics and developed sex reassignment procedures.

In addition to transsexuals, there are also people who identify as transvestites (cross dressers) or drag queens/kings, so the term *transgender* evolved to encompass a broad range of gender identities. Based on the work of several scholars, Rankin (2005) defined transgender as "individuals whose gender identity conflicts with biological sex assignment or societal expectations for gender expression as male or female" (p. 29). Douglas (2008) describes how transgender people have slowly been accepted and included by people in gay and lesbian communities. Today, when scholars refer to this diverse group of people, they usually employ the LGBT acronym.

Another issue related to sexual orientation emerged for people who openly identified themselves as bisexual (attracted to sexual partners of either gender). Bisexual people appear to receive the least attention of all groups within the LGBT community, perhaps because their sexual orientation may be viewed as disconcertingly fluid and ambiguous. Young (2004) discusses how lesbian and gay activists resisted adding "bisexual" to the names of their organizations or to the titles of their conferences. Young interviewed a gay man who admitted that he used to identify himself as bisexual, but he felt that he had to make a choice because: "Nobody likes bisexuals" (2004, p. 394). For that reason, many bisexuals are in the closet, "passing" as a gay man or lesbian when interacting with homosexuals and as straight when interacting with heterosexuals.

AFTERWORD

One of the most important changes needed in the United States is to establish policies and practices that promote tolerance for people across the spectrum of sexual orientations, so that all LGBT people feel safe being open at school, at work, and in their neighborhoods. Some LGBT individuals are trying to change the language of hate by choosing the term "**queer**" to describe this group of people with diverse gender identities, including those who are gay or lesbian, bisexual, transsexual, and transgender. They argue that the term helps to simplify a discussion of the issues affecting this diverse group. As one gay man said in an interview with the *New York Times,* "When you're trying to describe the community you have to list gays, lesbians, bisexuals, drag queens, transsexuals (post-op and pre), it gets unwieldy. Queer says it all" (Duggan, 2004, p. 59). On the other hand, Goldman (2004) articulates two opposing reactions to the term from LGBT people: ". . . many people employ the term queer because it blurs—and some would argue erases—boundaries" (p. 85). Despite the differences of opinion about the term, Queer Studies programs are appearing on many college campuses as scholars examine and disseminate information about issues in the lives of LGBT people.

Changing cultural attitudes will take a long time, but if it becomes more acceptable to be open about sexual identity, it is more likely that heterosexuals will find that they know someone who is homosexual. Simon (1998) has reported that when people know someone who is a gay man or a lesbian, they tend to be less homophobic and to have a more positive attitude about the issue of sexual orientation and homosexuality. Change is possible if conditions are created to allow it. Accepting homosexuality is an ethical challenge confronting nations around the world, and every American institution and individual must decide how to meet it.

myeducationlab

Now go to Topic #8: **Sexual Orientation** in the MyEducationLab (www.myeducationlab.com) for your course, where you can:

- Find learning outcomes for this topic along with the national standards that connect to these outcomes.
- Complete Assignments and Activities that can help you more deeply understand the chapter content by viewing classroom video and ABC News footage.
- Apply and practice your understanding of the core teaching skills identified in the chapter with the Building Teaching Skills and Dispositions learning units.

TERMS AND DEFINITIONS

Bisexual A normative category of sexual identity referring to lifelong sexual desires and/or erotic relations with members of both genders

Coming out When gay and lesbian youth publicly announce their sexual orientation

Cultural heterosexism The societal promotion of negative beliefs and practices that reinforce dominant culture traits that define heterosexuality as the norm and anything else as deviant and unacceptable; the assumption of superiority of heterosexuals over those who are not heterosexual

Domestic partnership An intimate, committed relationship between two individuals of legal age who are financially and emotionally interdependent, share the same residence, and intend to remain together indefinitely (Badgett, 2001)

Gay, Gays A term in reference to homosexuality in general, but specifically to male homosexuals

Gay bashing Physical assault on an individual who is perceived as being gay, which is motivated by the individual's sexual orientation

Gay rights The demand that gay men and lesbians be able to openly identify their sexual orientation and not be discriminated against with regard to the civil rights available to all other citizens

Greek love The nineteenth-century code phrase invented by boys at British boarding schools to describe their sexual activities with other boys

Heterosexism The systematic oppression and exploitation of bisexuals, lesbians, gay men, and transgender individuals, especially policies and practices reinforcing heterosexuality as the only option for relationships and families

Heterosexual A normative category of sexual identity referring to exclusive lifelong sexual desire and erotic relations with the opposite gender

Heterosexual assumption The assumption that every human being is born a heterosexual

Homophobia The culturally influenced fear and hatred of homosexual persons, acts, and events

Homosexual A normative moral category of sexual identity referring to exclusive lifelong sexual desire and erotic relations with the same gender

Individual heterosexism Prejudiced attitudes and behavior against others based on the assumption that sexual orientations other than heterosexual are unnatural; this is demonstrated whenever someone responds by saying or doing something degrading or harmful about persons who are not heterosexual

Institutional heterosexism Established laws, customs, and practices in a society that allow systematic discrimination against people or groups who are not heterosexual

In the closet The concealment of sexual orientation from colleagues, heterosexual friends, and/or family

LGBT An acronym identifying a group defined by sexual orientation and consisting of lesbians, gay men, bisexuals, and transgendered people

Pedophiles Adults who desire sexual contact with children

Queer Generic term used to refer to people who are gay, lesbian, bisexual, transgender, and transsexual (LGBT)

Sexual orientation The sexual identity of an individual based on lifelong sexual fantasies, desires, and practices

Transgender A person whose gender identity or gender expression does not conform to concepts conventionally associated with his or her biological gender

DISCUSSION EXERCISES

Exercise #1 Testing Your Knowledge about Homosexuality

Directions: Misconception and myth often obscure facts regarding sexual orientation. Decide if each statement below is true or false.

Are the following statements true or false?

	True	False
1. Most homosexuals want to be members of the opposite sex.	_____	_____
2. A person becomes a homosexual—develops homosexual orientation—because he or she chooses to do so.	_____	_____
3. Sexual orientation is established at an early age.	_____	_____
4. 60% of preadolescent males report at least one homosexual experience.	_____	_____
5. A majority of homosexuals were seduced in adolescence by a person of the same sex, usually several years older.	_____	_____
6. There is a good chance of changing homosexual persons into heterosexual men and women.	_____	_____
7. Homosexual activity occurs in many animal species.	_____	_____
8. According to the American Psychological Association, homosexuality is a mental illness.	_____	_____
9. In most states, sexual relations between two people of the same sex is a criminal act.	_____	_____
10. Homosexual males are more likely to molest young boys than heterosexual males are to molest young girls.	_____	_____
11. Gay men are at least four times more likely to be victims of criminal violence as members of the general public.	_____	_____
12. Some church denominations have condemned the legal and social discrimination against gay men and lesbians.	_____	_____

Adapted from James T. Sears, *Coming Out of the Classroom Closet*

Exercise #2 Integration in the Military

Directions: The statements below represent some original responses to the proposed U.S. military policy of racial integration. Rewrite each statement by substituting *homosexual* for *racial* or *Negro,* and *heterosexual* for *white.* Each statement will reflect a current argument concerning the integration of gay men and lesbians into the military. As you change the statements, decide whether the argument could be considered a legitimate concern with regard to integrating gay men and lesbians into the military today.

1. **The opinion of soldiers:** Army studies show that 80% of the *white* soldiers oppose *racial* integration in the armed forces.
2. **The opinion of generals:** Respected generals such as Dwight David Eisenhower and current military leaders have been and remain staunchly opposed to *racial* integration in the armed forces.
3. **Objections based on unit cohesion:** According to the Secretary of the Army, *racial* integration would undermine unit cohesion—"Effective comradeship in battle calls for a warm

and close personal relationship within a unit"; an Army Report opposing *racial* integration argued—"The soldier on the battlefield deserves to have, and must have, utmost confidence in his fellow soldiers."

4. **Objections based on opposition to using the military for social reforms:** As one general has said, "the Army is not out to make any social reforms." It will change its policy on *racial* integration "when the Nation as a whole changes . . . experiments within the Army in the solution of social problems are fraught with danger to efficiency, discipline and morale."
5. **Objections based on privacy:** A Georgia Senator says *racial* integration in the armed forces would compromise the privacy rights of the *white* soldiers—"There is no more intimate relationship known to men than that of enlisted men serving together at the squad level. They eat and sleep together. They use the same facilities . . . They are compelled to stay together in the closest association."
6. **Objections based on health concerns:** The Senator from Georgia went on to say he had statistics "which will show that the incidence of (all venereal diseases) is appallingly higher among *Negroes* than among *whites*."
7. **Objections based on religious beliefs:** A Congressman from Alabama has argued that *racial* integration in the armed forces would lower not just the morale but the "morals" of soldiers.
8. **Objections based on the will of the majority:** The Department of Defense has taken the position that *racial* integration in the armed forces would erode public confidence in the military—"The Army can under no circumstances adopt a policy which is contrary to the dictates of a majority of people (because) to do so would alienate the people from the Army and lower their morale."

REFERENCES

Abel, G., & Harlow, N. (2001). *The stop child molestation book.* Philadelphia, PA: Xlibris.

Analyzes responses from over 4,000 adults who had sexually molested children to determine characteristics of child molesters and to develop recommendations to curb child molestation.

Badgett, M.V.L. (2001). *Money, myths, and change: The economic lives of lesbians and gay men.* Chicago, IL: University of Chicago Press.

Describes economic myths and workplace discrimination against lesbians and gay men by examining various studies and analyzing statistical data.

Bérbubé, A. (1989). Marching to a different drummer: Lesbian and gay GIs in World War II. In M. Duberman, M. Vicinus, & G. Chauncey, Jr. (Eds.), *Hidden from history: Reclaiming the gay and lesbian past* (pp. 456–476). New York, NY: Meridian.

Discusses the emergence of the gay political movement in the United States as a consequence of military policies attempting to manage the homosexual behavior of soldiers during World War II.

Blumenfeld, W.J. (Ed.). (1992). *Homophobia: How we all pay the price.* Boston, MA: Beacon.

Addresses myths about homosexuality in many of the essays, and identifies twelve of these myths in the appendix.

Boswell, J. (1994). *Same-sex unions in pre-modern Europe.* New York, NY: Villard.

Reviews historical evidence for acceptance of same-sex relationships in Greek and Roman cultures and translates documents from Vatican archives suggesting that the Catholic Church sanctioned same-sex marriages during its early years.

Broadus, K.W. (2006). The evolution of employment discrimination protections for transgender people. In P. Currah, R.M. Juang, & S.P. Minter (Eds.), *Transgender rights* (pp. 93–101). Minneapolis, MN: University of Minnesota Press.

Reviews court cases pertaining to protecting employee rights in response to allegations of discrimination against transgender people, especially transsexuals.

Chauncey, G., Jr. (1989). Christian brotherhood or sexual perversion? Homosexual identities and the construction of sexual boundaries in the World War I era. In M. Duberman, M. Vicinus, & G. Chauncey, Jr. (Eds.), *Hidden from history: Reclaiming the gay and lesbian past* (pp. 456–476). New York, NY: Meridian.

Discusses the navy's investigation of the Newport naval training station (1919–1920) in terms of the social context and the self-awareness of sailors accused of homosexual behavior.

Christian Century Foundation. (1997). Accept gay orientation, say Catholic Bishops. *Christian Century, 114*(29), 936–937.

Highlights the pastoral statement "Always Our Children: A Pastoral Message to Parents of Homosexual Children and Suggestions for Pastoral Ministers" by the Catholic Bishops.

Crompton, L. (1998). *Byron and Greek love: Homophobia in 19th century England.* Swaffham, U.K.: Gay Men's Press.

Examines the influence of homoeroticism on Lord Byron and the homophobia of his time as revealed in sources such as the popular press, court documents, and parliamentary debates.

Cushner, K., McClelland, A., & Safford, P. (2008). Education in a changing society. In *Human diversity in education: An integrative approach* (6th ed.). New York, NY: McGraw-Hill.

Describes changes in American society and the implications of these changes for schools.

D'Augelli, A.R. (1998). Developmental implications of victimization of lesbian, gay, and bisexual youth. In G. Herek (Ed.), *Stigma and sexual orientation: Understanding prejudice against lesbians, gay men and bisexuals.* Thousand Oaks, CA: Sage.

Reviews research that explores the psychological impact of verbal and physical abuse directed against adolescents who are lesbian, gay, or bisexual.

D'Emilio, J. (1989). Gay politics and community in San Francisco since World War II. In M. Duberman, M. Vicinus, & G. Chauncey, Jr. (Eds.), *Hidden from history: Reclaiming the gay and lesbian past* (pp. 456–476). New York, NY: Meridian.

Describes factors that attracted gay men and lesbians to San Francisco following World War II and how the development of the gay community promoted political activism.

Douglas, E. (2008, Nov.). An uneasy alliance. *The American Prospect 19*(11), 30–33.

Describes how the efforts of mainstream gay activists have gradually become inclusive of transgender issues since the 1990s.

Doupe, G.E. (1982). True to our tradition. In W. Blumenfeld (Ed.), *Homophobia: How we all pay the price* (pp. 187–204). Boston, MA: Beacon.

Analyzes and rejects the biblical justification used to denounce gay men and lesbians and provides an alternative Christian response grounded in biblical principles.

Duberman, M., Vicinus, M., & Chauncey, G. Jr. (Eds.). (1989). *Hidden from history: Reclaiming the gay and lesbian past.* New York, NY: Meridian.

Consists of essays from more than twenty scholars describing the historical experiences of gay men and lesbians in China, Japan, Russia, and South Africa as well as the United States and Europe.

Duggan, L. (2004). Making it perfectly queer. In D. Carlin & J. DiGrazia (Eds.), *Queer cultures* (pp. 51–67). Upper Saddle River, NJ: Pearson Prentice Hall.

Examines the potential represented by such evolving concepts as Queer Nation and Queer Theory for creating community and for identity development in LGBT people.

Edwards, C. (2003, December 15). Coming out in corporate America. *Business Week*, p. 64.

Describes gay sensitivity training at corporations and other developments indicating the growing acceptance of gays and lesbians in the corporate world.

Franklin, K. (1998). Unassuming motivations: Contextualizing the narratives of antigay assailants. In G. Herek (Ed.), *Stigma and sexual orientation: Understanding prejudice against lesbians, gay men and bisexuals* (pp. 339–363). Thousand Oaks, CA: Sage.

Analyzes the motivations provided in interviews with three young men who engaged in gay bashing, taken from the author's research on anti-gay attitudes and behaviors.

Galeano, E. (2004, January). The heresy of difference. *The Progressive, 68*(9), 16–17.

Provides a brief history of the persecution of homosexuals and recent events from various nations that suggest a growing global acceptance of gay men and lesbians.

Gilgoff, D. (2004). The rise of the gay family: Special report. *U.S. News & World Report, 136*(18), 40–45.

Examines issues related to same-sex couples in the United States raising children.

GLSEN (2008). The 2007 national school climate survey. *The Gay, Lesbian and Straight Education Network.* Retrieved June 5, 2009, from http://www.glsen.org

Reports the findings of a survey of 6,209 LGBT youth from 50 states and the District of Columbia.

Goldman, R. (2004). Who is that *queer* queer? Exploring norms around sexuality, race, and class in queer theory. In D. Carlin & J. DiGrazia (Eds.), *Queer cultures* (pp. 83–98). Upper Saddle River, NJ: Pearson Prentice Hall.

Analyzes articles on queer theory to identify and address conflicting ideas expressed by scholars contributing to queer theory.

Gould, S.J. (1983). How the zebra gets its stripes. In *Hen's teeth and horse's toes* (pp. 366–375). New York: W. W. Norton.

Addresses genetic issues related to striping patterns on zebras.

Griscom, J.L. (2009). The case of Sharon Kowalski and Karen Thompson: Ableism, heterosexism, and sexism. In P. Rothenberg (Ed.), *Race, class, and gender in the United States: An integrated study* (7th ed., pp. 496–504). New York: Worth.

Describes an eight-year ordeal as a father opposed efforts of his daughter's lesbian partner to provide needed physical therapy following a traffic accident.

Halperin, D.M. (1989). Sex before sexuality: Pederasty, politics, and power in classical Athens. In M. Duberman, M. Vicinus, & G. Chauncey, Jr. (Eds.), *Hidden from history: Reclaiming the gay and lesbian past* (pp. 37–53). New York, NY: Meridian.

Explains how homosexuality and heterosexuality are modern cultural categories that are alien to the cultural perspective of the ancient Greeks.

Herdt, G. (1997). *Same sex, different cultures. Exploring gay and lesbian lives.* Boulder, CO: Westview.

Reviews anthropological and cross-cultural evidence on attitudes toward lesbians and gay men.

Herek, G.M., & Berill, K.T. (Eds.). (1992). *Hate crimes: Confronting violence against lesbians and gay men.* Newbury Park, CA: Sage.

Includes essays examining statistical data, exploring the cultural context, analyzing motivations of perpetrators, and featuring first-person accounts of anti-gay violence.

Hollier, G.D. (2004, July). *Sexual orientation issues in today's workplace.* Paper presented at the International Diversity Conference at UCLA, Los Angeles, CA.

Defines key terms, explains myths and realities about gay men and lesbians, and provides data concerning management issues related to gay men and lesbians in the workforce.

Holthouse, D. (2005, Winter). The fabulist. *Intelligence Report,* pp. 11–15.

Describes the career of Paul Cameron, focusing on his anti-gay activities.

Johnson, S.M., & O'Connor, E. (2002). *The gay baby boom: The psychology of gay parenthood.* New York, NY: New York University Press.

Reviews previous psychological studies of gay and lesbian families and discusses results from the author's "National Study of Gay and Lesbian Families."

Jones, G.R., & George, J.M. (2009). Managing diverse employees in a diverse environment. In *Contemporary Management* (6th ed.). Hightstown, NJ: McGraw-Hill.

Describes increasing diversity among consumers and in the workforce and provides strategies for managers to work effectively with diverse employees.

Kantor, M. (1998). *Homophobia: Description, development, and dynamics of gay bashing.* Westport, CT: Praeger.

Analyzes homophobia as an emotional disorder and describes possible causes of homophobia as well as common traits and suggested therapy for homophobes.

Katz, J. (1985). *Gay American history: Lesbians and gay men in the U.S.A.* New York, NY: Harper Colophon.

Provides documentary evidence of lesbians and gay men in America from the colonial period to the present with specific chapters devoted to Native Americans and women.

Kinsey, A.C., Pomeroy, W.B., & Martin, C.E. (1948). *Sexual behavior in the human male.* Philadelphia, PA: W.B. Saunders.

Analyzed information collected from 18,000 male subjects concerning their sexual behavior and developed a continuum to describe the variety of sexual behavior reported.

LeVay, S. (1996). *Queer science: The use and abuse of research into homosexuality.* Cambridge, MA: University of Massachusetts Press.

Reviews research on sexual orientation with attention to the influence of the social context. Discusses findings of hormonal and brain mechanisms in Chapters 5 and 6.

Marcus, E. (1992). *Making history: The struggle for gay and lesbian equal rights, 1945–1990.* New York, NY: HarperCollins.

Presents biographical descriptions of over forty individuals who played a significant role in assisting efforts of American lesbians and gays to combat heterosexism.

Massachusetts Governor's Commission on Gay and Lesbian Youth. (1994). Making Schools Safe for Gay and Lesbian Youth: Breaking the silence in schools and in families. In G. Remafedi (Ed.), *Death by denial: Studies of suicide in gay and lesbian teenagers* (pp. 151–205). Boston, MA: Alyson.

Presents the results of the commission's investigation into harassment and violence against gay and lesbian youth in Massachusetts schools, with specific recommendations.

McLeod, A., & Crawford, I. (1998). The postmodern family: An examination of the psychosocial and legal perspectives of gay and lesbian parenting. In G. Herek (Ed.), *Stigma and sexual orientation: Understanding prejudice against lesbians, gay men and bisexuals* (pp. 211–222). Thousand Oaks, CA: Sage.

Examines issues related to lesbian and gay couples such as the desire to have and raise children, including the results of public polls and relevant court decisions.

Money, J. (1988). *Gay, straight, and in-between: The sexology of erotic orientation.* New York, NY: Oxford.

Reviews research to describe the current state of knowledge about what determines human sexual orientation, including studies of the influence of prenatal hormones on animals.

Palmer, A. (1997). The military ban on gays and lesbians is based on prejudice. In T. Roleff (Ed.), *Gay rights* (pp. 126–131). San Diego, CA: Greenhaven.

Describes the experience of countries recruiting lesbian and gay soldiers in an attempt to refute arguments that having gays in the military will cause problems for morale and discipline.

Pillard, R.C. (1977). The search for a genetic influence on sexual orientation. In V. Rosairo (Ed.), *Science and homosexualities* (pp. 226–241). New York, NY: Routledge.

Reviews genetic research and anthropological studies to discuss the role of heredity and environment in determining sexual orientation.

Rankin, S.R. (2005, Fall). Campus climates for sexual minorities. In R. Sanlo (Ed.), *Gender identity and sexual orientation: Research, policy and personal perspectives,* No. 111 (pp. 17–23). San Francisco, CA: Jossey-Bass.

Describes the author's national study on harassment and discrimination of LGBT students in higher education involving more than 1,000 LGBT college students.

Rowse, A.L. (1977). *Homosexuals in history: A study of ambivalence in society, literature and the arts.* New York, NY: Dorset.

Describes the lives of many famous lesbian and gay individuals in the history of Europe, and the homophobic context in which they had to live their lives.

Sears, J.T. (1992). Educators, homosexuality, and homosexual students: Are personal feelings related to professional beliefs? In K. Harbeck, *Coming out of the classroom closet: Gay and lesbian students, teachers and curricula.* Binghamton, NY: Harrington Park Press.

Discusses survey data from school counselors, prospective teachers, and lesbian and gay young adults from the southern United States.

Shilts, R. (1987). *And the band played on: Politics, people and the AIDS epidemic.* New York, NY: St. Martin's Press.

Provides an account of the development of AIDS in the United States and the reactions of people, especially politicians, to the disease.

Simon, A. (1998). The relationship between stereotypes of and attitudes toward lesbians and gays. In G. Herek (Ed.), *Stigma and sexual orientation: Understanding prejudice against lesbians, gay men and bisexuals* (pp. 62–81). Thousand Oaks, CA: Sage.

Reviews research on the influence of stereotypes on attitudes of heterosexuals toward lesbians and gays, concluding with a discussion of strategies for prejudice reduction.

Sontag, S. (1989). *AIDS and its metaphors.* New York, NY: Farrar, Straus, and Giroux.

Analyzes the myths and prejudices associated with HIV and people with AIDS.

Steakley, J.D. (1989). Iconography of a scandal: Political cartoons and the Eulenberg affair in Wilhelmine Germany. In M. Duberman, M. Vicinus, & G. Chauncey, Jr. (Eds.), *Hidden from history: Reclaiming the gay and lesbian past* (pp. 233–263). New York, NY: Meridian.

Describes the Eulenberg Affair and provides political cartoons from the period that not only illustrate public anxiety but also the connection of homophobia with other prejudices.

Stein, E. (1999). *The mismeasure of desire: The science, theory, and ethics of sexual orientation.* Oxford, England: Oxford University Press.

Reviews and critiques scientific studies on sexual orientation and also examines questions stemming from theoretical and ethical considerations related to sexual orientation.

Sullivan, N. (2003). *A critical introduction to queer theory.* Washington Square, NY: New York University Press.

Discusses origins of and issues pertaining to the evolution of queer theory.

Van Den Bergh, N. (2003). Getting a piece of the pie: Cultural competence for GLBT employees at the workplace. In M. Sullivan (Ed.), *Sexual minorities: Discrimination, challenges, and development in America* (pp. 55–73). New York, NY: The Haworth Press.

Identifies challenges at the work site for LGBT employees stemming from the absence of federal legislation prohibiting discrimination based on gender identity/sexual orientation.

Williams, W.L. (2001). Benefits for non-homophobic societies: An anthropological perspective. In W. Blumenfeld (Ed.), *Homophobia: How we all pay the price* (pp. 258–274). Boston, MA: Beacon.

Describes benefits gained for children, families, friendships, religion, and for the society as a whole based on studies of cultures that are not homophobic.

Young, S. (2004). Dichotomies and displacement: Bisexuality in queer theory and politics. In D. Carlin & J. DiGrazia (Eds.), *Queer cultures* (pp. 83–98). Upper Saddle River, NJ: Pearson Prentice Hall.

Discusses why the topic of bisexuality makes not only heterosexuals uncomfortable but is avoided in the LBGT community as well.

Zeldin, T. (1994). *An intimate history of humanity.* New York, NY: HarperCollins.

Examines private lives and relationships but expands to explore a universal human history through a variety of perspectives, employing a wide range of knowledge.

Zemsky, B., & Sanlo, R.L. (2005). Do policies matter? In R. Sanlo (Ed.), *Gender identity and sexual orientation: Research, policy and personal perspectives,* No. 111 (pp. 7–15). San Francisco, CA: Jossey-Bass.

Examines the effect of nondiscriminatory policies that include sexual orientation and gender identity on college campuses, in business, and at the state level.

CHAPTER 11

Classism: Misperceptions and Myths About Income, Wealth, and Poverty

"The greatest of evils and the worst of crimes is poverty."

George Bernard Shaw (1856–1950)

Classism refers to attitudes and discriminatory actions toward others based on their low socioeconomic status. It is nearly impossible to grow up in the United States without being affected by pervasive cultural messages that engender antagonism and sometimes contempt for poor people. In our American capitalist economic system, which emphasizes competition for opportunity and reward, there are winners and there are losers. Americans are encouraged to admire winners. Stories of winners are told daily in newspapers and magazines, and we applaud their success. Americans do not tend to identify with losers. Poor people are usually perceived as losers. Historically, our culture has produced many negative messages asserting that people living in poverty are deficient and inferior; these negative cultural messages represent **cultural classism,** and they constitute one factor influencing the process by which Americans have learned to devalue poor people.

Cultural Classism

When colonists came to the New World, they had a well-established tradition that caring for the poor was both a local responsibility and a religious obligation. Historically, the European Catholic Church provided food to the hungry, shelter for the homeless, and care for the sick; the legacy can still be found in Catholic and Protestant hospitals and social service agencies today. Problems of poverty remained local, affecting a small percentage of people, and church resources were adequate to the task. But in fourteenth- and fifteenth-century Europe, the number of poor people increased dramatically. Plagues, wars, and various economic changes dispossessed rural families of their livelihoods and land, forcing them to search for employment elsewhere, usually in major cities.

What was the response in England to people in poverty?

In England, the local response to poverty was termed *outdoor relief,* where food, funds, and other assistance were distributed to people as needed. However, because of the increasing numbers of people whose poverty did not seem temporary, vagrancy laws were created that proscribed punishment for beggars and vagrants: public whippings, then exile, forced labor, and, for people who persisted in being poor and making a nuisance of themselves, execution. Another strategy involved auctioning groups of poor people to the lowest bidder—the person who offered to care for the group for the fewest tax dollars. The purpose of punishment, banishment, auctions, and executions was not to address problems of poverty, but to be rid of the poor, and English colonists in particular brought these attitudes and strategies with them.

What was the response to poverty in America during the colonial period?

In the colonies, outdoor relief included sharing food, providing common grazing land (and "town cows"), building shelters for homeless families, and caring for sick persons in their homes when they had no family to help them. To reduce burdens of poverty in a community, potential settlers often were required to prove they could care for themselves. If they weren't convincing or if they failed to take care of their own needs as promised, they could be *warned out*—notified that they must leave the community. Komisar (1977) reported that in 1790, one Massachusetts community warned out almost a third of its population.

Meanwhile, English poorhouses providing food and shelter became an alternative to outdoor relief. People living in poorhouses were required to work to pay for their care, thereby reducing the need for local revenue. According to Katz (1986), Boston established the first colonial poorhouse in 1664; later, others were established in Philadelphia (1732), New York (1736), and Baltimore (1773). Although poorhouses were never intended to offer compassionate care, they were "the best means of frightening the able bodied into going to work and discouraging people from applying for aid" (Komisar, 1977, p. 21). The physical conditions in many poorhouses were atrocious: too many people crowded together, many with contagious diseases and often too little food or medical care. Poorhouses also included people with additional problems such as mental illness and alcoholism. Even when poorhouses had decent conditions, people were reluctant to live there because of the stigma associated with them. Because anyone applying for outdoor relief could be referred to a poorhouse, it was hoped that the threat of referral would reduce relief applications. For many years in both America and England, sending people to the poorhouse was a major strategy for dealing with poverty. (See Figure 11.1.)

What happened to the "religious obligation" to help the poor?

Ironically, Christian faith in America was a major contributor to increasingly harsh attitudes toward the poor. Many colonial Protestants believed that poverty was a consequence of sin and slothfulness. They assumed the rich were rewarded for their thrift and virtue, whereas the poor were sinners needing reform. Americans often expressed their belief that anyone who wanted to work could find a job, as Matthew Carey noted in 1828:

FIGURE 11.1

If you were in a poorhouse, you might be able to let family and friends know where you were by sending a postcard like this one from the County Poor House in Burlington, Iowa, early 1900s.

Source: Courtesy of the Poorhouse Lady

> Many citizens entertain an idea that in the present state of society . . . every person able and willing to work may procure employment . . . [and that] the chief part of the distresses of the poor arises from idleness, dissipation, and worthlessness. (Katz, 1986, p. 7)

Carey believed that poverty was not a consequence of personal failure as much as it was low wages, poor working conditions resulting in accidents or illness, and the impact of economic downturns. Those who actually worked with poor people understood that many were industrious and virtuous, but still lived in poverty because of circumstances beyond their control. Despite the efforts of Carey and other advocates for poor people, negative attitudes prevailed, not only toward paupers but also toward the working poor who lived perilously on the brink of poverty.

Why were people who had a job so close to poverty?

Komisar (1977) described an 1833 economic analysis of a construction worker's salary that concluded it was hardly sufficient to support a wife and two children. A continuing flow of immigrants exacerbated the problems of the poor by increasing competition for jobs; this allowed employers to keep wages low or even reduce them. Schwarz (2000) quotes social reformer Joseph Tuckerman explaining that wages in 1830 were so low "because the number of laborers [was] essentially greater than the demand for them" (p. 17). Because unemployment remained high, poorhouses never lacked occupants even though conditions were usually unsanitary and unhealthy, filled as they were with people who were undernourished and often ill. Even so, Komisar provided an excerpt from a Massachusetts report in 1833 that complained of poor people who regarded poorhouses as their "inns":

> Here they find rest, when too much worn with fatigue to travel, and medical aid when they are sick. And as they choose not to labor, they leave these stopping places when they have regained strength to enable them to travel; and pass from town to town *demanding* their portion of the State's allowances for them as *their right.* (pp. 21–22)

In reality, poorhouses included so many children, elderly, and people with disabilities or illness that there were in fact few able-bodied residents. Komisar referred to an 1848 report of a Philadelphia poorhouse where only 12% of the residents were capable of working. In some communities, poorhouses were built on farmland in the hope that residents could pay for their care by operating the farm, yet "poor farms" often hired people to do the work because there were not enough healthy able-bodied people in residence. Men who could work stayed out of poorhouses and tried to find work; it wasn't easy.

Why was it so difficult to find work?

The rapid development and use of machines throughout the second half of the nineteenth century contributed to unemployment, even in rural areas where hand threshing was eliminated by threshing machines. In urban areas, unskilled factory workers replaced skilled artisans, diminishing the satisfaction derived from work. Schwarz (2000) quoted a social reformer commenting on the dehumanizing aspect of factory jobs:

> [Factory work] tends to dwarf the intellectual powers, by confining the activity of the individual to a narrow range, to a few details, perhaps to the heading of pins, the pointing of nails, or the tying together of broken strings. (p. 15)

Although working wages were low for men, they were lower for women. Even children worked to help cover family expenses. If everyone in the family worked and everyone stayed healthy, it was possible to save money to be self-sufficient in old age. Retirement was rare: Workers didn't usually retire, but worked as long as they could. When they could no longer work, they typically lived with their adult children, who often could not afford to keep that parent without outdoor relief. Elderly who could not stay with children usually lived in poorhouses.

Why did people think poorhouses were the solution to poverty?

In the early 1800s, institutions were promoted as a solution to social problems: prisons for criminals, mental hospitals for the insane, orphanages for children, reform schools for juvenile delinquents, and poorhouses for the poor. In addition to rehabilitating inmates, these institutions were supposed to require minimal tax dollars from state and local governments. By 1850, many people had been placed in institutions; however, expenses proved more costly than anticipated. To make matters worse, Katz (1986) noted the realization that "Mental hospitals did not cure; prisons and reform schools did not rehabilitate; . . . and poorhouses did not check the growth of outdoor relief or promote industry" (p. 25). In fact, from the beginning, institutions tended to provide primarily custodial care to protect society from deviant individuals within.

> It is the function of religion to teach society to value human life more than property.
>
> **Walter Rauschenbusch (1861–1918)**

Because of public opposition to providing relief to able-bodied men, the few men still in poorhouses in the late 1800s were expelled. They moved to cities to find work and often sought lodging with other poor families who were eager for the extra money lodgers would pay. Social activists were appalled because lodging indigent men gave them sexual access to women in the home. Katz (1986) explains that the word *lodger* became a derisive term; still the housing need could not be ignored, and lodging houses, later nicknamed *flophouses,* evolved to provide inexpensive rooms for single itinerant men. Shortly after men were barred from poorhouses, children were removed as well, and poorhouses evolved into nursing homes for elderly people without families to care for them.

Why were children removed from poorhouses?

Social activists believed that poverty was caused in part by *hereditary pauperism,* as if being poor was a genetic defect. They argued that adult paupers were beyond help, but that children in poverty could be saved. In state after state, legislation was passed mandating that children be removed from a parent or parents admitted to a poorhouse and placed in orphanages. By 1875, the majority of children in orphanages were not orphans; they had living parents who were poor.

Consequently, adoption patterns began to change. Low-income families had adopted children old enough to work outside the home or to assist with domestic chores, but middle- and upper-class families were increasingly adopting children based on the assumption that these infants would remember nothing of their impoverished origins and could be "saved" by being raised in good homes. Katz (1986) explains how social reformers defended the practice of taking children away from poor parents: "Only by snapping the bonds between pauper parents and their children could they prevent the transmission of dependence from one generation to another" (p. 106). Such negative attitudes were characteristic of this era, resulting in a minimal response to the needs of poor people.

What was the response to the needs of poor people?

In the late 1800s, charitable organizations including the *Association for Improving the Condition of the Poor* sent "friendly visitors" to homes of poor people to offer spiritual advice and to promote a Protestant work ethic, the notion that hard work is essential and that rewards come from one's willingness to work. Komisar (1977) reports that charitable organizations viewed a poor person asking for money to pay rent or purchase food as a "failure of character" (p. 33). Organizations provided minimal financial or material aid, believing people would work only if they were choosing between work and starvation. American society of the 1880s and 1890s tended to regard poverty as proof of moral misconduct; organizations denied aid to drunkards and would only help their families if the wife and children left the drunkard.

By the late 1890s, studies began to suggest that misconduct, especially alcohol abuse, was *not* a major cause of poverty. Data from one study suggested that alcohol abuse and other forms of misconduct affected only 10% to 30% of families living in poverty, but that circumstances beyond anyone's control accounted for 65% or more of families who were poor. Schwarz (2000) described social reformers such as Josephine Lowell defending poor people "who are not drunken and shiftless, but who lead lives of . . .

heroic self-sacrifice and devotion" (p. 101). Social reformers began to challenge Christians to demonstrate a more altruistic attitude by helping people in poverty, and reformers often identified capitalists as the true cause of suffering among the poor.

By the early 1900s, attitudes had evolved to the point that social reformers no longer supported the practice of taking children from poor parents. Buttressed by new child development theories, they denounced orphanages as harmful to children and advocated foster parent placement and care as an alternative. They lobbied for outdoor relief to keep poor families together, reasoning that the presence of children was an incentive for parents to work. In response to studies, speeches, and arguments of social reformers, states began to initiate programs of financial assistance to single-parent mothers regardless of whether they had been abandoned by their husbands or had given birth to children without being married.

Financial support was necessary because it was hard for single women to make enough money to cover their own expenses, and even more difficult if they had children: Women were paid considerably less than male workers. Perhaps women's low pay was the reason they were the first to form unions and to initiate strikes demanding wage increases and better working conditions. Most early labor strikes were unsuccessful because impoverished women workers desperately needed money and could not afford to be out of work for long. Nevertheless, women workers—and men as well—continued to organize into unions throughout the 1800s as their best option to stop exploitation by employers.

What did workers do to protest employer exploitation?

In the early 1870s, 20,000 unemployed workers in Chicago marched to City Hall demanding food, clothing, and shelter; textile workers went on strike in Massachusetts; and coal miners struck in Pennsylvania. Despite union activism, railroad owners drastically cut worker wages in 1877, causing strikes in several states; the owners hired newly arrived immigrants to break many of the strikes, fueling anti-immigrant sentiments among workers. Local citizens often supported strikers, but railroad owners had the law on their side. As strikers barricaded buildings and blocked tracks, police and state militias were called in to drive striking workers away, with many injuries resulting from the violent confrontations.

Zinn (1999) described solidarity between local people and striking workers during the Pittsburgh strike against the Pennsylvania Railroad in 1877. Owners believed local militias would not fire at the strikers for fear of killing them and demanded that local officials call federal troops from Philadelphia. When troops arrived, the workers refused to be intimidated. In the first confrontation with strikers, the federal troops killed ten people; Pittsburgh residents responded angrily, surrounding the troops as they retreated to the nearest building, which was a railway roundhouse. Although the citizens surrounded the roundhouse and set fire to the building, the troops managed to escape and left the city.

How did unions ultimately help workers to gain higher salaries?

Despite union organizing and strikes, wages remained low. Komisar (1977) identified a 1904 economist who calculated that an annual salary of $460 was required to support a wife and three children. Most railroad workers made less than $375 a year. Out of all the jobs studied, the economist reported that a third of them paid less than $300 a year. If more than one person in the family worked and the family was frugal, they might manage to save money, but instead of receiving praise for being thrifty, their savings would often be used against them. Schwarz (2000) explained how: "When employers discovered that their workers earned enough to put something by, they concluded that they had been overpaying them" (p. 43).

In addition to low wages, laborers often toiled in dangerous workplaces. In 1908, the federal government reported that every year, over 35,000 workers were killed and 536,000 were injured on the job. The U.S. rates for worker injuries and deaths were much higher than those in most European countries. Although workers did not often convince employers to raise wages, they did persuade state legislators to address the issue of workplace risks. Katz (1986) reported that 43 of 45 states passed workers' compensation laws between 1909 and 1920, over the objections of employers who complained of the financial burden of compensating workers for injuries sustained at work. Americans continued to debate what was fair for employees and employers until the Great Depression of the 1930s, when widespread unemployment demanded an aggressive response from the federal government.

> The test of our progress is not whether we add more to the abundance of those who have much; it is whether we provide enough for those who have too little.
>
> **Franklin Roosevelt (1882–1945)**

How did the federal government address unemployment in the 1930s?

By the spring of 1931, Komisar estimated 5 million unemployed U.S. workers; for the following year, he estimated a total of 8 million. By 1933, when Franklin Roosevelt began his first presidential term, between 12 and 15 million workers were unemployed, a third of the U.S. labor force. Federal programs were installed as New Deal activities from Roosevelt's campaign pledge to offer a "new deal" for workers in America. When Roosevelt signed a Federal Emergency Relief Act (FERA) to provide assistance for people suffering from poverty, he ended a tradition of local and state governments having exclusive responsibility for the poor. FERA distributed $250 million to the states based on a formula of $1 of federal money for every $3 the state spent for relief or economic assistance to individuals; another $250 million was given to states with the most severe poverty problems. In some states, 40% of the people were on relief. To add insult to injury, laws in fourteen states prevented people who received relief from voting.

In addition to providing money for relief, the federal government became an employer. The Civilian Conservation Corps recruited 250,000 young men (but no women) to work on projects to prevent floods, fires, and soil erosion, and to develop recreational areas. The Works Progress Administration (WPA) employed about 2 million men, a fourth of the workforce, to build roads or to construct bridges, public buildings, and parks. Some Americans did not support these actions; Komisar (1977) quoted a bank president who said, "I profoundly believe that society does not owe every man a living" (p. 56).

Although federal employment programs provided jobs, the numbers of unemployed continued to be significant, and employers took advantage of the oversupply of labor to keep wages low and (again) even reduce them, resulting in more worker protests and strikes. In response to this turmoil, the Wagner Act passed in 1935 created a National Labor Relations Board (NLRB) and granted unions legal status as collective bargaining agents for workers. The intent was that the NLRB would encourage peaceful resolutions of labor disputes by negotiation rather than through strikes and disruptive activities that often ended in violence.

What was the outcome of the New Deal?

Because of employment demands during World War II, the "make-work" New Deal programs were dismantled. Although European countries had been enacting social insurance programs since 1833, conservative critics had accused Roosevelt of aspiring to become a dictator and attacked his poverty programs, saying they would "threaten the integrity of our [capitalist] institutions" (Komisar, 1977, p. 62). Despite opposition, programs such as unemployment insurance and the social security and welfare programs that were created by the Economic Security Act of 1935 have been maintained to provide basic protection and support for people in need. A 1939 Gallup poll reported that 70% of Americans believed that the federal government should address the needs of unemployed people, and the same 70% approved the amount of relief available to the poor. Programs continue to function today because they have been successful, are still considered necessary, and enjoy widespread public support.

The legacy of Roosevelt's New Deal was not only social programs but also the principle of federal government involvement in poverty issues. The Civilian Conservation Corps, which is no longer in existence, was the forerunner of the Peace Corps and AmeriCorps and other programs that recruit young people to work on community projects locally and globally (see Figure 11.2.). Politicians may wish to reform the welfare program or propose privatizing social security, yet few would question the

FIGURE 11.2

The Civilian Conservation Corps (CCC) gave young men jobs in the 1930s when jobs were scarce (top photo). The federal government (bottom photo) continues to engage young adults to work on conservation projects, but unlike the CCC, the Student Conservation Association's diverse membership also includes women.

Source: Courtesy Franklin Delano Roosevelt Library (top photo) and Student Conservation Association (bottom photo)

need for such programs or the appropriateness of the federal government providing them. Because of federal remedies to economic challenges of the 1930s, American culture developed new perceptions of poverty and the role of government in response to it. Unfortunately, some Americans cling to old attitudes and persist in accusing poor people of deficiencies as a cause of their poverty.

Individual Classism

Individual classism refers to attitudes and discriminatory actions stemming from prejudice against poor people (see Figure 11.3.). According to a Harris poll, Taylor (2000) reports that 77% of Americans believe most unemployed people could find a job without much difficulty if they made an effort, an interesting assertion in a capitalist society. Unlike most Americans, economists understand that capitalism requires that a certain percentage of unemployed workers exist to keep wages low and to control inflation. Europeans seem to understand this economic principle better than Americans. In a 1990 survey of citizens from twelve European countries, 17% believed poverty was related to laziness or lack of will power, but 66% said poverty resulted from social injustice, from personal misfortune, or from changes in the modern world (Wilson, 1996).

In contrast to European attitudes, Wilson also reported surveys finding Americans more likely to blame poor people for being poor stemming from factors such as lack of effort, lack of ability, or loose morals. Ironically, our American penchant for blaming the victim overlooks the fact that children represent the largest percentage of poor people in the United States and that their numbers continue to increase. Further, a cross-cultural study found that the socioeconomic status of America's children was a better predictor of school performance than it was in European countries such as Denmark, the Netherlands, or France (Scott & Leonhardt, 2005). This would suggest that such countries are making an effort to address at least some of the needs of children living in poverty. Yet when Americans acknowledge poor children, all too often we blame them for not working harder in school to lift themselves out of poverty.

How are children from low-income families disadvantaged in schools?

Although Americans may argue that poor children should use free education provided in public schools to escape from poverty, Kozol (2005) and others have described the appalling conditions in the schools attended by those living in poverty. Among the world's industrialized nations, the

FIGURE 11.3

The Southern Poverty Law Center (SPLC) is dedicated to combatting individual and institutional classism by providing impoverished people with legal assistance. SPLC offices are located in Montgomery, Alabama, across the street from the Civil Rights Memorial designed by Maya Lin, visited by thousands each year.

Source: Photo courtesy of Timothy Hursley, Southern Poverty Law Center.

United States is the only one without universal preschool and child support programs. Wilson (1996) described an alternative approach: French child care programs of infant care, nursery schools, paid leave for parents of newborns, and medical care that includes a preventive care system for children and public health nurses to monitor children's health. The French support system sends a clear message that France values all children, not just middle- or upper-class children.

By 2010, Owen and Doerr (1999) predicted that 40% of American children will experience poverty at some time in their lives, and poor children tend to have greater needs than middle- or upper-class children. Anyon (2001) reports that 25% of U.S. urban school budgets are typically expended to respond to the psychological and social needs of students from low-income families, yet Americans often seem oblivious to the impact of poverty. Pipher (2002) provides this comment about American attitudes: "We were born on third base and we think we hit triples" (p. 21).

> For every talent that poverty has stimulated it has blighted a hundred.
>
> **John Gardner (1912–2002)**

The consequences of educational advantages for children of the middle and upper classes can be ascertained by analyzing student SAT scores in relation to family income. According to multiple studies, higher family income in all races—socioeconomic standing—translates into higher scores on SAT tests (Berliner, 2005). Owen and Doerr (1999) argued that the power of socioeconomic standing should not be surprising because studies also report that low-income families seldom have computers in their homes and that students from low-income homes rarely can afford fees paid by other students for coaching sessions to improve SAT scores. Despite the obvious explanation for their children's higher scores on SAT tests, Owen and Doerr described how SAT scores provided middle- and upper-class families with:

> A scientific-sounding justification for the advantages they enjoyed. The wealthy lived in nice houses because they were smart; the poor were hungry because they were stupid. American society was just after all. (p. 175)

How can schools make a difference in the lives of poor children?

Herrnstein and Murray (1994) reported the same pattern concerning socioeconomic standing and IQ test scores as reported for SAT tests and concluded that genetic differences exist and therefore IQ disparity could not be reduced by improving education for poor children. Yet in a study comparing IQ scores of black and white children, IQ differences were almost completely eliminated when adjustments were made for poverty-related factors such as economic conditions and learning experiences available in home environments (Brooks-Gunn, Klebanov, & Duncan, 1996). Similarly, researchers in France tracked a group of children who had come from abusive homes, foster care, or institutional settings after the children were adopted by financially secure parents. At the time of the children's adoption, they were regarded as borderline for a diagnosis of mental retardation with an average IQ score of 77. Just nine years after their adoption, the IQ scores for all of these children had improved significantly, with the highest increases appearing in those children who were adopted into the most affluent families (Kirp, 2007). Other studies report that children from low-income families initially learn at a rate similar to middle- and upper-class children but fall behind when they start school, and then lose further ground during summers when middle- and upper-class children take advantage of opportunities to travel, visit museums, and attend camps—activities that promote children's social and intellectual development (Entwhistle, Alexander, & Olson, 2001). If the federal and state governments provided aggressive intervention strategies, they could significantly improve the cognitive development of children from low-income families.

How has the federal government addressed the disadvantages for low-income students?

For the 2003 renewal of the Elementary and Secondary Education Act, President George W. Bush promoted and signed the No Child Left Behind (NCLB) Act, which requires rigorous testing of students, and identifies those students who do not achieve designated test scores. Those schools with student scores below the Adequate Yearly Progress (AYP) benchmarks for two consecutive years are labeled as "failing" (softened to "in need of improvement"). In 2006, more than a fourth of all public schools failed to reach their AYP (Karp, 2006). If these schools fail to meet their benchmark again in the following year, they are added to the list of schools *in need of improvement* and are in jeopardy of losing their federal funding. If schools remain on the list for four or five years, they must choose from drastic options such as (1) replacing all or most of their staff, (2) extending their school year or school day, or (3) contracting with an outside entity (or with the state) to operate the school (in violation of our longstanding principle of local control of schools).

Many educators have criticized NCLB for its reliance on standardized tests to determine student learning. Even makers of standardized tests admit that these tests measure only a portion of what a child learns, and that multiple measures are necessary for authentic assessment of learning. Yet the NCLB plan forces teachers to reduce their curriculum content to prepare students for the tests, including students learning English as a second language, at-risk students, and special education students. In addition, NCLB makes no distinction between students attending underfunded, deteriorating schools with inadequate facilities in areas of poverty and students attending well-maintained schools with state-of-the-art facilities in wealthy suburbs. They all have to pass the same tests (Mathis, 2003).

If NCLB were achieving its goal, educators and parents would be applauding it; instead, all fifty states have introduced legislation rejecting all or parts of NCLB. According to a study by the Harvard Civil Rights project, NCLB has failed to improve student scores on reading and math achievement tests, and it has made no progress on reducing achievement gaps between students based on differences of income or race (Lee, 2006). As Karp (2006) explains, the primary lesson to be learned from NCLB is that "tests, more tests, and punitive sanctions that create a systematic and misleading impression of failure . . . (hurts) public education" (p. 13). Even those in Congress who supported NCLB are concerned that President Bush did not request funding adequate for the implementation of NCLB. Furthermore, the 14 to 15 million American children living in poverty only spend about thirty hours per week in school for two thirds of the weeks in a year; that's five times as many hours out of school as in school. Advocates for children living in poverty increasingly insist that disadvantaged children need to have the problems that they encounter outside of school addressed if they are to perform more effectively in school.

Why should problems outside of school affect a child's performance in school?

As Kozol (2005) has documented, schools in the United States are segregated not only by race, but even more by social class. Segregated inner-city schools typically include as many as 75% or more students eligible for free or reduced-cost meals. Berliner (2005) noted "thousands of studies showing correlation between poverty and (low) academic achievement" (p. 11). Berliner suggested a number of reasons to explain the correlation: (1) Children living in poverty are less likely than other children to receive appropriate nutrition on a regular basis. In 2003, for example, 36 million Americans experienced "food insecurity," with 25% of them actually going hungry at some point during the year and 3 million facing chronic hunger; (2) Children living in poverty are less likely than other children to have stable home lives that promote financial and personal security; and (3) Children living in poverty are more likely to suffer from environmental deficiencies that often lead to health problems and are less likely to receive appropriate medical care.

Asthma has reached epidemic proportions among poor children in America, causing them to miss from 20 to 40 days of school. Reporting on lead poisoning, the Centers for Disease Control and Prevention (CDC) estimates that 450,000 American children between the ages of one and five have sufficient lead in their blood to impair cognitive development. Children referred to by the CDC are usually poor, with the majority being children of color. In addition, a 2001 study found that 50% of children living in poverty had a vision deficiency that could be corrected except their families could not afford the cost (Berliner, 2005).

Schwartz-Nobel (2002) emphasized that other countries have addressed problems of poverty more aggressively than the United States has. There are 37 million Americans living in poverty, 40% are living on incomes that are about half of federally designated poverty level incomes; 14.5% of Americans living in poverty are permanently poor, the highest rate of permanent poor of any industrialized nation. In addition, 17% of children in the United States live in poverty, the highest rate of child poverty of any industrialized nation. In 2005, a UN charter on the rights of children was signed by all of its member nations to indicate their support except for two—Somalia and the United States (Berliner, 2005).

How do we know that addressing the social problems of children living in poverty will improve their academic achievement?

According to Schwartz-Nobel (2002), the bodies of undernourished children use food energy first to maintain critical organs, next for growth, and the remaining energy is for cognitive development. Even short-term nutritional deprivation diminishes the ability to learn. "Children who come to school hungry are known to have shorter attention spans. They are unable to perform as well as their peers" (p. 139). Schwartz-Nobel cites a study of low-income children in which some participated in a school breakfast program and others did not. Participating students achieved significantly higher standardized test scores than students not participating.

As for living in a stable home, multiple studies report that being poor places great psychological stress on adults as well as children. DiAngelo (2006) described the stress she felt as a child living in poverty:

> We were evicted frequently. . . . If (the children) got sick, my mother would beat us, screaming that we could not get sick because she could not afford to take us to the doctor. . . . My teacher once held my hands up to my fourth-grade class as an example of poor hygiene. . . . I used to stare at the girls in my class and ache to be like them. (p. 51)

Overcoming poverty can diminish psychological stress and lead to behavioral changes. Berliner (2005) cites studies reporting decreases in the frequency of psychiatric symptoms when families escaped poverty. Consequences for children of families that improved their economic status included increased school attendance and higher academic achievement. By the fourth year of economic security, children who had been poor demonstrated psychological symptoms comparable to children who had never experienced poverty.

Multiple studies over several decades have reported that environmental factors leading to health problems have adverse effects on learning, and that learning can be improved when social problems are addressed. In 1970, Stein and Susser engaged in a review of considerable data that included cross-cultural research and reported,

> Improvement in the social environment of groups at a marked social disadvantage can bring about a substantial improvement in IQ levels and a decline in the frequency of mild mental retardation . . . the greatest advantage will come from a serious attack on poverty . . . unemployment, deteriorated housing, physical environment, and poor and inappropriate schooling. (p. 64)

Berliner (2005) cites an IQ study that reported only 10% of the variation of IQ is related to genetic influence. Berliner also describes a longitudinal study of families over a three-year period. When families identified as poor became less poor, their children's academic performance became similar to that of the children who had never been poor. This was true even when parents of children who were never poor earned significantly higher salaries than the parents who had been poor. The researchers concluded, "rising incomes provide families with dignity and hope" (p. 30).

> Men in search of a myth will usually find one.
>
> **Pueblo Indian Proverb**

Schwartz-Nobel (2002) cites a projection that the U.S. labor force will lose "as much as $130 billion in future productive capacity . . . for every year that 14.5 American children continue to live in poverty" (p. 224). Research suggests that to improve the academic achievement of low-income students, especially those living in poverty, school reform will be effective only if it occurs in the context of social programs that improve environmental factors for these children and youth. The stakes are high, not only for poor people but for our society as well. because studies tell us that low-achieving students are more likely to drop out of school, and studies of high school dropouts report that workers without a high school diploma are twice as likely to be poor as those who graduate from high school (Haskins & Sawhill, 2007). However, the effort to persuade Americans to make a serious commitment to addressing problems of the poor is persistently sabotaged by myths and misunderstandings about poverty, especially about welfare recipients.

What are some myths about welfare recipients?

There is confusion in the United States about who qualifies for welfare assistance. Americans have historically believed that it was possible for able-bodied men to receive welfare. Weaver (2000) explains that aside from programs for widows, orphans, and people with disabilities, over 90% of social support comes through Transitional Assistance for Needy Families (TANF), a program that replaced Aid to Families with Dependent Children (AFDC) in 1996. As with AFDC, TANF assists single-parent families, rarely including men but typically consisting of women with dependent children; children represent two thirds of recipients.

Johnson (1998) and others identify a variety of other myths about welfare; many have been around for a number of years. The following list includes examples of myths that have fostered negative or even hostile attitudes and actions toward recipients; further information is included to provide a more accurate picture about people receiving social assistance.

Myth #1: Welfare rolls are increasing. This is a half-truth, and as the Yiddish proverb says, "A half truth is a whole lie." True, numbers of people on welfare are increasing, but so is the population. Since 1970, people receiving some form of social assistance as a percentage of overall population has been relatively stable, with increases or decreases reflecting economic conditions. Schorr (2001) explains that in good economic times, women find available jobs and leave welfare; during economic downturns, unemployment increases, as do applications for social assistance.

Myth #2: Welfare families are large. As the twentieth century ended, the average size of a family receiving social assistance included 2.9 children, down from 4.0 children thirty years earlier. Over 37% of all TANF families have one child; 27% have two children (U.S. Department of Health and Human Services, 2004). Weaver (2000) reports that the average size of families receiving assistance across the nation is about the same as the typical American family.

Myth #3: People on welfare have a comfortable life by abusing the welfare system. In seven states offering the most generous social assistance, family income—including food stamps received—is raised to meet the poverty level. In more than half the states, combined forms of social assistance only raise a recipient's gross income to 75% of the poverty level, and to 60% of the poverty level in twelve southern states. Despite such inadequate support, less than 2% of recipients have been documented as being engaged in welfare fraud. Yet Allison and Lewis (2001) report Internal Revenue Service estimates revealing a considerably higher percentage of fraud in the tax returns of middle- and upper-class Americans, and Kivel (2002) reports that corporate fraud exceeds $200 billion each year.

Myth #4: The government only helps people on welfare. The U.S. Congress has helped corporations in fiscal trouble such as Chrysler and Boeing, and it has offered assistance to corporations not in financial trouble. According to Kivel (2002), federal government policies in support of wealthy corporations amounts to more than $160 billion each year, costing each taxpayer about $1400 compared to $400 per taxpayer spent on welfare and food stamps for poor people. Critics of corporate welfare argue that U.S. government spending reduces competition by subsidizing a select few corporations, creating an uneven playing field by providing what they regard as unnecessary assistance for minimal economic benefits.

Myth #5: Welfare recipients are too lazy to get a job. Two thirds of Americans receiving social assistance are children, half of whom are five years old or less. Before TANF, most state assistance programs penalized enrolled mothers who were employed, deducting one dollar from their welfare check for every dollar they earned, and yet almost half of welfare mothers held at least part-time jobs. Mead (2000) found that one of the most generous states paid benefits of $673 per month to a welfare mother—regardless of the number of children—and required that she work a minimum of thirty hours per week with child care paid for by the state. However, if that mother were employed at minimum wages for forty hours a week she would earn $824 each month, but because she is not on welfare she would not qualify for child care benefits. The additional $150 a month earned at her minimum wage job would not cover the cost of quality child care and work-related expenses such as clothing and transportation. Further, minimum wage jobs frequently lack health insurance, and if insurance is provided, it is likely restricted to employees only, not their families. Welfare assistance includes health care for families. It is not surprising that many mothers, forced to choose between such options, decide to swallow their pride and apply for assistance for the sake of their children.

MYTH #6: Welfare recipients stay on welfare forever. Because so many people believed this myth, the 1996 U.S. welfare reform placed time limits on assistance to recipients. Historically, the AFDC program provided few incentives to leave, yet recipients tended to require only temporary assistance. Studies showed that more than 30% of recipients left welfare each year, and 75% left within five years. Less than half returned to welfare. Of those who returned, 65% to 75% left the program again within a year, and most of those left permanently (Isaacs & Lyon, 2000; Sandefur & Cook, 1998). Even for families considered "highly dependent" because they were on welfare for over seven years, more than 80% of the daughters never became single mothers who required welfare assistance (Bray, 2000).

Myths about social assistance have shaped American attitudes and caused negative actions against welfare recipients. Although the negative actions illustrate individual classism, the inadequacies of American social assistance programs illustrate institutional classism.

Institutional Classism

Individual prejudice based on socioeconomic status and negative behaviors rooted in that prejudice are especially problematic in a society with as wide a disparity in wealth and income as exists in the United States. Yet **institutional classism**—institutional policies and practices that exploit low-income people and benefit middle- or upper-class individuals—have contributed even more to the wealth and income disparity. The increased economic disparity in the United States has made it more difficult for individuals from one class to move up to a higher class, contradicting the belief in social mobility that is still central to the American Dream. As reported in a *New York Times* poll, 35% of Americans believe that they have the same opportunity as has always existed in the United States to become successful enough to move from one social class to a higher one, and 40% of Americans believe that it is even easier to move up than it has ever been (Scott & Leonhardt, 2005). Yet Callahan (2007) reviewed studies on social mobility and concluded that "class status at birth largely determines life chances, and . . . this correlation has actually intensified in recent years" (p. A12). According to a study by the Federal Reserve Bank of Boston, social mobility declined during each of the last three decades of the twentieth century, and that is reflected in cross-cultural studies that have reported less social mobility in America today than in Britain, France, or Canada (Scott & Leonhardt, 2005). Based on their review of social mobility studies, Scott and Leonhardt found that although social mobility still occurs in the United States, it requires a lot more time than in the past and there is far less overall social mobility than ever before. In addition, there is evidence that institutional practices and policies during those years contributed to the dramatic rise in the wealth and income disparity that has occurred since the 1980s.

Why is the disparity between the richest and poorest Americans increasing?

Federal policies have played a major role in diverting resources to the richest Americans. Some Americans regard income redistribution as a socialist scheme, yet each year the U.S. Internal Revenue Service collects income taxes—scaled according to income—to fund programs and projects approved by our elected representatives. Phillips (1990) estimates that during the 1980s, $160 billion collected from middle- and low-income taxpayers replaced funds lost from capital gains tax cuts benefiting wealthy Americans and funded programs such as providing subsidies for overseas corporate advertising. Social economists term such effects a *redistribution of income.* According to Hout and Lucas (2007), the United States surpassed France and Great Britain in the 1980s to become the leading nation in the world for disparity between incomes and wealth of families in the highest 20% and lowest 20% of our economy.

Income redistribution also occurs when federal and state governments offer tax breaks to wealthy individuals and corporations resulting in their taxes becoming a lower percentage of income than that of most Americans. Because of the tax cuts passed by Congress from 2001 to 2003, the top 1% of Americans kept an additional $79 billion from their tax payment. As Sheehan (2004) points out, that is enough money to fully fund NCLB, provide housing subsidies for a million working poor families, add 47 million low-income children to the Women, Infants and Children (WIC) nutrition program, add 11 million children to the Medicaid program, and fully fund Head Start so that the 40% of eligible children not being served could participate. The $79 billion could fund all of these improvements with money left over. Yet even such federal generosity to wealthy individuals and corporations is not sufficient; they are trying to reduce their tax payments even further.

According to the Internal Revenue Service (IRS), American corporations are supposed to pay 35% of their income in taxes, but the IRS estimates that over 400,000 businesses and individuals employ tax-dodging practices to avoid paying approximately $250 billion to $300 billion each year (Allen, 2004; Zuckerman, 2004a). The most popular tactic is to establish "headquarters" in a tax-free Caribbean island or another overseas location with few or no taxes assessed. In 1983, such tax havens accounted for $200 billion in wealth; in 2004, they accounted for $5 trillion. In the 1950s, corporate taxes constituted about 27% of income tax revenue, but the 2003 corporate tax payment was only 7.4%, the lowest percentage in over twenty years and second lowest since 1934 (Zuckerman, 2004a). Based on a study of tax receipts from 1996 to 2000, the General Accounting Office reported that over 60% of U.S. corporations paid no taxes at all. Noncompliant corporations that filed no tax reports and paid no taxes deprived the American people of $310 billion in 2004 alone (Allen, 2004).

Another indication of wealth and income disparity in the United States is the dramatic increase in billionaires. From the Reagan economic policies of the 1980s through the Internet expansion and economic boom of the 1990s, data document dramatic increases in wealth for the richest Americans and a contrasting decrease in resources for low-income Americans. Phillips (1990) reported two billionaires in the United States in 1980, but more than 50 by 1989, and Forbes (2009) identified over 400 billionaires currently, representing 60% of all the world's billionaires. As Sklar (2005) noted, someone could deposit $1 million a day, every day, for an entire year, but he or she would only have about half of what is necessary to be included in the Forbes 400. In the very near future only billionaires will be on this list. Bill Gates and Warren Buffet are currently at the top of the Forbes 400, but five of the top ten families are heirs of Sam Walton, whose combined wealth is over $100 billion. While the rich have increased their wealth, thanks to federal tax cuts, 80% of working Americans earning $65,000 a year or less have seen their incomes stagnate (Zuckerman, 2004b).

> Wealth is a power usurped by the few to compel the many to labor for their benefit.
>
> **Percy Bysshe Shelley (1792–1822)**

How have salaries in the United States been affected by recent economic changes?

Starting in 1950, hourly wages for workers increased each decade until the 1980s, then declined by almost $1 per hour in that decade. Wages dropped another 50 cents in the first five years of the 1990s, but the economy prospered in the late 1990s and the 50 cents was regained. According to data from the U.S. Department of Labor Statistics, full-time male workers in the year 2000 earned a median weekly wage of $646, less than the $678 per week earned in 1979, a finding consistent across income levels (Children's Defense Fund, 2001). As Wilson (1996) stated, "The wage gap between low-skilled men and women shrank not because of gains made by female workers but mainly because of the decline in real wages for men" (p. 27). Historically, white men have enjoyed an economic advantage resulting in their salaries being the highest in all worker categories, yet even wages for white men declined. In too many cases, having a full-time job no longer provides adequate financial support. Greenberg (2007) reports that 25% of the full-time jobs available in the United States do not provide compensation sufficient to keep a couple with two children above the poverty line. Of the people living in poverty in the United States, 11%—almost 3 million Americans—have full-time, year-round jobs, and among Asian American and Latino populations, 18% have such jobs (Spriggs, 2007). This situation is likely to become even worse. The Bureau of Labor Statistics has identified 30 jobs expected to experience the greatest future need for additional workers, but two thirds of those jobs pay either "low" or "very low" wages (Greenberg, 2007).

While wages for workers have declined, management has prospered. Sklar (1998) found that U.S. chief executive officer (CEO) salaries have climbed astronomically since 1980 when the average CEO earned 42 times the average worker's salary, which is more than generous when compared to German CEOs, who make an average of 14 times the average worker salary. By 1995, U.S. CEOs were paid a corporate average of 224 times what the average worker earned, making their salaries the highest in the world. By 2007, American CEOs were making an average of 344 times the average worker's salary. Whereas German, Japanese, and British CEOs earned average annual salaries of approximately a half million dollars, the average CEO salary in the United States was $2 million; add their stock options and their average total compensation is $10.4 million (American Federation of Labor, 2009). (See Table 11.1.) In 1988, the ten highest paid CEOs averaged $19 million; in 2000, their average compensation was $154 million (Phillips, 2003). Large executive salaries are another factor in the increased disparity of wealth and income in the United States.

TABLE 11.1 CEO Salaries in the Global Economy.
In comparison to the salaries on this chart, American CEOs earn 431 times the average worker's salary (American Federation of Labor, 2006).

Home Base of Corporations	Comparison to Average Worker's Salary
Brazil	57 times
Mexico	45 times
Hong Kong	38 times
Britain	25 times
Australia	22 times
China	21 times
Italy	19 times
Spain	18 times
France	16 times
Taiwan	16 times
Germany	11 times
South Korea	11 times
Japan	10 times

The data from *Business Week* was reported in the June 2003 edition of *The Hightower Lowdown*, edited by Jim Hightower and Philip Frazer.

How large is the disparity of wealth in the United States?

Income is generated by toil or investment; *wealth* refers to assets one already controls. Because wealth is an obvious means of designating upper class, that group controls much of our wealth. But what level of concentrated wealth results in excessive influence? Wealth controlled by the top 1% of U.S. families declined slightly in each of the four decades after 1940 until 1980. The slight decrease in assets, related in part to higher tax rates, helped fund valuable social programs such as the GI Bill, FHA loans, and college loans that provided economic assistance to middle- and low-income families, creating a larger and more robust middle class.

In 1959, the top 4% of Americans had as much wealth as the lowest 35%; through the 1980s, wealthy Americans acquired even more wealth. In 1989, the top 4% held as much wealth as the lowest 51%, and by 2002, the top 1% had more wealth than 90% of Americans. From 1992 to 2002, the Forbes 400 were doubling their average wealth, but the number of American households with a net worth of only $5,000 or less increased to 44.2% (Dollars and Sense, 2004). Schwartz-Nobel (2002) pointed out that the United States is currently the wealthiest nation in the world, and yet an American child is three times more likely to be poor than a French child, and six times more likely to be poor than a Danish or Swiss child. This is not merely because of wealth disparity but income disparity. According to a study by the Congressional Budget

Office, the income disparity between the rich and poor at the end of the twentieth century was greater than at any time in the previous 250 years (Schwartz-Nobel, 2002).

Why has there been so little protest from Americans about the tax cuts for the wealthiest people in our society that have contributed to this upward redistribution of wealth and loss of wealth for the middle class? Perhaps Americans feel they lack the power needed to succeed in a confrontation with such a powerful group as the wealthy, or perhaps too many Americans see these tax cuts as benefiting them now or in the future. According to one poll, 19% of Americans identify themselves as being in the top 1% of incomes, and another 20% believe they will be in the top 1% in the near future (Collins, 2003). There is obviously considerable confusion in our society about how much wealth exists in America and who controls it.

How do income levels determine social class in the United States?

The nature of wealth in America makes it difficult to define who comprises the middle-income class. According to Heintz and Folbre (2000), middle-class wealth is overwhelmingly represented by two possessions: homes and cars. Historically, some American politicians lobbying for economic relief for their so-called middle-class constituents have argued for extending tax cuts to those with annual earnings of up to $200,000 or higher. Bonilla-Silva (2001) reported that a 1992 Congressional Budget Office study defined "middle class" as a family of four with an annual income of $19,000 to $78,000. More than 70% of Americans were middle class according to this definition. Wolfe (1998) conducted a survey asking Americans how large an annual income would have to be for someone to be considered too rich to be middle class. The answers were diverse, but ultimately it caused Wolfe to define **middle class** not as a specific income range but as a combination of attitudes, beliefs, and practices that characterize someone who is "not too poor to be considered dependent on others and not too rich to be so luxuriously ostentatious that one loses touch with common sense" (pp. 2–3).

It is not difficult to define "low income." The federal government established criteria for determining poverty, including earnings and number of people in a family (see Table 11.2). As of June 2009, the federal definitions of **poverty levels** designate an income of $11,201 for a person living alone; $14,840 for a single person with one child; $17,346 for a single person with two children (U.S. Census Bureau, 2009). Keeping these poverty levels in mind, a full-time worker paid the minimum wage will earn $15,080 a year. Recognizing the inadequacy of the minimum wage, many U.S. communities are implementing a "living wage" to meet the needs of low-income families.

Who suffers most from poverty?

Studies indicate that gender becomes a significant factor since most single-parent families are headed by a female. A poverty rate of 31% has been reported for all female-headed households with no spouse present compared to a 13% poverty rate for male-headed households with no spouse. Even single women suffer the consequences of the gender gap in salaries as studies report that for single people living alone, 24% of the women fall below the poverty line, but only 18% of the men do so. Elderly women are also more likely than elderly men to live in poverty, in part from their greater reliance on Social Security. They were more likely to work in low-wage jobs, which results in less lifelong earnings and lower Social Security payments. These women were also less likely to have jobs offering pensions (Spriggs, 2007).

When mothers live in poverty, so do their children, and many social activists have argued that children are the group most adversely affected by poverty. In the United States, one out of five children lives in poverty; two out of three social assistance recipients are children; and one out of five newborns is born into poverty—the highest rate in the industrialized world (Children's Defense Fund, 2001, 2008). The problems these children face begin with inadequate or even nonexistent prenatal and postnatal care offered by the American health care system, causing the United States to rank twenty-second among industrialized nations in low birth weights and in infant mortality rates. Low birth weight means a baby is born weighing 5½ pounds or less. In the United States, a low birth weight baby is born every two minutes and a very low birth weight baby (weighing 3 pounds, 4 ounces or less) is born every nine minutes. Since a

TABLE 11.2 Official Poverty Levels in the United States

Members in Family	Annual Income
Single Person	$11,201
Single with One Child	$14,840
Single with Two Children	$17,346
Single with Three Children	$21,910
Two Adults with One Child	$17,330
Two Adults with Two Children	$21,834
Two Adults with Three Children	$25,694
Annual Income for Minimum Wage Earner ($7.25/hr) = $15,080	

Source: United States Census Bureau, 2009, Available at www.census.gov.

newborn baby in the United States dies every nineteen minutes, America ranks twenty-second in infant mortality rates. These babies tend to come from low-income families, and Americans pay a price for our neglect of these children. As Johnson (2007) reported, "More than one-third of the dollars spent in the U.S. on health care during the first year of life can be attributed to low birth weight, even though these infants account for less than 10 percent of all U.S. births" (p. A15). For the children from low-income homes who survive infancy despite inadequate health care and insufficient diets, their poor nutrition will affect brain development. Studies have found that these children will be more likely to drop out of high school and more likely to earn as much as 15% less than their normal birth weight peers (Johnson, 2007).

The U.S. federal government response to help children in poverty began with the Economic Security Act of 1935 that included Aid to Dependent Children (ADC), a program intended for mothers widowed or abandoned by their husband. In 1950, ADC was expanded to include any single parent with children and was termed Aid to Families with Dependent Children (AFDC). In 1964, food stamps were made available to low-income families. In 1996, Transitional Assistance for Needy Families (TANF) replaced AFDC. Rodgers (2006) notes, however, that the average value of TANF benefits in combination with food stamps was about the same as what low-income families received from AFDC alone in 1970.

In the late 1970s, studies assessed the impact of war-on-poverty programs initiated in the 1960s by President Lyndon Johnson, especially programs concerned with meeting nutritional needs of the poor. One study reported that hunger had been virtually eliminated (Edelman, 2001). However, the Children's Defense Fund (2008) estimated that in 2007, 13 million children were living in poverty and 2.5 million children were living in "extreme poverty," meaning those children faced frequent and regular occasions where they were not receiving proper nutrition. When children go to bed hungry in the richest nation in the world, it illustrates a failure of our institutions to fulfill their social obligations.

Despite social assistance programs such as TANF, Women, Infants and Children (WIC), food stamps, and Meals on Wheels, malnutrition exists primarily among the old and the young in the United States. Children who do not die from malnutrition may suffer brain damage related to protein-deficient diets and sometimes calorie-deficient diets. Brain damage resulting from malnutrition is just as devastating as physical violence because it is permanent; it cannot be reversed by free breakfasts or free lunches once a child starts school.

American health care systems also fail to provide adequate services to poor people because they are

The Lessons of Hurricane Katrina

As Hurricane Katrina approached New Orleans, people who owned automobiles and could afford to leave streamed out of the city. Although most of the city's residents evacuated prior to the storm, few of the 30% living below the poverty line could escape, especially 112,000 people without cars. Many of the poor had no identification; their fear was that if they walked out following the interstate, they would be arrested for hitchhiking. With few resources, many of the poor and elderly felt they could not leave without social security or welfare checks that would be available in two more days. So they stayed.

As the magnitude of the storm became obvious, Mayor Ray Nagin announced that buses would stop at twelve locations to take people to the Superdome. Long lines of people—many elderly, disabled, or ill—stood outside the Superdome in 93-degree heat waiting to be processed so they could enter. That Sunday, 10,000 were housed there.

Katrina hit New Orleans with high winds and heavy rains, an inch per hour. Eventually 80% of the city was under water. When the first levee broke, twenty-five to thirty corpses were found floating in the flooded neighborhood. Floodwaters became a toxic soup consisting of sewage, gasoline, spoiled food, chemicals, dead animals, and human corpses; the stench caused people's eyes to burn. Many of the dead were among the 1,700 people, primarily elderly, not evacuated from hospitals. Television cameras captured people in wheelchairs trying to leave but trapped by floodwaters; in badly flooded areas, people stood on rooftops as water surged around them. Such images of vulnerable people haunted many Americans.

Because so many police officers abandoned New Orleans, looting began as soon as the waters receded. Some looters were criminals, but many ransacked stores to find food and medicine for survivors. State and local leaders begged President Bush to send in the National Guard, and representatives from the Federal Emergency Management Agency (FEMA), but the federal response to this tragedy was agonizingly slow.

Many Americans began to wonder if the inept response of the federal government was related to the poverty of the victims. The population at the Superdome increased to 25,000, but they did not have enough food or medicine, and the toilets were not working. Over 2,400 children were desperately looking for their parents or other family members. Despite the media coverage, almost a week passed before troops and federal disaster relief (food and supplies) arrived.

When the bodies in Louisiana were finally counted, Hurricane Katrina took 1,100 lives; most of the dead were poor and black. Diverse American reactions to Hurricane Katrina mirrored societal attitudes toward poor people and black people.

Douglas Brinkley, *The Great Deluge* (2006)

based on ability to pay. Poor people may visit free or low-cost clinics, yet these clinics are likely to be inadequately staffed and underfunded. Although the United States leads the world in medical technology, it is one of the worst among industrialized nations in health care delivery. The United States and South Africa are the only two developed nations without a universal health care program for all citizens. The United States ranks second to last among all developed nations (Mexico is last) in the percentage of children living in poverty, and twenty-sixth in the world in child mortality rates for children under twelve (Rifkin, 2004). There is one other group of people significantly affected by poverty, and that is the elderly. Many Americans believe that the United States effectively addressed the problem of poverty for elderly Americans with the establishment of the Social Security system in 1935, and there is some truth to this perception. Social Security is a major reason why only about 10% of people living in poverty in the United States are senior citizens (Spriggs, 2007), but elderly Americans continue to encounter serious problems related to poverty and to a form of prejudice that scholars have identified by the term "ageism."

How do scholars define ageism?

Butler (2008) originally coined the term *ageism* in 1968, defining it as "a form of systematic stereotyping and discrimination against people because they are old" (p. 41). An emerging view among some social scientists argues for a broader definition of ageism, one that includes both the young and the elderly. Levy and Banaji (2002), two prominent researchers in the field, recently expanded societal perspectives on ageism to include "an alteration in feeling, belief, or behavior in response to an individual's or group's perceived chronological age" (p. 50). Ageism is a profound form of prejudice in the United States that can be as devastating as racism and sexism. Both the old and the young encounter consequences stemming from preconceived notions, prejudices, and myths associated with age, including serious economic implications for both groups. What should not be overlooked is that current information related to ageism appears in the context of one of the deepest recessions in the global economy. In order to better understand the reality of the poverty associated with ageism, it is necessary to explore a larger context involving the dynamics of implicit ageism in society and ageism in the media and advertising.

How does ageism manifest itself in society?

Similar to racism and sexism, ageism is marked by stereotypes and prejudice of an implicit nature. The research of Levy and Banaji (2002) noted that "one of the most insidious aspects of ageism is that it can operate without conscious awareness, control or intent to do harm" (p. 50). They suggest that most kinds of prejudice in relation to the elderly, for example, are not characterized by explicit emotions such as the kind of vitriolic bigotry directed against targeted communities; instead, they describe a unique dimension to ageism that requires further attention:

> There are no hate groups that target the elderly as there are hate groups that target members of religious and racial and ethnic groups. Even gender prejudice has produced the recognition that there are those who have explicit antipathy toward one or the other group (e.g., misogynists, male chauvinists, man haters). In contrast, social sanctions against expressions of negative attitudes and beliefs about the elderly are completely absent. The widespread occurrence of socially acceptable expressions of negativity toward the elderly has been well documented. This state of affairs stands in sharp contrast to other social groups where, at least in public discourse, there has been a notable change in the recognition of social disadvantage and the need for action to ameliorate its consequences. (Levy & Banaji, 2002, p. 50)

As has already been discussed, the power of language remains a critically important factor in understanding the roots of prejudice. Language, sometimes taking the form of cultural insults, can communicate negative images of aging. A new word recently entered the American social lexicon. The emergence of "Elderspeak" in the form of cultural insults demeans the elderly through saccharine and infantilizing expressions such as "sweetie," "dear," or "dearie" used in nursing homes or other settings. Leland (2008) described such implicit ageism when health care workers used what they thought illustrated the language of caring with expressions of "dear" or "sweetie," but the older adults interpreted these words to mean that the health care workers perceived their elderly clients as incompetent and infantile.

Another elderspeak scenario occurs when a store clerk addresses older persons slowly or in a loud voice, assuming that all of them are hard of hearing. In a restaurant, a waiter may ignore an elderly person dining with a younger friend by asking the younger person to order for the elderly customer. What emerges from recent health care and psychological studies is that elderspeak can have consequences for one's health. Levy recently completed a long-term survey of 660 people over the age of 50 in a small Ohio town. She concluded from the results that people who had positive perceptions of aging lived 7.5 years longer (Levy & Banaji, 2002). This represented a bigger increase in longevity than factors associated with exercise and the cessation of smoking. Other studies have concluded that there is an association between older adults who have been exposed to negative portrayals of aging with lowered performance on memory tests, slower walking, and higher levels of stress. These negative portrayals of the elderly can be found in the marketplace and in the media that advertises marketplace products.

How do the marketplace and the media portray elderly people in a negative way?

Americans today are living in an age of botox, face-lifts, and anti-aging creams, all of which reflect a pervasive denial of aging in our society. The multi-billion dollar cosmetics industry plays a significant role not only in creating the illusion of youth, but also in rejecting the reality of aging in human life. Since aging is so often associated with the natural and inevitable process of dying, attempts to look younger become a special point of focus for advertisers. Advertisements promoting the maintenance of a youthful appearance through the use of so-called "anti-aging medicines" imply that aging is a kind of "disease" that can be "cured." Even more insidious is the implication that normal signs of aging—like balding or graying hair, wrinkles, or changes in vision or hearing—are ugly or objectionable (Palmore, 2005).

During Senate testimony on the image of aging in media and advertising, Emmy award-winning actress Doris Roberts challenged the senators to recognize what she felt were the heavy costs of age discrimination for society as a whole:

> I'm in my seventies and at the peak of my career, at the height of my earned income and tax contribution. When my grandchildren say I rock, they're not talking about a rocking chair. Yet society considers me discard-able: my opinions irrelevant, my needs comical and my tastes not worth attention in the marketplace. My peers and I are portrayed as dependent, helpless, unproductive, and demanding rather than deserving. In reality, the majority of seniors are self-sufficient, middle-class consumers with more assets than most young couples and substantial time and effort to offer society. This is not just a sad situation, Mr. Chairman. This is a crime. Age discrimination negates the value of wisdom and experience, robs us of our dignity and denies us the chance to grow and to flourish. (U.S. Senate, 2002, p. 4)

Roberts's criticisms of certain social norms on aging is emphasized in her condemnation of deeply rooted stereotypes portraying the elderly as *old fogeys, old coots, old codgers,* and *geezers.* That this has implications for Hollywood is certainly not lost in her testimony. She notes the pervasive worship of youth culture in Hollywood, resulting in the increased number of young actresses using the services of plastic surgeons, especially for botox injections that have become common for actresses in their twenties to prevent the possible development of wrinkles. One consequence of such concerns about signs of aging is illustrated in a demographic that clearly contradicts generational realities in the larger population. A Screen Actor's Guild employment survey concluded that there "are three times as many roles for women under forty as there are for women forty years old and older" (U.S. Senate, 2002, p. 7). This representation of women is obviously a distortion of the reality that was documented during this U.S. Senate hearing, noting that 42% of all Americans, both male and female, were older than forty. Yet as demeaning as these images, perceptions, and stereotypes are, the economic consequences of ageism for both aging adults and young people can be even more devastating.

What are some economic consequences of ageism for both the elderly and youth?

Although much of the information on ageism provided so far has been focused on older adults, one conclusion arising from the dynamics of ageism is that this form of prejudice and discrimination is harmful for young people as well as the elderly. Generally speaking, people in the United States are living longer. Between 1900 and 2000, life expectancy increased over 30 years, creating a kind of "longevity revolution" for which the United States is not quite prepared (Butler, 2008). At the same time, the gap between the rich and the poor continues to widen. The repercussions of the 2008 economic recession have resulted in an increase in the number of citizens living in poverty to levels surpassing those of recent memory. Just how much ageism will exacerbate the problem for people under conditions of rising unemployment remains to be seen.

In addition, the intersection of poverty with ageism and race reveals important gender issues. Women make up three fourths of the elderly poor, with the highest poverty rates existing among unmarried people. Exacerbated by unequal gender relations in work and family, many women receive an average of $200 less in monthly Social Security benefits compared to men. Racial and ethnic minority women, especially black women, suffer the highest poverty levels in old age. For one third of the ethnic minority population, social security comprises all of their income in old age, compared to 16% of income for white people (Calasanti & Slevin, 2001).

Demographic trends that impact the marketplace work to the disadvantage of elderly women through workplace sex discrimination on the job. Policies and practices based on the ageist assumption that increased age brings a decline in mental capabilities, slower reflexes, and less ambition can have a powerful negative influence, especially when combined with historic gender stereotypes. The traditional role in American culture of women as caregivers comes at a price. The consequences in the workplace resulting from the combination of age and gender means that the economic penalty paid by women for caregiving is much higher than that for men. As a result, a growing number of women cannot afford to retire under the present system (Barnett, 2005). Even as ageism forces aging women to pay a price, it also takes a toll on the economic fortunes of youth as well.

The evidence that the economic impact of ageism in the economy is not restricted solely to the elderly can be explored by anyone who conducts a Google search under the terms "ageism and young people." Although the Age Discrimination Employment Act of 1967 offers protection against job discrimination for people 40 years old and older, there is no similar law for young people. Yet media reports from the United States (*USA Today*, 2003) and Great Britain (*BBC News*, 2004) reflect a growing awareness that young people also suffer from various forms of job discrimination. A survey of 2,600 workers conducted by Mercer Resource Consulting in the United States revealed that only 44% of workers aged 18 to 24 felt they were treated fairly on the job as compared to 64% of the workers in the 45 to 55 age bracket (Lunn, 2005). In Great Britain, many younger workers believed that age discrimination stymied their job progression because of the perception by management that they were too young to take on extra responsibility (*Management Issues*, 2006). An increase in lawsuits filed by younger workers against alleged reverse age discrimination is now part of the legal landscape in both countries.

The deepening worldwide economic recession holds potential for an increase in explicit and implicit ageism, with negative effects for both the young and the elderly, and the workplace is only one aspect of this problem. The problem of ageism should be important to everyone because for those who live long enough, each generation becomes the elderly population for a new generation. Complex problems facing citizens in the twenty-first century include, but are not limited to, health care reform, social security, regulatory reform of the economy, global warming, and the formation of a stronger democratic society. Expectations that we will find appropriate solutions to such problems will probably remain unrealized unless a new and mutually supportive alliance emerges between the young and the elderly. It is possible that an intergenerational union might be able to confront not only the failure of institutions to meet their needs, but also the institutional exploitation that affects all people living in poverty.

How do institutions exploit poor people?

Financial institutions exploit poor families simply by enforcing policies meant to protect them from losses. **Redlining** refers to banks and other lenders identifying a deteriorating portion of a city, and then refusing to lend money for mortgages or business loans in that area. For low-income workers, such areas are most likely to offer the best opportunity to purchase affordable homes, yet when they apply for mortgage loans, their applications may be denied. In such cases, denial is not based on bad credit ratings or lack of skills to maintain and improve property; it results from the age and/or current condition of properties in the redlined area and the average income levels of its residents.

In addition, minority entrepreneurs interested in opening a business in a largely minority neighborhood cannot get the bank loans needed if the area is redlined. Banks insist that it is just good business practice not to invest in declining areas, but refusing to lend money for purchase or improvement of property makes it inevitable that an area will continue to deteriorate. The bank's prediction becomes a self-fulfilling prophecy. The federal government has attempted to stop redlining practices, and some corporations have even offered low-interest loans to promote minority-owned businesses in redlined areas, but they have not been able to overcome the difficulties that banks have created by this practice. Although the reason for redlining is supposedly based on objective economic factors, this practice has had a significant impact on low-income people of color. As Shorris (2001) observed, "Redlining by the bank has taken the economic heart out of Latinos, as it did (for) blacks" (p. 323).

> Nobody talks more of free enterprise and competition and of the best man winning than the man who inherited his father's store or farm.
>
> C. Wright Mills (1916–1962)

Another way financial agencies may discriminate against the poor is by insisting on a minimum balance of $150 or $200 for checking accounts, making it impossible for workers living from paycheck to paycheck to maintain checking accounts. Families are then forced to live on a cash-only basis—and most banks charge a fee for cashing payroll checks unless an individual has an account at the bank. Many workers find it more convenient to take their paychecks to a neighborhood check-cashing store, even though the convenience may cost them as much as 10% of the amount of the check.

Check-cashing stores have proliferated as banks have abandoned central cities, and fewer banks mean less money available for businesses and homeowners. Based on an analysis of twelve cities, Kane (1996) reported that there were approximately equal numbers of banks per 1,000 residents in white and minority (primarily inner city) areas in 1970, but by the 1990s, there were three times as many banks in white areas as in minority areas. A decline in numbers of banks has led to an increase in private financial companies legally permitted to charge interest rates higher than banks; these companies are also allowed to combine several high-interest loans and sell them to a bank for the interest owed. The bank owning the high-interest loans can then collect interest at a rate well above what it would normally be permitted to charge (Kane, 1996). And banks are not the only businesses involved in the exploitation of low-income families and individuals.

How do businesses discriminate against poor people?

According to Feagin and Feagin (1986), retail businesses serving low-income people may charge higher prices for products than stores in suburban areas with similar merchandise. As described next, merchants engage in a variety of practices to exploit the poor:

Blank price tags Blank price tags on merchandise force the customer to ask for the price of an item and allows merchants to quote higher prices to customers they feel may be particularly naïve.

Bait and Switch Although the practice is illegal, stores serving low-income customers may advertise a product at a low price to attract customers, who are then told that the product is of poor quality. Customers are encouraged to buy a similar product of better quality at a higher price.

Rent-To-Own Customers rent a product that they can own by making weekly payments over a specified time. Rent-to-own customers may pay up to four times more for merchandise; only 25% eventually own the rented product. Store owners are exempt from laws limiting interest rates; they insist that they are not charging interest but renting a product. One Virginia store rented a 20-inch Zenith television for $14.99 a week; the renter could own it after 74 payments totaling $1,109.26. Sears sold the same television for $329.99 (Hudson, 1996).

Pawnshops An expensive option for low-income families is to surrender a possession as collateral for a loan. Pawnshops have proliferated in recent years, with interest rates up to 20% a month—240% a year. Even when customers pay the interest and reclaim the property, the loan repayment does not go on their credit record, so the transaction does not improve their credit rating (Minutaglio, 1996).

> Of course I believe in free enterprise, but in my system of free enterprise the democratic principle is that there never was, never has been, never will be, room for the ruthless exploitation of the many for the benefit of the few.
>
> **Harry S. Truman (1884–1972)**

Poor people are exploited in other ways in America, but the preceding examples illustrate that exploitation occurs. One must overcome numerous economic obstacles to escape poverty, and no simple solutions exist. As was demonstrated in the 1930s, federal and state governments must address issues of poverty if any progress is to be made concerning the exploitation of and discrimination against poor people.

> Governments exist to protect the rights of the poor and minorities; the loved and the rich need no protection.
>
> **Wendell Phillips (1811–1884)**

What can federal and state governments do to assist families living in poverty?

Scholars Abelda, Drago, and Shulman (1997), Entwhistle, Alexander, and Olson (2001), Haycock (2001) and social activist organizations such as the Children's Defense Fund (2001) have made suggestions regarding the role government must play in assisting people in poverty or in supporting those struggling to stay out of poverty:

1. Provide services to address critical needs; subsidies for battered women's shelters would provide options for women in abusive situations.
2. Subsidize child care services for low-income women who are enrolled in education or training programs. Because of child care expenses, the best financial option for a single mother working at minimum wage is to quit her job and receive support from social assistance programs.
3. Raise the minimum wage and strive for a living wage. It is difficult to take care of individual needs with the current minimum wage, yet in many families both parents have minimum wage jobs. When the parents' combined salary is barely over $10 an hour, a family will still live in poverty. Jones and George (2003) concluded that for a family earning $10 to $15 an hour, "it is often difficult, if not impossible, for them to meet their families' needs" (p. 123).
4. Restructure public school funding so that taxes to support schools are collected by the state and disbursed to schools according to a variable per pupil funding formula that takes into account factors such as: (a) number of low-income

students in a given school; (b) amount of budget devoted to special learners; (c) mobility rate of students. In 1990, the New Jersey Supreme Court ruled that such plans are economically feasible and morally justified (*Abbott v. Burke*). Only by making a commitment to all children can we hope to nourish their talents and reap the benefits of these children becoming adults who know and use their abilities to the fullest.

5. Provide tax relief for low-income families. Tax relief for wealthy Americans exists as capital gains tax cuts and corporate exemptions from local property taxes for a specified number of years as incentive to locate. If tax relief is good for the wealthy, why not offer it to the poor? Some tax relief exists in the Earned Income Tax Credit (EITC) and child care allowances, although some politicians persist in proposing to eliminate these programs. Another form of tax relief for low-income workers might be to exempt home purchases to allow time to make improvements and save money in preparation for paying the resulting higher taxes assessed because of improvements.
6. Offer tax incentives for corporations to locate in inner cities, and tax incentives for corporations creating day care centers at the worksite if they allow low-income families in the area to place children in the centers. Wilson (1996) suggests that reduction of businesses in inner cities has been a major factor in the increase of drug use and crime, and the general deterioration of those communities.
7. Strengthen educational opportunity by increasing support for Head Start programs, and funding quality preschools and summer school programs for low-income children, especially during summers just before and after first grade, so children can experience similar educational gains as middle- and upper-income children during the summer. For middle school and secondary school low-income students, high expectations reflected in clearly articulated standards must be accompanied by a challenging curriculum. Teacher salaries could be subsidized to ensure higher salaries for experienced, quality teachers willing to be assigned to schools in low-income areas.
8. Increase the opportunity for affordable housing. Almost 5 million families use over half their income to pay rent, often for substandard housing. The federal government could add 300,000 more housing vouchers each year for the next ten years. In addition, the Low-Income Home Energy Assistance Program could be expanded so low-income families can meet rising energy costs.
9. Maintain reasonable regulation of the private sector concerning job discrimination, possibly with affirmative action policies focused on socioeconomic status. State and federal governments could review policies pertaining to multinational corporations that relocate outside the United States. Although inevitable in a global economy, there could be incentives to keep those corporate jobs in the United States and disincentives for locating elsewhere. At the present time, American corporations have more incentives to locate overseas than to remain in this country.

AFTERWORD

Oppression is an inevitable consequence when power and resources are concentrated in one group. During the 1930s, U.S. Supreme Court justice Louis Brandeis expressed his concern for the future of democracy in America by proposing that the United States could continue to be a democracy or it could continue to allow great wealth to be accumulated by a few people, but that it was not possible to accomplish both. Equity and justice depend on transferring resources and power to oppressed groups. People suffer the misery of poverty not because

> Until the great mass of the people shall be filled with the sense of responsibility for each other's welfare, social justice can never be attained.
>
> **Helen Keller (1880–1968)**

they deserve it, but most likely as a consequence of birth.

If needs of adults living in poverty are neglected, we will perpetuate a despair that often produces drug abuse, crime, and violence. In America today, one of every five babies is born into poverty. If the needs of children living in poverty are neglected, we will be guilty of abandoning American ideals and betraying the decency and compassion Americans have long associated with those ideals. If Americans reject our social conscience, we make achievement of social justice impossible. When we look at faces of poor children, we are not only confronted with a moral dilemma in the present, but with a question about what kind of society America will be in the years to come.

myeducationlab

Now go to Topic #6: **Class** in the MyEducationLab (www.myeducationlab.com) for your course, where you can:

- Find learning outcomes for this topic along with the national standards that connect to these outcomes.
- Complete Assignments and Activities that can help you more deeply understand the chapter content by viewing classroom video and ABC News footage.
- Apply and practice your understanding of the core teaching skills identified in the chapter with the Building Teaching Skills and Dispositions learning units.

TERMS AND DEFINITIONS

Ageism An alteration in feeling, belief, or behavior in response to an individual's or group's perceived age (Levy & Banaji).

Bait and switch An illegal strategy whereby a merchant advertises a cheap product and when the customer comes in to purchase it, he or she is persuaded to buy a more expensive product

Classism An attitude, action, or institutional structure that subordinates or limits a person on the basis of his or her low socioeconomic status

Cultural classism The societal promotion of negative beliefs and practices that tend to portray poor, less educated, or socially unacceptable persons as deficient, inferior, and responsible for their own situation; the assumption of superiority by people or groups based on wealth, employment, education, or social standing

Individual classism Prejudiced attitudes and behavior against others based on the perception of level of income, education, or status as inferior, demonstrated whenever someone responds by saying or doing something degrading or harmful about persons whose income, education, or social standing is looked on as unacceptable

Institutional classism Established laws, customs, and practices in a society that allow systematic discrimination against low-income individuals or groups to the benefit of middle- or upper-class individuals or groups

Middle class A socioeconomic status determined partly by income and primarily by a cluster of attitudes, beliefs, and practices of someone not too poor to be considered dependent on others but not living in an ostentatious manner associated with being wealthy

Pawnshops Businesses that receive individual possessions as collateral for loans

Poverty levels Income levels established by the federal government based on earnings and the number of individuals in a family

Redlining The practice of banks and other lenders of designating certain areas, especially inner-city neighborhoods (ghettoes or barrios), as "deteriorating," which means they are viewed as bad risks for mortgage loans

Rent-to-own Businesses that offer merchandise on a rental basis to customers who cannot afford the purchase price of that merchandise, stipulating that at the end of the rental period the merchandise will become the property of the renter

DISCUSSION EXERCISES

Exercise #1 Broadening the Wealth in America: Can We Avoid Economic Domination by the Wealthy?

The Plan: Ideas for a more equitable distribution of economic resources in the United States have been implemented including pension plans, profit sharing, the GI bill, FHA loans, and social security. Proponents argue that the money for the plan below could be raised by increasing income tax on the wealthiest 40% of Americans (those making $80,000 or more) by 2%.

Directions: Review the plan. Does it seem to be a reasonable way to obtain funding to fulfill its objective? What special considerations might need to be made in its implementation?

A Plan to Broaden the Wealth in America

Every American would have a "wealth account" of $80,000 established for him or her at birth. A person could have access to this account when he or she turned twenty-one, but *only* upon graduation from high school. For the rest of his or her life, a person could use this account to achieve desired goals, but anything taken from the account must be paid back. As an example of how the account could be used: eighteen-year-olds attending college would be permitted to access the account early to pay for college expenses (including the high school graduate trying to escape a violent and drug-ridden neighborhood); workers who are laid off from their job could live off the interest until they found a new job or they could pay for further training for a related or different occupation; a young couple who just had their first child and wanted to buy a house could use the money for a down payment; a truck driver could use the money to begin his or her own trucking company. Any of the interest or principal used from this "wealth account" would eventually be repaid so that when an individual died, the money plus interest from the wealth account would be reclaimed by the government and used to finance an account for another person. If an account did not have the full amount it should have, the government would get to make the first claims on whatever assets the dead person left behind in order to get the full amount repaid. (Adapted from Ackerman, B.A., & Alstott, A. (n.d.). $80,000 and a dream. *The American Prospect Online*. Retrieved December 22, 2003, from http://www.prospect.org/print/V11/16/ackerman-b.html)

Exercise #2 Economics American Style: Income, Wealth, and Poverty in the United States

Directions: Each of the questions below is followed by data regarding current American societal policy or practice. Develop your own comments or questions supporting and/or refuting those data, the legitimacy of the practice, and your feelings about the underlying concept.

1. Is work for pay balanced in the United States? In 1965, CEOs in major companies made 24 times more than the average worker. In 1980, CEOs made 40 times more than the average worker. In 2007, the average Fortune 500 Company CEOs earned 364 times an average worker's pay and over 70 times the pay of a four-star Army general.

   Source: Executive Excess 2007, p. 7, jointly published by Institute for Policy Studies and United for Fair Economy, August 29, 2007. 1965 data from: State of Working America 2004-2005, Economic Policy Institute.

2. How do Americans pay for their housing? Nationally, in order to rent a two-bedroom apartment, one full-time worker in 2008 must earn $17.32 per hour. In fact, 81% of renters live in cities where the Fair Market Rent for a two-bedroom rental is not even affordable with two minimum wage jobs.

   Source: Out of Reach: 2007–2008, National Low-Income Housing Coalition, April 7, 2008

3. What does it mean to be wealthy in the United States? According to the *Wall Street Journal*, the richest 1% of Americans earn 22% of the nation's adjusted gross income.

   Source: Jesse Drucker, "Richest Americans See Their Income Share Grow," *Wall Street Journal*, p. A3, July 23, 2008.

4. Does America have a homeless problem? On any recent given day, approximately 754,000 individuals are homeless, of which approximately 338,000 live on the streets, in cars, or in abandoned buildings. It is estimated that 415,000 homeless take refuge in shelters on any given night. The population of the city of San Francisco is about 739,000. HUD reports nearly one in four people in homeless shelters are children age 17 or younger.

   Source: U.S. Department of Housing and Urban Development (HUD), Annual Homeless Report to Congress: 2007, pp. iii, iv, and 23.

5. Are any U.S. veterans homeless? Figures suggest that over 100,000 veterans are homeless on any given night—about 18% of the U.S. adult homeless population—approximately the same number as the population of Green Bay, Wisconsin.

   Source: U.S. Department of Housing and Urban Development (HUD), 2007 Annual Homeless Report to Congress, p. 32.

6. How successful is our immigration program? At least 1,268 people have died along the border of Arizona and Mexico since 2004. The United States Border Patrol reported that along the entire U.S.–Mexico border more than 400 people died in fiscal 2006–2007, 453 died in 2004–2005, and 494 in 2004–2005. Over the 28-year history of the Berlin Wall, 287 people perished attempting to cross.

   Source: Associated Press, November 8, 2007.

7. Is the United States's penal system a success? The United States is said to jail 751 inmates per 100,000 people, the highest rate in the world. Russia is second with 627 per 100,000. England's rate is 151, Germany's is 88, and Japan's is 63. The United States has 2.3 million people behind bars, more than any country in the world.

   Source: Adam Liptak, "Inmate Count in US Dwarfs Other Nations." *New York Times*, April 23, 2008.

8. Should food grains be used to produce fuel? The grain needed to make enough ethanol to fill up a SUV tank could feed a hungry person for a year.

   Source: Lester Brown, CNN.Money.com, August 16, 2006.

Source: Bill Quigley. Human rights lawyer and law professor at Loyola University New Orleans quigley77@gmail.com

REFERENCES

Abelda, R., Drago, R., & Shulman, S. (2004). *Unlevel playing fields.* New York, NY: McGraw-Hill.

Describes the disadvantages faced by the poor in the game of economic survival in our society, and what could be done for the poor to make the competition more equal.

Allen, J.T. (2004). Who lobbies for the cheaters? *U.S. News & World Report, 136*(14), 42.

Describes successful tax evasion strategies of American corporations.

Allison, L., & Lewis, C. (2001). *The cheating of America: How tax avoidance and evasion by the super rich are costing the country billions and what you can do about it.* New York, NY: Morrow.

Describes how wealthy Americans avoid paying taxes by employing simple solutions such as utilizing cash transactions to complicated financial transactions that permit accounting experts to use legal tax loopholes.

American Federation of Labor. (2009). 2008 Trends in CEO Pay. *Executive Paywatch.* Retrieved June 5, 2009, from http://www.aflcio.org/corporatewatch

Provides data and descriptions of current trends in CEO compensation.

Anyon, J. (2001). Inner cities, affluent suburbs, and unequal educational opportunity. In J.A. Banks & C.M. Banks (Eds.), *Multicultural education: Issues & perspectives* (4th ed., pp. 85–102). New York, NY: John Wiley.

Compares the education offered by inner-city schools and suburban schools and describes the academic advantages of students in suburban schools.

Barnett, R. (2005, Fall). Ageism and sexism in the workplace. *Generations 29:* 25–30.

Provides demographic evidence to demonstrate the price that working women pay as a result of sexist attitudes and ageist thinking, penalizing women more as they grow older.

BBC News. (2004, September 19). Work ageism affecting the young. Accessed January 3, 2009, from http://www.news.bbc.co.uk/1/hi/business/3668320.htm

Explores an aspect of ageism in society often overlooked and largely unaddressed.

Berliner, D.C. (2005, August). Our impoverished view of educational reform. *TCRecord.* Retrieved January 2, 2006, from http://www.tcrecord.org

Discusses strategies to improve schools that go beyond school reform to take account of poverty issues that affect student learning.

Bonilla-Silva, E. (2001). *White supremacy and racism in the post–civil rights era.* Boulder, CO: Lynne Rienner.

Examines why blacks and other racial minorities remain behind whites financially, and in terms of occupation, health, educational attainment and other social indicators; the definition of *middle class* is given in the second footnote on page 14.

Bray, R. (2000). So how did I get here? In M. Adams, W.J. Blumenfeld, R. Castaneda, H.W. Hackman, M.L. Peters, & X. Zuniga (Eds.), *Readings for diversity and social justice* (pp. 425–429). New York, NY: Routledge.

Describes personal experiences with poverty and current realities of living in poverty.

Brinkley, D. (2006). *The great deluge: Hurricane Katrina, New Orleans and the Mississippi Gulf Coast.* New York, NY: Morrow.

Describes the lack of preparation for the hurricane, the destruction it caused throughout the affected area, and includes the stories of survivors during and after the storm.

Brooks-Gunn, J., Klebanov, P., & Duncan, G. (1996). Ethnic differences in children's intelligence test scores: Role of economic deprivation, home environment and maternal characteristics. *Child Development, 67,* 396–408.

Reports on the influence of poverty and home environment on the difference in IQ scores between black and white children and how that difference could be dramatically reduced.

Butler, R. (2008). *The longevity revolution: The benefits and challenges of living a long life.* New York, NY: Public Affairs.

Challenges readers to rethink their assumptions about the place of the elderly in society as well as positive developments in living a longer life.

Calasanti, T., & Slevin, K. (2001). *Gender, social inequalities, and aging.* New York, NY: Altamira Press, pp. 108–115.

Analyzes the role of gender in ageism and concludes that gender is at the heart of some of the most pernicious examples of ageism in U.S. society.

Callahan, D. (2007, May). False choices on poverty. *The American Prospect, 18*(5), A12–A13.

Explains why a combination of individual responsibility and government assistance is required to address poverty issues effectively.

Children's Defense Fund. (2008). *Annual Report 2007.* Retrieved May 9, 2009, from http://www.childrendefensefund.org

Provides data on children living in poverty in the United States and the programs that this organization has sponsored to address their needs.

Children's Defense Fund. (2001). *A Children's Defense Fund report: The state of America's children.* Boston, MA: Beacon.

Examines statistics from federal and state sources to identify issues affecting children and families living in poverty and makes recommendations to address these problems.

Collins, C. (2003). Tax wealth to broaden wealth. *American Prospect, 14*(5), A6–A7.

Explains how taxing the wealthy creates a more just tax system and a more stable society.

DiAngelo, R.J. (2006). My class didn't trump my race: Using oppression to face privilege. *Multicultural Perspectives, 8*(1), 51–56.

Describes how poverty was oppressive during the author's youth and yet how being white also protected her from oppression.

Dollars & Sense. (2004). Wealth inequality by the numbers. In *The Wealth Inequality Reader* (pp. 6–21). Cambridge, MA: Dollars & Sense—Economic Affairs Bureau.

Provides data, charts, and graphs to explain wealth inequality in the United States.

Edelman, M.W. (2001). Introduction. *A Children's Defense Fund report: The state of America's children.* Boston, MA: Beacon.

Focuses on data with regard to children in poverty today and explains why it is urgent for the United States to take immediate action to address their problems.

Entwhistle, D., Alexander, K., & Olson, L.S. (2001, Fall). Keep the faucet flowing: Summer learning and home environment. *American Educator, 47,* 10–15, 47.

Describes why low-income children have a greater learning loss during summer than middle- or upper-class children, and what steps could be taken to minimize that loss.

Feagin, J., & Feagin, C.B. (1986). *Discrimination American style* (2nd ed.). Malabar, FL: Robert E. Krieger.

Describes discrimination theories and practices with specific examples from research.

Forbes. (2009). *The Forbes 400.* Retrieved May 10, 2009, from http://www.forbes.com

Identifies the richest Americans and provides some data on their wealth. The list is updated each year and is available from this website.

Greenberg, M. (2007, May). Making poverty history. *The American Prospect, 18*(5), A3–A4.

Discusses the renewed political interest in the United States to address poverty issues and the barriers that must be overcome in order for the United States to deal with these issues effectively.

Haycock, K. (2001). Closing the achievement gap. *Educational Leadership, 58*(6), 6–11.

Compares data on the achievement of low-income students with middle- and upper-class students, and minority students with white students.

Haskins, R., & Sawhill, I. (2007, May). Using carrots and sticks. *The American Prospect, 18*(5), A13–A15.

Explains that poverty in the United States was reduced in the 1990s not because of welfare reforms but because of the economic boom and discusses what needs to be done now.

Heintz, J.S., & Folbre, N. (2000). Who owns how much? In M. Adams, W.J. Blumenfeld, R. Castaneda, H.W. Hackman, M.L. Peters, & X. Zuniga (Eds.), *Readings for diversity and social justice* (pp. 391–396). New York, NY: Routledge.

Describes the distribution of wealth in the United States with data on race and gender.

Herrnstein, R.J., & Murray, C. (1994). *The bell curve: Intelligence and class structure in American life.* New York, NY: The Free Press.

Analyzes research to argue that differences in intelligence stem from race/ethnicity and are genetically determined, and economic success or failure is determined by intelligence.

Hout, M., & Lucas, S.R. (2007). Narrowing the income gap between rich and poor. In P. Rothenberg (Ed.), *Race, class and gender in the United States: An integrated study* (7th ed.). New York, NY: Worth.

Reviews the gap between rich and poor and describes how *The Bell Curve* misled the public by claiming the gap is a result of inequality of ability.

Hudson, M. (1996). Rent to own: The slick cousin of paying on time. In M. Hudson (Ed.), *Merchants of misery: How corporate America profits from poverty* (pp. 146–152). Monroe, ME: Common Courage Press.

Explains how rent-to-own stores exploit low-income consumers.

Isaacs, J.B., & Lyon, M.R. (2000). *A cross-state examination of families leaving welfare: Finding from the ASPE-funded leavers studies.* Presented at the National Association for Welfare Research and Statistics Workshop, August, Scottsdale, AZ. Available at http://www.dhhs.gov

Describes preliminary outcomes for families in eleven states leaving welfare based on reports from studies funded by the Department of Health and Human Services.

Johnson, H.W. (1998). Public welfare and income maintenance. In *The social services: An introduction* (5th ed.). Itasca, IL: F. E. Peacock.

Discusses the nature and causes of poverty in the United States and examines several federal programs implemented to reduce poverty.

Johnson, R. (2007, December). From one generation to the next. *The American Prospect, 18*(12), A15–A16.

Examines how poverty affects children, especially children's poor health at birth, and explains how improving health care for children living in poverty would benefit society.

Jones, G.R., & George, J.M. (2008). Managing diverse employees in a diverse environment. *Contemporary management* (5th ed.). Boston, MA: McGraw-Hill.

Describes increasing diversity among consumers and in the work force and provides strategies for managers to work effectively with diverse employees.

Kaiser Family Foundation. (2007). Poverty rates by age, states (2006–2007), U.S. (2007). Accessed January 2, 2009, http://www.statehealthfacts.org/comparebar.jsp?ind=10&cat=1

Provides statistics on the extent of poverty for children and the elderly.

Kane, M. (1996). Fringe banks. In M. Hudson (Ed.), *Merchants of misery: How corporate America profits from poverty* (pp. 52–57). Monroe, ME: Common Courage Press.

Describes the decline of banks and the increase in check-cashing stores in poverty areas.

Karp, S. (2006). Band-Aids or bulldozers: What's next for NCLB? *Rethinking Schools, 20*(3), 10–13.

Discusses current outcomes of NCLB and why it has failed to achieve its goals.

Katz, M.B. (1986). *In the shadow of the poorhouse: A social history of welfare in America.* New York, NY: Basic Books.

Describes poverty programs in colonial America, why the poorhouse failed, and how social policies responded to the historic shifts in America's social and economic structure.

Kirp, D.L. (2007, December). Nature, nurture, and destiny. *The American Prospect 18*(12), A19–A21.

Discusses cross-cultural studies on the relationship of heredity to intelligence compared to environmental influences on intelligence.

Kivel, P. (2002). *Uprooting racism: How white people can work for racial justice* (rev. ed.). Gabriola Island, British Columbia: New Society Publishers.

Examines the dynamics of racism and white privilege in society and offers strategies to work for social justice.

Komisar, L. (1977). *Down and out in the USA: A history of public welfare* (rev. ed.). New York, NY: New Viewpoints.

Presents the history of American welfare including European antecedents, forms of relief established in the colonial period, and issues and actions taken up to the present.

Kozol, J. (2005). *The shame of the nation: The restoration of apartheid schooling in America.* New York, NY: Crown.

Examines evidence of segregation in American schools based on race and social class and discusses the moral and societal implications of maintaining this segregation.

Lee, J. (2006). *Tracking achievement gaps and assessing the impact of NCLB on the gaps: An in-depth look into national and state reading and math outcomes.* Cambridge, MA: The Civil Rights Project at Harvard University.

Compares scores on national and state assessments and concludes that high stakes testing and sanctions are not working.

Leland, J. (2008, October 7). "'Sweetie' and 'dear' a hurt beyond insult for the elderly." *New York Times,* pp. 1, 12.

Examines the harm caused by infantilizing terms and other language used to address the elderly in health care settings.

Levy, B., & Bahaji, M. (2002). Implicit ageism. In T. Nelson (Ed.), *Ageism.* London, England: MIT Press.

Discusses the unique nature of ageism as a form of prejudice and explains how ageism differs from sexism and racism.

Lunn, E. (2005, January 11). Ageism affects young and old. *Hindu Times,* p. 1.

Describes how ageism across generations has negative consequences for all of society.

Management Issues. (2006, August 10). Younger workers more at risk of age discrimination, p. 4.

Provides accounts of reverse age discrimination in the workplaces of Great Britain based on perceptions of how much responsibility young people can handle.

Mathis, W.J. (2003). No Child Left Behind: Costs and benefits. *Kappan.* Retrieved June 9, 2009, from http://www.pdkintl.org/kappan/k0305mat.htm, *Phi Delta Kappa International.*

Analyzes costs to explain how much federal financial support is required for schools to have a realistic chance of achieving the goals identified in the No Child Left Behind Act.

Mead, L. (2000). The twilight of liberal welfare reform. *Public Interest, 139,* 22–35.

Describes an experimental welfare program in Milwaukee called the New Hope Project and compares its effectiveness with the Wisconsin Works (W-2) welfare reform.

Minutaglio, B. (1996). Prince of pawns. In M. Hudson (Ed.), *Merchants of misery: How corporate America profits from poverty* (pp. 58–70). Monroe, ME: Common Courage.

Describes one highly successful pawnshop owner to discuss the growth of pawnshops and how they operate as an underground economy exploiting the financial needs of the poor.

Owen, D., & Doerr, M. (1999). *None of the above: The truth behind the SATs* (rev. ed.). Lanham, MD: Rowman Littlefield.

Describes the origin of standardized tests in America and biases in the current SAT tests.

Palmore, E. (2005). Anti-aging medicine. In E. Palmore, L. Branch, & D. Harris (Eds.), *Encyclopedia of ageism.* New York, NY: Haworth Pastoral Press, pp. 36–37.

Examines the role of advertising in selling illusions about extending youth and the avoidance of aging in the marketplace.

Phillips, K. (1990). Wealth and favoritism. In *The politics of rich and poor: Wealth and the American electorate in the Reagan aftermath.* New York, NY: Random House.

Describes how wealthy Americans exploited federal policies during the Reagan era.

Phillips, K. (2003). How wealth defines power. *American Prospect, 14*(5), A8–A9.

Compares the concentration of wealth since 1980 with that of the late 1800s and 1920s.

Pipher, M. (2002). *The middle of everywhere: The world's refugees come to our town.* New York, NY: Harcourt.

Describes the nature of recent immigration to America using some statistical data, but primarily based on interviews with immigrants.

Rifkin, J. (2004). *The European dream: How Europe's vision of the future is quietly eclipsing the American dream.* New York, NY: Jeremy P. Tarcher/Penguin.

Compares values, attitudes, and achievements of the United States and the European Union as the two major world powers and speculates on their future progress.

Rodgers, H. Jr. (2006). *American poverty in a new era of reform.* Armonk, NY: M.E. Sharpe.

Describes poverty in America, provides a history of the welfare system, and gives an analysis of the recent welfare reforms.

Sandefur, G.D., & Cook, S. (1998). Permanent exits from public assistance: The impact of duration, family and work. *Social Forces, 77*(2), 763–789.

Analysis of data to ascertain the length of time a woman receives welfare and the effect of marital status and work qualifications on the time an individual stays on welfare.

Schorr, A.L. (2001). *Welfare reform: Failure and remedies.* Westport, CT: Praeger.

Examines the successes and failures of previous efforts to reform welfare and the social forces that resulted in the 1996 welfare reform legislation.

Schwartz-Nobel, L. (2002). *Growing up empty: The hunger epidemic in America.* New York, NY: HarperCollins.

Discusses data and presents personal experiences with poverty and hunger in the United States.

Schwarz, J. (2000). *Fighting poverty with virtue: Moral reform and America's urban poor, 1825–2000.* Bloomington: Indiana University Press.

Examines the work of moral reformers with regard to poverty issues in the late 1800s and early 1900s and the implications for dealing with current poverty issues.

Scott, J., & Leonhardt, D. (2005). Shadowy lines that still divide. *Class Matters.* New York, NY: Times Books.

Analyzes data to examine the nature and extent of social mobility in America today and notes the absence of a "level playing field" due to advantages related to social class.

Sheehan, M. (2004). Tax breaks for the rich—or public programs for everyone? In Dollars & Sense (Ed.), *The Wealth Inequality Reader* (pp. 40–41). Cambridge, MA: Dollars & Sense—Economic Affairs Bureau.

Discusses the money lost from tax cuts for the richest Americans in terms of what public needs these tax dollars could have funded.

Shorris, E. (2001). *Latinos: A biography of the people.* New York, NY: W.W. Norton.

Provides a personal narrative of the diverse Latino groups in the United States.

Sklar, H. (2005, September). Growing gulf between rich and rest of America. *Raise the Floor.* Retrieved June 1, 2009, from http://www.ms.foundation.org

Examines the growing disparity of wealth in the United States and economic issues facing poor and middle-class families.

Sklar, H. (1998). CEO greed is out of control. *Z Magazine.* Retrieved June 10, 2009, from http://www.thirdworldtraveler.com

Describes the growing gap between average salaries of CEOs and workers, with specific examples of CEOs whose salaries increased while they released workers.

Spriggs, W. E. (2007, May). The changing face of poverty in America. *The American Prospect, 18*(5), A5–A7.

Examines the impact of policies and programs on the lives of people living in poverty.

Stein, Z., & Susser, M. (1970). Mutability of intelligence and epidemiology of mild mental retardation. *Review of Educational Research, 40,* 29–68.

Reviews research, including cross-cultural studies, and concludes that environmental conditions have a significant impact on student achievement. [*Note:* For a current perspective, refer to Desimone, L. (1999). Linking parent involvement with student achievement: Do race and income matter? *Journal of Educational Research, 93*(1), 1–31.]

Taylor, H. (2000, May 3). The public tends to blame the poor, the unemployed, and those on welfare for their problems. *Harris Poll #24.* Retrieved May 1, 2009, from http://www.harrisinteractive.com/harris_poll/index.asp?PID=87

Presents results of a Harris Poll on American attitudes concerning people living in poverty who are unemployed or on welfare.

USA Today. (2003, October 7). Young workers say their age holds them back, p. 3.

Reports on growing complaints among younger workers who resent the loss of promotions on the job because of their age and perceived inexperience.

U.S. Bureau of Labor Statistics. (2008). *Highlights of women's earnings in 2007.* Retrieved June 12, 2009, from http://www.bls.gov

Provides information and tables concerning women's and men's salaries in 2004.

U.S. Census Bureau. (2009). *Poverty thresholds/2008.* Retrieved June 13, 2009, from http://www.census.gov

Provides income levels defining poverty for families of various sizes.

U.S. Department of Health and Human Services. (2004, November). *6th annual report to Congress.* Office of Family Assistance. Retrieved May 15, 2009, from http://acf.hhs.gov/programs/ofa/data-reports/

Provides data on recipient of Temporary Assistance for Needy Families (TANF).

U.S. Senate. (2002, September 4). The image of aging in media and marketing. Hearing before the Special Committee on Aging. Statement of Doris Roberts.

Includes the social critique of an award-winning actress against Hollywood's promotion of youth culture and how implicit ageism severely impacts women in the entertainment industry.

Weaver, R.K. (2000). *Ending welfare as we know it.* Washington, DC: Brookings Institution Press.

Describes the former welfare system and the arguments for the need to change it and analyzes the most recent welfare reform.

Wilson, W.J. (1996). *When work disappears: The world of the new urban poor.* New York, NY: Knopf.

Examines causes of inner-city unemployment and makes recommendations to address the problem.

Wolfe, A. (1998). *One nation, after all: What middle-class Americans really think about God, country, family, racism, welfare, immigration, homosexuality, work, the right, the left, and each other.* New York, NY: Viking Penguin.

A team of researchers interviewed and gathered information from middle-class families living in suburban areas across the United States.

Zinn, H. (1999). *A people's history of the United States.* New York, NY: HarperCollins.

Provides a detailed account of the history of union organization and employer resistance beginning with Chapter 10, "The Other Civil War."

Zuckerman, M.B. (2004a). America's high anxiety. *U.S. News & World Report, 130*(9), 84.

Discusses how economic trends are affecting middle-class American families.

Zuckerman, M.B. (2004b). An intolerable free ride. *U.S. News & World Report, 136*(17), 80.

Describes how corporations avoid paying taxes and the cost to American taxpayers.

CHAPTER 12

Ableism: Disability Does Not Mean Inability

> "All governments treat disabled people badly. They all see us as a burden. All governments, whether capitalist or socialist, have separated us from the rest of society. . . . Until we are businessmen, politicians, community leaders, people at all levels of society, we will be marginalized and segregated."
>
> **Joshua Malinga (Contemporary)**

In 1993, members of the United Nations declared people with disabilities an oppressed minority group. Writers of the UN Human Rights and Disabled Persons Report documented that around the world, people with disabilities were being treated as outcasts and that the situation was getting worse as their numbers increased. The 1995 representatives at the World Summit on Social Development in Copenhagen described disabled people as "one of the world's largest minority groups facing poverty and unemployment as well as social and cultural isolation" (Ervelles, 2001, p. 93). Despite the statements of these global organizations, the concept of *ableism* (sometimes erroneously called *handicapism*) has yet to be accepted by many people in the United States and around the world.

Ableism has been defined by Linton (1998) as the negative determination of an individual's abilities based on his or her disabilities. Ableism promotes the belief that people with disabilities are inferior to able-bodied persons in order to justify discrimination against them. Linton's definition asserts that the dominant group oppresses people with disabilities, as do other minority groups. Many people, including some people with disabilities, reject that assumption. Hahn (1988) observed,

> Unlike other minorities . . . disabled men and women have not yet been able to refute the implicit and direct accusations of biological inferiority that have often been invoked to rationalize the oppression of groups whose appearance differs from the standards of the dominant majority. (p. 26)

Why should people with disabilities be considered a minority group?

In 1973, the passage of the Rehabilitation Act was perhaps the first public acknowledgment that people with disabilities could be considered a minority group in need of civil rights protections. Section 504 of that act prohibited discrimination against people with a disability who had appropriate qualifications for jobs in federally funded programs (Longmore, 2003). In 1990, Congress acknowledged discrimination against disabled people by passing the Americans with Disabilities Act (ADA) to provide a legal recourse against discrimination. (See Figure 12.1.) Hahn (1994) argued that in a democratic society, policies and practices reflected people's attitudes, and that American social attitudes were a major

FIGURE 12.1

Like other minority groups, people with disabilities and their advocates have had to protest and demonstrate to draw attention to the discrimination against them.

Source: Courtesy of Richard B. Levine

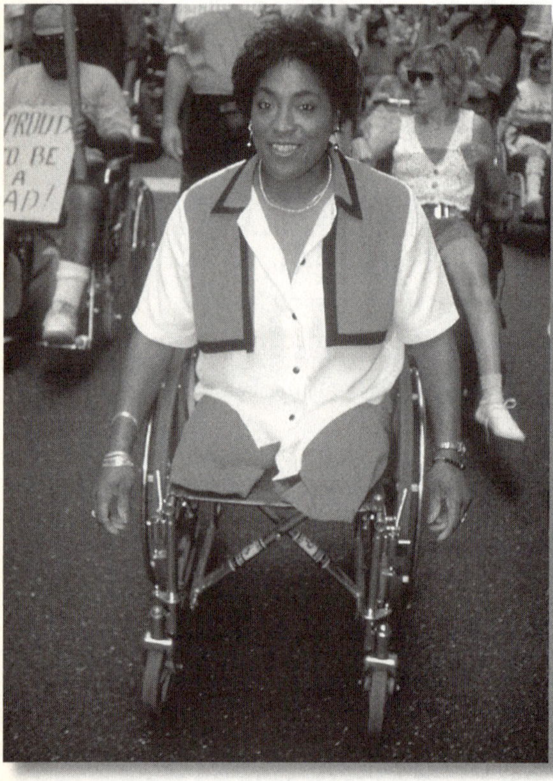

source of problems for people with disabilities. Nevertheless, some people still question the appropriateness of viewing persons with disabilities as a minority group.

The Fall 2001 issue of the *Journal of Disability Policy Studies* addressed the question of whether people with disabilities could be regarded as an oppressed minority. Although the contributors agreed that disabled people were oppressed, guest editor Andrew Batavia strongly disagreed. Although acknowledging problems in the past, Batavia argued that people with disabilities in the United States live in conditions "dramatically better" than those in other countries. Reacting to the high rate of unemployment for disabled people in the United States, Batavia said employers had the right to hire the most qualified person for a job regardless of disability, implying that disabled applicants were often not the most qualified.

Because of the efforts of disability rights advocates and with the passage of the Americans with Disabilities Act (ADA) in 1990, Batavia argued that people with disabilities no longer experience the regrettable discrimination that occurred in the past and therefore do not qualify as an "oppressed minority." Apparently Batavia had not reviewed recent statistics: A survey of people with disabilities reported that the percentage of unemployed adults had increased since the ADA became law, as had the percentage of people living in poverty (Wilson & Lewicki-Wilson, 2001). Batavia's denial rationalization that discrimination no longer affects people with disabilities today is unusual because such arguments are more likely to be expressed by a nondisabled person than someone like Batavia who has a disability.

Another argument denies that people with disabilities are oppressed because having a disability makes one part of the majority. According to the rationale of this argument, having a disability places a person on a continuum where mild physical disabilities, such as poor eyesight, can be corrected by wearing glasses, whereas a more severe physical disability may require someone to use a wheelchair. The logic continues that whether minimal or severe, almost all of us are disabled in one way or another and must learn to live with the condition. In response, Gill (1994) argues that to be a *person with a disability* means the disability has a significant impact on daily life: For example, the disability influences an individual's sense of identity, or others' perceptions of the disability have a significant influence on their reactions to the person, including the likelihood of negative attitudes of rejection or even discrimination. Our reactions reflect a similar rejection of or discrimination toward people from other minority groups.

Putnam (2005) argues that identifying people with a disability as a minority group is consistent with other acceptable models for disability because it defines the problems associated with disabilities as stemming from an inappropriate "fit" between the environment and the persons with disabilities and not emanating from the disabled individual. Having a disability would not present a problem "if a particular environment offered all of the resources a particular individual required to perform a task or activity" (p. 189). Putnam also cites research concluding that persons with disabilities share certain characteristics with other minority groups: "stigma, social distance, nonacceptance, negative stereotypes, prejudice, and discrimination" (p. 189).

Disability rights advocates argue that the concept of people with disabilities being an oppressed group would be more readily accepted if disability studies were included in secondary and higher education courses that examine women's issues, racial and ethnic problems, and negative social, cultural, and institutional experiences of other minority groups. Understanding experiences of people with disabilities requires recognition of dominant group privileges and power not shared. Linton (1998) suggests that such recognition could parallel that afforded other minority groups in viewing the dominant nondisabled group as "not the neutral, universal position from which disabled people deviate, rather, it is a category of people whose power and cultural capital keep them at the center" (p. 32).

> The disability rights approach views disability as a natural phenomenon which occurs in every generation, and always will. It recognizes people with disabilities as a distinct minority group, subject at times to discrimination and segregation . . . but also capable of taking our rightful place in society.
>
> **Laura Hershey (1962–)**

Cultural Ableism

Negative attitudes toward people with disabilities are not recent phenomena. Whether perceived as wicked, violent, or merely foolish, people with physical, emotional, or mental disabilities have been identified consistently as **deviant** because they were not *normal*, leading to negative and sometimes hostile behaviors. In the early 1900s, the U.S. Public Health Service categorized people with retardation as "defectives" along with criminals and delinquents, later labeling them "mental defectives" to distinguish them from the prostitutes, pimps, pickpockets, and paupers. But all such human beings were frequently placed together in institutions because they were nevertheless deviants, different from the norm, requiring their removal from communities. The historical record reveals a pattern of **cultural ableism,** images and beliefs perpetuated in society that promote the perception of people with disabilities as deviant or incompetent.

What are the historical perceptions of people with disabilities?

Understanding how societies have regarded people with various kinds of disabilities can explain not only negative individual attitudes, but also why different societies institutionalized people with disabilities. Wolfensberger (1970) explained some of the major historical perceptions of people with disabilities in the following categories.

A Subhuman Organism Although other groups (such as African Americans, Native Americans, and Jews) historically have been regarded as subhuman, the perception is still associated with people with disabilities, especially those labeled "mentally retarded" who have been occasionally referred to as "vegetables," alluding to medical terminology for performance of vital functions (heart rate, blood pressure) as vegetative functions. Logical thinking and other higher brain activity were assumed impossible for retarded persons. As late as the nineteenth century, "mental defectives" were housed in rooms not heated in winter nor cooled in summer because it was assumed that they were not sensitive to heat or cold like "normal" people. Even in the last half of the twentieth century, caregivers for institutionalized people with mental disabilities have been known to use cattle prods for control. Once we dehumanize a group to subhuman status, there are few limitations to what can be done. Another example of the subhuman perception was articulated in a 1960s *Atlantic Monthly* article suggesting that organs should be harvested from severely and profoundly retarded people, referred to by the author as "human vegetables," and donated to those on organ waiting lists to "increase the intellectual betterment of mankind" (Wolfensberger, 1970, p. 17).

Menace to Society This perception regards people with disabilities as evil. It is fostered in children's literature with villains such as Captain Hook, Long John Silver, and in fairy tales by an array of wicked goblins, giants, and other weird, frightening characters who are ultimately subjugated or eliminated (Fiedler, 1993). Winzer (1997) described how adult literature continues the pattern, portraying disabled people as criminal, homicidal, or maladjusted monsters who are often sexual deviants as well. Charles Dickens created a dwarf called Quilp to be the evil villain in pursuit of the innocent Nell in *The Old Curiosity Shop* (see Figure 12.2). Popular literature is often made into popular films, and there are several versions of *The Hunchback of Notre Dame* and *The Phantom of the Opera* to remind us that a person with a disability is a "monster" whose fearful features suggest "a disfigurement of personality and deformity of soul" (Longmore, 2003).

Object of Dread The origin of this perception is the medieval myth of the *changeling* where people believed that upon the birth of a normal child, evil spirits came in the night and stole the child, replacing it with a defective child such as one who was mentally retarded or with cerebral palsy. In Grimm's fairy tale "The Elves," a changeling with "fixed staring eyes" is substituted for the original baby. The belief that evil spirits were the source of changelings may have influenced Martin Luther's perception of defective children as spawn of Satan, denouncing them as a "mass of flesh" without a soul (Winzer, 1997). Today, some Christians regard deformity or disability as a sign of "moral failure" or as a visible stigma of sinfulness (Pelka, 1994). Some parents of children with disabilities regard the child as punishment from God; some mothers experience enough depression to seek therapy following the birth of such a child.

Object of Pity This perception may not seem negative because it appears to include compassion for disabled people, but it is a compassion seldom accompanied by respect. Fundraising campaigns by

FIGURE 12.2

One of the original illustrations by Phiz (Halbot K. Browne) depicting Quilp the dwarf, the villain in *The Old Curiosity Shop* by Charles Dickens.

Source: Michael Steig, *Dickens and Phiz.* Bloomington: Indiana University Press. Used with permission.

well-meaning organizations work to arouse pity with poster children or by having telethons that parade children with disabilities to stimulate viewers to make contributions. According to Charlton (1998), surveys conducted in the United States have concluded that more people form their attitudes about people with disabilities from telethons than from any other source. Because telethons tend to reinforce images of people with disabilities as helpless or dependent, the disability community in America has voiced objections to them, with some organizations responding by agreeing not to participate in telethons for fundraising purposes.

Diseased Organism This perception views a person's physical or mental disability as a temporary condition that can be cured by chemical or psychological treatments. Ancient Egyptians often regarded disability as a condition for which medical "cures" were prescribed. Egyptian doctors hoped to restore eyesight to blind people by applying a solution to their eyes made of copper, myrrh, Cyprus seeds, and other ingredients. Although many Greeks believed that supernatural forces caused disabilities, physicians including Hippocrates rejected superstition and attempted to identify physiological causes of disabilities (Winzer, 1997). In the United States today, national fund drives solicit money for research to find cures for disabilities, presenting people with that disability not only as an object of pity, but also as a diseased organism: The disability is perceived as "unhealthy" and the person is portrayed as needing to be cured. This medical view of people with disabilities is pessimistic because until a cure can be found, people with disabilities are regarded as having "incurable diseases." Because of such perceptions, people with disabilities have been placed in institutions, which penalize them for the crime of being disabled.

Holy Innocent/Eternal Child This perception is normally identified with one group: people labeled "mentally retarded." Viewed as incapable of sin, the Holy Innocent image can be found in most countries, religions, and cultures, and is often regarded as a benign view. The perception suggests that people with mental retardation need to be protected and sheltered, isolated from the outside world to perpetuate their innocent, childlike qualities. But encouraging people with mental retardation to maintain childish behaviors rather than learn adult behaviors is a barrier to their ability to live independently. Linton (1998) observed that when people with disabilities are viewed as "living in the body, not in the mind, [they] are configured as childlike, even infant like, acting on primary drives rather than engaging in purposeful behavior" (pp. 95–96). This perception can become a self-fulfilling prophecy, illustrated in reports of people with mental retardation who have been constantly treated as children even during adolescence who persist in childlike behaviors as adults, requiring constant care (Wehmeyer, 2000).

Object of Ridicule In literature, folk stories, and jokes, people with disabilities are subject to humiliation for the sake of humor. People with mental retardation have been portrayed as village idiots and ridiculed in moron jokes. According to Fiedler (1993), pagan practices of displaying freaks for public entertainment were revived in the Middle Ages by the Catholic Church, which displayed disabled or deformed "monsters" on feast days. In the nineteenth century, carnival side shows with magicians and sword swallowers also featured freaks: giants, dwarves, human skeletons, and other physically malformed or disabled people. Legendary showman P.T. Barnum popularized the freak show in the United States, exhibiting Chang and Eng (the original Siamese twins) and General Tom Thumb (a midget), along with anonymous pinheads and armless or legless wonders, now immortalized in wax at the Circus World Museum in Baraboo, Wisconsin. Living or dead, people with deformities or disabilities

> The point is, we are all one great big family, and any one of us can get hurt at any moment. . . . We should never walk by somebody who's in a wheelchair and be afraid of them or think of them as a stranger.
>
> **Christopher Reeve (1952–2004)**

are still perceived as odd, ridiculous, or bizarre—anything but human.

Each of these historical perceptions has stigmatized various disabilities and dehumanized people who had them. Today, many disability advocates in the United States (and elsewhere) are combating such negative images by insisting that people with disabilities are simply one cultural group among many others in a diverse society, that they have a disability culture that influences their development in different ways from the experiences that affect nondisabled Americans. According to Johnson and Nieto (2007), these arguments are being supported by an emerging discipline called Disability Studies, in which scholars examine "disability as an area of study in a manner similar to ethnic, linguistic, and women's studies" (p. 40). These scholars have identified characteristics that describe what advocates mean when they talk about a disability culture.

How do scholars describe a disability culture?

Because of past rejection, many people with similar disabilities have come together to support each other in their efforts to achieve the goal of living a normal life that includes a job, a home, a family, and so on. As a result of this collaboration, they have had similar experiences and developed cohesiveness based on common needs and shared aspirations. As Pai and Adler (1997) point out, a traditional concept of culture suggests that a group's historical experience together will create a "pattern of knowledge, skills, behaviors, attitudes and beliefs, as well as material artifacts" (p. 23). Using this kind of conventional definition for culture, Reagan (2005) argues that people with disabilities have created and continue to be influenced by a unique disability culture in the same way that individuals from racial and ethnic groups are shaped by their unique cultures.

Perhaps the clearest example of a disability culture is the deaf culture since it represents both cultural and linguistic diversity. Reagan (2005) agrees with scholars who describe many components of culture, but he identified four components that must be shared by all members of a culture: (1) historical knowledge and awareness, (2) a common language, (3) awareness of a cultural identity supported by cultural artifacts and identified by distinctive norms and patterns of behavior, and (4) a network of voluntary, in-group social organizations.

Scholars have provided evidence that deaf culture includes these components. With regard to the first component, much has been written in disability studies research about the shared historical experience that has shaped the deaf community and individual identities. As Padden and Humphries (1998) have noted: "(The) knowledge of Deaf people is not simply a camaraderie with others who have a similar physical condition, but is, like many other cultures . . . historically created and actively transmitted across generations" (p. 2). The issue of transmitting the culture leads to perhaps the most compelling argument for a deaf culture in the United States: the existence of American Sign Language (ASL). In the early 1970s, linguistic research concluded that ASL was a language characterized by its unique grammar and syntax, and that "manual language developed naturally in deaf children similarly to the way oral language developed in hearing children" (Hehir, 2005, p. 21). Deaf children usually become fluent in ASL early in their lives, and information being transmitted by this language becomes what Padden and Humphries (1998) describe as "the heart of the culture" (p. 5). This is the reason that many deaf people advocate for a bilingual/bicultural approach in classrooms educating deaf children and youth. In addition to recognizing deaf culture, this pedagogical approach should challenge the historic perspective of deafness as a deficit and enhance the goal of helping deaf children learn Standard English. Deaf advocates also argue that hearing students could benefit from learning about historical events that have affected the deaf community as well as some of the issues confronting deaf people today. These arguments are the same ones made by other cultural groups who advocate for bilingual/bicultural education for their children.

As for the two remaining components for culture, deaf people frequently express their sense of a shared cultural identity. Padden and Humphries (1998) and Reagan (2005) have reported about their distinctive cultural artifacts in communications with the Telecommunications Device for the Deaf (TDD) combined with a Teletypewriter (TTY) —a computer with a keyboard input and printer or display output; in television (closed-caption programming); and other personal devices such as doorbells connected to lights in their homes. These cultural artifacts exist to assist deaf people in functioning more effectively in their everyday lives. As for patterns of behavior, Reagan (2005) identified cultural patterns among deaf people such as a high rate of endogamous (in-group) marriage, and behavioral differences such as establishing eye contact or the acceptability of physical contact. These cultural norms for deaf people have sometimes created misunderstandings similar to what has been experienced by ethnic groups during cross-cultural interactions. Finally, the deaf community has established numerous social organizations related to sports, theater and the arts, and social clubs, as well as state and national organizations.

Many deaf people and disability advocates are working to remove the stigma historically associated with disabilities. In the United States, they are challenging people to reject the assumption that regards any disability as a deficit, and to understand disability as one more example of human diversity. Since 20% of Americans have some form of disability (Russell, 1998), it is surprising that so many individuals persist in maintaining negative attitudes about people with physical or mental disabilities. To understand this phenomenon, it is necessary to examine some factors that contribute to the perpetuation of these negative attitudes.

> Before I was paralyzed, there were 10,000 things I could do. Now there are 9,000. I could dwell on the 1,000 I lost or focus on the 9,000 I have left.
>
> **Walter Mitchell (Contemporary)**

Individual Ableism

Negative attitudes are reflected in the language we employ to identify disabled people. The word *disabled* implies inability; the prefix *dis* is generally regarded as signifying *not* or *no*. Derived from Latin, the prefix actually means *apart* or *asunder*, which is consistent with the historic practice of keeping disabled people apart from society.

People with disabilities are described as being "afflicted with" or a "victim of" a disability. Affliction is associated with disease, as is being a victim, so this language relates to the cultural image of the person with a disability as a diseased organism. Using words or phrases like *crippled, handicapped, impaired,* or *confined to a wheelchair* foster the belief that people with disabilities are incompetent or damaged, not capable of being independent. The term *confined to a wheelchair* is especially absurd. People in wheelchairs are not confined, but liberated by them. The wheelchair provides mobility to people who might be "confined" to their apartment or home if they did not have a wheelchair. Physical barriers can be identified easily, but it is much more difficult in America today to identify and overcome barriers created by **individual ableism**—prejudiced attitudes and actions toward people with a disability based on our assumptions about them.

What assumptions are made about people with disabilities?

Fine and Asch (2000) discussed five erroneous assumptions that nondisabled people commonly make about persons with disabilities:

1. **Disability is a biological problem of a particular individual.** This assumption is related to the medical model of disability, which views the disability as a problem and the solution is to find a cure for it. The assumption overlooks the influence of prejudices, stereotypes, and discrimination about disabilities. Individuals with disabilities react to their environmental circumstances. Putnam (2005) commented that the absence of disability accommodations by architects, urban planners, and public officials suggests to people with disabilities that they are not being recognized nor included as part of a community. That is not a problem created by their disability but by the thoughts and decisions of others.
2. **Any problems for a person with a disability must stem from the disability.** People with disabilities may have health problems like

anyone else, but they are not "unhealthy," nor is a disability a cause of disease. If a man with a disability is upset because he feels he has been discriminated against, it is discrimination and not the disability that is the cause of his anger. Being in a wheelchair is not necessarily frustrating, but a woman in a wheelchair may be frustrated when confronted with no curb cuts, no ramps for her to enter a building, or inaccessible rest rooms within the building.

3. **A person with a disability is a "victim."** This assumption may suggest a humane and even compassionate attitude, but it is steeped in pity and lacks respect for the person with a disability. Studies of people with disabilities often report that their subjects do not feel that they are victims but are more concerned about how to function effectively in their environment. In one study cited by Fine and Asch (2000), when questioned about their disability, a consistent response from people with disabilities was "it could be worse" (p. 323). Human beings want to live full, productive lives, and people with a disability are no different.
4. **Being disabled is central to self-concept and social comparisons for a person with a disability.** Although having a disability is usually a factor in shaping a person's sense of identity, self-concept refers to how a person feels about himself or herself. A person with a disability will develop his or her self-concept in ways similar to nondisabled people who tend to rely on factors such as academic achievement, honors and awards, aesthetic interests, good relationships with family and friends, demonstrating competence at work, and so on. As for social comparisons, people with a disability who have a job are not likely to compare their job performance only with other disabled workers but instead with all of their co-workers. Fine and Asch (2000) explain that a paraplegic woman "may be as likely to compare herself with other women her age, others of her occupation, others of her family, class, race or a host of other people and groups who function as (her) reference group" (p. 334).
5. **Having a disability means a person will need assistance.** This assumption comes from the history of "handicapped people" as helpless and dependent on others. In the 1930s, people with a disability were classified as "unemployable," preventing them from being considered for jobs in federal and local work relief programs (Longmore, 2003). Based on this assumption, disabled people are not viewed as responsible for their disability, nor are they seen as capable of resolving difficulties created by their disability. Yet people with disabilities are only as dependent as the environment makes them. The blind person on the elevator may ask someone to push the button for the right floor unless the elevator panel also has floor numbers in Braille. A wheelchair user will have to bring friends or ask strangers for help getting past a flight of steps if there is no ramp allowing wheelchair access. People with severe cerebral palsy may have trouble communicating with others if they are not given access to a computer and trained to use it. Because of assumptions like these, advocates for people with disabilities have had to defend them aggressively and demand that they be given opportunities to achieve their goals.

For example, a young woman who was born without arms chose to attend a large Midwestern university and enrolled in the nursing program. Although she had an excellent academic record, the nursing faculty was opposed to accepting her based on concerns that the young woman would not be able to perform physical tasks required of nurses. When a campus disability advocate became involved, a compromise was reached. The young woman was admitted to the nursing program but would not be allowed to take licensure exams. This resolution was acceptable to the young woman; she had hoped to earn a nursing degree because of her interest in the subject matter. After graduation, the young woman wrote articles for nursing journals, based on her research and observations, eventually becoming an editor. Nursing faculty had not focused on what the young woman could do, nor had they anticipated this outcome; their focus had been on tasks the disability would prevent the young woman from doing.

One more example: Sharisa Kochmeister was born with severe cerebral palsy. As a child she was also diagnosed as severely mentally retarded before she learned to use a computer. Initially someone held her hand while she hunted for letters on the keyboard; eventually, she could operate a computer independently. When she turned fifteen, her IQ was retested and her score was measured at 142. In a similar case, a teenager who had been diagnosed as mentally retarded was asked what it felt like before she learned to communicate with a computer. She replied, "(As if) I was a clown in a world that was not a circus" (Kliewer & Biklin, 1996, p. 90). These examples of change do not reflect a transformation in the ability of the people being labeled; rather, they reflect a change in opportunities for those who were labeled as well as a change in the assumptions of those responsible for the labeling.

What labels represent legitimate ways of identifying people?

Most Americans appear to believe that the "mentally retarded" label is a well-defined, scientifically determined, unambiguous way to categorize human beings: It is not. In the early 1900s, people with Down syndrome were considered profoundly retarded; today, it is estimated that 20% to 50% of people with Down syndrome are mildly retarded. In 1952, the American Psychological Association (APA) recommended institutionalization of people with IQs less than 50 who were considered severely retarded (Adelman, 1996). The current conclusion of the APA is that half of those with IQs of less than 50 can be considered moderately retarded and that neither moderate nor severely retarded individuals require continuous custodial care.

Another disability that professionals have been forced to reevaluate is cerebral palsy. In 1960, experts assumed that 75% of people with cerebral palsy were retarded. After some alternative methods of communication and assessment were developed, from adaptations for typewriters to special computers, assumptions of mental retardation diminished significantly (Kliewer & Biklin, 1996). These examples demonstrate why disability advocates are concerned about the labels given to people, especially children, and the consequences of such labeling.

What are some current controversies about labeling children?

Over the past forty years, studies have reported an overrepresentation of children of color among those labeled as needing special education services (Losen & Orfield, 2002). Overrepresentation means that children from a particular racial group are at least twice as likely to be labeled as white students are. For example, as we began the twenty-first century, African American children were still the most overrepresented racial group in diagnoses of mental retardation. According to Losen & Orfield (2002), black children were three times more likely to be given that label than white children. Parrish (2002) found that "In at least 45 states, black children in special education are extensively overrepresented in some categories" (p. 15). Parrish reported that American Indian children also tend to be overrepresented in special education, while Latino children are overrepresented in some states but underrepresented in others. As a further clarification, Parrish noted that when a racial group represents a significant part of a state's population, it is even more likely that children from this group will be overrepresented in special education classes. For example, although Asian American/Pacific Islander children tend to be underrepresented in all special education categories in the United States as a whole, in Hawaii, where these children comprise 59% of all K–12 students, Asian American/Pacific Islander children are almost three and a half times more likely to be labeled mentally retarded (Parrish, 2002).

In addition to the negative attitudes fostered by such labels, there is some evidence of significant differences by race in how these labeled children are treated in schools. According to Fierros and Conroy (2002), in school districts with a large number of racial minority students, among the population of students identified as needing special education services, black students were more likely than white students to be placed in restrictive settings rather than being placed in regular classrooms. In addition, Osher, Woodruff, and Sims (2002) report that black students labeled as having emotional and behavioral disorders (EBD) are far more likely to be suspended, expelled, or removed from schools. The consequences go beyond schools, as demonstrated by research on students labeled EBD in the United States finding that more than four times as many black students as white students end up in the juvenile justice system. In New Jersey alone, those black students labeled EBD were more than 16 times as likely to have had a "correctional placement" than white students labeled EBD (Osher, Woodruff, &

Sims, 2002). This disparity betrays the schools' fundamental purpose of providing a safe and appropriate setting for all students to learn. Students should come to school expecting to find an environment where they are encouraged to develop their abilities and receive support services when necessary to help them achieve academic success. When schools reinforce negative attitudes toward students with a disability, they reinforce the negative perceptions of those nondisabled people who continue to view disabled people as "not able."

How can negative attitudes be changed?

The first thing that can be done is create labels that promote a more positive image. The use of *people with disabilities* began to be widely accepted in the 1970s as a substitute for *the disabled* and *the handicapped* (Linton, 1998). The term places people first to emphasize the humanity of the group and retains the word "disability" to acknowledge an existing mental or physical problem. Linton (1998) defined **people with disabilities** as referring to "people with behavioral or anatomical characteristics marked as deviant . . . that makes them targets of discrimination" (p. 12).

Although there is no agreement regarding the acceptability of alternative terms, there is agreement on the offensiveness of negative terms such as *impaired, crippled,* and *handicapped.* These are words that contribute to the perception of people with disabilities being not just "disabled" but "unable," implying an inability to manage for themselves or to contribute to society. According to the World Health Organization, a disability is not a handicap. **Disability** refers to "a restriction of functional ability and activity caused by an impairment (e.g., hearing loss, reduced mobility)," whereas **handicap** generally is employed as a reference to "an environmental or attitudinal barrier that limits the opportunity for a person to participate fully in a role that is normal (depending on age, sex, and social and cultural factors) for that individual" (Bernell, 2003, p. 41).

> It is not the fact that [a person] cannot walk that is disabling but that society is organized for walking and not wheelchair-using individuals. [A person's] disability is not paraplegia but steps, pavement kerbs, buses and prejudiced shopkeepers.
>
> **Victor Finkelstein (Contemporary)**

Imagine a woman in a wheelchair approaching a building. Her legs do not function well enough for her to walk; the wheelchair provides mobility. As she nears the steps of the building, she discovers it has no access ramp. Now she is handicapped. She has found a way to be mobile, but because of the insensitivity or prejudice of the architect or building owners, the lack of a ramp is a barrier that denies her and any wheelchair user access to the building.

Institutional Ableism

Institutional ableism is a consequence of established laws, customs, and practices that systematically discriminate against people with disabilities. A unique consequence for this minority group has been their placement in institutions in the United States, comparable only to nineteenth-century poorhouses for paupers. Poorhouses and poor farms have come and gone; yet institutions for people who have mental or physical disabilities remain, despite efforts in recent years to close them and to place people with disabilities into communities.

Why were people with disabilities placed in institutions?

The first institutions charged with caring for people with disabilities were hospices built within monasteries. An early reported example comes in the fourth century: a hospice for the blind at a monastery in Caesarea, now Turkey. According to the legend of St. Nicholas, as bishop of Mya in southwestern Turkey, he provided care for "idiots and imbeciles." For his efforts he was named the patron saint of the mentally retarded, although that part of his history was lost in his transformation into the American Santa Claus (Winzer, 1997). As monasteries were built in Europe, many included hospices to care for poor, homeless, or disabled people. Using hospices to satisfy Christian mandates to care for "the least of these" continued into the sixteenth century, when turmoil over church reforms created a schism termed the Reformation, resulting in Protestant churches as alternatives to the Catholic Church.

Even before the Reformation, the Catholic Church contributed to an increasingly negative attitude toward people with disabilities. St. Augustine sowed seeds for religious rejection when he refused to allow deaf people to become church members because of his literal interpretation of St. Paul (Romans 10:17): "Faith comes by hearing." During the Middle Ages, as Europe was devastated by plague and pestilence, especially the Black Death, fear fostered a growing hostility toward people exhibiting strange appearances or odd behavior (Barzun, 2000).

With the Reformation, monasteries were abandoned or forcibly closed and inhabitants evacuated. Communities were confronted with the problem of disabled people and beggars wandering the streets. Not surprisingly, attitudes toward the newly released people became increasingly negative. Laws were passed that vagrants be whipped (Ribton-Turner, 1972). By the fifteenth century, the Catholic Church declared a virtual war on witches, which resulted in the arrests, torture, and deaths of a great many people who in some way were considered unusual or deviant. Evidence suggests that people who were mentally ill and people with disabilities were among the unfortunates serving as scapegoats.

The association with witchcraft often stemmed from people with mental retardation making odd comments or from mutterings of the mentally ill. Some citizens believed the strange talk was dialogue with the devil; others regarded the conversations as divinely inspired. Whether they talked with God or the devil, deviants were not tolerated on the streets. Some communities placed mentally retarded vagrants in the old city wall guard towers, which came to be called a "Fool's Tower" or "Idiot's Cage" (Winzer, 1997). In other communities, homeless people were charged with vagrancy, tortured, and expelled, or if they could work, they were forced into slavery (Ribton-Turner, 1972).

Reformation leaders John Calvin and Martin Luther did not question the prejudices behind this behavior; in fact, they contributed to them. According to Calvin, Satan possessed mentally retarded people; Luther believed Satan was responsible for fathering all mentally retarded children, and urged the parents of one mentally retarded child to drown it in a nearby river (Winzer, 1997).

When the centuries-old scourge of leprosy ended as the seventeenth century began, buildings used to quarantine lepers (leprosaria) became vacant. Communities found a solution to their dilemma of what to do with deviants: Europe initiated *the great confinement* to these newly christened "lunatic hospitals" (Foucault, 1989). Although the hospitals were initially used to house mentally ill people, they accepted "mental defectives," including people with various physical and mental disabilities, and eventually amassed a wide assortment of "defectives." Before long, only about 10% of inmates were considered insane in the average lunatic hospital. In addition to people with disabilities, other inmates included prostitutes, beggars, alcoholics, social dissidents, and people with syphilis (Winzer, 1997). Whereas hospices had protected disabled people from the wickedness of the world, lunatic hospitals protected the world from the wickedness of such morally, mentally, and physically deviant human beings.

It was apparent early on that hospitals could not provide treatment to rehabilitate inmates. The purpose of institutions was to remove defective people from society. Not surprisingly, the quality of "care" in such places was not good; rumors often circulated of inhumane treatment. In England, the Hospital of St. Mary of Bethlehem was referred to as "Bethlehem," which reduced to "Bedlam," coining a word to describe chaotic conditions there. By the nineteenth century, reformers visiting lunatic hospitals were appalled by the horrible conditions: some inmates wandering around naked and shivering, others chained to beds, some sitting in their own excrement, many bitten by rats or other vermin roaming the grounds. Reformers advocated for "moral treatment" of people in the institutions: eliminating chains, giving patients work, and treating patients with respect to develop self-esteem (Foucault, 1989).

Moral treatment involved not defining patients as deviant so much as regarding their defects as conditions requiring accommodations for them to function more effectively. Foucault (1989) tells the story of a mentally ill man who refused to eat because he thought he was dead and he was certain that dead people did not eat. One night, institutional staff came to the patient's bed looking pale, ashen, and dressed in clothing to simulate the look of a corpse. They brought in a table and some food, then sat down and began eating. When the patient asked why they were eating when they appeared to be dead, they replied that dead people had to eat like anyone else. They finished their meal and left. The next day the patient resumed eating. This approach was taken with patients who had mental or physical disabilities as well.

Instead of being defined as insurmountable deviance, *disability* gradually came to be regarded as a human condition; institutional staff began to provide accommodations to help individuals take better care of themselves and to function effectively with others. Although reforms were not universally applied, they constituted a practical alternative to the punitive treatment that had characterized previous institutional practices.

How were institutions for people with disabilities established in the United States?

When the United States entered the global community as a new nation, people with disabilities simply lived in communities, primarily cared for by their families, although some religious facilities also provided care. Their situations varied widely—from being employed to being the town fool or even a pariah whom the family hid from the community. In nineteenth-century America, attitudes toward people with disabilities were challenged. Americans were not to view people's disabilities as an act of God but instead in a biological context: Rehabilitation was emphasized as the appropriate response.

Following the Civil War, a transformation of public attitudes seemed to be demonstrated by the construction of numerous institutions and residential schools that were often dedicated to a particular kind of disability. Institutionalizing people with disabilities was especially popular in urban areas, indicating a shift in responsibility for care from families and communities to the state as the nation moved into the twentieth century. Based on a biological view of human disability, the institutions were usually administered by people with medical training who claimed to use rehabilitative strategies. In reality, the function of institutions was usually custodial care—monitoring and restraining patients—reflecting ongoing negative American attitudes toward disabled people.

> Progress, far from consisting in change, depends on retentiveness. . . . Those who cannot remember the past are condemned to fulfill it.
>
> **George Santayana (1863–1952)**

What evidence exists that negative attitudes prevailed in institutions and in society?

The negative attitude toward institutionalized patients is documented legal history. A 1913 Wisconsin law mandated the institutionalization of disabled people who constituted a "menace to society." A similar law passed the following year in Texas stated that people with disabilities mingling freely in the community was "a most baneful evil," describing people with disabilities as "defect(s)... [that] wound our citizenry a thousand times more than any plague . . . [they are] a blight on mankind" (Garrett History Brief, 2001, p. 72). Encouraged by the **eugenics** movement following World War I, every state in the United States passed laws singling out people with mental or physical disabilities for institutionalization. Some states went so far as to authorize the removal of children with disabilities from their homes, even against the wishes of parents.

With most disabled people confined to institutions, continuing prejudice was demonstrated in the 1930s when over thirty states enacted laws permitting involuntary sterilization of people in state funded institutions. Among the targets of this law were those identified as *feeble minded, idiots, morons,* and *mental defectives.* States justified their actions by claiming the need to eradicate the possibility of procreation for people who were such burdens on society (Garrett History Brief, 2001; Russell, 1998).

In Europe, German Nazis implemented a program of involuntary sterilization that was continued until the end of World War II. Subsequently, allies identified forced sterilization of people with disabilities for inclusion on the list of Nazi war crimes. Russell (1998) explained why it was deleted: "Allied authorities were unable to classify the sterilizations as war crimes, because similar laws had . . . recently been upheld in the United States" (p. 22).

People with disabilities who were institutionalized in the United States were largely ignored until 1972, when Geraldo Rivera exposed the appalling conditions at New York's Willowbrook State School where "one hundred percent of all residents contracted hepatitis within six months of entering the institution. . . . Many lay on dayroom floors (naked) in their own feces" (Linton, 1998, p. 40). The description parallels conditions denounced by "moral treatment" reformers a century earlier, yet ten years after the Willowbrook scandal, problems persisted in American institutions. Linton (1998) cites a 1984 *New York Times* article about a community facility for physically and mentally disabled people in California that described staff serving spoiled food, not repairing malfunctioning toilets, and physically and sexually abusing patients.

Are institutions for people with disabilities providing good care today?

Although reduced in number, institutions for physically and mentally disabled people still exist despite the fact that national and state political leaders know they are harmful to the people in them. In 1996, a federal General Accounting Office (GAO) investigation of public institutions for mentally retarded people warned Congress of serious deficiencies in quality of care: "insufficient staffing, lack of active treatment and deficient medical and psychiatric care" (Garrett History Brief, 2001, p. 72). The GAO report described harm to residents including injuries, unnecessary illnesses, and physical degeneration—in a few instances the institutional "care" contributed to a resident's death.

Some states attempted to eliminate institutions by passing "deinstitutionalization" laws, but this has not solved the problem. When institutions have closed, residents have often been relocated not to communities but to another form of institutional care—nursing homes. Care provided in nursing homes reportedly is no better, and is sometimes worse, than the care residents experienced in institutions (Russell, 1998).

What is the alternative to placing people with disabilities in institutions?

Instead of being placed in institutions, people with disabilities prefer to live in family homes or group homes in their communities. A 1996 federal court ruling found that some city zoning ordinances had limited or prevented the establishment of group homes in neighborhoods by including "density laws" restricting the number of "unrelated persons" in a house or the number of group homes within a certain area. Some cities have even passed so-called ugly laws that forbid people with an unsightly appearance from appearing in public (Garrett History Brief, 2001, p. 72). The irony of such ordinances is that placing disabled people in communities to receive care not only increases their quality of life, it is also more cost effective for taxpayers than providing care in nursing homes or institutions.

What is the cost of care for people with disabilities?

Taxpayers fund over 60% of the expenses for people with disabilities in nursing homes and institutions. Although people with disabilities overwhelmingly prefer to be cared for at home and require only minimal assistance, almost 2 million Americans with disabilities live in nursing homes at a cost of over $40,000 per person per year (Lefleur, 2009). According to Russell (1998), costs could total less than $10,000 per year to provide an individual with personal assistance services at home. State institutions are even more expensive: More than 75,000 people with developmental disabilities still live in state institutions at an average annual cost of

> If our brothers are oppressed, then we are oppressed. If they hunger, we hunger. If their freedom is taken away, our freedom is not secure.
>
> **Stephen Vincent Benet (1898–1943)**

more than $80,000 per person. Charlton (1998) estimated that the most expensive support system that could be created to provide adequate care for someone living in their own home within their community would cost no more than $30,000 per year.

Charlton (1998) reviewed numerous studies that consistently reported benefits for people with disabilities living in communities: "living at home, in a house or an apartment, is better psychologically, more fulfilling, and cheaper than living in nursing homes" (p. 47). By contrast, critics point out that nursing homes and institutions make substantial profits for private corporations while providing primarily low-wage jobs. As quoted in *Business First,* one private corporation providing "health care" said their three primary objectives were: "1. increase net profit, 2. increase net profit, and 3. increase net profit" (Russell, 1998, p. 103).

Advocates for **normalization** oppose confining disabled people in institutions. The concept refers to the implementation of policies and practices to help create life conditions and opportunities for disabled people that are at least as good as those of average citizens. Normalization promotes strategies for disabled people to live and work in communities, and it challenges nondisabled people to eliminate barriers that prevent disabled people from being involved in community life. Based on the concept of normalization, disability advocates help people with disabilities move out of institutions and into communities, and they have lobbied for legislation to protect the civil rights of disabled people living in communities. (See Figure 12.3.)

How do other countries respond to the needs of people with disabilities?

In 1995, the House of Representatives Ways and Means Committee reported that the United States spent less on long-term disability benefits than several European countries (Russell, 1998). Germany and Austria both provide cash benefits to disabled people regardless of their financial resources. Those receiving benefits can spend the money however they wish, including hiring family members to provide care. In Germany, cash benefits are half what can be obtained in service benefits, but it is at the discretion of the recipient to determine which kind of benefits to accept. Human services personnel pay random visits to recipients to assess the adequacy of their care. In 2000, Austria provided benefits for 310,000 people funded by general tax revenues,

FIGURE 12.3

Today people with a disability are just as likely to protest discrimination and demand their rights as any other minority group.

Source: Photo by Tom Olin

and Germany provided benefits for 1,280,000 people funded by a 1.7% tax on salaries and pensions, a cost shared by employers, employees, and retired workers (Batavia, 2002).

Austrian legislation has promoted hiring disabled workers, stipulating that for every twenty-five workers employed, one worker must be a person with a disability. If the company fails to meet this standard, it is assessed a fine of approximately $155 a month that it must continue to pay until it hires the required number of disabled workers. Money collected from fines is retained in an account from which employers can receive funds to make physical modifications necessary to employ workers with disabilities (Koppelman, 2001).

In France, benefits to people with disabilities are not as generous as in Austria and Germany, but they exceed those of the United States. Benefits are based on financial resources of recipients, with a maximum national benefit. Local French governments responsible for providing benefits are funded from general tax revenues that supported approximately 86,000 people in 2000. Local agency representatives make annual home visits to recipients to ensure that adequate services are being provided (Batavia, 2002).

How does the U.S. government provide support for people with disabilities?

European countries began providing social insurance and welfare assistance in the eighteenth and nineteenth centuries. In the United States, the federal social security program was established in 1935, although it did not include disabled people until the 1950s (Stone, 1984). Whereas European countries seem to have accepted their responsibility to provide care for disabled people, the United States has continually questioned its obligation. In 1996, Congress voted to add $320 million to the Social Security Administration, doubling the budget, but not to assist more disabled people. The budget increase was designated to fund reviews of recipients to determine if they could be removed from the list of those eligible for disability benefits. Ironically, that same year, Congress provided approximately $32 million for programs to protect disabled people from being discriminated against in hiring decisions (Russell, 1998).

The 1990 Americans with Disabilities Act (ADA) was enacted to prevent discrimination against people with disabilities. In the first four years after the law was passed, 3,600 complaints were filed, charging employer hiring practices with discrimination against workers with disabilities: The Equal Employment Opportunities Commission (EEOC) approved 28 to be pursued in court. By 2008, the EEOC reported over 19,000 complaints filed by people with disabilities concerning allegations of discrimination (EEOC, 2009).

How does the United States support people with disabilities who want to live independently?

In 1973, the Supplemental Security Income (SSI) program was created to assist people with disabilities. The means-tested program offers a range of $400 to $700 per month, but recipients must remain without other means of support to receive SSI funds. If recipients make extra money to be more financially secure, they are likely to lose the benefit.

In one case that exemplifies SSI policy, Lynn Thompson, a quadriplegic, was attempting to live on SSI payments of about $600 a month when she began earning extra income at home stuffing envelopes. After she reported her earnings, social security officials declared her income in excess of allowable limits and ordered her to return $10,000 of the benefits received or, if she couldn't pay the money, her benefits would be terminated until that amount was withheld. Termination of her benefits meant Thompson could no longer afford to hire a personal care attendant and she would need to leave her home and enter a nursing home. Thompson fought to overturn this decision, but the legal battle dragged on. Ms. Thompson committed suicide rather than be forced into a nursing home (Russell, 1998).

Is there discrimination against people with disabilities living in communities?

People with disabilities who are fortunate enough not to be institutionalized also encounter discrimination in the community. Hahn (1988) described the problems:

> Disabled persons have not only exhibited one of the highest rates of unemployment, welfare dependency, and poverty in the United States; but they also have experienced a more pervasive form of segregation in education, housing, transportation, and public accommodations than the most rigid policies of apartheid enacted by racist governments. (p. 26)

In addition to housing, already discussed, disabled people experience discrimination in four critical areas: jobs, mobility/accessibility, health care, and education.

Jobs Because of the shortage of men, women were hired for traditional male jobs during World War II; employment of people with disabilities also increased during the war. As was true for women workers, unemployment rates for disabled people increased after the war, as jobs were assigned to returning soldiers. The work performance of people with disabilities during the war proved that they not only wanted jobs, but they could perform their tasks competently. This lesson has apparently been lost on employers: Ongoing documentation reveals that people with disabilities continue to be discriminated against in hiring decisions.

According to the U.S. Census Bureau (2009), there are 41.2 million people with disabilities in the United States representing 15% of the total population. About 48% of disabled people were employed full time, yet a survey by the National Organization on Disability reported that 66% of working-age disabled adults want to work rather than rely on SSI benefits. Of disabled people who work, 80% are employed in sheltered workshops that hire only disabled workers for as little as 20% to 30% of the minimum wage, often earning as little as $11 a week. Although the unemployment rate was less than 4% in the late 1990s, unemployment for working-age disabled adults maintained the same range—from 65% to 71%—reaching a high of 80% in 2000 according to Harris poll data analyzed by Sowers, McLean, and Owens (2002).

> I am not broken! I am not broken! I am a representative of the diversity of the human race.
>
> **Norman Kunc (Contemporary)**

In a case illustrating the difficulties of finding work, a disabled man in Maine with a PhD in chemistry asked the state agency for assistance in finding a job. The agency sent him to the Goodwill store to be trained to sort socks. Another case occurred in Rhode Island where the vocational rehabilitation agency refused to provide further education to a quadriplegic man, arguing that he was adequately taken care of by SSI benefits (Garrett History Brief, 2001). Longmore (2003) cited a study in which 40% of people with a disability who were unemployed or working only part time identified "employer bias" as a major factor in their difficulty finding full-time employment. Even when they are employed full time, people with disabilities may still encounter discrimination by being paid less than their co-workers who have similar responsibilities or by being hired for a position with few responsibilities and little chance for promotion. Given this kind of discrimination, it should come as no surprise that in the United States, almost a third of working-age adults with disabilities are living in poverty.

Mobility/Accessibility The ability of people in wheelchairs to function effectively in the community is affected by the existence of ramps, elevators, curb cuts, and wheelchair lifts on public buses. According to a Harris survey, 60% of people with disabilities report that their social, recreational, and employment opportunities are substantially limited due to lack of accessible public transportation. Accessibility problems have been cited as the reason why 40% of disabled people say they cannot participate in community activities such as attending church. Even buildings with ramps are not necessarily accessible. Many ramps are too narrow, too steep, or lack handrails. Theaters, sports facilities and other public settings may provide wheelchair accessible spaces that are segregated from the other seats, not allowing wheelchair users to sit with friends or colleagues (Longmore, 2003). Accessibility problems can also impede a disabled citizen's right to vote. A 1996 study reported that almost 60% of New Hampshire's polling places were not accessible to disabled people, and a national study found that almost half of people with disabilities in their survey had experienced problems of accessibility at their polling places (Garrett History Brief, 2001).

Although the passage of the Americans with Disabilities Act (ADA) required public buildings to be accessible, most are still not accessible, and the ADA did not require accessibility for nonpublic buildings. A concept promoting accessibility to all buildings is termed "visitability"; advocates encourage the construction of homes, businesses, and other nonpublic buildings to accommodate people with disabilities. The primary accommodations required are level entryways, wide doorways, and an accessible bathroom. This concept not only benefits people with disabilities but their family, friends, and neighbors who want to interact with them (Kaminski et al., 2006). This idea is not new. In 1985, Mace proposed the **universal design** concept that advocates creating products capable of being used by all people and constructing environments that are accessible to everyone. A ramp instead of steps leading to the entrance of a building provides access for people with disabilities but also makes access easier for mothers with baby strollers or workers carrying heavy items. The concept of universal design is a means of improving a community for everyone.

Health Care According to Sulewski, Gilmore, and Foley (2006), people with disabilities spend more on health care than people without disabilities; therefore, access to health care is a major concern. People with disabilities often encounter difficulties in obtaining health insurance. The insurance industry openly uses personal health and genetic data in its review of potential clients. Russell (1998) cited one study reporting that 47% of applicants identified to be screened for "defects" were ultimately denied health insurance—even though no defects were found. In addition, Taylor (1998) found that disabled people are twice as likely as nondisabled people to report that they did not receive needed medical services during the previous year.

Because some people with disabilities need services and equipment not provided by private insurance, access to Medicaid is essential. Medicaid is the primary provider of health care for nearly 7 million people under age 65 who have disabilities (Sulewski, Gilmore, & Foley, 2006). People with disabilities often report that one of the main obstacles to seeking employment is the fear of losing Medicaid because taking a full-time job can jeopardize their federally funded health care. Once they are covered by an employer's health care plan, they can lose their federally funded medical benefits. Often, it takes up to two years to reclaim and receive federally funded health care if an individual with a disability loses his or her job. Many choose to not work or to only work part-time for a salary that keeps them eligible for Medicaid. According to a 1998

FIGURE 12.4

In the 1980s, Berke Breathed's "Bloom County" was one of the first comic strips to feature a character using a wheelchair.

Source: © 1982, The Washington Post Writer's Group. Reprinted with permission.

Harris poll, one third of all disabled people who are unemployed chose not to work rather than risk violating their eligibility for Medicaid (Sulewski, Gilmore, & Foley, 2006).

Education Since the United States began, children with disabilities were kept at home or sent to segregated institutions. From 1930 to 1960, the number of children and youth with a disability increased significantly, and so did research on their needs. By the 1950s, public schools were allowed to establish special education programs for these students, and from 1948 to 1956, schools providing such programs increased by 83% (Osgood, 2005). Even so, the assumption persisted that a segregated setting was the best way to teach these students. In the 1960s, researchers coined the term "learning disability" and identified various conditions that interfered with a child's ability to learn, and the ranks of disability activists grew. Following several court decisions and state legislation, the federal government passed the Education for All Handicapped Children Act (PL 94-142) in 1975, requiring public schools to educate students with a disability in the "least restrictive environment." Although the Act did not use the term "mainstreaming," the idea that students with disabilities should be educated in the least restrictive and most acceptable available environment had become the law of the land.

The problem that quickly emerged was that the concept of mainstreaming had different meanings for different people, including parents, teachers, and administrators. Some viewed mainstreaming as promoting the placement of students with disabilities into regular classes with support services to help them become academically successful; others argued that the "least restrictive environment" for academic achievement was occasionally a regular classroom, but more often a special education classroom where special accommodations could be made (Osgood, 2005). Research studies tended to support the position of disability advocates who insisted that students with physical and mental disabilities learned more when they were integrated into regular classes than when they were taught in separate classes (Hines, 2001; Kochhar, West, & Taymans, 2000). Yet the pace of change was slow, and the degree of ongoing segregation for special education students was documented in a 1987 Massachusetts report that included a comment from a student with a disability who had graduated from high school. Reflecting on his school experience, he stated that he and his disabled peers were "completely unprepared for the *real world* . . . Believe me, a segregated environment just will not do as preparation for an integrated life" (Osgood, 2005, p. 162).

In the 1990s, disability advocates began arguing for the merger of regular education and special education both in schools and in teacher preparation programs. They had abandoned mainstreaming to lobby for **inclusion** or "full inclusion"—calling for a total integration of students with disabilities in regular education classrooms (Kavale & Forness, 2005). Their efforts were assisted by a series of court decisions, influenced by civil rights laws, that ruled in favor of families with disabled children and ordered schools to adapt regular classrooms to meet the needs of students with a disability (Osgood, 2005). Despite these rulings, the debate has continued to the present. Opponents argue that disabled students demand too much time from teachers and that it is unfair to nondisabled students (Morse, 2005). Advocates counter that teachers can utilize aides, peers, and classroom strategies to ensure that all students receive appropriate educational experiences. Although Gliona, Gonzales, and Jacobson (2005) argue that alternate placements (i.e., segregation) may provide a better learning environment to meet the needs of some disabled students, Linton (1998) insists that inclusion is more than a teaching approach, and that it is not just "an educational plan to benefit disabled children. It is a model for educating all children equitably" (p. 61). Despite these arguments, the reality is that serious problems persist in educating students with a disability. Orfield, Losen, Ward and Swanson (2004) have reported that only 32% of students with disabilities are graduating from high school. Yet we should also acknowledge the progress that has been made over the last 40 years in educating students with disabilities. Osgood (2005) assessed the issue:

> Most of this progress has been recorded with children who have mild disabilities. Representing almost 90 percent of the overall special education population, children identified as mildly disabled have been the foot soldiers in efforts to integrate regular classrooms, as their academic needs and classroom behavior supposedly demanded less in

the way of classroom adaptations, classroom disruption, or teacher time. (p. 194)

Studies report that children are curious and interested in human differences, that they do not demonstrate a fear of differences unless they are taught to do so (Coleman, 2006). Even so, disability activists contend that most problems for people with disabilities stem from the attitudes of the nondisabled. When they advocate for inclusion, they not only argue that integration benefits students with disabilities by confronting stereotypes and stigmatizing labels, but that the presence of students with disabilities can benefit nondisabled students by providing opportunities to develop attitudes and skills that will enable them to work with people who may be different from themselves (Sapon-Shevin, 1999). Although the Americans with Disabilities Act (ADA) provided legal recourse against discrimination, disability advocates have argued that it is more effective to address the negative attitudes causing discrimination. For that reason, many believe that inclusion is the best strategy to improve attitudes and increase opportunities for people with disabilities.

How difficult is it to change people's attitudes?

As Fiedler (2008) wrote, "Perhaps the greatest obstacle to school change efforts is the attitudes of the individuals who must implement the change" (p. 258). The effectiveness of school change efforts has varied according to the attitudes of the teachers and administrators involved; this is true for community change efforts as well. Posner (1979) described an incident from Israel illustrating the difficulties involved in changing attitudes. Two villages did not have enough orange pickers at harvest time, so they arranged for young men at a nearby institution for the mentally retarded to help with the harvest. Before the young men arrived, researchers came to the villages and conducted an attitude survey. The researchers reported that 66% of villagers said there should be no contact between retarded people and children; 68% thought retarded people should be permitted to work only in sheltered workshops; 95% said institutions were the best place for retarded people; 58% believed that retarded people should be forbidden to marry.

When the retarded workers came, they picked oranges with great care and an enthusiasm not often displayed by other workers. Workers were told that if fallen oranges had not been bruised they could be used; only the retarded men inspected oranges that had fallen or been dropped. The retarded men climbed to the tops of ladders to pick oranges from high branches; no other workers were willing to climb so high. As the days passed, townspeople invited the workers to join them for lunch and the retarded men played with the children from the village. When the harvest was over, the young men returned to their institution.

The researchers returned to conduct a second attitude survey to see if changes had occurred in the attitudes of village residents. They found that the same 66% still believed there should be no contact between retarded people and children; the same 68% still thought retarded people should not work alongside others; the same 95% said retarded people should be in institutions, and the same 58% believed they should not marry. But please, all the villagers asked, will you make sure they send those nice young men back again next year?

> But in the ideal world, my differences, though noted, would not be devalued. Nor would I. Society would accept my experience as "disability culture," which would in turn be accepted as part of "human diversity.". . . In such a world, no one would mind being called Disabled.
>
> **Carol Gill (Contemporary)**

AFTERWORD

Our attitudes are resistant to change: Change occurs only when we first examine our attitudes for myths, misperceptions, or stereotypes. It is especially important for aspiring teachers to reflect on their attitudes because every teacher will teach children or youth with disabilities. But assessing personal attitudes is not only appropriate for teachers but for others as well: It is equally important for employers who have the choice of hiring a person with a disability and for employees who may work with that disabled person. According to Williams (2003), one out of five Americans—about 52 million people—has a disability. We can make a difference in the lives of people with disabilities who live in our communities. It is a choice each of us must make. If made wisely and compassionately, that choice will be a force for change.

myeducationlab

Now go to Topic #3: **Exceptionality** in the MyEducationLab (www.myeducationlab.com) for your course, where you can:

- Find learning outcomes for this topic along with the national standards that connect to these outcomes.
- Complete Assignments and Activities that can help you more deeply understand the chapter content by viewing classroom video and ABC News footage.
- Apply and practice your understanding of the core teaching skills identified in the chapter with the Building Teaching Skills and Dispositions learning units.

TERMS AND DEFINITIONS

Ableism The determination of an individual's abilities based on his or her disabilities; any policy or practice promoting the belief that disabled people are inferior to able-bodied persons to justify discrimination against people with disabilities

Cultural ableism The societal promotion of negative beliefs and images concerning people with disabilities that tend to portray the less able as deviant or incompetent; an assumption of superiority by people or groups based upon physical, mental, and emotional attributes

Deviant/Deviancy Someone whose appearance or behavior differs from the norm, from acceptable standards, in society

Disability A restriction of functional ability and activity caused by an impairment (such as hearing loss or reduced mobility) (Bernell, 2003)

Eugenics The study of agencies under social control that may improve or repair the racial qualities of future generations, either physically or mentally

Handicap An environmental or attitudinal barrier that limits the opportunity for a person to participate fully in a role that is normal (depending on age, sex, and social and cultural factors) for that individual (Bernell, 2003)

Inclusion Integration of all students with a disability into regular education classrooms

Individual ableism Prejudiced attitudes and behavior against others based on the assumption that one's level of ability is deviant from the norm, demonstrated whenever someone responds by saying or doing something degrading or harmful about persons whose ability is looked on as unacceptable

Institutional ableism Established laws, customs, and practices in a society that allow systematic discrimination against people with disabilities

Mainstreaming The responsibility of schools to educate all students, regardless of disability, in the least restrictive and most normally acceptable environment

Normalization Policies and practices that help create life conditions and opportunities for disabled people that are at least as good as those of average citizens

People with disabilities People with behavioral or anatomical characteristics marked as deviant, which identify them as targets for discrimination (Linton, 1998)

Universal design Designing and creating products and constructing environments that are accessible to everyone

DISCUSSION EXERCISES

Exercise #1 Group Home Discussion Activity

Directions: Imagine that you are a supervisor for people with various disabilities living in a group home. Identify activities listed below that a mentally retarded (MR), cerebral palsied (CP), epileptic (E), or physically disabled (PD) person should be permitted to do. Write the abbreviation for the particular disability next to each activity. If you feel that all people with the disabilities just listed should or should not be allowed to do the particular activity write "all."

Category/Activity

I. Interpersonal Relationships
  1. Date
  2. Engage in sexual activities
  3. Use birth control devices
  4. Marry
  5. Have and raise children

II. Lifestyle Concerns
  1. Choose their own clothing
  2. Dress and look the way they want
  3. Participate actively in the church of their choice
  4. Plan their own leisure time
  5. Engage in recreational activities of their choice

III. Economic Issues
  1. Choose the job they want
  2. Support themselves
  3. Be financially independent
  4. Enter into contracts
  5. Live where they choose

IV. Rights and Responsibilities
  1. Vote in political elections
  2. Drive a car
  3. Drink beer and/or liquor
  4. Have medical insurance
  5. Be educated to their fullest potential
  6. Be held responsible for their actions

Exercise #2 Disability Awareness Activity

What is a disability? How much do we know about disabilities? How prevalent are our disabilities?

Part One: List *all* the disabilities that you can think of; you will be reminded of additional disabilities as you listen to the suggestions of others. Attempt to identify at least 50 different disabilities. ("Paraplegic" may be combined with "quadriplegic" for example, in order for there to be room for a wide representation.)

Part Two: Sort your disabilities list into three principal groups: physical, emotional, or physiological. (For example, multiple sclerosis is a physical degeneration of one's muscular system; schizophrenia is commonly identified as a brain chemistry imbalance.) If you are uncertain of the category of a disability, discuss it with others. Recall from the chapter that disabilities may be permanent or temporary, evident and observable, or invisible.

Personal Insight Builder: Make three generalizations regarding how humans are different according to disability. Can you identify instances of unjustifiable discrimination against persons with disabilities? What attitudinal adjustments might be made within the general U.S. population regarding our attitudes toward persons with disabilities?

REFERENCES

Adelman, H.S. (1996). The classification problem. In W. Stainback & S. Stainback (Eds.), *Controversial issues confronting special education: Divergent perspectives* (pp. 29–44). Boston, MA: Allyn & Bacon.

Describes concerns, criticisms, and responses to labeling people in special education.

Barzun, J. (2000). *From dawn to decadence: 500 years of Western cultural life (1500 to the present).* New York, NY: HarperCollins.

Discusses significant historical events as well as the intellectual contributions of those individuals who have had a lasting impact on the culture of the Western world.

Batavia, A. (2001). The new paternalism: Portraying people with disabilities as an oppressed minority. *Journal of Disability Policy Studies, 12*(2), 107–113.

Critiques the other articles in this issue that provide evidence or analysis supporting the idea that people with a disability represent an oppressed minority group.

Batavia, A. (2002). Consumer direction, consumer choice, and the future of long-term care. In L. Powers (Ed.), *Journal of Disability Policy Studies, 13*(2), 67–73.

Describes home care as an alternative to institutional care in the United States and other nations.

Bernell, S. (2003). Theoretical and applied issues in defining disability in labor market research. *Journal of Disability Policy Studies, 14*(1), 36–45.

Reviews various definitions of disability and examines problems related to definitions and research methods in labor market research.

Charlton, J.I. (1998). *Nothing about us without us.* Berkeley: University of California Press.

Describes the status of people with disabilities in various cultures and compares it with the treatment that people with disabilities in the United States receive.

Coleman, L.M. (2006). Stigma. In L. Davis (Ed.), *The disability studies reader* (pp. 216–233). New York, NY: Routledge.

Discusses the origin of the concept of stigma and analyzes the reasons why some differences in human beings are valued and others are stigmatized.

EEOC. (2009). Disability discrimination. Retrieved September 28, 2009 from http://www.eeoc.gov/types/ada.html.

Provides information about the 1990 Americans with Disabilities Act and updated statistics on complaints filed.

Ervelles, N. (2001). In search of the disabled subject. In J.C. Wilson & C. Lewicki-Wilson (Eds.), *Embodied rhetorics: Disability in language and culture* (pp. 92–111). Carbondale: Southern Illinois University Press.

Explains how social differences such as disability, gender, race, and social class have been produced by and still operate within the context of global economic exploitation.

Fiedler, C. (2008). *Making a difference: Advocacy competencies for special education professionals.* Austin, TX: Pro Ed.

Discusses the need for teachers and parents to be advocates for people with disabilities and provides strategies, examples, and resources for being an effective advocate.

Fiedler, C., & Rylance, B. (Eds.). (2001, Fall). *Journal of Disability Policy Studies, 12*(2).

Addresses the question of whether or not disabled people constitute a minority group.

Fiedler, L. (1993). *Freaks: Myths and images of the secret self.* New York, NY: Anchor Books.

Provides a history of people with disabilities and deformities, describing how they were viewed in the past and how these perceptions have shaped contemporary attitudes.

Fierros, E.G., & Conroy, J.W. (2002). Double jeopardy: An exploration of restrictiveness and race in special education. In D.J. Losen & G. Orfield (Eds.), *Racial inequity in special education.* Cambridge, MA: Harvard Education Press.

Examined data from selected U.S. cities and found Latinos and Blacks overrepresented in special education and less likely to be educated in inclusive classrooms.

Fine, M., & Asch, A. (2000). Disability beyond stigma: Social interaction, discrimination, and activism. In M. Adams, W.J. Blumenfeld, R. Castaneda, H.W. Hackman, M.L. Peters, & X. Zuniga (Eds.), *Readings for diversity and social justice* (pp. 330–339). New York, NY: Routledge.

Examines reasons why people with disabilities are stigmatized, including explanations for widely held and erroneous assumptions about disabled people.

Foucault, M. (1989). *Madness and civilization: A history of insanity in the age of reason.* London, England: Routledge.

Describes perceptions of madness, the institutionalization of mentally ill people, and their treatment in such institutions from the Middle Ages to the eighteenth century.

Garrett History Brief. (2001). *Journal of Disability Policy Studies, 12*(2), 70–78.

Presents historical and contemporary evidence of discrimination against disabled people.

Gill, C.J. (1994). Questioning continuum. In B. Shaw (Ed.), *The ragged edge: The disability experience from the pages of the first fifteen years of "The Disability Rag"* (pp. 42–49). Louisville, KY: The Advocado Press.

Argues that placing all people at some point along a continuum of disability reflects a discomfort with differences and is an attempt to minimize them.

Gliona, M.F., Gonzales, A.K., & Jacobson, E.S. (2005). Dedicated, not segregated: Suggested changes in thinking about instructional environments and in the language of special education. In J.M. Kauffman & D.P. Hallahan (Eds.), *The illusion of full inclusion: A comprehensive critique of a current special education bandwagon*. Austin, TX: Pro-ed.

Argues that the common view of alternate placements as always restrictive and referring to them as "segregation" is harmful to the goal of educating children with special needs.

Hahn, H. (1988, Winter). Can disability be beautiful? *Social Policy, 18,* 26–32.

Examines cross-cultural perceptions of people with a disability and provides historic examples of disabled people being valued for their differences.

Hahn, H. (1994). The minority group model of disability: Implications for medical sociology. *Research in the Sociology of Health Care, 11,* 3–24.

Examines how public policy shaped the experiences and perceptions of people with disabilities.

Hehir, T. (2005). *New directions in special education*. Cambridge, MA: Harvard Education Press.

Describes the history of special education, its current practices, and recommends principles for making decisions regarding future directions for special education.

Hines, R.A. (2001). *Inclusion in middle schools.* (Report No. EDO-PS-01-13). Champaign, IL: ERIC Clearinghouse on Elementary and Early Childhood Education, Children's Research Center, University of Illinois. (ERIC Document Reproduction Service No. 459000)

Discusses research on inclusion and benefits for nondisabled and disabled students.

Johnson, J.R., & Nieto, J. (2007). Towards a cultural understanding of the disability and deaf experience: A content analysis of introductory multicultural education textbooks. *Multicultural Perspectives, 9*(3), 33–43.

Reports the findings of a content analysis of 11 multicultural textbooks with regard to the extent and nature of their inclusion of disability culture and deaf culture.

Kaminski, S.E., Mazumdar, S., DiMento, J.F.C., & Geis, G. (2006). The viability of voluntary visitability. *Journal of Disability Policy Studies, 17*(1), 49–56.

Presents a case study of a voluntary visitability program in Irvine, California.

Kavale, K.A., & Forness, S.R. (2005). History, rhetoric, and reality: Analysis of the inclusion debate. In J.M. Kauffman and D.P. Hallahan (Eds.), *The illusion of full inclusion: A comprehensive critique of a current special education bandwagon*. Austin, TX: Pro-ed.

Explores the history of efforts to integrate students with disabilities into regular education classes and discusses current issues pertaining to ongoing integration efforts.

Kliewer, C., & Biklin, D. (1996). Labeling: Who wants to be called retarded? In J. Stainbeck & S. Stainbeck (Eds.), *Controversial issues confronting special education: Divergent perspectives* (pp. 83–95). Baltimore, MD: Brookes.

Describes changes in labeling people as mentally retarded in the past and currently, and the changing perspectives on independent living for those individuals who have been labeled.

Kochhar, C.A., West, L.L., & Taymans, J.M. (2000). *Successful inclusion: Practical strategies for a shared responsibility.* Upper Saddle River, NJ: Prentice-Hall.

Describes the history and philosophy of inclusion and successful classroom practices; the benefits of inclusion are described in Chapter 9, pp. 37–40.

Koppelman, K. (2001). The only thing we have to fear. *Values in the key of life: Making harmony in the human community* (pp. 24–28). Amityville, NY: Baywood.

Uses a personal example to discuss the inadequate social services available in the United States, and compares U.S. social services with social services in Austria.

Linton, S. (1998). *Claiming disability: Knowledge and identity.* New York, NY: New York University Press.

Discusses the need for disability studies to understand the experience of disabled people as a minority group; defines ableism and other relevant terms in Chapter 2, pp. 8–33.

Longmore, P.K. (2003). *Why I burned my book and other essays on disability.* Philadelphia, PA: Temple University Press.

Discusses historical discrimination against people with disabilities in the media and in society and describes the evolution of the disability rights movement.

LaFleur, J. (2009, June 22). *Nursing homes get old for many with disabilities*. Retrieved September 28, 2009, from http://www.propublicorg/feature/nursing-homes-get-old-for-many-with-disabilities-621

Reports on numbers of people with disabilities in nursing homes and those who want to be placed in communities.

Losen, D.J., & Orfield, G. (2002). Introduction. In D.J. Losen & G. Orfield (Eds.), *Racial inequity in special education*. Cambridge, MA: Harvard Education Press.

Presents findings of past studies on overrepresentation of racial minorities in special education and summarizes issues related to this topic that are discussed in this book.

Morse, W.C. (2005). Comments from a biased viewpoint. In J.M. Kauffman & D.P. Hallahan (Eds.), *The illusion of full inclusion: A comprehensive critique of a current special education bandwagon*. Austin, TX: Pro-ed.

Challenges the advocates of inclusion by refuting some assumptions of the inclusion movement and describing difficulties inclusion can create for teachers and students.

Orfield, G., Losen, D., Wald, J., & Swanson, C. (2004). *Losing our future: How minority youth are being left behind by the graduation rate crisis*. Cambridge, MA: The Civil Rights Project at Harvard University. Contributors: Advocates for Children of New York and The Civil Society Institute.

Examines data revealing disparities of graduation rates for students of color compared to white students and includes narratives from students of color who dropped out of school.

Osher, D., Woodruff, D., & Sims, A.E. (2002). Schools make a difference: The overrepresentation of African American youth in special education and the juvenile justice system. In D.J. Losen & G. Orfield (Eds.), *Racial inequity in special education*. Cambridge, MA: Harvard Education Press.

Addresses issues related to overidentification of racial minorities in special education and the impact of effective and ineffective school interventions.

Osgood, R.L. (2005). *The history of inclusion in the United States*. Washington, DC: Gallaudet University Press.

Explores the origins and evolution of the inclusion concept and the growth of advocacy for inclusion in the United States.

Padden, C., & Humphries, T. (1998). *Deaf in America: Voices from a culture*. Cambridge, MA: Harvard University Press.

Presents numerous examples of the cultural life of deaf people and includes comments and anecdotes from individuals in the deaf community.

Pai, Y., & Adler, S. (1997). *Cultural foundations of education*, Upper Saddle River, NJ: Merrill/Prentice Hall.

Discusses concepts of culture in Chapter 2, "Culture, Education and Schooling."

Parrish, T. (2002). Racial disparities in the identification, funding, and provision of special education. In D.J. Losen & G. Orfield (Eds.), *Racial inequity in special education*. Cambridge, MA: Harvard Education Press.

Analyzes national data to consider under- and overrepresentation of students of color in special education and how this relates to funding of special education services.

Pelka, F. (1994, July/August). Hating the sick: Health chauvinism and its cure. *Humanist, 54*(4), 17–21.

Examines current evidence that attitudes in the United States reflect a "health chauvinist society" that is prejudiced against disabled people and blames them for having a disability.

Posner, B. (1979). Israel: A tale of two people. *Disabled USA, 2*(8), 16–17.

Describes negative attitudes in the United States toward people who are mentally retarded and uses an incident from Israel to illustrate the difficulty of changing such attitudes.

Putnam, M. (2005). Conceptualizing disability. *Journal of Disability Policy Studies, 16*(3), 188–198.

Presents a conceptual framework for understanding disability identity and uses this framework to analyze research on disabilities.

Reagan, T. (2005). A case study in cultural and linguistic difference: The DEAF-WORLD. In T. Osborn (Ed.), *Language and cultural diversity in U.S. schools*. Westport, CT: Praeger.

Defines the components of culture, then discusses evidence and provides examples of how the deaf community has created a culture reflecting these components.

Ribton-Turner, C.J. (1972). *A history of vagrants and vagrancy*. Montclair, NJ: Patterson Smith.

Describes the history of societal responses to vagrancy primarily in England, but with chapters on Russia, Turkey, and countries in Western Europe (first published in 1887).

Russell, M. (1998). *Beyond ramps: Disability at the end of the social contract*. Monroe, ME: Common Courage Press.

Examines historical examples of the oppression of disabled people and contemporary issues concerning poverty, institutionalization, and denial of civil rights.

Sapon-Shevin, M. (1999). *Because we can change the world: A practical guide to building cooperative, inclusive classroom communities*. Boston, MA: Allyn & Bacon.

Provides strategies and activities that reflect principles of multicultural education although primarily intended for creating cohesive classrooms in elementary schools.

Sowers, J., McLean, D., & Owens, C. (2002). Self-directed employment for people with developmental disabilities: Issues, characteristics, and illustrations. *Journal of Disability Policy Studies, 13*(2), 96–103.

Describes a customer-directed employment service system and provides an example of how such an approach can more effectively find employment for people with disabilities.

Stone, D.A. (1984). *The disabled state.* Philadelphia, PA: Temple University Press.

Discusses the complex issues affecting the medical basis for determining who is disabled and eligible for disability benefits and who is not.

Sulewski, J.S., Gilmore, D.S., & Foley, S.M. (2006, Winter). Medicaid and employment of people with disabilities. *Journal of Disability Policy Studies, 17*(3), 158–165.

Discusses the need for people with disabilities to rely on Medicaid for health care and how this can restrict their employment opportunities.

Taylor, H. (1998, October 14). Americans with disabilities still pervasively disadvantaged on a broad range of key indicators. *Harris Poll* 56. Retrieved May 12, 2009, from www.harrisinteractive/harris_poll/index.asp?PID=182.

Presents results of the Harris Poll on issues affecting people with a disability.

U.S. Census Bureau. (2009, May 26). *Facts for features* (press release). Retrieved June 15, 2009, from http://www.census.gov/Press-Release/www/releases

Provides most recent data on Americans with disabilities.

Wehmeyer, M. (2000, Summer). Riding the third wave. *Focus on Autism & Other Developmental Disabilities, 15*(2), 106–116.

Describes three waves of the disability movement with professionalism superseded by the parent movement that is now being challenged by those promoting self-advocacy.

Williams, C. (2003). Managing individuals in a diverse work force. In *Management* (2nd ed., pp. 434–471). Versailles, KY: Thompson Southwestern.

Explains why diversity is being promoted in the corporate world, the benefits of diversity, and principles for being an effective manager of diverse employees.

Wilson, J.C., & Lewicki-Wilson, C. (2001). Disability, rhetoric, and the body. In J.C. Wilson & C. Lewicki-Wilson (Eds.), *Embodied rhetorics: Disability in language and culture* (pp. 1–24). Carbondale: Southern Illinois University Press.

Examines the relationship between language and behavior and describes how rhetorical analysis can be an aid for people with disabilities as they define themselves.

Winzer, M.A. (1997). Disability and society before the eighteenth century: Dread and despair. In L. Davis (Ed.), *The disability studies reader* (pp. 75–109). London, England: Routledge.

Describes the experiences of disabled people from ancient times including how they were portrayed in literature and the evolution of institutions to care for them.

Wolfensberger, W. (1970). *The principle of normalization in human services.* Toronto: National Institute on Mental Retardation.

Analyzes the role of ideology and concepts of deviancy in shaping attitudes toward disabled people; describes how the principle of normalization could change human services.

The Challenge of Diversity to American Institutions

This section describes the changes in the United States that take advantage of American population diversity.

Elementary, middle, and secondary schools have historically been considered the vehicle by which we transmit our cultural values and knowledge to future generations, and Chapter 13 describes the philosophy and practices of school multicultural education curriculums. Following a brief review of America's traditional educational philosophy known as "essentialism," this chapter describes the changes necessary to create schools and classrooms where policies, practices, curriculum, and instruction reflect the purposes and goals of multicultural education. The chapter concludes with an explanation of why multicultural education represents an educational reform that needs to be pursued for the benefit of all our

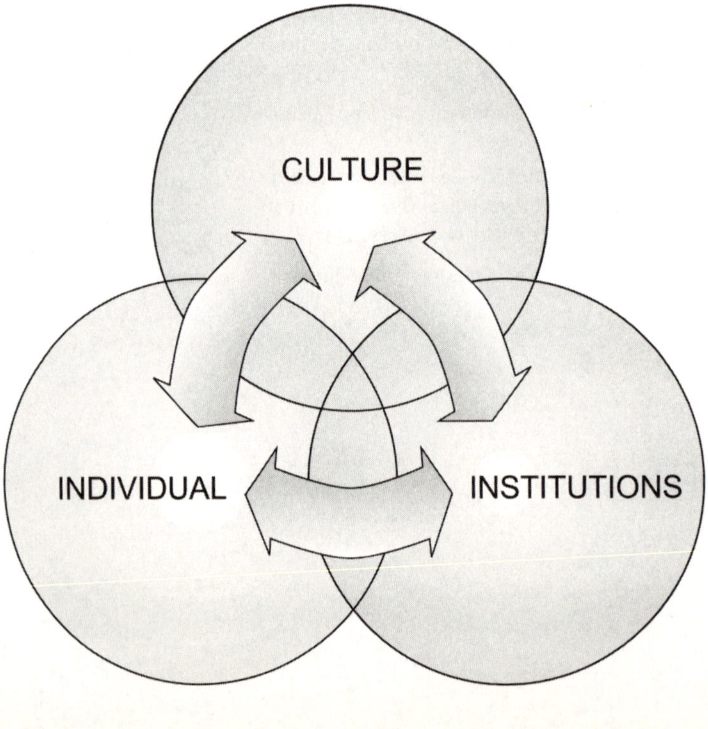

students and for the future of our diverse society.

Currently, considerable effort is being made to instill in the American workforce a more inclusive attitude toward diversity. Chapter 14 describes changes occurring in major institutions of our society that reflect the growing influence of pluralism as the preferred perspective in response to the ongoing and growing diversity of the American people. Our government continues to require affirmative action plans to ensure that opportunities are provided to members of groups that were discriminated against in the past and continue to be discriminated against. Higher education administrators have embraced the value of affirmative plans to broaden the diversity of faculty as well as student populations and to argue that such diversity enhances the education of all students.

In the corporate world, business leaders have recognized the growing diversity of the workforce and consumers and are increasingly implementing diversity training to take advantage of both. Mass media organizations have promoted diversity by placing more women and people of color in positions that have a high public visibility, and the diversity in this profession is likely to increase, given the significantly increasing numbers of women and people of color currently majoring in journalism or mass communication on college campuses. The military has taken aggressive action to promote gender and racial equality in its recruitment, in promotion policies and practices, and in its diversity training programs.

Change occurring in institutions across the United States reinforces the need to prepare new generations to appreciate and participate effectively in the unique and increasing diversity that defines our American society in the twenty-first century.

CHAPTER 13

Pluralism in Schools: The Promise of Multicultural Education

"Learning to read was, for slaves, not an immediate passport to freedom but rather a way of gaining access to one of the powerful instruments of their oppressors: the book."

Alberto Manguel (1948–)

Learning and schooling are critical for every person in any society. The future of our diverse society will depend on how schools educate the coming generations, and pluralism must be a significant factor in that education. During an interview for a college administrative position, an African American candidate asked about his views on diversity responded, "First, let me say that I'm a pluralist. After all, we had a diverse society when we had slaves." This is an important distinction. Many people refer to *diversity* and *pluralism* as if the two terms were synonymous, but **diversity** simply describes the existence of many different groups of people within a society, whereas **pluralism** describes a society in which diversity is accepted and supported. A pluralistic society is one in which diverse groups function together effectively with mutual respect. In a society that is diverse but not pluralistic, schools tend to teach principally about the dominant group—its influence on the evolution of society, and its literature, art, and music. In a diverse society committed to pluralism, schools would teach about all groups within the society, from most ancient to most recent.

Misunderstanding of terms occurs when we fail to clarify meanings and intentions. No study of human differences is complete without special terms, and precise communication exists only when everyone involved is clear about their meaning. So we must begin by clarifying our definition of multicultural education and explaining our vision of its importance for the future of our diverse society.

Defining Multicultural Education

Multicultural education is based on a commitment to pluralism; its guiding purpose is to prepare students to be active participants in a diverse, democratic society. There is confusion and considerable debate about multicultural education, even among educators who advocate for it. Some people regard multicultural education simply as the process of integrating issues and information about race and ethnicity into school curricula, but that describes what Banks (2006) defines as **multiethnic education.** In a study cited by Gayle-Evans and Michael (2006), some teachers regarded multicultural education as a curriculum for teaching about cultures around the world, but that is usually called **global (or international) education.** Others say multicultural education includes recognition of women, gays and lesbians, people with disabilities, and other minority groups; opponents to this idea argue that such groups do not constitute distinct cultures and therefore should not be included. This confusion raises many questions that must be answered before we can understand what multicultural education is and recognize schools that are engaged in an authentic form of this educational approach.

In addition to conflicting opinions about the definition of the term *multicultural education* and about who should be included, there are numerous perceptions about who benefits from it. Americans seem to agree that students of color benefit from multicultural education, especially in urban multiracial and multiethnic classrooms; yet many educators and parents in suburban or rural school districts consisting predominantly or exclusively of white students appear to believe that multicultural education provides no benefits. Gayle-Evans and Michael (2006) review several studies reporting that many teachers were uncomfortable incorporating multicultural issues into their content because they felt that the topics were "too sensitive"; educators also said they did not feel that their teacher education programs adequately prepared them to implement multicultural education practices. Some educators in elementary and secondary schools with predominantly white students have included the contributions of a few people of color into their curriculum, but such an addition does not represent an education that is genuinely multicultural.

What does it mean for education to be called *multicultural*?

As early as 1974, Hilliard wrote that **multicultural** refers to a society "made up of a number of cultural groups based upon race, ethnicity, religion, language, nationality, income, etc." (p. 41). Because income level is not usually regarded as representing a different culture—rich or poor, we're all Americans—Hilliard's comment is assumed to mean that the term *multicultural* includes other subordinate groups that he did not specifically identify, such as women, gays and lesbians, and people with disabilities.

As for the term *education,* we must distinguish between *education* and *training.* Some dictionaries suggest that education and training are synonyms, but people take classes to train them in a particular skill. A person can be trained to drive or cook, or even be trained to train a dog. Education is a broader concept. Partridge (1983) explained that *educate* derives from the Latin word *ducere,* which means to lead; "educere" means to lead out or bring forth (p. 169). By extrapolation, *education* means to bring forth the potential of an individual. In addition to developing cognitive skill and affective sensitivity, education entails developing an understanding of previous achievements in subjects such as history, literature, and science as a basis for making individual and societal choices in the future. Carse (1986) distinguished education from training:

> Education discovers an increasing richness in the past because it sees what is unfinished there. Training regards the past as finished and the future to be finished. Education leads toward a continuing self-discovery; training leads toward a final self-definition. (p. 23)

Multicultural education integrates information about past issues with achievements of diverse groups to describe how they have influenced our society. Children and youth from all groups are thereby provided with a sense of belonging to our society by understanding how their group has helped to shape what it is and by appreciating the potential they have for influencing what it will become.

What is an appropriate definition for multicultural education?

Multicultural education is a journey that leads students to self-discovery and to a sense of personal efficacy. Nieto (2008) provides a comprehensive definition and description of multicultural education that includes the components to be addressed in this chapter:

> **Multicultural education** is a process of comprehensive school reform and basic education for all students. It challenges and rejects racism and other forms of discrimination in schools and society and accepts and affirms the pluralism (ethnic, racial, linguistic, religious, economic, and gender, among others) that students, their communities, and teachers reflect. Multicultural education permeates the

FIGURE 13.1 Frank and Ernest

> schools' curriculum and instructional strategies, as well as the interactions among teachers, students, and families, and the very way that schools conceptualize the nature of teaching and learning. Because it uses critical pedagogy as its underlying philosophy . . . multicultural education promotes democratic principles of social justice. (p. 44)

Nieto's definition and description of multicultural education emphasizes that it is not a "business-as-usual" approach to schooling. It requires changes in teaching methods and perspectives on learning because of critical philosophical differences between traditional education and multicultural education.

Traditional Assumptions in American Education

The development of American schools has been based on a conservative philosophy that was eventually labeled *essentialism,* and essentialist assumptions are still in place. The term stems from the belief that an essential body of knowledge and essential human values that have stood the test of time can be identified and transmitted to students. Essentialists describe the purpose of schools as the transmission of the most significant accumulated knowledge and values from previous generations to the coming generation.

What body of knowledge have essentialists identified?

Essentialist scholars maintain that knowledge from four disciplines is essential: social studies, science, mathematics, and English language and literature; therefore these four subjects are emphasized in elementary, middle, and high school. Graduation requirements for high school students usually include a minimum of two years of course work, often three or even four, in social studies, science, mathematics, and English. To essentialists, subjects such as art, music, and physical education are accepted principally to make school more enjoyable, but they are regarded as additional rather than essential. When administrators consider budget reductions, programs in art, music, and physical education are scrutinized and are most likely to be reduced or eliminated. Similar assumptions continue into college, where general education programs often require students to choose among a selection of courses in social studies, science, math, and English literature and composition.

What essential human values do schools teach?

As indicated in Chapter 1, Myrdal (1944) identified core American values embraced by most citizens and taught in most schools. In addition, Americans presume that certain values represent the American middle class: promptness, honesty, hard work, competitiveness, and efficiency. Teachers implement traditional approaches to teaching values (see Chapter 1) to convince children and youth that the core values are worthwhile and should be adopted. Students may say they believe in these values because it's expected of them, even though their behavior often does not suggest that they have a genuine commitment to them.

How do essentialists define or describe learning?

Essentialists define learning as the acquisition of essential knowledge and values. Metaphors used by essentialists to describe learning portray knowledge as water and students as empty vessels to be filled or as sponges ready to absorb. To assess learning, essentialists favor objective tests with questions about factual information to ascertain if students absorbed the information. (If not, teachers may review the information and test students again.) In extreme cases, students may repeat a grade to have a second chance to learn material in the hope that the teacher, perhaps a different teacher, will be more successful helping them acquire the information. Maturity and readiness are considered secondary in this process.

> Teachers open the door, but you must enter by yourself.
>
> **Chinese Proverb**

What is the role of the essentialist teacher in helping students learn?

An essentialist teacher is supposed to be a skillful transmitter of information and an advocate for American values. Teachers are expected to be role models for our society's values—both inside and outside the classroom. As transmitters of information, teachers are expected to use technology to make information interesting and thereby promote acquisition of knowledge. Although teachers may select from a variety of pedagogical techniques, the goal is to motivate students to remember information provided in textbooks, lectures, and media. The problem is that few students can demonstrate that they are learning what teachers are teaching.

Why are students not learning in essentialist schools?

The first problem has to do with what has been considered essential. During the past several decades, research in various fields, especially the sciences, has generated what scholars have called a *knowledge explosion*. Given so much new knowledge, how is one to determine which facts are most important? Feminists and scholars of color have developed alternative interpretations of historical events that challenge conventional views; they believe their perspectives should be included in school curricula. Whereas women and writers of color were minimally represented in previous literature anthologies, advocates are increasingly demanding that their voices and ideas be acknowledged. Curriculum reformers suggest that most students regard traditional essentialist curriculum as inaccurate, irrelevant, and not at all motivational.

Another problem is that we know students learn at different rates. If teachers transmit information at the same rate, some students learn all of it, some learn most of it, and some retain very little of it; yet teachers often must proceed as if all students learned equally. The solution essentialists have developed to address incomplete learning is to group students according to ability, which is known as *tracking*. Studies of tracking have found that excellent students learn just as well in heterogeneous groups as in homogeneous groups where they are grouped by ability, but that the achievement of moderate and slow learners improves significantly when they are in mixed groups rather than when they are grouped according to academic ability (Kershaw, 1992; Oakes, 2005; Oakes & Wells, 1996; Oakes et al., 2000). Despite these consistent research conclusions, essentialist schools tend to continue to group students according to ability.

Perhaps the most significant obstacle to learning in essentialist schools is the problem of retention and transfer. **Retention** refers to student recall of knowledge; **transfer** is the ability of students to apply that knowledge both inside and outside the classroom. Students have long complained about cramming before taking exams that require them to memorize material. Studies have consistently found that when tested for retention of information, students tend to recall no more than 20% of what they had supposedly learned the first time they took the exam.

Assumptions of Multicultural Education

To resolve problems related to student learning, as parents or educators, we must change our assumptions about curriculum content, learning, teaching, and the purpose of schools. As described by Nieto (2008), Banks (2008), Sleeter (1996), and others, multicultural education challenges us to change those assumptions.

What assumptions do multicultural educators make about curriculum?

Nieto's widely accepted definition of multicultural education includes an affirmation of diversity that must permeate the curriculum to provide honest representations of diversity in American society. At present, textbooks continue to be dominated by the art, music, history, literature, perspectives, and images of white Americans. Sleeter and Grant (2003) reviewed forty-seven textbooks in social studies, reading, language arts, science, and mathematics for elementary and middle-level students. They reported that whites were featured predominantly in all of them. Although some improvements have been found in more recent textbooks, when people of color are included, the textbooks typically have provided:

> A sketchy account of Black history and little sense of contemporary Black life. Asian Americans appear mainly as figures on the landscape with virtually no history or contemporary ethnic experience. . . . Native Americans appear mainly as historical figures. (p. 22)

American elementary, middle, and secondary textbooks also tend to omit or provide only minimal representation of other groups: women, gays and lesbians, people with disabilities, and low-income families. School textbooks not only represent a problem for minority children but also are apt to teach white children a dishonest perspective of their society. As Baker (1994) explained, "Non-minority children are led to believe that their behavior, the ways they are taught to respond, are the only accepted ways of behaving" (p. 8). To present a realistic understanding of our multicultural society and the influence of diverse groups on our society, advocates support a multicultural curriculum for all students, not just for students of color.

A multicultural curriculum examines the influences of diverse groups on historical events, literary developments, musical styles, artistic expression, athletic achievements, and other facets of American society—but the goal is not simply to memorize facts. Appleton (1983) described multicultural curriculum as "a conceptual approach that provides a framework for understanding the experience and perspectives of all the groups" (p. 211). The need for a conceptual approach is another assumption about curriculum by multicultural educators.

> It is probably never really wise, or even necessary, or anything better than harmful, to educate a human being toward a good end by telling him lies.
>
> **James Agee (1910–1955)**

Why is it necessary to take a conceptual approach to curriculum?

Because of the knowledge explosion, it is impractical to emphasize memorization. It is not possible for us to remember all available information in every subject; we also know that much information soon will be obsolete or supplanted by new knowledge. In a multicultural curriculum, understanding broad concepts is preferable to memorizing facts. Gay (1977) described a multicultural curriculum design based on a thematic approach and a conceptual framework. In the thematic approach, students employ information from different disciplines to explore universal themes such as the search for identity, communication and conflict resolution, human interdependence, economics and exploitation, or the struggle for a just society.

Curriculum based on a conceptual framework also requires an interdisciplinary approach. Beginning with a concept such as power, alienation, or socialization, students could collect data from various sources addressing the concept, leading them to the identification and exploration of related concepts. Gay (1977) argued that both curriculum designs must be interdisciplinary because they require "the use of knowledge, concepts, and principles from many different disciplines" (p. 101). In either a thematic or a conceptual framework approach, students examine past and present experiences to develop an integrated understanding of principles and relationships between concepts.

Because multicultural curriculum is based on concepts rather than on specific content, students are involved in an ongoing and dynamic search for knowledge that is never finished, whereas the monocultural curriculum traditionally presented in schools is a finished product. As Nieto (2008) wrote,

> When reality is presented in schools as static, finished, and flat, the underlying tensions, controversies, passions and problems faced by people throughout history and today disappear. (p. 55)

Identifying concepts for students to analyze and discuss to clarify their understanding is the foundation of multicultural curriculum; to be effective, it is critical that the curriculum not be sabotaged by the hidden curriculum in school.

What is the hidden curriculum?

Pai and Adler (1997) define **hidden curriculum** as the indirect means by which schools teach students "the norms and values of their society" (p. 148). They describe the hidden curriculum as subtle messages learned from pictures displayed on bulletin boards or from school policies such as tardy slips and tracking. Messages may be intentional or unintentional; still, they have an impact on learners. Through the hidden curriculum, schools can promote such values as punctuality, assertiveness, or competitiveness. Pai and Adler suggest that the hidden curriculum may vary according to socioeconomic status, with upper-class children being taught leadership skills and having opportunities for creativity and problem solving in contrast to low-income students being taught to respect authority and receiving rewards for compliance and conformity.

Everyday situations reveal a hidden curriculum in school policies and practices, and subtle messages can even be found in formal curriculum. An education professor entered a Los Angeles high school English classroom, where 80% of the students were Hispanic; she noticed that only white authors were featured on wall posters. An unmarried high school student was expelled from the local chapter of the National Honor Society because she was pregnant. A student teacher in a fourth-grade classroom of predominantly white students wanted to make a "Black History Month" bulletin board for February, but her supervising teacher rejected the idea because she believed that the students were "too young" for that (Koppelman, 2001).

Teaching that Columbus discovered America tells children that Native Americans were irrelevant and can be ignored; perhaps it is no coincidence that the white majority ignores Native Americans who protest Indian mascots for school sports teams. Brigham Young took his followers to Mexican territory because of the oppression and violence Mormons had encountered in the United States. Teaching that Mormons settled in Utah instead of Mexican territory implies that religious groups have always been able to practice their beliefs freely in the United States and ignores the difficulty America has experienced living up to the principle of religious freedom. Teaching that Old World art refers only to ancient Greek and Roman cultures denies the artistic heritage of many—especially non-Western—countries. Nieto (2008) argued that presenting history only from the perspective of the dominant group teaches a skewed version of the truth. Educators implementing multicultural curric-

> The wise person can see a question from all sides without bias. The foolish person is biased and can see a question only from one side.
>
> **Confucius (551–479 BCE)**

ula must be especially sensitive to subtle messages provided by the hidden curriculum.

Why have schools implemented multicultural curriculum?

Many schools across the United States, especially in urban areas, have developed their own multicultural materials to supplement inadequate textbooks. Banks (2008) categorized the efforts into four approaches, two of which also satisfy Nieto's definition of multicultural education: the transformation approach and the social action approach (see Figure 13.2).

A *transformation* approach to multicultural curriculum design emphasizes concepts and themes. Students are presented with multiple perspectives on issues, and the goal is not to identify a "right perspective," but to understand how each perspective contributes to a richer understanding of issues. Critical thinking skills are emphasized as students develop their own insights and conclusions and logically justify them.

A *social action* approach to multicultural curriculum design encourages students to take action based on their ideas and conclusions. Students—individually or collectively—pursue projects at school and in their community to address problems they identify and study. The goal of a social action approach is to empower students and to demonstrate that learning is not a game of *Trivial Pursuit*. Knowledge can lead to social action and create positive change. By encouraging critical thinking and active learning, multicultural educators combine theory and practice about conditions necessary to promote effective learning.

How do multicultural educators describe learning?

Advocates for multicultural education rely on cognitive development theory to describe how people

FIGURE 13.2 Approaches to Multicultural Curriculum Reform

Source: From *Multicultural Education: Issues and Perspectives*, 9/e by James A. Banks and Cherry A. McGee Banks. Copyright © 2004. Reprinted with permission of John Wiley & Sons, Ltd.

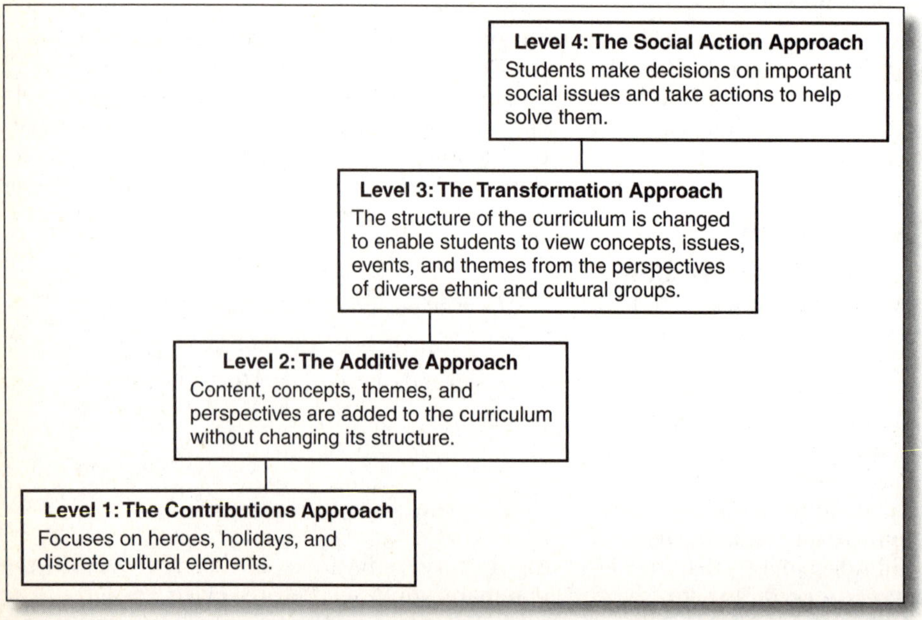

learn. In essence, learning is a process of meaning making. Learners organize ideas, information, and experiences they encounter to make sense of them. They may categorize, seek relationships, and simplify complex issues to achieve understanding. According to Sleeter and Grant (2003), "Learning is a process of constructing knowledge through the interaction of mind and experience" (p. 196). Piaget (1974) observed that children learn by interacting physically and intellectually with their environment. If students are provided information through lecture, they may attempt to extract relevant meaning from it, but if they perceive no relevance in the information, they are not likely to make the effort.

Learning results from the interaction learners encounter when they are required to be active. Learning also requires meaningfulness. Information regarded as meaningless will not be learned. Being an active learner promotes the development of competence and confidence, the basis for Dewey's insistence that children "learn by doing." Feeling competent and gaining self-confidence leads to a sense of power. As Hilliard (1974) wrote, "Learning is related to a sense of power over some of the forces which impinge upon our lives" (p. 47). If students feel powerless, they have little motivation to learn; when students are active, they develop skills and demonstrate abilities that reinforce self-confidence and give a sense of personal competence, and they acquire an enthusiasm for learning.

> In every child who is born, under no matter what circumstances, and of no matter what parents, the potentiality of the human race is born again; and in (that child) . . . and in each of us, our terrific responsibility towards human life; toward the utmost idea of goodness.
>
> James Agee (1910–1955)

With regard to skill development, learning must not be limited to basic academic skills—reading, writing, computing—but must include a multitude of skills related to critical thinking, creativity, decision making, problem solving, information accessing, interpersonal and cross-cultural communication, conflict resolution, visual literacy, and self-analysis. Gay (1977) argued that an education that "does not include the development of skills that will increase and enhance student's capabilities to live and function in a culturally pluralistic setting is incomplete" (p. 98). Although students may develop skills, an obstacle to facilitating skill development is that students have multiple ways of learning; therefore a single teaching strategy may be inadequate. Teachers committed to multicultural education must believe that all children can learn—if learning activities are designed to accommodate each child.

In what different ways do individuals learn?

Considerable research has been conducted to identify and explain styles of learning, but the result has been to categorize learning as a complex assortment of more than a dozen different learning styles. In more recent years, multicultural educators have been attracted to the work of Gardner (1993), whose theory of multiple intelligences is regarded by many as one of the best explanations of the diversity in learning. Gardner defines intelligence as the ability to process information and to generate solutions or products of value within a particular context.

Gardner originally identified seven distinct ways that people demonstrate intelligence (Gardner, 1993), but since then he has added an eighth category of intelligence (Gardner, 1999). According to Gardner, each person has the potential to engage in all eight means of processing information, although an individual is likely to be more competent in certain dimensions based on personal idiosyncrasies or the influence of his or her culture. (See Table 13.1.) The theory rejects the educational practice of recognizing and rewarding primarily two intelligences: logical-mathematical and linguistic. Gardner's theory describes a more complete means of understanding intelligence and identifying intellectual abilities. The challenge for teachers is to create instructional strategies and assessment procedures that accommodate more than one kind of intelligence. If teachers can meet this challenge, more students will have successful learning experiences, which will promote self-confidence.

TABLE 13.1 Descriptions of Multiple Intelligences

1. *Logical-Mathematical:* Ability to understand and solve logical problems, especially involving the use and manipulation of numbers.
2. *Linguistic:* Ability to understand nuances of meanings and multiple meanings of words, including a special appreciation for the sounds and rhythms of language.
3. *Bodily-Kinesthetic:* Ability to learn and master physical tasks involving motion and balance, and including manual manipulation of objects.
4. *Musical:* Ability to understand, reproduce, and appreciate musical sounds and rhythms in a range of musical expressions.
5. *Spatial:* Ability to understand spatial relationships in the environment and to cognitively modify those relationships for particular purposes.
6. *Interpersonal:* Sensitivity to nonverbal expressions of feelings and desires of other people and the ability to respond appropriately to them.
7. *Intrapersonal:* Ability for self-analysis, to understand clearly one's own feelings and desires and to apply that knowledge in one's choices and behaviors.
8. *Naturalist:* Ability to discern similarities and differences in plants and animals that leads to an enhanced understanding of established classifications.

Source: Gardner (1999).

Why is self-confidence necessary for learning?

Attitudes affect learning. It is generally understood that if students think they cannot learn something, they aren't likely to learn it. Combs (1979) claimed, "People behave in terms of what they believe about themselves. Whether we feel adequate or inadequate greatly affects how we approach a task" (p. 108). Research studies have confirmed that attitudes of teachers (and others) can positively or negatively affect student self-confidence. Research cited by Baker (1994) concluded, "There appears to be a high correlation between achievement in school and students' self-concept of academic ability as determined by the expectations and evaluations of significant others" (p. 9). By "significant others" Baker meant teachers and other school personnel. Although expectations should not be unrealistic, teachers must express high expectations for students to facilitate learning.

What must teachers do to implement a multicultural education approach?

Educators must determine which multicultural education approach they will implement. Sleeter and Grant (2003) identified five distinct approaches, two of which also satisfy the criteria included in Nieto's description: multicultural education and education that is multicultural *and* social reconstructionist (see Table 13.2). For purposes of clarity, the latter is referred to here as the *social reconstructionist approach.*

Principles underlying a multicultural education approach are reflected in a statement entitled "No One Model American" issued by the Commission on Multicultural Education (Hunter, 1974):

> Multicultural education values cultural pluralism. Multicultural education rejects the view that schools should seek to melt away cultural differences or the view that schools should merely

TABLE 13.2 Approaches to Multicultural Education

Teaching the Exceptional and the Culturally Different

GOALS: To help low-achieving students succeed within traditional education by building bridges between them and the curriculum, and providing special assistance.

CURRICULUM: Based on the traditional curriculum but incorporates students' experiences (especially those who are culturally different). Uses classroom materials that include meaningful contexts for the students.

INSTRUCTION: Implements English as a Second Language or transitional bilingual education for language minority students and culturally relevant teaching for culturally different students; provides remedial classes including special education placement for temporary but intensive remediation; displays images relevant to students on wall posters and bulletin boards.

Human Relations

GOALS: To maintain traditional educational assumptions but with an emphasis on reducing prejudice, developing positive student self-concepts, and promoting acceptance of individual diversity.

CURRICULUM: Based on the traditional curriculum but including content on prejudice and stereotypes, similarities and differences among groups and individuals, and societal contributions from members of diverse groups in society, especially those groups represented by the students in the school.

INSTRUCTION: Uses strategies that build student-student relationships such as conflict mediation, role playing, simulations that address interpersonal relationships, and cooperative learning; displays student work on walls and bulletin boards.

Single Group Studies

GOALS: To provide knowledge about a particular group (Women's Studies, Chicano Studies, etc.) including an examination of structural inequalities affecting members of this group and encouraging students to work for social change.

CURRICULUM: Provides information (for a unit or course) about cultural characteristics and historical experiences of a group with emphasis on perspectives of group members and how this group has been and still is oppressed.

INSTRUCTION: Responds to learning style differences of the group with accommodations for individual learning styles; incorporates media, music, performances, and guest speakers to address aspects of the culture or issues related to the group; wall displays and bulletin boards emphasize societal contributions from individual members of the group.

Multicultural Education

GOALS: To promote cultural pluralism by emphasizing respect for human differences, including individual lifestyles, equal opportunity for all in school and society, and the need for power equity among diverse groups in society.

CURRICULUM: Provides content on diverse groups and their contributions to society with emphasis on perspectives from members of each group; incorporates student experiences to enhance curriculum relevance, and emphasizes the need to be aware of and understand alternative

(*continues*)

TABLE 13.2 (*Continued*)

perspectives on issues; addresses "hidden curriculum" by including diversity in special events, holidays, school menus, etc.

INSTRUCTION: Responds to student learning styles and skill levels with emphasis on an analysis of curriculum content and critical thinking activities; promotes respect for and use of other languages and dialects while learning standard English; displays wall posters and bulletin boards that reflect human diversity represented by race, ethnicity, gender, disability, religion, and other diverse groups, as well as issues reflecting individual student interests.

Education That Is Multicultural and Social Reconstructionist

GOALS: To promote cultural pluralism and structural equality for diverse groups in our society, to prepare students to be active participants in our democratic society by understanding structural inequalities and promoting equal opportunity.

CURRICULUM: Provides content on current social issues of oppression and structural inequalities for diverse groups using perspectives of members of those groups including the perspectives of students and community members; emphasizes historic and contemporary life experiences for self-reflection, for analyzing oppression, and for understanding alternative perspectives; addresses "hidden curriculum" by including diversity in special events, holidays, school menus, etc.

INSTRUCTION: Responds to student learning styles and skill levels with emphasis on active student involvement in democratic decision making in the school; engages students in critical thinking and in problem solving to promote the development of social action skills that empower students; employs cooperative learning and group projects, especially those involving the community; avoids testing and tracking procedures that represent narrow views of student learning that label some students as failures; displays wall posters and bulletin boards that reflect cultural diversity, social action themes, and student interests.

Source: Sleeter and Grant (2003).

> tolerate cultural pluralism. Instead, multicultural education affirms that schools should be oriented toward the cultural enrichment of all children and youth through programs rooted to the preservation and extension of cultural diversity as a fact of life in American society. (p. 21)

A *multicultural education approach* insists that a diverse society can achieve unity through diversity; it need not eliminate cultural differences. Although some advocates of this approach focus on racial and ethnic groups, most promote an inclusive view of diversity by incorporating information on women, gays and lesbians, low-income families, and people with disabilities.

Multicultural education advocates support integration, inclusion, and "de-tracking" to create heterogeneous classrooms emphasizing skill development to gain knowledge and a better understanding of diverse groups in American society. Further, a multicultural education approach calls for curricular reform to correct omissions and distortions in textbooks concerning diverse groups, and provides multiple perspectives on important historical or contemporary events. Advocates have criticized visual images in textbooks for not representing diversity in

American society adequately and for continuing to depict certain groups in stereotypical ways. They urge teachers to use bulletin boards and media to provide accurate representations of diverse groups.

Advocates for the multicultural education approach challenge teachers to be sensitive to language that is derogatory toward any group and to model use of inclusive language. Teachers must study and understand diverse ways of learning and design or modify lessons to accommodate differences. In addition to having high expectations for students, multicultural teachers encourage cooperation between students in the classroom through group activities. Teachers need not strive to treat students equally—treating all students the same—but to address students equitably with responses based on the diverse needs of individual students.

A *social reconstructionist approach* shares many principles and practices of a multicultural education approach. Four major differences include: (1) attention to structural inequalities in America; (2) emphasis on democratic decision making in the classroom; (3) development of social action skills to empower students; and (4) use of an activist curriculum with student projects addressing problems in schools and communities.

Social reconstructionism has roots in the Progressive Education movement and in Dewey's 1920 book, *Reconstruction in Philosophy* that inspired the term. In the early 1930s, Counts and Rugg, leaders of a group called "Frontier Thinkers," were concerned about inequities in American society and urged that schools play a more active role in creating a more equitable society (Kneller, 1971). In his 1956 book, *Toward a Reconstructed Philosophy of Education,* Brameld became an influential advocate for reconstructionism, suggesting that schools create a new social order by fostering democratic principles and demanding more citizen control over major institutions and resources.

A social reconstructionist approach to multicultural education focuses less on awareness of cultural diversity and more on the ongoing struggles of diverse groups against oppression. The curriculum includes examples of successful resistance to oppression by subordinate groups and actions against injustice by individuals from the dominant group. This approach emphasizes democratic classroom practices to develop student decision-making skills and to encourage social action projects.

What does it mean to implement democratic practices in schools?

In describing schools employing democratic practices, Apple and Beane (1995) noted that all people in these schools must participate in governance issues and policymaking. In classrooms, students and teachers must work together to create learning environments responsive to student questions, interests, issues, and aspirations; however, as stated in Sleeter and Grant (2003), "Democratizing power relationships in the classroom does not mean turning all power over to the students" (p. 197). Teachers still represent adult authority and, like the state or federal government, they must take action if a majority of students makes decisions creating inequity or injustice in the classroom. In the history of the United States there have been numerous occasions when the majority was wrong, and as Griffin said, "Rule by majority is a great idea, but the majority has no right to rule wrong based on prejudice" (Terkel, 1980, p. 311). According to Michelli (2005), one major goal of a democratic classroom is to help students defend their beliefs while they also learn to be open to contrasting ideas and recognize when more effective arguments are being expressed.

In addition to emphasizing democratic practices, a social reconstructionist approach encourages students to analyze their own lives, reflecting Dewey's insistence that education take account of students' life experiences. Analyzing their own lives can lead students to a better understanding of their experiences with injustice, and provide a basis for developing constructive responses for future encounters. Self-analysis leading to action not only strengthens a student's self-concept, but also develops social action and interaction skills when coalitions are necessary to address issues. Social action projects can be as simple as examining the nutritional value of various fast foods or as complex as examining factors influencing a pattern of lower scores on standardized tests for females or students of color. By making curriculum personal, it becomes relevant; by emphasizing social action, it becomes empowering. Students are encouraged to regard citizenship in a democracy as active participation by individuals and groups to resolve personal and social dilemmas.

Engaging in democratic practices has enormous implications for a teacher's choice of instructional approaches. Before describing teaching strategies, it is important to recall an important point from Hilliard (1974), that teachers implementing multicultural education must believe "a multicultural orientation is beneficial to them personally" (p. 49). Howard (2006) argued that teachers have no choice about dealing with diversity; their only choice is how they will respond to diversity. If teachers implement strategies for multicultural education merely to *help* students, especially students of color, they are not likely to be effective.

What specific instructional strategies are recommended for teachers?

Sleeter (1996) insisted that implementing multicultural education effectively requires that teaching not be regarded as experimenting with a variety of classroom strategies; instead she described the importance of "listening to oppressed people, including scholars, with the aim of learning to hear and understand what is being said" (p. 134). By listening to students and their parents, teachers will develop appreciation for and understanding of their students, and will genuinely project high regard and high expectations for all students. As Nieto (2008) described it, "Becoming a multicultural teacher . . . means first becoming a multicultural person" (p. 424). Becoming a multicultural person means knowing about human differences and desiring to learn more; examining attitudes for biases, stereotypes, and prejudices; and understanding the need to look at issues from more than one perspective.

Advocates for either of the two multicultural education approaches just described agree that for a multicultural curriculum, teachers must employ **critical pedagogy.** Nieto (2008) describes critical pedagogy as a liberating experience that "encourages students to take risks, to be curious, and to question. Rather than expecting students to repeat teachers' words, it expects them to seek their own answers" (p. 56). Critical pedagogy is also illustrated by Sleeter's (1996) description of *Why? Papers:* In this activity students are assigned the task of asking a question about some issue involving race, social class, or gender. In doing research and writing their responses to the questions, students are asked to take the perspective of the oppressed group identified in the question. Examples of "Why?" questions include:

- Why are Mexican American children frequently absent from school?
- Why do Native American students drop out of school?
- Why are many African American males in prison? (p. 120)

According to Sleeter, taking the minority perspective has been effective because students talk with members of oppressed groups as they search for answers; this provides them with unique insights on the group's past experiences and their perspectives on problems addressed. Multiple insights and perspectives influence the analysis and conclusions students present in their papers:

> They framed concrete observations of inequality in terms of institutional discrimination and uncovered strategies oppressed groups use to cope with or attempt to advance from a minority position. (p. 123)

Appleton (1983) recommended process-oriented teaching strategies such as role playing, simulation games, using students as discussion leaders, and assigning individual or group projects based on student interests. Using the community to create learning experiences is essential for social action activities, but communities also have human resources—such as students' parents—who can be invited to the classroom to discuss the impact of past or current issues on the community. For students who struggle with nonstructured tasks, teachers might provide a mastery learning activity in which learning is partitioned into a series of sequential tasks and students can periodically evaluate themselves to determine when they achieve mastery. Effective multicultural teaching must allow for the flexibility to modify learning activities so that students will have the opportunity to be successful learners.

Maintaining such flexibility illustrates the point that the goal of multicultural teachers is not to think "I am fair because I treat all students equally." Cymrot (2002) argues that "equally" in this context usually means "the same," but each student is a unique person, in part because of lessons learned from his or her culture. Diller and Moule (2005) emphasize the need for teachers to be culturally competent. Although the dominant culture in the United States emphasizes individual achievement, other cultures place more value on the collective needs of the group. A teacher should avoid making assumptions about a student's behavior based on the norms of the teacher's culture. For example, it is easy to misinterpret the behavior of a child whose culture has taught him that possessions are to be shared and not used exclusively by one person. Having many different cultures represented in classrooms should not be viewed as a challenge but as a learning opportunity for teachers as well as students. In culturally diverse classrooms, Cymrot (2002) argues, "good teaching is about an exchange of cultures" (p. 17).

Because tracking practices have tended to diminish diversity in classrooms as well as academic achievement, multicultural educators deplore tracking and encourage the use of learning centers or cooperative groups as effective strategies in heterogeneous classrooms. Tiedt and Tiedt (2002) describe a learning center as a part of the classroom set aside for the study of a specific topic or for the purpose of developing a specific set of skills; it may be devoted to studying the issue of prejudice or filled with exercises requiring critical thinking. Before using a learning center, students are given directions concerning the center's activities and instructions for using equipment or materials. Students involved in learning center activities can proceed as individuals learning at their own pace or they can be organized into teams.

Cooperative learning strategies are especially attractive to advocates of multicultural education because they involve students of mixed abilities in learning tasks that have clearly defined responsibilities for each group member. Each person must complete his or her task in order for the group to complete the project. According to Sleeter and Grant (2003), research findings suggest that this strategy works well with children from diverse racial and ethnic groups, not only in terms of academic achievement but also in terms of developing positive interpersonal relationships. In reviewing research on cooperative learning, Kagan (2006) cites studies documenting that young children in schools with diverse student populations initially interact with others and choose their friends without regard to race, but by the end of their second grade year, self-segregation by race has begun and is dramatically apparent by the end of elementary school. Yet, research studies have also found that in classrooms that have implemented cooperative learning strategies, self-segregation was virtually eliminated. Based on his review of four decades of research, Kagan concluded: "Cooperative learning, when it includes heterogeneous teams and teambuilding, is the single most powerful tool this nation has for improving race relations" (2006, p. 53).

How can multicultural education help to reduce student prejudice?

Reducing prejudice and developing conflict resolution skills are important objectives in multicultural education. Referring to a review of prejudice reduction programs, Nieto (2008) reported that activities designed to reduce prejudice were more effective if students viewed cognitive learning as the primary objective. When prejudice reduction was the primary objective of an activity, students tended to feel as if they were being manipulated to "say the right thing," and they became defensive or resentful. The success of indirect approaches emphasizing cognitive tasks for reducing student prejudice may explain why studies have found cooperative learning strategies to be effective in this area.

Prejudice is not simply a black and white issue. Sheets (2005) cited a study of a school with diverse students in which African American children expressed negative attitudes toward children who were Asian American or Hispanic American, and there have been numerous incidents of interracial conflict between youth from diverse groups in schools and in communities. Based on the results of several studies, Stephan (1999) concluded that teaching conflict resolution skills can reduce the influence of prejudice on intergroup relations in schools. One study reported that helping students develop conflict resolution skills "improved students' abilities to manage conflicts, increased their social support from other students, and decreased

> Prejudices, it is well known, are most difficult to eradicate from the heart whose soil has never been loosened or fertilized by education; they grow there, firm as weeds among stones.
>
> **Charlotte Bronte (1816–1855)**

victimization by others" (p. 70). Stephan added that teaching conflict resolution skills to students had a positive effect on decreasing student anxiety, increasing self-esteem, and improving intergroup relations. Engaging students in prejudice reduction activities and developing their skills in conflict resolution to improve intergroup relationships is a persuasive rationale for all educators. In addition, teachers are increasingly being challenged to teach in ways that take into account the diverse cultures from which their students come. This approach has been called "culturally responsive teaching."

Multicultural Education as a Context for Culturally Responsive Teaching

Multicultural education incorporates the idea that all students—regardless of their gender, social class, ethnic, racial, or cultural differences—should have an equal opportunity to learn in school (Banks & Banks, 2003). However, the public school system in the United States is plagued with vast inequalities, and on virtually every measure, students of color and students from lower economic classes achieve below the level of their white and middle-class counterparts. This disparity in outcomes is called "the achievement gap." Mainstream explanations tend to blame the achievement gap on uninformed assumptions about families and communities (i.e., "they just don't value education"), but advocates for multicultural education have examined the ways schools are structured, and they report that institutional characteristics of schools systematically deny some groups of students equal educational opportunities (Banks & Banks, 2003). For example, in the early grades, the academic achievement of students of color is nearly the same as that of white middle-class students, but the longer students of color stay in school, the more the achievement gap widens (Banks, 2004). Students in high poverty, high minority schools are routinely provided fewer resources, fewer qualified teachers, fewer advanced level courses, and higher levels of policing in their schools than their more affluent white peers. As a result, they experience lower academic achievement, lower rates of high school graduation, and more interaction with the criminal justice system (Orfield, Losen, Wald, & Swanson, 2004). Thus, a major goal of multicultural education is to improve the academic achievement of students who are traditionally marginalized in school by considering several interconnected aspects of schooling itself. Many multicultural educators advocate culturally responsive teaching as a key strategy to achieve some of their major goals.

How does culturally responsive teaching address multicultural education goals?

Culturally responsive teaching addresses the goal of changing school practices that marginalize nontraditional students. Culturally responsive teaching is grounded in the perception of schooling as linked to social forces in the broader society. Schooling is a primary site of socialization, and, as such, schools play a key role in sorting students into predetermined places within a society that is hierarchical and socially stratified: Schools prepare students to occupy roles in society that have unequal value, for example, vocational training versus college preparation or special education versus honors courses (Anyon, 2003; Oakes, Wells, Jones, & Datnow, 1997). Because schools are such a powerful site of social reproduction, all aspects of schools are inherently political. Knowledge is never neutral; it is infused with the implicit cultural assumptions, frames of reference, biases, and interests of those who hold the power to determine which aspects of knowledge are valid and how they will be measured. Yet schools present the cultural norms, styles, and perspectives of dominant social groups as objective and reward those who fit these norms and penalize those who don't.

Other aspects of schooling that contribute to the achievement gap include standardized testing, culturally biased curriculum, ability tracking, unequal funding between urban and suburban schools, low expectations for students of color, and zero tolerance policies that criminalize minority students and channel them from school into the prison system (Clark, 2007). As defined and promoted by multicultural education advocates, culturally responsive teaching seeks to interrupt these inequitable aspects of schooling (Banks & Banks, 2003; Ladson-Billings, 1995; Nieto, 1999). While challenging these structural inequities will take time and society-wide effort, multicultural education advocates argue that individual teachers can make an immediate difference in their classrooms by infusing culturally responsive teaching.

Gay (2000) defines culturally responsive teaching as using the cultural knowledge, prior experiences, and performance styles of diverse students to make learning more appropriate and effective for them. Rather than viewing these students as deficient, culturally responsive pedagogy teaches to their specific strengths. According to Gay (2000), culturally responsive teaching has the following characteristics:

- It acknowledges the legitimacy of the cultural heritages of different ethnic groups, both as legacies that affect students' dispositions, attitudes, and approaches to learning and as worthy content to be taught in the formal curriculum.
- It builds bridges of meaningfulness between home and school experiences as well as between academic abstractions and lived sociocultural realities.
- It uses a wide variety of instructional strategies that are connected to different learning styles.
- It teaches students to know and praise their own and each others' cultural heritages.
- It incorporates multicultural information, resources, and materials in all the subjects and skills routinely taught in schools (p. 29).

Culturally responsive teaching is an all-encompassing and ever-present "lens" through which teachers view their practice; at its core is the expectation that all students can experience academic success while developing the critical consciousness to challenge the inequity of the status quo.

What are some current issues that make culturally responsive teaching difficult?

Despite the common belief that racial segregation is a practice of the past, our schools are more segregated than ever before (Kozol, 2005; Villegas & Lucas, 2002). Most students of color and lower income students are concentrated in urban areas, whereas most middle class and white students attend suburban schools in which they have very little authentic interaction with students who are different from them. In addition, the teaching force is getting *more*, not less, homogeneous. Trends continue to indicate that the teaching force is becoming increasingly white and middle class (Gordon, 2005), while at the same time, the student population is getting more diverse (National Center for Education Statistics, 2005). Over one third of U.S. public school students are children of color, whereas fewer than 16% of teachers are educators of color (Kearney, 2008; Stevens, Hamman, & Olivarez, 2007). The vast majority of teachers are white, and they also tend to come from segregated suburban schools and neighborhoods. In addition, they are challenged in their understanding of children from backgrounds different from their own. Howard (2003) states that "Teachers need to understand that racially diverse students frequently bring cultural capital to the classroom that is oftentimes drastically different from mainstream norms and worldviews" (p. 197). Because teachers and students often come from dissimilar backgrounds, teachers must "construct pedagogical practices in ways that are culturally relevant, racially affirming, and socially meaningful for their students" (p. 187).

Although urban schools may indeed be located in cities and be composed predominantly of low-income students and students of color, "urban" does not necessarily indicate location. In more affluent cities such as Seattle, San Francisco and Boston, schools located inside the city limits that are primarily white are not labeled "urban"; the term *urban* is used as the dominant culture's code for indicating the existence of a percentage of students of color that is "too high" for white families to feel comfortable with. Johnson and Shapiro (2003) found that perceptions of white parents regarding "good schools" were often based on the racial demographics of the school; the whiter the student body, the better the school was perceived to be. They concluded that race may be not just a factor in school choice for white families, but rather *the primary factor*. Schools that are not perceived as "good" because of the presence of a percentage of students of color are labeled "urban" (or "inner-city"). In turn, these schools are abandoned by white families and have unequal funding and resources, which perpetuates the cycle (Kozol, 1991; Kozol, 2005).

Although these factors complicate the efforts of teachers to engage in culturally responsive teaching, they also provide reasons for engaging in such practices to help students.

What students benefit from culturally responsive teaching?

Because race appears to be a key issue in decisions white people make when choosing schools and neighborhoods, one could easily argue that *all* students and *all* teachers could benefit from culturally responsive teaching, regardless of the overall racial demographics of their schools or neighborhoods. White children attending segregated schools need to be prepared, perhaps more so than any other group, to interact in a culturally diverse society (DiAngelo, 2006). Culturally responsive teaching builds a foundation for all students to engage in the critical tasks of empathetic and equitable engagement with the diversity that is so often lacking in their immediate world because of pervasive segregation in our schools and neighborhoods (Derman Sparks & Ramsey, 2004). The bigger question is not who benefits from culturally responsive teaching, but what is required for an individual teacher to successfully implement culturally responsive teaching.

What characteristics are necessary to be a culturally responsive teacher?

The following characteristics of culturally responsive teachers are adapted from Villegas and Lucas (2002) and Gay (2000). Culturally responsive teachers are those who:

- Understand teaching as a contextual and situational process in which students' prior experiences, community settings, cultural backgrounds, and ethnic identities are acknowledged and infused into the curriculum.
- Are familiar with their students' prior knowledge and beliefs, derived from both personal and cultural experiences and well-designed instruction that builds on what students already know while stretching them beyond the familiar.
- Have sociocultural consciousness; they recognize that the ways people perceive the world, interact with one another, and approach learning are deeply influenced by such factors as race/ethnicity, social class, and language.
- Are aware that they also are sociocultural beings, with a particular and limited cultural viewpoint: They know that no human is objective and they consistently engage in self-reflection and self-examination of their beliefs, values, and assumptions about those who are different from them.
- Have a positive perspective on students and families who are from diverse backgrounds, seeing resources for learning in all students rather than viewing differences as deficiencies, or problems to be solved.
- Communicate high expectations for all children.
- Have a sense that they are capable of and responsible for bringing about educational change that will make schooling more responsive to students from diverse backgrounds.

The characteristics outlined above involve ongoing education and self-awareness, particularly for those who have not grown up in environments that offered consistent and sustained opportunities to build relationships with people different from themselves in key social areas, such as race and class. Because culturally responsive teaching challenges our conventional worldviews and our sense of self in relation to others, it develops over a lifetime and is not achieved in the short term. At the same time, educators can't grow into culturally responsive teachers without practice, trial and error, and risk-taking. Although a school-wide commitment is necessary for authentic transformation in education (Villegas & Lucas, 2002), individual teachers may infuse culturally responsive teaching into their classroom practice without waiting for support or encouragement from outside of their classroom.

What actual classroom experiences illustrate culturally responsive teaching?

A social studies teacher with the non-Western first name of Özlem begins her class by explaining how her name is written and pronounced, and what it means in her first language, Turkish. She has students practice writing and saying her name. She explains how in North America the "dots" are often absent from the "O," and then tells her name's "story." She talks about the script change from Turkish to English and wonders aloud how the change in the spelling of her name affects her cultural identity. She shares why the Turkish spelling of her name is significant to her as someone whose family immigrated to Canada from Turkey. After this brief discussion, she invites each student to teach the class how to pronounce and spell his or her name and to "tell us the story of your name." If needed, she provides prompts such as "Who named you? What does your name mean? Do you have a nickname you prefer to be called? If so, how did you get it? Do you know the roots of your name?" She doesn't move on to the next student until the last student to share his or her name is satisfied that everyone has learned to pronounce it correctly. This exercise builds community by affirming cultural diversity as represented by the names of students in her class, allowing students to claim their names and tell their stories, and providing a culturally relevant framework for issues that will be discussed in the class, such as the following.

- *The cultural dimensions of names and the connections between religion and culture.* Students will find that many names are influenced by religion; for example, the middle names "Kaur" (for girls) and "Singh" (for boys) indicate Sikh heritage, just as Paul and John have religious significance for families of Christian heritage.
- *The cultural connections that have been lost by institutional practices that shortened or "corrected" immigrants' names.* Upon their arrival in the United States an immigrant with a name such as *Yih-Shue* could be changed to *Sherry*. The inability to make or represent certain sounds in different languages; the power relations imbedded in whose names are adapted or modified upon immigration; and the politics of who decides how that will be done are some of the issues students could discuss.
- *The impact of marriage on names, and the norms for patriarchal versus matriarchal societies.* Students could discuss who changes their surname when they get married, and why? Further, how are naming norms changing over time, with gender roles evolving and the legalization of same-sex marriages in some states in the United States and Canada?

This activity also illustrates a key tenet in multicultural education: recognition of the individual *as well as* the society in which the individual is embedded. Following this exercise, students make decorative nameplates for their desks. As new students join the class, the sharing of names is repeated to include the newcomers (adapted from Sensoy, 2009).

Another teacher, Ms. Walker, infuses culturally responsive teaching into a history lesson on heroes. Instead of asking students to stand outside of their own lives and write in the third person about people chosen for them by their textbooks, she asks her students to choose a "hero" from their community who works for social justice and interview that person. If a student is having trouble identifying a hero, Ms. Walker offers a range of possibilities based on her knowledge of leaders in the child's community and the interests of the child. The students generate questions that might include: What accomplishments are you proud of? What challenges did you face in achieving your goals? What methods did you use to affect change? What do you regret? What advice do you have for others? The students' community heroes are then invited to be guest speakers in the class so that all students may meet and learn from them. If students' heroes are not available for interviews, the students write essays as if they were the hero reflecting on the same questions at the end of his or her life. This lesson humanizes heroes, and rather than presenting overwhelmingly white and male figures from the dominant culture with the same few sanitized exceptions of Susan B. Anthony, Martin Luther King, Jr., and Rosa Parks, it affirms the range of communities from which the students come. The students' communities are brought directly into the classroom and utilized as a resource for everyone, and mainstream definitions of what makes a hero are challenged.

As Jana Dean (2007) has shown, even a math teacher can incorporate culturally responsive teaching in a lesson by using typical wages in her students' community to build a bridge between her students' lives and algebra; the mathematics in this lesson are clearly culturally relevant. Her students calculate and graph daily and monthly incomes in service sector jobs, using a day's wages and a month's wages for four full-time service industry occupations that many in their community hold—for example, a retail clerk at Wal-Mart, a security guard, a fast food restaurant cook, and a home nursing aide. Her students graph four linear relationships on the same coordinate grid and write equations for each. Along the way, they discuss questions such as: What is a minimum wage and who gets to set it? She says, "Following an example that I had prepared in advance, students worked together to draw an *x*- and *y*-axis on 11 by 17-inch graph paper. I told them that they would be graphing one day's wages, or eight hours, and that the size of one's paycheck depends on the number of hours worked; therefore, money—the dependent variable—belongs on the *y*-axis. The independent variable, however, will be the same for everyone: You are all going to work an eight-hour day."

After students complete the graphs, she introduces the variables *x* and *y*. In this case, *y* represents the paycheck and *x* stands for the number of hours worked. Ms. Dean also challenges her students to write an equation for each line that would show the relationship between time and earnings, and they arrive at equations to represent the lines on their graphs. She then asks her students to respond in writing to the following prompt: "How does the rate of pay affect the shape and steepness of the lines on your coordinate grid? Describe the shape of a graph for the wage of a job at $20 per hour. Describe the shape of a graph for the wage of a job at the federal minimum of $5.15 per hour." The prompt leads students to observe that the steeper the line, the higher the wage, and that each of the situations produces a straight line. Both observations pave the way for introducing the term "slope," meaning the rate of increase, and "linear," meaning a relationship that graphs as a straight line. This prompt also serves to identify the coefficient of *x* or the number that multiplies *x* as the value that determines the steepness of the line. Once students recognize linear relationships, Ms. Dean introduces the concept of *y*-intercept by having students make a table showing pay minus expenses for the first ten hours of work. This gives students a real-world context for operating with negative numbers. Other dimensions of her "living algebra" lesson include calculating the cost of housing and other expenses, comparing state and national minimum wages, and learning about the activism and organizing effort behind her state's highest-in-the-nation minimum wage (adapted from Dean, 2007).

What other strategies for culturally responsible teaching have been advocated?

Some strategies can be quite simple as long as the teacher understands the goal of the strategy. As Nieto (1999) explains, whether it's an informal chat as the parent brings the child to school, or through phone calls, home visits, and newsletters sent home in the first language of the families, teachers can begin a genuine dialogue that results in learning about each of the families represented in their classroom community. At Brown University, a consortium of educators called the Education Alliance is committed to enhancing the ability of teachers to work effectively and equitably with English Language learners. They have identified numerous culturally responsive teaching strategies, and some examples are provided below (2006):

1. **Learn about students' cultures**
   - Have students share artifacts from home that reflect their culture
   - Have students write about traditions shared by their families
   - Have students research different aspects of their culture
   - Have members of the community speak to students on various subjects
   - Ask members of the community to teach a lesson or give a demonstration (in their field of expertise) to the students
2. **Promote positive perspectives on parents and families**
   - Conduct home visits in which parents are able to speak freely about their expectations and concerns for their children
   - Send weekly/monthly newsletters (in the home language) informing parents of school activities
   - Host family nights at school to introduce parents to concepts and ideas children are learning in their classes and to share interactive journals

- Research the cultural background of students' families
- Visit local community centers to find out about cultural activities and beliefs of the students

3. **Bridge cultural differences through effective communication**
   - Teach and talk to students about differences between individuals
   - Show how differences among the students make for better learning
   - Attend community events important to the students and discuss the events with the students
   - See your classroom as a community of learners, rather than as individuals learning separately from one another
   - Use cooperative learning strategies

4. **Promote student engagement**
   - Have students generate lists of topics they wish to study and/or research
   - Allow students to select their own reading material
   - Share responsibility of instruction with students and community members
   - Have students lead discussion groups or reteach concepts
   - Create classroom projects that involve the community

5. **Provide culturally mediated instruction using diverse teaching strategies**
   - Use role-playing strategies
   - Assign students research projects that focus on issues that apply to their own community or cultural group
   - Ask educators who come from the same cultural background as the students about effective ways to teach them
   - Allow the use of the student's first language to enhance learning
   - Use classroom management techniques that are culturally familiar to students

6. **Reshape the curriculum**
   - Use resources other than textbooks for study
   - Have students research aspects of a topic within their community
   - Encourage students to interview members of their community who have knowledge of the topic they are studying
   - Provide information to the students on alternative viewpoints or beliefs about a topic
   - Allow students to set their own goals for a project

Although culturally responsive teaching requires extra effort and may even seem daunting, it is no more difficult than any strategy promoting successful classroom practices that are effective with diverse students. Good teaching is never easy, but in the history of education, including our current era, there have always been numerous teachers who have been effective in the classroom, so we know it's not impossible. This should be the response to the complaints from some critics who feel that culturally responsive teaching in particular and multicultural education in general are too idealistic to work in the "real world" of challenges inherent in the everyday task of classroom teaching.

Is multicultural education too idealistic?

The purpose of multicultural education is to prepare children and youth to be active, positive participants in a diverse, democratic society. Although this chapter can only provide an overview of multicultural education, the intent is to provide a framework that describes schools committed to multicultural education and teachers who have implemented multicultural education in their classrooms. Educators may not achieve the ideals of multicultural education, but they can have a significant impact on students by engaging in efforts consistent with the purpose of multicultural education. If teachers address that purpose with students now and in the future, this diverse nation we live

> Ideals are like stars: you will not succeed in touching them with your hands, but like the seafarer . . . you choose them as your guides and following them you reach your destiny.
>
> **Carl Schurz (1829–1906)**

in will make progress toward achieving two related goals: more effective schools for all students and a more accepting society.

Elementary, middle level, and secondary educators committed to principles of multicultural education have implemented strategies and activities described in this chapter. The National Education Association (NEA) has promoted multicultural education since the 1960s, and the National Council for Accreditation of Teacher Education (NCATE) requires teacher education programs to address diversity issues and to include principles and practices of multicultural education to receive accreditation for the preparation of teachers. Professional organizations advocate pluralism not just as a response to diversity but to meet our needs as a democratic society. Pai and Adler (1997) succinctly state the relationship between democracy, diversity, and multicultural education:

> In a truly democratic society, no single group rules over others because of the implicit faith in the human capacity for intelligent behavior. Democracy requires a method of resolving conflicts by inquiry, discussion, and persuasion rather than by violence. Hence, the kind of education that cultivates reflective thinking and conflict resolution through discussion and persuasion is essential. (p. 110)

> **The role of the teacher remains the highest calling of a free people. To the teacher, America entrusts her most precious resource, her children; and asks that they be prepared, in all their glorious diversity, to face the rigors of individual participation in a democratic society.**
>
> **Shirley Hufstedler (1925–)**

AFTERWORD

Diversity is not just an issue for K–12 schools; most universities and colleges mandate diversity courses in their general education programs, and corporations implement policies promoting diversity and provide diversity training for managers and employees. Churches, community organizations, and civic groups already articulate pluralistic mission statements about the value of diversity in our society. Idealistic or not, multicultural education is likely to become increasingly influential in American schools in the twenty-first century. Fortunately, we have many excellent resources that describe teaching strategies based on principles of multicultural education (Derman-Sparks & Ramsey, 2004; Ladson-Billings, 2001; Pasternak, 1986; Sapon-Shevin, 1999; Shade, Kelly, & Oberg, 1997; Sleeter & Grant, 2009; Tiedt & Tiedt, 2002).

The challenge confronting us today is how to become multicultural individuals. In the teaching profession, that question will be answered primarily by white middle-class people—primarily women. As our schools increasingly consist of students from subordinate groups—students of color, students from low-income families, children and youth who are not Christian, gay and lesbian youth, learners with disabilities—teachers continue to enter the profession from our dominant societal group. Cochran-Smith (2003) cites demographers analyzing 2000 census data and reporting that 86% of all teachers are white; students of color constitute almost 40% of the school population (p. 4); although the percentage of white teachers is predicted to re-

TABLE 13.3 U.S. Public School Teachers

Category	Percentage
Gender	
Female	79
Male	21
Race	
White	84.3
Black	7.6
Hispanic	5.6
Highest Degree	
Bachelor's	61.9
Master's	23.1
Years of Experience	
Less than 10	41.7
10–20	28.5
More than 20	29.8

Source: U.S. Department of Education. (2006). National Center for Education Statistics.

main stable, the percentage of students of color is predicted to be 57% by 2035 (see Table 13.3).

Pang (2005) has urged white teachers to engage in self-analysis to understand how being white has shaped their identity, and how oppression has affected and shaped the identities of members of subordinate groups in our society. Self-analysis is part of the journey toward becoming a multicultural teacher; it may often feel uncomfortable, but if pursued, it can also be liberating. In the end, white teachers can develop a profound appreciation for both diversity and democracy—and the need to be pluralistic to promote and sustain both in our schools and in our society.

myeducationlab

Now go to Topics #11, 12, 13: **Curriculum, Strategies,** and **School-wide Diversity Issues** in the MyEducationLab (www.myeducationlab.com) for your course, where you can:

- Find learning outcomes for these topics along with the national standards that connect to these outcomes.
- Complete Assignments and Activities that can help you more deeply understand the chapter content by viewing classroom video and ABC News footage.
- Apply and practice your understanding of the core teaching skills identified in the chapter with the Building Teaching Skills and Dispositions learning units.

TERMS AND DEFINITIONS

Critical pedagogy Providing opportunities for students to analyze perspectives and use their analysis to understand and act on perceived inconsistencies

Diversity The presence of human beings with perceived or actual differences based on a variety of human characteristics

Global (International) education Teaching about the cultures of nations around the world

Hidden curriculum Indirect means by which schools teach the norms and values of a society

Multicultural Any society composed of a number of subordinate groups based on race, ethnicity, religion, language, nationality, income, gender, sexual orientation, and degree of physical, mental, or emotional ability

Multicultural education A process of comprehensive school reform that rejects discrimination in schools and society and accepts and affirms pluralism

Multiethnic education Integrating issues and information about race and ethnicity into school curricula

Pluralism The equal coexistence of diverse cultures, institutions, and/or individuals within a mutually supportive relationship within the boundaries of one nation

Retention The ability of students to recall knowledge they have been taught

Transfer The ability of students to apply retained knowledge to situations occurring inside and outside the classroom

DISCUSSION EXERCISES

Exercise #1 The Hidden Curriculum: American Indians

Directions: Might children and youth be learning lessons that we aren't aware they are being taught? Through misunderstanding or lack of adequate knowledge of facts, curriculums may be teaching American children to be biased or to stereotype others. The statements below were originally developed as an elementary punctuation exercise [which is why they have no punctuation marks at the end of each statement].

Explain in what way each phrase or sentence is biased. Underline the word or words that you judge need replacement.

Other than learning correct punctuation, what else might children completing this exercise have learned that wasn't intended?

1. Indians lived in our country many years before the white man
2. Have you ever seen an Indian
3. Indians belong to the red race
4. Their skin is of a copper color
5. Most of the men are called warriors
6. The women are called squaws
7. Do they live in wigwams and tepees
8. The red man's name for corn was maize
9. Were bows and arrows used for hunting by the Indians
10. A group of Indians living together is called a "tribe"
11. Do little Indian girls and boys play games
12. The squaws carried their babies on their backs
13. What does each Indian tribe call its "leader"
14. The leader of each tribe is called a "chief"
15. A few Indian tribes still live in the western part of our country

Exercise #2 Whom would you hire? Selecting Elementary Teachers

Introduction: Being fair to schoolchildren and youth involves providing the best teachers to help them. Imagine that you are a committee member with responsibility for hiring new teachers. You have four positions open in grades 1 to 3 and eight applicants from whom to choose. You have interviewed all eight, and each has impressed you favorably.

Directions: Read the brief descriptions below and select the four you would hire.

Candidate 1: Forty-year-old woman, single, lives alone with eighteen years outstanding experience; highly successful with typically unsuccessful children. Possibly in a lesbian relationship.

Candidate 2: Twenty-four-year-old man, single, two years experience in a ghetto school. A near genius, he brings outstanding recommendations. Leader of local black power group; his students use African names and openly reject "slave" names.

Candidate 3: Thirty-five-year-old man, married, father of six. Community minded, interested in Cub Scouts. Known for having very well-organized planned lessons and classes. Ten years of experience. Native American heritage.

Candidate 4: Forty-year-old man, single, living with elderly parents. The candidate has extensive experience from being a local business entrepreneur before returning to college for credentials. Just completed requirements and received a $20,000 grant to work with junior high school students in distributive education. Native of India; practicing Catholic.

Candidate 5: Twenty-six-year-old woman, divorced, supports self and three small children. Highly creative; three years of experience; outstanding recommendations on professional capability. Native of Puerto Rico.

Candidate 6: Fifty-eight-year-old man, highly respected former Episcopal minister who left pulpit to work full time with children. Has just completed teaching credentials.

Candidate 7: Forty-eight-year-old woman, widowed. Twenty-five years of experience, including three years in the Infants School of England. Wants to incorporate Infant School concepts here. Independently wealthy through both her own and her spouse's families.

Candidate 8: Twenty-two-year-old woman, single, a year of experience, excellent recommendations. Voluntarily tutored all four years in college, including full time in summers. Living openly in the community with a man of another race.

Follow-up: Discuss the selections of each committee member. When your group has selected four teacher candidates for the jobs, post your selections and compare your choices with those of other groups.

REFERENCES

Anyon, J. (2003). Inner cities, affluent suburbs, and unequal educational opportunity (pp. 85–102). In J.A. Banks, & C.M. Banks, (Eds.), *Multicultural education: Issues & perspectives* (4th ed.). New York: John Wiley & Sons.

Presents statistical data and curriculum examples to address the disparities in education children receive based on the economic status of their families and communities.

Apple, M.W., & Beane, J.A. (Eds.). (1995). *Democratic schools.* Alexandria, VA: Association for Supervision and Curriculum Development.

Includes narratives written by those involved in reform efforts in four schools and describes how educators and students established democratic policies and practices.

Appleton, N. (1983). *Cultural pluralism in education: Theoretical foundations.* New York, NY: Longman.

Examines how the United States has become pluralistic, how American education has responded to pluralism, and what our pluralistic society might look like in the future.

Baker, G.C. (1994). *Planning and organizing for multicultural instruction.* Reading, MA: Addison Wesley.

Presents a conceptual approach to multicultural education and practical suggestions for implementing multicultural education in curriculum and instruction.

Banks, J.A. (2008). *An introduction to multicultural education* (4th ed.). Boston, MA: Pearson Allyn & Bacon.

Explains major concepts, principles, theories, and practices in multicultural education.

Banks, J.A. (2006). *Cultural diversity and education: Foundations, curriculum and teaching* (5th ed.). Boston, MA: Allyn & Bacon.

Discusses the evolution of multiethnic, pluralistic education and analyzes curricular issues and teaching strategies for implementing multiethnic content.

Banks, J.A. (2004). Multicultural education: Characteristics and goals (pp. 3–27). In J.A. Banks, & C.M. Banks, (Eds.), *Multicultural education: Issues & perspectives* (5th ed.). New York: John Wiley & Sons.

Updates text by including emergent issues post 9/11 and new chapters on diversity in religion, socio-economic class, and recruiting gifted students from unrepresented racial and ethnic groups.

Banks, J.A. (2003). Multicultural education: Characteristics and goals (pp. 3–30). In J.A. Banks, & C.M. Banks, (Eds.), *Multicultural education: Issues & perspectives* (4th ed.). New York: John Wiley & Sons.

Provides an overview of multicultural education in general, and discusses specific issues pertaining to various culturally diverse groups.

Bazron, B., Osher, D., & Fleischman, S. (2005). Creating culturally responsive schools. *Educational Leadership, 63*(1), 83–84.

Discusses how a culturally responsive approach to education can make classroom instruction more congruent with the cultural value system of a diverse student population.

Brameld, T.B.H. (1956). *Toward a reconstructed philosophy of education.* New York, NY: Dryden Press.

Advocates for school reform promoting a more democratic society.

Carlisle, L.R., Jackson, B.W., & George, A. (2006). Principles of social justice education: The Social Justice Education in Schools project. *Equity & Excellence in Education, 39,* 55–64.

Argues for an approach to multicultural urban education based on social justice principles to increase equity and student achievement.

Carse, J. (1986). *Finite and infinite games: A vision of life as play and possibility.* New York, NY: Free Press.

Describes two philosophical orientations toward life, one collaborative and the other competitive, and explains their divergent responses to life experiences.

Clark, C. (2007). *Understanding neoliberalism and its impact on education.* NAME Conference, Baltimore, November 2007.

Explains how educational standardization undermines ideals of democratic engagement and critical thinking and creates a "school to prison pipeline" for minority students.

Cochran-Smith, M. (2003). Standing at the crossroads: Multicultural teacher education at the beginning of the 21st century. *Multicultural Perspectives, 5*(3), 3–11.

Describes three issues of critical interest to U.S. educators: teacher/student demographic data and trends, competing school reform agendas, and criticisms of educational research.

Combs, A.W. (1979). *Myths in education: Beliefs that hinder progress and their alternatives.* Boston, MA: Allyn & Bacon.

Analyzes many myths about values, human nature, and education that influence educators and students and interfere with students learning and being successful in school.

Cymrot, T.Z. (2002). What is diversity? In L. Darling-Hammond, J. French, & S.P. Garcia Lopez (Eds.), *Learning to teach for social justice* (pp. 13–17). New York, NY: Teachers College Press.

Examines the concept of diversity and teachers' reluctance to acknowledge differences.

Darling-Hammond, G. (2002). Learning to teach for social justice. In L. Darling-Hammond, J. French, & S.P. Garcia Lopez (Eds.), *Learning to teach for social justice* (pp. 1–7). New York, NY: Teachers College Press.

Explains how Stanford Teacher Education Program faculty assist teacher preparation students to become educators teaching for social change.

Darling-Hammond, L., French, J., & Garcia-Lopez, S.P. (2002). *Learning to teach for social justice.* New York, NY: Teachers College Press.

Examination of experiences and concerns of student teachers committed to teaching about social justice.

Dean, J. (2007). Living algebra, living wage. *Rethinking Schools* Vol. 21 #4, pp. 31–35.

Describes in detail a lesson plan for incorporating students' lived experiences related to work, pay, costs of living, and budgeting into an algebra lesson.

Derman Sparks, L., & Ramsey, P. (2004). *What if all the kids are white?: Anti-bias multicultural education with young children and families.* New York, NY: Teachers College Press.

Provides strategies for teachers to engage young children in anti-racist learning; Chapter 4 provides a rationale for culturally responsive teaching and explains how teachers can implement this approach in primarily white and suburban schools.

DiAngelo, R. (2006). "I'm leaving!": White fragility in racial dialogue. In B. McMahon & D. Armstrong (Eds.), *Inclusion in urban educational environments: Addressing issues of diversity, equity, and social justice* (pp. 213–240). Centre for Leadership and Diversity. Ontario Institute for Studies in Education of the University of Toronto.

An analysis of the impact of racial segregation on white students' ability to withstand the discomfort of talking about race with students of color.

Diller, J.V., & Moule, J. (2005). *Cultural competence: A primer for educators.* Belmont, CA: Wadsworth.

Describes cross-cultural teaching using numerous classroom examples.

The Education Alliance Brown University (2006). Principles for culturally responsive teaching. Retrieved May 6th, 2009, from http://www.alliance.brown.edu/tdl/tl-strategies/crt-principles.shtml.

Promoting educational change and advocating for populations whose access to excellent education has been limited or denied, this website is filled with practical resources, including curriculum guides, publications, and access to diversity consultants.

Gardner, H. (1999). *Intelligence reframed: Multiple intelligences for the 21st century*. New York, NY: Basic Books.

Explains the theory of multiple intelligences, examines three possible additions to the theory, addresses myths and realities concerning the theory and its practical applications.

Gardner, H. (1993). *Multiple intelligences: The theory in practice.* New York, NY: Basic Books.

Reviews earlier theories of intelligence and discusses the evidence in support of the existence of a number of intelligences and the implications of this theory for educators.

Gay, G. (2000). *Culturally responsive teaching: Theory, research, & practice.* New York, NY: Teachers College Press.

Provides insights from theory, research and classroom practice to show that the performance of underachieving minority pupils is improved when teaching is filtered through their cultural experiences and frames of references.

Gay, G. (1977). Curriculum design for multicultural education. In C.A. Grant (Ed.), *Multicultural education: Commitments, issues, and applications* (pp. 94–104). Washington, DC: Association for Supervision and Curriculum Development.

Describes a philosophy of multicultural education as a basis for developing specific objectives and organizational principles for designing a multicultural curriculum.

Gayle-Evans, G., & Michael, D. (2006). A study of pre-service teachers' awareness of multicultural issues. *Multicultural Perspectives, 8*(1), 44–50.

Reviews research on teacher awareness of multicultural issues and presents results of their study on the awareness of preservice teachers to these issues.

Gordon, J.A. (2005). In search of educators of color: If we make school a more positive experience for students of color, they'll be more likely to continue with their education, and perhaps select teaching as a profession. *Leadership, 35*(2), 30–36.

Argues that culturally responsive teaching can make school a more positive experience for students of color and motivate more students of color to enter the teaching profession.

Hilliard, A. (1974). Restructuring teacher education for multicultural imperatives. In W.A. Hunter (Ed.), *Multicultural education through competency-based teacher education* (pp. 40–55). Washington, DC: American Association of Colleges for Teacher Education.

Provides definitions, rationale, general aims, methods, and content for a multicultural preparation of teacher education students.

Howard, G.R. (2006). *We can't teach what we don't know: White teachers, multiracial schools* (2nd ed.). New York, NY: Teachers College Press.

Discusses issues such as social dominance and racial identity development in relation to helping teachers, especially white teachers, become effective multicultural educators.

Howard, T. (2003). Culturally relevant pedagogy: ingredients for critical teacher reflection. *Theory into Practice 42*(3), 195–202.

Outlines theoretical and practical considerations for culturally relevant teaching and argues that the development of culturally relevant teaching strategies is dependent upon the ability of teachers and students to reflect critically on their race and culture.

Hunter, W.A. (1974). Antecedents to development of and emphasis on multicultural education. In W.A. Hunter (Ed.), *Multicultural education through competency-based teacher education* (pp. 11–31). Washington, DC: American Association of Colleges for Teacher Education.

Provides a historical overview of intergroup relations in the United States, the rise of cultural pluralism, and the need and support for multicultural education.

Johnson, H.B., & Shapiro, T.M. (2003). Good neighborhoods, good schools: Race and the "good choices" of white families. In A.W. Doane & E. Bonilla-Silva (Eds.), *White out: The continuing significance of race*. New York: Routledge.

Presents racist beliefs of white parents in a study in which these parents identified race as the primary factor in choosing schools for their children.

Kagan, S. (2006, Fall). The power to transform race relations. *Teaching Tolerance*, 30, 53.

Provides a brief review of research on the influence of cooperative learning on race relations.

Kearney, J.E. (2008). Factors affecting satisfaction and retention of African American and European American teachers in an urban school district: Implications for building and maintaining teachers employed in school districts across the nation. *Education and Urban Society, 40*(5), 613–627.

Describes how an urban school district recruited and retained minority teachers and examines data on factors that increase or decrease minority teacher satisfaction.

Kershaw, T. (1992). The effects of educational tracking on the social mobility of African Americans. *Journal of Black Studies, 23*(1), 152–170.

Analyzes criteria used to determine student placement in tracking systems; explains how black students are discriminated against and the negative consequences of such decisions.

Kneller, G.F. (1971). *Introduction to the philosophy of education* (2nd ed.). New York, NY: Macmillan.

Examines the intellectual foundations for five contemporary educational philosophies.

Koppelman, K. (2001). Like a whale. In *Values in the key of life: Making harmony in the human community* (pp. 57–63). Amityville, NY: Baywood.

Examines the difficulty that Americans have accepting human diversity.

Kozol, J. (2005). *The shame of the nation: The restoration of apartheid schooling in America.* New York, NY: Crown.

Examines evidence of race and class segregation and the inadequacy of facilities for low income students in urban schools.

Kozol, J. (1991). *Savage inequalities: Children in America's schools.* New York, NY: HarperPerennial, 1991.

Discusses documented disparities in education between schools of different classes and races and includes observations of various classrooms in urban public school systems.

Ladson-Billings, G. (2001). *Crossing over to Canaan: The journey of new teachers in diverse classrooms.* San Francisco, CA: Jossey-Bass.

Describes the experiences of eight teachers starting their careers in urban elementary schools and their use of student cultures to enhance academic achievement.

Ladson-Billings, G. (1995). Toward a theory of culturally relevant pedagogy. *American Educational Research Journal, 32* 3, 465–491.

Describes the teaching practices of eight exemplary teachers of African American students and offers a way to define and recognize culturally relevant pedagogy.

Laosa, L. (1974). Toward a research model of multicultural competency-based education. In W. Hunter (Ed.), *Multicultural education through competency-based education.* Washington, DC: American Association of Colleges for Teacher Education.

Discusses the value of cultural diversity and the need for competency-based programs to prepare teachers for working with culturally diverse students.

Michelli, N.M. (2005). Education for democracy: What can it be? In N.M. Michelli & D.L. Keiser (Eds.). *Teacher education for democracy and social justice* (pp. 3–30). New York, NY: Routledge.

Examines limitations often imposed on the concept of citizenship, the barriers to an appropriate education for citizens of a democracy, and hopeful signs for the future.

Myrdal, G. (1944). *An American dilemma: The Negro problem and modern democracy.* New York, NY: Harper & Row.

Describes values and contradictions in American culture and how they relate to the pervasive prejudice in American society.

National Center for Education Statistics. (2005). The nation's report card: Mathematics 2005 (No. NCES 2006453). Washington, DC: U.S. Government Printing Office.

Presents results of the National Assessment of Educational Progress (NAEP) 2005 in fourth- and eighth-grade mathematics assessments for U.S. students showing that math scores have increased overall.

Nieto, S. (2008). *Affirming diversity: The sociopolitical context of multicultural education* (5th ed.). Boston, MA: Pearson Allyn & Bacon.

Provides a comprehensive analysis of how schools are failing to meet the needs of students of color and suggests strategies for more effective teaching based on research and practice.

Nieto, S. (1999). *The light in their eyes.* New York, NY: Teachers College Press

Describes teaching and learning as a social as well as an academic pursuit and provides many examples of teachers practicing multicultural education.

Oakes, J. (2005). *Keeping track: How schools structure inequality.* (2nd ed.). New Haven, CT: Yale University Press.

Documents how tracking practices have perpetuated racial and social class inequalities.

Oakes, J., & Wells, A.S. (1996). *Beyond the technicalities of school reform: Policy lessons from detracking schools.* Los Angeles, CA: UCLA Graduate School of Education and Information Studies.

Describes problems affecting students in tracked classes and strategies for detracking schools.

Oakes, J., Selvin, M., Karoly, L., & Guiton, G. (1992). *Educational matchmaking: Academic and vocational tracking in comprehensive high schools.* Santa Monica, CA: RAND.

Examines tracking practices in five high schools in terms of curriculum, consequences, and participation by race and gender.

Oakes, J., Quartz, K.H., Ryan, S., & Lipton, M. (2000). *Becoming good American schools: The struggle for civic virtue in school reform.* San Francisco, CA: Jossey-Bass.

Describes the effort of sixteen schools in five states to move away from tracked classes and implement other reforms to improve the education of all students.

Orfield, G., Losen, D., Wald, J., & Swanson, C. (2004). *Losing our future: How minority youth are being left behind by the graduation rate crisis.* Cambridge, MA: The Civil Rights Project at Harvard University. Contributors: Advocates for Children of New York, The Civil Society Institute.

Explores the increasing drop in high school graduation rates for students of color and challenges policymakers to address this as an urgent educational and civil rights crisis.

Oakes, J., Wells, A.S., Jones, M., & Datnow, A. (1997). Detracking: The social construction of ability, cultural politics, and resistance to reform. *Teachers College Record, 95* (3), 482–510.

Presents results from a 3-year longitudinal study of 10 racially and socio-economically mixed secondary schools participating in detracking reform; explores how broadly held conceptions of intelligence intervene in efforts to detrack schools.

Pai, Y., & Adler, S. (1997). *Cultural foundations of education* (2nd ed.). Upper Saddle River, NJ: Merrill Prentice Hall.

Examines education as a cultural phenomenon, the implications for schooling, and provides information about curriculum and pedagogy as a foundation for multicultural education.

Pang, V.O. (2005). *Multicultural education: A caring-centered, reflective approach.* (2nd ed.). Boston, MA: McGraw-Hill.

Presents stories and classroom examples to illustrate concepts of culture, discrimination, and social justice, explaining how teachers can effectively address these concepts. Uses actual experiences to illustrate major concepts in multicultural education and explains how these concepts can be incorporated into school classrooms.

Partridge, E. (1983). *Origins: A short etymological dictionary of modern English* (p. 92). New York, NY: Greenwich.

Citation notes that the Latin *ducere* means to lead and is the basis for Duke, p. 169.

Pasternak, M.G. (1986). *Helping kids learn multi-cultural concepts: A handbook of strategies.* Champaign, IL: Research Press.

Describes activities developed for an urban school system to create a multicultural environment for a multiethnic student population.

Piaget, J. (1974). *The language and thought of the child* (Rev. ed.). New York, NY: New American Library.

Includes a collection of preliminary studies on the exchange of thought between children, their verbal understanding, and how social conditions affect the development of thought.

Sapon-Shevin, M. (1999). *Because we can change the world: A practical guide to building cooperative, inclusive classroom communities.* Boston, MA: Allyn & Bacon.

Provides strategies and activities that reflect principles of multicultural education, although it is primarily intended for creating cohesive classrooms in elementary schools.

Sensoy, Ö. (in press, 2009). It's all in your name: Seeing ourselves in historical and cultural context. In E. Heilman, R. Fruja, & M. Missias (Eds.), *Social studies and diversity teacher education: What we do and why.* New York, NY: Routledge.

Describes in detail a culturally responsive lesson using student names, and provides an in-depth analysis and rationale for the lesson.

Shade, B.J., Kelly, C., & Oberg, M. (1997). *Creating culturally responsive classrooms.* Washington, DC: American Psychological Association.

Examines the impact of culture on learning and suggests strategies to motivate students from diverse cultural groups in the United States.

Sheets, R.H. (2005). *Diversity pedagogy: Examining the role of culture in the teaching-learning process.* Boston, MA: Pearson Education.

Discusses the significance of culture for student learning and explains how teachers can engage in classroom practices to take advantage of cultural differences.

Sleeter, C.E. (1996). *Multicultural education as social activism.* Albany: State University of New York Press.

Explores the value of multicultural education for white people and the impact of the connections between race, gender, and class in the struggle for social justice.

Sleeter, C.E., & Grant, C.A. (2003). *Making choices for multicultural education: Five approaches to race, class, and gender* (4th ed.). New York, NY: John Wiley.

Examines how concepts of race, class, and gender are presented to students and how students are asked to respond in five different approaches to multicultural education.

Sleeter, C.E., & Grant, C.A. (2009). *Turning on learning: Five approaches for multicultural teaching plans for race, class, gender, and disability* (5th ed.). Hoboken, NJ: Wiley.

Provides lesson plans consistent with each of the five approaches to multicultural education the authors identified in previous research.

Stephan, W. (1999). *Reducing prejudice and stereotyping in schools.* New York, NY: Teachers College Press.

Reviews theories of prejudice and stereotyping, examines conditions to promote changes in negative attitudes and describes techniques for improving race relations in schools.

Stevens, T., Hamman, D., & Olivarez, A. (2007). Hispanic students' perception of white teachers' mastery goal orientation influences sense of school belonging, *Journal of Latinos and Education, 6*(1), 55–70.

Presents a study finding that Hispanic students were more likely to feel a sense of belonging in school when white teachers held high expectations for them.

Terkel, S. (1980). *American dreams: Lost and found.* New York, NY: Ballantine.

Includes interviews with diverse people about their perceptions of America, including the author of *Black Like Me,* John Howard Griffin.

Tiedt, P.L., & Tiedt, I.M. (2002). *Multicultural teaching: A handbook of activities, information, and resources* (6th ed.). Boston, MA: Allyn & Bacon.

Provides strategies for thematic studies and learning modules with specific multicultural lessons in various disciplines for teachers in elementary and middle level classrooms.

Tobin, K., & Roth, W-M. (2005). Implementing co-teaching and cogenerative dialoguing in urban science education. *School Science and Mathematics, 105,* 313–322.

Describes the preparation of science educators to teach in urban schools by decreasing teacher isolation, mitigating turnover and retention, and addressing contradictions that may arise from the cultural and ethnic diversity of students and teachers.

Villegas, A., & Lucas, T. (2002). *Educating culturally responsive teachers: A coherent approach.* New York: State University of New York Press.

Offers a conceptual framework and practical strategies for preparing teachers for culturally responsive teaching in schools with increasingly diverse racial and ethnic student populations.

CHAPTER 14

Pluralism in Society: Creating Unity in a Diverse America

> "How many goodly creatures are there here!
> How beauteous mankind is!
> O brave new world,
> That has such people in't."
>
> **William Shakespeare (1564–1616)**

All around us, a brave new world is indeed taking shape in America. Despite a wealth of **diversity,** America has not yet become a pluralistic society. **Pluralism** entails perceiving human differences as enriching, and valuing that diversity in our society. Yet Americans are still wary of one another, and fearful when conflicts occur between groups. Nevertheless, changes are taking place that encourage us to become more accepting of others and more pluralistic. It is obvious that students in K–12 schools and colleges today will shape our society in the future; yet many Americans don't realize that almost 40% of all K–12 children and youth are students of color. According to 2000 census data, students of color in California and Texas comprise 50% of the K–12 population. Immigrants constitute 12% of the American workforce, and 20% of all K–12 students are foreign-born or have foreign-born parents (Cochran-Smith, 2003; Pipher, 2002). U.S. trade agreements guarantee that these figures will increase.

The diversity and location of racial and ethnic groups have changed dramatically: for example, more than 600 Somali refugees live in Owatonna, Minnesota. And although our media still tend to present U.S. diversity as principally African American, Hispanic Americans have become the largest ethnic minority group. As these societal changes occur, they are reflected in organizations such as the American military: More than 1,400 Muslims and 1,240 Buddhists serve in the U.S. Armed Forces. One out of every five soldiers recruited by the army is a woman, and half are African American (Katzenstein & Reppy, 1999; Matthews, 1999).

To capitalize on these unprecedented demographic changes, Americans must realize the need for new approaches to living and working together and must create new partnerships with people in their communities. In Billings, Montana, a Jewish family decorated their home for Hanukkah and placed a menorah by their front window. After a vandal threw a cinder block through their window, thousands of Christian families put pictures of menorahs in their windows so vandals could not identify for certain which homes in their community had Jewish families (Eck, 2001).

America is the most diverse society in our diverse world: The global presence of major U.S. corporations requires sensitivity to diverse global issues and cultures. Americans come from almost every country on the planet; our diversity is represented by differences not only in geographical origins (ethnicity) but also in religion, social class, disabilities, gender, sexual orientation, age, region, and dialect, as well as individuals in multiple categories.

Psychologist Howard Gardner (2006) identified five categories of mental abilities that will be increasingly necessary in the future, not just in the United States but globally, and he argues that schools and professional training programs need to be cultivating these skills now. He calls one of these categories "The Respectful Mind," and it is characterized by a person's ability to encounter others without being threatened by their individual or cultural differences, but rather to respond to them with acceptance and respect. Gardner believes this mental ability can be taught, especially when teachers successfully model this behavior, but the lessons cannot come from teachers alone: "Messages of respect or disrespect, tolerance or intolerance, are signaled throughout a society" (p. 111). Gardner insists that simply tolerating differences is an inadequate response to the human diversity that is increasing in societies around the world; he rejects the idea of ignoring differences such as pretending to be "color-blind," but advocates for fostering pluralistic attitudes that enable people to interact and collaborate more effectively with the diverse individuals they will inevitably encounter in schools, while shopping, at recreational activities, at work, and even in neighborhoods as intolerance and old patterns of racial segregation finally begin to break down.

> For each age is a dream that is dying. Or one that is coming to birth.
>
> **Arthur O'Shaughnessy (1844–1881)**

Forces at work in all areas of society increasingly recognize pluralism as a preferred alternative to the Anglo conformity demanded in the past. Although the transformation from America's preference for conformity to an unequivocal acceptance of human differences will not be resolved for decades to come, we must be aware of recent changes and prepare for future challenges. This chapter reports on five major societal areas—the federal government, higher education, business, mass media, and the military—and how each is making conscious and deliberate efforts to respond positively to diversity in the United States. The information provided is based on these three questions:

How do advocates promote pluralism?
How do detractors oppose pluralism?
What changes illustrate progress toward pluralism?

Regardless of the profession chosen, most individuals starting their careers are likely to encounter some form of the challenges and changes described in this chapter.

Federal Government

President John F. Kennedy first used the phrase **affirmative action** when he issued Executive Order 10025 mandating that the federal government aggressively recruit and hire African Americans (Painter, 2005). Title VII of the 1964 Civil Rights Act expanded this concept to include people of color and women being employed by private companies contracted to do work for the federal government. Companies had to file affirmative action plans with hiring goals and timetables for those goals. By mandating affirmative action, the federal government began a major initiative to promote pluralism by reducing acts of discrimination and providing opportunity for women and people of color. Title VII stated that if a court rules a finding of discrimination is justified, the court might order an employer "to take such affirmative action as may be appropriate." A 1972 Title VII amendment added "or any other equitable relief as the courts deem appropriate" (Greene, 1989, p. 15). Title VII has been controversial from the moment the Civil Rights Act became law, consistently keeping the issue of equal opportunity for all Americans in the public eye.

According to the Civil Rights Act, affirmative action plans represent voluntary programs unless a court orders that an affirmative action plan be designed and implemented. Determining the need for an affirmative action plan begins by analyzing the diversity of employees at a business or agency, or the student population at a university. If population variation is similar to that of available applicants, there is said to be no equity problem. If disparities exist, however, each phase of the application and selection process is evaluated for bias that may advantage some applicants and disadvantage others.

The Affirmative Action Debate

Debate concerning affirmative action has resonated from the public square to the U.S. Supreme Court.

The crux of the debate concerns whether affirmative action was intended only to redress victims of intentional discrimination or if it mandates that programs create a more just distribution of women and minorities in the workforce and in higher education. In the business community, the principal emphasis has been on compensating victims of discrimination; institutions of higher education have implemented admissions policies designed to increase the numbers of women and minorities admitted.

Affirmative action advocates argue that aggressive action is required to address inequities in hiring and college admissions. Proponents insist our society must guarantee equal opportunity to every citizen, and they argue that ample evidence demonstrates our failure to achieve this goal. Because a college education is required to become qualified for certain jobs, policies and practices of college admission are scrutinized, just as businesses and corporations are monitored to ensure that women and minorities have the same opportunity as white men to work and to receive promotions. Affirmative action advocates explain that monitoring is not intended as punitive, but rather that it meets a broader goal of strengthening our society by creating racial, gender, and ethnic unity. Greene (1989) argued that if white men "continue to hold positions of power and prestige to the exclusion of other groups . . . divisions will continue to exist" (p. 10).

Affirmative action opponents counter that equal opportunity programs have created greater American disunity. They denounce affirmative action plans as racist when race is emphasized to create quotas, establishing what they term "preferential treatment." Opponents also claim that businesses and schools have often been forced to accept women and minorities who are less qualified than the rejected white men. They say it is ironic that affirmative action with a goal of reducing discrimination is engaging in "reverse discrimination"—decreasing opportunity for qualified white men. Eastland (2000) expressed gratitude for reverse discrimination lawsuits because they remind us of the principle "that no one in America should be discriminated against on account of race" (p. 175). Opponents also suggest that affirmative action plans have an adverse effect on society because quality and competence are being compromised, making the "solution" worse than the problem.

Judicial Limitations on Affirmative Action

Quality and competence were the focus of the *Griggs v. Duke Power* case heard by the U.S. Supreme Court in 1971. Job applicants at the Duke Power Company were required to have a high school diploma or passing scores on a specific standardized test. Lawyers argued that the requirement excluded a higher percentage of blacks than whites because unequal educational opportunities and other inequities prevented more black than white youth from earning high school diplomas. The U.S. Supreme Court ruled that any hiring practice that was intended to select the most qualified candidates was legitimate. Companies could not be held accountable for past discrimination that adversely affected individuals in the present. As long as job requirements were related to work performance, they could not be labeled discriminatory. But Duke Power did not demonstrate that the diploma/test requirement was related to successful work performance; therefore the use of this requirement was discriminatory.

Based on the same concept, the U.S. Supreme Court also upheld the *seniority system* to determine layoffs during economic downturns. Because of past discrimination against women and minorities, adhering to **seniority system** priorities required employers to lay off people with least seniority: "last hired is the first fired." Although the procedure seemed race neutral, lawyers provided evidence that the majority of women and minority employees had low seniority and were most likely to be dismissed. Supreme Court justices acknowledged the problem but consistently have found the seniority system constitutional because it does not represent intentional discrimination. The Court has ruled with the same consistency on cases where the affirmative action plan appears to include a racial quota, that is, a specific number of people hired or accepted based on race.

Affirmative Action and Quotas

Whenever **racial quotas** have been employed, the U.S. Supreme Court has always ruled against them, declaring that Title VII never mandated racial (or other) quotas. Indeed, the justices are correct. There is no mention of quotas in Title VII, nor anything to suggest that employers must hire unqualified applicants; as Greene (1989) noted, section 703 (j) of Title VII states:

> Nothing contained in this title shall be interpreted to require any employer, employment agency, labor organization, or joint labor-management committee subject to this title to grant preferential treatment to any individual or group. (p. 60)

One of the clearest judgments against racial quotas was the Supreme Court's ruling in the case of *Regents of California v. Bakke.* In 1970, 80% of the 800 students of color attending medical school in the United States were enrolled in programs at two historically black universities. Because minorities were never more than 3% of students at the University of California–Davis Medical School, the university decided to reserve eight of their admissions places (16%) for minority applicants. For two consecutive years, Alan Bakke was rejected by UC–Davis despite having a grade-point average and Medical College Admissions Test scores higher than those of several minority applicants admitted. Ball (2000) explained the strategy of Bakke's lawyers in arguing relentlessly against the concept of racial quotas while UC–Davis lawyers argued that the university only accepted academically qualified applicants to their medical school and that preferential treatment of minorities was necessary to increase the numbers of minorities in professions "from which minorities were long excluded because of generations of pervasive racial discrimination" (p. 92).

> One who gains strength by overcoming obstacles possesses the only strength which can overcome adversity.
>
> **Albert Schweitzer (1875–1965)**

The final decision on *Bakke* in 1978 fragmented the Court. Four justices approved UC–Davis affirmative action procedures, and four justices rejected them, arguing that race should play no role whatsoever on admission decisions. Justice Powell cast the deciding vote. In his written opinion, Powell declared that racial quotas were an unconstitutional strategy for achieving affirmative action goals, but that race could be used as one factor among others in considerations of college applicants.

Affirmative Action for Minority-Owned Businesses

Another affirmative action strategy rejected by the courts was the practice of setting aside a certain percentage of tax-funded projects for minority-owned businesses. In 1983, the city of Richmond, Virginia, was 50% African American, but in the previous five years, less than 1% of funds spent on city projects had been paid to minority-owned businesses. The Richmond city council approved an affirmative action plan to require recipients of city construction projects to subcontract at least 30% of the dollar value of these projects to minority-owned businesses. When J.A. Croson Company insisted it could not find any suitable minority-owned businesses and asked for a waiver of the subcontracting requirement, the city refused and informed the company that it would resubmit their part of the project for new bids. The company brought the case to federal court, and the Supreme Court ruled on the case in 1989.

Writing for the majority in the *City of Richmond v. J.A. Croson Co.,* Sandra Day O'Connor criticized Richmond's **set-aside program** for its apparently arbitrary determination of the 30% figure and for not providing evidence demonstrating that previous major contractors had intentionally discriminated against minority-owned businesses. O'Connor said the Richmond City Council could have implemented effective, race-neutral strategies rather than establishing set-aside quotas. The court affirmed the right to remedy past discrimination, but again rejected racial quotas as a legitimate constitutional strategy (Crosby & VanDeVeer, 2000).

The Future of Affirmative Action

In 1995, the National Employment Lawyers Association issued a position paper citing a number of studies in support of affirmative action to substantiate their contention that affirmative action had "significantly reduced job discrimination and improved occupational status and mobility for minorities and women" (2000, p. 711). Yet because of ongoing criticism of affirmative action, during that same year, President Clinton appointed a task force to review all federal affirmative action programs. Although some changes were recommended, the task force concluded that programs reviewed did not include quotas, did not mandate preferences for unqualified individuals, and did not engage in reverse discrimination. Instead, the programs were designed to remedy past discrimination and "lead the nation toward the goal of equal opportunity" (Ball, 2000, p. 163).

California voters did not agree. In 1996, they voted to approve **Proposition 209,** prohibiting preferential treatment to individuals or groups in hiring, awarding public contracts, and college admissions. According to Ball (2000), African American admissions to California law schools dropped 72% the year after the proposition was approved, and admission of all students of color to UC–Berkeley dropped 50%. The following year, UCLA and Berkeley reported continuing decreases in numbers of students of color. In response to complaints of increased segregation on state university campuses, California legislators voted to guarantee admission to any California university campus to all high school students graduating in the top 4% of their class. Critics said the vote represented a cynical recognition of racial segregation in California high schools. Although other states such as Oregon have passed propositions similar to Proposition 209, advocates argued that eliminating affirmative action was premature, and most would agree with the perspective expressed by Clayton and Crosby (2000):

> When the goals of true equality have been reached . . . affirmative action will be unnecessary. We have not yet reached such a happy state of being. Sexism and racism are still strong forces in American society, and both hostility toward and stereotypes about women and people of color influence decisions. (p. 88)

Higher Education

Since the 1960s, colleges and universities have implemented affirmative action plans to increase the numbers of students of color on their campuses. Although many administrators initially viewed affirmative action as unnecessary interference, in recent years administrators have displayed a pluralistic attitude, arguing that diversity of all kinds benefits

FIGURE 14.1

Source: Courtesy of *The Daily Cardinal,* University of Wisconsin.

the entire student population. Administrators, faculty, and student leaders on college campuses have consistently supported setting diversity goals. Musil (1996) summarized their perspective:

> To invite that diversity onto campus is not simply an act of charity. It is an act of raw self-interest. . . . it will make higher education better than it is. It expands our notion of learning. It widens what we study and how we study it. It improves our pedagogy. It adds to our resources in human capital. (p. 225)

Criticism of Diversity Goals in Higher Education

Affirmative action plans in higher education and the increased diversity they have helped produce have been the subject of much criticism. Even some people of color say affirmative action has stigmatized students of color, as white students question their academic ability and believe they are admitted through lower standards. Some faculty blame affirmative action for a perceived decline in academic standards and for promoting a multicultural curriculum that has caused a decline in the rigor of traditional college education.

Critics persist in denouncing changes in traditional curriculum, accusing faculty who are creating a more inclusive curriculum of having a "political agenda" rather than purely academic objectives. However, it would seem equally appropriate to accuse advocates for the preservation of a curriculum emphasizing white people as having a political agenda as well. One persistent criticism is that there has been widespread elimination of traditional Western civilization courses by universities in response to pressure from "multiculturalists." According to a 1999 survey, almost 60% of college faculty believed that Western civilization courses are the foundation of undergraduate education, and more than half of all U.S. colleges still require Western civilization courses (Yamane, 2001).

The critics are correct in insisting that feminists and people of color are challenging the lack of relevance and inclusiveness in college curricula. Duncan (2002) noted that women and students of color in college courses encounter minimal information written by or about their groups, and often the information provided misrepresents or distorts the group being described. Even worse, Duncan claimed that students of color find "both explicit and subtle racist themes in what they . . . study" (p. 45). What is included in college curricula is a critical issue, as Groff and Cain explained: "Curriculum is a microcosm of the culture: its inclusions and exclusions are an index of what the culture deems important" (Yamane, 2001, p. 6).

Diversity in College Faculty and Course Content

In addition to the omission of people of color in curriculum, few faculty of color are represented at most universities. Tusmith and Reddy (2002) reported that people of color constitute less than 15% of higher education faculty, and that the majority were nontenured lecturers or instructors. Browne-Miller (1996) quoted an Asian American student observing that the teaching styles of her white professors were "geared to white middle-class males, overlooking the fact that this may not be the most effective . . . with non-white students and women" (p. 90). Courses taught by faculty of color would benefit all students, including white students, by presenting perspectives they are not likely to have encountered. Reddy (2002) noted,

> Students—especially but not exclusively white students—arrive in our college classrooms with predictable baggage. Prepared by virtually every element of the society in which we live, they come ready to accept white authority, intelligence and rightness while discounting the views and experiences of people of color. (p. 54)

Because of Reddy's "predictable baggage," it is not inevitable that positive outcomes will occur if white students and students of color are brought together on a college campus; they may or may not enjoy each other or learn from each other. (See Figure 14.1.) Almost a century ago, journalist John Reed observed that participating in a diverse community may bring "pain, isolation of separateness, [or] intellectual exhilaration, greater self-knowledge and . . . human reconciliation" (Lowe, 1999, p. 22). To ensure productive interactions between members of diverse groups, colleges sponsor frequent diversity workshops and seminars, require all students to take at least one course on diversity, encourage relevant academic departments to include at least one course with significant content on diversity issues in their majors and minors, and encourage all faculty to integrate content about diversity issues into the courses they teach.

Since the 1960s, professors in numerous institutions of higher education have created scholarly courses focusing on one or more diverse groups. As these professors have grappled with diversity issues, their efforts have been learning experiences for themselves as well as their students. To struggle with diversity issues is to engage in an evolutionary process of change. According to Musil (1996), colleges cannot assume that they can "simply add diversity and stir and think the recipe will not be fundamentally altered" (p. 224). To illustrate, Musil went on to describe the limitations of initial courses developed to examine diversity issues, and what professors and students involved in those courses learned:

> Black studies were typically about only men. Women's studies were typically only about white women. Gay and lesbian studies had no practicing Christians or Jews. And none of the three paid much attention to those in the group who were old, working class or disabled. Today it is largely commonplace in the most influential texts . . . in these kinds of courses to recognize the reality of our multiple identities. (p. 228)

Unfortunately, enrollment figures indicate that only a few white students take ethnic studies courses, and there have been few men enrolled in women's studies courses. Duncan (2002) believes that most white students, especially white males, are so accustomed to white experience being the focus of curriculum that they feel strange, defensive, and uncomfortable as they struggle to understand information that focuses on experiences of women or people of color. Despite these difficulties, colleges and universities continue to promote the goal of students gaining knowledge about diverse groups. Although designed to heighten student acceptance of diverse populations, courses on diversity have tended to be an addition to rather than a replacement for traditional curriculum. Kolodny (1998) addressed the importance of adding diversity content to the traditional curriculum:

> We are expanding our students' repertoire of reading and interpretive strategies, teaching them to comprehend and appreciate the aesthetic rules and cultural practices governing the Zuni story of emergence as well as those governing the composition of a Shakespeare play. (p. 49)

In 1989, the University of Wisconsin System—consisting of 13 four-year and 12 two-year institutions of higher education—implemented a **Design for Diversity** plan mandating changes in policies and practices on all campuses to make them more welcoming places for students of color. Across America, universities have instituted changes to create positive environments for the increasingly diverse college student population. Humphreys (2000) presented results of a survey finding that 63% of colleges and universities either have at least one diversity course as a graduation requirement or they are developing such a course; 42% require more than one course; 25% have had such a requirement for more than ten years.

Results and Possibilities

Diversity courses not only provide greater understanding of diverse groups, but they also help students appreciate the benefits of diversity. In Browne-Miller (1996), one student learned "More diversity allows for more possibilities, be it knowledge, friends, understanding between people" (p. 83). In a society as diverse and democratic as the United States, colleges and universities must actively facilitate understanding between diverse groups. Ball (2000) commented, "For democracy to flourish, college students have to be able to interact with other students who are different from them" (p. 13). In a series of diversity reports, the American Association of Colleges and Universities (AACU) argued that diversity challenges democratic commitments: "instead of creating fragmentation and alienation . . . [AACU] asserts that only through diversity can we achieve a deeper and lasting national unity" (Musil, 1996, p. 226).

Diversity does not only refer to obvious differences of race, ethnicity, gender, or disabilities. Diversity includes other changes taking place in students attending college today: Almost 50% of all college students are over twenty-four years old, more than 50% are the first in their family to attend college, and students with learning disabilities are the fastest growing category of disabled students on our campuses. Individuals accepted today may require modifications of and accommodations within traditional policies and practices governing campuses. Yet as demographic developments and affirmative action plans change the face of our campuses, opponents struggle to maintain the status quo. White students filed suit against both graduate and undergraduate admissions programs at the University of Michigan for including race in their admissions procedures. In 2003, the Supreme Court's ruling on this case maintained its consistent position of allowing race to be used as a factor in admissions procedures while rejecting approaches that appear to establish racial quotas. Although there are likely to be further cases, this ruling affirmed the university's argument that having a diverse student body benefited all students at the University of Michigan; in addition, the justices provided further clarification concerning how universities can include race as a factor in admissions procedures.

> Democracy is a way of life . . . a vibrant, living sweep of hope and progress which constantly strives for the fulfillment of its objective in life—the search for truth, justice, and human dignity.
>
> **Saul Alinsky (1909–1972)**

Corporate and Small Business

It surprised some opponents of affirmative action to discover that several Fortune 500 corporations filed amicus briefs in support of Michigan's program; for the past two decades, the private sector has been in support of affirmative action. In the early 1980s, many corporations opposed the Reagan administration's efforts to reduce the demand for contractor compliance on federal projects. According to responses from Corporate Executive Officers (CEOs) reported by Reskin (2000), 122 of 128 major corporations would "retain their affirmative action plans [even] if the Federal government ended [required] affirmative action" (p. 111). On surveys, CEOs tend to agree that affirmative action has improved hiring, marketing, and productivity. According to Harvard business professor David Thomas, a diverse workforce is an "inescapable reality" for any corporation with over 100 employees no matter where it is located (Hymowitz, 2005).

In recent years, American business has become more attentive to diversity. They have to be. White men represent only 35% of the workforce today, and by 2010 people of color will constitute 40% of those entering the workforce (Daft, 2003). In a 2005 article for the *Wall Street Journal,* Hymowitz stated, "If companies are going to sell products and services globally, they will need a rich mix of employees with varied perspectives and experiences" (p. R1). Business leaders understand that responding positively to diversity by implementing pluralistic policies and practices is necessary because not only is the work force becoming more diverse, but so are the customers. Mor-Barak (2005) rejects the old workplace model requiring workers to conform to established organizational values and norms reflecting the dominant culture; instead, she argues for promoting a respect for "all cultural perspectives represented among its employees" (p. 8).

The numbers of women and people of color in the workforce mirror the percentage they represent as consumers, one certain to increase. In 2000, Secretary of Commerce Norman Mineta predicted, "America's population will increase 50% over the next 50 years, with almost 90% of that increase in the minority community" (Williams, 2003, p. 442). When people have money to spend, they command attention from American business. Williams claimed that people of color represent almost $800 billion of purchasing power, and 134 million American women have $1.1 trillion of purchasing power (see Table 14.1). One corporate president has insisted that more women must be appointed to corporate boards of directors primarily because "Women either control or influence nearly all consumer purchases" (Jones & George, 2003, p. 118).

Corporate Litigation

American demographic changes represent compelling reasons for corporate America to value di-

TABLE 14.1 Diversity and Purchasing Power Among U.S. Consumers

Group	Population Numbers	Purchasing Power
Gays and lesbians	20 million	$608 billion
People with disabilities	51 million	$220 billion
African Americans	34 million	$646 billion
Asian Americans	10 million	$296 billion
Hispanic Americans	35 million	$580 billion
Women	144 million	$1.1 trillion

Source: Census Bureau (2006) at www.census.gov and Cultural Access Group (2006) at www.accesscay.com

versity. Discrimination litigation has also provided motivation. In the 1980s and early 1990s, Denny's Restaurants were the sites for several alleged racist incidents such as one involving 21 secret service agents en route to Annapolis to make security preparations for a presidential visit. When they stopped at a Denny's restaurant to eat supper, the white agents were given what they ordered, but the black secret service agents were never served any food. Despite being one of the largest restaurant chains in the United States, Denny's hired few minority employees, and none of its major suppliers was a minority-owned firm. At the time of its purchase by Advantica Corporation, Denny's had just paid $54 million out of court to settle discrimination claims. According to Williams (2003), Advantica's CEO said the lawsuits had turned Denny's into "a poster child for racism" (p. 467).

Advantica took aggressive action to change the Denny image. As the twenty-first century began, 42% of Denny's employees were minorities, as were 33% of its managers. Nearly 20% of its suppliers were minority-owned firms, and 35% of its franchises were minority owned. Denny's commitment to diversity was recognized by *Fortune* magazine, which identified it as one of the top ten companies in its support of minorities. (see Table 14.2.)

In 1998, Arab American workers and managers alleged discrimination in decisions on promotions and pay raises in a class action lawsuit filed against Detroit Edison, the largest electric utility in Michigan. Detroit Edison representatives began negotiations immediately and promised changes. They kept their promises. They recruited and hired an Arab American widely known throughout the state to serve as vice president, and their contracts with suppliers included an increased number of businesses owned by people of Middle Eastern descent. In response, the Arab American community commended Detroit Edison, and its CEO accepted an invitation to serve on the advisory board of the Michigan chapter's Arab-American Anti-Discrimination committee (Millman, 2005).

Denny's and Detroit Edison's experiences are not isolated incidents. Shoney's Restaurants paid $132.8 million to settle a claim of racial discrimination in hiring; Edison International paid $11 million for the same offense. Bell Atlantic Telephone paid $500 million for discrimination against blacks in employee promotions. After making significant changes in policies and practices, all three companies are now listed among *Fortune* magazine's top 50 companies for their support of minorities (Williams, 2003). Global corporations such as Nike have also changed their policies and practices in response to accusations of discrimination or exploition (see the box on page 359).

Workplace Diversity

Most businesses do not address diversity issues in response to legal action, but rather because they recognize the advantages of promoting workplace diversity. In areas with significant Hispanic populations, Sears and Target Stores have profited by accommodating Hispanic consumers, as have Darden's Restaurants by providing Spanish menus (Jones & George, 2003). Furthermore, having diverse managers and employees increases the likelihood of appropriate responses to customer needs. To recruit a more diverse workforce, businesses use tactics such as (1) providing college scholarships and workplace mentors, (2) disseminating information on available jobs to local churches and Spanish-language radio and television stations, (3) sponsoring seminars on diversity for managers, (4) establishing a full-time position as diversity coordinator, or (5) sponsoring community events such as Cinco de Mayo or a Gay Pride march (Hymowitz, 2005).

> This country will not be a good place for any of us to live in unless we make it a good place for all of us to live in.
>
> **Theodore Roosevelt (1858–1919)**

Having a positive work environment to accommodate diversity improves productivity and reduces turnover costs. The Employment Management Association estimates the average costs for hiring a new employee is $10,000 (Jones & George, 2003). According to Griffin (2002), one pharmaceutical corporation saved $50,000 by lowering its turnover rate among women and minorities. The creation of positive work environments for diverse employees may be one reason why 62% of job seekers said they would prefer to work for organizations demonstrating a commitment to diversity (Daft, 2003).

Creating a positive work environment is not a simple task, but it must be done. In discussing current issues, Griffin (2002) stated that a fundamental trend in business "is that virtually all organizations . . . are becoming more diverse" (p. 169). Businesses define diversity as not only the obvious differences of race and gender, but also less obvious differences including status as single parents or dual-career couples. To accommodate diversity, some U.S. companies have created day care centers at their work sites or have instituted flexible working hours. Benefits packages have been structured to address the diverse needs of employees. Being flexible does not have to be expensive, even when providing accommodations for people with disabilities. According to Williams (2003), the average cost of accommodating workers with disabilities was $250; 20% of accommodations involved no direct cost.

Diversity Training Programs

Diversity training programs are not new, but older programs have been considered largely ineffective because they tended to use one of two approaches: sensitivity training, which appeared to have little practical value, or a confrontational approach that antagonized white men. Current diversity training covers a broader range of topics, focuses on a pragmatic business rationale for promoting diversity,

TABLE 14.2 America's Best Companies for Minorities

Company	Board of Directors	Officials and Managers	Total Workforce
McDonald's, Oak Brook, IL	2 of 16	36%	53%
Fannie Mae, Washington, D.C.	5 of 17	33%	44%
Denny's, Spartanburg, SC	3 of 9	29%	47%
Union Bank of CA, San Francisco, CA	3 of 12	39%	55%
Sempra Energy, San Diego, CA	4 of 12	29%	48%
Southern Cal Edison, Rosemead, CA	2 of 11	28.5%	44%
SBC Communications, San Antonio, TX	3 of 21	21.7%	38%

Source: *Fortune*, June 24, 2003

From Exploitation to Exemplary Practice
Critics of America's involvement in the global economy have expressed concerns not just about outsourcing jobs to other countries but also about the exploitation of workers of color in those countries. When Nike Corporation was founded in the 1960s, executives wanted to experiment with the idea of focusing on marketing shoes, but not manufacturing them. The shoes were designed in the United States, but the final product was purchased from independent contractors in Asian or Southeast Asian countries where wages were low. This innovative approach became so profitable that it soon became the norm for American corporations.

Beginning in the 1990s, national and local media published news reports about inhumane labor conditions at Nike's overseas factories. When consumers expressed outrage, Nike executives insisted that they only purchased the shoes, and it was not their responsibility to tell the Asian or Southeast Asian factory owners how to run their businesses. News coverage continued to reveal disturbing allegations, especially concerning child labor abuses, and Nike's stock value dropped. Eventually Nike executives recognized that they had to take action to counter the bad press, so they implemented programs to ensure better monitoring of labor conditions at the factories making Nike products.

Today, Nike pre-screens factories before signing contracts with a supplier, and the company has become a role model for other corporations because of its careful monitoring of worksite conditions. Nike publishes the names and addresses of all factories producing its products and publicly discloses its workplace monitoring activities. Nike has now become such a leader in this area that its web site (www.nikebiz.com) has been acknowledged as an excellent resource on international labor standards (Frank, 2008).

and develops specific skills in communication and management. Many businesses are implementing intensive diversity training programs not only to improve work relations between diverse employees and managers, but also to ensure that employees will interact effectively with diverse customers. At the conclusion of diversity training, some businesses engage in evaluations of how employees and managers respond to diversity (Egodigwe, 2005). A quarterly survey of Allstate Insurance employees included a "diversity index" for evaluating managers on diversity issues: 25% of a manager's bonus pay was determined by that score (Daft, 2003).

To promote a positive environment for diversity at the worksite, some U.S. companies have instituted **diversity training** programs for managers and employees. Training programs may include **diversity pairing,** where people from diverse backgrounds are paired to provide them with opportunities to interact and become better acquainted. Such pairs may be combined with mentoring as when a white male manager is paired with an employee of color or a woman. Many businesses create multicultural teams for more effective problem solving; these terms also provide an opportunity for workers to learn more about their colleagues. (See Figure 14.2.)

Jones and George (2003) described the diversity training program at United Parcel Service (UPS) that requires upper-level managers to participate in community programs for a full month. Approximately 40 managers per year work in organizations such as homeless shelters, Head Start centers, migrant farm worker assistance groups, and detention centers. Since 1968, over 800 managers have been involved in the program, and UPS believes it has had a positive impact on the abilities of its managers to respond more effectively to diversity issues.

Some U.S. corporations have been especially aggressive in their commitment to diversity. In 1995, the CEO at International Business Machines (IBM) was concerned that his senior executive team had minimal diversity, despite IBM's affirmative action efforts. He implemented a new diversity initiative, which over a ten-year period resulted in an increase of five times the number of female senior executives and tripled the number of those who were U.S.-born minorities. In 2000, IBM had no women as country managers for its overseas operations, but by 2005, the company had hired nine women general managers for such countries as France, Spain, Thailand, New Zealand, and Peru. IBM also increased its activities with women and minority-owned businesses with revenues rising from $10 million in 1998 to $40 million in 2001 (Hymowitz, 2005). IBM's efforts illustrate a comment from a CEO of another multinational corporation: "Affirmative action brings people in the door, and the inclusion piece brings people to the table. You really need both to be successful" (Egodigwe, 2005, p. R4).

Lingering Problems

Diversity problems still arise in the business community. Jones and George report that women and minorities continue to be disadvantaged because of the way they are regarded by white colleagues, especially at work sites where they are a numerical minority. Daft (2003) cited two studies; one reported that 59% of minority managers believed there was a "racially motivated double standard in the delegation of assignments" (p. 443). Another study found that employees of color believed they had to work longer hours and make extra efforts to be given the same respect as white co-workers. Salary data documents that women and minorities still earn substantially less money than white men and that minorities are still underrepresented in management. Although African Americans and Hispanics constitute 26% of the U.S. population, they represent only 13% of managers—8% and 5%, respectively (Daft, 2003).

Women hold 49.5% of managerial positions and appear to be fairly represented, but the **glass ceiling** prevents them from rising as high as their abilities should permit. Jones and George (2003) reported on evidence of women's managerial ability, with one study concluding that female executives outperformed males on listening, motivating others, communicating effectively, and producing high-quality work. Another study of 425 top executives assessed 52 skills and found that women received higher ratings than men on 42 of them; yet women remain underrepresented in top executive positions. Williams (2003) reported that 90% of women executives said the glass ceiling had restricted their career growth; 80% indicated that they left their last job because the glass ceiling hurt their chances for promotion. Studies show that women are increasingly leaving organizations to start their own businesses because of their perception of a glass ceiling at work.

Corporate leaders know that problems arising from human differences must be resolved if U.S. businesses are to remain competitive in the global economy. Multinational corporations with headquarters in nations other than the United States have openly promoted diversity and implemented policies to assure that diverse workers receive fair treatment in the workplace. As Mor-Barak (2005) has written: "The second half of the twentieth century witnessed an unprecedented global trend in antidiscrimination and equal opportunity legislation" (p. 17). To match the efforts of their global counterparts, corporate leaders in the United States are likely to continue to publicly promote diversity, hire job seekers who appreciate corporate commitments to diversity, and provide diversity training to create a positive work environment for diverse employees. As Williams (2003) stated,

> The general purpose of diversity programs is to create a positive work environment where no one is advantaged or disadvantaged, where "we" is everyone, where everyone can do their best work, where differences are respected and not ignored, where everyone feels comfortable. (pp. 438–439)

FIGURE 14.2

The cartoon illustrates why many corporations and businesses believe it is necessary to engage in diversity training for employees.

Source: © Tribune Media Services, Inc. All rights reserved. Reprinted with permission.

Mass Media

Ellmore (1991) defines **mass media** as "The various vehicles used for sending information to a mass audience: radio, television, CATV, newspapers, magazines, books, discs" (p. 351). The best evidence of mass media promoting pluralism is the increasing involvement of women and minorities. Because it is a visible medium, increased presence of people of color on television has been noticeable. In the 1950s and 1960s, few television programs cast minority characters; of those who were featured, most appeared in stereotypical roles. Stereotypes in television remain, but Americans also see people of color as news reporters, as anchors on local and network news programs, and as actors on television and in films. In 2002, Oscars for best performances by an actor and actress were both awarded to African Americans. Media spokespersons explain that diversity is promoted and appreciated in media because the industry understands the economic advantages of rewarding talent, regardless of gender, race, or ethnicity.

Actually, a weakness of the media industry argument is suggested in the representation of human diversity in media: People of color constitute 28% of the population, yet Popper (2000) found that people of color occupied 11.6% of the positions on newspaper staffs. And although diversity is represented on television and theater screens, the vast majority of jobs in television are behind the camera—writers, producers, camera operators, and technicians. According to Larson (1999), a study of U.S. news stations reported that in the top 25 markets, 81% of the news staff was white. Of the 19% minority staff, 9% was African American, 7% was Latino, 3% was Asian American, and 1% was Native American. In the 26–50 top markets, 91% of the news staff was white; in the 51–100 top markets—which included cities like Las Vegas, Nevada, and Jackson, Mississippi—94% of the staff was white. Popper (2000) responded to the question of future changes: "Most industry people expect on-air staff to remain diverse, since that's what the audience sees. What happens behind the scenes is less clear" (p. 67).

In entertainment programming, Johnson (2000) identified 55 African Americans among 839 writers for prime time shows—6.6% of the total—with 45 of the 55 writing for black-themed shows. Only one black writer was employed by a white-themed show, a seemingly blatant form of segregation suggesting that black writers can't write scripts for white actors even though white writers have written for black actors for years. In reference to segregation, the majority of black-themed shows are on the cable networks.

Increasing Media Representation of Human Diversity

According to data from the 2000 census, 12.5% of Americans are Latino, blacks constitute 12.3% of the population, Asian Americans are 3.6%, and American Indians are 0.9%. Yet fewer than 2% of reporters for network news are Hispanic Americans compared to 17% for African Americans, 3% for Asian Americans, and 2% for Native Americans (Ramos, 2002). Representation of diversity on television programs continues to be inadequate, and the NAACP, as well as Children Now, an advocacy group, are lobbying the entertainment industry to increase diversity on television programs. The Latino community includes 35 million potential television viewers, but Ramos cites a study conducted by Children Now that identified about 2% of the characters in prime-time shows as Hispanic: 47 of 2,251 characters examined.

Because of underrepresentation of people of color among television employees, the Federal Communications Commission (FCC) disseminated ambitious requirements for affirmative action plans to be submitted by communications corporations, but in 1998, a federal appeals court overturned the FCC requirements. Affirmative action advocates were encouraged, however, when the fifteen largest broadcast networks agreed to follow FCC requirements as guidelines in developing their affirmative action plans (Childs, 1998).

Media Presentation and Language

Another area of concern is how American media report diversity issues such as affirmative action. Reviewing media coverage of affirmative action controversies, Gabriel (1998) found a tendency to reinforce misperceptions such as "affirmative action = quotas = lowering standards = discrimination against white males = racism" (p. 87). Gabriel also reported that media coverage typically stated or implied that affirmative action benefited people of color at the expense of white men, yet only peripherally recognized that white women have been major beneficiaries of affirmative action programs.

Jackson (2000) referred to a study that revealed the media's tendency to portray poor people in the United States as African American. Although black people constitute about a third of Americans living in poverty, they accounted for 65% of the images of poor people presented on network news. African Americans were also featured in 62% of the pictures of Americans living in poverty published in major news magazines such as *Time, Newsweek,* and *U.S. News and World Report.* Similarly, Ferguson (1998) discussed a study of television news programming in twenty-nine North American cities that reported a tendency for newscasts to engage in both positive and negative stereotypes by covering successful black athletes and entertainers and providing frequent images of blacks as criminals, welfare mothers, and others representing a range of antisocial behaviors.

Bacon (2003) found a double standard in news coverage of black public figures. Although social activist Jesse Jackson ran two credible campaigns for the president of the United States, reporters and columnists frequently describe him as a "publicity hound" and "a race hustler." Betraying a total lack of understanding and respect for African American oral traditions, one Boston columnist chided Jackson because he "regularly substitutes rhyme for reason" (p. 27). Although professor Cornel West has consistently engaged in social justice issues, newspaper articles have referred to him as "a con man" and a "clownish minstrel." Some reporters have excerpted difficult passages from West's scholarly writing to illustrate their contention that West is impossible to understand. By creating such distractions, reporters have avoided addressing substantive issues being raised by Jackson and West. In Bacon's conclusion, she asks,

> Why do mainstream media approach progressive African American leaders with such evident contempt? . . . Why are they so reluctant to engage in arguments, preferring instead to ridicule and misrepresent them? (p. 29)

Perhaps part of the answer stems from white dominance of mainstream media. To grow up white in America is to believe in a world defined by white perspectives that are reinforced in schools and in media. As Ferguson (1998) stated, "Whiteness, and the power that goes with it, have been represented as so utterly normal that any other possibility seems like an aberration" (pp. 180–181). Gabriel (1998) cites June Jordan's reflection on media use of language to frame issues and images in stereotypes familiar to their white audience:

> I came to recognize media constructions such as "The Heartland" or "Politically Correct" or "The Welfare Queen" or "Illegal Alien" or "Terrorist" . . . for what they were: Multiplying scattershots intended . . . to establish and preserve white supremacy. (p. 11)

Media has the power to provide positive images of people and promote social change. In 1984, Levi Jeans aired the first advertisement providing a positive portrayal of a person with a disability. The energetic wheelchair user "popped a wheelie" to demonstrate his enthusiasm for Levi Jeans. The positive response to this advertisement caused a few more businesses to use people with disabilities in their advertisements. Although their presence remains minimal, people with disabilities were no longer completely absent from television. In the six years following that Levi Jeans commercial, more than 200 businesses produced over 2,600 advertisements with closed captions for hard-of-hearing people (Riley, 2005). Such changes are not simply altruistic. According to Corkery (2005), people with disabilities have $220 billion of purchasing power, and their inclusion in corporate advertising may influence not only their consumer choices but also the choices of their families and friends.

Representation of Diversity in Media: Present and Future

The creation of positive or negative images is not restricted to news reporting or television. Films have portrayed women and people of color in both positive and negative ways. Although American films have featured female characters overcoming obstacles, filmmakers have long been criticized for consistently producing films that link sex and violence. Similarly, although people of color have been portrayed as admirable and heroic individuals, we are still offered more negative images of people of color as drug dealers, thieves, and violent criminals.

When filmmakers depict oppression, the result often seems self-serving. Gabriel (1998) observed that films like *To Kill a Mockingbird* (1962) and *A Time to Kill* (1996) are part of a pattern of films that denounce racism but present blacks as powerless, requiring white people to save them. *Mississippi Burning* (1988) incensed people who knew that many black men, women, and children in Mississippi had courageously defied racist authorities and been jailed—some were killed—while the FBI did little to help them, instead tapping Martin Luther King, Jr.'s telephone to gather evidence that might prove a communist connection. For the film to portray white FBI agents as heroes saving frightened blacks was an outrageously racist revision of historical truth.

> **We are now at the point where we must decide whether we are to honor the concept of a plural society which gains strength through diversity or whether we are to have bitter fragmentation that will result in perpetual tension and strife.**
>
> **Justice Earl Warren (1891–1974)**

Media critics suggest that increasing the diversity of people writing and producing mass media in the United States will be the best way to reduce bias and stereotypes. Data show that women and people of color are entering media professions in increasing numbers. McQueen (2002) reported that 61% of journalism and mass communication students were female and that 27% were students of color. McQueen also noted that only 35% of journalism and mass communication faculty was female and 15% were faculty of color. By 2035, experts predict that 40% of students in journalism and mass communication will be students of color. In mission statements, media organizations often claim to reflect the diversity of their community. That does not describe the reality, but it should be the goal.

Military Services

Diversity in the armed forces of the United States is not a new issue; it is only the nature of the diversity that has changed. Although the military kept no records in its earliest years, there is anecdotal evidence that ethnic diversity in society was reflected in its military, and we know of at least one woman—Deborah Sampson—who disguised herself as a man and engaged in combat during the Revolutionary War (Craft-Fairchild, 1997).

Starting in 1856, records exist showing a significant percentage of ethnic immigrants serving in the army—a shortcut to being granted citizenship—but they also reveal problems. During the Mexican-American War, many Irish Catholic soldiers were reluctant to kill Mexican Catholics, and a number of them deserted to avoid doing so (Johnson, 1999). Nevertheless, diversity continued to exist in the U.S. Army. According to Buckley (2001), at the end of the Civil War there were 140 black regiments with over 100,000 soldiers, and the army continued to recruit blacks and immigrants. Johnson (1999) cited an 1896 army report documenting that 7% of that year's recruits were black and 33% were ethnic immigrants.

Significant differences concerning diversity in the military today include racial desegregation, inclusion of women, and exclusive reliance on volunteers. Each difference has created unique problems for military leadership to address, parallel to similar problems stemming from race and gender in the larger society. Dansby, Stewart, and Webb (2001) wrote, "In many ways the military has always been a mirror of American society, reflecting back the scars and blemishes as well as the face of the nation" (p. xvii). Although diversity problems have not yet been resolved, the U.S. military has made substantial progress, even more than society in general has made, according to sociologists Moskos and Butler (1996).

FIGURE 14.3

Military Desegregation

Desegregation in the military began with a research project during World War II. Black army platoons were integrated into white infantry companies and the social experiment was carefully monitored. The research team found that no unusual problems occurred and that all soldiers functioned effectively. Despite positive results, military leaders continued to oppose racial desegregation, even after President Truman issued an executive order mandating military racial desegregation. Because of racist attitudes among military leaders, the executive order was not fulfilled until the Korean War when desegregation became necessary for the sake of efficiency.

Dansby, Stewart, and Webb (2001) described problems with desegregation that came to the forefront during the Vietnam War. African Americans protesting against unequal treatment rioted at Fort Dix, Fort Bragg, on two aircraft carriers, and at Travis Air Force base. As the Vietnam War was ending in the early 1970s, General Creighton Abrams testified that poor race relations had had a negative impact on combat effectiveness. Complicating matters further, in 1973, Congress ended the draft and established an all-volunteer army. Recruiting and retaining quality soldiers would be affected by how the army addressed issues of race relations.

The army's response was to create a Defense Race Relations Institute charged with the responsibility of creating a race relations training program. The initial program lasted for six weeks; it was later expanded to include sexual harassment and discrimination, and now has become one of the army's most ambitious programs. Dansby and Landis (2001) report that the current training program lasts 16 weeks and, according to the American Council on Education, is equivalent to 23 undergraduate semester college credits. A major objective is "To create an environment that values diversity and fosters mutual respect and cooperation" (p. 9).

Integration Problems

Johnson (2001) evaluated the Defense Race Relations program and concluded that the training had an immediate positive effect on participant attitudes and improved subsequent work performance. Even so, problems with race relations in the U.S. military persist. Katzenstein and Reppy (1999) referred to a 1996 task force that found evidence of racism at 4 of 19 military facilities evaluated. Individual soldiers have been involved in incidents of racial violence; some continue to be members of extremist groups promoting racism or white supremacy, even though military policy prohibits active participation in such groups. Waldman (1996) explained the reason for that policy: "The nature of the military means that anything that gets in the way of mission accomplishment is unacceptable. Racism gets in the way" (p. 27).

Sexism gets in the way as well. Prior to the establishment of the all-volunteer army, fewer than 2% of recruits were women, with 90% of them receiving medical or administrative assignments (Katzenstein & Reppy, 1999); to maintain recruitment standards, however, the pool of candidates was expanded (see Figure 14.3.). According to Peterson (1999), female recruits have tended to be better educated, to have higher scores on aptitude tests, and to be less likely to cause disciplinary problems. According to Katzenstein and Reppy (1999), women represent approximately 14% of enlisted personnel, 14% of officers, and 20% of those in basic training. Peterson (1999) concluded, "The Army fields the highest quality force in its history owing to the gains brought about by the all-volunteer force" (p. 100).

Increasing the role of minorities and women in the military has challenged male recruits because of cultural messages some men have internalized about masculinity. Katzenstein and Reppy (1999) explain, "Cultural ideas of masculinity encourage recruits to prove their fitness for military life by flaunting their masculine prowess in bigoted and sexist behavior" (p. 2). Military leaders did not understand this cultural influence at first. Defense directives about **sexual harassment** had been in place for many years before the 1991 Tailhook incident, in which drunken navy pilots forced female officers to walk through a gauntlet while they were groped and verbally humiliated. The chief of naval operations said later, "Until Tailhook we dealt too often with sexual harassment . . . one case at a time, rather than understanding it as a cultural issue" (Katzenstein & Reppy, 1999, p. 2). The problem was intensified five years later when rape charges were brought against drill sergeants at the Aberdeen Army base. In 2002, cadet women of the Air Force Academy reported allegations of sexual assault, indicating the ongoing challenge for the U.S. military to address male concepts of power and gender superiority.

> Injustice anywhere is a threat to justice everywhere. We are caught in an inescapable network of mutuality, tied in a single garment of destiny. Whatever affects one directly affects all indirectly.
>
> **Martin Luther King, Jr. (1929–1968)**

Diversity Policy and Gender

As military leaders study the gender problem, they realize that rules are not always being observed. Kier (1999) reported that no action was taken for 56% of all sexual harassment complaints. Women had reported sexual harassment for years but had been ignored or encouraged to drop their complaint; some encountered hostile reactions from their male superiors. Katzenstein and Reppy (1999) conclude, "It was not a failure to have rules; [these] are problems emerging out of a culture at odds with [military] institutional policy" (p. 3). The 2002 and 2003 allegations of sexual harassment and even sexual assault at the Air Force Academy (AFA) demonstrated that more must be done to resolve these problems. Almost half of female AFA cadets reported that they had personally experienced sexual harassment, 64% heard derogatory remarks based on gender, and 66% reported being discriminated against because of their gender. Despite this evidence, AFA leaders denied that there were any serious gender issues at the Academy, causing the authors of the 2003 report to conclude that gender problems at the AFA were a consequence of "a lack of leadership at the Academy and at the highest levels of the Air Force itself" (Zeigler & Gunderson, 2005, p. 121).

Some people opposed to women in the military argue that sexual harassment is a reaction to double standards that allow women to perform at lower levels of competence. The army's response is that levels are adjusted to take account of physiological differences for men as well as for women. Roush (1999) pointed out that for soldiers of the same height, men are allowed to weigh 30 pounds more than women before being required to enter weight control programs. In areas where no weight adjustment is necessary, women and men compete on an equal basis. Women soldiers have demonstrated excellent marksmanship by winning the army's highest awards, and have participated on marksmanship teams at the Olympics (Carter, 2002). Shooting skills are only part of women's impressive record of achievement that has opened doors to new responsibilities.

During the 1970s and 1980s, the U.S. Army employed a **risk rule** that measured how close certain roles would bring a participant to battle and did not assign women to roles that would bring them into combat. Carter (2002) observed that the 1989 Panama invasion altered the rules when women soldiers engaged in battle while working in support units that were fired on. Women driving convoy trucks and flying helicopters to transport wounded men to safety were fired on and women in military police units assisted with cordoning off neighborhoods in search of guerrillas. Some women would have earned medals if their assignments had officially listed them as combatants.

In 1991, Desert Storm provided another opportunity for women to prove their combat readiness. Despite predictions of critics, mixed-gender units displayed as much cohesiveness as single-gender units. Because of their performance in the Gulf War, women are now assigned to command military police companies, pilot helicopters, and serve in artillery units. The 2003 Iraq war placed thousands of women in battle zones, and actual combat assignments no longer seem unthinkable. Perhaps the performance of women soldiers under fire is one reason why a survey of Reserve Officer Training Corps (ROTC) cadets conducted by Zeigler and Gunderson (2005) found that almost 60% of ROTC cadets said that women should be allowed to volunteer for combat and should be assigned to combat roles just as men are.

In a survey of civilians, 53% agreed that women should be permitted to serve in combat, but a survey of military leaders revealed that 62% of them did not favor using women in diverse combat roles (Zeigler & Gunderson, 2005). Guenther-Schlesinger (2001) reported that 70% of women want to be assigned to combat roles because major promotions are more likely to be given to those who prove themselves on the battlefield. Kier (1999) believes women will never be treated as equals in the military culture as long as their names are "missing from the rostrum of heroes, stories, and myths" arising from combat (p. 49).

Having studied demographic predictions, military leaders expect the percentage of women and minorities in the armed forces to increase; they are prepared to do much more recruiting from the growing pool of Hispanic American and Asian American candidates. Although there will be twice as many African Americans in the candidate pool by 2050, half of the U.S. population growth from 2000 to 2050 will occur among Latinos, with a smaller yet significant growth of Southeast Asians. Recruiters are encouraged by 1997 data showing that more Hispanics joined the military than any other ethnic group, but a major concern is the high dropout rate: Army policy requires that 90% of all recruits must have high school diplomas. According to a 1996 study by the National Center for Educational Statistics, 30% to 35% of Hispanic students drop out of high school, the highest rate of all groups included in their study (Diaz, 1999).

Religion and Sexual Orientation

Racial, ethnic, and gender diversity is only the beginning. The American military now has procedures for accommodating religious differences. And although the issue of lesbians and gays in the military is still debated, there is a growing sentiment that openly gay men and lesbians should be allowed to serve their country: "To be denied the right to serve is to have one's citizenship denied, and to be restricted in one's form of military service is to have one's citizenship restricted" (Segal, Segal, & Booth, 1999, p. 225).

Gay Americans have always fought in this country's wars, but their sexual orientation was not an issue until World War I, when military regulations excluded openly gay men from military service. Even so, there were gay men in uniform when World War II began, including gay sergeants responsible for training the massive numbers of new soldiers enlisted after the attack on Pearl Harbor (Estes, 2007). The formation of the Women's Army Corps (WACs), the Women Accepted for Volunteer Emergency Service (WAVES), and the admission of women into the Marines in 1943 brought lesbians as well as straight women into military service. The presence of lesbians was well known to military leaders, who waited until the war was over before purging lesbians from the ranks by giving them dishonorable discharges. As for gay men, although psychiatrists involved in screening procedures rejected slightly less than 5,000 recruits perceived as gay, it is estimated that as many as 650,000 of the 16 million American troops were gay men (Estes, 2007). From an interview with one of those soldiers, Estes quotes the veteran: "We were not about to be deprived of the privilege of serving our country in a time of great national emergency by virtue of some stupid regulation about being gay" (p. 5).

Although military leaders continue to express opposition to gay and lesbian soldiers, Matthews (1999) reported results of a survey of 270 male soldiers, finding only 36% strongly opposed to serving with gay soldiers; twice as many women soldiers said they would serve with lesbians as those who said they would not. Opponents to gays and lesbians serving in the military say the army is not the place for social experiments, but Katzenstein and Reppy (1999) note that the army and other units of America's armed forces have always been affected by societal changes: "The American military has at different times trailed, led or simply mirrored efforts to combat prejudice, but it has never been isolated from those prejudices" (p. 10).

Military Leadership

As military recruiters make contact with an increasingly diverse pool of candidates, they must offer evidence that advancement is possible. According to Stewart and Firestone (2001), minorities are underrepresented at the general officer level. Jones (1999) recommended that military services immediately identify and attract more minority officer candidates to function as a "source of inspiration" for minority soldiers. Sayles (1999) discussed the importance of women and minority role models at all levels in the military organizational structure to provide women and minorities proof of genuine opportunity for advancement in the military—rather than a glass ceiling. All branches of the service have been asked to address the need for minority officers in their affirmative action plans; as an example, the navy goal is to commission at least 7% black and 4% Hispanic officers each year. Jones (1999) stated, "Commitment to diversity and equal opportunity is the keystone to our entire value structure" (p. 62).

> One of the most successful institutions in American society in dealing with racial integration has been the United States Army. At the other extreme . . . (public) schools are among the most segregated associations in the country.
>
> **Eugene Y. Lowe, Jr. (Contemporary)**

AFTERWORD

In his discussion of diversity issues in the military, Jones (1999) commented, "Americans tend to be ignorant about other societies and even about subcultures within their own society" (p. 62). His comment echoes a concern multicultural education advocates have expressed for several years: that too many K–12 schools do not address diversity issues adequately. This book was written to address diversity issues with college students, but the issues need to be addressed in K–12 classrooms as well. Schools in rural or suburban areas with predominantly white students tend to offer too little information about diversity. White teachers are often uncomfortable with controversies related to diverse groups, some insisting that they don't need to address diversity because there are no—or few—students of color in their schools!

If white students rarely encounter people of color, it is even more important for teachers to provide accurate cognitive information about history, contributions, and issues affecting diverse populations in this country both historically and today. Further, this is not just a need for white students: Jones's comment referred to American recruits from diverse groups. African American students may know little about cultures or experiences of Native Americans; Native American students may only know about the "model minority" and have little knowledge of the past oppression, achievements, and current barriers of Asian Americans. Latino students may not understand why Somali students are in their school, and Somali students may have learned negative stereotypes about Latinos. Middle-class students need to understand the realities for low-income families; nondisabled students must confront misperceptions about people with disabilities; heterosexual students can unlearn myths they have been taught about gays and lesbians. In a diverse society, everyone needs to learn more about the diverse groups of people calling themselves Americans.

This book has offered an array of information about diverse groups of people and intergroup relations, but does acquiring new information change a person's beliefs and attitudes? For those who are interested in exploring their own attitudes about diversity, go to the MyEducationLab web site (www.myeducationlab.com) and respond to the selected statements in the Attitude Inventory. Your responses to these statements should clarify your beliefs or attitudes about the diverse issues being addressed, and for those who responded to the Attitude Inventory previously, consider how and why your current answers may be different from your earlier responses.

During the debate over ratifying the U.S. Constitution, some state leaders focused on the many differences dividing the states and argued that they could never be melded into a single union but should remain independent states. Alexander Hamilton rejected the argument, insisting that a unified nation encompassing those diverse cultures had already formed, and the Constitution would simply reflect the shared values and vision of that union (Chernow, 2004).

Today, people living in our fifty states are not defined as much by the state where they live as by their membership in social groups determined by race, gender, disability, social class, and sexual orientation; yet we are all Americans. We live in a nation that adopted the motto "E Pluribus Unum" in 1782, originally meaning: "from many states, one nation." The motto has also been a metaphor for the people in a nation built on foundations established by Native Americans, profiting from import of Africans, and exploiting the labor of immigrants and women: Each group has struggled to find its place in the kaleidoscope of changing images and altered realities. Their achievements were based on an American dream of a good life for themselves and their families, of a nation where they had freedom to work, worship, and live as they pleased among diverse people who were also guaranteed equal rights and equal opportunities.

That American dream has always been an ideal. Some groups were granted this ideal more readily than others, but all have sought it. America's history is a history of that struggle. We are farther along than ever today, yet we still have much to do to bring the dream closer to reality for all Americans. Pluralism represents a vehicle to move us forward. Committing ourselves to being pluralistic represents a commitment to the American dream, a

> When we dream alone, we are merely dreaming; but when we dream together, that's the beginning of reality.
>
> **Brazilian Proverb**

commitment to make our nation's motto—"out of the many, one"—a description of the nation we are becoming. That is a dream worth dreaming.

TERMS AND DEFINITIONS

Affirmative action A written plan required of businesses and institutions of higher education to reduce discrimination in hiring, public contracting, and college admissions

Design for Diversity A Wisconsin program that mandates changes in policies and practices on all thirteen UW System campuses to make them more welcoming places for diverse students

Diversity The presence of human beings with perceived or actual differences based on a variety of human characteristics

Diversity pairing A diversity training strategy where two people from diverse backgrounds are paired to provide them with opportunities to interact and become better acquainted

Diversity training Programs designed by businesses to promote a positive environment for diverse employees and managers at the worksite

Glass ceiling An informal upper limit that keeps women and minorities from being promoted to positions of greatest responsibility in work organizations

Mass media The various vehicles employed to provide information to a mass audience: radio, television, cable TV, newspapers, magazines, books, CDs, and so on

Pluralism The equal coexistence of diverse cultures in a mutually supportive relationship within the boundaries of one nation

Proposition 209 A California statute prohibiting preferential treatment to individuals or groups in hiring, awarding public contracts, and college admissions

Racial quota Designation of a specific number of applicants to be hired or admitted based on their race

Risk rule An army practice of measuring how close certain roles would bring a participant to combat and not assigning women to any role that would bring them too close

Seniority system Requires employees with least seniority to be laid off work if the employer needs to release a certain number of employees

Set-aside program Requiring contractors to hire a certain percentage of minority subcontractors if they are awarded a project funded by tax dollars

Sexual harassment Deliberate and repeated behavior that has a sexual basis and is not welcomed, requested, or returned

DISCUSSION EXERCISES

Exercise #1 Enhancing Unity in America Discussion: What Should We Do Next?

Directions: America today demonstrates its diversity in our military, marketplace, and manufacturing, in our media, and in federal, state, and local governments. The following questions ask for your speculation to resolve current issues for our future well-being.

1. Should our federal government eliminate, or modify, the current affirmative action program?
   - If you believe it should be eliminated, explain why.
   - If you believe it should be modified, explain how and why.
2. Do you agree that increased diversity among students on a college campus strengthens the education of all students?
   - How many—or what type—of diversity-related courses should all students be required to take?
   - What should be the outcome of any study of American cultural, racial, and societal human differences?
3. Assume that you have majored and matriculated in some aspect of business; following graduation you receive two job offers: one with a company that has a good reputation for having a positive environment for diversity; the other offers a higher salary with better benefits but with little or no record of attention to attracting a diverse workforce.
   - Which one would you choose, and why?
   - How can a diverse workforce create unity in America?
4. Now that women are approximately half of all managers, why are women still being excluded from a proportional share of top management positions?
   - What will it take to eliminate this glass ceiling?
   - How might business and industry change if women were adequately represented in leadership roles?
5. If the predictions are correct and twenty years from now print and broadcast media employ significantly greater numbers of women and people of color, how will it make a difference in the following areas:
   - What news stories are covered by print and broadcast journalists
   - How new stories are covered
   - What stories are presented by news programs (e.g., *20/20* and *Dateline*)
   - Which images and text are presented in advertisements
   - What content and diversity of characters is available in prime-time programming
6. Simply requiring that American societal institutions establish policies against sexual harassment has not been effective.
   - What must the military services do to eliminate the problem of sexual harassment?
   - Business and manufacturing?
   - Nonprofit and religious institutions?

Exercise #2 A Personal Post-Test Self Check: What Will You Be?

Directions: Respond to each of the items below with brief remarks; be sure to explain your responses *and* to hear and comment on the responses from your partners.

A Personal Post-Test Self Check

1. List what you believe personally are three of the most important human differences.
2. Explain one instance where you have witnessed racism as the belief that some human population groups are inherently superior or inferior to others. Tell your personal suggestion of how that situation could have been avoided.
3. Give an example of a situation that illustrates cultural blindness. Explain how it could be remedied.
4. Describe a real or imagined situation in which you might confront "ethnocentrism."

5. List three terms that you think are acceptable replacements for "handicapped" or "disabled."
6. Describe your current ability at cultural communication.
7. List four recommendations for how one might better recognize cultural and ethnic heritage when communicating.
8. Suggest two or more ways that you could be an active advocate for diversity.
9. Name several ways that current American culture—workplace and personal—affects women, disabled, or any other minority groups.
10. Tell what one practice you have resolved to adopt to be an active pluralist within our diverse America.

Adopted from Evelyn Harden. *Rural Health Care: Cultural Competency Training Workbook.* National Rural Health Association, 2002

REFERENCES

Bacon, J. (2003). Disrespect, distortion and double binds: Media treatment of progressive black leaders. *Extra, 16*(2), 27–29.

Analyzes media treatment of three black social activists and describes a pattern of remarks reflecting personal attacks without responding to the issues they raise.

Ball, H. (2000). *The Bakke case: Race, education, and affirmative action.* Lawrence: University Press of Kansas.

Examines law and politics providing a context for the Bakke case, presents key arguments from both sides, and reviews more recent events stemming from the Bakke decision.

Browne-Miller, A. (1996). *Shameful admissions: The losing battle to serve everyone in our universities.* San Francisco, CA: Jossey-Bass.

Discusses college admissions policies and practices and how they help or hinder fair access to equal opportunity for all applicants and what happens after a person is accepted to college.

Buckley, G. (2001). *American patriots: The story of blacks in the military from the Revolution to Desert Storm.* New York, NY: Random House.

Includes statistics and stories about African Americans who fought in America's wars.

Carter, P. (2002). War dames. *The Washington Monthly, 34*(12), 32–37.

Reviews recent history of women in the military and how their role has evolved from serving only in support units to having responsibilities that bring them into combat.

Chernow, R. (2004). *Alexander Hamilton.* New York, NY: Penguin.

Describes Hamilton's life with emphasis on his activities as one of the leading intellects shaping the new nation of the United States.

Childs, K. (1998). Media affirmative action pact. *Editor & Publisher, 131*(32), 11.

Describes the reaction of broadcast networks to a federal court's ruling against affirmative action requirements established by the Federal Communications Commission.

Clayton, S.D., & Crosby, F.J. (2000). Justice, gender, and affirmative action. In F.J. Crosby & C. VanDeVeer (Eds.), *Sex, race, and merit: Debating affirmative action in education and employment* (pp. 81–88). Ann Arbor: University of Michigan Press.

Explains the purpose of affirmative action, examines the denial of discrimination by victims of discrimination, and discusses the future of affirmative action.

Cochran-Smith, M. (2003). Standing at the crossroads: Multicultural teacher education at the beginning of the 21st century. *Multicultural Perspectives, 5*(3), 3–11.

Describes three issues of critical interest to U.S. educators: teacher/student demographic data and trends, competing school reform agendas, and criticisms of educational research.

Corkery, M. (2005, November 14). A special effort. *Wall Street Journal* (p. R8).

Describes Starbucks Corporation's commitment to hiring employees with disabilities and making the workplace welcoming to customers with disabilities.

Craft-Fairchild, C. (1997, Fall). Women warriors in the 18th century. *St. Thomas,* 32–35.

Describes eighteenth-century women who dressed as men in Great Britain or the United States, in some cases becoming soldiers, to have the advantages of men.

Crosby, F.J., & VanDeVeer, C. (Eds.). (2000). *City of Richmond* v. *J.A. Croson Co.* In *Sex, race, and merit: Debating affirmative action in education and employment* (pp. 280–293). Ann Arbor: University of Michigan Press.

Contains a brief introduction by the editors and presents an abridged version of Sandra Day O'Connor's text explaining the court's decision with comments from other justices.

Daft, R.L. (2003). Managing diverse employees. In *Management* (4th ed., pp. 436–468). Versailles, KY: Thompson Southwestern.

Discusses the current status of affirmative action, various dimensions of diversity in the workforce, and how corporate culture is changing to accommodate diversity.

Dansby, M.R., & Landis, D. (2001). Intercultural training in the United States military. In M.R. Dansby, J.B. Stewart, & S.C. Webb (Eds.), *Managing diversity in the military: Research perspectives from the defense equal opportunity management institute* (pp. 9–28). New Brunswick, NJ: Transaction.

Describes the background, philosophy, and status of intercultural training in the military.

Dansby, M.R., Stewart, J.B., & Webb, S.C. (Eds.). (2001). Overview. In *Managing diversity in the military: Research perspectives from the defense equal opportunity management institute* (pp. xvii–xxxii). New Brunswick, NJ: Transaction.

Summarizes the role of women and minorities in military history as a context for the essays in this book and explains the organization of the book.

Diaz, R.F. (1999). The Hispanic market: An overview. In L.J. Matthews & T. Pavri (Eds.), *Population diversity and the U.S. Army* (pp. 87–98). Carlisle, PA: Strategic Studies Institute.

Describes the current location and predicted growth of Hispanics and strategies for effectively recruiting Hispanics at the present time and in the future.

Duncan, P. (2002). Decentering whiteness: Resisting racism in the women's studies classroom. *Race in the college classroom: Pedagogy and politics.* In B. Tusmith & M.T. Reddy (Eds.), *Race in the college classroom: Pedagogy and politics* (pp. 40–50). New Brunswick, NJ: Rutgers University Press.

Describes conflicting racial perspectives between white students and students of color in college and how professors often behave as if white students are of primary concern.

Eastland, T. (2000). Ending affirmative action: The case for colorblind justice. In F.J. Crosby & C. VanDeVeer (Eds.), *Sex, race, and merit: Debating affirmative action in education and employment* (pp. 174–175). Ann Arbor: University of Michigan Press.

Argues that affirmative action has failed by harming those it was intended to help.

Eck, D.L. (2001). *A new religious America: How a "Christian country" has become the world's most religiously diverse nation.* New York, NY: HarperCollins.

Examines the growth of diverse religions in the United States, especially with regard to immigration patterns since 1965, and describes its impact and its potential.

Egodigwe, L. (2005, November 14). Back to class. *Wall Street Journal,* p. R4.

Describes how corporate diversity training programs have changed along with the rationale for implementing them.

Ellmore, R.T. (1991). *NTC's mass media dictionary.* Lincolnwood, IL: National Textbook.

Includes definitions of numerous terms related to mass media.

Estes, S. (2007). *Ask & tell: Gay and lesbian veterans speak out.* Chapel Hill, NC: The University of North Carolina Press.

Interviews gay and lesbian veterans of diverse races and ethnicities who participated in World War II or in wars since then.

Ferguson, R. (1998). *Representing "race": Ideology, identity and the media.* London, England: Arnold.

Reviews research to discuss relationships between racism and media representations of reality, and analyzes the ideology employed in maintaining racial hierarchies.

Frank, T. A. (2008, April). Confessions of a sweatshop inspector. *The Washington Monthly 40*(4), 34–37.

Explains the difficulties involved in monitoring workplaces in overseas factories to detect and address abuses of sweatshop workers.

Gabriel, J. (1998). *Whitewash: Racialized politics and the media.* London, England: Routledge.

Focuses on case studies to analyze media dissemination of language that normalizes white privilege and creates a racialized discourse influencing political and economic change.

Gardner, H. (2006). *Five minds for the future.* Boston, MA: Harvard Business School Press.

Describes five mental abilities increasingly necessary for the future: a disciplined mind, a synthesizing mind, a creating mind, a respectful mind, and an ethical mind.

Greene, K.W. (1989). *Affirmative action and principles of justice.* New York, NY: Greenwood.

Analyzes the philosophical and legal issues related to affirmative action and responds to the emotional reactions created by the affirmative action debate.

Griffin, R. (2002). The cultural and multicultural environment. In *Management* (7th ed., pp. 162–191). Boston, MA: Houghton Mifflin.

Discusses how trends in diversity affect the corporate environment, advantages of diversity, and suggests strategies for effective management of diversity.

Guenther-Schlesinger, S. (2001). Persistence of sexual harassment: The impact of military culture on policy implementation. In M.F. Katzenstein & J. Reppy (Eds.), *Beyond zero tolerance: Discrimination in military culture* (pp. 195–212). Lanham, MD: Rowman & Littlefield.

Reviews the history of sexual harassment in the military and identifies unique aspects of military culture that enable sexual harassment to persist.

Humphreys, D. (Ed.). (2000, Fall). National survey finds diversity requirements common around the country. *Diversity Digest*, pp. 1–2.

Presents results from a survey of 543 colleges and universities from every region of the country and representing an array of types of institutions.

Hymowitz, C. (2005, November 14). The new diversity. *Wall Street Journal*, pp. R1, R3.

Discusses how the global economy is influencing attitudes in American corporations about diversity and provides efforts of specific corporations to be more inclusive.

Jackson, D.Z. (2000). Lazy lies about welfare. In J. Birnbaum & C. Taylor (Eds.), *Civil Rights since 1787: A reader on the black struggle* (pp. 803–804). New York, NY: New York University Press.

Describes the role of media in promoting stereotypes of African Americans living in poverty and collecting welfare.

Johnson, D. (1999). The U.S. Army and ethnic diversity: A historical overview. In L.J. Matthews & T. Pavri (Eds.), *Population diversity and the U.S. Army* (pp. 45–56). Carlisle, PA: Strategic Studies Institute.

Describes the ethnic composition of the U.S. army in the past, reasons why ethnic groups joined the army, and issues related to the historic diversity of the American army.

Johnson, J.L. (2001). Local effects and global impact of Defense Equal Opportunity Management Institute Training. In M.R. Dansby, J.B. Stewart, & S.C. Webb (Eds.), *Managing diversity in the military: Research perspectives from the defense equal opportunity management institute* (pp. 178–188). New Brunswick, NJ: Transaction.

Evaluates effectiveness of DEOMI training in terms of local effects (mastery of content, development of skills and attitudes) and global impact (subsequent work performance).

Johnson, S.D. (2000, June). Keep the pressure on. *Essence, 1*(2), 184.

Discusses the participation of African American writers in prime-time television shows.

Jones, G.R., & George, J.M. (2003). Managing diverse employees in a diverse environment. *Contemporary Management* (3rd ed., pp. 112–149). New York, NY: McGraw-Hill.

Describes increasing diversity among consumers and in the workforce and provides strategies for managers to work effectively with diverse employees.

Jones, J.C. (1999). Diversity in the 21st century: Leadership issues. In L.J. Matthews & T. Pavri (Eds.), *Population diversity and the U.S. Army* (pp. 57–68). Carlisle, PA: Strategic Studies Institute.

Analyzes predicted demographic trends for implications on future recruitment and the importance of having more women and minority officers to enhance recruitment.

Katzenstein, M.F., & Reppy, J. (Eds.). (1999). Introduction: Rethinking military culture. In *Beyond zero tolerance: Discrimination in military culture* (pp. 1–21). Lanham, MD: Rowman & Littlefield.

Describes American military culture, how it has functioned as a social laboratory, and why it needs to change because of the increasing numbers of women and minorities.

Kier, E. (1999). Discrimination and military cohesion: An organizational perspective. In M.F. Katzenstein & J. Reppy (Eds.), *Beyond zero tolerance: Discrimination in military culture* (pp. 25–32). Lanham, MD: Rowman & Littlefield.

Uses knowledge from organizational theory to discuss the military's organizational culture and how that culture must change to end discrimination against women, gays, and lesbians.

Kolodny, A. (1998). *Failing the future: A dean looks at higher education in the twenty-first century.* Durham, NC: Duke University Press.

Describes issues in higher education, especially in a public research university, from perspectives of students, teachers, and administrators, and recommends changes.

Larson, M. (1999, November). News hues. *Brandweek, 40*(43), 4043.

Discusses participation of racial minorities in news stations at various market levels.

Lowe, E.Y., Jr. (Ed.). (1999). Promise and dilemma: Incorporating racial diversity in selective higher education. *Promise and dilemma: Perspectives on racial diversity and higher education* (pp. 3–43). Princeton, NJ: Princeton University Press.

Examines the history of societal efforts to accommodate racial diversity and identifies recurring phenomena that have helped or hindered these efforts.

Matthews, L. (1999). Introduction: Primer on future recruitment of diversity. In L.J. Matthews & T. Pavri (Eds.), *Population diversity and the U.S. Army* (p. 116). Carlisle, PA: Strategic Studies Institute.

Discusses issues affecting future recruitment, such as accepting gay and lesbian soldiers, increasing religious diversity in the army, and women engaging in combat.

McQueen, M. (2002, July/August). What about diverse faculty? *Quill, 90*(6), 19–22.

Discusses the presence of women and minorities as students and faculty in journalism/mass communication departments in higher education.

Millman, J. (2005, November 14). Delayed recognition. *The Wall Street Journal,* p. R8.

Describes the response of Detroit Edison to resolve a discrimination lawsuit brought by Arab Americans.

Mor-Barak, M.E. (2005). *Managing diversity: Toward a globally inclusive workplace.* Thousand Oaks, CA: Sage Publications.

Explains the benefits of implementing inclusive practices in the workplace and refers to case studies from businesses both within and outside of the United States.

Moskos, C.C., & Butler, J.S. (1996). *All that we can be: Black leadership and racial integration in the army.* New York, NY: Basic Books.

Provides evidence and arguments in support of their thesis that racial integration has been successfully achieved in the U.S. Army.

Musil, C.M. (1996 November/December). The maturing diversity initiatives on American campuses. *American Behavioral Scientist, 40*(2), 222–232.

Describes the increasing value for diversity expressed in corporate culture and in higher education and how the two mutually reinforce each other.

National Employment Lawyers Association. (2000). Position paper on affirmative action. In J. Birnbaum & C. Taylor (Eds.), *Civil Rights since 1787: A reader on the black struggle* (pp. 708–713). New York, NY: New York University Press.

Presents information and arguments in support of affirmative action.

Painter, N.I. (2005). *Creating Black Americans: African-American history and its meaning, 1619 to the present.* Oxford, England: Oxford University Press.

Describes historical and aesthetic developments, using artwork by blacks, to explain how certain people and events shaped black Americans.

Peterson, M.J. (1999). Women in the U.S. military. In L.J. Matthews & T. Pavri (Eds.), *Population diversity and the U.S. Army* (pp. 99–106). Carlisle, PA: Strategic Studies Institute.

Describes characteristics of women in the military, issues affecting them, and how their presence has enhanced the quality of the army.

Pipher, M. (2002). *The middle of everywhere: The world's refugees come to our town.* New York, NY: Harcourt.

Presents stories about a variety of recent immigrants, the conditions that forced them to immigrate, and the difficulties they encounter trying to adjust to American culture.

Popper, B. (2000). Minority hiring may be facing retrenchment. *USA Today Magazine, 128*(2658), 66–67.

Discusses the participation of racial minorities in newspapers and television news.

Ramos, J. (2002). *The other face of America.* New York, NY: Rayo.

Provides statistics and describes studies focusing on the contributions of Latinos and the implications of Latino immigration to the United States.

Reddy, M.T. (2002). Smashing the rules of racial standing. In B. Tusmith & M.T. Reddy (Eds.), *Race in the college classroom: Pedagogy and politics* (pp. 51–61). New Brunswick, NJ: Rutgers University Press.

Examines strategies—and describes the mixed outcomes—for dealing with presumptions of authority based on whiteness and for decentering whiteness in the classroom.

Reskin, B.F. (2000). The realities of affirmative action in employment. In F.J. Crosby & C. VanDeVeer (Eds.), *Sex, race, and merit: Debating affirmative action in education and employment* (pp. 103–113). Ann Arbor: University of Michigan Press.

Compares employers with and without affirmative action plans, and examines how affirmative action affects the workplace and the people it was designed to help.

Riley, C.A. II. (2005). *Disability and the media: Prescriptions for change.* Lebanon, NH: University Press of New England.

Provides examples to critique the media's presentation of people with disabilities and disability issues and gives suggestions for improvement.

Roush, P.E. (1999). A tangled Webb the navy can't afford. In M.F. Katzenstein & J. Reppy (Eds.), *Beyond zero tolerance: Discrimination in military culture* (pp. 81–100). Lanham, MD: Rowman & Littlefield.

Responds to James Webb's arguments against women being in the military.

Sayles, A.H. (1999). Person to person: The diversity challenge for the Army after next. In L.J. Matthews & T. Pavri (Eds.), *Population diversity and the U.S. Army* (pp. 107–124). Carlisle, PA: Strategic Studies Institute.

Discusses the benefits of diversity in the military and describes a program called Consideration of Others that is designed to enhance appreciation for diversity.

Segal, D.R., Segal, M.W., & Booth, B. (1999). Gender and sexual orientation diversity in modern military forces: Cross-national patterns. In M.F. Katzenstein & J. Reppy (Eds.), *Beyond zero tolerance: Discrimination in military culture* (pp. 225–250). Lanham, MD: Rowman & Littlefield.

Discusses issues affecting the acceptance of women, gay men, and lesbians in the military and the role of the "citizenship revolution" in promoting change in the military culture.

Stewart, J.B., & Firestone, J.M. (2001). Looking for a few good men: Predicting patterns of retention, promotion, and accession of minority and women officers. In M.R. Dansby, J.B. Stewart, & S.C. Webb (Eds.), *Managing diversity in the military: Research perspectives from the defense equal opportunity management institute* (pp. 231–256). New Brunswick, NJ: Transaction.

Reviews the literature on officer promotion, explains the issue of white male dominance, and makes recommendations to increase the numbers of women and minority officers.

Tusmith, B., & Reddy, M.T. (2002). Introduction: Race in the college classroom. In B. Tusmith & M.T. Reddy (Eds.), *Race in the college classroom: Pedagogy and politics* (pp. 1–3). New Brunswick, NJ: Rutgers University Press.

Defines affirmative action, summarizes the main arguments in the debate over affirmative action, and describes the organization of the book.

Waldman, A. (1996, November). GIs: Not your average Joes: What the military can teach us about race, class, and citizenship. *The Washington Monthly,* pp. 26–33.

Discusses the military's historic role in assimilating immigrants for future success in society and how the military has now achieved the same result for people of color.

Williams, C. (2003). Managing individuals and a diverse work force. In *Management* (2nd ed., pp. 434–471). Versailles, KY: Thompson Southwestern.

Explains why diversity is being promoted in the corporate world, the benefits of diversity, and principles for being an effective manager of diverse employees.

Yamane, D. (2001). *Student movements for multiculturalism: Challenging the curricular color line in higher education.* Baltimore, MD: Johns Hopkins University Press.

Addresses the problem of the color line in higher education curriculum and the process by which students have challenged this color line by demanding multicultural courses.

Zeigler, S.L., & Gunderson, G.G. (2005). *Moving beyond G. I. Jane: Women and the U.S. military.* Lanham, MD: University Press of America.

Summarizes and analyzes issues affecting women in the military, especially sexual harassment and assigning women to combat roles.

Index

Appendix I

Additional Course Materials

"Why" Paper
Instructions

The multiple purposes of this paper is to one, practice investigating alternative perspectives regarding why something is happening, looking particularly at perspectives of people of at least one cultural group other than your own. Two, learn how to access and begin an inquiry process into another group perspectives via scholarly educationally research and/or primary sources. Three, understand how in-group and out-group perspectives provide different perspectives to a particular issue. And finally to learn from communities that are different than your own.

Identify something you have seen happening in an educational or work experience, in a past field experience/observation, or something In the community, that involves another racial group, lower social class people, a language minority group, individuals with disabilities, and/or generic GLBT issues. It must be an event or occurrence that you do not understand. It should also be something that happens periodically rather than a one-shot event that may never happen again.

Here are a few concept questions.

> *Luis comes from a Spanish-speaking home you have been told. You have taken Spanish, and whish to talk with him in Spanish. One day in class you address him in Spanish and he refuses to answer. Finally, he tells you to talk normal, and insists that he doesn't talk that stupid stuff.* ***You wonder; If he (and possibly other Spanish speaking students) speaks Spanish at home, why in school does he deny being able to speak Spanish?***
>
> *In a forth grade class, you have noticed Robert, a nice-looking African American boy scowling at you. You decide to try to befriend him, so one day you start a conversation with him (you are a white woman). He answers at first with one-word replies, then declares that no white woman can teach a young Black man, so you might as well forget trying.* ***You wonder: Why did he say this, and what should you do?***
>
> *Jenny comes from a single-parent family, in which her mother (you have heard) is on AFDC. When Jenny comes to school, her long hair is often dirty and her clothing, although fully clean, is sometimes not appropriate for the weather. IN fact, it appears that Jenny has a total of about five uncoordinated outfits in her entire wardrobe. The teacher has tried to get Jenny's mother to come to school for a conference, but without luck.* ***You wonder: Why does her mother not come to school and why doesn't she take better care of Jenny?***
>
> *You have noticed that everyone on the local city council and school board is white, in spite of the fact that the community is racially diverse.* ***You wonder: Why do white people keep getting elected, if everyone can vote?***

Topics for inquiry might also develop from GLBT teen issues, oppressive stereotypes, white privilege, male privilege, class privilege, affirmative action, impact of the media on the representation of certain communities, juvenile justice/delinquency, teen dating, violence/domestic violence, teacher expectations, socioeconomic class issues, issues facing English language learners, student tracking, and high stakes testing. Students will identify at least six different sources in order to find out why this kind of event happens. **Your sources should include at least two different racial groups; they should include at least one interview and at least one article or book. In addition, at least three sources should have a background similar to the person or group of people you are wondering about.** An example would be, if you are wondering about why Luis refuses to speak Spanish, try to locate at least three Spanish speaking people or authors; if you are wondering why Robert said what he said, at least three sources should be African-American men of African American Male authors).

Paper should not extend beyond 7 pages. Each student must complete a concept map and get permission for their chosen question from the instructor before beginning the assignment. **A written description "Why" questin must be turned in**. Each student must **complete the finding sources table** (non-online students must meet in the library, *on-line student have the option of going to the library as well as a direct discussion linkk to the class librarian*).

Your grade will be based mainly on the appropriateness of your sources for the problem you selected, and the degree to which you accurately capture perspectives that authentically represent a group other than your own. The easiest sources are not necessarily the most appropriate.

In your paper, write a summary of what each source said. Also, attach your references. You can synthesis sources that agreed with each other, but they may contradict each other, or simply address different aspects of the situation in which case you will need to present them separately. You must also list your sources in the text.

Based on your investigation, why do you think the event happens? Explain why you think so. Try to take into account the perspectives of the person or people you did not understand when you started. At this point, you may need to critique your various sources, especially if your conclusions differ from some of them. Remember to always think in the term: What did you learn from this?

Created by Christine Sleeter
Professor Emeritus
California State University Monterey Bay

Appendix II

Taken from: *Multicultural Education in a Pluralistic Society*, Eighth Edition,
by Donna M. Gollnick and Philip C. Chinn

Evaluation Criteria	Target (conforms to 89% or better)	Acceptable (Conforms to 71-88 %)	Unacceptable (Conforms to 70% or less)	Score and Comments
Mechanics (20 pts possible)	5-7 pages Typewritten. Minimal grammar, punctuation & spelling errors (19-20)	5-7 pages Typewritten Grammar, punctuation & spelling errors do not detract from readability (14-18)	Less than 5 pages Typewritten Numerous grammatical, punctuation & spelling errors detract from readability (0-13)	
Structure (25 pts possible) Sections: • Abstract • Set Up • Introduction • Research & Analysis • Opinion • Conclusions • References • Presentation handout	All sections included Uses appropriate transition sentences to aid flow (22-25)	All sections included Transitions are implied but not explicitly linked (17-21)	Missing sections Connections between sections are missing (0-16)	
Question (10 pts possible)	Paper adds new insights in addresses the question Related to classroom / school setting (9-10)	Overall paper adequately addresses the "why" question Related to school / classroom setting (7-8)	Paper does not adequately address the "why" question Question is not related to school/ classroom setting (0-6)	
Evaluation (25 pts possible)	Discussion in paper emphasizes evidence & reasoning Clearly identifies and	Discussion in paper inconsistently uses evidence in development of	Discussion based on opinion rather than evidence Fails to identify insider	

Instructor: ______________ Section #: ________ Name: ______________

	investigates insider and outsider perspectives and shows understanding of diverse perspectives Integrates thoughtful analysis demonstrating students' understanding of course concepts related to "why" question. Conclusion reiterates and answers question, synthesizing sources with own experience (22-25)	argument Appropriately identifies and investigates insider and outsider perspectives and shows some understanding of diverse perspectives. Analysis of "why" question is not consistently tied to course concepts. Conclusion reiterates and answers the question (17-21)	and outsider perspectives. Minimal integration of course concepts in analysis of "why" question Conclusion tangentially related to "why" question. (0-16)	
References (20 pts possible)	Sources directly related to "why" question 6 or more sources Appropriate use of in-text citations Minimal citation errors Consistent citation style (19-20)	Sources inconsistently related to question 6 or more sources Minimal use of in-text citations Minor citation errors Inconsistent use citation style (14-18)	Sources minimally related to question Less than 6 sources Failure to use in-text citations Citations contain numerous errors Failure to use a citation style (0-13)	

Instructor: ____________ Section #: ________ Name: ____________

Resource Table Evaluation Rubric

Evaluation Criteria	Target	Acceptable	Unacceptable	Points Earned
Contextual Description	Well written weaves components together for a coherent and cohesive composite (1-2)	Includes most or all components but description lacks a sense of coherence and cohesiveness. Seems more like cataloging (1)	Narrative not present or poorly written, vague and general (0)	
Accuracy	Includes detailed and engaging interview narrative which reveals rich information about culture or diversity Presentation is not in transcript form (2-3)	Includes general and cursory interview narrative which reveals some information about culture and diversity (1-2)	Includes very general and cursory interview narrative which reveals little or contradictory information about the culture or diversity Presentation may be in transcript form or even missing (0-1)	
Analysis	Includes principles, concepts, and essential questions from class in analysis Analysis includes not only impressions but conclusions Personal impressions and evidentiary conclusions (3-5)	Generally analyzes data presented in the project but fails to go beyond descriptions. Evidence and conclusions scant or lacking (2-3)	Analysis missing entirely. May mistake presentation of data for the analysis (0-2)	10 Total

Resource Table Evaluation Rubric

Your library assignment Source Table will be evaluated against the following criteria. Your table is due Week 12.

Evaluation Criteria	Target	Acceptable	Unacceptable	Points Earned & Comments
Completeness	Completed entire table. Identified three sources from three different information locations. (i.e. databases, UNLV library catalog, web, personal communication, etc.). (5 pts)	Completed most of table (1-3 cells were left blank) Identified three sources. However they did not come from three unique locations (i.e. different databases, UNLV catalog, web, etc.). (3-4 pts.)	Completed only part of table (4 or more cells left blank). (0-2 pt)	
Accuracy	Identified the voice/perspective and insider and outsider perspectives of all sources correctly. Citations were correctly documented using APA style guidelines. Minimal errors (1-2) if any in punctuation, capitalization, syntax, etc.). (5 pts)	Identified the majority of voice/perspective and outsider and insider perspectives correctly. Most citations were correctly documented using APA style guidelines. Some minor errors (2-4 errors in punctuation, capitalization, syntax, etc.). (3-4 pts)	Misidentified or failed to identify majority of voice/perspective and outsider and insider perspectives correctly. Citations contained numerous errors (5 or more) according to APA guidelines. (0-2 pts)	
Evaluation of sources' usefulness	For each source, evaluated its usefulness & provided 2 or more *sound*	For majority of sources, evaluated their usefulness & provided 1-2 sound reasons as	Provided superficial and/or inaccurate reasons for the usefulness of the	

	reasons as justification (i.e. author credibility, currency, bias, scope, accuracy) (8-10 pts)	justification (i.e. author credibility, currency, bias). (4-7 pts)	source. Inaccuracies were evident in 2 or more of the sources evaluated. (0-3 pts)	

Annotated Bibliography

Evaluation Criteria	Target	Acceptable	Unacceptable	Points Earned
	Less than two errors	Between two to 5 errors	More than 5 errors	10 Total

Chapter 1

FOUNDATIONS OF MULTICULTURAL EDUCATION

Equality is the heart and essence of democracy, freedom, and justice.

A. PHILIP RANDOLPH, Civil Rights Leader, 1942

You are just beginning your first teaching position in a nearby urban area. Like many new teachers in an urban area, you were offered the job only a few weeks before school started. You had never been to that part of the city but were sure you could make a difference in the lives of students there. You quickly learn that many students have single parents, many of whom work two jobs to make ends meet. Almost all of the students are eligible for free lunch. The families of some students do not speak English at home, but the principal says the students speak English. You are disappointed in the condition of the school, and your classroom in particular, but have been assured it will be repainted during one of the vacation periods.

When students arrive on the first day, you are not surprised that a large proportion of them are from families who immigrated from Central America during the past two decades. The population includes some African American students and a few European American students. You did not realize that the class would include a student who had just moved from Bulgaria and spoke no English and that the native language of two students was Farsi. You have taken a few Spanish courses but know little or nothing about the language or cultures of Bulgaria and Iran. You wonder about the boy with the black eye but guess that he has been in a fight recently.

Reflections

1. What assumptions about these students and their academic potential did you make as you read this brief description?
2. How has your own cultural background prepared you to teach this diverse group of students?
3. What might you want to learn about students' cultures to assist them in learning?
4. What kind of challenges are you likely to confront during this year?
5. What do you wish you had learned in college to help you be a better teacher in this school?
6. Where should you go for assistance in working with students whose native language is not English?
7. Are you glad that you accepted this teaching assignment? Why or why not?

Diversity in the Classroom

Educators today are faced with an overwhelming challenge to prepare students from diverse populations and backgrounds to live in a rapidly changing society and a world in which some groups have greater societal benefits than others because of race, ethnicity, gender, class, language, religion, ability, geography, or age. Schools of the future will become increasingly diverse. Demographic data on birthrates and **immigration** indicate that the number of Asian American, Latino, and African American children is increasing. More than four of 10 students in P–12 schools today are students of color (U.S. Department of Education, 2006). By 2020, they are projected to be nearly half of the elementary and secondary population. However, the race and sex of their teachers match neither the student population nor the general population; 84% of the teachers are European American and 75% are female (U.S. Census Bureau, 2006).

Latinos, Asian Americans, American Indians, and African Americans already comprise more than half of the student population in Arizona, California, the District of Columbia, Hawaii, Louisiana, Mississippi, New Mexico, and Texas (Snyder, Tan, & Hoffman, 2006). European Americans make up less than one fourth of the student population in many of the nation's largest school districts (Dalton, Sable, & Hoffman, 2006). Although the U.S. Census Bureau (2006) reports that only 17% of U.S. children live below the official poverty level, 41% of the fourth graders are eligible for free or reduced-price lunch programs in the nation's schools (U.S. Department of Education, 2006). African American and Latino students are more likely than other students to be concentrated in high poverty schools (U.S. Department of Education, 2006). The number of students with disabilities who are being served by special programs has increased from 4.3 million in 1987 to 6.7 million or nearly 14% of the school population in 2005 (U.S. Department of Education, 2006).

See Chapter 2 for more information about students from diverse ethnic groups and Chapter 3 for details on students from low-income families.

It is not only ethnic and racial diversity that is challenging schools. During the past 35 years, new waves of immigrants have come from parts of the world unfamiliar to many Americans. With them have come their religions, which seem even stranger to many Americans than the new immigrants. While small groups of Muslims, Hindus, Buddhists, and Sikhs have been in the country for many decades, only recently have they and their religions become highly visible. Even Christians from Russia, Hong Kong, Taiwan, Korea, and the Philippines bring their own brand of worship to denominations that have strong roots in this country. The United States has not only become a multicultural nation, it has also become a multireligious society. In earlier years, most religious minority groups maintained a low and almost invisible profile. As the groups have become larger, they have become more visible, along with their houses of worship (Eck, 2000).

For more information on the religions that students bring to schools, see Chapter 7.

These religious differences raise a number of challenges for educators. The holidays to be celebrated must be considered, along with religious codes related to the **curriculum,** appropriate interactions of boys and girls, dress in physical education classes, and discipline. Immigrant parents value the importance of education for their children, but they do not always agree with the school's approaches to teaching and learning, nor accept the public school's secular **values** as appropriate for their family. Values are the qualities that parents find desirable and important in the education of their children, and include areas such as morality, hard work, and caring, often with religious overtones. Working collaboratively with parents and communities will become even more critical in providing education equitably to all students.

Pause to Reflect 1.1

To work effectively with the heterogeneous student populations found in schools, educators need to understand and feel comfortable with their own cultural roots. How would you describe your cultural background?

- From what countries did you or your ancestors come?
- How long has your family lived in the United States?
- How would you describe the experiences your family has had in the United States?

Go to the *Homework and Exercises* section in Chapter 1 of MyEducationLab at *www.myeducationlab.com* and select *Pause to Reflect 1.1* to answer these questions.

Educators also must understand the cultural setting in which the school is located to develop effective instructional strategies. They must help their students become aware of cultural differences and inequalities in the nation and in the world. One goal is to help students affirm cultural differences while realizing that individuals across **cultures** have many similarities.

Teachers will find that students have individual differences, even though they may appear to be from the same cultural group. These differences extend far beyond intellectual and physical abilities. Students bring to class different historical backgrounds, religious beliefs, and day-to-day experiences that guide the way they behave in school. The cultures of some students will be mirrored in the school culture. For others, the differences between home and school cultures will cause dissonance unless the teacher can integrate the cultures of the students into the curriculum and develop a supportive environment for learning. If the teacher fails to understand the cultural factors in addition to the intellectual and physical factors that affect student learning and behavior, it will be difficult to help students learn.

Multicultural education is an educational strategy in which students' cultures are used to develop effective classroom instruction and school environments. It supports and extends the concepts of culture, diversity, equality, social justice, and democracy into the school setting. An examination of the theoretical precepts and practical applications of these concepts will lead to an understanding of the development and practice of multicultural education.

Multicultural Education

Not all students can be taught in the same way because they are not the same. Their cultures and experiences influence the way they learn and interact with their teachers and peers. They have different needs, skills, and experiences that must be recognized in developing educational programs. Each student is different because of physical and mental abilities, gender, ethnicity, race, language, religion, class, sexual orientation, geography, and age. Students behave differently in school and toward authority because of cultural factors and their relationship to the dominant society. As educators, we behave in certain ways toward students because of our own cultural experiences within the power structure of the country. Multicultural education is a concept that incorporates the diversity of students and equality in education. **Equality** ensures that students are provided the same access to the benefits of society regardless of their group memberships.

When educators are given the responsibilities of a classroom, they need the knowledge and skills for working effectively in a diverse society. The following fundamental beliefs and assumptions support multicultural education, a strategy for accomplishing this goal:

- Cultural differences have strength and value.
- Schools should be models for the expression of human rights and respect for cultural and group differences.
- **Social justice** and equality for all people should be of paramount importance in the design and delivery of curricula.
- Attitudes and values necessary for the continuation of a democratic society can be promoted in schools.
- Schooling can provide the knowledge, skills, and **dispositions** (i.e., values, attitudes, and commitments) to help students from diverse groups learn.
- Educators working with families and communities can create an environment that is supportive of multiculturalism.

Many concepts support multicultural education. The relationships and interactions among individuals and groups are essential to understanding and working effectively with students from groups different than the teachers. Educators should understand **racism, sexism,** prejudice, discrimination, oppression, powerlessness, power, inequality, equality, and stereotyping. Multicultural education includes various components that often manifest themselves in courses, units of courses, and degree programs. They include ethnic studies, global studies, bilingual education, women's studies, human relations, special education, and urban education. Let's examine how multicultural education evolved over the past century.

Evolution of Multicultural Education

Multicultural education is not a new concept. Its roots are in the establishment of the Association for the Study of Negro Life and History. Through their research and books on the history and culture of African Americans, Carter G. Woodson, W. E. B. DuBois, Charles C. Wesley, and other scholars were the pioneers of ethnic studies. Woodson founded the *Journal of Negro History* and the *Negro History Bulletin* to disseminate research and curriculum materials. These materials were integrated into the curricula of segregated schools and the historically black colleges and universities, allowing these students to be empowered by the knowledge of their own history (J. A. Banks, 2004).

By the 1920s some educators were writing about and training teachers in intercultural education. The intercultural movement during its first two decades had an international emphasis with antecedents in the pacifist movement. Some textbooks were rewritten with an international point of view. Proponents encouraged teachers to make their disciplines more relevant to the modern world by being more issue oriented. One of the goals was to make the dominant population more tolerant and accepting toward first- and second-generation immigrants in order to maintain national unity and social control (C. A. M. Banks, 2004). However, issues of power and inequality in society were ignored. The interculturalists supported understanding and appreciation of diverse groups, but did not promote collective ethnic identities that were the focus of ethnic studies.

Following the Holocaust and World War II, tensions among groups remained high. Jewish organizations such as the Anti-Defamation League and the American Jewish Committee provided leadership for improving intergroup relations and reducing the anti-Semitic sentiment that existed at the time. National education organizations and progressive educational leaders such as Hilda Taba and Lloyd A. Cook promoted intergroup relations in schools to develop tolerance for new immigrants, African Americans, and other groups of color. Like the earlier intercultural movement, many intergroup educators had adopted the goal of assimilating immigrants and people of color into dominant society (J. A. Banks, 2004). Some programs focused on understanding the "folk" culture of these groups. Others were directed at native-born European Americans and their prejudice and discrimination against other groups. There was disagreement among the supporters of intergroup relations about the degree that they should promote an understanding of the culture and history of ethnic groups (C. A. M. Banks, 2004). Historian David Tyack (2003) found this movement to be one in which "oppression became reduced to stereotyping and separate ethnic identity was to be dissolved as painlessly as possible" (p. 81).

By the 1960s desegregation was being enforced in the nation's schools. At the same time, cultural differences were being described as deficits. Students of color and whites from low-income families were described as culturally deprived. Their families were blamed for not providing them with the **cultural capital** or advantages such as wealth and education that would help them succeed in schools. Programs like Head Start, **compensatory education**, and special education were developed to make up for these shortcomings. Not surprisingly, those classes were filled with students of color, in poverty, or with disabilities—the children and youth who had not been privileged in society and whose own cultures seldom found their way into textbooks and the school's curriculum.

In the 1970s oppressed groups were described as culturally different to acknowledge that they had a culture but that it was different from the culture of the **dominant group.** The goal of this approach was to teach the culturally different to develop the cultural patterns of the dominant society so that they could fit into the mainstream (Sleeter & Grant, 2006). Students with disabilities were still primarily segregated from their able-bodied peers.

The civil rights movement of the 1960s and 1970s brought a renewed interest in ethnic studies, discrimination, and intergroup relations. Racial and ethnic pride emerged from oppressed groups, creating a demand for African American and other ethnic studies programs in colleges and universities across the country. Similar programs were sometimes established in secondary schools. However, students and participants in ethnic studies programs were primarily members of the group being studied. Programs focused on their own ethnic histories and cultures with the objective of providing students with insights to and instilling pride in their own ethnic backgrounds. Most of these programs were ethnic-specific, and only one ethnic group was studied. Sometimes the objectives included an understanding of the relationship and conflict between the ethnic group and the dominant population, but seldom was a program's scope multiethnic.

Concurrent with the civil rights movement and the growth of ethnic studies, emphasis on intergroup or human relations again emerged. Often, these programs accompanied ethnic studies content for teachers. The objectives again were to promote intergroup, and especially interracial, understanding to reduce or eliminate stereotypes. This approach emphasized the affective level—teachers' attitudes and feelings about themselves and others (Sleeter & Grant, 2006).

With the growth and development of ethnic studies came a realization that those programs alone would not guarantee support for the positive affirmation of diversity and differences in this country. Students from the dominant culture also needed to learn the history, culture, and contributions of other groups. Thus, ethnic studies expanded into multiethnic studies. Teachers were encouraged to develop curricula that included the contributions of oppressed groups along with those of the dominant group. Textbooks were rewritten to represent more accurately the multiethnic nature of the United States and world. Students were to be exposed to perspectives of diverse groups through literature, history, music, and other disciplines integrated throughout the general school program. Curriculum and instructional materials were to reflect multiple perspectives, not just the single master narrative of the dominant group.

During this period, other groups that had suffered from institutional discrimination called their needs to the attention of the public. These groups included women, persons with low incomes, persons with disabilities, English language learners (ELL), and the elderly. Educators responded by expanding multiethnic education to the more encompassing concept of multicultural education. This broader concept focused on the different groups to which individuals belong, with an emphasis on the interaction of race, ethnicity, class, and gender in their cultural identities. It also called for the elimination of discrimination based on group membership. No longer was it fashionable to fight sexism without simultaneously attacking racism, classism, homophobia, and discrimination against all children, the elderly, and persons with disabilities.

CRITICAL INCIDENTS IN TEACHING

Celebrating Ethnic Holidays

Esther Greenberg is a teacher with Asian and African American students in an alternative education class. Ms. Greenberg's college roommate was Chinese American and she remembers fondly her visit to her roommate's home during the lunar New Year. She remembers how the parents and other Chinese adults had given all the children, including her, money wrapped in red paper, which was to bring all of the recipients good luck in the New Year. Ms. Greenberg thought that it would be a nice gesture to give the students in her class the red paper envelopes as an observance of the upcoming lunar New Year. Since she was unable to give the students money, she took gold-foil covered coins (given to Jewish children) and wrapped these coins in red paper to give to her students.

Unfortunately, on the lunar New Year's Day, all of the African American students were pulled out of class for a full day of testing. All of the remaining students were her Asian students. When she passed out the red envelopes, the students were surprised and touched by her sensitivity to a cherished custom.

When her administrator was told what Ms. Greenberg had done, he became enraged. He accused her of favoritism to the Asian students and of deliberately leaving out the African American students. When she tried to convince him otherwise, he responded that she had no right to impose Asian customs on African American students. She responded that this was an important Asian custom, and that the Asian students had participated in the observance of Martin Luther King's birthday. However, he continued his attack saying that this was Asian superstition bordering on a religious observance. She was threatened with discipline.

Questions for Classroom Discussion

1. Were Esther Greenberg's actions inappropriate for a public school classroom? If so, why? If no, why not? Was this a violation of the principles of church and state?
2. Did Ms. Greenberg create problems for herself by giving out the red envelopes when the African American students were absent from class? Did this create an appearance of favoritism of one racial group over the other?
3. How could Ms. Greenberg have handled the situation to make it a pleasing experience to all concerned?
4. Was the administrator the one who was out of line, and was Ms. Greenberg simply a victim?

Building Teaching Skills

Go to the *Building Teaching Skills* section in Chapter 1 of MyEducationLab at *www.myeducationlab.com* and select *Critical Incidents in Teaching: Celebrating Ethnic Holidays* to complete this exercise.

Multicultural Education Today

The 1990s were characterized by the development of standards, which led to debates between fundamentalists and multiculturalists. The fundamentalists argued that history standards should stress what they believed are the foundations of democracy—patriotism and historical heroes. The multiculturalists promoted the inclusion of diverse groups and multiple perspectives in the standards. The U.S. Senate was drawn into the history standards fray in 1995, voting 99 to 1 to abort the history standards developed by a widely respected group of historians who had promoted the inclusion of diverse groups (Symcox, 2002). In English language arts, groups disagreed about the literature to which students should be exposed, some arguing for multiple perspectives and others arguing that such literature might promote values they could not support.

Multicultural education is sometimes criticized as focusing on differences rather than similarities among groups. On the other side it is criticized for not adequately addressing issues of power and oppression that keep a number of groups from participating equitably in society. At least three schools of thought push multiculturalists to think critically about these issues: critical pedagogy, antiracist education, and critical race theory (Sleeter & Bernal, 2004). Critical pedagogy focuses on the culture of everyday life and the interaction of class, race, and gender in contemporary power struggles. Antiracist education is the strategy supported in Canada and a number of European countries to eliminate racist practices such as tracking, inequitable funding, and segregation in schools. Critical race theory also focuses on racism in challenging racial oppression, racial inequities, and white privilege (Ladson-Billings, 2004). Multicultural education as presented in this text attempts to incorporate critical pedagogy, antiracist education, and critical race theory as different groups are discussed. Multicultural education includes **critical thinking** about these and other issues to ensure that education serves the needs of all groups equitably.

Still, after eight decades of concern for civil and human rights in education, racism persists. Educators struggle with the integration of diversity into the curriculum and provision of equality in schools. Some classrooms may be desegregated and mainstreamed, and both boys and girls may now participate in athletic activities. However, students are still labeled

Although the Supreme Court ruled that schools should be desegregated in 1954, students in many classrooms today are from the same racial, ethnic, or language group.

as at risk, developmentally delayed, underprivileged, lazy, and slow (Tyack, 2003). They are tracked in special classes or groups within the classroom based on their real and perceived abilities. A disproportionate number of students who are African American, Mexican American, Puerto Rican, American Indian, and some Asian/Pacific American groups score below European American students on national standardized tests. The number of students of color, low-income students, and girls participating in advanced science and mathematics classes is not proportionate to their representation in schools. They too often are offered little or no encouragement to enroll in advanced courses that are necessary to be successful in college.

Some reformers are calling a good education a fundamental civil right (Spring, 2001; Tyack, 2003). In a country that champions equal rights and the opportunity for an individual to improve his or her conditions, educators are challenged to help all students achieve academically. At the beginning of the twenty-first century, the standards movement focused on identifying what every student should know and be able to do. The federal legislation for elementary and secondary schools, *No Child Left Behind* (NCLB), requires standardized testing of students to determine how effective a school is in helping students learn. It mandates that test scores be reported to the public by "race, gender, English language proficiency, disability, and socio-economic status" (U.S. Department of Education, 2001, p. 10). The goal of NCLB is to improve the academic achievement of all students. Students in low-performing schools may transfer to a higher-performing school to improve their chances of passing tests if their school is low-performing for three years.

A large number of students who are not European American or are from low-income families are not meeting proficiency standards in the current high-stakes testing environment. Only 42% of African American, 46% of Latino, and 48% of American Indian fourth graders scored at the basic level or higher on the reading test of the National Assessment of Educational Progress (NAEP) in 2005 as compared to 76% of the white fourth graders (NAEP, 2007). Forty-six percent of low-income students scored at the basic level or higher as compared to 77% of students from families with higher incomes. The pattern is similar on the eighth-grade mathematics test as shown in Figure 1.1.

Multicultural Proficiencies for Teachers

States and school districts expect teachers to have **proficiencies** or the specific knowledge, skills, and dispositions related to multicultural education by the time they finish a teacher education program. With *No Child Left Behind*, they are obligated to hire teachers who can help low-income students, students of color, English language learners, and students with disabilities meet state standards.

State standards for teacher licensure reflect the national standards in Table 1.1, which were developed by the Interstate New Teacher Assessment and Support Consortium (INTASC). Each of the 10 INTASC standards is further explicated by statements of the knowledge, dispositions, and performances that new teachers should be able to demonstrate for a state license to teach. Many of these multicultural proficiencies are discussed in this text; others will be addressed in other teacher education courses. For example, the INTASC standards (1992) that address multicultural proficiencies state that new teachers should:

- Know about areas of exceptionality in learning—including learning disabilities, visual and perceptual difficulties, and special physical or mental challenges. (Standard 3)
- Know about the process of second language acquisition and about strategies to support the learning of students whose first language is not English. (Standard 3)

FIGURE 1.1 NAEP 8th Grade Mathematics 2005 by Race and Ethnicity.

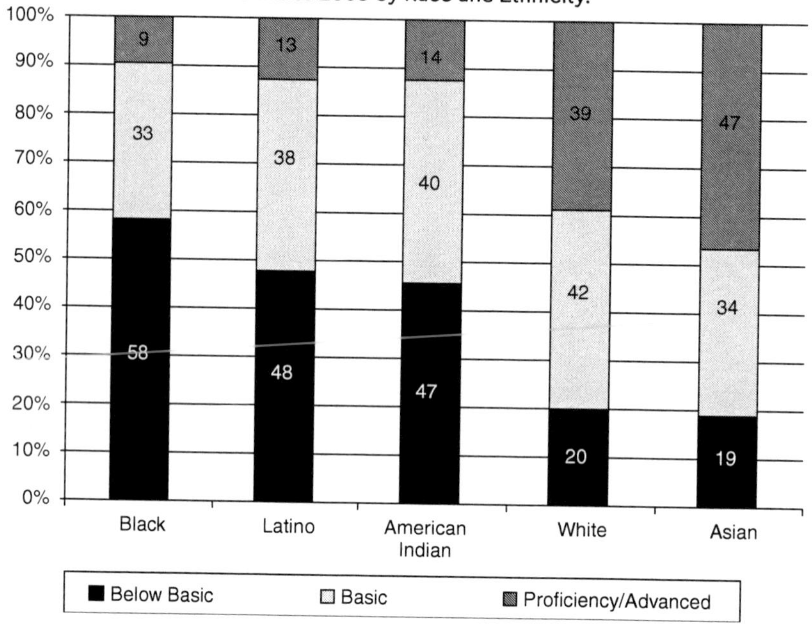

Data from the National Assessment of Educational Progress. (2007). Washington, DC: National Center for Education Statistics, U.S. Department of Education. Retrieved on May 20, 2007, from www.nces.ed.gov/nationsreportcard/nde/viewresults.asp

- Understand how students' learning is influenced by individual experiences, talents, and prior learning, as well as language, culture, family, and community values. (Standard 3)
- Have a well-grounded framework for understanding cultural and community diversity and know how to learn about and incorporate students' experiences, cultures, and community resources into instruction. (Standard 3)
- Understand how cultural and gender differences can affect communication in the classroom. (Standard 6)
- Understand how factors in the students' environment outside of school (e.g., family circumstances, community environments, health and economic conditions) may influence students' life and learning. (Standard 10)

In working with students who come from different ethnic, racial, language, and religious groups than the teacher, the development of dispositions that are supportive of diversity and differences is important. Students quickly become aware of the educators who respect their cultures, believe they can learn, and value differences in the classroom. Examples of dispositions that the INTASC standards (1992) expect teachers to have developed include:

- Appreciating multiple perspectives and conveying to learners how knowledge is developed from the vantage point of the knower. (Standard 1)
- Believing that all children can learn at high levels and persisting in helping all children achieve success. (Standard 3)
- Being sensitive to community and cultural norms. (Standard 3)
- Making students feel valued for their potential as people, and helping them learn to value each other. (Standard 3)

TABLE 1.1 INTASC* Standards for New Teachers

1. The teacher understands the central concepts, tools of inquiry, and structures of the discipline(s) he or she teaches and can create learning experiences that make these aspects of subject matter meaningful for students.
2. The teacher understands how children learn and develop, and can provide learning opportunities that support their intellectual, social, and personal development.
3. The teacher understands how students differ in their approaches to learning and creates instructional opportunities that are adapted to diverse learners.
4. The teacher understands and uses a variety of instructional strategies to encourage students' development of critical thinking, problem solving, and performance skills.
5. The teacher uses an understanding of individual and group motivation and behavior to create a learning environment that encourages positive social interaction, active engagement in learning, and self-motivation.
6. The teacher uses knowledge of effective verbal, nonverbal, and media communication techniques to foster active inquiry, collaboration, and supportive interaction in the classroom.
7. The teacher plans instruction based upon knowledge of subject matter, students, the community, and curriculum goals.
8. The teacher understands and uses formal and informal assessment strategies to evaluate and ensure the continuous intellectual, social, and physical development of the learner.
9. The teacher is a reflective practitioner who continually evaluates the effects of his/her choices and actions on others (students, parents, and other professionals in the learning community) and who actively seeks out opportunities to grow professionally.
10. The teacher fosters relationships with school colleagues, parents, and agencies in the larger community to support students' learning and well-being.

Reprinted with permission from Council of Chief State School Officers. (1992). Model standards for beginning teacher licensing, assessment, and development: A resource for state dialogue. Washington, DC. http://www.ccsso.org/content/pdfs/corestrd.pdf

- Understanding how participation supports commitment, and being committed to the expression and use of democratic values in the classroom. (Standard 5)
- Appreciating the cultural dimensions of communication, responding appropriately, and seeking to foster culturally sensitive communication by and among all students in the class. (Standard 6)
- Being committed to using assessment to identify student strengths and promoting student growth rather than denying students access to learning opportunities. (Standard 8)

As a new teacher, you should be able to demonstrate in your teaching the knowledge and dispositional proficiencies outlined above. The portfolio activities at the end of each chapter will provide opportunities for you to begin to collect artifacts related to your proficiency for working with a diverse student population and delivering education that is multicultural. The portfolio activities at the end of each chapter indicate the INTASC standard for which the activity may provide evidence. These artifacts could become part of the portfolio that you are developing in your teacher education program. They may be a valuable part of the portfolio that you present to a future employer, showing that you have developed the knowledge, skills, and dispositions appropriate for working effectively with a diverse student population. Finally, you may be able to further develop and refine these portfolio entries for national certification later in your teaching career.

Most state licensure tests include questions related to multicultural education in a combination of short-answer and multiple-choice questions. The Praxis II series of tests by the Educational Testing Service (ETS) include a test of your knowledge of (1) the subject that

Pause to Reflect 1.2

As you progress through your teacher education program, you will be expected to work with students from diverse groups in field experiences, student teaching, and/or your own classroom. How close are you to meeting the following INTASC proficiencies related to multicultural education?

Proficiency	Already Met	Partially Met	Not Met
• Know about areas of exceptionality in learning—including learning disabilities, visual and perceptual difficulties, and special physical or mental challenges.	☐	☐	☐
• Know about the process of second language acquisition and strategies to support the learning.	☐	☐	☐
• Understand how students' learning is influenced by language, culture, family, and community values.	☐	☐	☐
• Know how to learn about and incorporate students' experiences, cultures, and community resources into instruction.	☐	☐	☐
• Understand how cultural and gender differences can affect communication in the classroom.			
• Appreciate multiple perspectives.			
• Believe that all children can learn at high levels.	☐	☐	☐
• Be sensitive to community and cultural norms.	☐	☐	☐

Go to the *Homework and Exercises* section in Chapter 1 of MyEducationLab at *www.myeducationlab.com* and select *Pause to Reflect 1.2* to answer these questions.

you plan to teach and (2) learning and teaching. The second test addresses four categories: students as learners, instruction and assessment, communication techniques, and teacher professionalism. Each of these four categories includes content related to multicultural education. Some states have developed their own licensure tests with National Evaluation Systems (NES) or another testing company, but they address similar categories related to professional and pedagogical knowledge. At the end of each chapter you will have the opportunity to practice a test item that is similar to one that you may find on the licensure test that you will be required to pass before you can teach.

Reflecting on Multicultural Teaching

Throughout these chapters you will have the opportunity to pause and reflect on issues related to diversity and multicultural education. You may want to respond to the questions in your journal or on the book's Homework and Exercises section of MyEducationLab at www.myeducationlab.com. Teachers who reflect on and analyze their own practice report that their teaching improves over time (National Board for Professional Teaching Standards, 2001). You are encouraged to begin to develop the habit of reflecting on your practice now and to include in that reflection the multicultural proficiencies mentioned above.

From the first day of student teaching, you should begin to reflect on your effectiveness as a teacher. Are you actually helping students learn the subject and skills you are teaching? An important part of teaching is to ask what is working and what is not. Good teachers are able to change their teaching strategies when students are not learning. They do not leave any student behind, drawing on the experiences and cultures of their students to make the subject matter relevant to them. Self-reflection will be a critical skill for improving your teaching.

You can begin to develop skills for reflection while you are preparing to teach. Many teacher education programs require teacher candidates to keep journals and develop portfolios that include reflection papers. Videotaping lessons that you teach will allow you to critique your knowledge of the subject matter, interactions with students, and managing a class. The critique could be expanded to look for multicultural proficiencies. You may find it valuable to ask a colleague to periodically observe you while you are teaching and provide feedback on your multicultural proficiencies. Honest feedback can lead to positive adjustments in our behavior and attitudes.

Multicultural education requires an understanding of five basic concepts that support it: culture, cultural identity, pluralism, equality, and social justice. These foundational areas are discussed in the remaining sections of this chapter.

Culture

Until early in the twentieth century, the term culture was used to indicate the refined ways of the elite and powerful. People who were knowledgeable in history, literature, and the fine arts were said to possess culture. No longer is culture viewed so narrowly. It helps define who we are. It influences our knowledge, beliefs, and values. It provides the blueprint that determines the way we think, feel, and behave. What appears as the natural and only way to learn and to interact with others is determined by our culture. Generally accepted and patterned ways of behavior are necessary for a group of people to live together. Culture imposes order and meaning on our experiences. It allows us to predict how others will behave in certain situations.

Culturally determined norms guide our language, behavior, emotions, and thinking; they are the do's and don'ts of appropriate behavior within our culture. Although we are comfortable with others who share the same culture because we know the meaning of their words and actions, we often misunderstand the cultural cues of persons from different cultures. Culture is so much a part of us that we do not realize that not everyone shares our way of thinking and behaving. This could be, in part, because we may never have been in cultural settings different from our own. This lack of knowledge often leads to our responding to differences as personal affronts, rather than simply cultural differences. These misunderstandings may appear insignificant to an observer, but they can be important to participants. Examples include how loud is too loud, how late one may arrive at an event, and how close one can stand to another without being rude or disrespectful.

Pause to Reflect 1.3

It is normal for people to experience some cultural discontinuity when they visit another country or a new city or a neighborhood in which the inhabitants are ethnically different from themselves.

- In what settings have you found that you did not know the cultural norms and were at a loss as to how to fit in?
- How often have you been in such settings?
- Why did you feel uncomfortable?
- How were you able to overcome your awkwardness?
- How could you become more comfortable in cultural settings different than your own?

Go to the *Homework and Exercises* section in Chapter 1 of MyEducationLab at *www.myeducationlab.com* and select *Pause to Reflect 1.3* to answer these questions.

Characteristics of Culture

We all have culture, but how did we get it? One of the characteristics of culture is that it is learned. We were born into the culture of our parents or caretakers. The way a baby is held, fed, bathed, dressed, and talked to is culturally determined and begins the process of learning the family's culture. The process continues throughout life as we interact with members of our own and other cultures.

Two similar processes interact as one learns how to act in society: **enculturation** and **socialization.** Enculturation is the process of acquiring the characteristics of a given culture and becoming competent in its language and ways of behaving and knowing. Socialization is the general process of learning the social norms of the culture. Through this process, we internalize social and cultural rules. We learn what is expected in social roles, such as mother, husband, student, and child, and in occupational roles such as teacher, banker, plumber, custodian, and politician.

Enculturation and socialization are processes initiated at birth by parents, siblings, nurses, physicians, teachers, and neighbors. These varied instructors may not identify these processes as enculturation or socialization, but they demonstrate and reward children for acceptable behaviors. We learn how to behave by observing and participating in society and culture, learning the patterns of the cultures in which we are raised.

Because culture is so internalized, we tend to confuse biological and cultural heritage. Our cultural heritage identity is not innately based on the culture in which we are born. For example, Vietnamese infants adopted by Italian American, Catholic, middle-class parents will share a cultural heritage with middle-class Italian American Catholics, rather than with Vietnamese. Observers, however, will continue to identify these individuals as Vietnamese Americans, because of their physical characteristics and a lack of knowledge about their cultural experiences.

A second characteristic of culture is that it is shared. Shared cultural patterns and customs bind people together as an identifiable group and make it possible for them to live together and function with ease. An individual in the shared culture is provided with the context for identifying with the group that shares that culture. Although there may be some disagreement about certain aspects of the culture, there is a common acceptance and agreement about most aspects. Actually, most points of agreement are outside our realm of awareness. For example, we do not usually realize that the way we communicate with each other and the way we raise children are part of culture.

Third, culture is an adaptation. Cultures accommodate environmental conditions and available natural and technological resources. Thus, Eskimos who live with extreme cold, snow, ice, seals, and the sea develop a culture different from that of Pacific Islanders, who have limited land, unlimited seas, and few mineral resources. The culture of urban residents differs from that of rural residents, in part, because of the resources available in the different settings. The culture of oppressed groups differs from that of the dominant group because of power relationships within society.

Finally, culture is a dynamic system that changes continuously. Some cultures undergo constant and rapid change; others are very slow to change. Some changes, such as a new word or new hairstyle, may be relatively small and have little impact on the culture as a whole. Other changes have a dramatic impact. For instance, the introduction of technology into a culture has often produced changes far broader than the technology itself. Such changes may also alter traditional customs and beliefs. For example, the use of the computer has led to changes in the way we communicate with each other for business and personal purposes. It has even changed the way a number of people meet each other. Instead of blind dates, they are matched by a computer dating service with people they may want to meet.

Our cultures are adapted to the environments in which we live and work. While the environment in rural areas is characterized by space and clean air, urban dwellers adapt to smog, crowded conditions, and public transportation.

New York Convention & Vistors Bureau

Manifestations of Culture

The cultural patterns of a group are determined by how the people organize and view the various components of culture. Culture is manifested in an infinite number of ways through social institutions, lived experiences, and the individual's fulfillment of psychological and basic needs. To understand how extensively our lives are affected by culture, let's examine a few of these manifestations.

Our values are initially determined by our culture. They influence the importance of prestige, status, pride, family loyalty, love of country, religious belief, and honor. Status symbols differ across cultures. For many families in the United States, accumulation of material possessions is a respected status symbol. For others, the welfare of the extended family is of utmost importance. These factors, as well as the meaning of morality or immorality, and the use of punishment and reward, and the need for higher education are determined by the value system of the culture.

Culture also manifests itself in nonverbal communication patterns. The meaning of an act or an expression must be viewed in its cultural context. The appropriateness of shaking hands, bowing, or kissing people on greeting them varies across cultures. Culture also determines the manner of walking, sitting, standing, reclining, gesturing, and dancing. We must remind ourselves not to interpret acts and expressions of people from a different cultural group as wrong or inappropriate just because they are not the same as our own. These behaviors are culturally determined.

Observe and Learn Lessons in Action

Manifestations of Culture

Go to the *Homework and Exercises* section in Chapter 1 of MyEducationLab at *www.myeducationlab.com* and select *Observe and Learn: Lessons in Action* to view the video "School Uniforms and Freedom of Expression" and answer the accompanying questions. In this lesson, students discuss the ways in which clothing reveals a person's culture and identity as part of a debate on the issues surrounding schools uniforms.

1. How do students in the video connect clothing and dress to elements of personal identity?
2. What elements of your own identity and/or culture do you express through your dress?
3. Have you ever felt that one of your students was inappropriately dressed in school? What about one of your colleagues? If so, what—if anything—did you say/do?
4. How might your views regarding dress in school affect what you do in your future classroom?

Language itself is a reflection of culture and provides a special way of looking at the world and organizing experiences that is often lost in translating words from one language to another. Many different sounds and combinations of sounds are used in the languages of different cultures. Those of us who have tried to learn a second language may have experienced difficulty in verbalizing sounds that were not part of our first language. Also, diverse language patterns found within the same language group can lead to misunderstandings. For example, one person's "joking" is heard by others as serious criticism or abuse of power; this is a particular problem when the speaker is a member of the dominant group and the listener is a member of an oppressed group or vice versa.

Although we have discussed only a few daily patterns determined by culture, they are limitless. Among them are relationships of men and women, parenting, choosing a spouse, sexual relations, and division of labor in the home and society. These patterns are shared by members of the culture and often seem strange and improper to nonmembers.

Language is discussed in more depth in Chapter 6.

Ethnocentrism

Because culture helps determine the way we think, feel, and act, it becomes the lens through which we judge the world. As such, it can become an unconscious blinder to other ways of thinking, feeling, and acting. Our own culture is automatically treated as innate. It becomes the only natural way to function in the world. Even common sense in our own culture is naturally translated to common sense for the world. Other cultures are compared with ours and are evaluated by our cultural standards. It becomes difficult to view another culture as separate from our own—a task that anthropologists attempt when studying other cultures.

This inability to view other cultures as equally viable alternatives for organizing reality is known as **ethnocentrism.** Although it is appropriate to cherish one's culture, members sometimes become closed to the possibilities of difference. These feelings of superiority over other cultures can become problematic in interacting and working effectively and equitably with members of other cultures. The inability to view another culture through its cultural lens, rather than through one's own cultural lens, prevents an understanding of the second culture. This inability can make it difficult to function effectively in a second culture. By overcoming one's ethnocentric view of the world, one can begin to respect other cultures and even learn to function comfortably in more than one cultural group.

Chapter 10 includes recommendations for becoming familiar with cultural groups other than your own.

Cultural Relativism

Never judge another man until you have walked a mile in his moccasins. This North American Indian proverb suggests the importance of understanding the cultural backgrounds and experiences of other persons, rather than judging them by our own standards. The principle of cultural relativism is to see a culture as if WE are a member of the culture. In essence, it is an attempt to view the world through another person's cultural lens. It is an acknowledgement that another person's way of doing things, while perhaps not appropriate for us, may be valid for him or her. This ability becomes more essential than ever in the world today as countries and cultures become more interdependent. In an effort to maintain positive relationships with the numerous cultural groups in the world, we cannot afford to ignore other cultures or to relegate them to an inferior status.

Within our own boundaries are many cultural groups that historically have been viewed and treated as inferior to the dominant Western European culture that has been the basis for most of our institutions. These intercultural misunderstandings occur even when no language barrier exists and when large components of the major culture are shared by the people involved. These misunderstandings often happen because one group is largely ignorant about the culture of another group and gives the second culture little credibility. One problem is that members of one group are, for the most part, unable to describe their own cultural system, let alone another. These misunderstandings are common among the various groups in this country and are accentuated by differential status based on race, gender, class, language, religion, and ability.

Cultural relativism suggests that we need to learn more about our own culture than is commonly required. That must be followed by study about, and interaction with, other cultural groups. This intercultural process helps one know what it is like to be a member of the second culture and to view the world from that point of view. To function effectively and comfortably within a second culture, that culture must be learned.

Cultural Identity

Groups in the United States have been called **subsocieties** or **subcultures** by sociologists and anthropologists because they exist within the context of a larger society in which political and social institutions are shared along with some traits and values of the dominant culture. These groups provide the social identity for their members, allowing them to have distinctive cultural patterns while sharing others with members of the dominant culture. At the same time, there is no essential or absolute identity such as female or male, American or recent immigrant, or Buddhist or Jew. Our identities in any single group are influenced by our historical and lived experiences and membership in other groups.

Numerous groups exist in most nations, but the United States is exceptionally rich in the many distinct groups that make up the population. Group identity is based on traits and values learned as part of our ethnicity, religion, gender, sexual orientation, age, class or socioeconomic status, native language, geographic region, place of residence (e.g., rural or urban), and abilities or exceptional conditions, as shown in Figure 1.2. Each of these groups has distinguishable cultural patterns shared with others who identify themselves as members of that particular group. Although they share certain characteristics of the dominant culture with most of the U.S. population, members of these groups also have learned cultural traits, discourse patterns, ways of learning, values, and behaviors characteristic of the groups to which they belong.

Individuals sharing membership in one group may not share membership in other groups. For example, all men are members of the male culture, but not all males belong to the same ethnic, religious, or class group. On the other hand, an ethnic group may be composed of both males and females with different religious and socioeconomic backgrounds.

The interaction of these various group memberships within society begins to determine an individual's cultural identity. Membership in one group can greatly influence

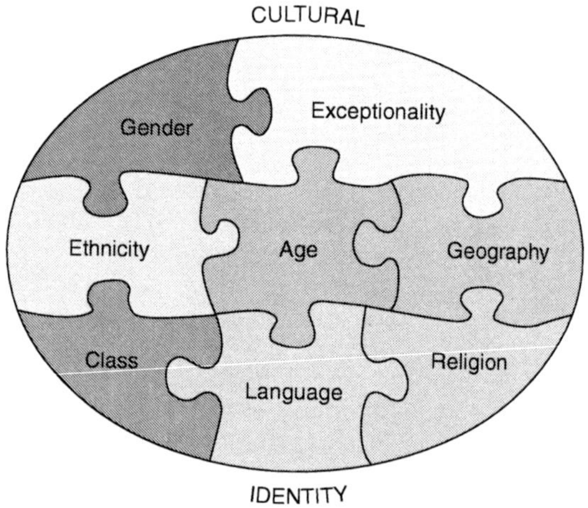

FIGURE 1.2 Cultural identity is based on membership in multiple groups that continuously interact and influence each other. Identity within these groups is affected by interaction with the dominant group and power relations among groups in society.

the characteristics and values of membership in other groups. For instance, some fundamentalist religions have strictly defined expectations for women and men. Thus, membership in the religious group influences, to a great extent, the way a female behaves as a young girl, teenager, bride, and wife, regardless of her ethnic group. One's economic level will greatly affect the quality of life for families, especially the children and elderly in the group.

This interaction is most dynamic across race, ethnicity, class, and gender relations. The feminist movement, for example, was primarily influenced early on by white, middle-class women. The labor movement had an early history of excluding workers of color and women, and their causes; in some areas, this antagonism continues. Membership in one group often conflicts with the interests of another as is the case when people feel forced to declare their primary identity by race rather than gender, class, or sexual orientation.

One cultural group may have a greater influence on identity than others. This influence may change over time and depends on life experiences. We can shed aspects of our culture that no longer have meaning, and we can also adopt or adapt aspects of other cultures that were not inherent in our upbringing. Identity is not fixed. Alternative views of self and culture can be learned as **cultural borders** are crossed (Kuper, 2000).

The degree to which individuals identify with the groups of which they are members and the related cultural characteristics determines, to a great extent, their individual cultural identities. For example, a 30-year-old, middle-class, Catholic, Polish American woman in Chicago may identify strongly with being Catholic and Polish American when she is married and living in a Polish American community. However, other group memberships may have a greater impact on her identity after she has divorced, moved to an ethnically diverse neighborhood, and becomes totally responsible for her financial well-being. Her femaleness and class status may become the most important representations in her identity as portrayed in Figure 1.3.

The interaction of these cultural groups within society is also important. Most political, business, educational, and social institutions (e.g., the courts, the school system, the city government) have been developed and controlled by the dominant group. The values and practices that have been internalized by the dominant group also are inherent within these institutions. Members of oppressed groups are usually beholden to the dominant group to share in that power.

Assimilation policies to force children to adopt the dominant culture have been promoted in schools as the values of the dominant group are reflected in school rules and the **informal curriculum** that guides the expected behaviors and attitudes of students. The children of immigrants and persons of color are expected to learn the dominant culture. To be successful in school they are expected to communicate and behave according to the dominant cultural norms. In the past, Americanization programs for immigrants have not only taught English, but also reinforced the meaning of being American. The virtues of being American and being patriotic continue to be reinforced in many schools, especially in times of crisis such as 9/11 and conflicts with other nations.

Understanding the importance of your group memberships to your identity helps answer the question "Who am I?" An understanding of other groups will help answer the question "Who are my students?" The various groups that educators are likely to confront in a classroom are examined in detail in Chapters 2 through 9.

FIGURE 1.3 Cultural identity is adapted and changed throughout life in response to political, economic, educational, and social experiences that either alter or reinforce one's status or position in society. Membership in some cultural groups may take on more importance than others at different periods of life, as shown here for a woman when she was 30 years old and married, and again when she was 35, divorced, and a single mother.

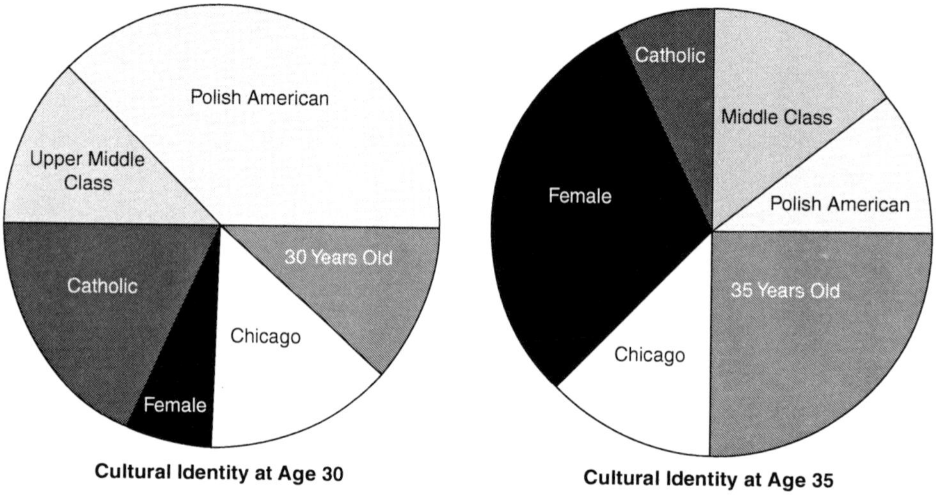

Pause to Reflect 1.4

Think about the cultural groups to which you belong. How important is your membership in the groups discussed above in your cultural identity? Identify their importance by drawing a circle similar to Figure 1.3 and indicating the degree of importance each has. After you have completed your circle, answer the following questions:

- What cultural groups are most important in your identity? Why?
- Why do some groups have little importance to your identity at this time?
- How has discrimination or the lack of it impacted the group memberships that are most important to you? Why?

Go to the *Homework and Exercises* section in Chapter 1 of MyEducationLab at *www.myeducationlab.com* and select *Pause to Reflect 1.4* to answer these questions.

FOCUS YOUR CULTURAL LENS: DEBATE

Should Patriotism Be a School Requirement?

What does it mean to be an American? Many schools are revitalizing the teaching of patriotism in elementary schools. First graders in some schools are being taught to love their country along with reading and writing. Greenbriar East Elementary School in Fairfax County outside of Washington, DC, hosts an annual Patriotic Salute in which their diverse student population sings "God Bless America," "This Land Is Your Land," and "We're Glad We Live in the U.S.A." Patriotic programs have included essay contests on being an American and assemblies to honor veterans. Other schools avoid interjecting patriotism into their curriculum, viewing it as a personal responsibility.

At times of crisis such as 9/11 and armed conflicts with other nations, state legislators and school board members are sometimes inclined to require students to recite the Pledge of Allegiance, sing the national anthem, or participate in patriotic activities on a daily or regular basis. However, these practices begin to infringe on the rights of groups and do not have unanimous support in all communities. For instance, the Supreme Court declared early last century that Jehovah Witness students could not be forced to say the Pledge of Allegiance.

Do you think patriotism should be required in schools?

For

- Students need to understand what it means to be American.
- Schools have an obligation to help students embrace American democracy.
- Students need to learn to appreciate the United States.

Against

- Civics instruction should be about personal responsibility, not instilling patriotism.
- Democracy is about making informed, thoughtful choices.
- Loving your country is not something that should be indoctrinated.

Questions

1. Why do some school districts feel obligated to push patriotism in their schools?
2. How might schools address issues of good citizenship without offending parents who find the focus on patriotism inappropriate?
3. What do you think is an appropriate balance between helping students be good citizens and overt patriotism?

Go to the *Homework and Exercises* section in Chapter 1 of MyEducationLab at *www.myeducationlab.com* and select *Focus Your Cultural Lens* to answer these questions.

Adapted from Kalita, S. M. (2004, June 8). A blending of patriotism, native pride: In diverse Fairfax school, civics starts in 1st grade. *The Washington Post*, p. B. 01.

Cultural Borders

Each of us belongs to multiple cultures (e.g., ethnic, religious, and socioeconomic groups) that help define us. As long as those differences have no status implications in which one group is treated differently from another, conflict among groups is minimal. Unfortunately, cultural borders are often erected between groups, and crossing them can be easy or difficult. What is valued on one side of the border may be denigrated on the other side. For example, speaking both Spanish and English may be highly rewarded in the community, but using Spanish in some schools is not tolerated.

Educators establish cultural borders in the classroom when all activity is grounded in the teacher's culture alone. As we learn to function comfortably in different cultures, we may be able to move away from a single perspective linked to cultural domination. We may be able to cross cultural borders, bringing the students' cultures into the classroom as well.

Biculturalism and Multiculturalism

Individuals who have competencies in, and can operate successfully in, two or more different cultures are border crossers; they are bicultural or multicultural and are often bilingual or multilingual as well. Having proficiencies in multiple cultures allows a broad range of abilities on which to draw at any given time, as determined by the particular situation.

Because we participate in more than one cultural group, we have already become proficient in multiple systems for perceiving, evaluating, believing in, and acting according to the patterns of the various groups in which we participate. We often act and speak differently when we are in the community in which we were raised than when we are in a professional setting. We behave differently on a night out with members of our own sex than we do at home with the family. People with competencies in several cultures develop a fuller appreciation of the range of cultural competencies available to all people.

Many members of oppressed groups are forced to become **bicultural** to work or attend school and participate effectively in their own ethnic community. Different behaviors are expected in the two settings. To be successful on the job usually requires proficiency in the ways of the dominant group. Because most schools reflect the dominant society, students are forced to adjust (or act white) if they are going to be academically successful. In contrast, most middle-class whites find almost total congruence between the culture of their family, schooling, and work. Most remain monocultural throughout their lives. They do not envision the value and possibilities of becoming competent in a different culture.

Becoming knowledgeable of other cultural groups is discussed in Chapter 10.

In our expanding, diverse nation, it is critical that educators themselves become at least bicultural. Understanding the cultural cues of several ethnic groups, especially oppressed groups, improves our ability to work with all students. It also helps us to be sensitive to the importance of these differences in teaching effectively.

Pluralism in Society

Although many similarities exist across cultures, differences exist in the ways people learn, the values they cherish, their worldviews, their behavior, and their interactions with others. There are many reasonable ways to organize our lives, approach a task, and use our languages and dialects. It is when we begin to see our cultural norms and behaviors not just as one approach, but as superior to others, that differences become politicized.

Differing and unequal power relations have a great impact on individuals' and groups' ability to define and achieve their own goals. These differences among and within groups can lead not only to misunderstandings and misperceptions, but also to conflict. Cultural differences sometimes result in political alliances that respond to the real and perceived realities of domination or subordination faced by the group. The result may be strong feelings of patriotism or group solidarity that expand into armed conflicts across nations, tribes, religious communities, or ethnic groups. Feelings of superiority of one's group over another are sometimes reflected in anti-Semitic symbols and actions, cross burnings, gay bashing, and sexual harassment.

Conflicts between groups are usually based on the groups' differential status and value in society. The alienation and marginalization that many powerless groups experience can lead them to accentuating their differences, especially to separate themselves from the dominant group. Groups sometimes construct their own identities in terms of others. For example, European Americans often do not think of themselves as white, except as different from blacks. Males define themselves in opposition to female. Many European American men have been socialized to see themselves as being at the center of a world in which they are privileging themselves in relation to others—women and African Americans.

In developing an understanding of differences and **otherness,** we can begin to change our simplistic binary approaches of us/them, dominant/subordinate, good/bad, and right/wrong. We begin to realize that a plurality of truths are as reasonable as our own. We seek out others for dialogue and understanding, rather than speak about and for them. We can begin to move from exercising power over others to sharing power with them.

The Dominant Culture

U.S. political and social institutions have evolved from an Anglo-Saxon or Western European tradition. The English language is a polyglot of the languages spoken by the various conquerors and rulers of Great Britain throughout history. The legal system is derived from English common law. The political system of democratic elections comes from France and England. The middle-class value system has been modified from a European system. Even our way of thinking, at least the way it is rewarded in school, is based on Socrates' linear system of logic.

Formal institutions, such as governments, schools, social welfare, banks, and businesses, affect many aspects of our lives. Because of the strong Anglo-Saxon influence on these institutions, the dominant cultural influence on the United States also has been identified as Anglo-Saxon, or Western European. More specifically, the major cultural influence on the United States, particularly on its institutions, has been White, Anglo-Saxon, and Protestant (WASP). But no longer is the dominant group composed only of WASPs. Instead, most members of the ethnically diverse middle class have adopted traditionally WASP characteristics and values that provide the framework for the dominant culture.

Although most of our institutions still function under the strong influence of their WASP roots, many other aspects of American life have been influenced by the numerous cultural groups that have come to comprise the U.S. population. Think about the different food we eat, or at least try: Chinese, Indian, Mexican, soul food, Italian, Caribbean, and Japanese. Young people of many cultures choose clothing that is influenced by hip-hop and black culture. But, more important are the contributions made to society by individuals from different groups in the fields of science, the arts, literature, athletics, engineering, architecture, and politics.

Although the United States has an agrarian tradition, the population now is primarily located in metropolitan areas and small towns. The country has mineral and soil wealth,

Members of Congress do not yet represent the diversity of the nation's population.

elaborate technology, and a wealth of manufactured goods. Mass education and mass communication are ways of life. Americans are regulated by clocks and calendars, rather than by seas and the sun. Time is used to organize most activities of life. Most Americans are employees whose salaries or wages are paid by large, complex, impersonal institutions. Work is done regularly, purposefully, and sometimes grimly. In contrast, play is fun—an outlet from work. Money is the denominator of exchange. Necessities of life are purchased, rather than produced. Achievement and success are measured by the quantity of material goods purchased. Religious beliefs are concerned with general morality.

The overpowering value of the dominant group is **individualism,** which is characterized by the belief that every individual is his or her own master, is in control of his or her own destiny, and will advance and regress in society only according to his or her own efforts (Bellah, Madsen, Sullivan, Swidler, & Tipton, 1996). This individualism is grounded in the Western worldview that individuals can control both nature and their destiny. Traits that emphasize this core value include industriousness, ambition, competitiveness, self-reliance, independence, appreciation of the good life, and the perception of humans as separate from, and superior to, nature. The acquisition of such possessions as the latest technology gadget, cars, boats, and homes measures success and achievement.

Another core value is **freedom,** which is defined by the dominant group, however, as not having others determine their values, ideas, or behaviors (Bellah et al., 1996). Relations with other people inside and outside their group are often impersonal. Communications may be very direct or confrontational. Many members of the dominant group rely more on associations of common interest than on strong kinship ties. The nuclear family is the basic kinship unit. Values tend to be absolute (e.g., right or wrong, moral or immoral), rather than range along a continuum of degrees of right and wrong. Personal life and community affairs are based on principles of right and wrong, rather than on shame,

Pause to Reflect 1.5

How much do you know about the power you have because of your race? Circle your responses to the following questions?

• Can you turn on the television or open the newspaper and see people of your race widely represented?	Yes	No
• Can you speak in public to a male group without putting your race [or gender] on trial?	Yes	No
• Can you perform well on a project without being called a credit to your race?	Yes	No
• Are you ever asked to speak for all people of your race?	Yes	No
• Can you be reasonably sure that if you ask to talk to "the person in charge," you will find a person of your same race?	Yes	No
• When you are stopped for a traffic violation, do you have to worry that you have been racially profiled?	Yes	No
• When you shop, are you followed around by a clerk or security person?	Yes	No

Go to the *Homework and Exercises* section in Chapter 1 of MyEducationLab at *www.myeducationlab.com* and select *Pause to Reflect 1.5* to answer these questions.

Adapted from McIntosh, P. (2004). White privilege: Unpacking the invisible knapsack. In M. L. Anderson & P. H. Collins (Eds.), *Race, class, and gender* (pp. 103–108.). Belmont, CA: Wadsworth.

dishonor, or ridicule. Youthfulness is emphasized in advertisements and commercials. Men and women use Botox and have plastic surgery to try to maintain their youthfulness. Many U.S. citizens, especially if they are middle-class, share these traits and values to some degree. They are patterns that are privileged in institutions such as schools. They are values to which the dominant society expects all citizens to adhere.

Privilege. Most male members of the dominant group do not usually think about themselves as white, financially secure, Christian, English-speaking, or heterosexual. They have not seen themselves as **privileged** in society and do not view themselves as oppressors of others. Most schools and teachers do not recognize the inequality, racism, and powerlessness that work against the success of students of color, girls, English language learners, non-Christians, students from low-income families, and students with disabilities. Most members of the dominant group have not had the opportunity to explore their own European ethnicity and privileged position in society. They often have not studied or interacted with groups to which they do not belong. Therefore, they have been unable to locate themselves within the continuum of power and inequality in society.

In contrast to whites, members of oppressed groups are constantly confronted with the difference of their race, language, class, religion, gender, disability, and/or homosexuality. The degree of identification with the characteristics of the dominant culture depends, in part, on how much an individual must interact with society's formal institutions for economic support and subsistence. The more dependence on these institutions, the greater the degree of sharing, or of being forced to adopt, the common traits and values of the dominant group.

These opposing perspectives are situated in one's real or perceived position of privilege or lack of privilege in society. They have led, in recent years, to public debates on college campuses about affirmative action to ensure diversity as well as diversity in the common core of the college curriculum. Members of oppressed groups argue that their cultures are not reflected in a curriculum that includes primarily the great books of Western European thought. The traditionalists, who are predominantly representatives of the dominant group, often invoke nationalism and patriotism in their calls to retain the purity of the Western **canon** and promote homogeneity in society. However, proponents of a common core curriculum that includes the voices of women, people of color, and religions other than Christianity also include many members of the dominant group who value differences and multiple perspectives.

The question appears to be whose culture will be reflected in the elementary and secondary, as well as college, curriculum. Those who call for a curriculum and textbooks that reflect only their history and experiences view their culture as superior to all others. Thus, they and their culture become privileged over others in schools. They do not see themselves as different; to them, diversity refers only to members of other groups in society. To be successful, members of the dominant group are not required to learn to function effectively in a second culture as are members of oppressed groups. The privileged curriculum reinforces this pattern. It is the members of the oppressed groups who must learn the culture and history of the dominant group without the opportunity to study their own cultural group or to validate the importance of their own history and lived experiences. It is as if they do not belong. This feeling may lead to **marginalization** and **alienation** from school as students are not accepted by the dominant group and do not feel a part of the school culture.

See Chapter 10 for strategies for incorporating diverse groups and multiple perspectives into the curriculum.

Acculturation. Many groups that immigrated during the twentieth century have become acculturated or adopted the dominant group's cultural patterns. Although some groups have tried to maintain the original culture, it is usually in vain as children go to school and participate in the larger society. Continuous and firsthand contacts with the dominant group usually result in subsequent changes in the original cultural patterns of either or both groups. The rapidity and success of the **acculturation** process depends on several factors, including location and discrimination. If a group is spatially isolated and segregated (whether voluntarily or not) in a rural area, as is the case with many American Indians on reservations, the acculturation process is very slow. Unusually marked discrimination such as that faced by oppressed groups, especially African Americans, American Indians, and Mexican Americans, deprives group members of educational and occupational opportunities and primary relationships with members of the dominant group (Alba & Nee, 2003; Rumbaut & Portes, 2001). The discrimination makes it more difficult to acculturate if they choose to do so.

It is important to note that acculturation is determined, in part, by the individual or family as they decide how much they want to dress, speak, and behave like members of the dominant group. After conducting a longitudinal study of immigrants in southern California and southern Florida, Rumbaut and Portes (2001) found three acculturation patterns among immigrants: consonant, dissonant, and selective. In consonant acculturation, parents and children learn the language and culture of the community in which they live at approximately the same time. In dissonant acculturation, children learn English and the new culture while parents retain their native language and culture, often leading to conflict within the family and decreasing parental authority. Fluent bilingualism in the second generation is an outcome of selective acculturation in which the children of immigrants learn the dominant culture and language, but retain significant elements of their native culture.

Members of many groups, however, have little choice if they want to share the American dream of success. Many people have had to give up native languages and behaviors or hide them at home. However, acculturation does not guarantee acceptance by the dominant group. Most members of oppressed groups, especially those of color, have not been permitted to assimilate fully into society even though they have adopted the values and behaviors of the dominant group.

Assimilation

Assimilation occurs when a group's distinctive cultural patterns either become part of the dominant culture or disappear as the group adopts the dominant culture. **Structural assimilation** occurs when the dominant group shares primary group relationships with the second group, including membership in the same cliques and social clubs; members of the two groups intermarry; and the two groups are treated equally within society. Assimilation appears to be relevant for voluntary immigrants, particularly if they are white, but does not apply to **involuntary immigrants** who were forced to come to this country through slavery or conquest of the area in which they lived. These families have been in the country for generations and not allowed to fully assimilate, especially at the structural level.

White European immigrants usually become structurally assimilated within a few generations after arriving in this country. Marriage across groups is fairly common across white ethnic groups and Judeo-Christian religious affiliations. Nearly one of three Asian Americans and 30% of Latinos marry outside of their group. However, only 2% of whites and 4% of African Americans were marrying outside their group at the end of the twentieth century (Alba, 2000). Acculturation has neither eliminated prejudice and discrimination nor led to large-scale intermarriage with the dominant group. If the assimilation process is effective, it leads to the disappearance of a cultural group that is distinct from the dominant group, and, in the process, changes the dominant group as well.

When Portes and Rumbaut (2001) studied the second generation of recent immigrants, they found that the degree of their assimilation differed. The history and experiences of the first-generation immigrant varied across and within groups. The pace of acculturation among parents and children as described above influenced assimilation with consonant acculturation being the most rapid. A critical factor is the cultural and economic barriers faced by second-generation youth. Young people who can see upward mobility in their future are more likely to assimilate. Some groups have greater family and community resources for confronting the barriers that society establishes for immigrants. "In a high-technology society, immigrant families who bring large volumes of human and cultural capital obviously have an advantage over low-wage laborers with little formal schooling" (Alba & Nee, 2003, p. 15).

Governmental support of new immigrants also has an influence on a group's desire and ability to assimilate (Portes & Rumbaut, 2001). Some groups have been actively encouraged to immigrate and have been warmly welcomed by society. Favored refugee groups include the Vietnamese and Cubans. Other immigrant groups such as Chinese, Middle Easterners, and Europeans have been passively accepted by society without favoritism, but also with limited discrimination. Discrimination based on race has made it difficult for many Haitians, Mexican Americans, and Central Americans to easily assimilate into the dominant culture. The immigrants and their children in this last group are likely to confront segmented or downward assimilation in which they are not able to improve their economic status (Alba & Nee, 2003; Rumbaut & Portes, 2001). Low educational attainment of immigrant children in these excluded groups is affected by the persistence of racial discrimination, the growing inequality of workers, and the consolidation of oppressed populations in the inner city (Portes & Rumbaut, 2001).

Some immigrant groups try to preserve their native cultures; others have assimilation as their goal. Nevertheless, assimilation does not characterize the contemporary U.S. scene. We are a nation of many cultural groups distinguished by our ethnicity, gender, class, language, age, and religion. At the same time, America's desire to assimilate different cultural groups affects the nation's political, social, and educational policies and practices.

Cultural Pluralism

A society organized according to a theory of **cultural pluralism** allows two or more distinct groups to function separately and equally without requiring any assimilation of one into the other. Refusing or not being permitted to assimilate into the dominant American culture, many immigrants and ethnic groups maintain their own unique ethnic communities and enclaves. For most oppressed ethnic and religious groups, primary-group contacts have been maintained within the group, rather than across cultural groups as required in structural assimilation. Cross-cultural contacts occur primarily at the secondary level in work settings and political and civic institutions. Members of oppressed groups develop institutions, agencies, and power structures for services within their ethnic communities—enclaves such as Little Italy, Chinatown, Harlem, Korea Town, East Los Angeles, and Amish and Hutterite communities. In some places, persons who are blind or deaf have established communities in which they feel comfortable with others who have the same disability.

The commitment to the value of cultural pluralism is not broadly supported by individuals and groups in society. American Indian nations within the United States come the closest to reflecting cultural pluralism in that they have their own political, economic, and educational systems. For most American Indians, however, the economic, political, and educational opportunities do not approach equality with the dominant group. In a cultural pluralistic society, the retention of diverse ethnic and religious groups would be promoted in schools and society. In a culturally plural society, power and resources would be shared somewhat equitably across groups.

The problem is that dominant groups are not usually willing to share their power and wealth with others. Some critics of the system believe that the dominant group uses a strategy of divide and conquer to keep ethnic groups segregated and fighting among themselves for the few resources available. Others believe that a societal goal should be the integration of diverse groups and the promotion of more equality across groups through a united front. Still others believe that individuals should be able to maintain their ethnic identities while participating in the common culture. These beliefs are not necessarily discrete from one another; for example, society could be integrated, but members would not be required to relinquish their ethnic identities. At the same time, an integrated society can lead to greater assimilation in that primary contacts across cultural groups are more likely.

Equality and Social Justice in a Democracy

The United States is a **democracy** in which people participate in their government by exercising their power directly or indirectly through elected representatives. Schools and the mass media teach us that our democracy is one to be emulated by the rest of the world. A democracy should promote the good of all its citizens. Thus, the Constitution was fashioned with a coherent set of "checks and balances" to limit the systematic abuse of power. **Egalitarianism**—the belief in social, political, and economic rights and privileges for all people—is espoused as a key principle on which democracy is based. All citizens are expected to have a voice. Power should be shared among groups, and no one group should continuously dominate the economic, political, social, and cultural life of the country. Society and government, though not perfect, are promoted as allowing mass participation and steady advancement toward a more prosperous and egalitarian society.

One strength of a democracy is that citizens bring many perspectives, based on their own histories and experiences, to bear on policy questions and practices. Thus, to disagree is acceptable as long as we are able to communicate with each other openly and without fear of reprisal. Further, we expect that no single right way will be forced on us. For the most part, we would rather struggle with multiple perspectives and actions and determine what is best for us as individuals within this democratic society.

At the same time, a democracy expects its citizens to be concerned about more than just their own individual freedoms. In the classic *Democracy and Education,* philosopher and educator John Dewey (1916/1966) suggested that the emphasis should be on what binds us together in cooperative pursuits and results, regardless of the nation or our group alliance and membership. He raised concern about our possible stratification into separate classes and called for "intellectual opportunities [to be] accessible to all on equitable and easy terms" (p. 88).

The emphasis on individualism in the dominant culture provides a dilemma for educators who promote democratic practice. In many classrooms, individualism is supported through competitive activities in which individual achievement is rewarded. A democratic classroom promotes working together across groups. Responsibility and leadership are shared by students and teachers as students practice being active participants in a democratic setting.

Democratic classrooms are discussed in more depth in Chapter 10.

Both individualism and equality have long been central themes of political discourse in a democratic society. The meaning of equality within our society varies according to one's assumptions about humankind and human existence. At least two sets of beliefs govern the ideologies of equality and inequality. The first accepts inequality as inevitable and promotes **meritocracy,** which is a system based on the belief that an individual's achievements are due to their own personal merits and that the people who achieve at the highest levels deserve the greatest social and financial rewards. It stresses the right of access to society's resources as a necessary condition for equal rights to life, liberty, and happiness. The focus is on individualism and the individual's right to pursue happiness and obtain personal resources. The second set of beliefs supports a much greater degree of equality across groups in society. Persons who believe in equality care about people who have fewer resources and develop policies that allow more people to share in the nation's wealth.

Meritocracy is also discussed in Chapter 3.

This dilemma forces some people to promote some equality while preventing any real equity from occurring. Affirmative action, for example, is viewed by its critics as evidence of group welfare gaining precedence over individual achievement. The outcry against affirmative action suggests that racism no longer exists and that decisions about employment, promotion, and so forth are no longer influenced by racism and sexism. Whites filing reverse discrimination cases believe that their individual rights to an education at a select school, a promotion, or a job should be based solely on their individual achievement. They believe that other factors such as income (or lack of), ethnicity, race, or gender should not be valued in the process. They overlook the fact that they have been privileged throughout their lives because of their race and family income. Even though egalitarianism is an often-espoused goal of democracy in the United States, the inequities that actually exist in society are continually overlooked.

Individualism and Meritocracy

Proponents of meritocracy accept the theories of sociobiology or functionalism or both, in which inequalities are viewed as natural outcomes of individual differences. They believe that everyone has the opportunity to be successful if they just work hard enough. They give little credit to family conditions, such as being born in a wealthy family, as a head start for success. Members of oppressed groups usually are seen as inferior, and their hardships blamed on their personal characteristics rather than societal constraints or discrimination.

For more information on racism, see Chapter 2. The overrepresentation of some students in special education is discussed in Chapter 5.

The belief system that undergirds meritocracy has at least three dimensions that are consistent with dominant values. First, the individual is valued over the group. The individual has the qualities, ambitions, and talent to achieve at the highest levels in society. Popular stories promote this ideology as they describe the poor immigrant who arrived on U.S. shores with nothing, set up a vegetable stand to eke out a living, and became the millionaire owner of a chain of grocery stores.

The second dimension stresses differences through competition. IQ and achievement tests are used throughout schooling to help measure differences. Students and adults are rewarded for outstanding grades, athletic ability, and artistic accomplishment.

Students do not start life with an equal chance to succeed. Because of family income and wealth, some students have access to resources and experiences in their homes, communities, and often schools that are not available to most low-income students.

© Masterfile Royalty Free Division

The third dimension emphasizes internal characteristics, such as motivation, intuition, and character that have been internalized by the individual. External conditions, such as racism and poverty, are to be overcome by the individual; they are not accepted as contributors to an individual's lack of success.

Equal educational opportunity, or equal access to schooling, applies meritocracy to education. All students are to be provided with equal educational opportunities that supposedly will give them similar chances for success or failure. Proponents of this approach believe it is the individual's responsibility to use those opportunities to his or her advantage in obtaining life's resources and benefits. Critics of meritocracy point out that children of low-income families do not start with the same chances for success in life as children from affluent families. Even the most capable of these students do not have equal educational opportunities if the schools they attend lack the challenging curriculum and advanced placement classes typically found in middle-class and affluent communities. Thus, competition is unequal from birth. The chances of the affluent child being educationally and financially successful are much greater than for the child from a low-income family. Those with advantages at birth are almost always able to hold onto and extend those advantages throughout their lifetimes.

Observe and Learn Lessons in Action

Equality

Go to the *Homework and Exercises* section in Chapter 1 of MyEducationLab at *www.myeducationlab.com* and select *Observe and Learn: Lessons in Action* to view the video "The 14th Amendment and Our Schools" and answer the accompanying questions. In this lesson, students take a firsthand exploration of constitutional rights by exploring the 14th Amendment and applying it to their own school context.

1. What issues did students in the video raise after reading the two Supreme Court cases? Did any of the students' comments surprise you? If so, which ones?
2. Do you agree with school choice? Why or why not?
3. What was your own high school context like in terms of socioeconomic status and class?
4. How might your views regarding school choice and the socioeconomic status of your students affect what you do in your future classroom?

Equality

With the persistence of racism, poverty, unemployment, and inequality in major social systems such as education and health, many persons have found it difficult to reconcile daily realities with the publicized egalitarianism that characterizes the public rhetoric. These persons view U.S. society as comprised of institutions and an economic system that represents the interests of the privileged few, rather than the pluralistic majority. Even where institutions, laws, and processes have the appearance of equal access, benefit, and protection, they are almost always enforced in highly discriminatory ways. These patterns of **inequality** are not the product of corrupt individuals as such, but rather are a reflection of how resources of economics, political power, and cultural and social dominance are built into the entire political-economic system.

Even in the optimistic view that some degree of equality can be achieved, inequality is also expected. Not all resources can be redistributed so that every individual has an equal amount, nor should all individuals expect equal compensation for the work they do. The underlying belief, however, is that there need not be the huge disparities of income, wealth, and power that currently exist. Equality does suggest fairness in the distribution of the conditions and goods that affect the well-being of all children and families. It is

VIDEO INSIGHTS

School Busing

For decades the remedy for segregation has been school busing. The goals of integrating schools have been racial balance and access to better schools, new equipment, and new opportunities for all students. Now some African American families are criticizing the busing experiment as a failure and are requesting a "separate but equal" education for their children in their own neighborhoods.

In this video segment, you will see proponents of this movement in Oklahoma City and in other cities across the country say their children have been subjected to segregated settings within integrated schools. African American children are often assigned to remedial classes or lower academic tracks and do not get exposure to the services and resource that other students receive. In addition, because these schools are not close to home, it is difficult for parents to be involved or even present if there is a problem or an emergency at school.

1. After viewing this video segment, how have your views on busing changed?
2. Are the people who support this movement to neighborhood schools forsaking the efforts of the countless individuals who have worked so hard for integration in our schools?
3. History has shown us that "separate but equal" has not worked. Is this because separate, by definition, is not equal?
4. What are your views on the issue of "separate but equal"?
5. Do you think we now have the resources, support, and technology to make "separate but equal" a reality?

Go to the Video Insights DVD and watch the *School Busing* video segment. Then, go to the *Homework and Exercises* section in Chapter 1 of MyEducationLab at *www.myeducationlab.com* and select *Video Insights: School Busing* to answer these questions.

fostered by policies for full employment, wages that prevent families from living in poverty, and child care for all children.

Critics decry the perceived socialism as being against the democratic foundations that undergird the nation. They believe that equality of resources and societal benefits would undermine the capitalist system that allows a few individuals to acquire the great majority of those resources. They warn that equality of results would limit freedom and liberty for individuals.

Equality is more than just providing oppressed group members with an equal chance or equal opportunity. One proposal is that equal results should be the goal. These results might be more equal achievement by students of both oppressed and dominant groups and similar rates of dropping out of school, college attendance, and college completion by different ethnic, racial, gender, and class populations.

Traditionally, the belief has been that education can overcome the inequalities that exist in society. The role of education in reducing the amount of occupation and income inequality may be limited, however. School reform has not yet led to significant social changes outside the schools. Equalizing educational opportunity has had very little impact on making

Pause to Reflect 1.6

How do you view equality in society and schooling? Check the statements below that best describe your perceptions.

- The ablest and most meritorious, ambitious, hardworking, and talented individuals should acquire the most, achieve the most, and become society's leaders.
- The individual is more important than the group.
- The U.S. economic system represents the interests of a privileged few, rather than those of the pluralistic majority.
- Huge disparities of income, wealth, and power should not exist in this country.
- It is the student's responsibility to get as much out of school as possible.
- Differences measured on standardized tests are more important than similarities.
- External conditions, such as racism and poverty, should be overcome by the individual.
- Students from all cultural groups can be academically successful.
- Tracking of students promotes inequality.
- Teachers can make a difference in the academic success of students.

Which of these statements are most related to a belief in meritocracy, and which to a belief in equality?

Go to the *Homework and Exercises* section in Chapter 1 of MyEducationLab at *www.myeducationlab.com* and select *Pause to Reflect 1.6* to answer these questions.

adults more equal. Providing equal educational opportunities for all students does not guarantee equal results at the end of high school or college. It does not yet provide equal access to jobs and income across groups. It may be that programs for equal educational opportunity have not overcome the academic and economic disparities that existed among families. To ensure equality in schools students in impoverished schools would be guaranteed to have teachers who are as highly qualified as the teachers in wealthy school districts. Equality requires financial support for providing quality instruction in environments that are conducive to learning by all students. More, not less, money may be needed to ensure equity in educational results by the children of dominant groups and other groups.

Social Justice

Social justice is another element of democracy that expects citizens to provide for those persons in society who are not as advantaged as others. Dewey (1966) called for social justice when he said, "What the best and wisest parent wants for his [or her] own child, that must the community want for all of its children. Any other ideal for our schools is narrow and unlovely; acted upon, it destroys our democracy" (p. 3). In schools, social justice requires a critique of practices that interfere with equity across groups. Social and economic inequities that prevent students from learning and participating effectively in schools must be confronted (Apple, 2004).

Observe and Learn Lessons in Action

Social Justice

Go to the *Homework and Exercises* section in Chapter 1 of MyEducationLab at *www.myeducationlab.com* and select *Observe and Learn: Lessons in Action* to view the video "The Universal Declaration of Human Rights" and answer the accompanying questions. In this lesson, students examine the role of the United Nations in promoting human rights, diversity, international understanding, and humanitarian affairs through its U.N. Convention—the Universal Declaration of Human Rights (UDHR). Violations of human rights in the form of lack of freedoms and economic and social inequalities are addressed.

1. What kinds of issues did the students document in their posters? Were most of the issues local or global? Why do you think this was the case?
2. What are some of the human rights issues that most interest/trouble/concern you at this time?
3. How might your understanding of various human rights issues affect what you do in your future classroom?

Enormous disparities exist between the very wealthy and the very poor. The very wealthy have accumulated vast resources while the very poor cannot even meet their basic needs. They are unable to obtain the barest essentials for shelter, food, or medical care. Some suffer from lack of heat in the winter and lack of cooling in very hot summers. Every year, there are reports of elderly, low-income people who die from exposure to excessive heat or cold. This reality is inconceivable for many Americans who simply turn their thermostats to the precise temperature that will meet their comfort level. Every day children from poor families come to school with insufficient sleep because of the physical discomforts of their homes, with inadequate clothing, and with empty stomachs. Tens of thousands suffer from malnutrition and no dental care. When they are sick, many go untreated. Under these conditions, it is difficult, at best, to function well in an academic setting.

Civil unrest has almost always been precipitated by the disenfranchised who have no realistic hope of extricating themselves from lives of despair. Children of affluent members of society do not typically form street gangs; they are usually too busy enjoying the good life that prosperity brings. The street gangs of New York, Chicago, and Los Angeles are comprised almost exclusively of young individuals who are poor, embittered, and disenfranchised.

Those who have the power to bring about meaningful change in society are usually the more affluent. They have the resources and connections to make things happen. To bring about truly meaningful change requires paradigm shifts. Even the middle class may be reluctant to make changes if a change in the status quo diminishes their position. Changes are usually supported only if they provide benefits to the dominant group or do not affect them negatively.

Meaningful change in society requires a universal social consciousness. It requires, to some extent, a willingness of the citizenry to explore the means of redistributing some of the benefits of a democratic society. Effective redistribution would require that some who have considerable wealth provide a greater share in the effort to eliminate poverty and its concomitant effects. The end result could be a society in which everyone has a decent place to sleep, no child goes to school hungry, and appropriate health care is available to all.

Obstacles to Equality and Social Justice

Prejudice and **discrimination** stem from a combination of several factors related to us and them. Persons who are prejudiced have an aversion to members of a group other than their own. Discrimination leads to the denial of the privileges and rewards to members of oppressed groups. Prejudice can result when people lack an understanding of the history, experiences, values, and perceptions of groups other than their own. Members of groups are **stereotyped** when others apply to them generalizations about the group without consideration of individual differences within the group.

Prejudice. Prejudice manifests itself in feelings of anger, fear, hatred, and distrust about members of a certain group. These attitudes are often translated into fear of walking in the group's neighborhood, fear of being robbed or hurt by others, distrust of a merchant from the group, anger at any advantages that others may be perceived as receiving, and fear that housing prices will be deflated if someone from that group moves next door.

Some members of all groups possess negative stereotypes of others. For example, many African Americans and Latinos believe that whites are bigoted, bossy, and unwilling to share power. In a two-year study of teachers in a staff development project, Sleeter (1992) found that many white teachers "associated people of color—and particularly African Americans and Latinos—with dysfunctional families and communities, and lack of ability and motivation" (p. 162). These negative stereotypes may describe some members of a group, but have been unfairly extended as characteristics of all members of the group.

Although prejudice may not always directly hurt members of a group, it can be easily translated into behavior that does harm them. An ideology based on aversion to a group and perceived superiority undergirds the activities of groups such as the neo-Nazis, Ku Klux Klan, skinheads, and other white racist groups. A prejudiced teacher may hold high academic expectations for students of one group and low expectations for students of another group. Such prejudice could lead to inappropriate placement of students in gifted or special education programs.

The overrepresentation of students of color in special education is discussed in Chapter 5.

Discrimination. Whereas prejudice is based on attitudes, discrimination focuses on behavior. Discrimination occurs at two levels: individual and institutional. Individual discrimination is attributed to, or influenced by, prejudice. Individuals discriminate against a member of a group because they have strong prejudicial, or bigoted, feelings about the group, or they believe that society demands they discriminate. For example, realtors, personnel managers, receptionists, and membership chairpersons all work directly with individuals. Their own personal attitudes about members of certain groups can influence whether a house is sold, a job is offered, a loan is granted, an appointment is made, a meal is served, or a membership is granted. The action of these individuals can prevent others from gaining the experiences and economic advantages that these activities offer.

An individual has less control in the other form of discrimination. Institutional discrimination cannot be attributed to prejudicial attitudes. It refers to inequalities that have been integrated into the system-wide operation of society through legislation and practices that ensure benefits to some groups and not to others. Laws that disproportionately limit immigration to people from specific countries are one example. Other examples include practices that lead to a disproportionately large number of African Americans being incarcerated, single low-income mothers being denied adequate prenatal care, and children in low-income neighborhoods suffering disproportionately from asthma as a result of poor environmental conditions in their neighborhoods.

We have grown up in a society that has inherently discriminated against persons of color and women since the first European Americans arrived. Throughout our lives, we have participated in societal institutions, including schools, Social Security, transportation, welfare, and housing patterns. We often do not realize the extent to which members of different groups receive the benefits and privileges of these institutions. Because we may believe that we have never been discriminated against, we should not assume that others do not suffer from discrimination.

Many individuals might argue that institutional discrimination no longer exists because today's laws require equal access to the benefits of society. As a result, they believe that individuals from all groups have had equal opportunities to be successful. They fight against group rights that lead to what is perceived as preferential treatment of the members of one group over them as individuals. The government is usually accused of going too far in eliminating discrimination against historically oppressed groups by supporting affirmative action, contracts set aside for specific groups, special education, and legislation for women's equity. Opponents to these programs charge that such programs lead to reverse discrimination.

However, criteria for access to the "good life" are often applied arbitrarily and unfairly. A disproportionately high number of persons of color have had limited opportunities to gain the qualifications for skilled jobs or college entrance or have the economic resources to purchase a home in the suburbs. As businesses and industries move from the city to the suburbs, access to employment by those who live in the inner city is limited. A crucial issue is not the equal treatment of those with equal qualifications, but the accessibility to the qualifications and jobs themselves.

The consequences are the same in individual and institutional discrimination. Members of some groups do not receive the same benefits from society as the dominant group. Individuals are harmed by circumstances beyond their control because of their membership in a specific group. The role of teachers and other professional educators requires that they not discriminate against any student because of his or her group memberships. This consideration must be paramount in assigning students to special education and gifted classes and in giving and interpreting standardized tests. Classroom interactions, classroom resources, extracurricular activities, and counseling practices must be evaluated to ensure that discrimination against students from various groups does not occur.

Summary

Multicultural education is an educational strategy that incorporates cultural differences and provides equality and social justice in schools. For it to become a reality in the formal school situation, the total environment must reflect a commitment to multicultural education. The diverse cultural backgrounds and group memberships of students and families are as important in developing effective instructional strategies as are their physical and mental capabilities. Further, educators must understand the influence of racism, sexism, and classism on the lives of their students and ensure that these are not perpetuated in the classroom.

Culture provides the blueprint that determines the way an individual thinks, feels, and behaves in society. We are not born with culture, but rather learn it through enculturation and socialization. It is manifested through society's institutions, lived experiences, and the individual's fulfillment of psychological and basic needs.

Historically, U.S. political and social institutions have developed from a Western European tradition and still function under the strong influence of that heritage. At the same time, many aspects of American life have been greatly influenced by the numerous cultural groups that make up the U.S. population. The dominant culture is based on its White, Anglo-Saxon, Protestant roots and the core values of individualism and freedom with which many middle-class families identify. Assimilation is the process by which groups adopt and change the dominant culture. Schools have traditionally served as the transmitter of the dominant culture to all students regardless of their cultural backgrounds.

Individuals also belong to a number of groups with cultural patterns that differ from that of the dominant group. Cultural identity is based on the interaction and influence of membership in groups based on ethnic origin, race, religion, gender, sexual orientation, age, class, native language, geographic region, and abilities. Membership in one of those groups can greatly affect one's identity with the others. Some religions, for example, dictate the norms for the behavior of men and women, children and adults, as well as the treatment of members of other groups. The theory of cultural pluralism promotes the maintenance of the distinct differences among cultural groups.

A democracy provides social justice for all of its people. Egalitarianism and equality have long been espoused as goals for society, but they are implemented from two perspectives. The emphasis on individualism is supported in a meritocratic system in which everyone is alleged to start out equally, but the most deserving will end up with the most rewards. Equality, in contrast, seeks to ensure that society's benefits and rewards are distributed more equitably among individuals and groups. Prejudice and discrimination continue to be obstacles to equality.

PROFESSIONAL PRACTICE FOR EDUCATORS

Questions for Discussion

1. How does multicultural education differ from multiethnic studies and intercultural or intergroup education?
2. What is the danger of stereotyping students on the basis of their membership in only one of their cultural groups?
3. Why is multicultural education as important to students of the dominant culture as to students of other cultures?
4. What impact does culture have on the way one lives?
5. How does ethnicity, gender, and religion interact in determining one's cultural identity? Why might one's cultural identity change over time?
6. What are the implicit and explicit differences between dominant and oppressed groups?
7. How might an understanding of cultural borders help teachers understand differences in classroom settings?
8. How do meritocracy and individualism conflict with the ideal of equality?

Portfolio Activities

1. Write a reflective paper that describes your cultural identity and the social and economic factors that have influenced it. Refer to your circle of cultural identity (Pause to Reflect 1.4) to get you started.
2. Develop a lesson plan for the subject and level you plan to teach that presents the topic from multiple perspectives. Include a summary of the perspectives to be presented, why they were selected, and how the different perspectives strengthen the lesson. (INTASC Standard 1)

3. Select one of the schools in which you are observing this semester to develop a case study of the cultural norms prevalent in the community served by the school. In your case study indicate the diversity of the community and the cultural norms that are reflected in the school. Teachers, parents, and students should be interviewed during the development of the case study. In addition, your observations of students should inform your case. (INTASC Standard 3)

Licensure Test Prep

The following passages are taken from a debate about the advantages and disadvantages of multicultural education. Read the two sides of the debate and answer the two questions that follow.

Why multicultural education is desirable

Multicultural education is a strategy that builds on the cultural backgrounds of students and their families to engage them in learning. It includes the experiences and histories of their cultures as well as the dominant culture of the country. It helps students develop their own self-esteem as well as linking their knowledge and backgrounds to the subject being taught. Multicultural education is not just for new immigrants and students of color as many people think. It is also important that middle-class European American students know about the histories, struggles, and contributions of other groups. In multicultural education the cultures of all students are respected and valued and drawn upon by teachers to plan lessons. The different learning styles of students are considered as lessons are planned and their work is assessed with the goal of helping all students learn at high levels.

Why multicultural education is misguided

When educators stress differences among groups rather than similarities, as they do in multicultural education, the approach is misguided. The focus of education should be to ensure that students learn English and understand the history and culture of the United States to unify the population. Focusing on differences and conflicts between the government and American Indians, African Americans, Latinos, Asian Americans, women, gays and lesbians, Jews, Muslims, low-income families, and English language learners will only divide the country into competing groups. A good teacher can help all students learn regardless of their cultural differences. Adapting instruction to different groups of students only limits the amount and quality of instruction that the average student receives in the classroom.

1. The first passage suggests which of the following is an essential element of multicultural education?
   A. The development of students' self-esteem.
   B. The inclusion of students' cultures throughout the curriculum and instruction.
   C. The maintenance of students' native languages.
   D. The acceptance of European American culture.
2. The second passage regards which of the following goals as essential for a good education?
   A. Accommodating instruction to students' learning styles and needs.
   B. Providing accurate information about the diverse groups that comprise the U.S. population.

C. Focusing on similarities among diverse groups.
D. Ensuring that students learn the common culture of the United States.

Go to the *Homework and Exercises* section in Chapter 1 of MyEducationLab at *www.myeducationlab.com* and select *Licensure Test Prep* to complete this exercise.

Suggested Readings

Apple, M. W. (2004). *Ideology and curriculum* (3rd ed.). New York: RoutledgeFalmer.
The politics of the school curriculum are the focus of this insightful account of the cultural, political, and economic influences on education. This edition includes a chapter on the challenges facing schools after 9/11.

Au, W., Bigelow, B., & Karp, S. (2007). *Rethinking our classrooms: Teaching for equity and justice.* Milwaukee, WI: Rethinking Schools.
This handbook for educators includes creative teaching ideas, compelling classroom narratives, and hands-on examples of ways teachers can promote the values of community, justice, and equality while building academic skills. It includes essays, poems, student handouts, and annotated resources.

Banks, J. A., & Banks, C. A. M. (Eds.). (2004). *Handbook of research on multicultural education* (2nd ed.). San Francisco: Jossey-Bass.
This comprehensive handbook provides broad coverage of the history as well as current trends, research issues, and knowledge construction of multicultural education. Well-known scholars address ethnic groups, immigrants, language issues, academic achievement, intergroup education, higher education, and international perspectives.

hooks, b. (1994). *Teaching to transgress: Education as the practice of freedom.* New York: Routledge.
Using passion and politics, this teacher promotes education that helps students cross racial, sexual, and class boundaries in the practice of freedom.

Tyack, D. (2003). *Seeking common ground: Public schools in a diverse society.* Cambridge, MA: Harvard University Press.
Beginning with the establishment of public schools in each township in the eighteenth century, this historian traces the debates that have guided the incorporation of diverse populations in schools into the twenty-first century.

References

Alba, R. D. (2000). Assimilations' quiet tide. In S. Steinberg (Ed.), *Race and ethnicity in the United States: Issues and debates* (pp. 211–222). Malden, MA: Blackwell.

Alba, R., & Nee, V. (2003). *Remaking the American mainstream: Assimilation and contemporary immigration.* Cambridge, MA: Harvard University Press.

Apple, M. W. (2004). *Ideology and curriculum* (3rd ed.). New York: RoutledgeFalmer.

Banks, C. A. M. (2004). Intercultural and intergroup education, 1929–1959: Linking schools and communities. In J. A. Banks & C. A. M. Banks (Eds.), *Handbook of research on multicultural education* (2nd ed., pp. 753–781). San Francisco: Jossey-Bass.

Banks, J. A. (2004). Multicultural education: Historical development, dimensions, and practice. In J. A. Banks & C. A. M. Banks (Eds.), *Handbook of research on multicultural education* (2nd ed., pp. 3–29). San Francisco: Jossey-Bass.

Bellah, R. N., Madsen, R., Sullivan, W. M., Swidler, A., & Tipton, S. M. (1996). *Habits of the heart: Individualism and commitment in American life.* Berkeley, CA: University of California Press.

Dalton, B., Sable, J., & Hoffman, L. (2006). *Characteristics of the 100 largest public elementary and secondary school districts in the United States: 2003–04* (NCES 2006-329). Washington, DC: U.S. Department of Education, National Center for Education Statistics.

Dewey, J. (1966). *Democracy and education: An introduction to the philosophy of education.* New York: Free Press. (Original work published 1916)

Eck, D. L. (2000). Religious pluralism in America in the year 2000. In E. W. Linder, *Yearbook of American and Canadian churches 2000.* Nashville, TN: Abingdon Press.

Interstate New Teacher Assessment and Support Consortium. (1992). *Model Standards for Beginning Teacher Licensing, Assessment, and Development: A Resource for State Dialogue.* Washington, DC: Council of Chief State School Officers.

Kuper, A. (2000). *Culture: The anthropologists' account.* Cambridge, MA: Harvard University Press.

Ladson-Billings, G. (2004). New directions in multicultural education: Complexities, boundaries, and critical race theory. In J. A. Banks & C. A. M. Banks (Eds.), *Handbook of research on multicultural education* (2nd ed., pp. 50–65). San Francisco: Jossey-Bass.

National Assessment of Educational Progress. (2007). Washington, DC: National Center for Education Statistics, U.S. Department of Education. Retrieved on May 20, 2007, from http://nces.ed.gov/nationsreportcard/nde/viewresults.asp

National Board for Professional Teaching Standards. (2001). *The impact of national board certification on teachers: A survey of national board certified teachers and assessors.* Arlington, VA: Author.

Portes, A., & Rumbaut, R. G. (2001). *Legacies: The story of the immigrant second generation.* Berkeley, CA: University of California Press.

Rumbaut, R. G., & Portes, A. (2001). *Ethnicities: Children of immigrants in America.* Berkeley, CA: University of California Press.

Sleeter, C. E. (1992). *Keepers of the American dream: A study of staff development and multicultural education.* London: Taylor & Francis.

Sleeter, C. E., & Bernal, D. D. (2004). Critical pedagogy, critical race theory, and antiracist education. In J. A. Banks & C. A. M. Banks (Eds.), *Handbook of research on multicultural education* (2nd ed., pp. 240–258). San Francisco: Jossey-Bass.

Sleeter, C. E., & Grant, C. A. (2006). *Making choices for multicultural education: Five approaches to race, class, and gender* (5th ed.). New York: John Wiley & Sons.

Snyder, T. D., Tan, A. G., & Hoffman, C. M. (2006). *Digest of education statistics 2005* (NCES 2006-030). U.S. Department of Education, National Center for Education Statistics. Washington, DC: U.S. Government Printing Office.

Spring, J. (2001). *Protecting cultural and language rights: An educational rights amendment to the U.S. constitution.* Keynote Presentation at Annual Meeting of the National Association for Multicultural Education in Arlington, VA.

Symcox, L. (2002). *Whose history? The struggle for national standards in American classrooms.* New York: Teachers College Press.

Tyack, D. (2003). *Seeking common ground: Public schools in a diverse society.* Cambridge, MA: Harvard University Press.

U.S. Census Bureau. (2006). *Statistical Abstract of the United States: 2006* (126th ed.). Washington, DC: U.S. Government Printing Office.

U.S. Department of Education. (2001). *No Child Left Behind Act of 2001.* (www.ed.gov/nclb/overview/intro/presidentplan/proposal.pdf). Washington, DC: U.S. Government Printing Office.

U.S. Department of Education, National Center for Education Statistics. (2006). *The condition of education 2006* (NCES 2006-071). Washington, DC: U.S. Government Printing Office.

Appendix III

Taken from: *Teaching Strategies for Ethnic Studies*, Eighth Edition by James A. Banks

REFLECTION AND ACTION ACTIVITIES

Respond to the following ethnic literacy test and discuss your responses, giving reasons for them, with your classmates or colleagues. Determine your ethnic literacy score by comparing your responses with the answers given at the end of the test. How might you use this test with your students to stimulate research and discussion? What sources might they use to check their responses? Administer this test, in part or whole, to your class. Adapt it to your students' reading and grade levels. How well did they do on the test? Why?

Ethnic Literacy Test

Directions: Indicate whether each of the following statements is true or false by placing a T or F in front of it.

1. The U.S. Census projects that people of color will make up about 50% of the United States population by 2050.
2. The first Chinese immigrants who came to the United States worked on the railroads.
3. In 2005, the population of African Americans in the United States exceeded the national population in Canada as well as that of Australia.
4. Puerto Ricans on the island of Puerto Rico became U.S. citizens in 1920.
5. In 2000, Mexican Americans made up 59% of the Hispanics in the United States.
6. Between 1820 and 1930, 15 million immigrants came to the United States.
7. White Anglo-Saxon Protestants are the most powerful ethnic group in the United States.

8. Rosh Hashanah, which in Hebrew means "end of year," is a Jewish holiday that comes early in the fall.
9. While most Arabs are Muslims, Arabs make up no more than 20% of the Muslims in the world.
10. The first law to limit immigration to the United States was passed in 1882 to restrict the number of African immigrants.
11. Puerto Ricans in New York City tend to identify strongly with African Americans in that city.
12. In the 2005 American Community Survey of the U.S. Census, about 5.5 million people, or 2% of the population, identified with two or more racial groups.
13. Most African Americans came from the eastern parts of Africa.
14. The internment of the Japanese Americans during World War II was opposed by President Franklin D. Roosevelt.
15. The 2000 U.S. Census indicated that the Hispanic population slightly exceeded the African American population.
16. Between 1990 and 2000, the Chinese population increased more than any other group of Asian Americans.
17. Congress passed a Removal Act that authorized the removal of Indians from the east to west of the Mississippi in 1830.
18. A Japanese settlement was established in California as early as 1869.
19. The United States acquired a large part of Mexico's territory under the terms of the Treaty of Guadalupe Hidalgo in 1848.
20. Agriculture dominates the economy of the island of Puerto Rico.
21. The first Africans to arrive in North America came on a Dutch ship that landed at Jamestown, Virginia, in 1619.
22. Whites made up about 72% of the U.S. population in 2000.
23. *Paper sons* is a custom that is associated with Chinese Americans.
24. There were fewer than two million American Indians, Eskimos, and Aleuts in the United States in 2000.
25. Some of the bloodiest riots involving African Americans and Whites occurred in the early 1900s.
26. Between 1991 and 2004, over 600,000 immigrants came to the United States from Africa.
27. The United States acquired the island of Puerto Rico from Spain in 1898.
28. There are only 438 Japanese surnames.
29. Chinese immigrants to the United States became distinguished for their outstanding work on truck farms.
30. The 2000 U.S. Census indicated that 11.4% of Latinos were Central, South, and Dominican Americans, which was larger than the percentage of Puerto Ricans.
31. A third-generation Japanese American is called a *sansei*.
32. About 56,800 Iraqis immigrated to the United States between 1991 and 2004.
33. About 64% of Native Americans lived outside tribal areas in 2000.
34. Most Chinese immigrants to the United States came from western China.
35. Eleven Italian Americans were lynched in New Orleans in 1892.
36. Nativism directed against southern and eastern European immigrants was intense when the Statue of Liberty was dedicated in 1886.
37. In 2000, there were more than three million Cubans living in the United States.

38. Approximately 255,500 Haitians immigrated to the United States between 1991 and 2004.

Answers to Ethnic Literacy Test

1. T 2. F 3. T 4. F 5. T 6. F 7. T 8. F 9. T 10. F
11. F 12. T 13. F 14. F 15. T 16. F 17. T 18. T 19. T 20. F
21. T 22. T 23. T 24. F 25. T 26. T 27. T 28. F 29. F 30. T
31. T 32. T 33. T 34. F 35. T 36. T 37. T 38. T